The Capital Budgeting Decision

Economic Analysis of Investment Projects

Sixth Edition

Harold Bierman, Jr.

*The Nicholas H. Noyes Professor of
Business Administration,
Graduate School of Management,
Cornell University*

Seymour Smidt

*The Nicholas H. Noyes Professor of
Economics and Finance,
Graduate School of Management,
Cornell University*

Macmillan Publishing Company
New York
Collier Macmillan Publishers
London

Macmillan Publishing Company
866 Third Avenue, New York, New York 10022

Collier Macmillan Canada, Inc.

Library of Congress Cataloging in Publication Data

Bierman, Harold
  The capital budgeting decision.

  Includes index.
  1. Capital investments—Evaluation.   2. Capital
budget.   I. Smidt, Seymour.   II. Title.
HG4028.C4B54   1984   658.1'52   83–7949
ISBN 0–02–309940–2

Printing: 2 3 4 5 6 7 8   Year: 4 5 6 7 8 9 0 1 2
ISBN   0-02-309940-2

Preface to the Sixth Edition

This edition follows the direction set by the previous revisions. When the first edition was published in 1960, we were convinced that the net present-value method was superior to other methods of making investment decisions. We still believe this. In the important area of uncertainty, however, our attitudes have undergone some changes that were first incorporated in the second edition. The greatest change from the first edition will be found in the choice of the rate of discount and general method of incorporating uncertainty in the investment decision process.

We continue to advocate the net present-value method, using a default-free discount rate to compute the present value. A dollar risk adjustment is added or subtracted from the present value of the expected cash flows. Thus investments with internal rates of return less than the firm's weighted average cost of capital may be considered to be acceptable. The procedure is more desirable than evaluating investments on the basis of the cost of capital implicitly combining a risk discount and a measure of time-value preference. For some investments the firm's borrowing rate may be a good minimum hurdle rate, if the cash flows of these investments are not uncertain.

We also continue to advocate the use of a default-free rate of interest as the basic tool to take the time value of money into consideration. The cost of capital cannot be used as a universally correct tool for evaluating investments. The cost of capital is a useful concept in handling the capital mix question, but it is not useful in evaluating all investment alternatives.

This edition differs from the fifth edition in the arrangement of material. We have moved all basic material into parts one and two and the more complex material into part four. Other changes include the addition of a substantial number of new problems and the addition of the cases found in Part Five. Some of the cases are complex and could easily be used more than once. Suggestions for using the cases are contained in the solutions manual which is available from the publisher to instructors who adopt the text. Many problems have been relocated so that there is a closer relationship between the contents of a chapter and the problems that follow it. The solutions manual contains problem locator tables that enable one to determine the present location of every problem that appeared in the Fifth Edition, and the source of every problem appearing in the present edition.

We have attempted to present intuitive solutions in the early chapters. An understanding of this basic material will avoid certain types of errors in evaluating investments. Even though it will not give exact answers to the types of complex problems that require more sophisticated mathematics, it will help improve decision making.

Preface to the First Edition

Businessmen and economists have been concerned with the problem of how financial resources available to a firm should be allocated to the many possible investment projects. Should a new plant be built? Equipment replaced? Bonds refunded? A new product introduced? These are all to some extent capital budgeting decisions to which there are theoretically sound solutions. The purpose of this book is to express the solution of the economist in the language of the business manager.

Decades ago, economists such as Böhm-Bawerk, Wicksell, and Irving Fisher laid the theoretical foundation for a sound economic approach to capital budgeting. In recent years the technical literature has contained articles (such as those by Dean, Solomon, Lorie, Savage, and Hirshleifer) that have significantly increased our understanding of what is required for sound capital budgeting decisions. However, these works have not been directed toward business managers and, until recently, the work of these men has had no perceptible influence on the way businessmen actually made capital investment decisions. Businessmen have tended to make capital budgeting decisions using their intuition, rules of thumb, or investment criteria with faulty theoretical foundations and thus have been likely to give incorrect answers in a large percentage of the decisions.

The purpose of this book is to present for an audience that may be completely unfamiliar with the technical literature on economic theory or capital budgeting a clear conception of how to evaluate investment proposals.

The authors are convinced that the "present-value" method is superior to other methods of evaluating the economic worth of investments that have been discussed in the business literature. They recognize that considerations other than that of economic worth are also important in making investment decisions. The early pages of the book show that "cash payback" and "return on investment" may give incorrect results. The "yield" or "investor's method" is shown to be inferior to the present-value method, especially where there are several alternative investments available. The explanation of the reasons for the inferiority of yield to present value is particularly timely, since popular business magazines have carried many articles praising the yield method without mentioning its important drawbacks.

The first four chapters present an over-all picture of the method of analysis advocated in this book that would be a suitable introduction for management at any level who need to be informed about the ideas involved in evaluating capital investments, but who are not directly involved in preparing investment evaluations. The remainder of the book elaborates on the basic description of the first four chapters and gives material that will assist a person in actually preparing the analysis of investments.

Book one is divided into two parts, enabling us to establish those conditions in which the suggested decision rules are relatively effective and those in which their effectiveness is limited. In Part I we treat decisions under certainty in a perfect capital market. Although these assumptions are not descriptive of the world, they do enable us to suggest solutions for some types of problems and to introduce the basic concepts of time discounting. In Part II we introduce imperfect capital markets and uncertainty, under which conditions the suggested solutions of Part I must be adjusted. We find under uncertainty that it is necessary to consider many attributes of the investment rather than only one. The more nearly unique the investment, the less reliable are the conventional guides for action that use the cost of capital as a hurdle rate.

We wish to thank the many persons in government, academic, and business areas, as well as our colleagues Jerry Hass, Vithala Rao, and John McClain, who have raised questions and made suggestions that have advanced our thinking.

HAROLD BIERMAN, JR.
SEYMOUR SMIDT

Ithaca, New York

Contents

PART ONE

Sirs:
The Indian who sold Manhattan for $24.00 was a sharp salesman. If he had put his $24 away at 6% compounded semiannually, it would now be $9.5 billion and could buy most of the now-improved land back.

—*S. Branch Walker, Stamford, Conn., Life, Aug. 31, 1959.*

In the first seven chapters of this book we present a theoretically correct and easily applied approach to decisions involving benefits and outlays through time, that is, capital budgeting decisions. Essentially, the procedure consists of a choice of a rate of discount representing the time value of money, and the application of this rate of discount to future cash flows to compute their net present values. The sum of all the present values associated with an investment (including immediate outlays) is the net present value of the investment.

In the first seven chapters it is assumed that the cash flows associated with an investment are known with certainty, that there are markets to borrow or lend funds at the rate of interest used in the time discounting, and that there are no constraints preventing the firm from using these markets. The objective of the discounting process is to take the time value of money into consideration, but it includes no adjustment for risk.

We advocate the use of the net present value method to evaluate investments, both because of its simplicity and its theoretical soundness.

CHAPTER **1**

Capital Budgeting

The New York Times on January 17, 1964, reported the following exchange between Alfred P. Sloan, former Chairman of General Motors, and a reporter:

One questioner asked Mr. Sloan if he had made any mistakes in 40 years as a top executive of General Motors and added: "Think of one." "I don't want to keep you up all night." Mr. Sloan snapped. "The executive who makes an average of 50–50 is doing pretty good.'

The controller points to the ancient, gray, six-story structure and says with pride, "This is one reason we can keep our costs down. Our plant is fully depreciated, so we don't have the large depreciation charges our competitors have."

Another company in the same industry sells a relatively new plant because it is not large enough for a three-shift operation. Rather than operate what is considered to be an inefficient production line (the production line had been completely overhauled within the last twelve months), a new plant is being constructed in another state.

The investment philosophies of the two companies making these decisions were vastly different. One was reluctant to invest money in plant and equipment. The other wanted to operate only the latest in plant and equipment. Which of the two companies was right? Maybe each company was following a policy that was correct for it, or perhaps they were both making faulty decisions. We cannot decide here because the necessary facts are not available to us. But the facts should be available to the responsible executives in both these companies, and these facts should be arranged in a useful manner and then interpreted correctly.

Consider the statement of a steel company executive that Japanese steelmakers were lucky in having their obsolete plants destroyed in World War II. It enabled them to start fresh with efficient plants and equipment. Were the Japanese really "lucky" to have had their productive capacity destroyed? We think not. Good decision making is more effective (and humane) than bombs.

Investment decisions may be tactical or strategic. A tactical investment decision generally involves a relatively small amount of funds and does not constitute a major departure from what the firm has been doing in the past. The consideration of a new machine tool by Ford Motor Company is a tactical decision, as is a buy or lease decision made by Mobil Oil Company.

Strategic investment decisions involve large sums of money and may also result in a major departure from what the company has been doing in the past. Acceptance of a strategic investment will involve a significant change in the company's expected profits and in the risks to which these profits will be subject. These changes are likely to lead stockholders and creditors to revise their evaluation of the company. If a private corporation undertook the development of a supersonic commercial transport (costing over $4 billion), this would be a strategic decision. If the company failed in its attempt to develop the commercial plane, the very existence of the company would be jeopardized. Frequently strategic decisions are based on intuition rather than on detailed quantitative analysis.

The future success of a business depends on the investment decisions made today. That business managers are generally aware of this is indicated by the requirement that important investment decisions must be approved by the chief operating executive or the board of directors. In spite of this fact, the procedures used to help management make investment decisions are often inadequate and misleading. Few manufacturing concerns would sign a long-term contract for supplies of an important raw material without carefully investigating the various sources of supply and considering the relative advantages of each in terms of price, service, and quality. Yet occasionally management groups approve investments without a careful consideration of available alternatives. Even when there is an investigation of alternatives, the information obtained sometimes does not lead to effective decisions, because managements may not organize the information in a way that will help them make better decisions.

Business organizations are continually faced with the problem of deciding whether the commitments of resources—time or money—are worthwhile in terms of the expected benefits. If the benefits are likely to accrue reasonably soon after the expenditure is made, and if both the expenditure and the benefits can be measured in dollars, the solution to such a problem is relatively simple. If the expected benefits are likely to accrue over several years, the solution is more complex.

We shall use the term *investment* to refer to commitments of resources made in the hope of realizing benefits that are expected to occur over a reasonably long period of time in the future. Capital budgeting is a many-sided activity that includes searching for new and more profitable investment proposals, investigating engineering and marketing considerations to predict the consequences of accepting the investment, and making economic analyses to determine the profit potential of each investment proposal. The primary purpose of this book is to help business management analyze the profit potential of investments in plant and equipment, marketing programs, research projects, and the like.

The Role of Strategy in Investment Decision-Making

The investment strategy of a firm is a statement of the formal criteria it applies in searching for and evaluating investment opportunities. Strategic planning guides the search for projects by identifying promising product lines or geographic areas in which to search for good investment projects. One firm's strategy may be to seek opportunities for rapid growth in emerging high technology businesses; another may seek opportunities to become the low-cost producer of commodities with well-established technologies and no unusual market problems; a third firm may look for opportunities to exploit its special knowledge of a particular family of chemicals. A strategy should reflect both the special skill and abilities of the firm (its comparative advantage) and the opportunities that are available as a result of dynamic changes in the world economy.

Strategic planning leads to a choice of the forest; project analysis studies individual trees. The two activities should complement and reinforce each other. Project analysis may provide a feedback loop to verify the accuracy of the strategic plan. If there are good opportunities (high net present value projects) where the strategic plan says they should be found, and few promising opportunities in lines of business which the strategy identifies as unattractive, confidence in the strategic plan increases. Alternatively, if attractive projects are not found where the plan had expected them, or if desirable projects appear in lines of business that the strategic plan had identified as unattractive, a reassessment of both the project studies and the strategic plan may be in order.

Present Value and Productivity

Productivity is defined as a ratio of output to input. There are many productivity indices since there are many ways to measure output or input. By any reasonable measure, productivity increases were an important source of economic growth for the United States for at least the first three-quarters of the twentieth century. As the data in Table 1-1 demonstrates, in the late 1960's and even more noticeably in the 1970's, there has been a significant drop in the rate of increase of productivity. This has been a source of concern to policy-makers in the business and public sectors. Many attempts have been made to explain this rather sudden change in the rate of growth of productivity. Scholars who are experts in the subject can account for some of the factors that appear to be causing the decline in productivity; one such explanation is the rapid rate of growth of the labor force during this period. But a substantial portion cannot be explained. According to the 1982 *Economic Report of the President*:

There have been concerted efforts to explain the measured slowdown. These efforts have met with only limited success. While there are a number of possible explanatory variables, available studies suggest that none separately nor in combination is capable of explaining more than half of the decline.[1]

While scholars cannot explain fully the surprising decline in productivity, some authors have offered ad hoc explanations. Among the suggested explanations is

[1] *Economic Report of the President*. Washington: Government Printing Office, February, 1982, p. 114.

TABLE 1-1. *Average annual growth rates of real GNP, total factor productivity, and factor inputs, 1959–79 (percent)*

Period	Real GNP	Total factor productivity	Capital	Labor
		Total GNP		
1959 to 1965	4.3	2.5	3.8	0.9
1965 to 1969	4.0	1.9	4.1	1.2
1969 to 1973	3.6	2.3	3.5	.4
1973 to 1979	2.8	1.2	2.5	1.6
		Private nonfarm nonhousing GNP		
1959 to 1965	4.4	2.5	4.1	1.0
1965 to 1969	4.0	1.3	5.8	1.3
1969 to 1973	4.1	2.4	4.2	.7
1973 to 1979	2.8	.6	3.2	1.8

Sources: Department of Commerce (Bureau of Economic Analysis); Gollop, Frank and Jorgenson, Dale, "U.S. Productivity Growth By Industry 1947–1973"; and Council of Economic Advisers. Reproduced from the *Economic Report of the President*, February 1982, p. 113.

the idea that the extensive use of present-value techniques is responsible for a decline in capital expenditures, which in turn has caused the decline in productivity. The following quotation represents this point of view:

As these techniques have gained ever wider use in investment decision making, the growth of capital investment and R&D spending in this country has slowed. We believe this to be more than a simple coincidence. We submit that the discounting approach has contributed to a decreased willingness to invest for two reasons: (1) it is often based on misperceptions of the past and present economic environment, and (2) it is biased against investment because of critical errors in the way the theory is applied. Bluntly stated, the willingness of managers to view the future through the reversed telescope of discounted cash flow is seriously shortchanging the futures of their companies.[2]

In fairness to the authors quoted above, a careful reading of the quotation, and of the article in which it appears, indicates that it is the "misuse" of net present value (NPV) which results in the undesirable effects, not the "use". Unfortunately, the last sentence of the quotation, and the subtitle of the article in which it appears, give the impression that there are some inherent flaws in the NPV or discounted cash flow (DCF) method that inevitably bias against investment.

---

[2] Robert H. Hayes and David A. Garvin. "Managing as if tomorrow mattered: Investment decisions that discount the future may result in high present values but bleak tomorrows." *Harvard Business Review*, May–June 1982, pp. 71–72.

Our position is summarized in the following propositions:

1. The DCF or Present-Value framework is the best available framework for analyzing investment cash flows. But it is only a tool and any tool can be misused. There is no inherent bias in the tool. It can be misused to produce bias against investments that are desirable or to cause bias in favor of investments that are undesirable. It is not a substitute for good judgment or for effective business strategic planning, but it is an aid to implementing these processes. The main objective of this book is to explain how to use this tool in an effective manner.

2. We do not claim to be able to explain the substantial drop in productivity, though we doubt that it is caused by the widespread adoption of present value techniques. Certainly there is no substantial evidence to support this proposition: decision makers in Japan and West Germany have been using present value techniques as long as their American counterparts.

We think it is at least as plausible to argue that the decline in the competitive position of the economy in the United States is due to the more effective use of DCF methods by our international competitors. Previous editions of this book have been translated into at least five foreign languages, and more copies have been sold overseas, in English and in translation, than have been sold in the United States. The first foreign language in which the book was published was Japanese.

Is there any connection between productivity and the use of DCF technology at an industry level? There certainly could be. Lacking concrete evidence, we cannot give DCF the credit for preventing an even larger decline in productivity. Nor can the DCF method receive the blame for the decline that has actually occurred. We do argue that the DCF method is the best decision tool available. Managers should learn to use it effectively. That is what this book is about.

Investments as Cash Flows

To focus attention on the problems of economic analysis, we begin by assuming that we have investment proposals worthy of preliminary consideration and that for each investment proposal the necessary engineering and marketing research has been completed. We assume that these studies will enable us to measure the dollar value of the resources expended and the benefits received from the investment during each future interval of time. In the early chapters of this book we assume that these dollar values can be estimated in advance with certainty. Later we relax this assumption and consider the additional complications that arise when decision makers are uncertain about the amounts and timing of the cash flows that will result from an investment.

Many investments cannot be described in terms of the certain (or uncertain) cash flows they will generate in each interval of time. We exclude these investments from exact analysis. Even business organizations, which carry further than most other organizations the attempt to measure all costs and benefits in dollar terms, find that the costs or benefits of many investments cannot be completely described in terms of dollars. Consider an advertising program designed to build up the prestige associated with the name of a corporation. This is an investment, because the expenditures are made in the hope of realizing benefits that will continue long after the advertising expenditures have been made. But it is difficult to estimate in dollar terms the exact value of the benefits that will accrue from the advertising program.

In nonprofit organizations, whether private or public, investments whose costs and benefits cannot be measured reasonably well in dollar terms are made even more frequently than in business. Nevertheless, investment proposals for which both the cost and benefits can be measured in dollar terms do arise in all these organizations, and the quantity of resources involved in such investments is considerable. In designing a building, for example, the architect or engineer is frequently faced with alternative means of accomplishing the same objective. The design of the heating or lighting systems are but two examples. Frequently one alternative will have a high initial cost but low maintenance or operating expenses, whereas another alternative will have low initial costs but high operating or maintenance expenses. A choice between the two alternatives is in essence an investment decision.

Thus, although not all the investment decisions in an organization can be described in terms of the dollar value of the expenditures or benefits, important decisions that can be described in these terms seem to occur in all organizations in modern society. As we increase our ability to forecast the consequences of our decisions, the number of investments that can be described reasonably well in dollar terms will also increase.

In this book we shall be mainly concerned with the economic analysis of investments from the point of view of a profit-seeking enterprise. Nevertheless, many of the methods of analysis described apply to investment decisions arising in private nonprofit organizations or in local or national governments, if the investment can be described in terms of cash flows. In these latter organizations, the appropriate definition of the cash flow may be different. For example, in considering whether an investment was worthwhile, a private business would not try to take into account the additional profits that might be earned by other businesses as a result of its investment. A government engaged in economic planning would normally try to consider such profits. We shall consider these questions briefly in Chapter 20. Also, the costs and methods of finance available to business enterprises are often significantly different from those available to governments or private nonprofit institutions. A government cannot sell common stock; a business firm cannot levy taxes to finance the investments it would like to undertake. In other respects the methods of analysis that apply in business organizations are usually applicable in governments as well.

Frequently, an investment proposal will involve both benefits and expenditures during one or more time periods. When this occurs it will be convenient to combine the dollar estimates of the benefits and expenditures for each period of time. If, during a specific period of time, the benefits exceed the expenditures, we may speak of the net benefits or cash proceeds; if the expenditures exceed the benefits, we may refer to the net expenditures or cash outlays. We shall adopt the convention of referring to cash proceeds or outlays during a given period of time by using positive or negative dollar amounts, respectively. We shall refer to the entire series of net proceeds and net outlays associated with an investment as the cash flow stream of the investment.

If some of the proceeds are subject to taxation, we shall measure the proceeds after taxes. A business corporation is subject to taxes on its income, and this income in turn depends on the amount of depreciation charges that can be used to offset revenues in computing taxable income. The amount of cash proceeds resulting from an investment in any future year will depend upon the regulations or laws established by the tax authority. These laws or regulations will determine the kinds of expenditures that can be charged immediately to expense and those that must be capitalized and written off in subsequent years by depreciating the asset. Nonprofit organizations and governments are not subject to income taxes, and therefore the proceeds they receive from an investment do not depend upon their depreciation accounting method.

It should be stressed that the definition of net benefits or cash proceeds given above is *not* identical with the income concept used in corporate accounting. The major difference is that, in estimating cash proceeds, depreciation charges and other amortization charges of fixed assets are not subtracted from gross revenues because no cash expenditures are required. The cash outlays associated with the investment are subtracted at the time of investment and these substitute for the depreciation expenses. Corporate accounting computes the income of each year and thus must allocate the cost of the investment over its life. For decision purposes we are interested in the overall effect of the investment on the wellbeing of the firm and its investors and do not have to measure its effect on the income of any one year.

We shall define *conventional* investments as those having one or more periods of outlays followed by one or more periods of cash proceeds. Borrowing money is a kind of "negative investment" in which one or more periods of cash proceeds are followed by one or more periods in which there are cash outlays. *Loan-type* investments have positive cash flows followed by periods of cash outlays. There are also *nonconventional* investments that have one or more periods of outlays (proceeds) interspersed with periods of proceeds (outlays). With nonconventional investments there is more than one sign change in the sequence of the cash flows.

The possibilities may be illustrated as follows:

	Sign of Flow for Period:			
	0	1	2	3
Conventional investment	−	+	+	+
Loan type of flows	+	−	−	−
Nonconventional investment	−	+	+	−
Nonconventional investment	+	−	−	+

These examples do not exhaust the possibilities. For example, a conventional investment may have many periods of outlays.

Any decisions involving measurable cash flows over one or more periods may be implemented by using the capital budgeting procedures to be developed in this book.

Estimate of Cash Proceeds

It is frequently stated that refinements in capital budgeting techniques are a waste of effort because the basic information being used is so unreliable. It is claimed that the estimates of cash proceeds are only guesses, and that to use anything except the simplest capital budgeting procedures is as futile as using racing forms to pick winners at the track or complicated formulas to determine which way the stock market is going to move next.

It is true that in many situations reliable estimates of cash proceeds are difficult to make. Fortunately, there are a large number of investment decisions in which cash proceeds can be predicted with a fair degree of certainty.

But even with an accurate, reliable estimate of cash proceeds, the wrong decision is frequently made because incorrect methods are used in evaluating this information.

When it is not possible to make a single estimate of cash proceeds that is certain to occur, we do not believe it follows that incorrect methods of analysis are justified. If it is difficult to predict the outcome of an investment with certainty, and if the investment is large, the use of a careful and comprehensive analysis is justified, even if this means that the analysis will be more complicated and costly. With small tactical investments, somewhat less involved methods might be used because a more complex analysis would not be necessary, but again there is no need to use inferior methods that decrease the likelihood of making correct investment decisions.

Application of Capital Budgeting Techniques

Many different decisions may be thought of as investments and hence incorporated into the capital budgeting process. We shall illustrate in this section some of the situations of this nature.

Replacement Decision

A company is currently using three pieces of equipment that cost $10,000 each and are 70 percent depreciated. They can be replaced with one unit of equipment that would cost $20,000. It is expected that at normal activity the new machine would save $40,000 a year in labor, maintenance, and so on, for a period of five years. Should the machines be replaced?

Size of Plant

A company must choose between a small plant that would cost $1 million and a large plant which would cost $1.5 million. The earnings of both plants are computed, and it is found that the small plant would yield a return of 20 percent and the large plant a return of 17 percent. Which plant should be chosen?

Lease or Buy
A company can either buy data-processing equipment or rent it. The cost of the equipment is $300,000 and the rental fee is $10,000 per month. It is estimated that improvements will make this equipment obsolete within five years. Should the company lease or buy?

Refunding of Debt
A company currently has $10 million debt outstanding, bearing a coupon rate of 10 percent. The debt was issued at a discount, which is still unamortized to the extent of $500,000. The company can currently issue bonds to yield 9 percent. The costs of issuing the new bonds would be $200,000, and there would be a call premium on the old bonds of $300,000. The old bonds have twenty years remaining until they become due. Should the bonds be refunded?

Although none of the preceding examples contains all the facts that would be necessary for a decision, they illustrate well the kind of problem that will be considered. The analytical methods that will be suggested in this book are applicable for all these examples.

For many purposes it is helpful to be able to use one or two words to describe a class of investments or investment decisions. We shall suggest several classification schemes.

Methods of Classifying Investments

Any useful scheme of controlling investments must be based on a classification of types of investments. Different kinds of investments raise different problems, are of different relative importance to the firm, and will require different persons to evaluate their significance. By classifying types of investments, each investment proposal will receive attention from persons qualified to analyze it.

Investments may be classified according to the following categories:

1. The kinds of scarce resources used by the investment. For example, whether or not the investment requires important amounts of cash, of floor space, of the time of key personnel (and personnel may also be classified: sales, production, research, top management, legal staff, and so on).
2. The amount of each of the resources that is required. For example, with respect to the amount of immediate cash outlays required, we could classify investments as requiring less than $500, between $500 and $5,000, and over $5,000.
3. The way benefits from the investment are affected by other possible investments. Some investments stand on their own feet. Others will be improved if supplementary investments are made; still others will be useless if competing investments are accepted. For example, the worth of another fork-lift truck may depend on whether or not the plan for adding an automatic conveyor system is accepted.

4. The form in which the benefits are received. Thus investments may generate greater cash flows, reduce the risks associated with poor business conditions, reduce the accident rate, improve employee morale, or eliminate a community nuisance such as excessive smoke or noise.
5. Whether the incremental benefits are the result of lower cost or increased sales, or whether the investments merely prevent a decline in sales or market share.
6. The functional activity to which the investments are most closely related. Thus an oil company may classify investments according to the following activities: exploration, production, transportation, refining, or marketing.
7. The industry classification of the investment. Thus the manager of a conglomerate may want to know if the investment being considered has to do with its professional football team, producing steel, or space activities.
8. The degree of necessity. Some investments are necessary in the sense that if they are not undertaken the entire operation stops (the stoppage may be desirable, thus the *necessity* may not be absolute). Other investments are highly optional and move the firm in directions it does not have to go in order to keep operating.

Many other methods of classification could be suggested (e.g. energy saving, new products, maintaining market share, capacity expansion, pollution control). Clearly no single scheme of classification will be equally valid for all uses or for all companies. The essential task is to develop a classification system for investments that is appropriate to the activity of the business and the organizational structure of the particular company.

In this book we are first concerned with investments for which both the resources used and the benefits to be received can be measured to an important degree in terms of cash flows. Second, the analytical methods developed in this book will be most useful for investments that are important enough to the firm to warrant a relatively careful study of their potential profitability. Next we shall consider a classification of investments that is based on the way the benefits from a given investment are affected by other possible investments.

Dependent and Independent Investments

In evaluating the investment proposals presented to management, it is important to be aware of the possible interrelationships between pairs of investment proposals. A given investment proposal may be economically independent of, or dependent on, another investment proposal. The first investment proposal will be said to be *economically independent* of the second if the cash flows (or more generally the costs and benefits) expected from the first investment would be the same regardless of whether the second investment were accepted or rejected. If the cash flows associated with the first investment are affected by the decision to accept or reject the second investment, the first investment is said to be economically dependent on the second. It should be clear that, when one investment is dependent on another, some attention must be given to the question of whether decisions about the first investment can or should be made separately from decisions about the second.

Economically Independent Investments

In order for investment A to be economically independent of investment B, two conditions must be satisfied. First, it must be technically possible to undertake investment A whether or not investment B is accepted. Thus it is *not* possible to build a school and shopping center on the same site, and therefore the proposal to build the one is not independent of a proposal to build the other. Second, the net benefits to be expected from the first investment must not be affected by the acceptance or rejection of the second. If the estimates of the cash outlays and the cash inflows for investment A are not the same when B is either accepted or rejected, the two investments are not independent. Thus it is technically possible to build a toll bridge and operate a ferry across adjacent points on a river, but the two investments are not independent because the proceeds from one will be affected by the existence of the other. The two investments would not be economically independent in the sense in which we are using the term, even if the traffic across the river at this point were sufficient to operate profitably both the bridge and the ferry.

Sometimes two investments cannot both be accepted because the firm does not have enough cash to finance both. This situation could occur if the amount of cash available for investments were strictly limited by management rather than by the capital market, or if increments of funds obtained from the capital market cost more than previous increments. In such a situation the acceptance of one investment may cause the rejection of the other. But we shall not then say that the two investments are economically dependent. To do so would make all investments for such a firm dependent, and this is not a useful definition for our purposes.

Economically Dependent Investments

The dependency relationship can be further classified. If a decision to undertake the second investment will increase the benefits expected from the first (or decrease the costs of undertaking the first without changing the benefits), the second investment is said to be a *complement* of the first. If the decision to undertake the second investment will decrease the benefits expected from the first (or increase the costs of undertaking the first without changing the benefits), the second is said to be a *substitute* for the first. In the extreme case where the potential benefits to be derived from the first investment will completely disappear if the second investment is accepted, or where it is technically impossible to undertake the first when the second has been accepted, the two investments are said to be *mutually exclusive*. It is also possible to define an extreme case for investments that are complements. Suppose that the second investment is impossible (technologically) or would result in no benefits whatsoever if the first invest-ment were not accepted. Then the first investment can be said to be a *prerequisite* of the second.

It may be helpful to think of the possible relationships between investments as being arrayed along a line segment. At the extreme left we have the situation where investment A is a prerequisite to investment B. In the center of the line we have a situation where investment A is independent of investment B. At the extreme right-hand end of the line we have the situation where investment A is mutually exclusive with respect to investment B. As we move to the right from the left-hand side of the line, we have varying degrees of complementariness, decreasing as we proceed to the right. Similarly, on the right-hand side of the line we represent varying degrees of substitutability, increasing as we proceed outward to the right. The following is a graphic representation.

Prerequisite		Independent			Mutually exclusive
↓	Strong complement	Weak complement ↓	Weak substitute	Strong substitute	↓

One additional complication in connection with complementary investments should be mentioned here. The complementary relationship need not be sym-metrical. Suppose that we consider the building of a new factory as one invest-ment and the purchase of an air-conditioning unit for the factory as the second investment. The two investments are clearly complementary. But the relationship need not be symmetrical, because the new factory may be profitable without air conditioning. With air conditioning, worker efficiency may go up, so that the factory is even more profitable. The additional efficiency resulting from the addi-tion of air conditioning may properly be called the return or benefits resulting from the expenditure on air-conditioning equipment. But the air-conditioning equipment by itself is useless unless there is a factory in which it can be used. The factory is a prerequisite to the investment for the air-conditioning equipment, but the air conditioning is not a prerequisite to the investment in the factory building.

Statistical Dependence

It is possible for two or more investments to be economically independent but statistically dependent. Statistical dependence is said to be present if the cash flows from two or more investments would be affected by some external event or happening whose occurrence is uncertain. For example, a firm could produce high-priced yachts and expensive cars. The investment decisions affecting these two product lines are economically independent. However, the fortunes of both activities are closely associated with high business activity and a large amount of discretionary income for the "rich" people. This statistical dependence may affect the risk of investments in these product lines, because the swings of profitability of these two products lines will be wider than those of two product lines having less statistical dependence. Statistical dependence is defined and its importance for investment decisions discussed in Chapter 22.

Administrative Implications

The number of possible relationships that may exist between pairs of complementary investments is very large. In dealing with investments that are complementarily related, the most effective technique is to combine sets of investment proposals in such a way that the new proposal is either an independent proposal or one of a set of mutually exclusive proposals. In the preceding example, instead of considering two complementary investment proposals, a factory and the air-conditioning equipment for the factory, we can reformulate the problem as one involving a choice between mutually exclusive investment alternatives—a factory with air conditioning or a factory without air conditioning.

In most large organizations, operating procedures require that proposals for capital investment which exceed specified limits must be submitted by the sponsor to higher executive levels for review and approval before actual expenditures can be authorized. Except in unusual circumstances such proposals should consist of independent investment proposals for which an accept or reject decision is appropriate; or they should comprise a set of mutually exclusive proposals, such that either the whole set must be rejected or only one of the mutually exclusive alternatives can be accepted.

No system of controlling capital expenditures can operate effectively if management finds that, after having approved a seemingly highly profitable investment, additional investments that do not generate any profits on their own account are presented as being absolutely necessary to implement the profit potential of the initial investment proposals.

Example

The research and development section of a large chemical manufacturing firm submitted technical data on a new product to one of the firm's operating divisions. After investigation of the product by the engineering, production, and sales staffs, the operating division management decided that the product should be added to their line. Because existing facilities were not adequate for the production of the new product, a capital appropriation request for the new plant and equipment was submitted for review and approval to the firm's executive committee. On review by the executive committee the following deficiencies were uncovered: (1) The appropriation request did not include an estimate of the working capital requirements that would be required to operate the new plant and market the resulting product; (2) one of the raw materials required in the new process would be purchased from another operating division of the company, and the increased output of that division would have required additional plant and equipment expenditures by the supplier division; (3) the new product was partially competitive with one of the company's existing products, and the decline in the profit potential from this existing product had not been taken into consideration; (4) distribution of the new product would require acquisition of additional storage facilities, because demand for the product was seasonal, but efficient production would require a steady rate of production. The proposal was returned to the operating division for further study. After additional investigation it was determined that the company could most effectively develop the new product by licensing other manufacturers to produce and market it.

In developing an investment proposal to be submitted to higher levels for review and approval, the sponsor should normally include as a part of the single package whatever complementary investments seem necessary or desirable. Similarly, if the proposed investment will serve as a partial substitute for any investments to which the firm is already committed or which are under consideration, this fact should be noted in submitting the proposals.

If some of the choices involved in planning the investment are considered sufficiently important that the final decision must be made by top management, the investment proposals should be submitted in the form of a set of mutually exclusive alternatives. Examples would be the decision on the location of a new plant or the possibility of including an important piece of auxiliary equipment. This procedure has the advantage of enabling top management to examine in an orderly fashion the major alternatives involved. It also enables management to make decisions at a stage in the planning of the expenditure where the special knowledge, experience, and insight of the senior executives can be effectively brought to bear on the proposal. Too often such choices are not presented to management until previous commitments have largely foreclosed the opportunity to exercise choice, and management is presented in effect with a *fait accompli.*

Ordinarily, the cost figures contained in an investment proposal submitted to top management will be based on a careful but necessarily preliminary estimate of the final cost of the proposed project. On major projects the expensive step of preparing detailed specifications and working drawings should be deferred until the project has actually been approved. Once approval has been obtained, management will proceed with the detailed planning of the project. At this stage a great many decisions will have to be made on such questions as the type of materials to be used in construction, the choice of equipment, and even the location of a plant if no definite decision on this point was made in the preliminary plans. Given the general approval for the project as a whole, these choices are mainly among different ways of accomplishing the same objective—that is, the alternatives are mutually exclusive. Although the most important of these choices, such as plant location, may be submitted to higher management levels, many of the less important decisions will necessarily be made by lower levels of management or by staff personnel.

To ensure coordination when decision making is decentralized, it is necessary to set up means of communicating information about the policies and objectives of the organization so that decisions made independently in various parts of the organization will contribute to the goals of the organization. When the decentralized decision-making powers grant authority to make investment—type decisions, the procedures recommended in this book can provide an important means of assuring that uniform standards of choice consistent with overall organizational goals are available to the many separate decision-making centers.

As could be expected, these problems occur not only in business organizations but also in nonprofit organizations, both public and private. The following example is based on a situation that occurred in a university.

Example

The head of the buildings and grounds department of a large university obtained approval to replace and modernize the lighting system in one of the university gymnasiums. The old lighting system had been installed thirty years earlier, when the building was built. It was expensive to maintain, and the quality of the lighting was definitely low by modern standards. The detailed job of designing the new lighting system was turned over to a lighting engineer in the Office of the University Architect. Three types of lighting equipment were initially considered. Of these, one was eliminated on the basis of having excessive glare for this application. The two remaining possibilities were both capable of producing satisfactory light conditions, and therefore an attempt was made to choose between the two on the basis of cost. The cost analysis disclosed that system A would require a high initial outlay but would have low maintenance and operating costs. System B would require lower initial outlays but higher maintenance and operating costs than system A. As a result, the lighting engineer felt that no clear choice could be made on the basis of cost; therefore, the final decision was made on the basis of admittedly unimportant differences in the quality of the light produced by the two systems. If the engineer had applied the discounted cash flow approach, taking into account the fact that the university was able to earn a 9.5 percent return on its funds, it would have been clear that system A had a very decided cost advantage.

Measures of Investment Worth

In the next chapter we shall introduce some methods of evaluating the worth of investments that are in common use or have been frequently recommended as desirable. If we take a group of investment proposals and rank them by each of these methods, we shall find that each method will frequently give a different ranking to the same set of investment proposals. In fact, it can be said that the different measures will only accidentally give identical rankings to a set of investment proposals. Although we shall not be able to rank economically independent investments in a useful manner, we shall normally be able to make decisions without such rankings.

Various executives faced with the same set of investment possibilities, but using different measures of investment worth, will tend to make dissimilar investment decisions. Clearly, all the measures that will be described here cannot be equally valid. We shall attempt to determine which of the measures have some legitimate reason for use and to isolate the circumstances under which they will tend to give satisfactory results.

In current business practice, each of the methods selected has advocates, and frequently one is used in combination with another. Because investment proposals are rarely accepted by top management solely on the basis of such analysis, it may be argued that the choice of method is of little significance because the investment decision is likely to be influenced by many different factors. Insofar as the executives making the final decision are aware of the risks involved and are intimately familiar with the proposals, know the possible technical or operating problems that may be encountered, and realize the potential erosion of earnings resulting from competitive action or changing technology, this criticism may very well be valid. In most large organizations, however, it is impossible for the top management officials, who must finally approve or disapprove investment proposals, to be intimately familiar with the details of each and every proposal presented to them. To the extent that this intimate knowledge is impossible or impractical, these executives must rely upon the evaluation of the recommendations from their subordinates. To make reasonable choices in weighing alternative investments, it is increasingly necessary that various proposals be evaluated as nearly as possible on some uniform, comparable basis. In such circumstances, although the measure of economic worth of an investment should never be the sole factor considered in making a final decision, it may play an increasingly important part in the investments under consideration by the firm.

Accordingly, that various measures give different rankings and indicate different accept or reject decisions to identical sets of investment proposals is a matter of concern. Substantial improvements in efficiency and income may result if a more adequate measure can be discovered and widely adopted. Any such progress requires first a more general agreement about the desirable characteristics to be possessed by a good index of the economic worth of an investment. We therefore turn to consider the various criteria that can be used in evaluating the adequacy of a measure of the economic worth of an investment proposal.

Criteria for Evaluating Measures of Investment Worth

As anyone who has ever attempted the task will recognize, it is difficult to develop an explicit statement of the goals of an organization. The task becomes even harder if, as in the present instance, the purpose of the statement of goals is to provide a test of the extent to which activities and programs are appropriate for the organization. In the case of business organizations the measures of investment worth that have been proposed and that are developed in this book concentrate on a form of the profit-maximization goal, but attempt to include equally important conditions, such as the risks associated with the investments undertaken and the future structure of assets and liabilities that will be determined in part by the investment decisions currently being made.

To be a reasonable criterion, profit maximization has to consider the size of the investment employed and the alternative uses of the funds invested (including the possibility of returning these funds to the stockholders). One way of stating the objective of the investment decision procedure is to describe it as tending to maximize the current market value of the stockholders' holdings in the firm. Although not an exact criterion (for example, it does not help decide between a decision that elevates the value of a stock now but depresses it later and a decision that depresses the stock now and elevates it later), maximization of the value of the stockholders' holdings is a reasonable description of what we would like our measure of investment worth to accomplish.

It is recognized that a complete statement of the organizational goals of a business enterprise would embrace a much wider range of considerations, including such things as the prestige, income, security, freedom, and power of the management group, and the contribution of the corporation to the overall social environment in which it exists and to the welfare of the labor force it employs. Insofar as the attainment of profits, without unnecessary risks or an unduly awkward financial structure, does not conflict with the other goals mentioned, the assumption that the pecuniary objectives are the proximate goals of a business organization is tenable.

The measure of investment worth that best describes the profit potential of a proposed investment is the net present value of the cash flows associated with the proposed investment. It is more consistent with furthering the stockholders' interests than straight maximization of income, because the accounting measures of income do not take into consideration alternative uses of the funds that would be tied up in investments. The present-value method, however, does not necessarily provide a useful measure of the additional risks to which the owners of a business will be exposed as a result of accepting an investment. Methods of incorporating such risks into the analysis are discussed in Chapter 11 and subsequent chapters.

Budget Process and Planning

Frequently we think of the budget of a firm as being part of the cost-control apparatus and forget that it is an important tool for planning. The capital budget for the coming period will affect the cash budget and will be affected in turn by sales forecasts; thus the capital budget must be incorporated into the budgetary process.

The timing of cash flows resulting from capital expenditures is extremely important to the corporate officer attempting to plan the cash needs of the firm. Information is needed on the specific days the bills will have to be paid and when cash will begin to be generated by the investment. Of course, it will hardly ever be possible to predict these events with certainty, but it should be possible to make reasonable estimates that will be useful.

Some firms will prepare a five-year capital budget. If an attempt is being made to project other financial data over one or more years, the composition of the capital budget will affect the nature of the other planning budgets. For example, if an automobile company is planning to enter the steel industry, this would be disclosed in the capital budget and would certainly affect all other budgets.

The capital budget should be an integral part of the budget and planning process. The officer in charge of the capital budget must be in effective communication with the budget officer of the firm (if the positions are separate), because the decisions they make will result in a considerable amount of interaction.

Time Value of Money

This book is founded on the concept of the "time value of money" and the relevance of the timing of cash flows to making investment decisions. We shall find that we want to compute the present equivalent of future sums of money as a basic part of our investment analysis. To accomplish this transformation of future sums into present equivalents, we shall make use of present-value tables.

Consider a situation where a firm is to receive $10,000 at time 2 and wants to know the present-value equivalent of the $10,000. Assume the firm's discount rate is .10.

Appendix Table A at the end of the book gives the present value of $1 due n periods from now. The present value $1 due two periods from now discounted at .10 is .8264. The present value of $10,000 due at time 2 is

$10,000(.8264) = \$8,264.$

The $8,264 is the economic present-value equivalent of $10,000 at time 2. The .10 interest factor represents the rate at which funds can be lent and borrowed by the firm. If the firm invested $8,264 to earn .10 per year, the following would occur:

Original investment	$8,264.00
Interest of year 1	826.40
	9,090.40
Interest of year 2	909.04
Amount at time 2	$9,999.44

Aside from a rounding-off error, the $8,264 grows to an amount equal to $10,000. The firm would be indifferent to receiving $10,000 at time 2 or $8,264 at time 0.

Using Table A to collapse future dollars back to the present we can place all dollars to be received (or paid) in the future on a comparable basis so that they can be added and subtracted. We can add time 0 dollars. We cannot add a time 0 dollar and a time 2 dollar without first transforming the time 2 dollar back to time 0 by computing its present-value equivalent.

In addition to finding present-value equivalents, we can also find future-value equivalents. For example, if the firm currently has $10,000 to invest, it might want to know how much it will have at the end of two time periods if the invested funds can earn .10. One method of solution is to divide the $10,000 by the entry from Table A:

$$\frac{10,000}{.8264} = \$12,100.$$

The appendix to this chapter gives an alternative method of obtaining an equivalent solution to this problem using the accumulation factor $(1 + r)^n$ where r

is the interest rate and n the number of time periods. For the example we have $(1.10)^2 = 1.21$ and the future value of $10,000 is again $12,100.

Annuities

We can describe an annuity as a series of equally spaced payments of equal amounts. Appendix Table B gives the present value of $1 a period for n periods discounted at r rate of interest, the first payment being received (or paid) one period from now and the last payment n periods from now.

Example: Finding the Present Value of an Annuity

Assuming an effective interest rate of .05, we want to find the present value of annual interest payments of $100,000 a year. The first payment is one year from now and there will be twenty payments. Using Appendix Table B and an interest rate of .05 we find that the present value of a $1 period for twenty periods is $12.4622. The present value of the interest payments is

$100,000 \times 12.4622 = $1,246,220.$

In the previous example, Appendix Table B was used to find the present value of an annuity. The same table can also be used to find a series of annual equivalent cash flows for n periods that has a given present value. Depending on the context, these annual equivalents may represent costs, revenues, or profits.

For example, the table can be used to compute the amount that has to be paid at the end of each period to repay a loan.

Example: Finding an annual equivalent payment

Assume the A Company borrows $34,710 from the bank at an annual cost of 10 percent.

The company wants to repay the loan in two equal installments at the end of each of the following two years.

Let R represent the amount of the annuity that has the same present value as $34,710. Table B indicates the present value of $1 a year for two years at .10 is $1.7355. Thus R must satisfy the following relationship:

$1.7355R = 34,710,$

and

$R = $20,000$

is the annual payment to be paid at the end of each of the two years after the date of the loan. The debt repayment schedule is as follows:

Period	Amount Owed Beginning of Period	Interest	Total Owed	Payment	Amount Owed End of Period
1	34,710	3,471	38,181	20,000	18,181
2	18,181	1,818	19,999	20,000	0

Rate of Discount

We shall use the "time value of money" as a discount rate. This can be defined to be the rate of interest associated with default-free securities and does not include an adjustment for risk. In some situations it is convenient to use the firm's borrowing rate (the marginal cost of borrowing funds). The objective of the discounting process is to take the time value of money into consideration. We want to find the present equivalent of future sums, neglecting risk considerations. Later, we shall introduce a technique to adjust for the risk of the investment.

Although the cost of capital is an important concept that should be understood by all managers and is useful in deciding on the financing mix, we do not advocate its general use in evaluating investments. Our justifications for this position are presented in Chapter 12.

Assumption of Certainty

In the first part of this book there is an assumption that the cash flows are known with certainty. This assumption may be somewhat difficult to accept, since it is well known that there are few cash flows associated with real investments that are actually known with certainty. There are two reasons for proceeding in this manner. First, we have to "walk through our plays" before starting to run. There are sufficient difficulties in just taking the time value of money into consideration without also incorporating risk factors. Second, when the cash flows are finally allowed to be uncertain, we shall suggest the use of a procedure that is based on the initial recommendations made with the certainty assumption, so nothing is lost by initially making the assumption of certainty.

Appendix: Basic Mathematical Relationships for Time Discounting

For these introductory examples the reader should assume either that the cash flows are not subject to income taxes, or that they are measured on an after-tax basis. Tax effects will be considered explicitly later in this volume. Also, the formulas derived in this appendix are all based on the assumption that the time value of money will be the same in all future periods. The formulas presented here could be generalized to take into account any changes that the decision maker believes will occur in the rate of interest. Let

A = initial sum of money;
r = time value of money per period;
n = number of time periods;
S_n = future value of a sum of money to be received in the nth period from now.

If A is invested for one period to earn r, we would have at the end of the one period

$$S_1 = A + Ar = A(1 + r).$$

At the end of two periods, if the initial investment and the accumulated interest continue to earn at the rate r, we would have

$$S_2 = A(1 + r) + [A(1 + r)]r = A(1 + r)^2.$$

At the end of n periods, under the same assumptions, we would have

$$S_n = A(1 + r)^n.$$

The term $(1 + r)^n$ is called an *accumulation factor*. Solving for A by dividing both sides by $(1 + r)^n$,

$$A = \frac{S_n}{(1 + r)^n} = S_n(1 + r)^{-n}.$$

The term $(1 + r)^{-n}$ is called a "present-value factor." If S_n is equal to \$1, we can solve for the present value of \$1:

$$A = (1 + r)^{-n} = \frac{1}{(1 + r)^n}.$$

See Appendix Table A for values of $(1 + r)^{-n}$. We will define $A(n, r)$ to be the present value of \$1 due in n periods discounted at r time value of money. Thus,

$$A(n, r) = (1 + r)^{-n}.$$

An annuity is a series of equal payments that occur at equally spaced intervals for a predetermined period of time. In this book the symbol $B(n, r)$ is used to represent the present value of an annuity of \$1 per period, for n periods, with the first payment one period from now and with an interest rate of r percent per period. The present value of such an annuity could be obtained from Appendix Table A by going to the column headed r percent and adding up the first n entries in the table. Since the present value of an annuity is used so frequently in present-value calculations, however, the present values are presented in a separate table, Appendix Table B. If the annuity pays some amount other than \$1 per period, the present value of the annuity can be obtained by multiplying the annuity factor from Table B by the actual amount involved.

Instead of using Table B or adding up the entries from an appropriate column of Table A, the present value of an annuity of \$1 per period can also be obtained by using the following formula:

$$B(n, r) = \frac{1 - (1 + r)^{-n}}{r}.$$

The following paragraph explains how this formula is derived.

In the following table each row in column 1 gives the present value of \$1 received at the end of the period indicated in the column headed *Time*. The sum of the items in this column is $B(n, r)$. Each row in column 2 of this table gives the item in that row of column 1 multiplied by $(1 + r)$. The sum of the items in this column is $(1 + r)B(n, r)$. Note that $(1 + r)^0 = 1$, and that all except two of the amounts are in both columns. Taking the difference between the sum of the two columns and solving for $B(n, r)$ gives the formula we wish to derive.

Time	Col. 1	Col. 2
1	$(1+r)^{-1}$	$(1+r)^0$
2	$(1+r)^{-2}$	$(1+r)^{-1}$
3	$(1+r)^{-3}$	$(1+r)^{-2}$
$\vdots$	$\vdots$	$\vdots$
$n-1$	$(1+r)^{-n+1}$	$(1+r)^{-n+2}$
n	$(1+r)^{-n}$	$(1+r)^{-n+1}$
	$B(n, r)$	$(1+r)B(n, r)$

Column 2 minus column 1:

$$(1 + r)B(n, r) - B(n, r) = 1 - (1 + r)^{-n}$$

Simplifying the left-hand side,

$$rB(n, r) = 1 - (1 + r)^{-n},$$

and, dividing by r,

$$B(n, r) = \frac{1 - (1 + r)^{-n}}{r}.$$

Appendix Table B gives the values of $B(n, r)$. $B(n, r)$ is the present value of an annuity of \$1 per period. If the annuity is for \$$R$, we multiply the value obtained from the table by R.

If n is very large (let n approach infinity), we have the present value for a perpetuity of \$1 per period:

$$B(\infty, r) = \frac{1}{r}.$$

Questions and Problems

1-1. Assume a firm is given the choice between receiving \$1,000 three years from now or some amount now. The firm's discount rate is .10. What amount now would cause the firm to be indifferent?

1-2. Assume that you are given the choice between \$100 now and \$100 one year from now and that both payments are certain. Which would you choose?

Explain. How large would the amount one year from now have to be for you to be indifferent between the two choices? What does the answer to this question imply as to your rate of interest (time value of money) during this time period?

1-3. Assume a .05 per year time value of money. Use the tables in the Appendix to compute the value of $100 (a) received one year from now; (b) received immediately; (c) received at the end of five years; (d) received at the beginning of the sixth year; (e) received at the end of fifty years; (f) received at the end of fifty years, but the interest rate is .10; (g) received at the end of each of ten periods.

1-4. Assume a .05 time value of money. Use the tables in the Appendix to compute the value of the following series of payments of $100 a year received for (a) five years, the first payment received one year from now; (b) five years, the first of five payments received immediately; (c) ten years, the first payment received one year from now; (d) ten years, the first of ten payments received immediately.

1-5. Assume a .05 time value of money. The sum of $100 received immediately is equivalent to what quantity received in ten equal annual payments, the first to be received one year from now? What would be the annual amount if the first payment were received immediately?

1-6. Assume a .05 time value of money. We have a debt to pay and are given a choice of paying $1,000 now or some amount X five years from now. What is the maximum amount that X can be for us to be willing to defer payment for five years?

1-7. We can make an immediate payment now of $10,000 or pay equal amounts of R for the next five years (first payment due one year from now). With a time value of money of .05, what is the maximum value of R that we would be willing to accept?

1-8. Assume that you are given a choice between incurring an immediate cost (and outlay) of $10,000 and having to pay $2,310 a year for five years (first payment due one year from now); the time value of money is .05. What would be your choice? Explain.

1-9. Assume a bank charges .01 interest per month. You borrow $50,000 to be paid by equal payments over a 35-month period, first payment one month from now. How much will you have to pay each month?

1-10. Assume the O-I Company has outstanding $10,000,000 of 4 percent bonds, maturing in 20 years (paying $400,000 of interest per year). The current interest rate is .10. What is the present value of the debt?

1-11. Assume the I-O Company has outstanding $10,000,000 of 10 percent bonds maturing in 20 years (paying $1,000,000 of interest per year). The current interest rate is .04.
   a. What is the present value of the debt?
   b. If the bonds can be called at a price of $10,500,000, how much could the firm pay to accomplish the refunding? Assume zero taxes.

1-12. Compute the present value for a bond that promises to pay interest of $50 a year for thirty years and $1,000 at maturity. The first interest payment is one year from now. Use a rate of discount of .05.

1-13. Estimate the present value of a bond that promises to pay interest of $30 a year for thirty years and $1,000 at maturity. The first interest payment is one year from now. Use a .03 rate of discount. After estimating the present value, compute it using the present-value tables.

1-14. A twenty-year $1,000 bond promises to pay .045 interest annually. The current interest rate is .05. How much is the bond worth now? How much is the bond worth if the current interest rate were .04?

1-15. Exactly twenty years from now Jones will start receiving a pension of $10,000 a year. The payments will continue for thirty years. How much is the pension worth now, assuming money is worth .05 per year?

1-16. Assume a .05 interest rate. How much is a perpetuity of $1,000 per year worth?

1-17. Assume a .10 interest rate. How much is a perpetuity of $1,000 per year worth?

1-18. Assume a .10 interest rate (you can borrow and lend at that rate). Specify which you would prefer:
   a. $10,000 in cash or
   $1,000 per year for perpetuity (first payment received at the end of the first period).
   b. $10,000 in cash or
   $1,100 per year for perpetuity (first payment received at the end of the first period).
   c. $10,000 in cash or
   $900 per year for perpetuity (first payment received at the beginning of the first period).

Discussion Questions

1-A. The ABC Company has to make a choice between two strategies:
   Strategy 1: Is expected to result in a market price now of $100 per share of common stock and a price of $120 five years from now.
   Strategy 2: Is expected to result in a market price now of $80 and a price of $140 five years from now.
   What would you recommend? Assume that all other things are unaffected by the decision being considered.

1-B. It has been said that few stockholders would think favorably of a project that promised its first cash flow in 100 years, no matter how large this return.
   Required: Comment on this position.

1-C. Each of the following is sometimes listed as a reasonable objective for a firm: (a) maximize profit (accounting income); (b) maximize sales (or share of the market); (c) maximize the value of a share of common stock t time periods from now; (d) ensure continuity of existence; (e) maximize the rate of growth; (f) maximize future dividends.

Required: Discuss each item and the extent of its relevance to the making of investment decisions.

1-D. Explain what is meant by conventional and nonconventional investments. Why is it important to know whether you are discussing a conventional or nonconventional investment?

1-E. Classify each of the following types of business decisions as conventional investments, loan-type investments, or nonconventional outlay–benefits–outlay investments. Explain the reason for your classification in each case.

    a. To enhance the attractiveness of its cars, an automobile manufacturer is considering giving a guarantee to purchasers that certain parts will be replaced if they become defective within a five-year period.

    b. A young student who has just earned a bachelor's degree is trying to decide whether to accept an attractive job offer or to enroll in a two-year graduate program.

    c. The patent on a highly successful product will expire in three years. The company is considering an immediate and drastic price reduction to discourage competitors from entering the market after the patent protection has expired.

    d. To attract a key executive, a company is planning to offer a five-year contract guaranteeing a minimum of $80,000 per year. The company is obligated to pay this salary even if the executive is fired before the end of the five-year period.

    e. A city is considering using a recreation field for an exposition. The exposition will last three years and then the fields will be converted back to their original use.

1-F. Prepare an example or an explanation that indicates why each of the following is an insufficient description of the goals of a profit-seeking organization: (a) maximize profits or earnings per share; (b) maximize the price per share of the common stock now; (c) maximize the price share of the common stock in the future; (d) maximize sales (or percentage of the market).

Answers to Selected Questions

1-1. $751.30   **1-3.** (*a*) $95.24 (*b*) $100 (*c*) $78.35 (*d*) $78.35 (*e*) $8.72
(*f*) $.85 (*g*) $772.17   **1-5.** $12.95 and $12.33   **1-7.** $2,310   **1-9.** $1.700
1-11. (*a*) $18,154,300 (*b*) $7,654,300   **1-13.** $1,000   **1-15.** $60,829
1-17. $10,000

CHAPTER **2**

Illustrating the Measures of Investment Worth

How far the majority of our agricultural and industrial plants lag behind the most progressive model establishments in their own fields! And even the latter, in all probability, fall just as far short of the ideal of truly perfected equipment.

—*Eugene von Böhm-Bawerk, "Capital and Interest," Vol. II, Positive Theory of Capital (South Holland, Ill.: Libertarian Press, 1959; first published in 1888), p. 85.*

In this chapter we shall describe and illustrate the applications of four different measures of investment worth chosen either because they are used in current business practice or because logical arguments in favor of their use have been advanced. These measures by no means exhaust the possible investment measures. Others, in many cases variations of those discussed, have been suggested or are known to be used by one or more firms. After studying this chapter, you should be able to analyze and evaluate for yourself the probable performance of other measures of investment worth you encounter.

We shall first introduce the two primary discounted cash-flow investment evaluation procedures, net present value and internal rate of return. After a brief discussion of these two measures of investment worth, we shall describe a series of four hypothetical investments. The four hypothetical investments have been designed so that for two selected pairs it is possible to decide that one investment is clearly preferable to the other. If a measure of investment worth indicates that one investment is better than a second, when it is obvious that the second investment is actually better, then clearly there is a danger in using that measure. Of the four measures considered, we shall find that two can easily be eliminated as general decision rules because in some situations they give obviously wrong answers and another measure gives the "right" answer. We shall conclude that the net present value method is at least as useful as the other possible methods.

Net Present Value

We offer two proposed measures of investment worth that employ different methods for evaluating the timing of future cash proceeds. As a group these could

28

be called the *discounted cash flow measures*. Before proceeding to analyze them, it is desirable to explain again the concept of the present value of a future sum, because in one way or another this concept is utilized in both these measures.

The present value of $100 payable in two years can be defined as that quantity of money necessary to invest today at compound interest in order to have $100 in two years. The rate of interest at which the money will grow and the frequency at which it will be compounded will determine the present value. We shall assume that funds are compounded annually. The manner in which a rate of interest will be chosen will be discussed later. For the present, let us assume that we are given a 10 percent rate of interest. Let us examine how the present value of a future sum can be computed by using that rate of interest.

Suppose that an investment promises to return a total of $100 at the end of two years. Because $1 invested today at 10 percent compounded annually would grow to $1.21 in two years, we can find the present value at 10 percent of $100 in two years by dividing $100 by $1.21. This gives $82.64. Therefore, a sum of $82.64 that earns 10 percent interest compounded annually will be worth $100 at the end of two years. By repeated applications of this method, we can convert any series of current or future cash payments (or outlays) into an equivalent present value. Because tables are available that give the appropriate conversion factors for various rates of interest, the calculations involved are relatively simple.

The net present value method is a direct application of the present-value concept. Its computation requires the following steps: (1) Choose an appropriate rate of discount; (2) compute the present value of the cash proceeds expected from the investment; (3) compute the present value of the cash outlays required by the investment; (4) add the present value equivalents.

If all the cash outlays required by the investments are made at the beginning of the first period, then, of course, the present value of these outlays is equal to the actual amount expended.

The sum of the present values of the proceeds minus the present values of the outlays is the net present value of the investment. The recommended accept or reject criterion is to accept all independent investments whose net present value is greater than or equal to zero and to reject all investments whose net present value is less than zero.

Because the net present value of an investment will depend upon the rate of discount used, there is not one present-value measure but a schedule of measures, depending on what rate of interest is chosen. This should not be interpreted as meaning that this approach provided purely arbitrary indications of the worth of an investment.

With zero taxes the net present value of an investment may be described as the maximum amount a firm could pay for the opportunity of making the investment without being financially worse off. Because usually no such payment must be made, the expected present value is an unrealized capital gain from the investment, over and above the cost of the investment used in the calculation. The capital gain will be realized if the expected cash proceeds materialize. Assume an investment that costs $10,000 and returns $12,100 a year later. If the rate of discount is 10 percent, a company could make a maximum immediate outlay of $11,000 in the expectation of receiving $12,100 a year later. If it can receive the $12,100 with an actual outlay of only $10,000, the net present value of the investment would be $1,000. The $1,000 represents the difference between the actual outlay of $10,000 and the present value of the proceeds $11,000. The company would have been willing to spend a maximum of $11,000 to receive $12,100 a year later.

The following example illustrates the basic computations for discounting cash flows, that is, adjusting future cash flows for the time value of money, using the net present-value method.

Assume that there is an investment opportunity with the following cash flows:

	Period		
	0	1	2
Cash flow	−$12,337	$10,000	$5,000

We want first to compute the present value of this investment using .10 as the discount rate. Appendix Table A gives the present value of $1 due n periods from now. The present value of

$1 due 0 periods from now discounted at any interest rate is 1.000.
$1 due 1 period from now discounted at .10 is .9091.
$1 due 2 periods from now discounted at .10 is .8264.

The net present value of the investment is the algebraic sum of the three present values of the cash flows:

Period	(1) Cash Flow	(2) Present-Value Factor	(3) Present Value Col. 1 × Col. 2
0	−$12,337	1.0000	−$12,337
1	10,000	.9091	9,091
2	5,000	.8264	4,132
		Net present value	$ 886

The net present value is positive, indicating the investment is acceptable. Any investment with a net present value equal to or greater than zero is acceptable using this single criterion. Since the net present value is $886, the firm could pay an amount of $886 in excess of the cost of $12,337 and still break even economically by undertaking the investment. The net present value calculation is a reliable method for evaluating investments.

Internal Rate of Return Method (IRR)

Many terms are used to describe the same concept. Among these terms are yield, interest rate of return, rate of return, return on investment, present-value return on investment, discounted cash flow, investor's method, time-adjusted rate of return, and marginal efficiency of capital. In this book, IRR and internal rate of return are used interchangeably.

The internal rate of return method utilizes present-value concepts but seeks to avoid the arbitrary choice of a rate of interest in evaluating an investment proposal. The procedure is to find a rate of discount that will make the present value of the cash proceeds expected from an investment equal to the present value of the cash outlays required by the investment. Such a rate of discount can be found by trial and error. For example, with a conventional investment set of cash flows, if we know the cash proceeds expected and the cash outlays required by an investment in each future year, we can start with any rate of discount and find for that rate the present value of the cash proceeds and the present value of the cash outlays. If the present value of the cash proceeds exceeds the present value of the outlays, then some higher rate of discount would make them equal. By a process of trial and error, the approximately correct rate of discount can be determined. This rate of discount is referred to as the internal rate of return of the investment, or its IRR.

The IRR method is commonly used in security markets in evaluating bonds and other debt instruments. The yield to maturity of a bond is the rate of discount that makes the present value of the payments promised to the bondholder equal to the market price of the bond. The yield to maturity on a bond having a coupon rate of 5 percent will be equal to 5 percent only if the current price of the bond is $100. If the current price is greater than $100, the IRR to maturity will be something less than the coupon rate; if the current price is less than $100, the IRR will be greater than the coupon rate.

The internal rate of return may also be described as the rate of growth of an investment. This is more easily seen for an investment with one present outlay and one future benefit. For example, assume that an investment with an outlay of $1,000 today will return $1,331 three years from now.

This is a .10 internal rate of return and it is also a .10 growth rate per year:

Time	Beginning of Period Investment	Growth of Period	Growth Divided by Beginning of Period Investment
0	$1,000	$100	$100/1,000 = .10
1	1,100	110	110/1,100 = .10
2	1,210	121	121/1,210 = .10
3	1,331	—	

The internal rate of return of a conventional instrument has an interesting interpretation that may be referred to at this point. It represents the highest rate of interest an investor could afford to pay, without losing money, if all the funds to finance the investment were borrowed and the loan (principal and accrued interest) was repaid by application of the cash proceeds from the investment as they were earned. It should be remembered that all investments being considered in this chapter are conventional investments, consisting of periods of outlays followed by periods of proceeds. For other patterns of cash flows, the interpretation of rate of return given here may not apply. (See Chapter 3.)

We will illustrate the internal rate of return calculation using the example of the previous section where the investment had a net present value of $886 using .10 as the discount rate.

We want to find the rate of discount that causes the sum of the present values of the cash flows to be equal to zero. Assume our first choice (an arbitrary guess) is .10. In the preceding situation we found that the present value using .10 is a positive $886. We want to change the discount rate so that the present value is zero. Should we increase or decrease the rate of discount for our second estimate? To decrease the present value of the future cash flows, we should increase the rate of discount (thus causing the present value of the future cash flows that are positive to be smaller).

Let us try .20 as the rate of discount:

Period	Cash Flow	Present-Value Factor	Present Value
0	−$12,337	1.0000	−$12,337
1	10,000	.8333	8,333
2	5,000	.6944	3,472
		Net present value	−$ 532

The net present value is negative, indicating that the .20 rate of discount is too large. We shall try a value between .05 and .20 for our next estimate. Assume that we try .16:

Period	Cash Flow	Present-Value Factor	Present Value
0	−$12,337	1.0000	−$12,337
1	10,000	.8621	8,621
2	5,000	.7432	3,716
		Net present value	0

The net present value is zero using .16 as the rate of discount, which by definition means that .16 is the internal rate of return of the investment.

Present Value Profile

The present value profile is one of the more useful devices for summarizing the profitability characteristics of an investment. On the horizontal axis we measure

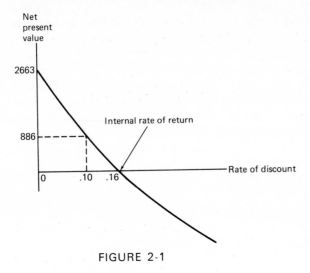

FIGURE 2-1

different discount rates and on the vertical axis the net present value of the investment. The net present value of the investment is plotted for all discount rates from zero to some reasonably large rate. The plot of present values will cross the horizontal axis (have zero present value) at the rate of discount that is called the internal rate of return of the investment.

Figure 2-1 shows the net present value profile for the investment discussed in the previous two sections. If we add the cash flows, assuming a zero rate of discount, we obtain

$$-12{,}337 + 10{,}000 + 5{,}000 = 2{,}663.$$

The $2,663 is the intersection of the graph with the Y axis. We know the graph has a height of $886 at a .10 rate of discount and crosses the X axis at .16, since .16 is the internal rate of return of the investment. For interest rates greater than .16 the net present value is negative.

Note that for a conventional investment (minus cash flows followed by positive cash flows) the present-value profile slopes downward to the right.

We shall now consider four different investment opportunities and will apply four different investment criteria to these investments.

Four Investments

In Table 2-1 a series of four hypothetical investments are described in terms of the initial cost of each and the net cash proceeds expected during each year of earning life. The salvage value or terminal value of each is assumed to be zero. We shall illustrate the ranking that may be given to these investments by each measure of investment worth under consideration.

Some comments on the interpretation of these hypothetical investments are in order. In the first place, nothing has been said about the risk characteristics of the various investments. An evaluation of the risk or uncertainty associated with an investment is a crucial part of the investment decision process. The concepts of risk or uncertainty are complex, however, and need to be clarified before they can be discussed intelligently. It has seemed advisable to take these problems up separately later in the book, and for present purposes the reader may assume that the hypothetical investments described in Table 2-1 are completely riskless; thus there is no basis of choice between them on risk grounds. We could also assume that the figures presented are mean values, and it is appropriate to use mean values in computing the worth of an investment.

TABLE 2-1. *Cash Flows of Hypothetical Investments*

Investment	Initial Cost	Net Cash Proceeds per Year	
		Year 1	Year 2
A	$10,000	$10,000	
B	10,000	10,000	$1,100
C	10,000	3,762	7,762
D	10,000	5,762	5,762

Second, the question of income taxes needs clarification. It is commonly recognized that investment proposals should be evaluated on an after-tax basis. The discussion of income tax adjustments is deferred to Chapter 6, however. In the present instance, the explicit introduction of income taxes would complicate the task of describing the various hypothetical investments and of illustrating the rankings that would result from the use of each of the various measures. Moreover, an explicit consideration of income taxes would not change, in any of their essentials, the conclusions we reach. For this reason we shall assume in the present chapter that corporate income taxes have already been taken into consideration and that the net cash proceeds used in the computations are proceeds after deducting the income tax of the period.

The outlays are made at the beginning of the first year, and proceeds are earned at the end of each year. Each investment is of a conventional nature—that is, there are one or more periods of outlays followed by one or more periods of positive cash proceeds. If there were nonconventional investments, for example, more than one period of outlays interspersed with periods of positive cash flows, the internal rate of return method would require additional refinements, because with nonconventional cash flows a higher internal rate of return may indicate a less desirable investment opportunity.

Ranking by Inspection

It is possible in certain limited cases to determine by inspection which of two or more investments is more desirable. The two situations in which this is true are as follows:

1. Two investments have identical cash flows each year through the final year of the short-lived investment, but one continues to earn cash proceeds in subsequent years. The investment with the longer life would be more desirable. Thus investment B is better than investment A, because all factors are equal except that B continues to earn proceeds after A has been retired.
2. Two investments have the same initial outlay and the same earning life and earn the same total proceeds. If at the end of every year (during their earning life) the total net proceeds of one investment are at least as great as, and for at least one year are greater than, the total for the other investment, then the first investment will always be more profitable. Thus investment D is more desirable than investment C, because D earns $2,000 more in year one than investment C does; investment C does not earn this $2,000 until year two. The earning of $2,000 more in the earlier year leads to the conclusion that investment D is more desirable than investment C.

Payback Period

The payback period is one of the simplest and apparently one of the most frequently used methods of measuring the economic value of an investment. The payback period is defined as the length of time required for the stream of cash proceeds produced by an investment to equal the original cash outlay required by the investment. If an investment is expected to produce a stream of cash proceeds that is constant from year to year, the payback period can be determined by dividing the total original cash outlay by the amount of the annual cash proceeds expected. Thus if an investment required an original outlay of $300 and was expected to produce a stream of cash proceeds of $100 a year for five years, the payback period would be 300 divided by 100, or three years. If the stream of expected proceeds is not constant from year to year, the payback period must be determined by adding up the proceeds expected in successive years until the total is equal to the original outlay.

Ordinarily, the administrator would set some maximum payback period and reject all investment proposals for which the payback period is greater than this maximum. Investigators have reported that maximum payback periods of two, three, four, or five years are frequently used by industrial concerns. The relatively short periods mentioned suggest that different maximum payback periods are required for different types of investments because some kinds of investments (construction, for example) can seldom be expected to have a payback period as short as five years.

Assume that the payback period is also used to rank investment alternatives with those having the shortest payback periods being given the highest ranking. The investments described in Table 2-1 are ranked by this method in Table 2-2.

TABLE 2-2.   *Payback Period*

Investment	Payback Period (Years)	Ranking
A	1	1
B	1	1
C	1.8	4
D	1.7	3

Let us check the reasonableness of the ranking given the investments by the cash payback approach. Investments A and B are both ranked as 1, because they both have shorter payback periods than any of the other investments, namely one year. But investment A earns total proceeds of $10,000, and this amount merely equals the cost of the investment. Investment B, which has the same rank as A, will not only earn $10,000 in the first year but also $1,000 in the next year. Obviously, investment B is superior to A. Any ranking procedure, such as the payback period, that fails to disclose this fact is deficient.

Consider investments C and D modified so as to cost $11,524. Both would be given identical rankings because both would return their original outlay by the end of the second year. The two investments are in fact identical, with the single exception that, out of identical total returns, more proceeds are received in the first year and less in the second year from investment D than is the case with C. To the extent that earnings can be increased by having $2,000 available for reinvestment one year earlier, D is superior to investment C; but both would be given the same ranking by the payback period measure.

Thus the cash payback period measure has two weaknesses: (1) It fails to give any consideration to cash proceeds earned after the payback date; (2) it fails to take into account the differences in the timing of proceeds earned prior to the payback date. These weaknesses disqualify the cash payback measures as a general method of ranking investments.

Return on Investment

The methods described in this section are commonly referred to as "rate of return analysis" or "return on investment analysis." Terminology is a problem, because both these terms are also used to describe other procedures. We will consistently use "internal rate of return" only when we refer to a discounted cash flow calculation and "return on investment" to refer to an income divided by investment calculation.

In attempting to get a measure of efficiency, analysts frequently use the ratio of the firm's income to the book value of its assets. Some companies also use this measure as a means of choosing among various proposed internal investments. When this measure is used, the average income is computed after depreciation. If the denominator in the ratio is the book value of the investment, the value of both the numerator and the denominator will depend on the depreciation method used. An alternative procedure is to divide the average income by the cost of the investment (the accrued depreciation is not subtracted).

The ratio of income to book value is a common and useful measure of performance, but it is less useful as a device for ranking investments. Table 2-3 shows that the same rankings are given to investments C and D, although D is preferable to C. This procedure fails to rank these investments correctly, because it does not take into consideration the timing of the proceeds.

TABLE 2-3. *Average Income on Book Value*

Invest-ment	Average Cash Flows	Average Depre-ciation*	Average Income (Cash Flow Less Depreciation)	Average Book Value†	Income on Book Value (%)	Ranking
A	$10,000	$10,000	$ 0	$5,000	0	4
B	5,550	5,000	550	5,000	11	3
C	5,762	5,000	762	5,000	15	1
D	5,762	5,000	762	5,000	15	1

* Assuming straight line depreciation.
† Investment divided by 2.

An alternative procedure (see Table 2-4) is to divide income by the cost of the investment (accumulated depreciation not being subtracted). For purposes of measuring performance and computing return on investment, the use of undepreciated cost will give lower measures than the use of book value. Both measures illustrated fail to take into consideration the timing of the cash proceeds. It is this failing that leads to incorrect rankings from the use of either of the two methods.

TABLE 2-4. *Average Income on Cost*

Investment	Cost	Average Income	Average Income on Cost (%)	Ranking
A	$10,000	$ 0	0	4
B	10,000	550	5.5	3
C	10,000	762	7.6	1
D	10,000	762	7.6	1

Use of Discounted Cash Flow Methods

We have considered payback and return on investment as methods for measuring the value of an investment. In the case of each proposed measure, we have been able to find at least one pair of investments in which it was obvious that one of the pair was more desirable; yet the proposed measure of investment worth gave either the same ranking to both investments or a higher ranking to the less desirable of the pair. On the basis of such evidence we have been able to reject both of the proposed measures of investment worth because of their undesirable characteristics.

One flaw that eliminated from consideration the above two measures has been the inability of the measure to take proper account of the timing of cash proceeds from the investments. The payback period represents one extreme in this regard, because all the proceeds received before the payback period are counted and treated as equals, and all the proceeds received after the payback period are ignored completely. With the return on investment, the proceeds were related by simple averaging techniques to such things as the original cost of the investment or its book value. Neither of these methods succeeded in bringing the timing of cash proceeds into the analysis.

We have seen that the measures of investment worth previously considered may give obviously incorrect results because they fail either to consider the entire life of the investment or to give adequate attention to the timing of future cash proceeds. The discounted cash flow concept provides a method of taking into account the timing of cash proceeds and outlays over the entire life of the investment. We now return to the two measures of investment worth already introduced that incorporate present-value concepts.

Internal Rate of Return

In Table 2-5 we show the internal rate of return for each of the investments listed in Table 2-1 and the ranking of investments that would result if this method were used.

TABLE 2-5. *Internal Rate of Return (IRR) of the Investments*

Investment	IRR (%)	Ranking
A	0	4
B	10	1
C	9*	3
D	10	1

* Approximate measure.

It is instructive to examine the rankings given by this method applicable to each of the pairs of investments in this list for which we were earlier able to determine the more desirable investment of each pair.

We previously compared two pairs of investments and decided that investment B was preferable to A and D to C. In each case, if preference had been determined by using the internal rate of return of an investment method, the pairs would be given the correct ranking. This is the first method that we have used which gives the correct rankings of both pairs.

A, 0%   C, 9%
B, 10%   D, 10%

Net Present Value

It is instructive to note the rankings that will be given to the hypothetical investments of Table 2-1 by the present-value method, using two sample rates of discount. In Table 2-6 we present the results of using the present-value method and a 6 percent rate of discount.

In discussing the measures of investment worth that do not use the discounted cash-flow method, we pointed out that the relative ranking of certain pairs of these four investments was obvious. That is, it is obvious from examining the cash flows that investment B is preferable to A, and D is preferable to C. The reader may note that in each case the present-value method using a 6 percent rate of discount ranks these investment pairs in the correct relative order.

TABLE 2-6. *Present Values of the Investments Rate of Discount: 6 percent*

Investment	Present Value of Cash Flows	Present Value of Outlay	Net Present Value	Ranking
A	$ 9,430	$10,000	−$570	4
B	10,413	10,000	+ 413	3
C	10,457	10,000	+ 457	2
D	10,564	10,000	+ 564	1

In Table 2-7 the same investments are ranked by the present-value method, using a 30 percent rate of discount instead of 6 percent. The relative ranking of investments C and D does not change with the change in the rate of discount. Investment C, which was ranked second when a 6 percent rate of discount was used, is ranked fourth when the 30 percent discount rate is used. The ranking of investment D is changed from first to second by the change in the rate of discount. The higher rate of discount results in the proceeds of the later years

TABLE 2-7.   *Present Values of the Investments Rate of Discount: 30 percent*

Investment	Present Value of Cash Flows	Present Value of Outlay	Net Present Value	Ranking
A	$7,692	$10,000	−$2,308	3
B	8,343	10,000	− 1,657	1
C	7,487	10,000	− 2,513	4
D	7,842	10,000	− 2,158	2˙

being worth less relative to the proceeds of the early years; thus the ranking of B goes from 3 to 1, but D is still ranked ahead of C.

Even with a 30 percent rate of interest, the present-value method maintains the correct ordering of each of the two pairs of investments for which an obvious preference can be determined. Thus we still find investment B preferred to A, and D preferred to C. This result is not an accident resulting from the specific choice of hypothetical investments and discount rates used in our examples. Whenever it is possible to determine obvious preferences between pairs of investments by the methods described earlier, the present-value method will rank these investments in the correct order, no matter what rate of discount is used to compute the present value, as long as the same rate of discount is used to determine the present value of both the investments. Thus we are justified in concluding that, in the sense that it will not make certain kinds of obvious errors, the present-value method even when used with the "wrong" rate of discount will give better results than measures that do not incorporate the discounted cash flow method.

Summary of Rankings

The rankings given by each measure of investment worth for each of the hypothetical investments described in Table 2-1 are summarized in Table 2-8.

TABLE 2-8.   *Summary of Rankings*

Measure of Investment Worth	Investment			
	A	B	C	D
Payback period	1*	1*	4	3
Average income on book value or cost	4	3	1*	1*
Internal rate of return (IRR)	4	1*	3	1*
Net present value: at 6%	4	3	2	1
at 30%	3	1	4	2

* Indicates a tie between two investments.

The most striking conclusion to be drawn from Table 2-8 is the tendency for each measure of investment worth to give a different ranking to the identical set of investments. This emphasizes the need to give careful consideration to the choice of measures used to evaluate proposed investments. All four measures cannot be equally valid. By considering specific pairs of investments, we have shown that the measures of investment worth that do not involve the use of discounted cash flow method can give rankings of investments that are obviously incorrect. For this reason these measures will be excluded from further consideration.

The rankings given the investments by the present-value measures are not identical with that given by the internal rate of return of an investment measure. Neither of these rankings can be eliminated as being obviously incorrect; yet, because they are different, they could lead to contradictory conclusions in certain situations. In Chapter 3 we shall continue our investigation in an attempt to determine whether the present value or the internal rate of return measure is more useful to a decision maker.

Limitation of Investment Rankings

In this chapter we discussed the ranking of four investments and showed that given a carefully defined set of investments we can make definite statements about the relative desirability of two or more investments. If the investments are not restricted to this set, we would find our ability to rank investments to be very limited.

For the remainder of this book we shall not be concerned with the "ranking" of investments; instead, we shall be attempting to

1. Make accept or reject decisions for investments that are independent (that is, if we undertake one investment, the cash flows of undertaking the other investments are not affected).
2. Choose the best of a set of mutually exclusive investments (that is, if we undertake one, either we would not want to undertake the other or we would not be able to because of the characteristics of the investments).

Although the objectives we are setting are somewhat more modest than the objective of ranking investments, we shall still encounter difficulties. There is nothing in our recommendations, however, that will preclude a manager from applying qualitative criteria to the investments being considered to obtain a ranking. The ranking that is obtained is likely to be difficult to defend. Fortunately, for a wide range of decision situations a manager can make decisions without a ranking of investments. We shall return to ranking procedures later in the book.

Discounted Payback

Instead of computing the length of time required to recover the original investment, some analysts compute the length of time required until the present value

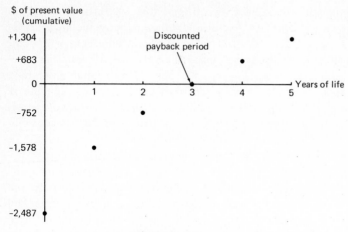

FIGURE 2-2

turns from being negative to positive. This computation gives a break-even life of the asset or a discounted payback period. If the life of the asset exceeds this break-even life, the asset will have a positive present value.

Figure 2-2 shows the cumulative present values (with a discount rate of 10 percent) for an investment with the discounted payback period indicated, and Table 2-9 shows the calculations, assuming a 10 percent rate of discount.

TABLE 2-9. *Present Values for Different Lives*

	Net Present Value	Cash Flows and Present Values Period:					
Period i	for Life of i	0	1	2	3	4	5
		−$2,487	$1,000	$1,000	$1,000	$1,000	$1,000
0	−$2,487	−2,487					
1	− 1,578	−2,487	909				
2	− 752	−2,487	909	826			
3	0	−2,487	909	826	752		
4	683	−2,487	909	826	752	683	
5	1,304	−2,487	909	826	752	683	621

Relationship Between Payback Period and Internal Rate of Return

If an investment is expected to earn equal proceeds each year of its life and if the life of the investment is known, it is possible to construct a theoretically correct payback period that will lead to the same accept or reject decisions as the present-value rule. Because of the limiting assumptions, especially equal annual proceeds, this formula has limited usefulness in making decisions, but it does illustrate the weakness of certain payback conventions. In particular, it shows that the longest acceptable payback period depends on the life of the investment and the time value of money.

The payback period is defined as the period of time required to recover the initial investment, or as the cost of the investment divided by the proceeds per period. In equation form, with equal proceeds per period,

$$\text{Payback period} = \frac{\text{Cost of investment}}{\text{Proceeds per period}}.$$

The present-value rule is that an investment should be accepted if the sum of the present values of the proceeds from the investment is greater than the cost of the investment. The symbol $B(n, r)$ stands for the present value of an annuity of $1 per period for n periods (the life of the investment) discounted at a rate of r per period. We assume that r is known and is the appropriate discount rate for the firm. With equal annual proceeds we would accept the investment, using the present-value rule, if the following inequality is satisfied:

(Proceeds per period) $\times$ $B(n, r) \geq$ Cost of investment.

If the proceeds per period are positive, we can divide both sides of the preceding inequality by the proceeds per period without changing the sense of the inequality sign. When we do this, the right-hand side becomes cost of investment divided by proceeds per period, which is the payback period. This leads to the following formulation of the present-value rule:

$B(n, r) \geq$ Payback period   or   Payback period $\leq B(n, r)$.

This shows that an investment with positive equal annual proceeds over its n year life will have a positive NPV if and only if its payback period is less than $B(n, r)$. As the life of the investment increases, so does the maximum acceptable payback period. As the life tends to infinity, the maximum acceptable payback period approaches an upper limit of $1/r$.

Sometimes we may not be sure what life we can expect for an investment. In this case the preceding formula can also be used to find the minimum acceptable life for an investment whose payback period is known. To do this we find the smallest value of n for which $B(n, r)$ is greater than the investment's payback period. The values of $B(n, r)$ are listed in Appendix Table B.

Example

The ABC Company requires a two-year payback period or less before accepting equipment. A piece of equipment is being considered that costs $5,000 and is expected to earn cash proceeds per year of $1,000 for a life of ten years. The relevant discount rate is 10 percent per year. Should the equipment be purchased?

The equipment has a payback period of five years; thus it seems to be undesirable in view of the company's two-year payback criterion. Because it has a life of ten years, however, it could have a payback period up to six years $B(10, .10) = 6.1446$) and would still be acceptable.

Now assume that the equipment has a perpetual life. The reciprocal of the payback period of five years is .2. This is also the internal rate of return of the investment:

$$\text{Internal rate of return} = \frac{\text{Income}}{\text{Investment}} = \frac{1,000}{5,000} = .2.$$

If, instead of a perpetual life, we had assumed a very long life, the reciprocal of the payback period would have approximated the IRR of the investment.

The Roll Back Method

Using a naïve hand calculator (one where there is no present-value button) it is sometimes convenient to use a roll back method of calculation to compute the present value of an investment. One advantage of this procedure is that the present values at different moments in time are obtained. Consider the following investments:

Time	Cash Flow
0	−7,000
1	5,000
2	2,300
3	1,100

Assume the discount rate is .10.

The first step is to place the cash flow of period three ($1,100) in the calculator and divide by 1.10 to obtain $1,000 the value at time 2. Add $2,300 and again divide by 1.10 to obtain $3,000 the value at time 1. Add $5,000 and divide by 1.10 to obtain $7,273 the value of time 0. Subtract $7,000 to obtain the net present value of $273. The common divisor, 1.10, can be stored in the calculator's memory (if it has one) and recalled as needed. This eliminates keystrokes and increases accuracy.

Where We Are Going

There are many different ways of evaluating investments. In some situations several of the methods will give identical decisions. In this book we will consistently recommend the net present-value method as the primary means of evaluating investments.

The net present-value method ensures that future cash flows are brought back to a common moment in time called *time zero*. For each future cash flow a present value equivalent is found. These present-value equivalents are summed to obtain a net present value. If the net present value is positive the investment is acceptable.

The transformation of future flows back to the present is accomplished using the mathematical relationship $(1 + i)^{-t}$ which we will call the present-value factor for i rate of interest and t time periods.

In cases of uncertainty, additional complexities must be considered, but the basic framework of analysis will remain the net present-value method.

Appendix

Net Present Value and Internal Rate of Return

The basic mathematical relationships for the present value and the internal rate of return of an investment follow.

Let

X_t = cash flow of period t;
i = time value of money of the firm;
r = internal rate of return of the investment;
V = net present value of the investment;
n = life of the investment.

Then the net present value of an investment is

$$V = \sum_{t=0}^{n} X_t(1 + i)^{-t}.$$

The internal rate of return of an investment is found by solving the following equation for r:

$$\sum_{t=0}^{n} X_t(1 + r)^{-t} = 0,$$

or, equivalently,

$$\sum_{t=1}^{n} X_t(1 + r)^{-t} = -X_0.$$

X_0 is the outlay and is negative. The equation is solved by a trial-and-error procedure, as illustrated in the section on the Internal Rate of Return Method in this chapter.

Questions and Problems

2-1. Compute the net present value for each of the following cash flows. Assume a cost of money of 10 percent.

Investment	Period					
	0	1	2	3	4	5
A	($1,000)	$100	$100	$100	$100	$1,100
B	(1,000)	264	264	264	264	264
C	(1,000)					1,611

2-2. Compute the internal rate of return for each of the cash flows in problem 2-1.

2-3. Compute the payback for each of the cash flows in problem 2-1. Assume the maximum acceptable payback period is four years. Which (if any) of the cash flows would be accepted as a desirable investment?

2-4. Assume a cost of money of 5 percent. Compute the net present value of the cash flows of problem 2-1.

2-5. Assume a cost of money of 15 percent. Compute the net present value of the cash flows of problem 2-1. Compare with the results obtained from problems 2-1 and 2-4.

2-6. The Arrow Company is considering the purchase of equipment that will return cash proceeds as follows:

End of Period	
1	$5,000
2	3,000
3	2,000
4	1,000
5	500

Assume a cost of money of 10 percent. What is the maximum amount the company could pay for the machine and still be financially no worse off than if it did not buy the machine?

2-7. Mr. Smith wants to save enough each year for twenty years so that he can consume $100,000 per year for perpetuity starting at time 21. How much should he save if the first payment is due one year from today? The appropriate interest rate is .10.

2-8. Compute the net present value (use a cost of money of .15) and the internal rate of return for each of the following investments:

Investment	Period 0	Period 1	Period 2
A	($1,000)		$1,322
B	(1,000)	$ 615	615
C	(1,000)	1,150	

2-9. Recompute the present values using (a) a cost of money of .20, (b) a cost of money of .05 for each of the investments of problems 2-8.

2-10. Prepare a schedule showing that, with a rate of growth of .15 per year, $1,000 will grow to $1,322 in two years.

2-11. Determine the internal rate of return of the following investment:

Period	Cash Flow
0	($ 9,120)
1	1,000
2	5,000
3	10,000

2-12. How much could you pay in excess of the indicated cost for the investment of problem 2-11 if you had a cost of money of .10?

2-13. Assume that you can only invest in one of the three investments of problem 2-8.

   Required: (a) Using the internal rates of return of the three investments, which is preferred? (b) Using the present-value method and a cost of money of .05, which is preferred?

2-14. A company uses a 10 percent discount rate. Assume equal annual cash proceeds. What should be the maximum acceptable payback period for equipment whose life is five years? What are the maximum acceptable paybacks for lives of ten, twenty, and forty years, and infinite life?

2-15. Assume that the discount rate is 5 percent and answer problem 2-14.

2-16. Assume that the discount rate is 6 percent. A new machine that costs $7,000 has equal annual cash proceeds and a payback period of 7.0 years. What is the minimum number of full years of life it must have to be acceptable?

2-17. Compute the internal rate of return of the following investments:

Investment	Period 0	1	2	3
A	−$10,000	$4,747	$4,747	$ 4,747
B	− 10,000			17,280

Compare the two investments. Which do you prefer? Are you making any assumption about the reinvestment of the cash flows?

2-18. Determine the internal rate of return of the following investment:

Period	Cash Flow
0	-$15,094
1	10,000
2	10,000
3	1,000

2-19. Draw the present-value profile for the investment of problem 2-18. Using a hand calculator and the roll back method described in the chapter, compute the net present value using a discount rate of .10.

2-20. Assume a discount rate of 3 percent and a machine that generates a constant annual amount of savings. What is the maximum acceptable payback period if the life of the machine is five years? What if the life of the machine is ten years? Fifteen years? Twenty years?

2-21. Assume interest rates of 6 percent and 12 percent and answer problem 2-20.

2-22. Assume a discount rate of 3 percent and a machine that generates a constant annual amount of savings. If the machine has a payback period of five years, what is the minimum acceptable life? What are the minimum acceptable lives for machines with paybacks of eight, twelve, and twenty years?

2-23. Assume a discount rate of 12 percent and answer problem 2-22.

2-24. Find the net present value at a 5 percent discount rate for each of the following three investments:

	Period		
Investment	0	1	2
A	-$18,594	$10,000	$10,000
B	- 18,140	0	20,000
C	- 19,048	20,000	0

2-25. Assume a discount rate of 5 percent from time 0 to time 1 and of 7 percent from time 1 to time 2. Find the net present value of each of the three investments in problem 2-24.

2-26. Assume a discount rate of 5 percent from time 0 to time 1 and of 3 percent from time 1 to time 2. Find the net present value of each of the three investments in problem 2-24.

2-27. An investment costing $31,699 will earn cash flows of $10,000 a year for eight years. The rate of discount is 10 percent. What is the discounted payback period?

2-28. An investment costs $100,000 and is expected to generate cash flows of $20,000 per year for perpetuity.

a. What is the payback period?

b. What is the internal rate of return of the investment?

c. How are the answers to parts a and b linked to each other?

2-29. An investment costs $10,000 and will generate cash flows of $12,900 at time 1.4 years. The firm uses a discount rate of .124.

Compute the net present value (use a hand calculator which has y^x where y equals 1.124 and x equals 1.4).

2-30. Assume two investments have the following sets of cash flows. Based on the analysis it is decided that A is more desirable. Evaluate the conclusion.

	0	1	2
A	−19,008	10,000	12,000
B	−19,008	12,000	10,000

	A		B	
	1	2	1	2
Revenue	10,000	12,000	12,000	10,000
SL Depec.	9,504	9,504	9,504	9,504
Income	496	2,496	2,496	496
Ave. Inv.	14,256	4,752	14,256	4,752
ROI	.03	.50	.17	.11
Average ROI	.26		.14	

Discussion Questions

2-A. Can the internal rate of return method be used for accept or reject decisions on an investment when the interest rate is not the same in all future time periods?

2-B. The Ithaca Machine Company has a maximum two-year payback period for equipment and a nine-year requirement for buildings. The cost of money for the firm is considered to be 10 percent. Equipment commonly lasts between ten and twenty years. Buildings are expected to last in excess of twenty years. Do you consider the company's criteria to be useful? Explain.

2-C. The Super Company used a ROFE (return on funds employed) method of evaluating investments. The income of each period is divided by the average assets used during the period. This is done for each period and then an average ROFE is computed of all the ROFE's.

The controller of the Super Company defends the procedure since it is consistent with the performance evaluation procedures that are used after the investment is acquired.

The company is currently evaluating two investments (A and B).

	0	1	2
A	−20,000	+11,000	+12,100
B	−20,000	+12,100	+11,000

	A		B	
	Year 1	Year 2	Year 1	Year 2
Revenue	11,000	12,100	12,100	11,000
Depreciation	10,000	10,000	10,000	10,000
Income	1,000	2,100	2,100	1,000
Average				
Investment	15,000	5,000	15,000	5,000
ROFE	.067	.420	.140	.200
Average ROFE		.24		.17

The firm requires a .20 return for an investment to be acceptable.
The firm acquired investment A.
Required:
a. Which investment is more desirable?
b. Is either investment acceptable?

Answers to Selected Questions

2-1. NPV = $0   **2-3.** A, 4.5 years   B, 3.8 years   C, 4.6 years

2-5. NPV = $\dfrac{A}{-168}$ $\dfrac{B}{-115}$ $\dfrac{C}{-199}$ **2-7.** $17,454

2-9.

	NPV .05	NPV .20
A	199	−82
B	144	−60
C	95	−42

2-11. .25   **2-13. (a)** Indifferent   **(b)** A has highest present value

2-15. $n = 5$, 4.3 years $n = 10$, 7.7 years $n = 20$, 12.5 years $n = 40$, 17.16 years
$n = \infty$, 20 years   **2-17.** Both have an internal rate of return of .20.
2-20. and **2-21.**

Life of Machine	Discount Rate		
	3%	6%	12%
5	4.6	4.2	3.6
10	8.5	7.4	5.7
15	11.9	9.7	6.8
20	14.9	11.5	7.5

2-25. A, NPV $= -169$ B, NPV $= -338$ C, NPV $= 0$
2-27. The PV is $31,699 for four years. The discounted payback period is four years.

CHAPTER 3

Net Present Value Versus Internal Rate of Return

Long-range investing under rapidly changing conditions, especially under conditions that change or may change at any moment under the impact of new commodities and technologies, is like shooting at a target that is not only indistinct but moving and moving jerkily at that.

—*J. A. Schumpeter, Capitalism, Socialism, and Democracy (New York: Harper & Row, Inc., 1947), p. 88.*

In the preceding chapter we saw that neither of the discounted cash flow procedures for evaluating an investment are obviously incorrect. In many situations the internal rate of return procedure will lead to the same decision as the net present-value procedure. There are also situations where the internal rate of return may lead to different decisions from those obtained by using the present-value procedure. When the two methods lead to different decisions, the present-value method tends to give better decisions.

It is possible to use the internal rate of return method in such a way that it gives the same results as the present-value method. For this to occur it is necessary that the rate of discount at which it is appropriate to discount future cash proceeds be the same for all future years. If the appropriate rate of interest varies from year to year, even if that pattern of variation is known in advance, then the two procedures may not give identical answers.

If they are used correctly, either one of the two methods is acceptable. *If*, however, is the biggest two-letter word in the English language. It is easy to use the present-value method correctly. It is much more difficult to use the internal rate of return method correctly—more difficult to describe what comparisons are appropriate for a given decision, and more difficult to carry out the required calculations. For both these reasons this book will consistently recommend the use of the present-value method. In this chapter we shall explain why we believe the internal rate of return method is inferior, and in the process we shall show how that method could be used correctly to arrive at the same answers as are obtained by the present-value method.

Accept or Reject Decisions

Frequently, the investment decision to be made is whether or not to accept or reject a project where the cash flows of the project do not affect the cash flows of other projects. We speak of this type of investment as being an independent investment. With the internal rate of return procedure the usual recommendation with conventional cash flows is to accept an independent investment if its IRR is greater than some minimum acceptable rate of discount. If the cash flow corresponding to the investment consists of one or more periods of cash outlays followed only by periods of cash proceeds, this method will give the same accept or reject decisions as the present-value method, using the same discount rate. Because most independent investments have cash-flow patterns that meet the specifications described, it is fair to say that in practice the internal rate of return and present-value methods would give the same recommendations for independent investments.

Consider an investment with an immediate outlay of $100 and benefits of $115 one year from now. Its present-value profile is shown in Figure 3-1. With discount rates less than 15 percent the present value is positive; with rates larger than 15 percent the present value is negative. At 15 percent the present value is zero; the investment has an internal rate of return of 15 percent.

Figure 3-1 shows a situation where an investment has an internal rate of return of 15 percent. If the required rate is less than 15 percent the investment is acceptable using the IRR method, and the figure shows that the net present value will be positive if the discount rate is less than 15 percent. With a conventional investment the present-value method and the IRR method will lead to consistent accept and reject decisions.

It is sometimes suggested that one of the advantages of the internal rate of return procedure is that it may be utilized without deciding on a minimum acceptable discount rate, whereas the present-value method requires that this rate be incorporated into the computations. The weakness of this position becomes

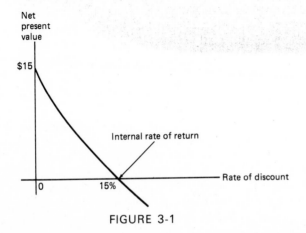

FIGURE 3-1

evident when we consider the accept or reject type of investment decision. To reach a decision, the internal rate of return of an investment must be compared with the minimum acceptable discount rate. The discount rate is no less important to IRR than to present value, although it enters at an earlier stage in the computations of the present-value method.

Mutually Exclusive Investments

If undertaking any one of a set of investments will decrease the profitability of the other investments, the investments are substitutes. An extreme case of substitution exists if undertaking one of the investments completely eliminates the expected proceeds of the other investments. Such investments are said to be *mutually exclusive.*

Frequently, a company will have two or more investments, any one of which would be acceptable, but because the investments are mutually exclusive, only one can be accepted. For example, assume that a company is trying to decide where to build a new plant. It may be that either of two locations would be profitable. But the company will have to decide which one is likely to be the more profitable, because only one new plant is needed. An oil company may need additional transport facilities for its products. Should it build a pipeline or acquire additional tankers and ship by water? Either of these alternatives may result in a net profit to the firm, but the company will wish to choose the one that is more profitable. Suppose that it has decided to build the pipeline. Should a 6- or 10-inch diameter pipeline be installed? Again the problem is to choose the more profitable of these alternatives. In all these situations, the choice is between mutually exclusive investments.

Mutually exclusive investment alternatives are common. The situation frequently occurs in connection with the engineering design of a new installation. In the process of designing such an installation, the engineers are typically faced at a great many points with alternatives that are mutually exclusive. Thus a measure of investment worth that does not lead to correct mutually exclusive choices will be seriously deficient. In this light, the fact that the two discounted cash flow measures of investment worth may give different rankings to the same set of mutually exclusive investment proposals becomes of considerable importance.

Incremental Benefits: The Scale Problem

The internal rate of return method gives less correct recommendations for mutually exclusive investments than those that result from the application of the present-value method because it reflects the average rather than the incremental cash flows. It thereby fails to consider the size of the investment. Let us assume that we must choose one of the following investments for a company whose discount rate is 10 percent: investment A requires an outlay of $10,000 this year and has cash proceeds of $12,000 next year; investment B requires an outlay of $15,000 this year and has cash proceeds of $17,700 next year. The internal rate of return of A is 20 percent and that of B is 18 percent.

TABLE 3-1

Investment	Cash Flows 0	Cash Flows 1	Internal Rate of Return (%)
A	−10,000	12,000	20
B	−15,000	17,700	18
Incremental (B − A)	− 5,000	+ 5,700	14

A quick answer would be that A is more desirable, based on the hypothesis that the higher the internal rate of return, the better the investment. To see why this answer may be wrong, consider that an internal rate of return of 1,000 percent on an investment of a dime for one year is a poor substitute for a rate of 15 percent on $1,000 if only one of the investments can be undertaken, and if the time value factor is less than 15 percent.

When only the IRR of the entire investment is considered, something important is left out—the *size* of the investments. The important difference between investments B and A is that B requires an additional outlay of $5,000 and provides additional cash proceeds of $5,700. Table 3-1 shows the IRR of the incremental investment is 14 percent, which is clearly worthwhile for a company that can obtain additional funds at 10 percent. One can take the $5,000 saved by investing in A and earn $5,500 (a 10 percent return). This is inferior to the $5,700 earned by investing an additional $5,000 in B.

Figure 3-2 shows both investments. It can be seen that investment B is more desirable (has a higher present value) as long as the discount rate is less than 14 percent.

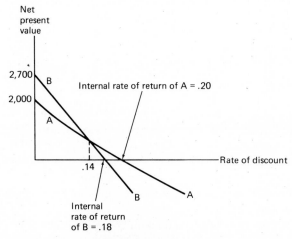

FIGURE 3-2

We can identify the difficulty just described as the "scale" or "size" problem that arises when the internal rate of return method is used to evaluate mutually exclusive investments. Because the IRR is a percentage, the process of computation eliminates size.

Timing

The scale problem is sometimes more difficult to identify than in the preceding example. Assume that there are two mutually exclusive investments having different internal rates of return, but both requiring the same initial outlay. This case seems to be different from the one we have just discussed because there is no incremental investment. Actually, the difference is superficial. Consider investments Y and Z described in Table 3-2. Suppose that they are mutually exclusive

TABLE 3-2

	Cash Flows for Period			Internal Rate of Return (%)	Net Present Value at 5%
Investment	0	1	2		
Y	−$100.00	$ 20.00	$120.00	20	$27.89
Z	− 100.00	100.00	31.25	25	23.58

investments for a company whose cost of money was 5 percent. The internal rate of return of Y is 20 percent, whereas that of Z is 25 percent. If we take the present value of each investment at 5 percent, however, we find that the ranking is in the opposite order. The present value of Z is less than the present value of Y. Neither investment can be said to be obviously superior to the other, and both require the same cash outlays in the first year.

Suppose that we attempt to make an incremental comparison, as follows:

Period 0	0	Cash flows identical
Period 1	−$80.00	Cash flow of Y less than of Z
Period 2	$88.75	Cash flow of Y exceeds that of Z

We see that the cash flow of Y is $80 less in year 1, and $88.75 more than Z in year 2. As before, we can compute the IRR on the incremental cash flow. An outlay of $80 that returns $88.75 one year later has an IRR of 10.9 percent. An investment such as this would be desirable for a company whose cost of money is only 5 percent. Again we are really dealing with a problem of the scale of the investment, but in this case the opportunity for the additional investment occurs one year later.

The same result can be reached by a somewhat different route if we ask how much cash the company would have on hand at the end of the second year if it accepted investment Y or if it accepted investment Z. Both investments give some

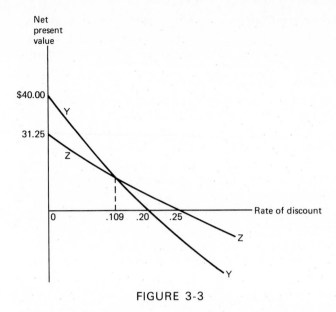

FIGURE 3-3

cash proceeds at the end of the first year. The value of the investment at the end of the second year will depend on what is done with cash proceeds of the first year. Assume that the cash proceeds of the first year could be reinvested to yield 5 percent. Then investment Y would result in a total cash accumulation by the end of the year of $141 (105 percent of $20 plus $120). Investment Z would result in a cash accumulation of only $136.25 (105 percent of $100 plus $31.25).

Figure 3-3 shows that investment Y is to be preferred as long as the appropriate discount rate is less than .109. If the rate is in excess of .109 then Z is to be preferred.

One disadvantage associated with the use of the internal rate of return method is the necessity of computing the IRR on the incremental cash proceeds in order to determine which of a pair of mutually exclusive investments is preferable. If there are more than two mutually exclusive investments, we shall have to conduct an elimination tournament among the mutually exclusive investments. Taking any pair, we compute the internal rate of return on the incremental cash flow and attempt to decide which of the two investments is preferable. The winner of this round would then be compared in the same manner with one of the remaining investments until the grand-champion investment were discovered. If there were 151 investments being considered, there would have to be 150 computations, because 150 investments would have to be eliminated.

Reinvestment Assumption

It is frequently claimed that the present-value method assumes reinvestment at the rate of discount, and that the internal rate of return method assumes reinvestment at the internal rate of return. (These are equivalent in the sense that the rate of discount in both cases is the assumed reinvestment rate.) At best this assumption is inexact. In the first place the internal rate of return of an investment can be computed without any assumption about the utilization of the funds generated by the investment. For example, an investment generating cash flows which are consumed will have the same internal rate of return as an investment whose cash flows are invested, if the cash flows of the two investments are identical.

In general the cash flows from an investment may be reinvested in some productive investment, or consumed, or saved (which usually means acquiring a liability issued by another economic unit), or used to reduce outstanding liabilities. It is hoped that they will be allocated to the most valuable of these alternatives. Similarly, the cash inflows required to make the investment may be obtained by foregoing some other investment, by reducing consumption or by increasing outstanding liabilities. It is hoped that the cash will be obtained from the least costly of these alternatives. It is not even necessary to know the cost of the cash used or the value of the cash produced by an investment to calculate its internal rate of return. But these costs and values are necessary to decide if an investment is acceptable.

If we are comparing two mutually exclusive investments that have the same internal rate of return, then the relevant opportunity cost for cash will affect the choice. We would be indifferent if the opportunity cost were equal to the internal rate of return (thus the conclusion that the reinvestment rate is equal to the internal rate of return). If the mutually exclusive investments have different internal rates of return the opportunity cost (investment rate) is again relevant to the choice, and we cannot assume that funds are reinvested at the internal rate of return of either investment.

The statement that the internal rate of return calculation assumes that funds are reinvested at the internal rate of return is not likely to be harmful, but it is not exactly correct.

It is sometimes stated that the internal rate of return method implicitly assumes reinvestment at a rate of interest equal to the internal rate of return of the investment. Assume the following investment:

0	1	2	3
−$1,000	$80	$80	$1,080

In this example, the internal rate of return is .08. This IRR is not dependent on any assumption about reinvestment opportunities. For example, the $80 of periods 1 and 2 could be consumed or reinvested at .05 and the internal rate of return of the investment would still be .08. Although we do not need to know the reinvestment rate to compute the IRR of an investment, if we are comparing two mutually exclusive investments, we do not need to know the opportunity cost of funds to decide between the alternatives. For example, the following investment also has an IRR of .08.

0	1	2	3
−$1,000	$388	$388	$388

To decide between the two investments we would have to know the uses of the extra $308 in periods 1 and 2 (or equivalently the cost of obtaining $308). The incremental analysis would be as follows:

		Period			Internal Rate of Return
	0	1	2	3	
I	−$1,000	$ 80	$ 80	$1,080	.08
II	− 1,000	388	388	388	.08
I − II		−308	−308	692	.08

The term *internal rate of return* emphasizes that the value of this measure depends only on the cash flows from the investment and not on any assumptions about reinvestment rates.

Assume a bank can invest $100 in a one-month note yielding 26.8 percent on an annual basis (2 percent per month compounded twelve times) or, it can invest in a twelve-month security yielding 16 percent. The bank wants to invest the funds for one year.

To make the choice we have to know or estimate the return to be earned for the eleven months after the one-month security matures. Assume the bank will be able to earn 1 percent per month or 12.7 percent per year. The note matures in one month and at the end of the year the bank will have:

$100(1.02)(1.01)^{11} = \$113.80$

This total is less than that which the twelve-month security yielding 16 percent will return. The reinvestment opportunity must be considered.

Consider three investments:

	A	B	C
0	−1,000	−1,000	−1,000
1	+ 100		+1,100
2	+1,100	+1,210	

The internal rates of return of the three investments are all .10. This is independent of the cash flow reinvestment. The $100 of time 1 for investment A can be consumed and the internal rate of return will remain .10. Let us assume the investor wants to consume at time 2. In this case a comparison of A, B, and C requires a reinvestment assumption. Assume that it is expected that one-period funds can be invested at time 1 to earn .20. The terminal values of the three investments using the forward rate of .20 are:

A	B	C
120		1,100
+1,100		+ 220
1,220	1,210	1,320

Investment C is the best of the three investments if the reinvestment rate for period 2 is larger than .10. Present values, instead of terminal values, can be used to reach an identical decision. Assume that the discount rate for period 2 is .20 and for period 1 is .10. We obtain the following present values:

$$A - 1,000 + \frac{100}{1.1} + \frac{1,100}{1.1 \times 1.2} = -152$$

$$B - 1,000 + \frac{1,210}{1.1 \times 1.2} = -83$$

$$C - 1,000 + \frac{1,100}{1.1} = 0$$

We conclude that one does not need to know the reinvestment rates to compute the internal rate of return. However, one may need to know the reinvestment rates to compare alternatives.

Loan-Type Flows

So far in this chapter we have discussed investment type of cash flows. Now let us consider loan type of cash flows (positive flows followed by negative flows or outlays). Instead of a negative slope the net present value profile will now have a positive slope. Consider a borrowing of $10,000 where $12,100 is to be repaid at time 2. The net present value using a zero rate of discount is a negative $2,100 and the present value is zero at 10 percent. Figure 3-4 shows the net present value profile of the borrowed funds. The maximum height of the profile is $10,000, the amount borrowed.

The characteristic of loan-type flows is that their present value increases with higher rates of discount. By contrast, with a pure investment type of cash flow the present value decreases with higher rates of discount.

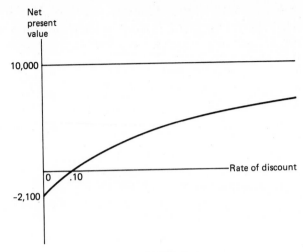

FIGURE 3-4

Multiple Internal Rates of Return

When the internal rate of return method is used, the ability to choose the best of two investments depends on whether a given series of incremental cash flows is like a conventional investment—in which case the higher the rate the better, or whether it is like a loan—in which case the lower rate or interest cost, the better. The following example illustrates a case in which the choice is not obvious. The cash flows represented by two mutually exclusive investments, R and S, are given in Table 3-3. The last line, labeled I, shows the incremental cash flows (that is, R − S). The cash flows, R and S, are conventional investments because they have outlays *followed by proceeds*. But for investment I, the outlays of period zero are followed by proceeds in period 1 and then by further outlays in period 2. With this kind of cash flow we cannot say, "The higher the internal rate of return, the better," or "The lower the internal rate of return the better."

Suppose that the mutually exclusive investments R and S are available to a company whose cost of money is 15 percent. If the IRR of the incremental cash flows I is 10 percent, should the company accept R or S? If the IRR of the

TABLE 3-3

	Cash Flows for Period			Internal Rate of Return
Investment	0	1	2	
R	−100	+ 30	+130	.30
S	0	−280	+350	.25
I	−100	+310	−220	.10 and 1.00

incremental cash flows I is 100 percent, should the company accept R or S? It turns out that the present value of the cash proceeds is equal to the present value of the cash outlays at a 10 percent rate of discount and at a 100 percent rate of discount. The internal rate of return of I is *both* 10 and 100 percent.

Interpretation of Multiple IRRs

To help illustrate the relationship between the internal rate of return of an investment and the present-value measure and to explain why multiple IRRs occur and how they should be interpreted, it is helpful to introduce a graph at this point. In Table 3-3 we described the three series of cash flows, R, S, and I. For R, S, and I in Figure 3-5 the vertical axis represents the net present value of the corresponding cash flow for various possible rates of interest, which are measured along the horizontal axis. By net present value we mean the algebraic sum of the present value of the proceeds and the present value of the outlays.

Because the IRR of a cash flow is defined as the rate of discount that makes the net present value zero, the IRR is the point at which the net present-value line crosses the horizontal axis (which measures the rate of discount).

For R the net present-value line drops as the rate of discount increases. At discount rates lower than 30 percent, the net present value is positive; at discount rates greater than 30 percent, it is negative. This general configuration typifies those conventional investments in which a series of cash outlays is followed by a series of cash proceeds. For such cash flows the internal rate of return represents the highest rate of discount at which the net present value would be positive and the investment desirable.

The first part of the graph for I is typical of that of a loan; the second has the downward slope typical of the ordinary investment. This series of cash flows would be worthwhile at rates of discount between 10 and 100 percent; outside this range it is not advisable. There is a corresponding inverted cash flow that could be obtained by subtracting R from S, thereby converting the proceeds to outlays and the outlays to proceeds. The resulting cash flows would be desirable only at interest rates that were less than 10 percent or greater than 100 percent.

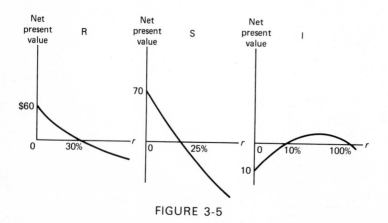

FIGURE 3-5

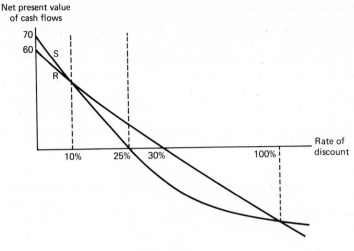

FIGURE 3-6

Thus we can compare the cash flows that would result from undertaking investment R instead of investment S and obtain a decision that R is more desirable than S at discount rates greater than 10 percent and less than 100 percent. Or we can compare the cash flows that result from undertaking S instead of R and obtain a decision that S is more desirable than R at discount rates less than 10 percent and greater than 100 percent. These are equivalent ways of saying the same thing.

In each case a simple calculation of the net present value of the investment at the correct rate of discount would have provided the correct answer and would have bypassed the problem of multiple internal rates of return. Figure 3-6 shows that investment R has a higher present value at rates of discount in excess of 10 percent. The two curves cross again at 100 percent.

The cash flows of the unconventional investment I can be broken down into two components, a one-period investment and a one-period loan. To do this we assign part of the cash proceeds of period 1 to the investment and the remainder to the loan. To test whether the investment is desirable if the cost of money is 15 percent, we divide the cash flows so that the internal rate of return on the investment is exactly 15 percent, and the loan consists of the rest of the cash flows.

	Cash Flows of Period		
	0	1	2
Investment I	−$100	+$310	−$220
"Investment"	− 100	+ 115	
"Loan"		+ 195	− 220

The investment is marginally desirable, since its rate of return is equal to the firm's cost of money. The loan of $195 at time 1 has a cost of .128, which is less than the .15 cost of money; thus the entire package, I, is acceptable.

If R had been subtracted from S, we would have obtained the cash flows of investment S − R which can be broken down into a loan costing 15 percent and an investment.

	Cash Flows of Period		
	0	1	2
Investment S − R	+$100	−$310	+$220
"Loan"	+ 100	− 115	
"Investment"		− 195	− 220

The loan costs 15 percent and is marginally desirable. The investment has a rate of return of .128 and is not acceptable with a .15 cost of money, however. Since the entire package (loan plus investment) must be accepted or rejected, we would reject the package, thus rejecting investment S − R.

The procedure we used was to set an initial investment or loan at the cost of money and then determine the internal rate of return of the remaining cash flows after the change in sign.

Converting Multiple IRRs to a Single IRR

If an upper level manager is told that an investment has two internal rates of returns, one of 0 percent and one of 100 percent, it is apt to be confusing. A 0 percent return is not acceptable, but a 100 percent return is outstandingly good. What decision should be made? We know that the use of net present value can solve the dilemma, but not everyone is willing to abandon the internal rate of return method even in situations where it cannot be used.

One solution is to adjust the cash flows so as to eliminate the possibility of multiple IRRs. Then a new internal rate of return is calculated from the adjusted cash flows. If this new internal rate of return is greater than the minimum acceptable cutoff rate, the investment can be accepted. Otherwise it can be rejected. The problem is to find a procedure for adjusting the cash flows that will eliminate the possibility of multiple rates of return but will not make undesirable investments seem desirable, or vice versa. There are a number of procedures that do this. All of them adjust the cash flows so that the present value of the adjusted cash flows is the same as the present value of the original cash flows using the minimum acceptable cutoff rate as a discount rate. The precise value of the new internal rate of return calculated from the adjusted cash flows will vary depending on which new adjustment method used. In each case, however, the value of the new internal rate of return will be greater than the cutoff rate if and only if the original cash flows had a positive present value at the cutoff rate.

Using one of these methods offers a solution to the multiple IRR problem. Based on reasonable assumptions, it offers a workable measure that can be compared to the minimum cutoff rate for accept or reject decisions. Given that the investment really does have two internal rates of return it would be surprising if we could wave our hands and convert a complex investment into an exactly economically equivalent investment with one internal rate of return. The adjusted investment is similar to the original investment, but not exactly equivalent. We will illustrate two methods for adjusting cash flows to eliminate multiple internal rates of return.

Let us consider the investment used above where there is outlay of $100 followed at time 1 by benefits of $310 and an outlay at time 2 of $220. This investment has two internal rates of return 10 percent and 100 percent and is graphed in Figure 3-5. Either of two procedures (they are other variations) may be used to obtain one IRR. With the first procedure the negative cash flows that follow positive flows are discounted back using the cutoff rate until they are at least balanced by positive cash flows of a prior period. Begin with the most distant cash outlays and continue until the adjusted cash flows are in the form of a conventional investment.

The second procedure is to proceed as if positive cash flows will be reinvested at the cutoff rate. They are accumulated forward in time until they eliminate all subsequent negative cash flows. Assume initially that the cutoff rate is 8 percent.

Using the first procedure, we discount $220 one period by 8 percent. This is a negative present value of $204 which when added to the cash flows of time 1 of $310 is $106. The new investment has an outlay of $100 and returns at time 1 of $106. This is a 6 percent internal rate of return. Reject the investment since 8 percent is required.

Using the second procedure we would accumulate $310 using 8 percent for one period and obtain $334.80 which is added to the $220 outlay to obtain a net of $115. An investment of $100 leading to benefits of $115 in two periods is an internal rate of return of approximately 7 percent. Again we should reject.

With an 8 percent cutoff rate both computational methods lead to a reject decision, since the unique internal rate of return in each case is less than the cutoff rate (even though the two IRRs of the unadjusted investment are both greater than 8 percent). Inspection of Figure 3-5 also indicates that with a time-value factor of 8 percent the investment should be rejected.

If the cutoff rate were raised to 12 percent we would then have $220 with a present value (discounted for one time period) of $196 which when subtracted from $310 gives $114. This is a 14 percent IRR on an outlay of $100 and the investment is acceptable, since 14 percent is larger than 12 percent.

If we had accumulated $310 by 12 percent we would have $347 at time 2 which must be reduced by the time 2 outlay of $220 to $127. This is a two-period 13 percent IRR on $100, and again the investment is acceptable. Inspection of Figure 3-5 indicates that with a 12 percent time-value factor the investment is acceptable.

If the cutoff rate being used to make the accept or reject decision is also used to convert the basic nonconventional cash flows to a conventional set of cash flows (with one internal rate of return) the accept or reject decision will not be changed. If the present value is positive before the adjustment, the present value .will be positive after the adjustment. If one rate of discount is being used as the cutoff rate (the hurdle rate) and another discount rate is used to convert the cash flows to conventional cash flows, however, then the investments can be changed from acceptable to nonacceptable or from nonacceptable to acceptable. Thus we return to the fact in evaluating nonconventional cash-flow streams one should compute and plot its net present value profile. From these techniques one should be able to make a reasonable accept or reject decision.

Significance of Nonconventional Cash Flows

In Chapter 1 we defined conventional investments (or loans) as those in which there were one or more periods of net cash outlays (or net proceeds) followed by one or more periods of net cash proceeds (or net outlays). It is important to determine whether a series of cash flows is conventional because *a conventional investment will have one and only one positive internal rate of return.*

If an investment is not conventional, we consider it to be a nonconventional investment. With a nonconventional investment, any of the following is possible:

1. The investment has *no* internal rate of return.
2. The investment has *one* internal rate of return.
3. The investment has *more than one* internal rate of return.

An example of a nonconventional investment with two internal rates of return was given in the preceding section. An example of a nonconventional investment with no internal rate of return would be an investment having cash proceeds of $100 and $150 in periods 1 and 3, respectively, and cash outlays of $200 in period 2. This "investment" does not have an internal rate of return, but it has a positive present value for all rates of discount.[1]

Index of Present Value

Some authors suggest dividing the present value of the cash proceeds by the present value of the investment type of outlays to obtain an index of present value (proceeds per dollar of outlay, both expressed in terms of present value).

The index-of-present-value method is a variant of the present-value method; its appeal lies in the fact that seemingly it can be used to rank investments. We shall attempt to show that the resulting ranking of mutually exclusive investments is frequently spurious. If our objective is limited to accept or reject decisions, the

---

[1] Mathematically, finding an internal rate of return for this series of cash flows is equivalent to finding a real number x that would satisfy the equation

$$0 = 100 - 200x + 150x^2.$$

But this equation has no solution in the domain of real numbers.

index of present value (accept all investments with an index greater than 1) will give results identical to those of the present-value method.

Example
The cost of money is 10 percent. Assume that an investment has the following cash flows:

0	1	2
−$1,500	$1,000	$1,000

The present value of the $1,000-a-period cash proceeds is $1,736. The index is 1.16.

$$\text{Present-value index} = \frac{1,736}{1,500} = 1.16.$$

One rule to use with an independent investment is the following: If the index is larger than 1, accept the investment.

This rule is sound. If the index is greater than 1, however, the net present value is also positive, and the computation of the present-value index is unnecessary.

A second rule is this: Evaluate mutually exclusive investments by their indexes; choose the investment with the highest index.

This rule may lead to correct decisions, but it may just as well lead to incorrect decisions because of two factors: scale of the investment and classification of cash flows.

Example (Scale)
Assume two mutually exclusive investments with the cash flows indicated. Which is the more desirable for a cutoff rate of 10 percent?

Investment	Period 0	Period 1	Period 2	Present-Value Index
X	−$1,500	$1,000	$1,000	1.16
Y	− 3,100	2,000	2,000	1.12

The index measure indicates that X is preferred to Y. A computation of present values will show that Y is better, however (a net present value of $371 for Y compared to $236 for X). The present-value index is a ratio of benefits to outlay. But it fails to consider the scale of the investment in the same manner as other ratio measures, such as return on investment and internal rate of return. This point can be seen more clearly if we look at the incremental investment consequent on moving from X to Y. We shall label that investment Y-X.

Investment	Period 0	Period 1	Period 2	Present-Value Index
Y-X	−$1,600	$1,000	$1,000	1.08

The index is greater than 1; thus the incremental investment is desirable. The problem of scale can be solved by comparing pairs of investments, but this is unnecessary because the problem can be solved more easily by using present value. Also the problem of the classification of cash flows still exists.

Example (Classification of Cash Flows)

The second difficulty with the present-value index is that it requires a distinction between deductions from cash proceeds and investment-type outlays. Assume the following two mutually exclusive investments and a 10 percent time-value factor:

	Period			Present-Value Index
Investment	0	1	2	
A Net flows	−$1,500	$1,000	$1,000	1.16
B Proceeds		2,000	2,000	1.07
Outlays	− 1,500	− 1,000	− 1,000	

Calculations:

$$\text{Present-Value Index (A)} = \frac{1,000(1.10)^{-1} + 1,000(1.10)^{-2}}{1,500} = \frac{1,735.54}{1,500.00} = 1.16$$

$$\text{Present-Value Index (B)} = \frac{3,471.08}{3,235.54} = 1.07$$

The index measure chooses A over B. Close inspection of the cash flows of the investments shows that the investment net cash flows are identical for both investments. The difference may be only a matter of classifying the $1,000 outlays of B as investments or as deductions from cash proceeds as with A. Any procedure that depends on arbitrary classifications rests on quicksand. For example, are advertising expenditures an expense or an investment? A partial solution to this problem is to use net cash flows.

A misconception about the present-value index is that it will rank independent investments. This ranking is not reliable. If the company does not intend to accept all independent investments with a positive present value (or an index greater than 1), the cost of money used will not be the appropriate rate of discount and the index ranking will not be reliable. It is not claimed here that the present-value method may be used to rank independent investments. It is claimed only that the present-value method will lead to more easily obtained decisions involving choices between mutually exclusive investments and will give equally correct accept or reject decisions when applied to independent investments.

Even Russia

Even Russia is not immune to the necessity of making capital budgeting decisions. In December 1980 the Soviet refused to pay 8 percent for debt money from European banks necessary to finance a twin gas pipeline from Siberia to Western

Europe. The twin pipeline would have cost $14 billion and would have generated $19 billion of revenue per year for twenty years. They considered 8 percent to be an excessively high cost of money.

In July, 1981 the Soviets arranged financing for a single pipeline. The loans cost between 9 and 10 percent. The single pipeline would generate revenues of about $10 billion annually and would cost about $9 billion.

It was planned to build the second pipeline on completion of the first line (in about three years). At that time the second pipeline would cost $6 billion.

The alternatives were as follows:

	0	3	4	5	6	...	24
Twin Pipeline	−14	+19	+19	+19	+19		+19
One Pipeline Followed							
by Second	−9	+10	+10	+10	+10		+10
		−6			+9		+9
Difference	−5	+15	+9	+9			

How much could the Soviets have paid for borrowed funds to finance the second pipeline immediately? It can be argued that the given estimates of costs and revenues are inexact. That is true (for example, the opportunity-cost of the gas should be included as outlays) but the magnitudes and the pattern of the cash flows give an indication of the direction in which the decision should be slanted. It would be interesting to know the exact numbers that were used.

Ranking Independent Investments

We can safely use the present-value method to choose the best of a set of mutually exclusive investments only when the rate of discount used is an appropriate opportunity cost. As soon as we use the present-value method to rank independent investments for the purpose of choosing a cutoff rate above zero present value (some investments with positive present values will be rejected), the rate of discount used in computing the present values becomes not the appropriate rate to use, because the true opportunity cost is higher than the rate chosen.

Example

The time value of money of the firm has been computed to be .10. There are two independent investments, C and D, with the following characteristics:

	Cash Flows for Period		Internal Rate of Return	Present Value (using .10)
Investment	0	1		
C	−$ 5,000	$10,000	1.00	$ 9,091 − 5,000 = $4,091
D	− 20,000	30,000	.50	$27,273 − 20,000 = $7,273

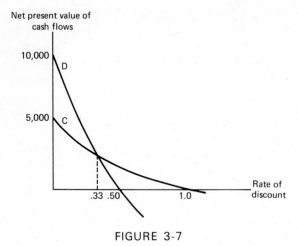

FIGURE 3-7

Using the net present values, we would choose D over C and reject C. Using as the opportunity cost the internal rate of return of the rejected investment C (1.00), we find the present values to be

Present value of C = $5,000 − 5,000 = 0,
Present value of D = $15,000 − 20,000 = −$5,000.

If we used the internal rate of return of the last investment accepted, D (.50), we would have as present values

Present value of C = $6,667 − 5,000 = $1,667,
Present value of D = $20,000 − 20,000 = 0.

With both of these rates of interest we find that C is preferred to D, but with an interest rate of .10, D is preferred to C. Figure 3-7 shows that as long as the appropriate time value factor is less than 33 percent the investor prefers investment D, but that if the discount factor is greater than 33 percent, investment C is preferred.

The problem becomes even more complex when we consider the opportunity costs of money for many time periods, and where we have many sets of mutually exclusive investments. The choice of the best of each set will depend on the opportunity cost that is chosen.

Thus we make no claim that the present-value method can be used to rank independent investments where that ranking will be used to eliminate some independent investments with positive present values. This problem will be taken up again in Chapter 8 when we discuss capital rationing.

Duration: A Sensitivity Measure

Assume there are two mutually exclusive investments with the same present value. Which is to be preferred?

Let us consider an approach similar to computing payback, for like payback it considers the entire life of the asset. Its name is "duration." The duration of an investment is its weighted average life where the weights are the present value of the cash flows received in the period (P_t):

$$\text{Duration} = \frac{\sum tP_t}{\sum P_t}.$$

An investment with a single cash flow of $330.99 in year three would have a present value of of $248.68 (with a discount rate of .10) and a duration of 3. Assume an investment has three equal cash flows of $100, first payment to be received one period from now. The discount rate is .10. The duration of this investment is:

$$\text{Duration} = \frac{1(100)(1.10)^{-1} + 2(100)(1.10)^{-2} + 3(100)(1.10)^{-3}}{100(1.10)^{-1} + 100(1.10)^{-2} + 100(1.10)^{-3}} = 1.94$$

Both investments have a present value of $248.60, but one has a duration of 1.94 and the other has a duration of 3. If we think that the rate of interest may increase, we might prefer the investment with the shorter duration, since its present value would decline by less as a result of the interest rate increase.

Summary

If a business knows its cost of money (at least approximately) and can either obtain additional funds from the market at that cost of money for desirable internal investments or invest any excess funds externally at that cost of money, then either of the two discounted cash flow procedures can be used to make correct investment decisions.

If the present-value method is used, the rules for making correct investment decisions are quite simple in principle. They are

1. For each investment proposal, compute the net present value of the proposal, using the cost of money as the discount rate.
2. If the choice is between accepting or rejecting the investment, accept it if its net present value is greater than zero, and reject it if the net present value is less than zero.
3. If a set of comparable mutually exclusive investment proposals is available and the present value of each investment is greater than zero, but only one can be accepted, accept the one for which the present value is the greatest. The comparability requirement complicates this analysis. In Chapter 7 we will give an explanation of the procedures to be followed when two mutually exclusive investments are not comparable because their lives are not equal.

The internal rate of return (IRR) method can also be used to make correct investment choices, provided the cost of money is the same in all future time periods. If properly used, this method will in fact lead to the same choices as the present-value method. But the rules that must be followed if the internal rate of return method is to be used properly are quite complex. The complexities arise from the following considerations:

1. A single investment may have more than one internal rate of return. The present value of the cash proceeds from an investment may equal the present value of the costs at x and at y percent. This may mean that the investment is profitable only if the cost of money is between x and y percent, or it may mean that the investment is profitable only if the cost of money is either less than x percent or greater than y percent.

2. If a group of two or more mutually exclusive investments is available, a direct comparison of their internal rates of return will not necessarily lead to the correct choice of the best alternative. It is necessary to analyze the investment proposals two at a time, decide which one of each pair is more desirable, and then compare the more desirable investment with one of the others to decide which of those two is more desirable, continuing until by a process of elimination the best one can be determined. By contrast, the present-value method indicates immediately which one of a group of mutually exclusive proposals is more desirable.

3. In interpreting the internal rate of return of a single investment, it is necessary first to determine whether the cash flows correspond to an ordinary conventional investment or to a loan from the point of view of the borrower.

4. It may not be possible to define the internal rate of return for a cash-flow series. In this case the easiest procedure is to interpret the cash-flow series using the present-value method.

5. If the cost of money is not expected to be the same in all future time periods, the internal rate of return method cannot be used to give the same decisions as the present-value method.

For most purposes the present-value method is simpler, safer, easier, and more direct. The remainder of this book will proceed in terms of this approach.

The "conflict" between present value and internal rate of return disappears if the graph of present values is used to comparing investments. The internal rate of return is the intersection of the graph and the X axis, and the present value is the vertical height from the X axis to the graph. Using the internal rate of return as the rate of discount, the net present value is zero. However, present value graphs are useful only if the cost of money is expected to be the same in all future periods.

Questions and Problems

3.1. Accept or reject the following independent investment proposals, using the internal rate of return and present-value procedures, and a cutoff rate of 10 percent.

	Period		
Investment	0	1	2
A	($10,000)	$ 2,000	$12,000
B	(10,000)	10,500	
C	10,000	(12,000)	

3-2. a. Assume that there are three mutually exclusive investments. Which of the three investments should be chosen? Assume a cutoff rate of 10 percent.

	Period				Internal Rate of Return
Investment	0	1	2	3	(%)
A	($ 1,000)	$ 505	$ 505	$ 505	24
B	(10,000)	2,000	2,000	12,000	20
C	(11,000)	5.304	5,304	5,304	21

b. Compute the incremental cash flow for investments B and C in problem 3-2(a). Compute the internal rate or rates of return of this incremental cash flow. Is investment B or C more desirable?

3-3. The Apple Company is attempting to choose between two different machines that accomplish essentially the same task (the machines are mutually exclusive). A comparison of the cash flows of the two machines shows that if the less expensive of the two machines is chosen, there will be a saving of $1,000 at the time of purchase, but there will be additional outlays of $333 per year over the five-year life of the machines. The cost of money of the Apple Company is 10 percent.

Required: Compute the internal rate of return of the incremental cash flows and determine whether or not the cheaper of the two machines should be purchased. Make the same decision using the present-value procedure.

3-4. There are two mutually exclusive investments. Assume a discount rate of 10 percent. Choose the better of the two investments.

	Period			Internal Rate of Return
Investment	0	1	2	(%)
A	($16,050)	$10,000	$10,000	16
B	(100,000)	60,000	60,000	13

3-5. There are two mutually exclusive investments. Assume an interest cost of 5 percent. Choose the better of the two investments.

Investment	Period 0	1	2	Internal Rate of Return (%)
A	($10,000)	$0	$12,100	10
B	(10,000)	5,762	5,762	10

3-6. Assume an interest rate of 15 percent. Choose the better of the two investments of problem 3-5.

3-7. There are two mutually exclusive investments. Assume an interest rate of 5 percent. Choose the better of the two investments.

Investment	Period 0	1	2
A	−$600	$500	$600
B	− 700	800	400

3-8. Compute the relative cash flows of investment (B-A) of problem 3-7. Comment on the computation of the internal rate of return of this investment.

3-9. There is an investment with the following cash flows:

Period 0	1	2
−$50	$150	−$100

Assume an interest rate of .05. Is the investment acceptable? What are the internal rates of return of the investment?

3-10. a. Compute the internal rates of return of the following two investments:

	X		Y
0	− 9,089	0	− 7,118
1	+ 1,000		
2	+10,000		
3	+ 1,000	3	+10,000

b. Compute the present values of the investments if the appropriate rate of discount is .10.

3-11. a. Compute the internal rates of return of the following three investments:

	0	1	2
A	−10,000	11,500	
B	−10,000	6,151	6,151
C	−10,000		13,226

b. Compute the amount the investor will have at time 2 if the funds received at time 1 can be reinvested to earn .15.
c. For each of the three investments graph the present value profile.
d. Which investment is to be preferred if the rate of discount is .10?

3-12. The ABC Company is considering undertaking an investment that promises to have the following cash flows:

0	1
−$50	$90

If the firm waits a year it can invest in an alternative (that is, mutually exclusive) investment that promises to pay

1	2
−$60	$100

Assume a time value of money of .05. Which investment should the firm undertake? Use the present-value and the internal rate of return methods.

3-13. The IBC Company is considering undertaking an investment that promises to have the following cash flows:

0	1	2	3
−$100	$150	$50	$50

If it waits a year it can invest in an alternative (that is, mutually exclusive) investment that promises to pay

1	2	3
−$150	$250	$50

Assume a time value of money of .05. Which investment should the firm undertake? Use the present-value method and the internal rate of return approaches. With the IRR approach, use the incremental cash flows.

3-14. The Arabian Oil Company is considering an investment that can be undertaken this year or postponed one year. The investment cash flows if undertaken now would be as follows:

Period	
0	1
−$100	$200

The cash flows if delayed one period would be as follows:

Period	
1	2
−$100	$200

Required: Assume a time value of money of .05. Should the company invest now or delay one year? First use the internal rate of return method and then use the present-value method.

3-15. The IBC Company is considering undertaking an investment that promises the following cash flows:

0	1	2
−100	80	80

If the company waits a year it can make the following investment:

1	2
−220	280

Assuming a time value of .10 which investment should the firm undertake? Use both the net present value and IRR approaches. With the IRR method use incremental cash flows.

3-16. Assume that there are two mutually exclusive investments. Which of the two investments would be chosen using the index of present value? Assume a cost of money of 10 percent. Evaluate the procedure.

Investment	Period 0	1
A	−$ 4,000	$11,000
B	− 20,000	33,000

3-17. Assume that there are two mutually exclusive investments. Which of the two investments would be chosen using the index of present value? Assume a cost of money of 10 percent.

Investment	Period 0	1
A	−$4,000	$11,000
B	− 4,000	− 10,000
		21,000

3-18. Assume that an investment has the following cash flows:

0	1	2
−$10,000	$21,600	−$11,600

This investment has IRRs of 0 and .16. Assume that the firm has a time value of money of .10 (it can borrow at .10). Divide the investment into two components, a fictitious investment of $10,000 at time zero and borrowing of $10,600 at time 1. Determine whether the basic investment is desirable.

3-19. Assume that an investment has the following cash flows:

0	1	2
$10,000	−$21,600	$11,600

The investment has IRRs of 0 and .16. Assume that the firm has a time value of .10 (it can borrow at .10). Divide the investment into two components, a fictitious borrowing of $10,000 at time zero and an investment of $10,600 at time 1. Determine whether the basic investment is desirable.

3-20. Assume that an investment has the following cash flows:

0	1	2	3
$10,000	$10,000	$10,000	−$29,000

The firm uses the internal rate of return method of evaluating investments and has a hurdle rate of .10. Is the investment desirable?

3-21. There are two mutually exclusive investments with the following cash flows:

Investment	Cash Flows for Period		
	0	1	2
R	−$162,727	$190,909	$60,000
S	− 90,000	20,000	160,000

Required: Which of the two investments do you prefer if the firm's time value of money is (a) .05; (b) .20; (c) .30?

3-22. The ABC Company can save $200,000 immediately by reducing its finished goods inventory. Lost sales due to stockouts will reduce profits by $30,000 per year as a result of the reduction, however. This decision offers a 15 percent internal rate of return. Should the change be accepted if the cost of money of the firm is 10 percent?

3-23. The controller of the A-Can Company is evaluating the status of a plant. Currently the plant is losing $1,000,000 per year (cash flow). These losses will continue unless some action is taken. If the plant is shut down there will be $5,000,000 of closing costs (out-of-pocket).

Another alternative is to modernize the plant at a cost of $10,000,000. This will cause the cash flow per year to be $500,000. Assume this cashflow will continue for perpetuity as will the $1,000,000 negative cash flow associated with doing nothing.

What should the company do? The company is not sure which discount rate it should use to evaluate this decision.

Discussion Questions

3-A. In 1978 Cornell University's Teagle Hall instituted a plan that reduced the inventory of gym wear by eliminating the "dead" inventory stored in the lockers. The new system did result in increased labor cost through time, however, since each customer now had to go through the service line twice, whereas before each customer went through the line once.

Assuming that the cash flows were computed for the decision to implement the system, and assuming that the internal rate of return was unique and equal to 30 percent, should Cornell adopt the new system?

The cash flows were calculated by assuming that students and professors waiting in line have zero value to their time.

3-B. Is the plant which offers the highest internal rate of return the most desirable plant (in a set of mutually exclusive alternatives)?

Answers to Selected Questions

3-1.

	IRR	NPV(.10)	
A	.20	1,735	Accept
B	.05	−454	Reject
C	.20	−909	Reject

3-3. The more expensive of the two machines is the more desirable.

3-5. A is better ($975 NPV)   **3-7.** B is better ($424 NPV)

3-9. The IRRs are 0 and 100 percent. The NPV = $2 using .05.

3-11. **(a)** .15 for all three.   **(b)** $13,226 at time 2.   **(d)** At .10, C is preferred.

3-13. The IRRs are 0 and 100 percent. The NPV is $4. Accept A now.

3-15. Using .10 doing the project now is to be preferred.

3-17. Index of PV (A) = 2.5.   Index of PV (B) = 1.46.   But same NPV.

3-19. The IRR of the investment is .094 which is less than .10 thus reject.

3-21. S is to be preferred at .05 and .30.

CHAPTER 4

The Meaning of Present Value

The theory is one of investment opportunity and human impatience as well as exchange.

—Irving Fisher, The Theory of Interest, As Determined by Impatience to Spend Income and Opportunity to Invest It (New York: Kelley & Millman, Inc., 1954), p. 149.

In the preceding chapters we have argued that measures of investment worth that do not utilize discounted cash flow concepts can frequently give incorrect evaluations of investment alternatives. But the fact that a measure of investment worth incorporates discounted cash flow concepts is no guarantee that it will give correct results in all cases. There are errors that can be introduced within the present value framework.

The thoughtful reader will have noticed that the argument up to this point has been largely negative. We have emphasized the shortcomings of the methods in common use. But we have not yet developed the arguments for preferring the discounted cash flow approach for measuring the value of an investment. In this chapter we shall attempt to present in a systematic and positive way our reasons for recommending the use of the present-value measure. We hope to make clear the advantages as well as the limitations of this method. It is by no means a cure-all for the problem of the manager harassed by the difficult problems of developing, evaluating, and choosing long-run investments.

We believe that the present-value method can make a definite and important contribution to the solution of the problems of making investment decisions. But it is vitally important that the users understand what it is they are accomplishing by discounting the cash flow of an investment, and what they are not accomplishing. Unfortunately some of those who have advocated use of this procedure have done so for the wrong reasons or have made claims for it that cannot be fulfilled. All of us recognize that the simple screwdriver is a useful tool when properly used. There is no need to revise that opinion because an inexperienced do-it-yourself enthusiast reports disastrous consequences from the attempt to use a screwdriver in a situation where a chisel was required.

A Bird in the Hand

Most managers will agree that a dollar in the hand today is more valuable to them than a dollar to be received a year from now. There are a variety of reasons for this preference. A survey may reveal the following answers to an inquiry, " Why is a dollar in hand today worth more to you than a dollar to be received in one year?"

Risk:

As a manager I live in an uncertain world. A dollar in the bank is something I can count on. A promise to pay me a dollar in one year is only a promise until I actually get the money. The promise may be made in perfectly good faith, but any number of things may occur between now and next year to prevent the fulfillment of the promise.

Immediacy:

Human nature naturally attaches more weight to present pleasures than to the more distant joys. Offer a young man the choice between a trip to Europe during the coming summer, or a trip five summers from now, and he will nearly always choose the earlier trip. We would always prefer to receive a given total amount of after-tax income as soon as possible.

Earning Opportunities:

A dollar received now is more valuable than a dollar to be received five years from now because of the investment possibilities that are available for today's dollar. By investing or lending the dollar received today, I can have considerably more than a dollar in five years.

We have suggested three separate reasons for attaching more weight to dollars on hand than to dollars that may be received in the future. Each reason is a correct one in important respects. But the last one of them by itself is sufficient justification for using discounted cash flow procedures in evaluating investment proposals. The other two reasons, insofar as they are appropriate in any situation, need to be taken into account in other ways. Let us consider each of the three reasons in turn.

Uncertainty

Our first hypothetical respondent stressed the fact that one can never be certain about the receipt of future cash. We would not disagree. In fact, we would generalize and say that one can never be certain about the future value of present cash held. It can be lost or stolen, the bank in which it is deposited might fail, or our ability to benefit from it may be impaired by death or injury.

It is not the need to allow for uncertainty that is in question, but the suitability of using the present-value approach to make this allowance. The inappropriateness of using high discount rates as a general method of allowing for uncertainty may be illustrated by cases in which there is great uncertainty about the cash flows in the near future, but relatively little uncertainty about the more distant cash flows. Suppose that we are considering investing in a building which, once it is built, could be rented on the basis of a long-term lease. The prospective lessee is willing to sign a contract now, and its credit standing is excellent, so that there is minimum uncertainty about the ability to meet the rental payments. There may be considerable uncertainty about how much it will cost to construct the building, however. In a situation such as this, it is difficult to justify using a high rate of discount applied to the relatively certain future cash receipts. There is considerable uncertainty about the magnitude of the cash outlays required to build the building, but varying the discount rate will have little effect on the present value of these outlays, because they will occur in the near future.

Some suggestions for handling data to improve the judgements of the risks involved in investments will be discussed later. No completely satisfactory and universally applicable method is known, however.

Subjective Time Preference

The second reason suggested as a justification for discounting future income is the time preference of the individuals involved. There are individuals who would prefer an additional $100 of consumption immediately to the opportunity of obtaining an additional $110 of disposable income available a year from now. Such individuals might be acting rationally if they rejected a riskless opportunity to invest $100 today in such a way that it would return $110 in one year, if acceptance of the investment requires a corresponding reduction in the investor's immediate consumption.

But acceptance of the investment will not require a reduction in immediate consumption if opportunities to borrow money at less than 10 percent are also available now. Suppose the individuals in question accept the investment and at the same time borrow $100 at 5 percent to maintain their immediate consumption. At the end of a year the proceeds from the investment will enable them to pay off the loan, plus its accrued interest, and still retain an additional $5.

In general, the subjective time preferences of the owners of a corporation do not need to be consulted in making investment decisions for that corporation, provided the corporation can obtain additional funds in the capital market and invest its excess funds, if any, on the capital market. It is only the rates at which the corporation can obtain or lend funds that are relevant. Accordingly, the purpose of a business enterprise in discounting expected future cash proceeds is not to take account of the subjective time preferences of the owners (unless the owners do not for one reason or another have access to the capital market).

The manager of a business owned by a small group of individuals may, and sometimes should, adjust the investment policy of the company to take into consideration the cash requirements of the owners. But the shareholders of a large corporation are usually a diverse group. They may pay marginal tax rates on dividends of anywhere from zero (for certain individuals and nonprofit institutions) to over 50 percent. At any given time, some shareholders will be reinvesting a part of their dividend receipts, while others will be reducing their portfolios. The large corporation cannot easily adjust its investment policy to the needs of individual shareholders.

Alternative Uses of Money

The purpose of discounting the cash flows expected from an investment is to determine whether the investment produces more cash than alternative uses of the same amount of money. In the case of an independent investment proposal in a firm not subject to capital rationing,[1] whose current dividend has been determined, the consequences of accepting the investment are to borrow more funds or to lend less outside the firm. If the costs of borrowing are the same as the rate that could be earned by lending elsewhere, the alternatives are equivalent. It should be mentioned that the term *borrowing* is used here in a very broad sense to include raising additional equity as well as the more conventional forms of debt.

Investment Financed by Borrowing

To illustrate the meaning of the present-value computation when the investment must be financed by borrowing we may use an investment that requires an initial outlay of $10,000 and offers proceeds of $11,506 at time one. At a 10 percent rate of interest the net present value of the investment is $460, and the present value of the proceeds are $10,460. The value of the proceeds expected from the $10,000 investment is sufficient to pay off the principal and accrued interest on a loan of $10,460 at 10 percent payable at time one. One way of interpreting the meaning of the present-value calculation is to realize that a firm could borrow a total of $10,460 at 10 percent. They could then apply $10,000 of the loan proceeds to buying the investment, and immediately distribute the remaining $460 as a dividend to the owners. The $11,506 of proceeds from the investment will be sufficient to repay the loan and interest.

We mentioned earlier that making allowances for the subjective time preferences with respect to receipt of income is not the purpose of the discounting process as long as the income recipient has access to the capital market. In the case of the preceding example we assumed that the owners of the firm chose to receive the profit resulting from the investment in the year it was made. Actually, any pattern of cash receipts, such that their present value was equal to $460, could have been selected. If some or all of the income withdrawals were deferred to time one, the actual withdrawals that could be made would exceed $460. Suppose the owners elected to borrow $10,000, the amount required to undertake the investment, and to withdraw their proceeds only after the initial loan had been repaid. Under these circumstances the owners would be enabled to withdraw $506 at the end of the year, because this amount has a present value of $460 with an interest rate of 10 percent.

Investment Financed Internally

So far we have considered the case where the investment within the firm was to be financed by obtaining additional capital from outside the firm. This may seem

---

[1] For a discussion of capital rationing, see Chapter 8.

to be an artificial comparison to a company whose past operations are generating enough cash to undertake all the worthwhile investments that seem to be available within the company. This situation is not uncommon. It is a mistake to assume that internally generated funds are "free," however, because there is the possibility of lending funds outside the firm. For example, if a riskless possibility of earning 10 percent from loans outside is available, then risk-free internal investments should be compared with these external profit opportunities; otherwise, the company may undertake internal investments that are not so profitable as those outside of its funds.

Consider the previous example. In the situation in which the funds to finance the investment were obtained from outside the firm, we said that we could interpret the fact that the investment had a net present value of $460 as meaning that a loan equal to the amount required to finance the investment, plus $460, could be negotiated, the excess over immediate needs ($460) withdrawn, and the proceeds from the investment then would be sufficient to repay the entire loan.

Assume that the firm has funds available from internal sources. The owner has estimated that by applying $10,000 of those funds to the internal investment the company could generate cash proceeds of $11,506 at time one. We could ask how much money the firm would have to lend outside at 10 percent in order to generate cash proceeds of $11,506. Because the present value of $11,506 at 10 percent is $10,460, it would require an external loan of that amount to generate the same cash proceeds that would be generated internally from an investment of only $10,000.

In the case where funds are available from internal sources, and external lending opportunities to earn 10 percent per year are available, the fact that an internal investment with a net present value of $460 is available means that $10,460 would have to be lent externally to generate the same cash proceeds as the internal investment of $10,000.

As in the previous case, the subjective time preferences of the owners should not affect the choice between the internal or external investment loan. If the owner wants to consume now, then up to $10,460 can be borrowed and up to $460 can be consumed now if the owner currently has zero assets. The investment generating $11,506 of proceeds can be used to repay the loan of $10,460 plus $1,046 of interest.

One further interpretation of the net present value of $460 of the investment is possible. The $460 is like an unrealized capital gain. For an expenditure of $10,000 we obtain the right to proceeds whose present value totals $10,460 and whose net present value is $460. Before investing, we have $10,000 in cash; after investing, we have prospects of cash proceeds whose present value is $10,460. Thus our asset position can be improved in terms of present values (by $460) by making the investment.

Present-Value Factors as Prices

To understand the approach to capital budgeting taken in this book, it is helpful to think of dollars that are received or paid at different times (dated dollars) as being different commodities. Present-value factors are the prices of these dated dollars.

An investment is essentially a production process in which near dollars are used up to produce distant dollars. To determine whether an investment is profitable we need to calculate whether the value of the distant dollars to be received is greater than the cost of the near dollars that are used to start the production process. To do this we multiply the quantity of each different dated dollar by its price. Prices of dated dollars are measured in present dollars just like the prices of oranges and grapefruits. If the value of the distant dollars produced by an investment is greater than the value of the near dollars used up, then we can say the investment is profitable. The magnitude of these profits is a measure of how desirable the investment is.

Whether two amounts can be treated as identical or must be distinguished depends on whether the market treats them as perfect substitutes. A rational person would give a firm a discount for making a loan payment a year early. That is, the lender would accept less than a dollar paid today to settle a payment of one dollar due in a year. A dollar now and a dollar a year from now are different if the interest rate is positive.

To illustrate these ideas, suppose that a business is considering an investment opportunity that requires an immediate outlay of $100 that would generate proceeds of $60 at the end of each of the next two years. If the decision-makers understood that dollars received at different times have different value, they would request more information to make the investment decision. The additional data needed are today's prices (or values) for dollars to be received one and two years from now. Today's price for a dollar to be received today is $1.00. If the price of a dollar to be received one year from now is $.9091, and the price of a dollar two years from now is $.8264 (reflecting a 10 percent time-value factor), the manager is in a position to evaluate the future cash flows. One can multiply the price of each of the three kinds of dollars involved by their quantities and find the net benefit in terms of today's dollars. Thus:

Value of second period's proceeds	$.8264 × 60 = $ 49.58
Value of first period's proceeds	$.9091 × 60 = 54.55
Total value of proceeds in terms of today's dollars	104.13
Less required outlay in today's dollars	100.00
Equals net value of the investment in terms of today's dollars (NPV)	$ 4.13

The example illustrates, first, that the process of making investment decisions involves using market prices (when possible) to put otherwise noncomparable quantities (dollars of different time periods) on a comparable basis in terms of today's dollars. Second, the net present value of an investment is equivalent to the net benefit from an investment in terms of today's dollars.

Intuitive Explanations of Present Value

Consider an investment that will generate cash flows of $10,000 one year from today and will cost $8,000. With a discount rate of 5 percent the investment has a net present value of $1,524 [that is, ($10,000 × .9524) − 8,000]. The $1,524 is the present value of the unrealized profit that the firm will earn if the expectations are realized by operations one period after the expenditure of the $8,000. The present value of the investment will be $9,524 and the cost is only $8,000, so there will be $1,524 of unrealized profit associated with the investment. An accountant would report $2,000 of income in period 1, but if 5 percent of $8,000 is subtracted, we obtain a net earnings after interest of $1,600. The present value of $1,600 is $1,524.

Revenues	$10,000
less:	
Depreciation $8,000	
Interest 400	8,400
Net Income	$ 1,600

The above income measure is after the capital cost ($400) on all capital and will equal the actual interest paid only if the investment is financed entirely with debt.

Another useful interpretation of the net present value of the investment is that the firm could afford to pay $1,524 more than the cost of the investment and still break even (on a present-value basis) on the investment. For example, if the firm paid $9,524 for the investment, 5 percent interest on $9,524 would be $476. Since the investment will earn $10,000, there will be enough cash to pay the original investment of $9,524 plus the $476 interest cost on the investment.

The previous example illustrated the fact that the net present value is equal to the present value of future incomes (after an interest cost on capital), but it was a one-period case. Now consider an investment with an outlay of $8,000 followed by benefits one year later of $1,000 and benefits two years later of $11,000. This investment has a net present value of $2,000 using a .10 rate of discount. Using straight line depreciation we get the following two income statements.

	Year 1	Year 2
Revenues	1,000	11,000
Depreciation	4,000	4,000
Income (Loss) before interest	(3,000)	7,000
Interest (.10)	800	400
Net Income	(3,800)	6,600

The present value of the income measures is

$$PV = -3,800(1.10)^{-1} + 6,600(1.10)^{-2} = \$2,000.$$

Again the present value of the incomes is equal to the net present value of the investment. If we changed the method of depreciation it would not change this relationship.

Describing the net present value of an investment as the amount that one could afford to pay in excess of the initial cost is helpful in giving management an estimate of the amount of room for error that is in the estimation of the cost of the investment. It is a useful intuitive definition of net present value. Nonzero taxes requires a tax adjustment.

Logical Basis for the Net Present-Value Method

In our discussions of the net present-value method we have chosen to present our explanation in terms that have a maximum intuitive appeal. If the desirability of the net present-value method depended only on its intuitive appeal, there would be the possibility that somebody might discover or invent another method that had even stronger intuitive appeal. Our confidence in the net present-value method is derived from the fact that it is at least as good as any other solution to the problem of measuring the economic worth of an investment under certain well-defined circumstances.

First, we assume that the owners of a firm want investment choices that offer the greatest satisfaction. The entity can be thought of as a single individual, a family unit, a business firm, or some other organizational entity. The satisfaction that the owner of the entity derives from the investment decisions depends upon the amount and timing of the cash flows that can be withdrawn from the business operations. It may be helpful to think of these cash flows as consumption. In a business organization the analogue to consumption on the part of an individual is dividends paid to stockholders.

The decision maker faces two sets of decisions that together determine the pattern of consumption the owner will be able to enjoy. One set of decisions concerns investment choices; the second determines how these investment choices will be financed.

Each possible investment alternative may be described by a series of cash flows representing the amount that would be paid out in each period or the amount that would be received in each period. The size and timing of the cash flows associated with each investment choice are assumed here to be known in advance and with certainty. The number of separate investment choices open to the decision maker may be small or extremely large.

It is assumed that there is a known market rate of interest at which the firm can lend as much as it wants or borrow as much as it wants. The only restriction on borrowing is that loans must be repayable out of future cash flows.

How should the decision maker select from among the available investment options in such a way that it will be possible to achieve the maximum attainable level of satisfaction? All the investment opportunities should be arranged into groups of mutually exclusive investments. Some of these groups may contain only one option; others may contain a large number of mutually exclusive options. From each mutually exclusive group select the investment whose net present value is algebraically the largest when the net present value is computed at the market rates of interest. If this investment has a positive net present value, accept it; otherwise, reject all the investments in that mutually exclusive group.

Now imagine that the decision maker has selected from among all the investment options the ones that have a positive net present value and that do not violate the restriction that no more than one of a set of mutually exclusive investments can be accepted. These investments will determine the amount of money the firm will receive or must pay out in each time period as a result of the investments.

Assume that the decision maker has two independent investment opportunities with the following cash flows projected:

	Period		
Investment	0	1	2
A	−$ 900	$1,000	
B	− 1,500		$2,000

The rate of interest (this is both the borrowing and lending rate) is assumed to be .05. All we need know to make the investment decisions is the net present value of these two investments ($52.40 for A and $314 for B). Because the two net present values are positive, the investments should be undertaken, and no further information or computations are required. The investor can borrow the funds at a cost of .05 and repay the debt using the cash flows from the investments. There is no question that the funds should be obtained to finance the investments. The conclusion not only holds for the two investments illustrated, but is valid for any investment with a positive net present value using the .05 borrowing rate. (Remember that there is no uncertainty; thus the cash flows of the investments are known.)

We can make the decision to undertake the investments without considering the consumption preferences of the owners. If $X is available these funds can be consumed, and $2,400 can be borrowed to finance the investments. The value of $X does not affect the investment decision. We assume, other things being equal, the owners prefer more consumption to less. Specifically, if two patterns of consumption are identical in all time periods except one, and if the first pattern of consumption results in more consumption in a given time period than the second pattern of consumption, the owners will prefer the first to the second.

Accepting investments A and B will enable the investors to finance any pattern of consumption they may desire, provided the present value of the amounts consumed does not exceed the sum of the net present values of the investments accepted, in this case $366.40. If the investors are presented with a third independent investment option whose net present value is positive, they should accept it. By doing so they will be able to increase the amount they consume in one or more periods without having to decrease consumption in any period. On the other hand, if the investors are presented with another investment option whose net present value is negative, they should reject it. Accepting it would require them to reduce, in one or more periods, the amounts consumed.

The details of the investors' consumption preferences do not need to be known in order to advise them about which investments to accept. One would need to know something about these consumption preferences in order to advise them about how to finance the investment—that is, what loans they should make and when they should be repaid. But the decision to invest is independent of consumption preferences as long as funds can be borrowed (obtained from external sources) or lent at the specified market interest rate.

Qualifications

The problem we have just described is not exactly the problem faced in practice by managers. There are two important ways in which managers might feel that the problems they face are different from the problem just described.

The managers may feel that the financial alternatives open to them are not considered in the preceding problem. They may feel that they are not able to obtain any additional funds, or if they borrow, the lender may impose undesirable restrictions on their actions, or they may not know for future dates what the cost of borrowing or the return from lending will be. In any of these circumstances the present-value method, as we have described it, is not strictly applicable. Second, the managers may not feel they are able to predict with perfect certainty the cash-flow consequences of their investment alternatives. Thus they cannot describe the outcome of making an investment in terms of a single set of cash flows. Rather, there may be a large number of possible cash flows, any of which could be the outcome of selecting the particular investment, and the managers do not know in advance which one of the possible outcomes will occur.

Later we shall consider what modifications should be made to the net present-value method to make it more useful as a method of selecting investments in these more general circumstances.

Net Terminal Value

The net present value of an investment transmits all the information that is needed from an economic point of view (if the net present value is positive the alternative is acceptable). If it is desired to make a point, however, it is frequently more impressive to switch to net terminal value. For example, assume a decision will save $10,000 a year for twenty years. The time-value factor is 10 percent. The present value of these savings is $85,136. After twenty years, however, the firm will have as a result of the savings $572,750 (assuming reinvestment at 10

percent). This latter number is more impressive than \$85,136 and might benefi-
cially be inserted into an argument.

Time Zero

We will generally assume the outlay takes place at time zero. When is time zero?
The choice of time zero will affect the magnitude of the net present value, but it
will not affect the decision. Essentially when we shift time zero forward or backward we are merely multiplying by $(1 + r)^x$ where the exponent x may be positive
or negative.

   If the internal rate of return is being computed, a change in time zero will have
no effect at all on the value of the internal rate of return. Since the net present
value of the cash flows is being equated to zero, multiplying by $(1 + r)^x$ will not
change the value of the solution.

Appendix: Continuous Cash Flows and Continuous Discounting

The assumption is made throughout this book that all cash flows occur instanta-
neously, usually at the end or beginning of a period, and that interest is compounded annually. Either or both of these assumptions may be varied. Interest
may be compounded monthly, weekly, daily, or continuously. Instead of
assuming that the cash flows occur at the end of a year, they may also be
presumed to occur monthly, weekly, daily, or continuously.

Continuous Compounding

To convert a nominal rate of interest j, which is compounded m times annually,
to an effective rate of interest r, compounded annually, we make use of the fact
that

$$(1 + r)^{-n} = \left(1 + \frac{j}{m}\right)^{-mn}, \text{ and solve for } r.$$

Because the present value of a dollar may be computed more easily by using
$(1 + r)^{-n}$, we can substitute it for the right-hand side of the equation. If m is
allowed to increase beyond bound (approach infinity), we have

$$\lim_{m \to \infty} \left(1 + \frac{j}{m}\right)^{-mn} = e^{-jn};$$

e is approximately equal to 2.71828 and is the base of the natural or Naperian
system of logarithms.

   Thus the present value of \$1 for n periods with interest compounded contin-
uously may be computed by using the nominal interest rate.

Example
Let

$$j = .02,$$

$$n = 1.$$

To compute the present value of a dollar, assuming that interest is compounded continuously,

$$e^{-jn} = e^{-.02},$$

$$e^{-.02} = (2.71828)^{-.02}.$$

We can make use of Appendix Table E for finding values of e^{-x}.

$$e^{-.02} = .9802.$$

The .9802 resulting from continuous compounding should be compared with .9804, which is the present value of a dollar, using 2 percent compounded annually. The difference between annual compounding and continuous compounding increases as the level of interest rates increase.

Continuous Payments
Instead of $1 being received at the end of each year, there may be k payments per year, each payment being an amount of $1/k$ dollars. The total received during each year is $1. The present value of a series of such payments extending over n years, with interest compounded continuously at a rate j, will be

$$\sum_{t=0}^{n \times k} \frac{1}{k} e^{-jt}.$$

As we let k become very large (so that we receive the $1 per year in a large number of small installments) the summation approaches a limit, which can be written as follows:

$$\lim_{k \to \infty} \sum_{t=0}^{n \times k} \frac{1}{k} e^{-jt} = \int_0^n e^{-jt} \, dt = \frac{1 - e^{-jn}}{j}.$$

Example
Compute the present value of $1 per period, assuming that interest is compounded continuously and the cash flows occur continuously.

$$j = .02$$

$$n = 1$$

$$e^{-jn} = e^{-.02} = .9802 \text{ (see preceding example)}$$

$$\frac{1 - e^{-jn}}{j} = \frac{1 - .9802}{.02}$$

$$= \frac{.0198}{.02} = .99.$$

The .99 should be compared with the .9802, obtained in the preceding example with continuous compounding but one instantaneous payment, and the .9804 of annual compounding and one payment.

We can convert from interest rates assuming annual compounding to equivalent interest rates assuming continuous compounding, and vice versa. Suppose that r is the rate assuming annual compounding and j is the equivalent continuous rate. Then the following relation must hold:

$$(1 + r) = e^j \quad \text{or} \quad r = e^j - 1.$$

To convert from a continuous rate j to the corresponding annual compounding rate, we use $r = e^j - 1$. Alternatively, taking the log of the first relation, we have $j = \ln(1 + r)$. Table 4-1 shows the continuous equivalents of some representative annual rates. For interest rates below 10 percent, the differences between continuous compounding and annual compounding are not of practical significance for most capital budgeting applications. When r or j becomes large the divergence between their values becomes large.

TABLE 4-1. *Continuous Interest Rates Equivalent to Various Annually Compounded Interest Rates*

Annual Rate	Equivalent Continuous Rate
r	j
.01	.00995
.02	.01980
.03	.02956
.04	.03922
.05	.04879
.10	.09531
.15	.13976
.20	.18232
.25	.22314
.30	.26236
.40	.33647
.50	.40547
1.0	.69315
11.00	2.48491
22,025.46	10.00000

Using the preceding analysis combined with Appendix Table E, we can obtain approximations to the entries in the longer Appendix Tables A or B.

To use Table E, we need the value of x, where x is equal to j times n.

Example

j (continuous interest rate)	n (number of periods)	x	Present Value (from Table E)
.05	1	.05	.951229
.05	2	.10	.904837
.05	3	.15	.860708
.15	1	.15	.860708
.075	2	.15	.860708

In place of Table E any calculator that includes the e^x and ln x functions could be used.

Questions and Problems

4-1. Assume a cost of money of 10 percent. How much could you afford to pay now for $1,000 per year (payable at the end of each year, with the first payment a year from now) for (a) five years; (b) ten years; (c) twenty years; (d) thirty years; (e) perpetuity?

4-2. It costs $20,000 to make a new machine that promises to return cash flows of $10,000 per year for five years. Assume a cost of money of 10 percent. How much could you pay the owner for the patent rights to this machine and still be no worse off than if the new machine were not made?

4-3. If the patent rights for the machine described in problem 4-2 could be purchased for $10,000, what is the largest extra dividend the company could declare immediately on the basis of the net cash flows expected from these transactions?

4-4. Assume the transactions described in problem 4-3 were financed by a "loan" costing 10 percent. How large a loan would be required? Set up a payment schedule for this loan so that the machine is self-financing.

4-5. If the "loan" described in problem 4-4 were to be repaid in a single payment (including "interest") at the end of five years, what financial arrangements would be required?

4-6. There are two investments that have different degrees of risk associated with them. With the first investment it is thought that a dollar to be received one period from now is worth $.9524 today (implying a 5 percent rate of discount). With the second investment it is though that a dollar to be received one period from now is worth $.9091 (implying a 10 percent rate of discount). Use the implied rates of discount to determine the value today of $1 to be received fifty years from now, for each of the two investments.

4-7. Mr. Jones can borrow $1,000 or more at a cost of 6 percent. He has an investment opportunity costing $1,000 that will earn 10 percent. Should his consumption preferences affect the amount he invests or borrows?

4-8. The ABC Company has an investment opportunity that costs $6,000, has a life of one year, and will return $10,000 one period from the time of the investment. Money can be borrowed at a cost of 5 percent.

Required: (a) What is the net present value of the investment? (b) Assume the company borrows $9,524 from the bank and purchases the investment. How much can it pay as immediate dividend and still repay the loan? (c) If the investment costs $9,524, what would be the IRR of the investment?

4-9. The ABC Company has an investment opportunity that requires an immediate outlay of $10,000 and will have a payoff of $12,155 four years from now. It can borrow short-term funds now for the investment at a cost of .04, and then at the end of the first year it will be able to issue a long-term debt at a cost of .06.

Required: Should the investment be undertaken?

4-10. An investment has the following cash flows:

0	−11,712
1	10,000
2	5,000
3	1,000

a. Compute the net present value using 10 percent and the internal rate of return.
b. Using straight-line depreciation, compute the present-value of the income after capital costs 10 percent.
c. Should the investment be undertaken?

4-11. Miss Jones has been offered a desirable investment opportunity that will cost $10,000 and will return 15% per year. She has $10,000 available, but has wanted to buy a new automobile that also costs $10,000.

What facts are relevant to the decision as to whether or not she makes the investment?

4-12. A decision will save $10,000 per year for twenty years. The time-value factor is 10%.

a. What is the present value of the savings?
b. What will the firm have after twenty years if the savings are reinvested?

4-13. Use the continuous discounting to compute the present value of $1,000 for the following situations:

	Annual Discount Rate j	Number of Years Until Receipt of the Cash n
1	.01	100
2	.10	10
3	.20	5
4	.25	4
5	.05	20
6	.05	40
7	.05	100

4-14. Use continuous discounting to compute the internal rate of return of the following investment:

Period	Cash Flow
0	−$15,094
1	10,000
2	10,000
3	1,000

4-15. The C-Can Company is evaluating the status of one of its plants. Currently the plant is losing $1,000,000 per year (cash flow). If the plant is shut down there will be $8,000,000 of closing costs (out-of-pocket).

Another alternative is to modernize the plant at a cost of $10,000,000. This will cause the cash flow per year to be $500,000. Assume this cash flow will continue for perpetuity as will the $1,000,000 negative cash flow associated with doing nothing.

What should the company do?

4-16. *The N Manufacturing Company*
A product is currently being manufactured with an old machine, and the costs of the product are as follows:

	Unit Costs
Labor, direct	$ 4.00
Labor, variable indirect	2.00
Other variable overhead	1.50
Fixed overhead	2.50
	$10.00

In the past year 10,000 units were produced and sold for $8 per unit. It is expected that with suitable repairs the old machine can be used indefinitely in the future, but it has no salvage or trade-in value. A new machine would cost $60,000 and the project costs associated with new machine are as follows:

Labor, direct	$2.00
Labor, variable indirect	3.00
Other variable overhead	1.00
Fixed overhead	2.25
	$8.25

The fixed overhead costs are allocations from other departments plus the depreciation of the equipment. It is not expected that the costs of these departments will be changed by the acquisition of the new equipment.

The new machine has an expected life of ten years.

The appropriate time discount rate for this company is .05.

It is expected that future demand of the product will remain at 10,000 units per year for the next ten years. After ten years the product will be obsolete.

Required: (a) Should the new equipment be acquired? (b) If the product can be purchased at a cost of $7 per unit from a reliable supplier, should it be purchased or made?

4-17. The ABC Company has a cost of money of 10 percent. It has an opportunity to invest in an asset that yields 8 percent and has the following cash flows:

Time	Cash Flow
0	−10,000
1	5,608
2	5,608

While this investment would ordinarily be rejected, the analyst has computed the return on reinvested funds to be 20 percent; accordingly, the $5,608 can be reinvested at time 1 to earn $6,730 at time 2. With $12,338 now being received at time 2, this is an 11 percent return. Thus the firm has decided to accept the investment.

Evaluate the decision.

4-18. Bank A promises to pay its depositors 8 percent interest *compounded continuously,* on one year time deposits.

Bank B makes the same payments to its depositors on one year time deposits, but describes itself as paying X percent interest compounded annually. X is _____ percent. (Show the formula you use to derive X.)

4-19. In the U.S. it is customary for bonds to pay interest semiannually. That is, a $1,000 face value bond is described as paying 8 percent if interest of $40 is paid every six months. In some countries it is customary to pay interest annually. In those countries a $1,000 face value bond is described as paying 8 percent if interest of $80 is paid every twelve months.

If you were willing to pay $1,000 for a bond that would pay $1,080 in one year, what would you be willing to pay for an otherwise identical bond that paid $40 in six months and $1,040 in one year?

4-20. *Long Range Financial Planning*

For this problem ignore income taxes. Assume money can be borrowed or lent at 12 percent per year.

a. Jacque and Jackie are very good friends. Together they have $100,000 in cash. If they did not work but were willing to use up their $100,000, what level annual rate of consumption could they afford for the next eight years? (At the end of year 8 they would be broke.)

b. What level rate of consumption could they afford if they wished to preserve their capital? (At the end of year 8 they would still have $100,000.)

c. Jacque and Jackie believe that if they both got jobs they would be able to earn $20,000 a year for the first four years, and $25,000 a year for the next four. What annual increase in consumption would be made possible if they work? (Consumption is to remain at the same level every year.)

d. Jacque and Jackie are actually planning to go into the retail sporting goods business for themselves. They first plan to open one store, and four years later, when it is established, they expect to open a second. They do not believe that they can handle more than two stores.

They estimate that it required an outlay of $100,000 (mostly for working capital) to start a store. The estimated cash proceeds and outlay for the first eight years are shown below:

End of Period	Outlays	Operating Proceeds
0	-100,000	0
1		10,000
2		20,000
3		30,000
4	-100,000	30,000
5		40,000
6		50,000
7		60,000
8		60,000
Present Values	-163,550	164,494

Assuming that the stores could be sold at the end of year 8 for the value of the working capital at that time ($200,000), what is the NPV of the investment? Use 12 percent as the discount rate.

4-21. What is the maximum possible level rate of consumption if Jacque and Jackie go into business for themselves, and preserve their capital? (Their net worth will be $100,000 at the end of year eight. See the Pro-Forma Balance Sheets.)

Now			
Cash	$100,000	Net Worth	$100,000

At End of Year 8 Balance Sheet Before Business is Liquidated			
Working Capital	200,000	Bank Loans	100,000
		Net Worth	100,000

4-22. The Town of Itheker has been planning some sewer improvements. The cost of constructing the improvements is $1,000,000. The improvements were to be financed by borrowing money to be repaid over a thirty year period. In answering parts a., b., and c. of this question, assume level repayments over the next thirty years.

a. What annual repayment would be required if interest rates are 6 percent?
b. What level annual payments would be required if the interest rates were 12 percent?
c. How much of the first payment referred to in b would go toward interest expense, and how much toward repayment of principal?
d. An obscure provision of the New York State Constitution has the effect of requiring that at least $25,000 of principal be repaid during each of the first two years. What would the total payment be in the first year if the principal repayment were exactly $25,000 and if interest rates were:
(1) 6 percent.
(2) 12 percent.

4-23. A pension fund manager (whose funds were not subject to taxation) considered that the appropriate cost of money for his fund was a continuously compounded rate of 12 percent. The manager had excess funds which he was planning to invest in a bond. He was considering two alternatives. Both bonds were of the very highest quality, and both promised to pay $1,000 at maturity in five years. The domestic bond promised to pay interest at six month intervals, each payment being $62. The first payment would be received in six months and the last at maturity. The other alternative was a Euro-dollar bond which promised to pay interest at annual intervals, each payment being $128. The first payment in this case would be received in one year and the last at maturity.

Which bond would you recommend that the pension manager purchase?

Answers to Selected Questions

4-1. (a) $3,791 **(b)** $6.145 **(c)** $8,514 **(d)** $9,437 **(e)** $10,000
4-3. $7,908   **4-5.** Invest proceeds to earn .10   **4-7.** No   **4-9.** No
4-11. If the cost of borrowed funds is less than 15% she can borrow and invest.
4-13. Answers 1–5: $367.88; 6: $e^{-2} = .13534$ Answer $135.34;
7: $e^{-5} = .00674$ Answer $6.74
4-15. If the discount rate is less than .15 the firm should modernize. If the discount rate is more than .15, "Continue as is" is most desirable.
4-17. Reject the investment.

CHAPTER 5

The Use of Cash Flows in Evaluating Investments

I really don't know one plane from the other. ... To me they are all marginal costs with wings.

—*Alfred E. Kahn, C.A.B. chairman. New York Times, April 23, 1978.*

In Chapter 1 an investment was defined as a commitment " of resources made in the hope of realizing benefits that are expected to occur over a reasonably long period of time in the future." According to this definition, neither the resources nor the benefits need be in the form of explicit cash flows. A decision to have an accounting executive spend a month studying the capabilities of various types of electronic data-processing equipment would be an investment in the sense of this definition. The executive's time is a scarce resource. The month could have been spent in other activities that are valuable to the firm. In the first instance, at least, the expected benefits will be increased knowledge by management of a relatively new technology. Thus there is no explicit cash outlay or cash inflow, but there is an investment.

We have argued that investments ought to be evaluated in terms of the present value of the cash flows expected from them, in preference to any other measures of investment worth that have been suggested. We have not given a complete or careful definition of the term *cash flows*, however. In the present chapter we shall attempt to do this and also to explain some of the difficulties that arise in applying a cash-flow analysis to investment proposals. In Chapter 6, the influence of income taxes on the calculation of cash flows will be discussed.

Cash Flows and Profits

Cash flows are not identical with profits or income. Changes in income can occur without any corresponding changes in cash flows. During a period of investment in plant and inventories, a corporation can even experience a decrease in cash at the same time that income is increasing.

The popular conception of an investment is typified by a one-period outlay of funds, followed by a series of periods in which incomes are earned. The incomes are then related to the investment, and some type of return on investment is computed. One main advantage of the cash-flow procedure is that it avoids difficult problems underlying the measurement of corporate income, which necessarily accompanies the accrual method of accounting. These problems include the following:

1. In what time period should revenue be recognized?
2. What expenses should be treated as investments and therefore capitalized and depreciated over several time periods?
3. What method of depreciation should be used in measuring income as reported to management and stockholders (as distinct from income measurement for tax purposes)?
4. Should LIFO (last in, first out), FIFO, (first in, first out), or some other method be used to measure inventory flow?
5. What costs are inventoriable? Should fixed, variable, direct, indirect, out-of-pocket, unavoidable, administrative, or selling costs be included in evaluating inventory?

There are disagreements as to the answers in each of these questions. Different approaches may lead to different measures of income. If income is used to evaluate investment worth, investments may look good or bad, depending on how income is measured. The utilization of cash flows minimizes many of these complications.

Why Cash Flows

In evaluating an investment we suggest that the cash flows of the investment be used in the analysis. We are not interested in the conventional "cost" of the investment, but rather in the cash outlays required and the timing of these cash flows. We are not using the earnings of period 1, but rather the cash flows of period 1. These distinctions can be important. A builder may tell us that a construction project will cost $1 million, but this is not sufficient information. We want to know when the outlays will be required. For example, if the outlays are made on completion of the building, the cost is truly $1 million. If the payment is required one year prior to completion, the true cost is $1 million plus the interest on the $1 million for one year. The use of expected earnings to measure the benefits of an investment would require a much more sophisticated accounting system than is currently being used by any corporation. The earnings figures resulting from current accounting practices are not usable. Also, even with improved measures of income, there would remain the question of whether the use of cash flows or earnings is more appropriate. If earnings are measured correctly, both measures should give identical results. The advantage of the use of the cash flow is that the receipt of cash is an objective, clearly defined event that leads to a significantly different situation than before the receipt of cash.

A sale on account is an economic event recorded by the accountant and affecting accounting income. But the firm has not yet received the cash, it cannot spend the cash, and the ultimate collection of the cash is uncertain. For purposes of investment analysis we are more interested in the moment when the cash is to be received. At that moment the firm reaches a new decision point. The cash may be returned to the stockholders by the payment of a dividend. It may be used to retire debt, increase the working capital, or to acquire new long-lived assets.

It might be suggested that to be correct the dollar of cash received in period 1 should be followed to its disposition at the end of the firm's life. However, we find it more convenient to take the receipt of cash associated with a specific asset to be a self-contained event, and we do not normally concern ourselves with the final disposition of the dollar. The assumption that the funds can be borrowed and lent at a given discount rate allows us to make this simplifying assumption.

Thus for purposes of investment analysis, unlike conventional accounting, we choose the receipt or disbursement of cash to be the crucial event. It should not be thought that a sale on account or other accruals are ignored. A sale on account in period 1 will affect the expected cash collection in period 2; hence it is brought into the analysis in the period in which the firm has the cash in hand and has reached a decision point.

Absolute and Relative Cash Flows

Every investment analysis involves a comparison of alternatives. If there are not at least two possibilities, there is no problem of choice. Usually the number of alternatives is large. The question may be whether the company is better off with investment A or without it, or whether investment A is better than investment B, or whether both A and B should be accepted or both should be rejected. In any case, because the investment analysis involves a comparison of two or more alternatives, it is not surprising to find that any estimate of cash flows must also be on a comparative basis.

Suppose that the question is whether to start a new business. After a careful analysis we arrive at an estimate of the net cash flows that we expect to occur in each future period after we start the business. Our estimate will tell us how much money we would have to invest during each period as the business got started and how much more money would be available after necessary expenses and additional investments in each period after it began to operate successfully. Perhaps we would plan to sell the business after five years if it were successful, and we would include as a cash flow the amount we would expect to receive for the business five years hence. The present value of the net cash flows might then be calculated, using a rate of discount of 10 percent. What comparisons are we making in analyzing the investment? What comparisons are we making in estimating the net cash flows?

If we say that the cash outlays in the first year are $100,000 (because that amount of money would have to be expended during that period, over and above any cash receipts), we are implicitly comparing the cash flows from operating the business with a cash flow of zero. When cash flows are being compared with zero cash flows, we shall speak of *absolute* cash flows. In evaluating the present value of these cash flows, using a 10 percent rate of interest, we are implicitly comparing this investment with an investment that would return 10 percent per year indefinitely for each net outlay.

Suppose now that the question is whether to start one kind of business or another, for example, a retail store or a wholesale distributorship. One possible analysis would be to estimate the absolute cash flows from each business and compute the present value of the corresponding cash flows. Again, in this case, we are comparing each business separately against a hypothetical investment that could earn 10 percent. Because the hypothetical standard of comparison is the same for both businesses, the two can be readily compared with each other by noticing which business would probably give a higher present value of cash flows. In practice, the final decision would depend on many other factors as well, such as the degree of risk involved in each business, the degree of confidence we feel in our estimates, and so on.

An alternative analysis would be to compare directly one business with the other. In looking at the cash flow estimates, for example, we can subtract (algebraically) the cash flows of the retail store from the cash flows in corresponding periods of the wholesale distributorship. If the difference is positive in a particular period, it will tell us how much better the cash flows from the wholesale business are than those from the retail business during that period. The cash flows, in this case, can be called *relative* cash flows; the wholesale business is being measured relative to the retail business. Again we can compute the present value of this series of relative cash flows. It can be shown that the present value of this series of relative cash flows will be the same as the present value of the absolute cash flows from the wholesale distributorship minus the present value of the absolute cash flows from the retail business. Thus the present-value method will lead to the same conclusion as to the relative worth of the two alternatives, whichever approach is used.

There is an important difference between the two series of cash flows, however. With the series of absolute cash flows, if the corresponding investment (the retail or wholesale businesses) were accepted and actually began to operate, we could compare, period by period, the actual cash flows with our forecasts. There is not, however, any similarly identifiable series of cash flows that could be compared with the relative cash flow estimates. If we decided to operate the wholesale business on the basis of a comparison of relative cash flows, and wished after a few periods to compare our actual results with those we had forecast earlier, we would need to know what assumptions had been made about the retail business in order to make this comparison.

Frequently, when we are considering investments to be made in a going business, it may be difficult to define the absolute cash flows that would result from the investment. It may be easier to use a relative cash flow concept in computing flows. Suppose, for example, that an automobile manufacturer is trying to decide whether to invest in the tools and dies necessary to make a particular modification in the body style of the product. It might compare what sales would be if it made the investment and what they would be if it did not make the investment. This may still be a very difficult estimate to make, because all sorts of other changes are taking place at the same time, both in the product and marketing strategy, and in those of its competitors.

Importance of Considering All Alternatives

Apart from those difficulties in making estimates of relative cash flows that are a by-product of the difficulties of estimating the incremental effects of various actions of the firm, there is an important conceptual danger that must be avoided in estimating relative cash flows. As explained, an estimate of relative cash flows always involves an implicit or explicit comparison of two alternatives. The size of the estimated relative cash flows from making a particular investment will depend upon the alternative that is used as a basis of comparison. *This means that almost any investment can be made to seem worthwhile if it is compared with a sufficiently bad alternative.* Consider a problem that was once faced by many railroads. Should the old coal-burning locomotive used on a particular passenger run be replaced with a modern and more efficient diesel? Assuming that the change would not affect passenger revenues, the natural basis of comparison would appear to be to take the present value of the extra outlays required to purchase the new engine (minus the scrap value of the old coal burner) and the cash savings resulting from the difference between the operating costs of the old and the new engines. On this basis it may seem that the investment in a new diesel engine would be quite profitable. But suppose, using the old coal-burner, that the revenues from the passenger run are insufficient to cover the incremental out-of-pocket costs of operating the train. In such circumstances the purchase of a diesel may serve to decrease the loss, but it may not convert the passenger run into a profitable operation. If there is no possibility of eliminating the passenger run, the decision to purchase the diesel may be wise. But if the passenger train could be eliminated, purchase of the diesel would not be justified. This situation could be handled by examining the absolute cash flows generated by the diesel—that is, by comparing the cash flows resulting from the passenger train with a diesel locomotive and the cash flows resulting from no train at all. When using relative cash flows, we must remember to consider all alternatives, including the alternative of continuing as we are now or abandoning the operation entirely, if these alternatives are both possible.

An investment should not be accepted unless the net present value of its relative cash flows are positive when compared with the next best alternative. Frequently, the analyst will be faced with a situation in which there are quite a number of possible alternatives whose relative advantages are not yet known. In such cases any one of the investments can be used as the standard of comparison, and the relative advantage of each estimate can be compared to this standard. If all the other alternatives have a negative present value when compared with the standard, the standard is the most advantageous insofar as explicit cost and revenue considerations are the determinants. In the railroad locomotive example, if continuing to operate the coal-burning locomotive were taken as the standard, it could turn out that discontinuing the passenger train altogether would give a higher present value than buying a diesel, although the latter is better than continuing to operate the coal-burning locomotive. As long as all feasible alternatives are considered, it makes no difference which alternative is tentatively accepted as the standard of comparison. The final answer will be the same in any case. The choice of a standard of comparison may lead to mistaken conclusions only if some advantageous alternatives (such as ceasing production entirely) are excluded from the analysis.

Example 1: Absolute and Relative Cash Flows
A new modernized store replacing an old store is expected to earn 25 percent. Should it be accepted if the firm has a 10 percent cost of money? The cash flows (a perpetuity) are

0	1	2
−1,000,000	+250,000	+250,000 $\cdots$

Conclusion: We have to know what the present store is earning.

Example 2 (*continuation of 1*)
Now assume the cash flows of Example 1 are absolute flows and the old store is currently earning $200,000 a year. The relative cash flows for "new minus old" are

0	1	2	3
−1,000,000	50,000	50,000 $\cdots$	

This is a 5 percent return and the new store is clearly not acceptable unless we add new information (such as a changing competitive situation).

Example 3 (*continuation of 1*)
Now assume the cash flows of Example 1 are relative cash flows and the old store is losing $200,000 per year:

	0	1	2	3
Continue Old		−200,000	−200,000	$\cdots$
New	−1,000,000	50,000	50,000	$\cdots$
New − Old	−1,000,000	250,000	250,000	$\cdots$

The 25 percent return is not valid, since the new is being compared to an unacceptable alternative. Both alternatives are unacceptable. If there are no better alternatives the store should be shut down.

Example 1 illustrates the fact that all the alternatives must be considered. Example 2 shows that if both alternatives are acceptable we cannot just consider the new. Example 3 shows that we cannot compare the new against an alternative that is not acceptable.

Opportunity Costs

Usually, the cash outlays included in the computation of net cash flows are the outlays incurred because of the investment; these would not be incurred otherwise. Outlays that would be incurred by the firm whether or not the investment is accepted should not be charged to a particular investment project. Thus the practice of allocating a share of general overhead to a new project on the basis of some arbitrary measure, such as direct labor hours or a fraction of net sales, is not recommended *unless* it is expected that general overhead will actually increase if the project is accepted.

On the other hand, in some instances an investment project may require the use of some scarce resource available to the firm, although the explicit cash outlays associated with using that resource may be nonexistent or may not adequately reflect the value of the resource to the firm. Examples are projects that require a heavy drain on the time of key executive personnel or that use valuable floor space in a plant or store already owned by the business. The costs of using such resources are called *opportunity costs*, and they are measured by estimating how much the resource (the executives' time or the floor space) would earn for the company if the investments under consideration were rejected.

It may appear that the practice of charging opportunity costs against an investment project when no corresponding cash outlay can be identified is a violation of, or exception to, the procedure of evaluating investments in terms of actual cash flows. Actually, including opportunity costs is not so much an exception to the cash-flow procedure as an extension of it. The opportunity cost charged should measure net cash flows that could have been earned if the project under discussion had been rejected. Suppose that one floor of a factory building owned by a business could either be rented out at $1,200 per month or used to produce a new product. After an initial outlay for equipment the new product could produce an absolute net cash inflow of $2,000 per month after taxes but before an allowance has been made for use of the factory space. The figure of $2,000 per month overstates the benefits to be derived from the new product, because the space required could otherwise be used to earn $1,200 per month. By charging a rental opportunity cost of $1,200 per month against the new product, a more meaningful measure of its actual value to the company is obtained. An alternative procedure would be to estimate the relative cash flow from the new product compared with that produced by renting the extra space and not producing the new product.

In some instances it will be extremely difficult to estimate opportunity costs. The temptation then is to use some other, more easily identifiable basis of charging for the use of such things as floor space or the time of key executives. This temptation must be viewed with some skepticism. The pro rata share of the costs of owning a building may be much higher or much lower than the true opportunity costs of using that space. When there is really no basis for estimating the opportunity costs associated with the use of a factor, such as the time of certain key executives, it may be preferable to note merely that the proposed project is likely to require considerably more or considerably less than the usual amount of attention from such key executives.

The only valid justification for the prorating of the out-of-pocket costs to the proposed project would be if the costs are a reasonable basis for estimating the opportunity cost. For example, if an additional executive can be hired for the same cost as a present executive, the opportunity cost of using some of the time of the present executive should not be greater than this current salary (a new executive could be hired). If it is felt that the managers are currently earning their salaries when they are doing the least profitable tasks, the cost should not be less. Thus we can correctly say that the opportunity cost of an executive's time is equal to the actual salary that would be paid to the next executive who could be hired.

Acquiring Assets Without Cash Disbursements

The term *cash outlay* is also applied to a transaction in which an asset is acquired by incurring a long-term debt or by issuing stock. Even though there may be no explicit borrowing of cash, receipt of cash, and disbursement of cash, these transactions are assumed to occur when an asset is acquired via a promise to pay in some distant time period, and the transaction is treated as if there has been a cash outlay as well as a source of new capital.

When an asset is acquired by the incurrence of a non-interest-bearing current liability, the convention is adopted in this book that it is the timing of the actual cash disbursement that is important. Thus, if the investment results in an increase in inventories of $100 and the source of capital is an increase in current liabilities of $100, the net cash outlay that is required in the period of inventory acquisition is zero. If the $100 increase in inventories required cash outlays of $20 and current liabilities increased by $80, then the net cash outlay in the period of inventory acquisition is $20.

Using Common Stock

Some investments are acquired by the issuance of common stock. In such a situation there is no disbursement of cash and there is a tendency to evaluate such opportunities as if there are no cash outlays. This tendency is wrong. The cash that could have been obtained by a public offering of the common stock is an opportunity cost and in an economic sense is a cash outlay. The method of analysis for an issuance of stock should be identical to the analysis used when there is an explicit cash outlay. The tax consequences may be different.

Excluding Interest Payments

Cash disbursed for interest is normally excluded from the cash-flow computation used in analyzing investments. The interest factor is taken into consideration by the use of the present-value procedures. To include also the cash disbursement for interest would result in double counting. Assume that the discount factor being used to take into consideration the time value of money is 6 percent. There is an investment that requires an outlay of $1,000 and promises to return $1,080 at the end of one period. This investment would seem to be desirable. Assume that we can raise money for this investment at a cost of 6 percent—that is, borrow $1,000 now and pay $1,060 a year from now. An incorrect analysis would show the $60 interest as a deduction from the cash flows of period 1:

	Year	
	0	1
Investment	−$1,000	$1,080
Interest		− 60
Net cash flows	−$1,000	$1,020

This series of cash flows would incorrectly lead to a reject decision, using higher than a 2 percent rate of interest because of a double counting of interest.

Including All Debt Flows

As stated previously, it is incorrect to include the interest payments in the cash flows. We can choose for certain purposes to inclue all cash flows of the debt-financing associated with an investment, however.

Continuing the preceding example, the cash flows of the investment and the cash flows of the debt would be as follows:

	Year	
	0	1
Investment	−$1,000	$1,080
Debt financing	1,000	−1,060
Net cash flows	0	20

An inspection of the table shows that the present value of the net of debt cash flows is positive for any choice of interest rate greater than zero. Whenever we allow the inclusion of the debt financing cash flows in the investment analysis with no limit on the amount of debt, by a suitable usage of debt we can make any conventional investment with an internal rate of return greater than the cost of debt have a positive present value (or an acceptable internal rate of return). If we were using the internal rate of return method we would say that the internal rate of return resulting after the subtraction of the debt cash flows would be the IRR on the stockholders' investment. In like manner, using the present-value method, we are computing the present value of the cash flows associated with the stockholders' investment. Because by combining suitable amounts of debt with the investment cash flows we can make investments with IRRs only slightly greater than the cost of debt have acceptable present values and acceptable IRRs, the method of analysis being illustrated should never be used arbitrarily for some investments and not for others.

The computation of the internal rate of return and present value of the cash flows associated with the stockholders' investment are interesting calculations. They follow naturally from the assumption that the stockholders are interested in the expected return (and risk) of their investment. However, they are more complex than the basic investment flows since their use requires either that the capital structure be kept constant through time, or a different discount rate be used each time period.

Salvage and Removal Costs

The salvage and removal costs introduce no real problem if we keep in mind that we are interested in the periods when cash outlays are made or when cash flows into the firm. In the following descriptive material, the term *salvage* refers to "net salvage"; removal costs have been subtracted.

Let us first consider the salvage value of the new investment. Any funds obtained from selling the new investment when it is retired will increase the flow of cash in the last period. Thus the salvage of the new investment will increase the cash flow of the last period of use.

When the investment is being made to replace an item of equipment currently being used, there are two additional salvage values to be considered: (1) the salvage value now of the old equipment, and (2) the salvage value that the old equipment would have had at the end of its physical or useful life (whichever comes first) if it were not replaced now. If the asset is replaced now, the present salvage will have the effect of increasing the cash flow of this period (or decreasing the required cash outlay). However, if the old equipment is being retired now, the salvage that would have been obtained at the end of its life will not be obtained. Thus there is a decrease in the relative cash flows of that last period because of the salvage which will not be obtained at that time. To summarize, the absolute cash flow effects are:

Salvage value of the new equipment: Increase the cash flow of the last year of use for the buy alternative.

Present salvage value of the old equipment: Increase the cash flow for this year (decrease the cash outlay) for the buy alternative.

Salvage value of the old equipment at time of normal retirement: Increase the cash flow of that year (because the salvage value would be obtained if the replace-ment did not take place). This cash inflow applies to the absolute cash flows of the "continue-the-old" alternative.

The cash flows arising from salvage of the old equipment would be treated in a somewhat different manner if the present values of the alternatives were com-puted individually. It would only increase the cash flows at the time of retirement.

The analysis of the cash flows arising from salvage is complicated by the fact that the cash-flow analysis may be made in terms of relative or absolute cash flows. The preceding description assumes that the cash flows are relative, that is, the cash flows from buying the new equipment minus the cash flows which would occur if the old equipment were retained. It is frequently reasonable to analyze the absolute cash flows of the several alternatives. Thus the cash flows of retaining the old would be computed, as would the cash flows of purchasing the new equipment. The present salvage value of the old equipment and the future salvage value of the new equipment would affect the cash flow of the alternative of purchasing the new equipment. The salvage value on retirement of the old would affect the cash flow of retaining the old equipment.

Example

Assume the present equipment has a salvage value now of $1,000 and an expected salvage value in five years of $400 (at which time the equipment would be physically unusable). The new equipment will have a salvage value at the time of its expected retirement of $650. All figures are on an after-tax basis. The cash flows arising from the salvage values would be as follows:

	Year		
	0	5	10
Absolute flows of			
Retaining the old		$ 400	
Purchasing the new	$1,000	_____	$650
Relative flows of			
replacing now	$1,000	$(400)	$650

Terminal Value

Salvage value is one form of terminal value. Another form of terminal value is the release of cash necessary to operate the investment. Other examples of items that may result in released cash at cessation of operations are collections of accounts receivable and reduction in required inventories. All these items gave rise to outlays of cash when they were purchased and then lagged in their generation of cash. When the outlays of cash cease, because the production is being phased out, the coming periods will have increases in cash flows resulting from the conversion of these noncash current assets into cash; similarly, reductions of current lia-bilities reduce cash.

Income Taxes and Cash Flows

The question of income taxes and cash flows is reviewed in detail in Chapter 6. It should be remembered that *the term* cash flows *in this chapter refers to flows after the deduction of income taxes.* The income taxes are computed by applying the expected tax rate for each period to the taxable income (excluding interest charges) of that period. The taxable income will not be equal to the cash flow of the period, and frequently the taxable income will not equal the income computed in accordance with generally accepted accounting principles. Thus no matter what method is being used to accept or reject investments, it will be necessary to compute the income for tax purposes.

Cash Flows and Uncertainty

Each computation of cash flows makes specific assumptions about the level of business activity, actions of competitors, future availability of improved models of machines, costs of factors of production, future sales, and the like. Because there is a large amount of uncertainty connected with each of these factors, it should be appreciated that computations using the present-value method are indications rather than numbers with 100 percent certainty and accuracy. A more detailed discussion of the consequences of uncertain estimates and some suggestions for making analyses when basic assumptions are subject to uncertainty are presented in later chapters. It should be stressed that any decision about investments must be based on as complete a consideration of all the relevant factors as it is possible to provide, and that the probable present value of an investment proposal is only one factor, although a very significant one, to be considered in arriving at a final decision.

Questions and Problems

5-1. The Bright Machine Tool Shop is considering replacement of the equipment in a section of its shop. The equipment performs a function that could be completely eliminated. A comparison of the present equipment being used with new equipment indicates that the following relative cash flows would result if the new machine were purchased instead of continuing with the old:

Period	
0	1
($10,000)	$12,000

The internal rate of return of the investment is 20 percent, and the cost of money is 15 percent. The net present value of the investment is $435. Based on the positive net present value, the decision was made to replace the present equipment.

In the period of operation the machine performed exactly as predicted, and all costs were as predicted. The absolute cash flows were as follows:

Period	
0	1
($10,000)	$11,000

Required: Comment on the investment decision made by the Bright Machine Tool Shop.

5-2. The Dotted Airline Company is considering replacement of its fleet of ten two-engined planes with five new-model jets. One jet can replace two of the present planes. The airplane company has prepared an analysis showing that each new plane will cost $343,000 and will earn cash proceeds of $100,000 per year for five years. Assume that after five years the salvage value will be zero for both the new and old planes. The analysis was based on the load and operating characteristics of the new plane and the past experience of the airline, as well as the number of passengers and the routes traveled, adjusted in a reasonable manner for additional passengers who will be attracted by the new planes.

The planes currently being used are considered to be safe workhorses, but are not as glamorous as the new planes. In competition with jets, they are expected to earn net cash proceeds of only $10,000 per year per plane. There is no discernible trend of earnings. The present planes now have a zero salvage value.

The cost of money of the Dotted Airline is 10 percent. Assume that the company has access to the necessary funds.

Required: Should the Dotted Airline purchase the new jets? Explain. What would be your recommendation if the salvage value is now $40,000 on an old plane?

5-3. The following facts relate to an investment that costs $10,000 being considered by the ABC Company:

	Period	
	1	2
Cash revenues	$12,000	$12,000
Depreciation	5,000	5,000
Net income	7,000	7,000

The company intends to declare dividends of $12,000 in period 1 and $12,000 in period 2 as a result of the investment. The company is not subject to income taxes.

Required: What are the cash flows of the two years for purposes of the analysis of the investment?

5-4. For problem 5-3, assume that all the sales were made on account, and collection lagged the sale by one period. The company will distribute dividends equal to the cash generation.

Required: What are the cash flows of each year?

5-5. An investment will require an increase in the following working capital items:

Cash	$1,000,000
Accounts receivable	3,000,000
Inventories	6,000,000

It is also expected that current liabilities will increase by $4 million.

Required: How will the preceding items affect the cash flows of the investment?

5-6. The increase in current liabilities referred to in the previous question includes $1 million of interest expense accrued but not yet paid. Revise your previous answer, if necessary, taking account of this information.

5-7. The ABC Company is considering an investment in a new product. The information for one year is as follows:

Sales	$200,000
Manufacturing costs of sales	80,000
(includes $20,000 of depreciation)	
Selling and administrative expenses	40,000
(directly associated with the product)	
Equipment purchases	10,000
Decrease in contribution of other products	5,000
Increase in accounts receivable	15,000
Increase in inventories	20,000
Increase in current liabilities	30,000
Income taxes associated with product income	12,000
Interest on bonds expected to be used in financing	18,000

Required: Compute the cash flow that can be used in the present-value computations of this investment.

5-8. A product is currently being manufactured on a machine that has a book value of $10,000 (it was purchased for $50,000 twenty years ago). The costs of the product are as follows:

	Unit Costs
Labor, direct	$ 4.00
Labor, variable indirect	5.00
Other variable overhead	2.50
Fixed overhead	2.50
	$14.00

In the past year 10,000 units were produced and sold for $10 per unit. It is expected that the old machine can be used indefinitely in the future.

An equipment manufacturer has offered to accept the old machine as a trade-in for a new version. The new machine would cost $80,000 after allowing $15,000 for the old equipment. The projected costs associated with the new machine are as follows:

Labor, direct	$ 2.00
Labor, variable indirect	3.50
Other variable overhead	4.00
Fixed overhead	3.25
	$12.75

The fixed overhead costs are allocations from other departments plus the depreciation of the equipment. Repair costs are the same for both machines.

The old machine could be sold on the open market now for $6,000. Ten years from now it is expected to have a salvage value of $1,000. The new machine has an expected life of ten years and an expected salvage of $10,000.

There are no corporate income taxes. The appropriate time discount rate for this company is .05. It is expected that future demand of the product will remain at 10,000 units per year.

Required: (a) Should the new equipment be acquired? (b) If the product can be purchased at a cost of $8 per unit from a reliable supplier, should it be purchased or made?

5-9. The ABC Company is considering an investment in a new product. The information for one year is as follows:

Sales (all on account)	$200,000
Manufacturing costs of sales	90,000
(include $20,000 of depreciation and $6,000 of fixed cost allocations from service departments)	
Selling and administrative expenses	40,000
(directly associated with the product)	
Equipment purchases	10,000
(purchased on account and not yet paid)	
Decrease in contribution of other products	5,000
Increase in accounts receivable	15,000
Increase in inventories	20,000
(includes $4,000 depreciation)	
Increase in current liabilities	30,000
Income taxes associated with product income	12,000
Interest on bonds expected to be used in financing	18,000
Uncollected accounts receivable expected to be written off	2,000
Increase in accumulated depreciation	19,000

Required: Compute the cash flow that can be used in the present-value computations of this investment.

5-10. Assume that the investment of problem 5-9 is financed partially by sinking fund bonds and there is a requirement to place $50,000 per year into a sinking fund. Does this additional information change the computation of the cash flows?

5-11. The Big Manufacturing Company (BMC) has a plant that is currently losing $1,000,000 of cash per year. This loss is expected to continue into the future unless either of two actions is taken.

The plant can be closed down at a one-time cost of $10,000,000 (there are large pension obligations). Alternatively $12,000,000 can be invested to earn $600,000 of cash flow per year (a perpetuity).

The analysts of the firm have concluded that the $12,000,000 should not be invested, since the investment will earn only 5 percent per year and the plant should be closed down. The firm has a weighted average cost of capital of 15 percent and a borrowing cost of 12 percent (it has debt outstanding). Its tax rate is zero.

Required:
a. What should BMC do?
b. What should BMC do if the investment opportunity is not available?

5-12. The A Company is currently earning $13,000,000 per year on $100,000,000 of stockholders' equity, or a return of 13 percent. One plant with a cost base of $10,000,000 earns $800,000 per year.

The Chairman of the Board has set a target ROI of 15 percent.

The Company has received an offer of $5,000,000 for the plant. The pro forma return on investment (assuming the $5,000,000 is returned to investors) is

$$\text{ROI} = \frac{12,200,000}{90,000,000} = 13.5\%.$$

Should the plant be sold?

5-13. The X Company will use a .10 discount rate in evaluating an investment that costs $1,500,000. For each year of its fifteen-year life the investment will have the same revenues and out-of-pocket expenses. The firm uses straight-line depreciation. The first year's income statement is:

Revenues	$280,000
Out-of-pocket expenses	30,000
Interest	150,000
Depreciation expense	100,000
Income	0

The company has a zero tax rate. Should the company undertake the investment?

5-14. Assume the cash flows of an investment are

0	−1,500,000
1–15	250,000

The rate of discount to be used is .10.

Should the company undertake the investment?

5-15. The MN Manufacturing Company (a modification of problem 4-16)

A product is currently being manufactured with an old machine, and the costs of the product are as follows:

	Unit Costs
Labor, direct	$4.00
Labor, variable indirect	2.00
Other variable overhead	1.50
Fixed overhead	2.50
	$10.00

The old machine has a book value of $20,000 (it was purchased for $55,000 ten years ago).

In the past year 10,000 units were produced and sold for $7 per unit. It is expected that with suitable repairs the old machine can be used indefinitely in the future. A new machine would cost $80,000 less $24,000 trade-in allowance for the old machine. The project costs associated with new machine are as follows:

Labor, direct	$2.00
Labor, variable indirect	3.00
Other variable overhead	1.00
Fixed overhead	2.25
	$8.25

Repair costs are the same for both machines, and are included in variable overhead. The old machine could be sold on the open market now for $6,000 and in ten years for $1,000.

The fixed overhead costs are allocations from other departments plus the depreciation of the equipment. It is not expected that the costs of these departments will be changed by the acquisition of the new equipment.

The new machine has an expected life of ten years, and expected salvage of $9,000.

The appropriate time discount rate for this company is .05. There are no income taxes.

It is expected that future demand for the product will remain at 10,000 units per year for the next ten years. After ten years the product will be obsolete.

Required:

a. Should the equipment be acquired?

b. If the product can be purchased at a cost of $6.90 per unit from a reliable supplier, should it be purchased or made?

5-16. The National Money Company, in deciding whether to make or buy, considers only direct labor and direct material as being relevant costs. The sum of these two costs factors is compared with the cost of purchasing the items, and a decision is made on this basis.

Required: Appraise the make or buy procedure of the National Money Company.

5-17. The Ithaca Manufacturing Company has excess capacity and is considering manufacturing a component part that is currently being purchased. The estimate of the cost of producing one unit of product is as follows:

Direct labor	$2.00
Material	3.00
Variable overhead	1.00
Fixed overhead (based on accounting procedures of a generally accepted nature)	2.50
	$8.50

The average increase in net working capital that will be required if the item is produced internally is $50,000.

The firm uses 100,000 of the parts per year. The unit cost of purchasing the parts is $6.05. Assume a zero tax rate.

Required: Should the company make or buy?

5-18. The Company has an investment opportunity that offers $1 million of cash flows a year for perpetuity. It requires a cash outlay of $19.6 million for plant and equipment and the necessary inventory. It is estimated that an additional $500,000 of cash will have to be carried as a compensating balance during the period of the investment. The company has a time value of money of .05.

Required: Is the investment acceptable?

5-19. A product is currently being manufactured on an old machine. The costs of the product are:

	Unit Costs
Labor, direct	0.20
Labor, indirect	0.20
Variable overhead	0.15
Fixed overhead	0.25
Total	0.80

In the past year, 100,000 units were produced and sold for $0.60 per unit. It is expected that the old machine could be used indefinitely.

A new machine is available that would cost $90,000 in cash with the old machine traded in. The projected costs with the new machine are:

	Unit Costs
Labor, direct	.10
Labor, indirect	.15
Variable overhead	.15
Fixed overhead	.45
Total	.85

The fixed overhead costs are allocations from other departments plus the depreciation of the equipment. Repair costs are the same for both machines.

The old machine could be sold on the open market now for $40,000. Eight years from now it is expected to have a salvage value of $15,000. The new machine has an expected life of eight years and an expected salvage of $60,000.

There are no corporate income taxes. The appropriate time discount rate for this company is .12.

It is expected that future demand of the product will remain at 100,000 units per year.

Should the new equipment be acquired? Justify your answer with specific calculations.

Discussion Questions

5-A. To make a new product, inventories must be increased by $5 million. Should this be considered a cash outlay?

5-B. Would you expect the relevant costs for decisionmaking (such as the make or buy decision) to be higher or lower than the accounting costs computed on an absorption costing basis?

5-C. In computing the cash flows of a period, should interest payments be included or excluded? Explain.

Answers to Selected Problems

5-1. The new machine should not have been purchased.
5-3. The cash flows are

Period 1	12,000
Period 2	12,000

5-5. The use of cash is $6,000,000.

5-7. Net cash flow = $68,000.

5-9. Net cash flow = $68,000.

5-11. (a) The investment is desirable. **(b)** The company should operate the plant.

5-13. NPV = $401,525.

CHAPTER **6**

Corporate Income Taxes and Investment Decisions

Ben Franklin:
A penny saved is a penny earned.
Accountant:
Wrong. An after-tax penny saved is equal to two pennies
before tax.

Accounting theory suggests three basically different methods of recording a cash outlay for an asset or cost factor; these in turn affect the measurement of income. The outlay may be considered to be an expense of the period in which it is incurred, or to represent the acquisition of a wasting asset that will be charged to expense over a number of future periods, or to represent the acquisition of a nonwasting asset, in which case it is never charged to expense. The first is typified by outlays for a sale executive's salary, the second by outlays for plant and equipment, and the third by outlays for land. For some outlays a reasonable case can be made for one or another accounting treatment. Thus outlays for research, certain types of advertising, and some kinds of maintenance may be treated as current expenses or capitalized and depreciated over a longer period; outlays for land may be treated as wasting assets if the important characteristics of the land are its possession of certain minerals or soil fertility, or as partially nonwasting if its site value is considered.

The accounting treatment accorded a particular outlay will influence the amount and timing of income measurement. But in the absence of income taxes, the choice of investments should not be influenced by the method of accounting for a particular outlay. The amount and timing of the cash outlays and the amount and timing of future cash proceeds are what is relevant to the choice of investments.

In the case of corporations subject to income taxes, the accounting treatment adopted for income tax purposes must be considered in evaluating a potential investment, because the choice will affect the amount and timing of income tax payments. Because income taxes do not affect all investments in the same manner, it is necessary to place cash flows associated with each investment on an after-tax basis before evaluating the investments. In this chapter we shall be concerned with the mechanics of computing the after-tax cash flows associated with investments. We shall consider separately the problems associated with depreciable assets, nondepreciable assets, and outlays chargeable to current expense.

Measuring the Effects of Depreciation Charges on Cash Flows

Suppose that we are considering the purchase of a new piece of equipment that is expected to have no salvage value on retirement. If there were no income taxes, the cash proceeds resulting from the use of the equipment could be estimated by subtracting the additional cash outlays required to operate the equipment from the additional revenues that result from acquiring it. That is,

Before-tax cash proceeds = revenues − expenses.   (1)

The term *cash proceeds* is used here to refer to the proceeds generated by operating the investment. It assumes that all revenues are accompanied by an immediate generation of cash equal to the revenues. It also assumes that all cash outlays, except the initial investment, are charged to expense—that is, none is charged to inventory—and that inventory is not reduced. Thus cash outlays are equal to the expenses (excluding depreciation) in this simple example. For a nonprofit hospital or government bureau this is the only calculation that would be necessary. For a business it is necessary to subtract the additional income tax liability that occurs because of the investment:

After-tax proceeds = revenues − cash outlays − income tax,   (2)

or

After-tax proceeds = revenues − expenses other than depreciation
− income tax.   (3)

The income tax liability is computed by applying the income tax rate to the additional taxable income. One allowable deduction for tax purposes is the depreciation of the investment. It is possible to express the determination of the income tax in the following way:

Income tax = (tax rate) × (taxable income),   (4)

and

Income tax = (tax rate)
× (revenues − expenses other than depreciation − depreciation).   (5)

From equation (5) it can be seen that the higher the depreciation taken for income tax purposes, the lower the income tax will be and the greater the after-tax cash proceeds. Substituting equation (5) in equation (3) and simplifying gives equations (6) and (7).

After-tax proceeds = (1 − tax rate)
× (revenues − expenses other than depreciation − depreciation)
+ depreciation,   (6)

or

After-tax proceeds = $(1 - \text{tax rate})$
$\times$ (revenues − expenses other than depreciation)
$+ (\text{tax rate} \times \text{depreciation}).$ (7)

Equations (6) and (7) are mathematically equivalent, and therefore give identical answers, although one or the other formula may be easier to use in a particular instance. Equation (7) is particularly useful, because it highlights the fact that the cash proceeds of the period are increased by the allowable tax depreciation times the tax rate. Thus we can compute the present value of the "tax savings" by multiplying the depreciation by the expected tax rate of each period and discounting that amount back to the present. For convenience we assume that the first depreciation deduction and the resulting tax saving takes place exactly one year after the single outlay associated with the investment. This is a simplification since the exact timing of the savings will depend on the timing difference between the investment outlays and the tax payments.

Example
A piece of new equipment costs $10,000. It can be depreciated for tax purposes in four years, and it has been decided to use the sum-of-the-years'-digits method. It is expected to have no salvage value on retirement. The company uses straight-line depreciation in its accounting. The equipment is expected to result in an increase in annual revenues (sales are all for cash) of $8,000 and additional annual costs requiring cash outlays of $4,000 (not including depreciation of the equipment). The income tax rate is 48 percent. The cost of money is 10 percent (after tax).

The first step is to compute the taxable income and income tax of each year. This is accomplished in Table 6-1.

TABLE 6-1.   *Computation of Income Tax*

Year	Revenues	Other Costs	Depreciation for Tax Purposes	Taxable Income	Tax Rate (%)	Income Tax
1	$8,000	$4,000	$4,000	$ 0	48	$ 0
2	8,000	4,000	3,000	1,000	48	480
3	8,000	4,000	2,000	2,000	48	960
4	8,000	4,000	1,000	3,000	48	1,440

It should be noted that the use of a tax rate of 48 percent for all years carries an assumption that the tax rate will not be changed. If a change is expected, the tax rates of the future years should be used.

The second step is to compute the cash proceeds of each year (Table 6-2.) It is important to note that the book depreciation does not enter into this computation at all, but the depreciation for tax purposes influences the income tax and thus does indirectly affect the proceeds.

TABLE 6-2. *Computation of Cash Proceeds*

Year	Revenue	Other Costs	Income Tax	Cash Proceeds
1	$8,000	$4,000	$ 0	$4,000
2	8,000	4,000	480	3,520
3	8,000	4,000	960	3,040
4	8,000	4,000	1,440	2,560

Using equation (6) to compute the cash flows of year 2, we would have

$$\text{After-tax proceeds} = (1 - .48)(8{,}000 - 4{,}000 - 3{,}000) + 3{,}000$$

$$= 520 + 3{,}000$$

$$= 3{,}520.$$

Using equation (7), we have

$$\text{After-tax proceeds} = (1 - .48)(8{,}000 - 4{,}000) + (.48 \times 3{,}000)$$

$$= 2{,}080 + 1{,}440$$

$$= 3{,}520.$$

The next step is to compute the present value of the cash flows, using 10 percent as the rate of discount (see Table 6-3).

TABLE 6-3. *Computation of the Present Value of Proceeds*

Year	Cash Proceeds	Discount Factor (Using 10 Percent)	Present Value of the Proceeds
1	$4,000	.9091	$ 3,636
2	3,520	.8264	2,909
3	3,040	.7513	2,284
4	2,560	.6830	1,748
			$10,577

The present value of the proceeds, $10,577, is greater than the cash outflows of $10,000; thus the investment is apparently desirable.

In the preceding example the "other costs" allowed for tax purposes were equal to the "other costs" for which cash outlays were made. It is possible for these two amounts to differ. For example, costs may be incurred that are not allowable for tax purposes because the cost factors are in inventory. The cash outlays are required, but they do not give rise to decreases in the income tax of the period.

TABLE 6-4. *Computation of Twice-Straight-Line Depreciation*

Year	Decreasing Balance	Depreciation Rate (%)	Depreciation of the Period	Accumulated Depreciation
1	$10,000	50	$5,000	$ 5,000
2	5,000	50	2,500	7,500
3	2,500	50	1,250	8,750
4	1,250	100*	1,250	10,000

* Assuming the asset is to be retired at the end of the fourth year.

A different schedule of depreciation deductions for tax purposes is obtained if the twice-straight-line, declining-balance method is used (Table 6-4). The company using this procedure for tax purposes has the option to switch to the straight-line procedure. When the depreciation charge following twice straight line becomes less than it would be following straight line, the company should switch to the latter procedure. This will result in $1,250 of depreciation for year 4. The next step would be to compute the taxable income, income tax, and cash proceeds for each year of the life of the investment so that the present value of the cash flows may be computed, just as was done when using the sum-of-the-years'-digits depreciation.

Choosing the Most Advantageous Depreciation Procedure

Under the internal revenue code, a company has had a choice (among other methods) of depreciating a new asset by using straight-line depreciation, sum-of-the-years' digits, or twice straight line on the declining balance. It has frequently been noted that the choice of depreciation method will affect the profitability of the investment. The best depreciation method for a company will depend upon the appropriate discount rate as well as upon the life of the investment and its expected salvage value. The present-value method can be put to use in making this decision. For this purpose equation (7) for computing the after-tax cash proceeds is most advantageous, because it divides the after-tax cash proceeds into two parts. The first part is independent of the depreciation method, and the second part depends only on the depreciation method. The depreciation method giving the highest present value should be chosen.

As is indicated in Table 6-5, the present value of the after-tax equivalent of $4,000 a year for four years is $6,594 when the tax rate is 48 percent and the discount rate is 10 percent. This part of the calculation is independent of the depreciation method used.

To determine the best depreciation method, we need to compute the present value of the tax saving resulting from the use of each possible depreciation method. These computations are shown in Table 6-6, assuming a 48 percent tax

TABLE 6-5.   *Present Value of After-Tax Cash Proceeds Excluding Depreciation*

Year	(1) Revenues Less Current Expenses	(2) After-Tax Equivalent (Col. 1 × .52)	(3) Discount Factor	(4) Present Value (Col. 2 × Col. 3)
1	$ 4,000	$2,080	.9091	$1,891
2	4,000	2,080	.8264	1,719
3	4,000	2,080	.7513	1,563
4	4,000	2,080	.6830	1,421
	$16,000	$8,320	3.1698	$6,594

TABLE 6-6.   *Present Value of Tax Savings from Different Methods of Depreciation, Assuming a 10 Percent Rate of Discount*

Year	Straight Line Allowable Expense	Saving (48%)	Present Value	Twice Straight Line Allowable Expense	Saving (48%)	Present Value	Sum-of-the-Years' Digits Allowable Expense	Saving (48%)	Present Value
1	$ 2,500	$1,200	$1,091	$ 5,000	$2,400	$2,182	$ 4,000	$1,920	$1,745
2	2,500	1,200	992	2,500	1,200	992	3,000	1,440	1,190
3	2,500	1,200	902	1,250	600	451	2,000	960	721
4	2,500	1,200	820	1,250	600	410	1,000	480	328
	$10,000	$5,200	$3,805	$10,000	$4,800	$4,035	$10,000	$4,800	$3,984

rate and a 10 percent rate of discount. We assume the firm has other taxable income to absorb the tax loss of year 1. It is clear from this table that the investment would be most advantageous if it could be used with the twice straight-line method of depreciation, because in that case the present value of the cash proceeds would be $10,629 ($6,594 + $4,035). The present value of the proceeds, when the sum-of-the-years'-digits method of depreciation is used, would be $6,594 plus $3,984, or $10,578, which is less than the $10,629 obtained previously.

In this example the present value of the savings from the most advantageous method of depreciation as compared with the next best method amounts to $51 with an initial outlay of $10,000. In the case of a similar investment whose initial cost was $10 million, the present value of the difference between the two depreciation methods would be $51,000. With a longer-lived asset the difference would be larger.

Accelerated Cost Recovery System (ACRS)

In August, 1981 the U.S. Congress passed a law that introduced a new method of tax depreciation expense calculation. Even the words depreciation expense were dropped, and "recovery allowances" were introduced. The objective of the legislation was to accelerate the tax deductions.

Capital assets were divided into five classes, with four of the classes defined in terms of a number of years. We have

Three-year property class: Tangible personal and other property with a life of four years or less (certain tools, research and development equipment, light-duty trucks and autos).

Five-year property class: Practically all machinery and equipment, petroleum storage facilities, and public utility property with lives between 4.5 and eighteen years.

Ten-year property class: Certain public utility property (with lives between 18.5 and twenty-five years), and a few other selected items (e.g., railroad tank cars).

Fifteen-year property class: Exclusive for public utility property with lives greater than twenty-five years.

Real estate: Mostly written off over fifteen years using 200% declining balance (for low income housing) or 175% declining balance with a switch to straight line (for other real estate).

When the asset (tangible personal property) is sold, any gain is treated as ordinary income to the extent of any prior capital recovery allowance. For example, if an asset costing $10,000 with a book value of $8,000 after one year is sold for $11,000 there would be $2,000 of ordinary income and $1,000 of capital gain.

The recapture provisions for real property are more complex (there are more exceptions to the treatment of the gain as ordinary income).

Investment Tax Credit

The three-year class has a 6 percent investment credit rather than the 10 percent available for the other classes (only depreciable property is eligible).

The investment tax credit may be recaptured if the asset is disposed of prior to the asset being fully depreciated for three-year property, or prior to the completion of five full years of use for five-, ten-, or fifteen-year property.

In 1982 the law was changed so that any regular investment tax credit that is taken reduces the tax basis for depreciation calculations by 50 percent of the tax credit. In lieu of reducing the tax basis, the investor can reduce the 10 percent credit to 8 percent and the 6 percent credit to 4 percent (for 3-year projects).

Tax Law Carryover

The tax loss carryover period was increased in 1981 to fifteen years for operating losses and as well as the various tax credits.

The following table gives the recovery allowances in effect as a result of the

TABLE 6-7.   *ACRS Depreciation Expense: Property*
Placed in Service after December 31, 1980

Ownership Year	Class of Investment			
	Three-Year	Five-Year	Ten-Year	Fifteen-Year Utility Property
	%	%	%	%
1	25	15	8	5
2	38	22	14	10
3	37	21	12	9
4		21	10	8
5		21	10	7
6			10	7
7			9	6
8			9	6
9			9	6
10			9	6
11				6
12				6
13				6
14				6
15				6
	100	100	100	100

1981 tax act as amended in 1982. The use of this table is mandatory except for real estate, and the use of straight-line depreciation (if straight-line is chosen it must be used for all assets acquired in that year in that class, except for fifteen-year real estate where the election may be made on a property-by-property basis).

Using Depreciation Tables to Evaluate Investments

The depreciation tables in the Appendix to this book enable us to take a short-cut in the calculations. Instead of computing the actual cash flows of each year we separate the calculation into several subcomponents. The steps in the calculations are:

1. Compute the present value of the after tax cash proceeds without considering the depreciation expense tax shield. This is an "incorrect" calculation that will be corrected by step 4.
2. Compute the investment tax credit.
3. Compute the present value of the depreciation tax savings using the appropriate tables.
4. Combine the cost of investment and the information from steps 1–3 to compute the net present value.

Example

Let us consider the acquisition of equipment that costs $1,000,000. There is a .10 investment tax credit and the asset can be depreciated using the five-year property class schedule for property put into service after 1980. The investment has a life of twenty years and will earn cash flows (before tax) of $167,000 per year. The corporate tax rate is .4. The firm has a .10 cost of money. Assume the investment tax credit does not reduce the asset's tax basis.

Analysis
1. The after tax cash flow (before considering depreciation) is 167,000(1−.4) or 100,000. The present value factor for the annuity is 8.5136 and the present value is $851,360.
2. The investment tax credit is $100,000 (do not reduce the tax basis).
3. The present value of depreciation per dollar of investment is .749784 or $749,784 for a $1,000,000 investment. The present value of the tax savings is .4 (749,784) or $299,914.
4. The net present value of the investment is

$$\text{NPV} = -1,000,000 + 100,000 + 299,914 + 851,360 = \$251,274$$

Additional Complications Affecting Choice of Depreciation Methods

The examples presented in the preceding section are intended primarily to illustrate the type of analysis that can be undertaken when it is considered worth the effort to determine the most advantageous method of depreciating a wasting asset. The examples chosen were deliberately oversimplified to bring out the point that the present-value approach can be used to determine the most advantageous method of depreciating an asset. A full treatment of the complications that arise in determining a proper and acceptable method of depreciation under the internal revenue code would require a book in itself and is beyond the scope of this chapter. Some of the more important complications that may arise in practice will be mentioned briefly, however.

In the examples presented it was assumed that the assets to be depreciated would have no salvage value at the end of their expected useful life. Following present tax laws, expected salvage value does not affect the recovery allowance.

Another complication is that many companies use the group method of depreciation instead of the unit method. Under the group method the rate of depreciation is based on the average life of many units of like items (for example, telegraph poles). This rate of depreciation is then applied to the balance of unretired units. As the units are retired, no loss or gain is recognized at the time of retirement. The depreciation of successive periods is based on the estimate of average life (which is computed by using mortality experience for this type of asset) and the number of units that are retired in each period. Thus the use of the group procedure of depreciation requires a forecast of the number of units in use in each period in order to compute the depreciation of each period as well as a rate of depreciation.

A final complication is the timing of tax payments and of tax savings resulting from depreciation. In the past years tax payments have lagged the earning of corporate income, but at present they have been advanced to such an extent that to assume that the tax payment (or the tax saving) occurs at the end of the period in which income is earned will generally do no great harm.

Working Capital

In focusing attention on outlays for plant and equipment it is possible to lose sight of the fact that the working capital needed to operate the investment project should also be included in computing the investment outlays. Because residual working capital is recoverable at the termination of operations, this leads to the investment having a net terminal value that should be taken into consideration. The term *working capital* is used here in a net sense, and applicable current liabilities are subtracted from the increase in current assets to compute the use of cash. It is assumed that the additional current liabilities do not change the proportion of current liabilities to other sources of capital.

An investment in plant assets will usually lead to funds being tied up in working capital. This will include the cash necessary to meet payroll and other bills, funds invested in the raw material, work-in-process and finished-goods inventory, and receivables from customers. The size of these items will depend on the exact nature of the capital investment, but all the previously mentioned fund requirements will usually accompany an investment in long-lived assets. The one possible exception would be an investment that would decrease the need for working capital by increasing efficiency. Examples of this nature are accounting machines that expedite the billing to customers or storage facilities and inventory-control devices that reduce the amount of inventory which must be kept on hand.

A working capital increase has the effect of increasing the investment outflow today. Ignoring this factor will lead toward the acceptance of investments that should be rejected. If the investment has a limited life and the working capital is expected to be recovered at the end of the life of the investment, the recovery of the working capital in the last period should be considered as cash proceeds and treated in the same manner as the other cash flows are treated. It should not be thought that ignoring the working capital investment and the recovery of working capital will balance each other out. The factor that must be considered is the required return on the working capital during the period of use.

Terminal Value and Taxes

If taxes are introduced into the analysis of working capital, strange things happen to the conclusions of the investment analysis. The presence of taxes in some situations can actually make terminal value undesirable.

High costs of money, high tax rates, and long-lived assets, combined with accelerated depreciation for tax purposes, can result in the presence of terminal value adversely affecting the desirability of an investment.

Example

Assume a discount rate of 10 percent, a 50 percent tax rate, a life of twenty years for the asset, and a tax depreciation scheme that allows a company to write off a depreciable asset in five years. In this case $100 of depreciable assets may be worth more than $100 of terminal value.

The present value of $100 of terminal value due in twenty years, assuming a rate of interest of 10 percent, is

$100 × .1486 = $14.86   (present value of salvage).

The $100 of additional depreciable assets (assuming no salvage value) will reduce taxes a total of $50, or $10 per year. The present value of an annuity of $1 per period for five periods, with an interest rate of 10 percent, is $3.7908.

$10 × 3.7908 = $37.91   (present value of the tax deductions).

With these facts, the tax deduction is worth more than the terminal value. Note that the facts of this situation are reasonable and close to reality: the corporate tax rate in recent years has been close to 50 percent; depreciable assets do frequently have lives of twenty years; 10 percent is not excessively high for a discount rate; and assets have frequently been written off for tax purposes over a period of sixty months.

The ideal situation from the point of view of the investor would be to write off the investment for tax purposes as if it had no salvage, and then wait and see if any salvage would develop. The taxpayer is going to be better off with a conservative estimate of salvage. This argument would be even more important if the gain on disposition of the investment were to qualify as a capital gain, thus receiving special tax consideration. There are provisions in the present internal revenue code that tend to result in such gains being taxed as ordinary income if the asset is held for a short period of time.

The preceding analysis leads to several interesting conclusions. First, with income taxes, situations can develop when, all other things being equal, it may be more desirable to accept a depreciable investment that has no terminal value than one which has terminal value. This conclusion must be tested by existing facts; it cannot be assumed. The factors that tend to make it valid are high tax rates, high discount rates, long-lived investments, and the privilege of writing off an investment for tax purposes at a faster rate than its actual service potential warrants. Not all these factors have to be present, but their presence leads to the conclusion that a depreciable asset that is deductible for tax purposes is more desirable than an asset that is not depreciable for tax purposes. Second, other things being equal, an expenditure that can be expensed immediately for tax purposes is more desirable than an expenditure that must be written off for tax purposes over a period of years. Thus, under the present tax code, increasing net revenues by research may be more desirable than increasing net revenues by the same amount through increasing plant and equipment, since research may be expensed immediately, but plant and equipment must be depreciated.

Changes in Inventories and Income Taxes

The computation of cash flows makes use of the cash expenditures for factors of production in the period of outlay when computing the amount of outlays. Some of the factors of production may be lodged in inventory at the end of the accounting period and thus not charged against the revenues of the period. This would affect the cash flows of the period, because the items would not be expensed for purposes of computing income taxes. The income taxes of this period will be higher than they would be if all cash expenditures were expenses for tax purposes. In some future accounting period, these items will be expensed and will result in taxes for that period being reduced, thus in effect increasing the cash flows (by decreasing taxes) in a period long after the cash expenditure was made. Thus buildups of inventory required by an investment will adversely affect the desirability of the investment by requiring an immediate cash outlay, whereas the cash flows, both by reducing income taxes and by generating revenues upon sale of the item, are delayed for one or more periods. The inventories must generate enough cash flows not only to recover the initial outlay of funds, but also to pay the interest costs of the differences in time of outlay and recovery of cash.

Taxes and Present Value

We have defined the net present value of an investment as the amount a firm could afford to pay for an investment in excess of its cost. This implicitly assumes a zero tax rate. With a corporate tax rate of t_c, the amount that a firm would be willing to pay for a stream of benefits must take into consideration the fact that the benefits will be taxed and that the amount paid for the investment generally will be deductible for tax purposes. If D is the present value of the depreciation deductions using sum-of-the-years'-digits (see Appendix Table C), the cost of an investment (C) net of the tax savings from depreciation is

$$C(1 - t_c D).$$

Setting this equal to the present value of the benefits of the investment, we can then solve for C, the amount we could afford to pay for the investment.

Example

An investment will result in cash proceeds of $10,000 per year before tax and $6,000 after tax ($t_c = .4$) for a period of ten years. The time value of money is .05 after taxes. If we use sum-of-the-years'-digits method of depreciation, how much could we pay for the investment?

The present value of the benefits are

$6,000 \times B(10, .05) = \$6,000 \times 7.72173 = \$46,330.$

The present value of depreciation deductions (from Appendix Table C) per dollar of investment is .82846.

$C(1 - t_c D) = 46,330$

$$C = \frac{\$46,330}{(1 - t_c D)} = \frac{\$46,330}{1 - .4 \times .82846} = \$69,292.$$

We could pay $69,292 for an investment that has cash flows with a present value of $46,330, because the tax depreciation deduction reduces the cost of the investment from $69,292 to $46,330. With a .10 investment tax credit that did not reduce the tax basis, we could afford to pay

$$C = \frac{\$46,330}{(1 - t_c D - .10)} = \frac{\$46,330}{1 - .331384 - .10} = \frac{\$46,330}{.568616} = \$81,479.$$

Timing of Tax Payments

The timing of income tax payments is relevant to the investment analysis if the payment of the tax occurs in a time period significantly later than the earning of the proceeds. We consider the cash outlay to occur when the actual cash disbursement occurs, not when the obligation to pay is created.

Example
Assume that a firm has an opportunity to invest $20,000 today in promoting a sport contest. The promised return to be received one year from today is $24,000. The income tax of $2,080 (assuming a 52 percent tax rate) is to be paid two years from today. The interest rate is 10 percent. The schedule of cash flows would be as follows:

Year	Cash Flows	Present-Value Factor	Present Value of Cash Flows
0	($20,000)	1.0000	($20,000)
1	24,000	.9091	21,818
2	(2,080)	.8264	(1,719)
			$ 99

The net present value is positive and therefore the investment should be undertaken.

If the income taxes were paid during period 1, the cash flows of that period would be $21,920, and the net present value of the cash flows, using a 10 percent rate of discount, would be a negative $73. This would indicate that the investment should not be undertaken.

Taxes and Investment Incentives

Governments have available many devices for encouraging or discouraging firms to undertake investments. Among the variables are the method of depreciation, the allowed life of assets, the treatment of salvage, and investment tax credits or investment allowances. Instead of investment tax credits, some countries use investment allowances or grants where firms are actually paid a percentage of the cost of the investment. Whatever the terminology, the economic effect is to reduce the cost of the investment.

The investment tax credit that has been used several times in the United States allows most corporations to deduct 10 percent of the cost of qualified investments from their federal income taxes.

Business managers should be knowledgeable as to the nature of the current tax laws and sensitive to changes in the laws. The tax laws are a powerful tool for governments to influence the level of investments. Businesses must make decisions that are consistent with the tax laws under which they will have to operate.

The Tax Shield of Interest

The interest on debt gives rise to a tax shield. How should this affect the investment analysis?

Consider an investment requiring an immediate outlay of $1,000 that will generate before tax benefits of $1,090. The tax rate is 46 percent. The asset will be financed 100 percent by debt.

If debt costs 10 percent and inspection of the cash flows reveals that the investment does not generate enough cash to pay the debt, this investment is not acceptable.

The after-tax cost of debt is 5.4 percent. Since the $100 interest tax shield is larger than the $90 of taxable income, there will be no taxes paid. The before-tax cash flows will be:

Time 0	Time 1	NPV (.054)
−1,000	+1,090	34.16

The calculation is incorrect since it double-counts the interest tax shield. The interest tax shield is used to compute the discount-rate and cash flows. The interest tax shield cannot be used in the discount rate calculation and to compute cash flows. The correct investment cash flows for time 1 are $1,090 minus the $41.40 tax on $90 or $1,048.60. Discounting this amount by 5.4 percent we obtain a negative net present value of $5.12, properly indicating that the investment should be rejected.

The Tax Rate

Let us assume that the statuatry tax rate is 48 percent and that we are making a capital budgeting analysis. What rate should be used if the tax expense divided by reported income is 30 percent and if the deferred tax expense item were excluded the percentage would be 10 percent?

The differences arise because of provisions in the tax code such as tax-exempt interest, investment tax credits, accelerated depreciation, and various other tax avoidance possibilities. A normal tax-paying corporate entity may have any tax rate from zero to 48 percent. What rate should be used?

We could argue that the rate applicable to the marginal investment should be used. If the rate is zero for the next investment because of a tax loss carryover, however, the tax rate might still change to 48 percent on a second investment.

A firm with tax losses that would otherwise not be used would be incorrect if it used 48 percent. If there is expectation that an investment for a zero tax firm will move a firm closer to a tax status of 48 percent, then there is some tax cost, however. If we could expect the firm to be able to keep itself in a zero tax status at no cost then the tax rate should be zero. But a zero tax rate tends to be unrealistic, since most companies are only temporarily zero tax and profitable investments tend to cause taxes. We advocate the use of a marginal tax rate applicable to the entire group of investments being considered. This rate would be between 0 and 48 percent. Remember it could be 48 percent when the average tax on the corporation's reported income is less than 48 percent if the tax rate on the incremental investments is 48 percent. If the appropriate marginal tax rate is uncertain at the time the decision is being made, the expected marginal rate may be appropriate.

Questions and Problems

6-1. Assume that the internal revenue code allows a tax credit of .07 of the cost of eligible investments to be deducted from the amount of federal income taxes payable. It also allows the use of accelerated depreciation.

Assume a marginal income tax rate of .4, and an after-tax discount rate of .03. (a) How much is $1 of tax credit worth today? (b) How much is the "right" to deduct $1 of depreciation today worth today? (c) Assume that we pay $1 million for equipment eligible for the tax credit. The equipment will be depreciated for tax purposes in ten years. What is the cost of the equipment? What is the cash flow of the period of purchase of the equipment? What do we know about the value of the equipment as of the beginning of the period after the taking of tax credit?

6-2. Assume a rate of discount of 5 percent. Prepare a set of rules for when to choose the straight-line, double-declining-balance, and the sum-of-the-years'-digits methods of depreciation, if the salvage value is zero. How does your rule change if the rate of discount is 10 percent?

6-3. Assume that a rate of discount is 5 percent and that a firm is making other income. It is considering an investment eligible for the investment credit that costs $1 million. The investment has an expected life of twenty years. Compute the present value of the cash flows that result because of the income tax and the income tax laws (assume a .40 tax rate).

6-4. Assume a tax rate of .4 and a rate of discount of .05 after tax. (a) If the firm is basically a profitable operation, what is the present value of $1 of tax-deductible expense incurred and paid for at the end of period 1? (b) If the firm is a loss operation, what is the present value of $1 of tax-deductible expense incurred and paid for at the end of period 1?

6-5. Compute the present value of the right to deduct $1 million in depreciation immediately compared with the right to deduct the $1 million in twenty years from now. The tax rate is .4 and the after-tax rate of discount is .05.

6-6. The AB has a borrowing cost of .10 and a tax rate of .4. It uses an after tax borrowing rate of .06 to evaluate riskless investments (cash flows are certain). It can invest $1,000 to earn $1,080 of net revenues (before tax) one period hence. The cash flows are cetain and the firm has taxable income. The following calculations have been done:

Revenue		1,080
Depreciation	1,000	
Interest	100	1,100
Tax Loss		$ 20
Tax Rate		× .4
Tax Saving		$ 8

The cash flows used were

Time 0	−1,000	
Time 1	+1,088	(including $8 tax savings)

The present value using .06 as the discount rate is

$$-1{,}000 + 1{,}088(1.06)^{-1} = -1{,}000 + 1{,}026 = +26.$$

The investment was accepted.
   Required: Evaluate the decision.

6-7. Manufacturers of heavy electric generating equipment have been arguing for years over the value of buying in advance of need. The following analysis was presented by one manufacturer in order to persuade utilities to order in advance under a "buy and store" plan.

Cost of boiler if purchased a year early and stored (90 percent of the purchase price would be paid immediately and 10 percent one year later, when the boiler is completed)	$1,000,000
Storage costs for one year (this amount would be paid two years from now)	$ 10,000

It is expected that there will be an 8.5 percent increase in cost ($85,000) if the purchase is delayed one year.
   Assuming a short-term interest rate of .04, the interest cost of buying early is $36,000, and with a .52 tax rate the after-tax interest cost is $17,200. Comparing the $85,000 of cost saving with the storage cost plus the interest indicates that it is desirable to purchase early.

Assume that the boiler is to be placed into use two years from now.

The after-tax cost of money of the company considering the purchase is 7 percent.

Required: Prepare an estimate of the incremental after-tax cash flows resulting from ordering a boiler immediately. The estimated cash flows should be suitable for determining the value of advance ordering, using a discounted cash flow approach. Assume that the boiler would be depreciated on a' straight-line basis over a twenty-year period from the date it is installed and ready to use. The 10 percent tax credit does not apply.

6-8. While discussing the pros and cons of an automated collator with an executive of a large corporation, the dean of a school in a large university said, "You are lucky; with a tax rate of .40 you pay only $6,000 for a $10,000 machine." Assume that there is a labor saving of $2,500 per year associated with the collator being considered. The expected life is ten years and the before-tax time value of money is .05 to both the university and the corporation.

Required: Who has more incentive to purchase the machine, the university or the corporation?

6-9. Continuing problem 6-8. Assume that a university and a corporation both are considering spending $5 million for an administrative office building. The expected life is fifty years. Take the 10 percent tax credit and depreciation into consideration; what is the net saving to each? The tax rate is .40 and the time value of money is .05 before taxes (.03 after taxes to the corporation). The alternative for both is to rent at a before-tax cost of $300,000 per year with a cancelable lease.

6-10. The Old Company is currently producing a product that sells for $7.00 per unit and the variable costs of manufacturing are $6.00 per unit. The company produces and sells 1,000,000 units per year and expects this level of production and sales in the future. The total market is 2,000,000 units. The fixed costs (including overhead) allocated to the product are $1,200,000 per year. The company has an opportunity to purchase new equipment costing $9,000,000 and having an expected life of twenty years. The IRS will accept the twenty year life for taxes. The equipment qualifies for the investment tax credit.

The equipment will reduce variable costs to $4.50 per unit. Because of the method of cost allocation the fixed costs allocated (including the equipment depreciation) will increase to $1,600,000 per year.

The tax rate is .48. There is a .10 investment tax credit. The appropriate rate of interest to be used in this type of investment decision has been determined by the company to be 6 percent. Maintenance expense will be constant throughout the equipment's life.

The board of directors of the company is very much concerned with an investment's payback, ROI and its effect on earnings per share. However, it does believe that all decisions should be made in the best interests of the firm's common stockholders.

Should the equipment be purchased? Explain.

6-11. The XYZ Company has an investment that costs $6,000 and has a life of three years. There is an investment tax credit of 5 percent. The tax rate is .48.

The asset will earn $10,000 the first year, $9,000 the second, and $7,000 the third. There are $5,500 of out of pocket expenses per year.

Working capital will be $1,000, then $1,600, then zero.

The time discount rate is 10 percent.

Use the sum of the year's digits method of depreciation.

Using the worksheet following, evaluate the investment.

WORKSHEET For Problem 6-11

	Period 1	Period 2	Period 3
Revenues or savings (cash and receivables)			
Out-of-pocket expenses	___	___	___
Income before taxes			
Taxes (.48)	$___	___	___
Income after taxes	$___	___	___
Plus: Net working capital decrease Less: Net working capital increase	___	___	___
Cash flow	$___	___	___
Present value factors			
Present values	═══	═══	═══

Total present value of savings $___

Cost of investment $___

Less: Investment
   Tax credit $___

   PV of dep. times
     Tax rate   ___
     Net cost   ___

Net present value   ___

6-12. *The NSV Manufacturing Company*

A product is currently being manufactured on a machine that is fully depreciated for tax purposes and has a book value of $10,000 (it was purchased for $30,000 twenty years ago). The costs of the product are as follows:

	Unit Costs
Labor, direct	$ 4.00
Labor, variable indirect	2.00
Other variable overhead	1.50
Fixed overhead	2.50
	$10.00

In the past year 10,000 units were produced and sold for $18 per unit. It is expected that with suitable repairs the old machine can be used indefinitely in the future. The repairs are expected to average $25,000 per year.

An equipment manufacturer has offered to accept the old machine as a trade-in for a new version. The new machine would cost $60,000 after allowing $15,000 for the old equipment. The projected costs associated with the new machine are as follows:

Labor, direct	$2.00
Labor, variable indirect	3.00
Other variable overhead	1.00
Fixed overhead	3.25
	$9.25

The fixed overhead costs are allocations from other departments plus the depreciation of the equipment.

The old machine could not be sold on the open market. The new machine has an expected life of ten years and no expected salvage at that time.

The current corporate income tax rate is .40. For tax purposes the cost of the new machine may be depreciated in ten years. The appropriate after-tax time discount rate for this company is .10.

It is expected that future demand of the product will stay steady at 10,000 units per year.

Required: (a) Should the new equipment be acquired? (b) If the product can be purchased at a cost of $7.80 per unit from a reliable supplier, should it be purchased or made? Explain.

6-13. *The XYZ Manufacturing Company*

A product is currently being manufactured on a machine that is fully depreciated for tax purposes and that has a book value of $10,000 (it was purchased for $30,000 twenty years ago). The costs of the product are as follows:

	Unit Costs
Labor, direct	$ 4.00
Labor, indirect	2.00
Variable overhead	1.50
Fixed overhead	2.50
	$10.00

In the past year 1,000 units were produced and sold for $18 per unit. It is expected that the old machine can be used indefinitely in the future. An equipment manufacturer has offered to accept the old machine as a trade-in for a new version. The new machine would cost $60,000 after allowing $15,000 for the old equipment. The projected costs associated with the new machine are as follows:

Labor, direct	$2.00
Labor, indirect	3.00
Variable overhead	1.00
Fixed overhead	3.25
	$9.25

The fixed overhead costs are allocations from other departments plus the depreciation of the equipment.

The old machine could be sold on the open market now for $5,000. Ten years from now it is expected to have a salvage value of $1,000. The new machine has an expected life of ten years and an expected salvage of $10,000.

The current corporate income tax rate is .40 and the capital-gain tax rate is .25. Any salvage from sale will result in a capital gain at the time of retirement. (For tax purposes the entire cost may be depreciated in ten years.) The appropriate after-tax time discount rate for this company is .10.

It is expected that future demand of the product will stay steady at 1,000 units per year.

Required: (a) Should the equipment be acquired? (b) If the product can be purchased at a cost of $7.80 per unit from a reliable supplier, should it be purchased or made? Explain.

6-14. *Con-Chem-Co.*

The company leaves out the .10 investment tax credit (ITC) in evaluating an investment. It requires a .26 internal rate of return.

a. Assume a life of one year (but still eligible for the ITC). What is the effective required return?

b. Assume a ten-year life and constant benefits. What is the effective required return?

c. Repeat part b. assuming a perpetual life.

d. Assume the benefits are decaying at a rate of .24 per year. What is the effective required return?

6-15. RST Corporation is considering introducing a new product. The product could be manufactured on a machine costing $15,000. The life of the product and machine is five years. Start-up costs (which can be expensed) are $5,000 in year 1, and $2,000 in year 2. Expected unit sales are 3,000 in years 1 and 5 and 5,000 in years 2, 3 and 4. The product would contribute 2.00 per unit before taxes towards fixed overhead and profit. The firm is subject to an income tax rate of 40 percent. Working capital of 5,000 would be required in year 1, and would be returned in year 5. The machine would be depreciated using the SYD methods for taxes. It has no salvage value and is not eligible for the investment tax credit. Working capital would be financed by a bank loan at a before-tax rate of 8 percent, which would be renewed each year. The firm expects to have taxable income from other operations in each of the next five years. Calculate the total after-tax cash flow per period that you would use in deciding whether to accept or reject this investment opportunity. Enter the totals in the last row of the table on this page. Use the other rows in the table to show the details of your calculations. Label each row if you use it.

RST Corporation Cash Flow Summary

Item	0	1	2	3	4	5
(1) Capital Outlay	−15,000					
(2)						
(3)						
(4)						
(5)						
(6)						
(7)						
(8)						
(9)						
(10) Total After-tax cash flow						

6-16. The Seymour Products Co. Inc. is currently bottling furniture polish on a machine that is fully depreciated for tax purposes. The old machine has a market value of $5,000 now, and it is expected that in ten years it would have a salvage value of $6,000 (inflation).

The old machine could be traded in on a new machine with an additional cash payment of $28,000. The new machine has an expected life of ten years and is expected to have a salvage value of $2,000 at that time.

The current corporate tax rate is 22 percent and the capital gain tax rate is 10 percent. The new machine would have a tax base of $34,000 and for tax purposes could be depreciated over a life of ten years. Straight line depreciation will be used.

It is expected that future demand for the product will stay steady at 10,000 units per year. Unit costs with the old and new machines would be as follows:

	Unit Costs	
	Old	New
Labor, direct	$0.70	$0.40
Labor, indirect	0.15	0.05
Raw materials	.30	.30
Fixed overhead	.15	.25

Fixed overheads are allocations from other departments and do not include depreciation of the equipment.

With either machine, unit revenues would be $1.25 per unit for the entire ten-year period. The appropriate after-tax cost of money for this company is 9 percent.

What action would you recommend to the management of this company? Justify your recommendation by calculating an appropriate measure of the benefits to be derived from each of the alternatives that you consider.

6-17. The XYZ Company has an investment that costs $6,000 and has a life of three years. There is an investment tax credit of 10 percent. The tax rate is .46. The asset will earn $10,000 the first year, $9,000 the second and $7,000 the third. There are $5,500 of out-of-pocket expenses per year. Working capital will be $1,000, then $1,600, then zero. The $1,600 of working capital will be worth $400 on termination. The time discount rate is 10 percent. Using the sum-of-the-year's-digits method of depreciation, the present value of the depreciation per dollar of asset is .855427, and with a depreciable cost of $6,000 the present value of depreciation is $5,133. The format on the following page should be used.

6-18. The New Company is currently producing a product that sells for $7.00 per unit and the variable costs of manufacturing are $6.00 per unit. The company produces and sells 1,000,000 units per year and expects this level of production and sales in the future. The total market is 2,000,000 units. The fixed costs (including overhead) allocated to the product are $1,200,000 per year. Of these costs $100,000 are incremental to the product and $1,100,000 are independent of whether the product exists. The company has an opportunity to purchase new

```
┌─────────────────────────────────────────────────────────────────────┐
│                 WORKSHEET For Problem 6-17                            │
│                                                                       │
│                              Period 1      Period 2     Period 3      │
│  Revenues or savings (cash and receivables)                          │
│    Out-of-pocket expenses         ____        ____        ____        │
│  Income before taxes                                                  │
│    Taxes (.46)                  $ ____        ____        ____        │
│  Income after taxes             $ ____        ____        ____        │
│  Plus:  Net working capital decrease                                  │
│  Less:  Net working capital increase                                  │
│                                   ____        ____        ____        │
│    Cash flow                    $ ____        ____        ____        │
│       Present value factors                                           │
│    Present values                                                     │
│                                  ════        ════        ════        │
│                                                                       │
│  Total present value of savings    $ ____                             │
│  Cost of investment          $ ____                                   │
│  Less: Investment                                                     │
│    Tax credit                  ____                                   │
│    PV of dep. times                                                   │
│      Tax rate                                                         │
│      Net cost                  ____                                   │
│                                       ____                            │
│  Net present value                                                    │
│                                ____                                   │
└─────────────────────────────────────────────────────────────────────┘
```

equipment costing $9,000,000 and having an expected life of twenty years. The IRS will accept the twenty-year life for taxes. The equipment qualifies for the investment tax credit.

The equipment will reduce variable costs to $4.50 per unit. Because of the method of cost allocation the fixed costs allocated (including the equipment depreciation) will increase to $1,600,000 per year. (The $100,000 described above stays constant.)

The tax rate is .48. There is a .10 investment tax credit. The appropriate rate of interest to be used in this type of investment decision has been determined by the company to be 6 percent. Maintenance expense will be constant throughout the equipment's life.

The board of directors of the company is very much concerned with an investment's payback, ROI, and its effect on earnings per share. However, it does believe that all decisions should be made in the best interests of the firm's common stockholders.

a. Should the equipment be purchased? Explain.

b. Would you change your answer if management said the discount rate should be 20 percent?

6-19. There is a marginal tax rate of .4 and an after-tax time-value factor is .06. Assume there are no other uses for the plant or equipment and their book value for taxes is $12,000,000. The annual out-of-pocket costs of making the product are $300,000. The annual costs of buying are $400,000.

If retained, the plant and equipment will be depreciated over 20 years, using the straight-line method of depreciation.

Should the product be made or bought?

Answers to Selected Questions

6-1. (a) $1 **(b)** $.40 **(c)** $930,000

6-3. Tax credit = $70,000.   PV of Depreciation = .717885 × 1,000,000 × .4

$$= 287,154$$

6-5. $249,240.   **6-7.** Conclusion: Buy a year from now.

6-9. University: PV of Savings $476,770 Corporation: PV of Savings $1,400,392.

6-11. The NPV = $778.

6-13. Purchase the product.   Buy. Buying is less than the cost of making, when the proceeds from selling the old equipment are taken into account.

7

Annual Equivalent Costs and Replacement Decisions

What is usually called a reasonable wage, or a reasonable profit, proves on investigation to be not so much "reasonable" as "usual," to be in fact the wage or profit determined by free competition under the prevailing conditions of time and place.

—*Knut Wicksell, Lecture on Political Economy, Vol. I (London: George Routledge and Sons, Ltd., 1946), p. 51.*

Investments tend to involve large expenditures that benefit many time periods, and to have lives longer or shorter than the time period for which the decision is being made. In these situations we find it useful to compute the annual equivalent cost of utilizing a long-lived asset. This concept has a large number of potential uses, including computing the cost of making a product and solving the decision problem when different alternatives or components have different lives.

Consider an investment that has an expected life of twenty years and that costs $2,000,000. It is easy to divide the $2,000,000 by twenty and obtain an annual cost of $100,000 per year. The difficulty is that this cost computation leaves out the capital cost (the interest factor) and is an incomplete calculation.

Annual Equivalent Cost

In the above illustration we assumed there was an outlay of $2,000,000 and the investment had a life of twenty years. We would like to replace the $2,000,000 outlay with a series of costs that have the same present value and thus are economically equivalent. Let us assume that the firm has 10 percent time value of money. Define R to be the annual equivalent cost of the initial outlay. Then,

$$B(20, .10)R = 2,000,000$$
$$8.5136R = 2,000,000$$
$$R = \$234,918.$$

The firm would be indifferent between the immediate outlay of $2,000,000 and an annual outlay of $234,918 occurring at the end of each time period. We would say that the annual equivalent cost is $234,918. Remember that, if we had divided the cost by the life, we would have obtained an annual cost of $100,000. The equivalent annual cost is about 2.35 times as large as the incorrect calculation that omits the interest cost.

Make or Buy Decisions

As an example of the use of the annual equivalent cost concept consider a simple make or buy decision. The CBD Corporation requires 10,000 units per year of a certain metal part used in several of its major products. Demand for the part will remain at this level for the next twenty years. CBD has been purchasing the part from a reliable outside supplier at a cost of $20.00 per unit. The purchasing manager has proposed that the company make the product itself at a saving of $5.00 per unit, and has justified the recommendation with the following data.

Cost of Making	Per Unit	Per Year
Labor and Material	$ 5.00	$ 50,000
Depreciation	10.00	100,000
Total	15.00	150,000
Cost of Buying	20.00	200,000

The depreciation results from the acquisition of a specialized machine at a cost of $2 million that will be needed if CBD is to make the part itself. The machine has no other applications and would have a life of twenty years. CBD Corporation has a long-term revolving credit arrangement with an insurance company under which it could borrow the $2,000,000 needed to acquire the machine at an interest cost of 10 percent per year. If CBD borrows it can arrange whatever repayment terms it wishes for the loan. Or if CBD has available excess funds, they could be applied to a partial repayment of existing loans under this revolving agreement, thereby saving interest of 10 percent per year, if the funds are not used for capital outlays.

The purchasing manager's analysis of the cost of making is incomplete in that it fails to consider the time value of money. The labor and material expense will not be incurred until future years, so that their present value will be less than the eventual outlay. But the payment for the machine is made at the start, so the annual equivalent cost is more than $100,000 per year. A complete analysis could easily be done using present value concepts.

Cost of Making	Outlays	Present Value Factors	Present Values
Labor and Material	$ 50,000 per year	8.5136	$ 425,680
Equipment cost	2,000,000	1.0	2,000,000
Total Present Value			2,425,680
Cost of Buying	$ 200,000	8.5136	1,702,720

While the above analysis is complete, it may not be as meaningful to executives who are not familiar with present-value calculations. Additionally, the present-value calculation does not provide a convenient means of evaluating the savings from buying on a per unit basis.

An alternative approach is to present the analysis in terms of annual equivalent costs. With this approach the annual equivalent cost per unit can easily be obtained by dividing the total annual equivalent cost by the number of units per year. The resulting annual equivalent cost per unit will be fully comparable to the $20.00 cost per unit of buying. The analysis might be presented as follows:

Cost of Making	Per Unit	Per Year
Labor and Material	$ 5.00	$ 50,000
Equipment (2,000,000/8.5136)	23.49	234,918
Total Cost of Making	$28.49	$284.918
Cost of Buying	20.00	200,000

With this approach the annual equivalent cost of the equipment can be explained (to persons not familiar with present-value discounted cash flow techniques) as the annual payment that would be required to amortize a 2 million dollar loan at 10 percent with twenty equal annual payments. Or, if the CBD uses available funds to buy the equipment, the $234,918 can be interpreted as the annual amount by which future debt service payments could have been reduced over the next twenty years if the 2 million had been paid to the equipment supplier at the time of acquisition.

Instead of assuming that the expenditure for the equipment cost takes place at the end of the period we could assume that the expenditure takes place at the beginning of the period. We would then have for the annual equivalent cost:

$$[1 + B(19, .10)]R = 2,000,000$$

$$9.3649R = 2,000,000$$

$$R = \$213,563.$$

A third possibility is to assume continuous outlays for the equipment. For this purpose we must use continuous discounting. If the nominal interest rate is $r = .10$ compounded annually the corresponding equivalent continuous interest rate j can be found from the following equality,

$$1 + r = e^j$$

Taking the natural logarithm of both sides (using an electronic calculator) we find for $r = .1$ that $j = .09531$.

We then have

$$R\left[\frac{1 - e^{-20j}}{j}\right] = 2,000,000,$$

$$R \left[\frac{1 - .14864}{.09531} \right] = 2,000,000,$$

$$R = 2,000,000/(8.93248) = 223,902.$$

One important application of annual equivalent costs occurs in situations where mutually exclusive alternatives have different lives. We will define this to be a problem of "comparability of life."

Comparability

The problem of comparability arises if the profitability of future investment proposals will be affected by decisions made currently. A group of investments will be said to be comparable if the profitability of subsequent investment possibilities will be the same, regardless of which investment is accepted or if all are rejected. A group of investments is mutually exclusive if at most one investment of the group can be accepted. Investment alternatives should be combined into groups that are both mutually exclusive and comparable before a final decision is made.

For example, a new plant could be heated by using forced hot air or steam. These are mutually exclusive alternatives. They are not comparable, however, if it seems likely that the installation of an air-conditioning system will become necessary at some time in the future. The air-conditioning system would cost less to install in a building already equipped with air vents, and the present value of this difference in expected costs should be taken into account when choosing the heating system.

This simple example brings out two points. First, it may not be practical to make a group of mutually exclusive investment alternatives exactly comparable. In designing a new plant, the number of possible changes that may be desirable at some future date (such as remodeling, installation of new machinery, and additions or extensions) is very large, and the cost of each such possible change will depend on the basic plant design originally adopted. In such circumstances, to make an analysis of truly comparable investments would require consideration of an unduly large number of alternatives.

Second, the importance of having mutually exclusive investments comparable is a matter of degree. In choosing a heating system for a new plant, the importance of the fact that future installation of air conditioning would be more expensive with steam heating will depend on the likelihood that air conditioning will eventually be required, the lapse of time until it may be required, the extent of the extra installation costs, and so on. In deciding whether a group of mutually exclusive alternatives is sufficiently comparable for practical purposes, one must apply a reasonable approach.

Mutually Exclusive Alternatives with Different Lives

Must mutually exclusive investment alternatives have the same lives in order to be comparable? The answer is no. In some instances investment alternatives with different lives will be comparable; in other instances equal future time periods are necessary to achieve comparability.

An example of comparable mutually exclusive alternatives not having the same life occurs in connection with deciding how to exploit a new patented product. One alternative is to sell the patent rights to another firm. This results in a single, lump-sum payment. The patent may also be exploited by manufacturing and selling the product.

In this example the two choices are comparable, although the expected cash proceeds from one would extend only one year, and from the second for a longer period of time. When this is the case, the two alternatives should be compared using the net present value of each over its own life. For example, if selling the patent rights would generate immediate cash proceeds of $2 million and manufacturing and selling the product would produce cash flows having a net present value of $1.5 million over a twelve-year period, the immediate sale is more desirable.

It is possible to compare these two alternatives using annual equivalent returns, but to do this we must divide the comparable net present values by an annuity factor for a common period. For example, suppose that the appropriate discount rate is 8 percent and we wish to find the annual equivalent return from each alternative for a twelve-year period. The annuity factor $B(12, .08)$ is approximately 7.5. The annual equivalent return from selling the patent rights is $2,000,000/7.5 = $266,667$. The comparable annual equivalent return from producing and manufacturing the product is $1,500,000/7.5 = $200,000$. Dividing the present values by 7.5 in both cases cannot change the decision.

When mutually exclusive investments have unequal lives, we have essentially three choices of assumptions that we can make.

1. We can assume that at the expiration of life of each asset the firm will invest in assets that earn the time value of money. In this case the alternatives are comparable even though their lives are unequal. Under uncertainty the assumption required is that at the expiration of the life of each asset the firm will invest in other assets whose expected rate of return is the minimum required for the risk involved.
2. We can assume that the firm will reinvest in assets of exactly the same characteristics as those currently being used.
3. We can make specific assumptions about the reinvestment opportunities that will become available in the future.

The present-value method will lead to a correct decision with all three assumptions as long as the facts of the decision are consistent with the method chosen.

In theory the third alternative is the best of the three and the easiest to describe. While it is easy in theory, it is the most difficult to implement in practice because it requires a great deal of forecasting about the future. The first alternative is the simplest of the three in practice, because it merely requires the computation of the present value of the first round of equipment with no further forecasts about the future (other than the implicit forecast that the time value of money will be earned). We shall consider in more detail the implementation of the assumption that the firm will reinvest in assets of exactly the same character-istics as those currently being used.

As an example, suppose that there are two mutually exclusive investments, A and B, with the following characteristics:

| Investment | Cash Flows for Period | | | |
	0	1	2	3
A	−$10,000	$12,000		
B	− 10,000	5,000	$5,000	$5,000

A and B may be different types of equipment that perform the same task, with A having a life of one year and B a life of three years. With a cost of money of 10 percent, the present values of the relevant cash flows of A and B with assumption 1 are as follows:

Investment	Present Value of Cash Flows
A	$ 909
B	2,434

Investment B would seem to be the more desirable investment; however, this analysis is incomplete if we instead assume (assumption 2) that after one year equipment of type A (or similar equipment) will again be purchased. Where it is likely that investment A will be repeated at the beginning of periods 2 and 3, the following cash flows would occur for investment A:

| Investment | Period | | | |
	0	1	2	3
A	−$10,000	−$10,000	−$10,000	
		12,000	12,000	$12,000
Total	−$10,000	$ 2,000	$ 2,000	$12,000

The present value of the cash flows as now presented is $2,488 for investment A; thus A is more desirable than B. When the mutually exclusive investments have unequal lives, we may want to take into consideration the possibility of reinvest-ing in a similar type of equipment.

If we choose assumption 3, we have to forecast the nature of the equipment available after one period and after two periods for investment A.

In most situations the lowest common multiple of the lives of the two invest-ment results in a length of time longer than the life of the longest-lived alternative. For example, if there are two types of equipment, one of which has a life of three years and the other of eight years, the lowest common multiple of lives is twenty-four years. In á situation of this nature the equivalent cost per year, the cost for perpetuity, or the present value of the costs for twenty-four years could be computed. The equipment with the lowest cost would be the most desirable alternative. The three methods of computation being discussed will all lead to the same decision. Each method implicitly adopts assumption 2.

Example:
Assume that two pieces of equipment have the following characteristics:

Equipment	Expected Life (Years)	Initial Cost	Operating Cost per Year
X	3	$10,000	$2,000
Y	8	30,000	1,500

This problem can be solved by taking the lowest common multiple of 8 and 3, twenty-four years, and by computing the costs for a twenty-four-year period.

Annual Equivalent Cost
An alternative procedure is to compute the annual equivalent cost of an outlay of $10,000 every three years, and the annual equivalent cost of an outlay of $30,000 every eight years.

$RB(3, .10)$

$RB(3, .10) = \$10,000$
$R \times 2.4869 = \$10,000$
　　　　$R = \$ 4,021$　Annual equivalent of an outlay of $10,000 every three years

$RB(8, .10) = \$30,000$
$R \times 5.3349 = \$30,000$
　　　　$R = \$ 5,623$　Annual equivalent of an outlay of $30,000 every eight years

The annual equivalent cost of using equipment X is $6,021 (that is, 2,000 + 4,021), and the annual equivalent cost of using equipment Y is $7,123 (that is, 1,500 + 5,623). On the basis of annual equivalent costs, X is the more desirable equipment.

To find the present value of the cost of using each type of equipment for twenty-four years we multiply the annual equivalent cost for each type of equipment by the annuity factor for twenty-four years. Since $B(24, .10) = 8.9847$ the present values are as follows:

X　　$6,021 \times 8.9847 = \$54,097$

Y　　$7,123 \times 8.9847 = \$63,998.$

Since both annual equivalent costs are multiplied by the same annuity factor, the relative merits of the two alternatives are not changed if we compare their present values instead of their annual equivalent costs. X remains more desirable than Y.

To find the cost of using the equipment forever, we multiply the equivalent cost per year by the present value of a perpetuity. The general formula for the present value of a perpetuity of $1 a period is

$$\text{Present value of a perpetuity} = \frac{1}{r},$$

where r is the appropriate rate of interest.

Since r is equal to .10, the factor in this example is 10. The present value of using equipment X forever is $10 \times \$6,021$, or $60,210. The present value of using Y is $71,230.

Replacement Chains

Suppose that a real estate company is considering whether to remodel a motel and to continue operating it for an additional ten years, or to raze the old motel and build a new one that would have an economic life of twenty years.

If the alternatives were comparable, we would compare the present value of expected cash outlays and proceeds from the two unequal-lived streams. In this instance, however, the two investments are not comparable. If the company chooses to remodel the existing motel now and scrap it after ten years, it will then have the options of selling the land, building a new motel, or using the land in some other way. These possibilities must be taken into account in making the present decision.

One possibility is to convert the two investments into annual equivalent cash flows. Suppose that the company has a cost of money of 10 percent and that remodeling the old motel would produce a net present value at 10 percent of $100,000 during the next ten years. To convert this into annual equivalent cash flows, we would find the annual amount for ten years that has a present value of $100,000. Similarly, if the expected net present value from building a new motel were $125,000, we would find the twenty-year annuity that has a present value of $125,000. At 10 percent the annual equivalent payments are $16,274 and $14,682. With this system the alternative having the largest annual equivalent cash flow is most favorable. See Table 7-1.

Note that, by using net present value, building a new motel is favored; by using annual equivalent returns, remodeling the present motel is better. Using net

TABLE 7-1. *Comparison of Present Value and Annual Equivalents for Motel Example*

Alternatives	Horizon Life	Present Value Over Horizon	Annual Equivalent Return Over Horizon
Remodel	10	100,000	16,274
Build New	20	125,000	14,682

present value, we ignore any profits that could result from using the land in years 11 through 20, when the present motel will be torn down if it is remodeled now. This creates a bias toward the alternative of building a new motel now. On the other hand, by converting to annual equivalent returns, we assume that an investment as profitable as remodeling the current motel will reappear ten years from now. Another possible assumption would be that ten years from now it will be possible to build a new motel that would be as profitable and long-lived as the new motel to be built now. Although it may turn out upon investigation in a particular case that this assumption is reasonable, we cannot assume that this will be the case.

If we considered ourselves sufficiently clairvoyant, we might attempt to estimate the cost of building a new motel ten years from now and also the cash proceeds that would be generated by operating this new motel. Even this would not solve the problem if this new motel is expected to last for more than an additional ten years, because the two alternatives would not then be comparable.

Sometimes a practical solution is found by putting an upper or lower limit on the value of potential future opportunities. For example, in the motel problem one can safely estimate that, if the motel is remodeled now, in ten years there will be a potential cash flow of at least equal to the value of the land at that time. It may turn out that even an optimistic estimate of the value of the land will not be sufficient to make the alternative of remodeling the old motel more attractive than the prospect of constructing a new motel.

Components of Unequal Lives

An investment alternative (possibly one of several mutually exclusive investments) may be made up of several components of unequal lives. For example, we may have a building with a life of fifty years costing $5 million, a furnace with a life of twenty-five years costing $4 million (exclusive of lining), and a furnace lining costing $1 million with a life of four years. With a time value of money of .05, the annual equivalent cost for the first four years of operation is

$$\frac{5,000,000}{B(50, .05)} = \frac{5,000,000}{18.25593} = \$273,884 \quad \text{Cost of building}$$

$$\frac{4,000,000}{B(25, .05)} = \frac{4,000,000}{14.09394} = 283,810 \quad \text{Cost of furnace}$$

$$\frac{1,000,000}{B(4, .05)} = \frac{1,000,000}{3.54595} = 282,012 \quad \text{Cost of furnace lining}$$

Total annual equivalent cost = $\overline{\$839,705}$

The expression $1/B(n, r)$ is called a *capital recovery factor*. When tax considerations are not a problem a simple rule for converting from the initial cost of an item of capital equipment to the corresponding annual equivalent cost is to multiply the initial cost of the equipment by the corresponding capital recovery factor. When this procedure is used to find the annual equivalent cost of a collection of equipment with varying lives there is the implicit assumption that each item of equipment will be replaced at the end of its useful life by another item having the same annual equivalent cost. This assumption would be satisfied if each item of equipment were replaced by another having the same cost and the same life.

Cost of Excess Capacity

It is incorrect to conclude that the use of excess capacity had no costs. Sunk costs are not relevant to incremental decisions but there may be incremental costs that are relevant. Assume that the ABC Chemical Corporation has extra boiler capacity and is considering the addition of a new product which will take one half of the extra capacity. How is the cost of the boiler brought into the analysis? The quick, easy answer is to say there is no boiler cost. Unfortunately, this conclusion may not be correct. Add the information that undertaking the new product and using one half of the excess capacity moves up the expected date of purchase of a new utility system from year five to year three in the future. This acceleration of purchase has costs, and these costs are part of the new-product decision.

The means of incorporating the cost of accelerating the acquisition are not obvious. Assume that the expected cost of the boiler acquisition is $2.595 million and it has an estimated life of fifteen years. With a cost of money of .05, the annual equivalent cost per year of use is

$$\frac{\$2,595,000}{B(15, .05)} = \frac{\$2,595,000}{10.38} = \$250,000.$$

Without the new product, years 4 and 5 will not have the cost of a new boiler. With the new product there is an additional equivalent cost of $250,000 for years 4 and 5.

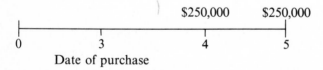

The present value at time 0 of the additional costs is $401,550.

.8227 × 250,000 = $205,675
.7835 × 250,000 =   195,875
                   $401,550

An advocate of the new product might argue that the cost should be less because the degree of utilization of the boiler during the first two years will be very low, and there will not be much wear and tear. If we assume no wear and tear (also no obsolescence), there would only be the interest cost of $129,750 (.05

of $2,595,000) occurring four and five years in the future. Just taking interest into account gives a cost of approximately $208,404 present value.

.8227 × 129,750 = $106,745
.7835 × 129,750 =   101,659
                   $208,404

Some amortization of cost for tax purposes and some decrease in value (that is, depreciation) should be recognized, however. Thus the exact present value of the cost of adding the product has not been determined. One estimate is $401,550, but it could be $208,404 if we assume the life of the new equipment is not shortened by the early purchase. Including either of these estimates is better than assuming that there is no cost associated with using the excess capacity.

We may want to include an analysis in which we did not include the capacity cost but rather dropped the product when capacity was reached and it was time to add new facilities. This possibility should be checked out, but generally it is appropriate to assume that once the product is added it will be produced in the future. This will tend to occur because of the momentum principle (it is difficult for a firm to change directions), and because after the costs of getting a product under way have been incurred, there is a good chance that an economic analysis would indicate the desirability of continuing the sale of the product and taking advantage of the goodwill that was created.

Conclusions

Although techniques such as those we are recommending force one to make difficult estimates in the face of imperfect and incomplete information, they have the advantage of focusing attention on the important unknowns. Simpler techniques achieve their simplicity by using general assumptions about the nature of future opportunities rather than conjectures tailor-made to a particular situation. They save time and effort but result in a less precise analysis of the decision-making situation.

Questions and Problems

7-1. The Roger Company has the choice between two different types of dies. One type costs less, but also has a shorter life expectancy. The expected cash flows after taxes for the two different dies are as follows:

	Period				
Die	0	1	2	3	4
A	($10,000)	$8,000	$8,000		
B	(12,000)	5,000	5,000	$5,000	$5,000

The cost of money of the firm is 10 percent.
Required: Choose the more desirable die. Explain.

7-2. Assume that there are two mutually exclusive investments that have the following cash flows:

Investment	Period 0	Period 1	Internal Rate of Return (%)
A	($10,000)	$12,000	20
B	(5,000)	6,100	22

Assume that either investment will require modification to the basic building structure, which will cost $1,000, and that this amount is not included in the preceding computations. The cost of money is 10 percent.

Required: (a) Compute the actual internal rates of return of the investments. (b) Does the additional $1,000 change the ranking of the two investments? Explain.

7-3. Consider the following two mutually exclusive investments.

Investment	Period 0	Period 1	Internal Rate of Return
A	($20,000)	$ 30,000	.50
B	(100,000)	130,000	.30

Required: Assuming a cost of money of .10, which investment is to be preferred?

7-4. An existing machine must be replaced. Two new models are under consideration. Both cost $15,000. Model X will generate savings of $10,000 per year and has a life of two years. Model Y will generate savings of $18,000 per year; it has a life of one year. The machine will be needed for two years. Which model should be purchased if the cost of money is .05?

7-5. Assume that two pieces of equipment have the following characteristics:

Equipment	Expected Life (Years)	Initial Cost	Operating Cost per Year
A	9	$20,000	$10,000
B	5	25,000	8,000

Required: Assuming a cost of money of .10, which equipment is the more desirable?

7-6. The A Corporation's computer currently has excess capacity. The controller would like to prepare and distribute a report that would take approximately one hour a day of the computer's time. The computer could do this task and still have excess capacity. The annual cost of this type of computer is $1 million a year. The discount rate is .05. The long-range planning group estimates that without the report the corporation would be shifting to a more powerful computer five years from now. With the report, they estimate the shift four years from now. The new computer will cost $1.5 million per year. Assume that the computer payments take place at the end of each year.

Required: What is your estimate of the cost of adding the report?

7-7. The New York State Utility Company is considering the construction of a new utility plant. It has accumulated the following cost information:

	Fossil Plant (Oil and Gas)	Nuclear Energy Plant
Initial outlay	$60,000,000	$100,000,000
Annual operating cost	15,000,000	20,000,000*

* This is the projected cost for year 1. It is expected that the operating costs will decrease by $2,000,000 per year and level off at $10,000,000. The expected decrease is a result of decreased fuel costs. Both plants have an expected useful life of fifty years.

Assume a time value of money of .05 per year.

Required: (a) Which plant should be built? (b) Assume that if the nuclear plant is not built the needed electricity can be purchased at a cost of $16 million per year. Should it be built?

7-8. Continuing part b of problem 7-7. Assume that the cost of the needed electricity is $17 million: (a) Should the nuclear plant be built now? (b) Compute the present value today of building (that is, completing) the nuclear plant six years from now when the operation costs would be $10 million per year, compared to buying electricity.

7-9. The A Corporation is considering the construction of a new plant to build a component part that it is currently purchasing. It has the following information:

	Cost	Expected Life
Plant	$20,000,000	Forty years
Utilities	10,000,000	Twenty years
Equipment	15,000,000	Ten years

The operating costs are estimated at $5 million per year, assuming an output of 1 million units of product per year.

The corporation uses a discount rate of .05. It can purchase the product at a cost of $10 per unit. Should the new plant be built (on a straight economic basis)?

7-10. A company is considering two alternative marketing strategies for a new product. Introducing the product will require an outlay of $15,000. With a low price the product will generate cash proceeds of $10,000 per year and will have a life of two years. With a high price the product will generate cash proceeds of $18,000, but will have a life of only one year. The cost of money for the company is .05. Which marketing strategy should be accepted?

7-11. Compare your answers to problems 7-4 and 7-10. Are the relevant cash flows the same in both problems? If not, why?

7-12. State Electric wants to decide whether to repair or replace electric meters when they break down. A new meter costs $30 and on the average will go twelve years without repair. It costs $18 to repair a meter, and a repaired meter will, on the average, go eight years before it again needs a repair. Repairs can be made repeatedly to meters because they are essentially rebuilt each time they are repaired. It costs $6 to take out and reinstall a meter. The time value of money is 0.5.

Required: Should the company repair old meters or buy new meters?

7-13. Assume an investment requires an initial outlay of $12,337 and that the revenues from the investment are $10,000 in year 1 and $5,000 in year 2. Assume an interest rate of .05 should be used.

Using annual equivalent revenues and costs, determine whether the investment is acceptable.

7-14. The following facts apply to an investment the ABC Company is considering:

Plant costing $10,000,000 with a life of 50 years.

Equipment costing $2,000,000 with a life of 20 years.

Annual fixed costs are $180,000, of which $100,000 are incremental with the decision (but excluding depreciation) and $80,000 are allocations from other departments and projects. These costs could be avoided if the product is discontinued in the future.

The net revenue contribution per unit sold is $2.

The cost of money of the firm is .10.

It is expected that 1,000,000 units of product will be used per year.

Required: If 1,000,000 units are produced, what will be the per unit fixed cost?

7-15. Continuing problem 7-14. Assume that the plant and equipment described have been purchased. One million units of the product are needed in the coming year. These units can be purchased at a cost of $1.20 per unit from a reliable supplier. The variable manufacturing costs per unit are $.20. If the units are purchased, the plant and equipment will be shut down (this can be done with little additional cost).

Should the units be made or bought? Assume that the probability of the product being supplied on time and the quality of the product are the same whether made or bought.

7-16. (*Refers to problem 7-15*). If the plant requires working capital of $1,500,000 (liquidation value), should the units be made or purchased?

7-17. Assume the plant and equipment of problem 7-15 have been purchased. There is a marginal tax rate of .4 and an after-tax time-value factor is .06. Should the units be made or bought? Assume there are no other uses for the plant or equipment and their book value for taxes is $12,000,000. The annual out-of-pocket costs of making the product are $300,000. (This includes the fixed costs that could be avoided if the product is not produced.) The annual costs of buying are $400,000.

If retained, the plant and equipment will be depreciated over twenty years using the straight-line method of depreciation.

Should the product be made or bought?

7-18.

	Relative Cash Flows (Millions of Dollars)				
Strategy	Periods				
*	0	1	2	3	4
A	−50	+40	+40		
B	−30	+20	+20	+20	+20

The P & A Corporation is considering marketing policy for its brand of deodorant. Two mutually exclusive advertising-strategy changes are under consideration. The cash flows associated with each are shown above. The cost of money to P & A Corporation is 10%.

a. Which of the two strategies would you prefer if each strategy can be repeated as often as desired? Justify your answer.

b. Which of the two strategies would you prefer if neither decision can be repeated (and future decisions are expected to have a net present value of zero)? Justify your answer.

c. P & A's deodorant brand is currently losing money at the rate of $15 million per year. Would this fact, if it were true, lead you to change your idea about what action would be desirable for P & A in the situation described in 1)? In the situation described in 2? Explain.

Answers to Selected Problems

7-1. Type A is more desirable.   **7-3.** Investment B is more desirable.

7-5. A is more desirable.

7-7. The nuclear plant has lower costs. Do not build now.

7-9. Build the new plant.   **7-11.** Reinvestment assumptions differ.

7-13. The investment is acceptable. Contributes $926 per year.

7-15. The relevant costs of making are $.30 versus $1.20 cost of buying.

7-17. Buying is more desirable than making.

PART TWO

All hope abandon, ye who enter here.

—*Dante Alighieri (1265–1321), Divine Comedy, Inferno, Canto III, Line 9. Translation from Oxford Dictionary of Quotations, 2nd ed. (New York: Oxford University Press, Inc., 1959).*

In Part I we described easily applied decision rules that use the present-value procedure. With conditions of certainty and no capital rationing, we are able to make accept or reject decisions involving independent investments or to choose the best of a set of mutually exclusive investments. In Part II we introduce capital rationing and uncertainty. Although the decision rules offered in Part II are analogous to those of Part I, they are more complex.

A business decision maker could possibly read Part II and then despair of ever finding an easily applied rational approach to making investment decisions. We hope that a knowledge of the complexities will lead to more reasonable procedures, if not exact simple rules.

We think it is important that the decision maker understand all aspects of the investment decision and realize the limitations of the present-value procedure as well as the advantages of this very useful tool for business decision making. The purpose of Part II is to ensure that the reader is able to analyze situations in which it is appropriate to supplement the simple decision rules of the present-value procedure with an analysis of risk. In Chapter 8 we introduce the problem of capital rationing (there are more dollars of investment than there is cash available to undertake them). Solutions to this problem are less satisfactory, but fortunately, the problem frequently can be bypassed completely. Chapter 9 discusses several approaches for evaluating investments given inflationary conditions. Chapters 10 and 11 attempt to offer some simplified approaches to the making of decisions when there is uncertainty. Chapter 12 describes the choices available in choosing a rate of discount, and Chapter 13 ties together the investment decision and accounting concepts. Chapter 14 is a guide for preparing an investment manual.

The chapters in Part II have the general characteristic of requiring the reader to have somewhat more patience with mathematics than in the first part of this book. We have attempted to keep the mathematics as simple as possible.

In any event, if you want a better understanding of decision making under uncertainty, you are encouraged to read this material.

CHAPTER 8

Capital Budgeting Under Capital Rationing

In practice we have tacitly agreed, as a rule, to fall back on what is, in truth, a convention. The essence of this convention—though it does not, of course, work out quite so simple—lies in assuming that the existing state of affairs will continue indefinitely, except insofar as we have specific reasons to expect a change.

—*J. M. Keynes, The General Theory of Employment, Interest and Money (New York: Harcourt, Brace & Company, 1936), p. 152.*

In the preceding chapters we concluded that under conditions of certainty, if a firm could borrow or lend funds at a given market rate of interest, it should accept independent investments when the investments have positive net present values at this market rate of interest. In this chapter we consider situations in which the assumption that a firm can borrow or lend any quantity of funds that it desires at a given market rate of interest is not valid. There are two distinctly different situations in which this assumption may not hold.

One of these situations arises because of a decision by management to limit arbitrarily the total amount invested or the kind of investments the firm undertakes, or to set acceptance criteria that lead it to reject some investments that are advantageous when judged by market criteria. For example, instead of using the market interest rate it might use some higher rate as a cutoff or hurdle rate.

A second situation that must be considered is when there is a difference between the market rate of interest at which the firm can borrow money and the market rate at which it can lend.

Both situations are frequently labeled *capital rationing*. To distinguish between them, we shall refer to the former situation as *internal capital rationing* and to the latter as *external capital rationing*. External capital rationing is actually the result of market imperfections or transaction costs.

Two observations should be noted. First, capital rationing in both the first and second form is present throughout the economy, but usually to a relatively minor degree, and thus may frequently not be incorporated into the analysis (although it should not be ignored without trying to estimate its impact). Second, when

161

capital rationing is present, there is no simple solution to the internal investment decision. Two possible approaches are offered. The first possibility is to make simplifying assumptions where appropriate and to recognize that the answer obtained is an approximation. The second approach is to use mathematical techniques to develop possible solutions, following different possible investment alternatives (including all possible combinations of investments through the succeeding years). This analytical technique may lead to a sound solution to the capital-budgeting decision under capital rationing, but it is complex and requires detailed knowledge of future investment alternatives that is frequently not available.

External Capital Rationing

In this chapter the term *borrow* is used when a firm obtains capital from the market by issuing any type of security. The term *lend* is used to mean the use of funds to purchase any type of security. We specifically assume that borrowing takes place in such a way that the borrowing firm's capital structure (the relative proportion of the various kinds of securities it has issued) is not changed. Thus *borrowing* would normally involve issuing both debt and equity securities. Similarly, we assume that *lending* means acquiring a portfolio of securities that has approximately the same average risk characteristics as the assets presently owned by the firm.

Under conditions of certainty the term *lending* could be interpreted literally, because there is no problem of risk. Under uncertainty we want to define lending so that the process does not change the risk characteristics of the firm's assets compared to expanding the firm's operations by investing internally. A firm is lending if it purchases the securities of other firms whose assets have the same risk characteristics as its own assets.

A firm may purchase its own securities in amounts proportional to their market value. Suppose that a firm has only equity shares outstanding and it buys some of its own shares. The effect is very nearly the same as if it had used the same amount of cash to pay a cash dividend. It differs from lending in that it is not expected that the funds will be returned to the corporation.

If capital markets were such that a firm could lend or borrow as much money as it desired at the going rate of interest, this rate of interest would be the same for both the borrowing and lending transactions. The goal of profit maximization would then require that the firm accept all independent investments whose present values were positive, using this rate of interest. With such capital markets the choice of investments would not be dependent on the amount of funds available to the firm, because by an appropriate combination of borrowing and lending, each firm could finance investments that had positive present values.

This theoretical situation is an ideal never encountered in practice. There will almost always be some divergence between the rates of interest at which the firm can lend surplus funds and the rates at which it can borrow funds. The size of the gap may vary for many reasons, including the effect of the underwriting costs of raising new money and the fact that there may be hidden costs or risks connected with one or another of the investments. Another reason is that money-lenders may prefer firms having certain characteristics, thus driving up the cost of borrowing by firms that lack these characteristics.

If the borrowing rate and the lending rate are almost equal, little is lost by neglecting the difference and speaking of a market rate of interest. If the difference is large, it cannot be ignored in determining the investment and financial policies of the firm. This gives rise to the situation we describe as external capital rationing.

A partial solution to the capital-budgeting process with external capital rationing can be described as follows: Assume that a schedule is prepared showing the total current net outlays required in period zero for investments having a positive present value at various rates of discount. Such a schedule will show greater current outlays at lower rates of interest, because some investments whose present values are negative at high discount rates will have positive present values at low discount rates. The schedules are shown by curves $I–I$ in Figures 8-1(a), (b), and (c). We let the distance $0Q_1$ represent the quantity of internally generated funds available for investment during the current period. Three situations are possible. In Figure 8-1(a) the vertical line drawn up from point Q_1 intersects curve $I–I$ at a rate of interest higher than r_2, the borrowing rate. This indicates that some investments which would be profitable at a cost equal to the borrowing rate could not be financed from internally generated funds. It would be profitable for the firm to borrow an amount Q_1Q_2 to enable it to accept all investments that would be profitable at the borrowing rate. It would not be profitable to borrow any more than this amount, because all remaining investments have negative present values at the borrowing rate of discount.

In Figure 8-1(b) the internally generated funds currently available are more than sufficient to enable the firm to undertake all the investments that would be profitable when evaluated at the lending rate of interest. Only $0Q_2$ dollars would be invested internally. The remaining funds, Q_1Q_2, would either be invested externally by buying the securities of other organizations or used to reduce the capitalization of the firm by returning the funds to the suppliers.

A third possibility is that the firm has sufficient funds to accept all independent investments whose present values are positive when evaluated at the borrowing rate, but that the firm does not have enough funds to accept all investments whose present values are positive when evaluated at the lending rate. This is illustrated in Figure 8-1(c). Under those circumstances the firm would neither borrow any additional funds nor lend any part of its present funds, and the proper rate of discount for investments would be lower than the borrowing rate, but higher than the lending rate.

Based on this analysis, an incomplete set of rules for dealing with individual investment projects can be derived. Consider independent projects for which accept or reject decisions are appropriate. Evaluate the present value of the cash flows from the project at the borrowing rate. If the present value is positive, the project should be accepted. Projects that meet this test will be worth accepting

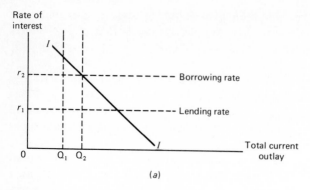

(a)

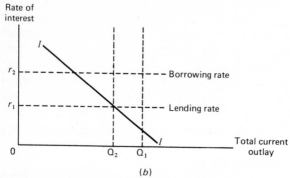

(b)

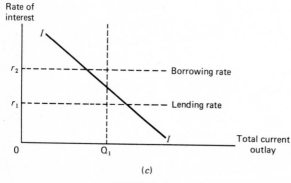

(c)

FIGURE 8-1

even if money must be borrowed to finance them. If the project is not accepted by this rule, evaluate the present value of the cash flows from the project at the lending rate. If the present value is negative, the project should be rejected. A project whose present value is negative at the lending rate should be rejected even if the firm has surplus funds.

These two rules will not lead to definite decisions for all projects. There may be some independent projects whose present values are negative at the borrowing rate and positive at the lending rate. For such projects no strict rules can be given. The final decision will depend partly on the firm's financial position and partly on management's objectives.

A similar set of tests can be applied to pairs of mutually exclusive alternatives, but in this case the cash flows that should be used are the incremental cash flows. If the best of a set of mutually exclusive alternatives can be identified utilizing these two tests, it is still necessary to consider whether this best alternative should be accepted or rejected when considered as an independent investment.

Strictly speaking, these rules are applicable only to conventional cash flows. Modifications to handle cases in which the cash-flow sequences alternate between outlays and proceeds are possible but are beyond the scope of this book.[1]

The analysis of this chapter assumes a capital market with a significant difference between the borrowing and lending rates. The solution suggested is only approximate, because we have not indicated what assumption is being made as to the probable lending and borrowing rates in the future, and the firm's position relative to them. The appropriate interest rates in future time periods are relevant to decisions made in the present because they affect the profitability of funds reinvested at those times. Cash flows expected in each future time period should be discounted at the rate of interest which will apply in that period. If we predict future lending and borrowing rates, we can assume that the appropriate rate of discount for each future period will lie somewhere between these upper and lower limits. Occasionally, a firm will have some basis for predicting whether in a given future year it is more likely to be operating somewhere near its borrowing rate or near its lending rate. If a firm, even in a growing industry, is faced with a temporary excess of capacity, it may feel safe in predicting that for the next few years it will have more internally generated funds than it needs for the available profitable investment alternatives. This can be reflected by using a rate of discount for these years that is relatively close to the lending rate. In other cases the firm may anticipate product improvements that are presently in the research and development state but which are expected to be perfected within a few years. If the introduction of these innovations will require large-scale capital investments, the firm may feel confident in predicting that it will be likely to be operating relatively close to its borrowing-rate point during the years these investments are being made. See Figure 8-1(c) and assume that curve *II* has shifted upward to the right (meaning there are more profitable investments) until the situation is described by Figure 8-1(a). In this situation the borrowing rate is applicable.

Although such predictions of future cutoff rates under external capital rationing are inevitably rather crude, they serve a useful purpose if the predicted rates are in the right general direction. By using a high rate of discount for a future year in which there is likely to be a shortage of internally generated funds relative to the available investment opportunities in that year, the firm is recognizing that the opportunity cost of funds may be higher in some periods than in others. Investment proposals that release funds for use in periods when the demand is

[1] On this point, see Gordon Pye, "Present Values for Imperfect Capital Markets," *Journal of Business*, **39**, Jan. 1966, pp. 45–51.

greatest will thus be preferred, all other things being equal, over investments that utilize funds in the periods of high demand. Similarly, if excess funds are likely to be available, the use of a lower discount rate will tend to lead toward the choice of investments that do not generate funds during these periods. The opportunity cost of funds during periods of excess funds is low; thus a low rate of discount is appropriate.

If a company is in a situation of external capital rationing, it may be useful for the top management to predict the appropriate cutoff rate that will apply in future years. By this means the investment planning in various parts of the organization can be coordinated in terms of the best available estimates of future cash needs and requirements for the company as a whole. If fluctuating cutoff rates are expected in the future, the company may wish to prepare and use present-value tables that show the appropriate discount factors to be used for each future period.

Example

Suppose a firm expects that the appropriate cutoff rate for it will be 5 percent for periods 1, 2, and 3, and 10 percent for periods 4 and 5. The firm is considering two mutually exclusive investment alternatives. Both require initial outlays of $100 now. Investment G will return $150 in year 3; investment H will return $200 in year 5. The present value of G's proceeds is $150 $(1.05)^{-3}$ = $150(.8638) = $130. The present value of H's proceeds is $200 $(1.05)^{-3}(1.10)^{-2}$ = $200(.8638)(.8264) = $200(.7138) = $143. Investment H with a net present value of $43 is preferred to G with a net present value of only $30.

Internal Capital Rationing

There are two types of internal capital rationing. In the first, the firm sets a cutoff rate for investments that is higher than the firm's cost of money. In the second type the firm decides to limit the total amount of funds committed to internal investments in a given year to some fixed sum, even though investments having positive present values at the firm's cost of money must be rejected as a result of this decision.

Consider the first kind of internal capital rationing. Suppose a firm requires that investments must have a positive present value at 15 percent, even though the firm's cost of money is only 10 percent. In this case, if the same cutoff rate is maintained from year to year, the cutoff rate in future years will be known, and the firm can evaluate all investments *as if* the cost of money were 15 percent. This will have some advantages compared to many other measures of investment worth. We have shown in Chapter 2 that whatever rate of discount is used, the present-value measures will avoid some errors in making investment decisions that could be committed if the pay-out period or other measures were used.

But, although a definite cutoff rate is available, the logic of using that rate to discount cash flows is no longer completely correct. The rate of discount used should measure the alternative uses of funds available to the firm. In the present instance, however, it indicates only that an investment of $1 now yielding less than 15 percent will not be undertaken. If next year the company has more internally generated funds than it is willing to invest following the 15 percent cutoff rule, then an extra dollar of funds that becomes available next year will have an opportunity cost that is less than 15 percent. How much less will depend on what use the firm makes of the "excess" cash that it will not invest. Usually, these excess funds are invested in short-term government securities.

Internal Capital Rationing and Dividend Policy

In the second type of internal capital rationing, the cutoff rate is not specified, but the maximum amount that will be invested is determined by top management, because it is unwilling to go to the market to obtain additional funds, even though there are desirable investments. This reluctance to go to the market may result from a wish to prevent outsiders from gaining control of the business, or from a feeling that there will be a dilution of earnings if additional equity funds are raised under the given market conditions.

In these circumstances, the correct amount and selection of investments will depend on the firm's dividend policy. One possibility is that the firm will maintain (over the life of the investments) the current level of dividends, regardless of any increases in earnings that may come about because of additional investment. Assume that past investments will support the dividend; then the net cash flows generated in future periods by the investments of the current period will be available for reinvestment in the period in which they are earned. The amounts of cash available for investment will vary from period to period, as will the desirability of investments (the demand schedule for investments may shift). This situation may result in the firm's rejecting internal investments with IRRs greater than the borrowing rate. For this reason it will be very difficult to make predictions of future cutoff rates (the opportunity costs for future cash flows).

A common dividend policy is that whereby the firm pays a dividend equal to a given fraction of its income (the income is measured by ordinary financial accounting techniques). In this case only a fraction of the future cash proceeds generated by current investments will be available for reinvestment. It is theoretically desirable to divide future cash flows generated by investments into that part which will be used as dividends and that part which will be available for reinvestment. The value of a dollar of reinvestible funds earned in future period t may be greater than the value of a dollar used for dividends in the same future period, if we ignore uncertainty and assume that the dollars will be reinvested in projects with positive net present values and that the market price of the stock will reflect this.

Even if the firm has an overabundance of cash, it should not invest the funds in investments with a negative net present value. Such investment would result in the reinvested dollars having less value than the dollars paid as dividends. It is unnecessary for the firm to accept investments whose IRRs are less than the IRRs of alternative opportunities available to the stockholders, because these same investments are generally available to the corporation.

Ranking of Investments

If management views a situation as being one of capital rationing it is apt to lead to a request to the investment analyst for the ranking of independent investments. The decision for the independent investments is no longer a matter of accept or reject decisions, but management wants to know the ranking of investments so that it might choose the best set of investments.

There are many procedures that seem to give a reliable ranking of investments, but that appearance is an illusion. There is no sure proof procedure for the ranking of independence investments. The problem is that ranking implies the use of a cutoff rate above the cost of money and a rejection of investments that would be acceptable except for the rationing situation. This implies that the use of the conventional cutoff rate as a discount rate is not valid, since the opportunity cost for funds will be higher. Also, the opportunity cost of future time periods may well be different than that of the present as the capital rationing either becomes more tight or less tight.

Let us consider the use of net present value as a ranking technique. First, the net present value does not tell us how much capital had to be committed to the investment. Two small investments may well be better than one large investment, even though the large investment has a larger net present value than either of the two small investments (but not larger than their sum). Second, the net present value is the result of an assumption about the time value of money that with rationing may not be appropriate. Neither of these difficulties is bothersome in the absence of capital rationing, but with capital rationing, they eliminate present value as an effective means of ranking investments.

The internal rate of return method is intuitively appealing but we already know that an investment with a lower internal rate of return might be more desirable than an investment with a higher internal rate of return. Figure 8-2 shows that investment B is preferred to investment A if the time value factor being used is less than r, even though the internal rate of return of A is larger than that of B.

A third popular method of ranking investments is the index of present value (present value of benefits divided by benefit of outlays). There are several difficulties in using this technique to rank independent investments. For example, the index depends on whether an outlay decreases the numerator (is deducted from benefits) or increases the denominator (increases the outlays). Since the classification is of necessity somewhat arbitrary, this is a severe weakness. A second problem is that the technique does require the use of a rate of discount in a situation where the ultimate choice of investments and rejection of investments will determine the opportunity cost of funds. A third problem is the fact that investments come in different sizes; thus we might not be able to undertake the mix of investments indicated by the ranking. The index of present value fails to consider effectively the size of the investment.

Recognizing that certain individuals have the audacity to pick a " Miss Uni-

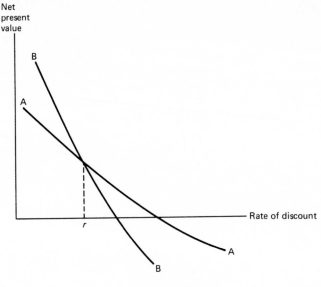

FIGURE 8-2

verse," we should be able to rank investments. And so we can, as long as the ranking is placed in somewhat the same perspective as the Miss Universe contest. A reasonable (not exactly correct) ranking can be obtained using either internal rate of return or index of present value. If desired, the present value of different sets of investments can be computed and an attempt made to maximize present value (but remember, the discount rate should represent the opportunity cost of funds).

In addition to the above complexities, if risk considerations are also brought into the analysis, then we must conclude that the ranking of independent investments for a capital rationing situation is truly more like choosing Miss Universe than it is an exact scientific technique.

Summary—Capital Rationing and Present Value

Capital rationing in one form or another exists to some extent in most corporations. We may distinguish among minor and severe cases of capital rationing. In the minor cases the present-value rules suggested in this book may be used with confidence. In the more severe forms of capital rationing, the present-value method may still be used, but it is now less correct to use a constant rate of discount for all future years. The rate of discount used for each future year must reflect the cost of obtaining additional funds, the value of external investments available to the firm, or the desires of the owners for present versus future proceeds.

Questions and Problems

8-1. The ABC Company is planning its investment budget. Currently, it can raise money at a cost of .06. It assumes that its stockholders are able to invest funds so as to earn .04. There are also opportunities for the company to lend its funds and earn .04 (a) Assume that the company expected a large amount of investment opportunities. What discount rate should it use in making investment decisions? (b) Assume that the company expected a large amount of cash compared to internal investment opportunities. What rate of discount should it use in making decisions? (c) Assume that the company expected a shortage of cash for the coming twenty-four months, but then expected a surplus amount of cash. What does this imply about the rate of discount to be used?

8-2. The ABC Company has a stable dividend policy ($2 per share a year). It also has a policy of not raising new capital from the market. The policy is to invest the available funds after payment of the dividends (excess cash is invested in marketable securities). What does this imply about the use of the present-value method of making investment decisions?

8-3. The ABC Company has more investment opportunities than it can use (it is unwilling to borrow or issue more common stock). Management estimated that the investment cutoffs for the next two years will be as follows:

Year	Cutoff
0–1	.20
1–2	.30

It is attempting to choose between two mutually exclusive alternatives both of which will require an initial outlay now and payoff at the end of two periods.

What discount rate should be used in evaluating the mutually exclusive investments? What rate would you use if the investments had a life of one year? [*Hint:* $(1 + R_n)^n = (1 + r_1)(1 + r_2) \cdots (1 + r_n)$, where r_i is the value of money of period i and R_n is the equivalent interest rate for the n periods.]

8-4. The president of the ABC Company wants a ranking of three investments. The firm considers its cost of money to be .05. The following three independent investments are ranked.

Investment	Cash Flows of Period 0	1	2	Present Net Value, Using .05	Ranking
A	−$1,000	$1,120		66.69	3
B	− 1,000		$1,210	97.47	1
C	− 1,000	400	775	83.89	2

The firm has $1,000 of uncommitted funds available (without borrowing) for investment. Based on the preceding ranking, the president decides to accept investment B. It is then revealed that because investment B has a IRR of .10 this could be considered to be the investment cut off rate (other investments already approved having higher IRRs).

Evaluate the decision process.

8-5. In answering the following questions assume that a dollar one year from now is worth $0.90 today, and a dollar two years from now is worth $0.75 today. Dollars can be bought and sold at these prices. There are no transaction costs.

A firm anticipates that it will have a surplus of dollars one year from now, but a shortage two years from now.

- **a.** The present value of the surplus of dollars that are forecast for one year from now is $2,000. What is the amount of the surplus in terms of dollars available in one year?
- **b.** By how much would the net present value of the firm change if all of the surplus year one dollars are sold (now) and the proceeds used to buy more year two dollars?
- **c.** How many year two dollars can be obtained in the transaction described in question b?
- **d.** What is the present value of an annuity of a dollar per year for two years at these prices?
- **e.** What is the interest rate the firm would have to pay on a one year loan, negotiated now, with the funds to be received one year from now, and paid back two years from now? That is, the cash flow from the point of view of the borrower would be as follows:

Time

Amount	0	1	2
	$\frac{0}{0}$	$\frac{}{+100}$	$\frac{}{-100(1+r)}$

Find r.

8-6. An investor can earn .05 (before taxes) in default-free investments. He is considering purchasing stock in a corporation that will pay a dividend of $10 a year for perpetuity (assume this information is known with certainty). The investor is in a marginal .7 tax bracket (a) Compute the value of the stock to the investor. (b) Compute the value of the stock, assuming that an investor has a marginal tax rate of .4. (c) Compute the value of the stock for the investors of parts (a) and (b). Assume that there are tax-exempt securities that can be purchased to yield .03.

8-7. Assume a situation where it is known that the dividend of $10 a year will not begin for eleven years and that the price at the end of ten years will be $200. The capital gains tax rate is .25; the after-tax opportunity cost to high tax investors is .03, and the after-tax opportunity cost to low tax investors is .05. (a)

How much would a high-tax investor be willing to pay for the stock now? Assume that he will sell at the end of ten years for $200. Why is this selling assumption reasonable? (b) How much would a low-tax investor (say zero tax) be willing to pay for the stock now? Would he sell at the end of ten years?

8-8. Recompute parts (a) and (b) of problem 8-7. Assume that the expected price at the end of ten years is $100.

8-9. Refer to problem 8-7. (a) How much would the high-tax investor be willing to pay for the stock at the end of year 9? How much would the low-tax investor be willing to pay? (c) How much would the high-tax investor realize in year 9 if she liquidated her investment at a price of $190? Assume that she paid $130 for the investment. (d) Compute the present value of the investment at the end of year 9. Assume that the high-tax investor intends to hold until year 10 and sell at $200.

8-10. The ABC Company prefers to finance investments internally to the extent possible. However it has adopted the following policies which are applied unless there are significant qualitative considerations that justify an exception for a particular project.

   a. Investments are not accepted unless they can earn at least 11.1 percent after taxes on a discounted cash flow (DCF) basis, even if excess funds are available.

   b. Investments are not rejected if they will earn 25 percent or more after-taxes on a discounted cash flow (DCF) basis, even if internally generated funds are not available.

The table below shows the cash flows for a series of independent investments. Use the ABC Company's criteria to classify each investment as:

A   Must Accept;
R   Must Reject;
U   Uncertain.

Show your calculations!

Investments	Cash Flows			Classification
D	−100	50	50	50
E	−100			200
F	−100	80	50	30
G	−100	30	50	80
H	−100	10	40	70

8-11. The ABC Company has opened 100 new stores. It has incurred a great deal of expenses associated with opening the stores, and the stores have not yet built up enough clientele to be profitable. However, the stores are operating at profit levels exceeding expectations and there are indications that they will be very profitable in the future. It is obvious that the stock market has not yet digested this latter fact, and the stock of the company is currently depressed compared to management's appraisal of value. The company has the opportunity to acquire an additional fifty stores this year, but to do so will require new stockholder capital acquired from the market (it has borrowed all it feels it is prudent to borrow and cannot obtain more capital from its current stockholders). Without the new capital the stockholders can expect to earn an equivalent annual yield of .15 on the current market value of their investment (assume that there is $100 million or 1 million shares of stock outstanding). The stock is currently selling at $100 per share and paying a $6 per share dividend. The earnings are $7.50 per share ($7.5 million in total).

The new investments would require $10 million to be obtained by issuing 100,000 new shares of common stock. The investment would return $1.2 million per year available for dividends for perpetuity. The stockholders desire a .08 return per year on their incremental investments.

Required: (a) Should the corporation issue the new shares and undertake the investment? (b) What would be your recommendation if the corporation had the necessary cash already available?

8-12. (*Continuing problem 8-11*). Change the statement of the problem so that the present stockholders can expect to earn dividends of $6 per share or an equivalent annual yield of .06 for perpetuity, unless the new investment is undertaken. Should the new investment be undertaken?

8-13. (*Continuing problem 8-11*). Change the statement of the problem so that the present stockholders can expect to earn $8 million, or an equivalent return of .08 per year on the current market value of their investment, if the new investment is not undertaken. Should the new investment be undertaken?

8-14. The ABC Company currently has outstanding $1 million of .05 debt with a maturity of two years. The only way it can finance a $500,000 investment would be by refinancing the $1 million with $1.5 million of .08 debt, also maturing in two years. The investment would pay $55,000 in year 1 and $555,000 in year 2 (the investment has a yield of .11). The firm has a cost of capital of .10:

Cost of equity	$.12 \times .5 = .06$
Cost of debt	$.08 \times .5 = \underline{.04}$
	$.10$

Should the investment be accepted?

8-15. The CDE Company can borrow and lend funds at an interest rate of .08. It can invest $11 million in a risky project that on the average will lead to net cash flows of $1 million per year. A consultant has suggested that the firm use its cost of capital of .10 in computing the present value of the investment. The investment's life is extremely long. Insurance can be purchased that will guarantee the $1 million per year. Should the investment be undertaken? How much could the firm afford to pay for the insurance?

8-16. *Production Line Problem*

Three new machines are required for a proposed improvement to the production line in the Charles Corporation main plant. Each has a life of five years and no salvage value. The proposed improvement requires all three machines. All data in this problem are already on an after-tax basis.

Machine A costs $400,000 to buy; it could be leased for $115,000 per year for five years. Machine B costs $1,000,000 to buy; it could be leased for $285,000 per year for five years. Machine C costs $500,000 and is not available for lease.

If all three machines are installed, there will be operating savings of $600,000 per year for each of the next five years. (There would be no benefit to installing just two of the machines.)

The cost of money for the Charles Corporation is 8 percent. (Money could be borrowed or lent at that rate.) The president, H. Arvard, seldom accepts investment proposals that have an internal rate of return of less than 20 percent.

    a. In your opinion, what decision in this matter is in the best interests of stockholders? (If your decision is to make the improvement specify whether A and/or B are to be bought or leased.) Why?

    b. Of the proposals that might be acceptable to the president, which one is best for stockholders?

Discussion Questions

8-A. Company X's reported net earnings have increased to $3 per share after having remained at the $2 per share level for a number of years. Dividend payments have been $1.20 per share for quite a few years. Its dividend payout has been somewhat more liberal than that of its industry.

Practically all the increase in earnings has resulted from consolidated earnings of new foreign subsidiaries and affiliated domestic companies. The earnings of these companies are available for Company X dividends only to the extent that Company Y receives dividends from them. The foreign companies and affiliates are relatively new and their capitalizations are highly leveraged, so a major portion of their net earnings is currently required to repay debt and provide funds for expansion, leaving only a small portion available for dividend payments to Company X.

The treasurer considers the general financial position of Company X to be quite satisfactory. Although cash is kept at the minimum amount necessary to run the business, long-term debt represents only 15 percent of total capitalization and could be increased readily to finance major capital expenditures. Depreciation is adequate to support replacement of worn-out and obsolete equipment, but not a significant expansion of plant and equipment. Long-term debt repayments are equivalent to approximately $.60 per share of net earnings.

Required: With the increase in reported earnings, management is receiving inquiries as to why the dividend has not been increased. Based on the information presented, the dividend could be increased by about $.20 per share from parent company earnings plus dividends from foreign subsidiaries and affiliates, which may average $.20 to $.30 per share over the next several years, but this would reduce or eliminate retained earnings for expansion.

The company's dividend policy is to maintain a dividend rate once established. The problem facing management is whether to increase the dividend or not, and, if so, how much and still provide adequately for future expansion.

8-B.

The United Fruit Company

During the annual stockholders' meeting held April 21, 1965, the following exchanges took place:

Question: When capital investment is being considered to reduce costs, what minimum rate of return is considered acceptable by the company?

M. Fox: To reduce costs, the minimum rate of return that we would be at all interested in would be about 11 percent after taxes, which is the target we are setting on our return for investments.

There are other considerations than just straight cost reductions. If they improved the quality of the product or improved the safety of our operations, these would also have to be considered. But by and large, anything that didn't enable us to have 11 percent after taxes would not get serious consideration.

Question: Is there a chance the company again may offer to buy its stock at $26 a share?

M. Fox: I think that what you are really asking here is: Are we contemplating acquiring a large amount of our stock and inviting tenders at whatever the price might be at that particular time?

We have better opportunities to broaden and expand this company by using our cash and our credit if need be to acquire other businesses. And rather than retrenching the company, I would like to see it expand. This, of course, would pretty much preclude a tender in the near future at least.

Question: Would you comment, sir, about our oil leases?

M. Fox: There is little to report. We have not made any major strikes and have ceased exploring. We would like to find some way to profitably dispose of these properties to someone who might like to proceed with them. The cost of exploring for oil is too big a gamble for this company to take.

Question: Has there been a tremendous investment of corporate assets in the oil explorations or is it relatively insignificant?

M. Fox: No, it has been insignificant.

Required: Discuss the preceding questions and answers.

8-C. A small oil company owns ten different oil-producing properties. It wants to raise capital for more drilling, but the owner does not want to dilute his ownership, and thus the firm cannot sell my common stock. It has borrowed up to its debt capacity.

What do you recommend?

8-D. In September, 1964 the Commonwealth Edison Company announced it would discontinue its stock dividend policy. The policy of the company had been to issue stock dividends of 1 to 2.4 percent for the earnings in excess of the cash dividends. The stated purpose of the stock dividends was to help finance expansion without public offerings of common stock. The dividends were stopped because it was feared that a further increase in the common stock equity ratio would increase the common stock equity ratio would increase the company's overall cost of money.

Required: Discuss the company's use of stock dividends.

9

Capital Budgeting and Inflation

Among the many misfortunes which bring ruin to entire
states ... four are the most serious: internal dissension, a
high death rate, poor harvests and the corruption of
money ....

—*Nicholas Copernicus, "A Method of Coining Money,"*
1528.

The basic principles of capital budgeting are applicable when there is a risk of
inflation as well as when the risk of inflation is negligible. However, it is not
always easy to apply these principles correctly when the risk of inflation is of
primary importance. The purpose of the present chapter is to offer some suggestions about how to consider inflation in an effective manner. When inflation is
possible, future cash flows may differ not only in their timing but in their purchasing power, and we may want to determine whether money flows or purchasing
power flows are more useful in describing the outcomes of an investment and in
making decisions about alternative investments. In addition, selecting an appropriate discount rate in the presence of inflationary risks is more complex. The
principal conclusion of this chapter is that investments can be analyzed using
either money cash flows or purchasing power flows, as long as the analysis is
done in a consistent manner.

What Is Inflation?

In a dynamically growing economy, price changes take place constantly. In the
highly organized markets for securities and for some commodities, it is normal
for prices to change from one transaction to the next. In other cases—for
example, most real estate leases—prices (rents, in the case of a lease) are fixed by
contract for a period of years. Sometimes the price of a particular good or service
may exhibit an upward or downward trend that can last for months, years, or
even decades.

The price changes that are the result of shifts in the supply or demand for
particular goods and services do not imply any change in the general price level.
Increases in the price of some goods or services may be offset by decreases in
others, so that the average level of prices can remain more or less constant. A

change in the average price level takes place if there is a strong tendency for many prices to move up (or down). Inflation is a rise in the average price level; deflation is a decline in the average price level. In the United States, price-level changes have tended to be inflationary during most of the last half-century; during the preceding half-century, the price-level changes tended to be deflationary.

Although the idea of an average price level is a useful tool, it is important to be aware of its limitations. The statisticians who construct price-level indexes must decide what goods to include in the index and what weight to assign to each. A commonly used index, the consumer price index, is designed to measure the average price of the goods consumed by an average-sized middle-income urban family. It is a reasonable measure for this purpose, but the price level it records may not accurately reflect the buying habits of a specific family or of a business enterprise. Many families and almost all business organizations will have important components of their revenues or expenses whose movements are not closely tied to the average price level of consumer goods. In these circumstances careful consideration of the prices of specific goods and services of particular importance to the decision makers is required. In evaluating capital budgeting decisions a manager must consider not only the possible effects of inflation, but also the effect of long-run trends in the relative prices of products and of important categories of expenditures.

This point is particularly important because the prices of many of the most important goods and services purchased by firms are not directly included in the commonly used price indexes. Labor is the prime example. Wage and salary payments are a major expense item for almost every business. Yet wage rates are not directly included in price indexes used to measure the rate of inflation or deflation. Labor costs, however, are reflected in the costs of the consumption goods and services that are included in the price indexes.

Real Cash Flows

Up to this point we have described investments in terms of cash flows. If the price level rises, the purchasing power of a dollar will decline. For some purposes it may be equally useful to measure the costs and benefits of an investment in terms of dollars of constant purchasing power. Suppose that an investment will return $100 this year and $100 next year. If the price level rises 4 percent between now and next year (the price index is 100 for this year and 104 for next year), the $100 to be received next year will have a purchasing power in terms of this year's dollar of $100/1.04 = R\$96.15$.

To distinguish in this chapter between cash flows measured in dollars and cash flows measured in terms of purchasing power, the former will be referred to as money cash flows and the latter as real cash flows. The symbol $R\$$ will be used to denote real cash flows. Thus, in the example used in the previous paragraph, $R\$96.15$ is the real cash flow of the investment next year.

Real Cash Flows and Money Flows

The process of analyzing a capital investment project involves at least two distinct steps. First, the costs and benefits of the project must be described in some meaningful way. Second, the costs and benefits must be evaluated in terms of the goals and objectives of the decision maker. In each of these steps the decision maker has a choice of whether money cash flows or real cash flows will be used.

It has long been recognized that one of the disadvantages of an unstable price level is that it makes the task of appropriately analyzing the economic advantages and disadvantages of different alternatives more difficult and complex. In the present chapter it is our intention to illustrate with specific examples techniques that may be used to take the possibility of inflation into account.

Although capital budgeting decisions may be made using either money or real flows, there may be differences in our ability to estimate the necessary inputs, the costs and benefits of an investment project. If revenues or costs are mainly determined by market forces in the period in which the outlays are made or the revenues received, estimates in terms of real cash flows may be more accurate than estimates of money flow. But if future costs and revenues are determined by long-term fixed-price contractual relationships, estimates in terms of money flows are likely to be more accurate.

Money values are converted into real values by dividing the monetary value by an appropriate price-index relative. For example, suppose that an investment promises to return $100 per year for the next two years and that the cash proceeds measured in money values are certain. At 9 percent, the present value of the monetary value is $175.91. Suppose that the price index for the current period is 140; it is expected to be 145.6 next year and 151.424 the following year. We wish to convert the money values in all three years to real values in terms of this year's price level. To do this the first step is to construct price-index relatives for each of the three years. A price-index relative is a ratio of two price-index values. The value in the numerator is the value of the price index for the year in which the cash flows will occur. The denominator is the price index of the base period (the real values are to be expressed in terms of the purchasing power of that period). The price relatives are $140/140 = 1$ for the current period, $145.6/140 = 1.04$ for next year, and $151.424/140 = 1.0816$ for the following year.

To convert money values to real values, the money values for a given period are divided by the price-index relative for that period. The real value of the $100 to be received next year is $R\$96.154$ ($100/1.04$) and the real value of the $100 to be received the following year is $R\$92.456$ ($100/1.0816$). If real cash flows are used it is not appropriate to use the nominal observed market costs of capital as a discount rate. A "real" cost of money must be estimated.

The Use of Specific Prices

Suppose that a firm is considering investing $10,000 in a machine that has a useful life of five years. For simplicity, assume that for tax purposes the original cost of the machine will be depreciated (zero salvage) on a straight-line basis over its life. With the machine, one worker using 2,000 pounds of raw materials per year can produce 1,600 units of product per year. In current prices the machine will cost $10,000, the worker, $8,000 per year, and the raw material $2 per pound. The firm is subject to a combined federal and state corporate income tax rate of 60 percent. The product can be sold for $10 per unit.

In each of the five years, if there are no changes in any of these prices, the cash flow will be as follows:

Revenues 1,600 × $10	$16,000
Labor expense	8,000
Raw material expense	4,000
Income taxes	1,200
Net cash flow	$ 2,800

These numbers are reproduced in column 1 of Table 9-1.

Even with no change in the general price level, specific prices may still change. For example, assume labor expense will rise by 10 percent if there is no change in the price level. This will increase labor expense by $800, reduce tax payments by $480, and reduce the cash flow by $320 to $2,480. The resulting cash flows are shown in column 2 of Table 9-1.

TABLE 9-1.   *Examples of Effects of Price Level and Labor Expense Changes on Money and Real Cash Flows*

	Column 1	Column 2	Column 3
Assumptions			
Real wages	No change	+10%	+10%
Price level	No change	No change	+10%
Money cash flows			
Revenues	$16,000	$16,000	$17,600
Expenses			
Labor expenses	8,000	8,800	9,680
Raw material	4,000	4,000	4,400
Income taxes	1,200	720	912
Net cash flow	$2,800	$2,480	$2,608
Real cash flows	R$2,800	R$2,480	R$2,371

Now suppose that the general price level increases by 10 percent and that this price-level change is reflected in strictly proportional changes in the product and raw material prices. Suppose also that real labor expense increases by an additional 10 percent in real terms to $9,680. Calculating the cash flow under these assumptions, we have the following:

Revenues: 1,600 × $11	$17,600
Labor expense	9,680
Raw material expense	4,400
Income taxes	912
Net cash flow	$ 2,608

The cash flows under these assumptions are shown in column 3 of Table 9-1.

Comparing the money cash flows of columns 2 and 3, a firm might conclude that despite a 10 percent increase in real wages inflation is to its advantage. The money cash flow is $128 higher with a 10 percent increase in the price level than without it ($2,608 compared to $2,480). But with a 10 percent inflation the money cash flow of $2,608 in year 5 is equivalent, in purchasing power, to (1/ 1.10) × ($2,608) = R$2,371. It is this amount that should be compared to $2,480, which will be received (real and money cash flow) without inflation. With inflation the firm's real cash flow is R$109 less than without inflation.

The three situations described above are summarized in Table 9-1. The table is intended to illustrate the importance of making realistic assumptions about how specific prices are likely to change with or without general price level inflation.

Real and Money Discount Rates

In previous sections we have stated that the cash flows from a project could be described in terms of money cash flows or real cash flows. In the present section we discuss the choice of a discount rate. The value of an asset should not depend on whether it is analyzed in monetary terms or in real terms as long as the appropriate discount rate is used in each case. With money cash flows the discount rate used should be the money discount rate. With real cash flows, the discount rate used should be a real discount rate. The failure to follow these apparently simple rules is a frequent source of errors in project evaluation.

To illustrate the relationships between the two discount rates, we first ignore tax effects. (Assume the decision maker is in the zero tax bracket.) With annual compounding, if j is the annual rate of inflation and i is the real rate of interest, then the corresponding money (nominal) rate of interest is

$$r = (1 + j)(1 + i) - 1 \qquad (1)$$

or equivalently

$$r = j + i + ij. \qquad (2)$$

For example, if we require a real rate of interest of .03 and expect a rate of inflation of .10, then the required money rate of interest to give an equivalent real return will be

$$r = .03 + .10 + .003 = .133.$$

The same relationship can also be used to solve for the real rate of interest, given the nominal rate and the expected rate of inflation. For example, suppose the expected rate of inflation is .10 and we observe a nominal rate of interest of 13.3 percent. What is the corresponding real interest rate? Solving equation (2) for i gives

$$i = (r - j)/(1 + j),\tag{3}$$

and substituting the assumed values gives

$$i = (.133 - .10)/(1.1) = .033/1.1 = .03.$$

In valuing an asset we have two choices. We can use money cash flows and the nominal rate of interest, or the corresponding real cash flows and real interest rate. Suppose under the conditions described above we observe a bond that promises interest payments of $133 per year for three years, with the principal of $1,000 to be repaid at the end of the third year. At the nominal discount rate of 13.3 percent, the present value of the bond should be $1,000. This presumption is verified in the following calculations:

Period	Money Cash Flow	Nominal Present-Value Factor (.133)	Present Value
1	$ 133	.8826	$ 117.39
2	133	.7790	103.61
3	1,133	.6876	779.00
			$1,000.00

The same present value would result if we first convert the money cash flows to real cash flows and discount these at the corresponding real interest rate of .03. This is illustrated in the following calculations.

Period n	Money Cash Flow (1)	Price Level Relative (2) = $(1+j)^n$	Real Cash Flows (3) = (1)/(2)	Real Present Value Factor (4) = $(1+i)^{-n}$	Present Value (5) = (3)(4)
1	$ 133	1.10	120.91	.9709	$ 117.39
2	133	1.21	109.92	.9426	103.61
3	1,133	1.331	851.24	.9151	779.00
					$1,000.00

In the above example we began with an asset that promised definite money cash flows. Now suppose that an asset is available that is expected to provide R$100 per year for three years, for example a lease with a price index escalator clause. What is the value of the lease? The easiest approach is to discount the real cash flows using the real interest rate of 3 percent. In this case we can use the annuity factor $B(3, .03) = 2.8286$. Therefore the value of the asset is $282.86. An alternative approach is to translate the real cash flows into money cash flows at the assumed 10 percent rate of inflation, and evaluate the money cash flows using the nominal interest rate. The calculations are shown below:

Period	Real Cash Flow	Price Level Relative	Money Cash Flow	Money Present Value Factor	Present Value
1	R$100	1.10	$110.00	.8826	97.09
2	100	1.21	121.00	.7790	94.26
3	100	1.331	133.10	.6876	91.51
					$282.86

We first used nominal cash flows and nominal discount rates and obtained a present value of $1,000. We then converted the money (nominal) cash flows to real cash flows and used a real discount rate to again obtain a present value of $1,000. If nominal cash flows are used it is important that a nominal discount rate be used. However, if real cash flows are used it is necessary to use a real discount factor. The real cash flows cannot sensibly be discounted using the nominal discount rate.

Tax Effects

The previous analysis did not take income taxes into consideration. Suppose an investor is subject to income taxes at a marginal rate of t on nominal income. Without inflation the real and nominal rates would be i and the after-tax real return would be $(1 - t)i$. Suppose the rate of inflation is j per year. We want to find the nominal rate that is required if the investor is to continue to earn an after-tax real return to $(1 - t)i$. The basic relationship analogous to $(1 + r) = (1 + j)(1 + i)$ is

$$1 + (1 - t)r = (1 + j)[1 + i(1 - t)].$$

Solving for r we have

$$r = i + ij + j/(1 - t). \tag{4}$$

For example, suppose that the real rate of interest before taxes would be 3 percent if there were no inflation, and that the marginal income tax rate is 30 percent. With an inflation rate of 6 percent per year investors in the 30 percent tax bracket would have to earn a nominal rate of 11.75 percent $= .03 + .0018 + .06/.7$ in order to have the same after-tax real return that they could have earned if the real rate were 3 percent and there were no inflation. Table 9-2 shows the nominal rates of interest that are equivalent to 3 percent before taxes without inflation for different rates of inflation and two different tax rates.

TABLE 9-2. Nominal Interest Rates Equivalent After Taxes to 3 Percent Return Before Tax Without Inflation

Rate of Inflation (%)	Investor Tax Rate	
	.3	.5
3	7.38	13.09
6	11.75	15.18
9	16.13	21.27
12	20.50	27.36
15	24.88	33.45

Conclusions

During periods of rapidly changing prices managers tend to question the use of dollar cash flows. The maintenance of purchasing power becomes an objective. Investments can be analyzed using either money cash flows or real cash flows, but the analysis must be done in a consistent manner. If real purchasing power units are used (dollars adjusted for purchasing power changes) the nominal (observed) discount rates cannot be used. If nominal dollars unadjusted for purchasing power changes are used the real rate of interest cannot be used.

While the maintenance of real purchasing power may be considered to be desirable, an investment may still be acceptable in the absence of uncertainty if its return is larger than the cost of money (e.g., the borrowing rate) without considering the purchasing power changes.

Questions and Problems

9-1. Assume that the price level is expected to increase by .05 in the coming year. What return do you have to earn on an investment of $100 to earn .06 on your investment in terms of real purchasing power?

9-2. A one-year $100 debt security is issued to yield .10. It is expected that there will be .08 inflation during the next year. What return, in real terms, will the security earn if the prediction of price-level change actually is fulfilled?

9-3. A three-year $100 debt security is issued to yield .10 ($133.10 will be paid after three years). It is expected that there will be .08 inflation per year during the time period. What return, in real terms, will the security earn if the prediction of price-level change actually occurs?

9-4. The ABC Company is building a plant that is expected to cost $10 million to service the capacity needs of the firm for the next three years. For another $2

million it can build excess capacity that is expected to fill the needs for an additional seven years. It is expected that it would cost $3 million to make the identical changes three years from now. The firm's cost of money is .10. Should the excess capacity be purchased?

9-5. The UVW Company is considering an investment costing $1 million. The expected IRR is .04. Debt funds can be obtained to finance this investment at a cost of .05. The justification offered for the investment is that there is expected to be inflation; thus there will be a gain at the expense of the bondholders (they will be holding fixed dollar claims). The .04 IRR of the investment includes appropriate adjustments in cash flows because of the expected inflation. The lives of the investment and the debt are comparable. Can the investment be justified?

9-6. Assume a firm expects a 9 percent per year increase in wage rates and in the price level, and a 10 percent time-value factor (costing of borrowing).

A piece of equipment costing $331,210 will save 5,000 hours of labor per year. Initially each hour is worth $20.

The life of the equipment is four years.

Should the equipment be purchased? There are zero taxes.

9-7. (*Continuing problem 9-6*). Assume the 9 percent increase in wage rates still applies to the firm, but there is a 15 percent inflation in the economy. The cost of borrowing is still 10%. The firm wants to translate future dollars into current purchasing power and make the following calculations:

100,000	$= 100{,}000 \times 1.10^{-1}$	$= 90{,}909$
$109{,}000 \times 1.15^{-1} =$	$94{,}800 \times 1.10^{-2}$	$= 78{,}347$
$118{,}000 \times 1.15^{-2} =$	$89{,}800 \times 1.10^{-3}$	$= 67{,}468$
$129{,}503 \times 1.15^{-3} =$	$\underline{85{,}200} \times 1.10^{-4}$	$= \underline{58{,}193}$
	369,800	294,917

The NPV $= -331{,}210 + 294{,}900 = -36{,}310$.   The investment was rejected. Evaluate.

9-8. An asset costs $10,000 now. It will return a perpetuity R$400 per year with no risk. (The dollar amount paid out will grow in proportion to the rate of inflation.) The time value of the money is 10 percent.

Is this a desirable investment if the expected rate of inflation is 8 percent? Explain. Ignore taxes. Illustrate your explanation with a simple numerical example, if possible.

9-9. Dr. M. Upham has $100,000 cash which she wants to invest. Her marginal tax rates are 60 percent for ordinary income, and 20 percent for capital gains. She expects the rate of inflation to be 12 percent. She can buy a high grade municipal bond costing $100,000 which pays interest of 9 percent ($9,000) per year. This interest is not taxable. There are no capital gains or losses.

a. If a high grade corporate bond were available that was just as safe as the municipal bond, what interest rate on the corporate bond is required so that Dr. Upham would be indifferent between the two bonds?

b. In fact, the comparable corporate bond available pays an interest rate of 15 percent ($15,000) per year. This interest is taxable as ordinary income. There are no capital gains or losses. What interest rate on the municipal bond is required so that Dr. Upham would be indifferent between the two bonds?

c. Dr. Upham has read that investments should be analyzed in real (purchasing power) terms. Dr. Upham's alternatives are either a nontaxable municipal bond paying 9 percent or a taxable corporate bond paying 15 percent. What is the best *real* rate of return that she can expect to earn? (Calculate your answer to the nearest 1/10 of one percent.)

d. In order to increase her real return, Dr. Upham consulted a real estate broker. He suggested a tract of land that was *worth* $113,700 which he said was sure to increase in value by the same percentage amount as the price level. Furthermore, the land could be picked up at a bargain price of $100,000 because the seller needed cash. The broker said the cash flows would be:

0	1	2	3
− 100,000	0	0	150,000

Dr. Upham realized that these were before-tax cash flows, and that the $50,000 profit would be taxable at the capital gains rate. Find the real NPV of this investment, using a real after-tax interest rate of one percent.

e. Find the real NPV of the investment described in part d, if the best alternatives available to the doctor are the bonds previously described.

9-10. *Con-Chem-Co. IV*

Con-Chem-Co. has specified standard methodology for evaluating investments. They specified in 1980 a 26 percent IRR "regardless of the project or division."

One of the directions given in the manual is "Deflate the current dollar cash flows to obtain the results in today's dollars." Annual deflators were supplied. The deflators to be used for the five years starting in 1980 are:

1980	1.00
81	.90
82	.80
83	.73
84	.68
85	.63

Assume that five-year debt costs Con-Chem-Co. .14 percent; there is a .46 tax rate; and the after tax cash flows (current dollars) of an investment are:

1980	−1,000
81	+ 200
82	+ 200
83	+ 200
84	+ 200
85	+1,200

The cash flows are certain.

Required:

a. Prepare the analysis as it would be prepared by Con-Chem-Co.

b. Should the investment be undertaken?

9-11. A company requires a 26 percent "real return." With a 15 percent inflation rate, what nominal (current dollar) return must the firm earn?

9-12. Assume a 9 percent inflation rate (with an equivalent increase in wage rates) and a 10 percent time value factor (cost of borrowing).

A piece of equipment costing $250,000 will save 4,000 hours of labor per year. Initially each hour is worth $20.

The life of the equipment is three years.

Should the equipment be purchased? There are zero taxes.

9-13. An investment costs $1,000 and with no inflation the expected cash flows are $1,100. With a 20 percent inflation the cash flows are expected to be $1,180.

Funds can be borrowed at a cost of 15 percent.

Required:

a. Using the borrowing rate, should the investment be undertaken?

b. What real return does the investment earn if inflation occurs?

c. Should investment be accepted?

9-14. Company A can borrow funds at 15 percent. It is considering an investment that has an outlay of $1,000 and $1,100 of benefits in real purchasing power terms at time one. A 20 percent inflation rate is forecasted.

Should the investment be accepted?

9-15. Assume investors want a real return of .04 percent and there is an inflation rate of 16 percent. What nominal return must be earned?

9-16. Assume there is a 16 percent rate of inflation. A $1,000 investment earns a return of 20.64 percent. What real return is earned?

9-17. Assume a firm has borrowed $1,000 and is paying 20.64 percent interest per year. There is a 16 percent inflation rate. What is the real cost of the borrowed funds?

9-18. Does a firm benefit from using debt instead of common stock during a period of inflation?

9-19. Miss Smith is currently earning $30,000, and is paying an average tax rate of .4 and a marginal rate of 70 percent.

With an inflation rate of 10 percent what pay increase does Miss Smith require to maintain her standard of living?

9-20. (*Continuation of 9-19*). Miss Smith would like to earn a real return of 4 percent before tax and $(1 - .7)(.04) = .012$ or 1.2 percent after tax.

What nominal interest rate would she have to earn if the marginal tax stays at .7 and if there is an inflation rate of .10?

9-21. What interest rate would you use to find the annual equivalent cost in constant (real) dollars of owning a home which could be purchased for $100,000 now? Assume the homeowner is in the 30 percent income tax bracket, that he expects the rate of inflation to be 6 percent per year, and that the home would be financed with a $80,000 mortgage at an interest rate of 10 percent. The remaining $20,000 would be obtained by selling securities, with an opportunity cost of 15 percent per year before taxes. The homeowner believes that there is no correlation between short-term changes in the rate of inflation and short-term changes in the rate of return on the stock market.

Discussion Question

9-A. Which is more risky, a mortgage bond or common stock of a large oil company? Explain.

CHAPTER **10**

Describing Uncertain Investments

Business men play a mixed game of skill and chance, the average results of which to the players are not known by those who take a hand. If human nature felt no temptation to take a chance, no satisfaction (profit apart) in constructing a factory, a railway, a mine or a farm, there might not be much investment merely as result of cold calculation.

—*J. M. Keynes, The General Theory of Employment, Interest and Money (New York: Harcourt, Brace & Company, 1936), p. 150.*

Up to this point we have assumed that an investment could be described as a unique sequence of cash flows. In the present chapter some essential concepts necessary for dealing with uncertainty are introduced. With uncertainty there may be many alternative sequences of cash flows that could occur if an investment were accepted. The decision maker does not know in advance which sequence will actually occur. The objective of the present chapter will be to consider methods of describing these uncertain outcomes.

Uncertain Events and Forecasts of Cash Flows

The difficulty of specifying unique cash flows derives from the fact that there are future events that will affect the cash flows. But we do not know in advance which of these events will occur. For each possible event, we have to make a somewhat different forecast of the cash flows from the investment. The uncertainty arises because we do not know with certainty which of the possible events will occur, and thus cannot be sure which cash flow will actually occur.

We shall use the term *event* to describe an observable outcome at a particular point in time. If there is uncertainty, more than one event is possible; but one and only one will actually occur. For some purposes it may be useful to combine fundamental occurrences to form a master event. For example, rain or snow may result in the cancellation of a game; hence we may use an event "bad weather" rather than one event "rain" and another event "snow."

To take a simple example, suppose that you have an opportunity to bet on the outcome of the flip of a coin. If the coin lands heads, you win $1; if the coin lands tails, you lose $1. The cash forecast is a plus $1 with one event and a $1 loss with

189

the other event. Before the toss you do not know whether the coin will land heads or tails. Only if you know that the coin is two-headed or two-tailed will the cash flows be known with certainty.

To take a more immediately relevant case, suppose that a firm is contemplating investing in a plant to produce a product whose demand is very sensitive to general business conditions. If general business conditions are good, the demand for the product is likely to be high and the plant profitable. If general business conditions are poor, the demand is low and the plant unprofitable. Again, in this case, uncertainty about the cash flows associated with the investment derives from uncertainty about some other event—general business conditions. If the future state of general business conditions could be perfectly forecast, the outcome of the investment could be predicted.

TABLE 10-1.   *Conditional Forecasts of Net Present Value of a New Product Investment*

Product Design	General Business Conditions	
	Favorable	Unfavorable
Popular design	$1,500,000	$1,400,000
Unpopular design	−250,000	−400,000

Table 10-1 illustrates the effect of business conditions and product design on the potential profits from introducing a new product. In this case, the state of business conditions has some effect on the present value of the investment; but product design is more important. If the product design turns out to be unpopular with customers, producing the new product will result in a loss, and only the exact size of the loss depends on general business conditions. However, if the product is popular with customers, it will be profitable; but profits will be somewhat better if business conditions are favorable than if they are unfavorable.

Events could be classified in a large number of ways, and no one classification will be useful for all purposes. We might consider as one category those events that affect the level of business activity generally. The international political situation, the monetary and fiscal policies of the government, and the general state of confidence of the business community might be considered to be factors that help determine the actual level of the business activity which occurs. Another category might be events that tend to affect all companies in an industry. For example, all companies in the steel industry would be affected by the outcome of the labor negotiations that determine the wage rates in the industry, by new important discoveries of iron ore, by changes in the cost of rail or water transportation and by excise taxes affecting steel. A third category would be events directly affecting a particular company, such as a change in its management or a natural disaster such as a flood or fire. A fourth category would be events affecting primarily one product category or one particular investment.

The classification of events is the first step in focusing attention on what is most relevant for a particular decision. The desirability of an investment is likely to be affected more by some events than by others. The purpose of the analysis and the point of view of the analyst will determine which category of events is most important. If the point of view is that of a manager whose future depends in an important way on the outcome of a particular project, then events affecting this project are likely to be more important to that manager. However, if the analysis is done for the benefit of stockholders, then the level of the general business condition may be more important. This will influence many different projects and assets in the same direction at the same time, thus greatly affecting corporate profitability.

A new product with a popular design would generate positive new profits even under unfavorable business conditions that would eliminate the profits for most of the other lines of activity. A product that could produce high positive profits under such conditions might be extremely attractive to a company. This has very important consequences in determination of the effect of the decision on the uncertainty of total profits for the company.

The considerations discussed suggest that, in evaluating a specific uncertain investment, we need to consider the outcomes of the investment in relation to the outcomes of the other investments that have been undertaken by the investor. Methods of evaluating the outcomes of a portfolio of investments will be considered in detail in later chapters. In the present chapter we concentrate on methods of describing the different possible events that can occur, the possible investment outcomes associated with those events and the likelihood of the events. These methods, which are applied in this chapter to individual investments, can also be applied to portfolios of investments.

The distribution of outcomes may be continuous. For example, the cash flows from a project might be related to the level of GNP. In this case, the level of GNP is the event and it is a continuous variable. For ease of illustration, most of the events discussed in this chapter will be discrete. But in practice, continuous events are frequently easier to handle.

Probability: A Measure of Likelihood[1]

Probability may be described as a measure of someone's opinion about the likelihood that an event will occur. If an event is certain to occur, we say that it has a probability of 1 of occurring. If an event is certain not to occur, we say that its probability of occurring is 0. All events have a probability of occurrence somewhere between 0 and 1. By convention, probabilities follow several rules. Among them are the following: (1) the probability assigned to each possible event

---

[1] Readers who are familiar with basic probability concepts may wish to skip ahead to the section on Tree Diagrams, later in this chapter.

must be a positive number between 0 and 1, where 0 represents an impossible event and 1 represents a certain event; (2) if a set of events is mutually exclusive and exhaustive (covers all possible outcomes), the probabilities of the events must total 1.

Suppose that we consider events associated with one flip of a coin. With a new, fairly machined coin that has a head on only one side, most of us would be willing to agree that the probability of landing a head on one fair toss is .5 and the probability of a tail is .5 (these two events are mutually exclusive and exhaustive, if we do not allow the coin to stand on its edge). If we did not know that the coin was fair (for example, if the coin were worn unevenly), there would be some question if the probability of landing a head would be exactly .5. One can easily imagine that different people might have different opinions about the probability in this case. If, however, we were to take such a two-sided coin and flip it in a fair manner a very large number of times, say 100,000 times, the ratio of the actual number of heads to the total number of flips would be a reasonable estimate of the probability of the event "heads" for that particular coin. The probability estimate is based on the objective evidence of 100,000 trials and is called an *objective probability*.

If the concept of probability were applicable only to events that could be repeated a large number of times under co·.trolled circumstances, the concept would be of relatively little use in analyzing business investment decisions. Most business decisions are either unique or are made a small number of times. One does not generally make the same decision in essentially the same circumstances a great many times and observe the outcome of each decision. Even when decisions are repetitive, conditions tend to change. If a manager is considering opening a drugstore, there may be a great deal of evidence that helps form a judgment about whether a drugstore in a particular location could be profitable. But there is no other location and period of time that is exactly the same in all respects as the location and time this person has in mind, and the manager cannot resort to an objective measure of probability to describe the events associated with the profitability of the drugstore.

Some statisticians have taken the position that it is not very useful to describe a business manager's beliefs in terms of probability (for example, to specify a probability that a drugstore opened at that location could be profitable). We believe that a useful measure of probability can be applied to such situations, provided it is kept in mind that the probability measure describes the state of belief of the decision maker, and that this measure is being used to cause the decision to be consistent with these beliefs. Probability measures that reflect the state of belief of a person rather than the objective evidence of a large number of trials are called *subjective probabilities*. The use of this concept will be illustrated by examples in the remainder of this chapter and in several of the following chapters. After reading these pages, and perhaps attempting to apply some of the ideas to decisions, each reader can determine whether subjective probability measures are useful.

Let us consider an election and ask ourselves the meaning of a statement such as the following: Mr. A has a .65 probability of winning this election. The election will not be repeated in exactly the same form, nor has it been held before, although there may be all sorts of evidence relevant to a belief about the outcome. If we say that there is a .65 probability that Mr. A will win the election, this statement implies a comparison of the following sort: Suppose that a jar is filled with 100 beads identical in all respects, except that 65 are blue and 35 are red. We mix the beads thoroughly and randomly draw out one bead. The statement that Mr. A has a .65 probability of winning the election means we believe that we are as likely to draw a blue bead as Mr. A is to win the election. Suppose that we were to be paid $10 if the bead drawn is blue and to pay $10 if it is not blue. If we believe the statement about the election, and are concerned only with how much we win or lose, we should be equally willing to enter a bet in which we would receive $10 if A won the election and lose $10 if A did not win the election. That is, we should be indifferent as to whether the outcome of the bet is determined by the actual outcome of the election or by drawing a bead from a jar of the nature described.

In the case of any unique event (like an election) all observers will not exactly agree on the probability that any particular candidate will win. The adjective *subjective* applied to probabilities suggests that the probabilities described are opinions or statements of belief held by individuals. The purpose of expressing an opinion about the likelihood that an event will occur in terms of a numerical subjective probability is to facilitate the development of decision-making procedures that are explicit and consistent with the decision maker's beliefs.

Expected Values, Variances, and Standard Deviations

In working with probabilities, the concepts of expected value, variance, and standard deviation are essential. These basic ideas will be introduced with an example.

In Table 10-2, column 1 lists six possible events, column 2 shows the net

TABLE 10-2. *Calculating the Expected Net Present Value of an Uncertain Investment*

(1) Possible Events	(2) Net Present Value for Each Event	(3) Probability of Event	(4) Expectation Col. 2 × Col. 3
a	−$100	.3	−$30
b	0	.1	0
c	50	.1	5
d	0	.2	0
e	50	.1	5
f	200	.2	40
		1.0	20

present value of a particular investment if the event in question occurs, and column 3 lists the probability of each event. We wish to calculate the "expected" net present value. To do this we multiply the probability in each row by the corresponding net present value. The products are shown in column 4 of the table. The sum of the amounts in column 4 is the expected net present value for this investment, which is a weighted average. Each possible net present value is weighted by the probability that it will occur.

In Table 10-2, two events, b and d, both result in net present values of zero. Although the two events lead to the same net present value, they are not necessarily indistinguishable. For example, assume that the cash flows for events b and d are as follows:

	Period		
	0	1	2
Event b	-$200	$110	$121
Event d	- 100	55	60.5

Both sets of flows have a zero net present value with a .10 discount rate.

If the only relevant characteristic of an event is the net present value to which it will lead, events that lead to identical net present values can be combined (by adding their probabilities). However, if the cash flows of specific periods are important, the events can be combined only if the cash flows of each period are identical.

A redescription of the events is shown in Table 10-3. The expected net present value is not changed by this recombination of the data; it is still $20.

TABLE 10-3. *Calculating the Expected Net Present Value of an Uncertain Investment*

(1) Possible Values of Net Present Value	(2) Probability of That Value	(3) Expectation (Col. 2 × Col. 3)
-$100	.3	-$30
0	.3	0
50	.2	10
200	.2	40
	1.0	20

Further insight into the meaning of an expected value can be obtained if we examine the differences between the net present values that can occur and their expected value. In Table 10-4, column 1 lists the possible net present values and column 3 the corresponding differences, or deviations, of each from the expected value. That is, each value in column 3 is the corresponding value in column 1 minus the expected value of 20. The values in column 4 are these deviations times the corresponding probabilities. The sum of the items in column 4 is the expected value of the deviations, and the sum of these deviations is zero. In fact, it could be proved that the expected deviation must always be zero.

TABLE 10-4. *Calculating the Expected Deviation Between Net Present Value and Expected Net Present Value*

(1) Possible Values of Net Present Value	(2) Probability of That Value	(3) Net Present Value Minus Expected Net Present Value	(4) Expectation (Col. 2 × Col. 3)
−$100	.3	−$120	−$36
0	.3	− 20	− 6
50	.2	30	6
200	.2	180	36
	1.0		0

This suggests another interpretation of the expected net present value. It is a number in the center of the possible values, in the sense that the sum of positive deviations from the expected net present value equals the sum of the negative deviations, provided both types of deviations are weighted by their respective probabilities.

TABLE 10-5. *Calculating the Variance of the Net Present Value of an Uncertain Investment*

(1) Possible Values of Net Present Value	(2) Probability of That Value	(3) Net Present Value Minus Expected New Present Value	(4) Squared Deviation	(5) (Col. 2 × Col. 4)
−$100	.3	−$120	$14,400	$ 4,320
0	.3	− 20	400	120
50	.2	30	900	180
200	.2	180	32,400	6,480
	1.0			Variance = 11,100

Standard deviation $= \sqrt{\$11,100} = \$105.36$

The variance and its square root, the standard deviation, are commonly used as measures of how concentrated the possible present values are around their expected value. The variance is calculated by squaring each deviation and taking the expected value of the squared deviations. The procedure is illustrated in Table 10-5. The first three columns in that table contain the same entries as in Table 10-4. Column 4 of Table 10-5 shows the square of the deviation, and column 5 the squared deviation multiplied by its probability. The sum of the items in column 5 is the variance. For some purposes it is more convenient to work with the standard deviation, since its units, dollars in this case, are the same as the units of the expected value. In this example, the variance of the net present value is 11,100 (dollars squared) and the standard deviation is the square root of 11,100 or $105.36.

Symbolic Notation for Random Variables and Their Expected Values

In the preceding paragraphs the concepts of expected value variances and standard deviation have been introduced, using the net present value of an uncertain investment as an example. These concepts, however, have a much more general applicability. If we can describe all mutually exclusive and exhaustive outcomes by assigning a numerical value to each uncertain event, the expected value and variance of these numerical quantities can be calculated. Whether the numerical quantities represent the number of units sold, the cash flow of the period, the cost of an investment, or the highest temperature for a day, the concepts of expected value, variance, and standard deviation are applicable.

If the specific value of a quantity, such as the net present value, depends on the outcome of an uncertain event, the quantity is called a *random variable*. The net present value of an investment might be denoted by the symbol X, where the specific numerical value of X depends on the outcome of an uncertain event. X is a random variable.

The symbol E is used to denote the process of finding the expected value of a random variable; the specific random variable whose expected value is being taken is placed in parentheses or brackets following the E. Thus in our example

$$E(X) = 20$$

could be used to summarize in symbolic terms, the results of the calculations shown in Tables 10-2 and 10-3. Although X is a random variable, note that $E(X)$ is just a number whose value depends on all the events that could occur.

Using this notation, the deviation of net present value from its expected value could be denoted as

$$X - E(X).$$

The quantity $X - E(X)$ is itself a random variable and we can calculate its expected value. The equation

$$E[X - E(X)] = 0$$

summarizes the results of the calculation shown in Table 10-4.

In Table 10-5 we illustrated the computation of the variance by squaring each deviation and then calculating the expected value of the squared deviations. In symbols, the variance could be described as

$$E[X - E(X)]^2 = 11,100.$$

In using this notation it is important to distinguish between

$$E(X)^2 = 20^2 = 400$$

and

$$E(X^2) = 11,500.$$

The first equation indicates that an expected value was found and then squared. The second equation indicates that each possible value of the random variable is first squared, and the expected value of these squared quantities is then found. It can be shown that the variance equals $E(X^2) - E(X)^2$.

We shall find it convenient to represent the expected value using $\bar{X}$ rather than $E(X)$. Thus we could write $\bar{X}^2 = 400$ instead of $E(X)^2 = 400$.

We shall have frequent occasion to utilize this notation in the remainder of this book.

Summarizing the Set of Possible Outcomes of an Uncertain Investment

Ordinarily, there are a large number of different possible events that are relevant to any uncertain investment. Corresponding to each distinct event, there is a unique set of cash flows associated with the investment. One way of describing an uncertain investment is to list all the possible events, the probability of each event, and the cash flows that would be associated with each event if the investment were accepted. This method of describing an uncertain investment has the advantage and the disadvantage of being detailed. The disadvantage is that the decision maker may be presented with more information than he or she can readily comprehend or evaluate.

In Table 10-6 an uncertain investment is described by listing all the possible events, the probability of each event, and the sequence of cash flows that would occur if the investment were accepted and that event occurred. In this example there are six possible events, and cash flows can occur in only three different periods, so the complete description is manageable. Nevertheless, the need for methods of summarizing the description of the investment should be apparent.

A number of possible strategies for summarizing the kind of information in Table 10-6 are possible and will be described next. In describing these different strategies we shall attempt to indicate some of the advantages and disadvantages

TABLE 10-6. *Alternative Cash Flows*
for an Uncertain Investment

Event	Probability of Event	Cash Flows in Period		
		0	1	2
a	.3	−$200	$110	$ 0
b	.1	− 200	110	121
c	.1	− 200	165	121
d	.2	− 100	55	60.5
e	.1	− 100	55	121
f	.2	− 100	110	242

of each. We shall not attempt to evaluate the different strategies at this point, however. Except in very special circumstances, any method of summarizing the outcomes of an investment decision will involve some loss of information. We would like to choose methods in which the information lost is relatively unimportant to the decision maker. But this requires a consideration of the objectives of the decision makers and the circumstances in which they operate.

Tree Diagrams

A common and very useful means of describing the information contained in Table 10-6 is a tree diagram. We will illustrate how tree diagrams can be used to show the interrelationships between sequences of events.

Table 10-6 shows the possible outcomes that are predicted for three periods from accepting an investment. Figure 10-1(a) shows a tree diagram of the forecasted outcomes at time zero. The two events possible at time zero are an outlay of $100 or of $200. Each outcome has a probability of one half, which can be determined by summing the probabilities of the corresponding rows in Table 10-6. In the tree diagram each event is depicted by a branch that ends above the point on the time line at which the events will be observable. All mutually exclusive events observable at a given time are arranged vertically above the appropriate point. The cash flow corresponding to the event is shown at the end of each branch and the probability that the event will occur is displayed in the middle of the branch. The sum of the probabilities of all branches originating from a common point must sum to 1.

In Figure 10-1(b) events that would be observable at time 1 have been added to the tree diagram. All of the outcomes that are possible from a given starting point are shown as branches radiating from that starting point. At the end of each branch are the cash flows that would occur, and in the middle of each branch is the probability of that branch, given the starting point at the left-hand end of the branch.

In Figure 10-1(c) the tree diagram is completed by adding the outcomes that

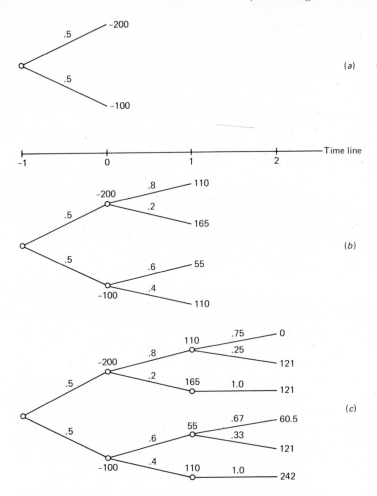

FIGURE 10-1. Tree diagrams of investment outcomes.

could occur at time 2. Tree diagram 10-1(c) and Table 10-6 contain identical information about the investment although the form of the presentation differs.

A limb in the tree diagram consists of a sequence of branches starting at the extreme left of the diagram and ending at the extreme right. Each limb corresponds to a particular sequence of events, one at each point in time. Such a sequence of events is referred to as a *state of nature* or a scenario. In Figure 10-1 each row corresponds to a different state of nature. To determine the probability of a scenario, multiply the probabilities of the corresponding branches.

The circles at the beginning of each split in the branches indicates that a stochastic event (an outcome subject to a probability distribution) follows.

In this simplified example in which there are only three periods and six scenarios it is possible to depict all the possible outcomes. In practice with a real investment this will not be possible. Suppose that cash flows occur at ten different times and that there are ten different outcomes that can occur at each time. Then a total of 10 billion different scenarios are necessary to describe completely an investment. Clearly a method of summarizing the possible outcomes is necessary. The next sections of the chapter briefly introduce some strategies that have been used to summarize the possible outcomes associated with an uncertain investment.

Period-by-Period Summaries

A common approach for summarizing the cash flows associated with an uncertain investment is for an analyst who has studied the investment to write down a single number for each time period to represent the cash flow that it is "estimated" will be associated with the investment. The estimated cash flow may be labeled an expected cash flow; but in practice it is more likely to be based on an educated guess by the analyst than a complete risk analysis. Many investment decisions are based on the expected present value with no further formal analysis of uncertainty. That is, the numbers reported will usually represent a judgment as to the magnitude of the cash flows rather than a detailed calculation based on a listing of alternative scenarios.

Another common approach is for the analyst to specify the assumptions that were used. In effect, the analyst describes a particular scenario, and estimates the cash flows that would result if that scenario occurred.

The estimated cash flows may be accompanied by a written report in which the analyst has an opportunity to describe in qualitative terms the conditions under which the estimated cash flows will or will not be realized and the extent of the discrepancies that might possibly occur. Occasionally the single set of estimated cash flows may be supplemented by some effort to indicate other possible outcomes that could occur, perhaps by providing cash flow estimates labeled optimistic or pessimistic. An example of this type of presentation is contained in lines 2 and 3 of Table 10-7. The first line is the "best" estimate of cash flows. The terms used in Table 10-7 do not have exact statistical interpretations.

TABLE 10-7.   *Period-by-Period Summary of the Cash Flows of an Uncertain Investment*

Line	Item	0	1	2
		Periods		
1	Best estimate of cash flows	−$150	$100	$100
2	Optimistic cash flow for each period	− 100	165	242
3	Pessimistic cash flow for each period	− 200	55	0

The estimated cash flows are ordinarily accompanied by a table that gives one or more summary measures of investment worth based on the estimated cash flows, as illustrated in Table 10-8.

TABLE 10-8. *Summary Measures of the Worth of an Uncertain Investment, Based on Estimated Cash Flows*

Measure	Value
Net present value at 10%	$23.55
Internal rate of return	21.5%
Payback	1.5 years
Return on average investment	33.3%

Sensitivity Analysis

The summary measures included in Table 10-8 may be estimates that are conditional on certain assumptions. For example, the net present value calculation assumes a discount rate of 10 percent. All of the measures calculated assume that the life of the investment will be two years and that the initial outlay will be $150. The purpose of a sensitivity analysis is to determine how varying the assumptions will affect the measures of investment worth. Ordinarily the assumptions are varied one at a time. The results of this type of analysis are illustrated in Table 10-9. In the first panel of the table the estimated cash flows are held constant, but the rate of discount used is varied. In the second panel the discount rate is assumed to be 10 percent, and the initial outlay is assumed to be $150; holding

TABLE 10-9. *Sensitivity Analysis*

Assumption Varied	Assumed Level of Variable	Net Present Value
A. Discount Rate	20%	2.78
	15%	12.57
	10%	23.55
	5%	35.94
B. Estimated Annual Proceeds	120	58.26
	100	23.55
	80	−11.16
C. Initial Outlay	200	−26.45
	150	23.55
	100	73.55

these assumptions constant, the effect of changing the assumed level of the estimated annual proceeds is determined. In the third panel of the table the effect of
changing the level of the initial outlay is illustrated if the discount rate is 10
percent and annual proceeds are $100 per period.

Risk Analysis: Simulation

Risk analysis is intended to give management a better feel for the possible outcomes that can occur, so that they can use their judgment and experience with
regard to whether or not the investment is acceptable. Because risk analysis is
relatively costly, it should be used only on the larger and more important investments. In practice, the number of possible outcomes is so numerous that listing
all of them is not feasible, even with the help of a large-scale computer. Instead
the analysis is based on a sample of the possible outcomes. This approach is
called simulation. If the process involves choosing outcomes randomly, the
process is sometimes called the "Monte Carlo" method.

The steps involved in producing a risk analysis can be briefly summarized as
follows: First, a measure of investment worth is selected; for example, net present
value or IRR. Second, for each set of decisions a computer program is devised
that will sample from all possible outcomes. For each outcome selected the
probability of the outcome and the value of the investment are computed. Third,
the outcomes of the simulation are summarized and presented to management.
The final summary might consist of drawing a histogram, or calculating the mean
and variance (or other measures of central tendency and dispersion) for whatever
measure or measures of investment worth have been selected in the first step. This
approach is called risk analysis.

Assume the outcomes for one set of decisions have been simulated a large
number of times (say 100,000). For 30,000 trials outcome *a* occurred. Table 10-10
assigns a .3 probability to outcome *a*.

Table 10-10 gives the net present value, using a 10 percent discount rate, to
compute the net present value for each state of nature *a* to *f*. This table is
consistent with the hypothetical investment of Table 10-6. Table 10-11 illustrates
some of the ways a set of net present values could be summarized for management using the information of Table 10-10.

Uncertainty and Repeated Trials

If the investment being considered has uncertainty characteristics similar to those
arising from the flipping of a coin, with the amount of possible winnings equal to
the possible loss, then definite statements may be made as to the possibility of
realizing profits. On any one toss there is a fifty-fifty chance of success in obtaining a selected side of the coin; thus there is .5 probability that we shall be
completely correct if we pick heads and an equally large chance that we shall be
completely wrong. If, however, there are going to be 100,000 tosses of the coin,
we can predict that heads will appear approximately half the time, and we have a

TABLE 10-10. Frequency Distribution of Net Present Values of an Uncertain Investment

Possible States of Nature	Probability of State	Net Present Value at 10%
a	.3	−$100
b	.1	0
c	.1	50
d	.2	0
e	.1	50
f	.2	200

TABLE 10-11. Risk Analyses of an Uncertain Investment Based on Net Present Value Using a 10 Percent Discount Rate

Expected net present value	$ 20.00
Modal net present value	0.50
Standard deviation of net present value	105.36
Maximum (with probability .2)	200.00
Minimum (with probability .3)	−100.00
Probability of zero or less	.6
Probability of $200 or more	.2

fair degree of confidence that we have chosen correctly. There is more uncertainty connected with predicting the percentage of heads with one toss than with 100,000 tosses of the coin. The number of heads, however, may differ significantly from the expected number of heads. The presence of different degrees and types of uncertainty may also be true in business.

Let us compare the profit potential of an oil company with the chance of success in tossing coins. If a group of investors organize for the purpose of drilling *one* oil well, they can hire statisticians, geologists, and other experts to compute the odds of finding oil and of finding oil in sufficient quantities to make a profit. In fact it would be possible to make a probability curve of the different possible profits and losses. The actual oil well may result in the maximum possible profits, the maximum possible loss, or something in between. Since only one event will occur, an accurate estimate of the probability of each possible event may help the investors decide whether or not to commit their funds to drilling the well. But knowing the probabilities will not eliminate the uncertainty as to the actual event that will occur, just as knowing the probability of a head will not eliminate the uncertainty as to the outcome on any one flip of a coin.

Now consider a large oil company that intends to drill fifty wells during the coming period. Assume that very small and very large oil companies have the same probability of finding a productive well and that this probability is 0.1. Assume also that for the large oil company, each well is being drilled in a different geological formation, so that knowing the outcome of any particular well would not enable the geologists to revise their estimates of the probabilities associated with other wells. (A statistician would describe this as a situation in which the outcomes of the different wells were statistically independent.)

The small oil company drilling one well has a .90 probability of not finding any oil and facing ruin. The large company has .9948 probability of finding at least some oil and a probability of .0052 of not finding any oil. The probability of not finding any oil is equivalent to the event "no oil" occurring fifty times. The probability of not finding oil on one drilling is .9 and the probability of not finding oil on fifty drillings is $.9^{50}$, or .0052. This example requires that the probability of finding oil on each drilling is statistically independent of the results of the other drillings.

The probability of a success for a single well is the same for both companies, but the probability of complete failure is greatly different. One consequence of repeated identical independent trials is that there will be a drastic reduction in the probability of extreme results, such as financial ruin on the one hand, or dazzling success on the other, and an increase in the probability of intermediate results.

In general, even though the outcome of a particular decision may be highly uncertain, if a large number of identical decisions are going to be made, it may turn out that we can predict the relative frequency of each possible outcome of the whole collection of decisions with little uncertainty. The proportion of wildcat wells that may be classified as being productive over a ten-year period for Mobil Oil and the average number of customers per store for A&P may be examples. If we can make reasonably good predictions of the relative frequency of each possible outcome of the whole collection of decisions, then uncertainty about the outcome of any particular decision decreases in importance. In a sense the individual decisions can be treated as components of some master decision whose outcome can be predicted with considerably more certainty.

An accurate statement of the conditions necessary for us to be able to predict these characteristics is too technical for this book. However, as a practical matter we shall obtain reasonable results if the investments are statistically independent; that is, the probabilities of possible outcome for each single investment are the same regardless of what outcomes occur for the other investments, and if for individual investments the probabilities of extremely good or extremely bad outcomes are not too high.

Though undertaking several investments tends to reduce the probability of extreme results, uncertainty will remain. There is less uncertainty about the amount of oil that will be discovered per dollar of investment if a given amount is invested in fifty separate drilling operations than if the same amount is invested in drilling one well. There is still some probability of finding no oil, however.

Also, the return on our investment will depend not just on how much oil is discovered but on how much the oil is worth. A change in the level of world oil prices will change the value of a given amount of oil reserves by nearly the same percentage, whether the oil has been obtained by drilling one well or fifty. The element of uncertainty is seldom if ever completely eliminated as a factor affecting business investment decisions.

Changing the Uncertainty

It is possible for a firm to follow courses of action that will decrease to some extent the degree of uncertainty connected with its operations. Increasing the information obtained prior to making a decision is one method of decreasing uncertainty. For example, a thorough job of market research may make the outcome of an investment in a new product much less uncertain than if the product were launched without the market research.

Another method of reducing uncertainty in some situations is by increasing the size of operations. A large oil company faces less risk of complete bust when it drills fifty oil wells than does a small group banded together to drill one well. On the other hand, a decentralized company may not make use of this fact if a division manager's performance is measured by using the operating data of the relatively small operation. In this case he or she may be in the same position as the manager of a small firm who fears risky investments because of the threat of insolvency.

Product diversification may also decrease the uncertainty, especially if two products compete with each other. Thus a combined gas and electric company servicing a metropolitan city would have less uncertainty than two separate companies, each specializing in either the electric or gas business. If major industrial users switch from electricity to gas, the fortunes of the specialized companies will be drastically affected, whereas if there were only one company there would be less of a change in the company's profits. Product diversification would also decrease uncertainty if the two products were differently affected by changes in business activity. For example, a combined grocery chain and machine equipment company would have less uncertainty than a specialized machine equipment manufacturer.

The interrelationships of two investments on each other to reduce or eliminate risk can be shown graphically. Assume that the horizontal axis of Figure 10-2 measures different possible states of business activity (for example, the percent of the work force unemployed or the different possible gross national products for the coming year). The vertical axis measures the mean cash flows of the investment for the year in question. The possible expected cash flows for two investments are plotted in Figure 10-2.

Taken individually both investments have risk. If a new investment A plus B is considered (adding the results of A and B), Figure 10-3 shows there is little risk with the joint investment. The objective of diversification is to dampen the swings

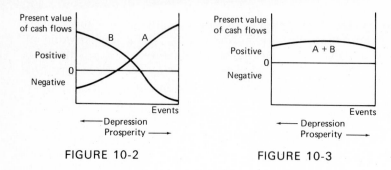

FIGURE 10-2   FIGURE 10-3

of the total investment portfolio, thereby, it is hoped, eliminating the possibility of zero or negative results.

Summary

Up to this chapter we proceeded on the assumption that an investment could be characterized by the cash flows that would occur if the investment were accepted. Uncertainty was bypassed by assuming that only one set of cash flows was possible. In this chapter the complication of uncertainty is introduced. An investment is uncertain if more than one set of cash flows can result from accepting the investment.

The concept of probability was introduced as a means of describing the likelihood of the different possible outcomes. If the outcomes are described in numerical terms, whether as cash flows, net present values, internal rates of return, or some other measure, the expected value, variance, and standard deviation can be used to help summarize the possible outcomes.

Using these concepts, two main strategies for summarizing the possible outcomes of an uncertain investment were presented. One strategy is based on looking at the cash flows on a period-by-period basis. The cash flows may represent a guess at the expected cash flows, or an estimate conditional on a particular scenario occurring. A sensitivity analysis is frequently used to supplement the period-by-period cash flow estimate. To produce a sensitivity analysis, the assumed value of one factor is varied and the resulting variations in estimated cash flows are recorded. A second strategy is to simulate the possible cash flows and summarize the results. This is called a risk analysis using simulation or the " Monte Carlo " method. The term " Monte Carlo " applies since outcomes are selected randomly.

Questions and Problems

10-1. An investment has two equally likely possible outcomes, $0 and $400.
   a. Compute the expected monetary value.

b. Compute the expected present value if outcomes occur at time 1 and there is a 10 percent time-value factor.

10-2. Using problem 10-1 as a guide, write a general formula for the expected present value of a cash flow received at time n. Let p_i be the probability of the X_i cash flow.

10-3. Compute the variance of the monetary values of 10-1 part a.

10-4. Compute the variance of the present values of 10-1 part b.

10-5. Based on research, your logic, or the results of problems 10-2 and 10-3, write a formula for the variance of the present value of an uncertain cash flow to be received in period n.

10-6. Assume that a small firm has enough funds to drill one oil well and the cost of drilling a well is $1 million. A large firm has enough funds to drill fifty wells. (a) What is the maximum loss of the small firm? (b) What is the maximum loss of the large firm? (c) Which of the two firms has more risk?

10-7. Assume that the average oil well returns a present value of benefits of $1.5 million for every well drilled (a well costs $1 million on the average to drill), resulting in a net present value of $500,000 per well. Assume that you are in charge of investing $1 million. You have the choice of investing in one well and owning it completely or investing in a series of ten wells and having .1 ownership. The probability of a successful well is .1. What decision would you make? Explain.

10-8. Assume that you have to predict the number of successful wells for a small firm that will drill one well and for a large firm that will drill 100 wells. Which prediction would you guess will be closer to the actual number of successful wells?

10-9. (*Continuation of 10-8.*) Assume that you are to estimate the proportion of successes for the two firms. Which estimate is likely to be closer?

10-10. An investment firm conducts a contest where the person who recommends twenty stocks that perform the best over a given period wins a prize.
What investment strategy would you recommend to win the contest?

10-11. Assume that you are approached about the possibility of investing in a Broadway play. After conducting some research you find that the expected profits are $800,000 per play and that approximately 25 percent of the plays that open on Broadway show a profit.
Required: Explain whether you would be willing to invest in a play being prepared for Broadway.

10-12. In 1972 a broker argued that although the Dow-Jones industrial average was high, there were still many stocks that were far from their own highs.
Assume that common stocks can be divided into sixteen groups and that each

firm in a group is independent of each other's movements (except for certain major events such as war or depression; which we shall assume have not occurred). Assume that the probability of each group hitting a high during a given period is .6.

What is the probability that all groups will hit a high during that period?

10-13. Answer the following three questions as you would if *you* were faced with the betting situations. Assume that the bets are legal and moral.

Situation 1: A fair coin will be tossed fairly. If a head appears, you will receive $5. If a tail appears, you will receive nothing. How much would you pay to participate in this game?

Situation 2: A coin whose characteristics you do not know will be tossed. You can call heads or tails. If you call correctly, you receive $5. If you call incorrectly, you will receive nothing. How much would you pay to participate in this game?

Situation 3: Two evenly matched basketball teams (say, U.C.L.A. and N.C. State) are playing this Saturday. You will receive $5 if you pick the winner, $0 otherwise. How much would you pay for this gamble?

10-14. If A is an event, which one or more of the following numbers could not represent the probability of A? Explain.

1.5, .6, .3, −.4.

10-15. Two events are said to be mutually exclusive if, at most, one of them can occur. Suppose A and B are two mutually exclusive events. For each of the following pairs of numbers if someone told you that "The first number represents the probability of A and the second the probability of B," could you believe that person? Explain.

  a. .5, .5   **d.** −.2, 1.2
  b. .4, .3   **e.** 0, .9
  c. .4, .7   **f.** 0, 1.0

10-16. Two events are said to be exhaustive if at least one of them must occur. Suppose C and D are exhaustive events. For each of the following pairs of numbers if someone told you that "The first number is the probability of C and the second number is the probability of D," could you believe that person? Explain.

  a. .5, .5   **d.** −.2, 1.2
  b. .4, .3   **e.** 0, .9
  c. .4, .7   **f.** 0, 1.0

10-17. Suppose the events E and F are mutually exclusive and exhaustive. If someone told you, "The first number is the probability of E and the second number is the probability of F," could you believe that person? Explain.

  a. .5, .5   **d.** −.2, 1.2
  b. .4, .3   **e.** 0, .9
  c. .4, .7   **f.** 0, 1.0

10-18. "Our research labs have just developed this great new product. We feel it almost has to be profitable. Unless, of course, business conditions are really bad; or if our sales engineers have drastically misjudged customer acceptance. With the stock market behaving the way it has been, we think the probability of really bad business conditions is only two tenths. Our sales engineers make drastic misjudgments of product-acceptance only three times out of ten."

Based on the above information, what is the maximum probability you would be willing to assign to the event that the new product will be profitable? What is the minimum probability you would assign to that event?

10-19. A new product has been proposed. In terms of after-tax net present values, introducing the new product will require initial outlays of $600,000 for specialized production facilities and promotional expenses. Over the lifetime of the product, the after-tax net present value of the proceeds could be any of the following.

Present Value of Proceeds	Probability
$1,000,000	.8
400,000	.1
200,000	.05
100,000	.05

Find the expected net present value and its standard deviation.

10-20. A proposed exploratory well for oil will cost $1,000,000 to drill. A large oil deposit would be worth $20,000,000, and a small oil deposit would be worth $2,000,000; the probabilities of these events are .04 and .10, respectively. If no oil is found, the drillers can collect $200,000 in dry hole money from the owners of nearby leases. What is the expected profit from drilling and its standard deviation?

10-21. In the table below, X, Y, and Z are three different investments, each with four different outcomes. The decision maker is free to accept or reject each investment.

Find the expected NPV and the standard deviation of NPV for each of the following:

a. X alone d. $X + Y$
b. Y alone e. $X + Z$
c. Z alone

Event	Probability of Event	NPV for Event		
		X	Y	Z
e_1	.25	1000	0	1000
e_2	.25	1000	0	0
e_3	.25	0	1000	1000
e_4	.25	0	1000	0

Discussion Questions

10-A. In 1965 the Boeing Airplane Company was faced with a major decision: to what extent should it independently develop a supersonic air transport?

The estimates of the cost of developing such a plane ranged from $1 to $4 billion. During the period of decision the English and the French were acting jointly in the development of such a plane, and the United States government considered undertaking a similar project.

Required: If you were advising the president of Boeing, what would you suggest? If you were advising the President of the United States, what would you suggest?

10-B. Through their subsidiaries the ABC Company and the XYZ Company are both currently distributing automobiles in the country of Acro. The profits per year of the two subsidiaries are currently as follows:

ABC	$10,000,000
XYZ	20,000,000

The ABC Company is considering establishing a manufacturing plant in Acro. An analyst has projected a profit of $38 million after the plant begins operations (this assumes that the XYZ Company continues to distribute but not manufacture in the country).

An analyst for the XYZ Company has heard of the plans of the ABC Company. If the plant by ABC is built, she projects XYZ's profits to fall to $4 million. If the XYZ Company builds a plant and the ABC Company does not, she anticipates profits of $38 million and a decrease in the profits of ABC to $4 million.

If both companies build plants it is expected that they would both earn $5 million per year.

Required: What course of action would you recommend for the ABC Company?

10-C. It has sometimes been argued that net present value is "more sensitive" than the IRR of an investment to variations in the cash-flow estimates. For example, suppose that an immediate outlay of $3.859 million produces proceeds of $1 million per year for fifteen years and an additional end-of-life salvage value that might be from $0 to $4.4 million. With a discount rate of 9 percent the net present values would range from $4.2 million to $5.4 million (a variation of about 25 percent). The IRR would range from 25 percent, if there is no salvage, to 26 percent if there is the maximum recovery of salvage (a variation of only 4 percent).

If sensitivity is measured by the percentage of variation in the measure of investment worth for a given range of variation in the cash-flow estimates, would you agree that in general net present value is a more sensitive measure of investment worth than IRR?

CHAPTER 11

Attitudes Toward Risk

Ten percent of what I teach is wrong and should be ignored. The problem is that I do not know which ten percent.

—*Cornell University Professor*

Attitudes toward risk are an important factor that must be taken into account when considering investment opportunities that are subject to uncertainty. A risk-adjustment factor is one component of a risk-adjusted present-value calculation. The value of future dollars depends on the states in which they will be realized.

To illustrate, let us suppose a potential investor has assets worth $5,800, all held in the form of a savings account earning 4 percent. The investor considers that the probability is 1 that the assets held in a riskless savings account for one year will be worth $6,032 one year from now. Now suppose there is an investment opportunity that would require an immediate outlay of $5,800 and would return either $1,300 (with probability .2) or $10,000 (with probability .8) one year from now. If this opportunity is accepted, the expected cash flow one year from now will be $8,260 (that is, .2 × $1,300 + .8 × $10,000). The expected rate of return on this one-year investment will be 36.9 percent. This is an attractive expected rate of return by ordinary standards. However, it may be that we cannot use the expected rate of return to decide the acceptability of this investment for this potential investor. It is necessary to establish attitudes toward risk before we can decide whether the investor should accept or reject the investment, if it must be financed with the investor's own funds.

The reader may be tempted to say that a reasonable way to make the decision is to compare the certain cash flow of $6,032 that would be realized if the investor kept the money in a savings account with the average or expected cash flow of $8,260 from accepting the risky investment. The difficulty with this approach is that it buries the fact that at the end of the year the investor will have $1,300 or $10,000 from the risky investment compared to the initial assets of $5,800. The question that our potential investor cannot avoid is whether the dissatisfactions associated with the possibility of having only $1,300 next year, when an investment in the bank would lead to a sure $6,032, outweigh the satisfactions associated with the possibility of having $10,000.

The ability to make a decision under uncertainty depends on such comparisons, and requires knowledge of attitudes toward risk. Different investors might answer such questions differently, in which case we shall say that they have different risk preferences. And clearly the same investor may have different risk preferences at different stages of life or under different circumstances. Other investments already undertaken, the state of health, the number of persons dependent on the outcome, and the chances of being unemployed next year are clearly factors that one must take into account in making the decision.

A description of an investor's risk preferences is called a *utility function*. Just as subjective probabilities can be used to describe a person's attitude about the likelihood that some outcome will occur, so a utility function may describe risk preferences.

A utility function assigns a number to each possible outcome of an uncertain event. The number assigned by a utility function can be interpreted as an index of the relative satisfaction the individual would derive if that outcome actually occurred. Table 11-1 illustrates the use of a utility function for the potential investor in the preceding example. For purposes of this simplified example we assume that there are only two possible states, a and b. In state b the risky investment pays off $10,000 and in state a it pays off only $1,300. We assume that the states are identical in all other respects to the investor and that the only two alternatives are to keep the money in the bank or to accept the risky investment and finance it by taking all the money out of the bank.

In Table 11-1 there are two panels. One analyzes the expected utility of the bank account. The other analyzes the expected utility of the risky investment. Column (1) in the table lists the different possible states. Column (2) lists the possible outcomes measured in terms of net present values. Column (3) lists the utility the investor assigns to each possible outcome. Since the states are identical except for the outcome of the investment, the utility assigned to the outcome of the bank account is the same for each state. With the risky investment the utility

TABLE 11-1. *Computation of Expected Utility*

(1) State	(2) Outcome: Values of Wealth Given State	(3) Utility of Outcome	(4) Probability of State	(5) Utility × Probability
	Bank Account Retained			
a	$6,032	1,906	.2	381
b	6,032	1,906	.8	1,525
		Expected utility of bank account		1,906
	Investment			
a	$ 1,300	500	.2	100
b	10,000	2,500	.8	2,000
		Expected utility of investment		2,100

assigned to a state is greater if the investment has a favorable outcome than if it has an unfavorable outcome.

If the utility function accurately describes the investor's risk preferences, the choice that provides the highest expected utility is optimum. The calculation for this risky investment is presented in Table 11-1. In column 4 we list the probability of each outcome if the investor accepts either the bank account or the risky investment. In column 5 we list the product of the probability of each outcome multiplied by its utility. The expected utilities or the sums of these products for the two alternatives are also given in column 5. For the example given in this table the investor would choose the risky investment in preference to the certain outcome, because the former has a higher expected utility than the latter.

Suppose that we multiplied each of the utility numbers in column 3 by some positive number. Would this change the decision? The answer is that it would not. If we multiply each utility number in column 3 by .5, the expected utility for the risky investment would become 1,050 and the expected utility for the riskless investment would become 953. But the relative magnitudes of the two alternatives, and therefore the decision, would not change. Similarly, if we add or subtract the same number to or from every utility value in column 3 we will not change the decision. This means that two apparently different utility functions may actually describe the same risk preferences, just as the Fahrenheit and centigrade scales both measure the same quantity, temperature. By a combination of adding and multiplying the appropriate constants, one can convert temperature readings from one of these scales to the other. In exactly the same way, if one utility function can be derived from another by adding and multiplying by appropriate constants, the two utility functions actually measure the same risk preferences.

The computations carried out in Table 11-1 are illustrated graphically in Figure 11-1. In that figure the curve through the points SXT represents the utility function. Point S represents the utility resulting from a wealth of $1,300, point T utility associated with a wealth of $10,000, and point X the utility associated with a wealth of $6,032.

The point labeled V on the straight line connecting points S and T represents the expected utility associated with accepting the risky investment. The coordinate of V on the terminal value axis is the expected terminal value of the investment, which is $(.2 \times 1,300 + .8 \times 10,000) = 8,260$. The coordinate of the V on the utility axis is the expected utility of the investment which is $(.2 \times 500 + .8 \times 2,500) = 2,100$. Since the utility of V exceeds the utility coordinate of X, the risky investment corresponding to V is preferred to the safe investment corresponding to X, assuming these are the only two alternatives available.

Equity Markets and Subjective Risk Preferences

It is typical of many productive investments that they are "lumpy" rather than marginal to the investors to whom they are available. If the only alternatives

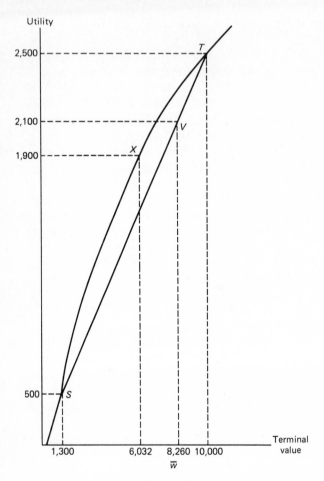

FIGURE 11-1

available to the investor were to reject the investment or to accept it and finance it without borrowing (perhaps by withdrawing funds from other liquid assets such as bank accounts), then the decision would depend on the subjective attitudes toward risk of the investor. In the previous example, the investor was willing to accept the risky investment. But another investor starting with the same wealth and faced with the same risky investment might decide to reject the investment because it was too risky. Thus there can be no single objective criterion for deciding which investments to accept and which to reject. The decision will depend on the investor's risk preferences, wealth, and on the risky investments already owned.

The decision-making circumstances are drastically changed if there exist securities markets to which the investor has access.

Complete Security Markets

In the above example the investor found the risky investment to be acceptable. But if there are complete security markets, even a very risk-adverse investor might find such an investment acceptable.

Assume that securities can be issued by the investor that pay off only if event b occurs (with event b the investor has large wealth and wants to strengthen the outcome associated with event a). Now if event a occurs the $1,300 payoff still occurs, but it is in this case supplemented by the proceeds of the securities issued by the investor, which only require a payoff if event b occurs.

Thus with complete security markets the investor can shift some of the desirable payoffs of event b to the weaker payoffs of event a. This can move the investment from being too risky to being an investment that has acceptable risk characteristics.

The investor can adjust the proportion of state a and state b dollars that will be received by engaging in appropriate security market transactions. When an investor can adjust the proportions of dollars to be received in every state by appropriate security market transactions, we say that security markets are complete. If security markets are complete, every investor's equilibrium subjective risk-adjusted present-value factor for every state will equal the market price of a dollar in that state. Therefore market prices can be used as objective criteria for deciding whether a particular risky investment is desirable. With complete markets, if the market based net risk-adjusted present value of an investment is positive, any investor should be willing to accept the investment. Personal differences in attitudes toward risk may affect how much of the investment the investor retains, and how much is financed by buying or selling various securities to reestablish the equality between a subjective appraisal of the value of a dollar in each state and the market price of those dollars.

When securities markets are not complete in the sense described above it is not necessarily true that investors will increase their expected utility by accepting investments whose market-based risk-adjusted net present value is positive. An added complexity is that investment decisions are made by corporations on behalf of groups of stockholders; it may happen that even if each investment accepted tends to increase the market value of the corporation's common stock, some of the investments may be considered to be undesirable by some stockholders. A corporation can minimize (but probably not completely eliminate) these conflicts of objectives among its stockholders by having a clearly defined investment and financial policy and by attracting stockholders who tend to agree with these policies.

Utility Functions and Business Decision Making

Under conditions of uncertainty, subjective attitudes toward risk bearing should play an important role in investment policy. However, the issue of whose risk attitudes are relevant for a corporation remains. Any ongoing business affects the interests of a variety of groups, among them the owners, managers, workers, customers, and suppliers. These groups may consist of separate individuals or there may be considerable overlap. In a small family store or farm, the owners, managers, and workers may all be members of the same family. In such a case it is clearly the family's attitude toward risk that will be considered. In a large corporation, there is typically less overlap.

The traditional point of view is that where the owners are a distinct group a business is run primarily in the interests of the owners, except insofar as their freedom to make decisions in their own interest has been limited by laws, customs, or contractual arrangements with other interested parties.

In many business situations it is not sufficient to refer simply to the owners. For example, we might distinguish three subgroups. First, there may be the group of owners who actually control the business. These controlling owners may own a majority of the shares, or they may have a minority interest but a larger block than any other organized group of shareholders. In addition to those who have a controlling interest, there may be a much larger group of persons who have an ownership interest in the business but who do not, or cannot, control it. This latter group has an interest in the financial results insofar as they affect stockholders. Finally, the concept of owners might usefully be expanded, for some purposes, to include not only the present stockholders but also potential stockholders—in effect, the entire financial community. For example, while some investment or financial policies that a firm adopts might reduce the appeal of the stock to some of its present owners, at the same time they might increase the stock market value by making it more attractive to persons who are not currently owners.

If attitudes toward risk are to be considered in deciding what investments should be accepted, decision makers need a clear idea of whose attitudes toward risk are relevant and to what extent they should be considered. Suppose that the group whose attitudes toward risk are relevant in selecting investments has been defined. There still remain important questions of how to implement the investment decision.

One difficulty with the current procedures of many firms for making decisions under uncertainty is that where there are operating divisions it is likely that different criteria for evaluating (or incorporating) risk are being used by different management groups. It may be that operating management is rejecting, as being too risky, investments that from the corporate standpoint would be very reasonable. One can imagine a credit officer of a bank rejecting a loan application because of the risk. From the point of view of the firm as a whole the loan may be a good investment, however. A second loan officer might be accepting loans that had too much risk from the point of view of the corporation. The element of personal judgment as to the likelihood of various events cannot be eliminated, but interpretation of the monetary consequences can at least be applied in a somewhat more consistent manner than is currently done.

If the group whose risk attitudes the decision makers wish to take into account is a relatively small, cohesive group with whom the decision makers can communicate directly (for example, if it were decided that investments should be selected in terms of the risk preferences of a small group of controlling stockholders or of an owner–manager or of the professional managers), the persons whose risk attitudes are relevant can be involved directly in the decision-making process. An attempt can be made to communicate the nature of the available risk alternatives and to obtain the reactions of the investors.

A second set of circumstances would obtain if it were decided that the relevant risk preferences were those of the present stockholders, but the stockholders were a large and diverse group with whom direct communication were not easily possible. Given present techniques we know of no one who has effectively implemented such an attempt.

A third possibility is that the relevant risk preferences would include those of all present or potential future owners. This is in some respects less difficult to implement than the second situation described, if we assume that all the stockholders have had ample opportunity to purchase the stock of other corporations (thus diversifying their portfolios, if they so wish).

If the controlling group whose risk preferences are to be taken into account is also in a position to provide the financing necessary to implement their preferences, the risk preferences of the financial community as a whole decrease in importance. The primary considerations are what the controlling group's preferences are with respect to investment and financial policy (the market opportunities will influence these preferences). The situation is not much different when a relatively small amount of debt financing is required, because it will usually be possible to arrange small amounts of debt financing without severe restrictions on the controlling group's freedom of action.

Even when a firm is effectively controlled by some group that wishes to establish policies that reflect its own risk preferences, the response of the financial community will be relevant whenever a significant proportion of outside financing will be required, either immediately or in the foreseeable future.

If there is no cohesive group of stockholders seeking to exercise a controlling interest, and if the managers of the firm attempt to operate it in the best interests of the stockholders, the tastes and preferences of the financial community as a whole will be controlling. Among any large group of stockholders there will be individuals whose interests and preferences conflict with those of other stockholders. Management cannot hope to satisfy every individual stockholder. Those who are dissatisfied will tend to exercise their privilege of selling their stockholdings. Management can best discharge its interests to a diverse group of stockholders by undertaking policies that tend to lead to the highest sustainable market value for the company's common stock.

Utility Analysis and Wealth Maximizing

The term *wealth maximizing* is an approximate description of a decision process that accepts investments that have a positive expected present value. The classic example used to discredit the use of the expected monetary value decision rule is the St. Petersburg paradox. A fair coin is tossed until the first head, the winnings being equal to 2^n, where n is the number of tosses required. The expected value of this gamble is infinite, but most of us would pay very little, say $8, for the right to gamble.

Whether you consider the use of expected utility to be inconsistent with the objective of wealth maximizing depends on your interpretation of wealth maximization under conditions of uncertainty. Say you could buy a lottery as described (the St. Petersburg paradox) for $100. The expected monetary value is positive, but the probability of winning more than the $100 is very low and the probability of losing is high. Are we serving the wealth-maximizing objective by rejecting this type of gamble?

A difficulty with a wealth-maximizing objective is that it is not clearly defined under conditions of uncertainty, unless it is defined in terms of expected value. But we know that expected value may be a poor guide to action.

In some situations the use of expected monetary value may be reasonable. Assume that a person of known repute approached you and proposed an investment that costs $1 and offers a payoff of $6 with a .5 probability and a payoff of $0 with .5 probability (the net expected monetary value of the investment is $2). Most of us would accept the investment. However, if the size of your investment were increased a millionfold, most of us would reject the investment. In the first situation the amounts are small, and we can easily absorb the possible loss. In the second case the amounts are large, and the possible loss could result in a mortgaging of our future for this and the next lifetime. With relatively small investments, statistically independent of other assets, and with a small variance of outcomes, the use of expected monetary value is a reasonable procedure. Some investments may turn out to be bad, but if the investments have positive net present values, and if they are small investments without too large a probability of loss, the use of expected monetary values may be a reasonable guide to action.

Now let us consider a large investment. This may be a machine-tool company of $200 million asset size that considers going into the automobile industry. In such a situation the use of expected monetary value may be misleading. If the investment does not turn out to be desirable, the entire future of the firm may be jeopardized. The distribution of possible events may be too spread out for the firm, despite a favorable expected value.

Essentially the same type of risk situation may develop with small investments if the investments are not statistically independent of each other. Consider a whole series of investments where each investment is $1, and we can undertake 1 million of these investments. The payoffs are $4 and $0 with .5 probability. If the investments are statistically independent, this is a very fine investment opportunity. If the investments are statistically dependent and we either win or lose on all one million investments, the risk of a large loss is much greater, and we might steer clear of this investment.

No matter how large the firm, there is some investment opportunity that it would not want to consider on a straight expected monetary value basis. The analysis of risk (that is, incorporating the consequences of the outcomes) could be performed by a utility analysis or by some other means, but it must be recognized that we cannot inspect one number (say, the yield of the investment or the expected monetary value) to make an investment decision. It is necessary to consider the range of outcomes and the probabilities of these outcomes. One method of systematically accomplishing this is a utility analysis.

For giant corporations it is sometimes difficult to imagine an investment that we could not judge on a straight expected monetary value basis. But even for such corporations there are investments (or classes of investments) of such magnitude that they give rise to the likelihood of events that could be disastrous to the firm. Incorporating this information into the analysis, rather than just using the maximization of wealth (or the expected monetary value criterion), can be done by the use of a utility analysis. Assume that an investment has the characteristic of resulting in a doubling of income or reducing income to approximately zero. Should this type of investment decision be made on an expected-value basis?

The expected-value decision criterion may at times be consistent with the wealth-maximization objective, but several things should be noted. The consistency holds true only in the long run and assuming we can repeat the trial many times. We are dealing with averages, and there is very little chance that the average event will actually occur on any trial (there may be no chance). In some cases, following the expected monetary value criterion will lead to bankruptcy (that is, ruin) and end of the "game." The possibility of this unhappy event is always present, and it is reasonable that this should affect our decision process. The objective "maximize the wealth of the owners" ignores the fact that this is a maximization of an average amount. This is not a sufficient description of the objectives of the investor. The maximization goal is reasonable, but the things being maximized should not be expected monetary values, but rather expected utility.

Investor diversification helps reduce the importance of the type of risk analysis described here; however, there are three important qualifications:

1. Not all investors in the corporation may have diversified portfolios; a risky decision may have a significant impact on the well-being of some of the stockholders. Management cannot assume that all stockholders possess well-diversified portfolios.
2. Even with the stock widely held, the corporation may encounter investments that the individual investor would reject if given the opportunity to invest in a proportion of the investment equal to the proportion of his or her investment in the firm. This can occur when the variance of the outcomes is large and there is a large probability of undesirable outcomes.
3. The management, workers, controlling stockholders, and communities where the major units of the firm are located all have an interest in the well-being of the corporation, and they may not be able to diversify to the same extent as the average stockholder.

These important qualifications all point in the direction of utility analysis or some other formal incorporation of risk attitudes.

An Illustration

Implementing investment decisions with uncertain outcomes can be very complicated. We shall illustrate a procedure, using an artificial situation, to make clear
the basic steps. Assume that the time value of money is .05 and that we have been
given the utility function of an individual. The following measures of utility of
wealth apply:

Present Value of Wealth	Utility of Wealth
$1,500	−1,200
1,900	−60
2,000	0
2,500	500
3,500	1,000
4,500	1,200

The investment is a two-period investment, with an immediate $500 outlay. At
the end of the first period there is .5 probability of $0 and .5 probability of $1,050.
At the end of the second period there is .8 probability of $0 and .2 probability of
$2,205. The tree diagram (Figure 11-2) shows the possible outcomes. The
expected net present value is $400.

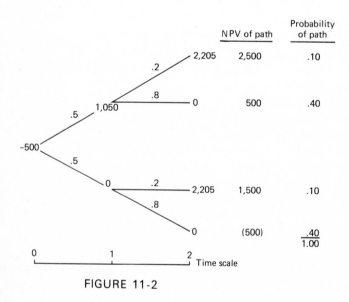

FIGURE 11-2

Net Present Value of Outcome		Probability		Expectation of Net Present Value
$2,500	×	.10	=	$250
500	×	.40	=	200
1,500	×	.10	=	150
−500	×	.40	=	−200
		Expected net present value		$400

Assume the investor currently has wealth of $2,000. We shall add each of the outcomes of the investment to $2,000 to determine the dollar outcomes. We will then convert the dollar outcomes to their utility counterparts to compute the expected utility of wealth if the investment is undertaken. If the investment is rejected the value of the investor's wealth will be $2,000 with a probability of 1.0, and a utility of zero. Thus the expected utility of doing nothing is zero.

Outcome in NPV's	Wealth in NPV's	Utility of Wealth	Probability	Expectation of Utility
$2,500	$4,500	1,200	.10	120
500	2,500	500	.40	200
1,500	3,500	1,000	.10	100
−500	1,500	−1,200	.40	−480
			Expected utility	− 60

The expected utility of wealth with the investment is less than the utility of $0 without the investment, and we would choose the action "do nothing" with zero utility compared to the choice "invest." The negative utility of a loss of $500 outweighs the expected consequences of the other events.

The utility function provides a means of calculating the amount of dollar risk premium a decision maker would attach to a particular investment. In the preceding example undertaking the investment has an expected utility of −60. If a certain loss of $100 also has a utility of −60, a dollar loss of $100 is the certainty equivalent of the investment. The expected net present value of the investment is $400. The risk premium for any investment is the expected monetary value of the investment less the certainty equivalent of the investment. In this case, the risk premium is $500 [400 − (−100)]. In a situation where there are a very large number of outcomes, we would shift to the use of continuous probability distributions.

Using this approach to decision making, we go beyond the application of intuition as a means of weeding the list of eligible investments. Attitudes toward risk are systematically incorporated into the analysis, and the procedure leads to a decision that is consistent with the feelings of the decision maker about the likelihood of the possible outcomes and the effect of the outcomes on the investor's financial position. The analysis as presented does leave out the value of immediate information about the outcomes compared with having to wait two periods for the final outcome. In the example which was illustrated, the investment would be rejected even if we assumed that we knew the results immediately. Thus it does not make a difference that we did not incorporate the information factor. If the investment had been marginally acceptable based on the expected utility computation, we would have had to incorporate a qualitative factor to take into account that we would have to wait two time periods before the final results were known.

In the preceding example we analyzed a situation in which there were four possible outcomes. Now assume that there are a large number of possible outcomes (possibly an infinite number of outcomes). This change would only modify the mechanics.

Derivation of a Utility Function

We shall illustrate one approach to deriving the utility function of an individual. The first step is to assign two arbitrary values of utility to two arbitrary amounts of money wealth. For example, we shall arbitrarily choose $0 and $1 million and assign utilities of 0 and 1,000 to these two money amounts. The choice of these two points determines the scale of the utility function as well as its location.

The second step is to set up a sample lottery consisting of one lottery offering $X for certain and a second lottery offering the two amounts arbitrarily picked, each with .5 probability of occurring.

Lottery A	Lottery B
$X for certain	$0 with .5 probability
	$1,000,000 with .5 probability

What amount X for certain causes you to be indifferent between lotteries A and B? If we set X equal to $50, most of us would prefer lottery B. If we set X at $5 million, all of us would prefer lottery A. After some introspection we might establish an amount for X equal to $10,000. We then have

$$U(A) = U(B)$$

$$U(\$10,000) = .5U(\$0) + .5U(\$1,000,000)$$

$$U(\$10,000) = .5 \times 0 + .5 \times 1,000 = 500.$$

Thus the utility of $10,000 is determined to be 500, and we have three points of the utility function. We can continue the process by substituting the $10,000 for the $1 million of lottery B. After obtaining several points, we may decide to find the utility of larger amounts by setting up the following two lotteries:

Lottery C	Lottery D
$1,000,000 for certain	$0 with .5 probability
	$X with .5 probability

Assume that for you to be indifferent to the two lotteries X in lottery D must be equal to $800 million.

$$U(\$1,000,000) = .5U(\$0) + .5U(\$800,000,000)$$

$$1,000 = .5 \times 0 + .5U(\$800,000,000)$$

$$U(\$800,000,000) = 2,000$$

The utility measure of $800 million is 2,000. We can continue the process to obtain the utility measures of still larger amounts.

We must still determine utility measures for negative amounts of wealth. Lotteries of type E and F accomplish this.

Lottery E	Lottery F
$0 for certain	$10,000 with .5 probability
	$X with .5 probability

If X were equal to or greater than $0, we prefer lottery F; therefore, for us to be indifferent to E and F, X must be negative. Say X is equal to $-\$200$. We then have

$$U(\$0) = .5U(\$10,000) + .5U(-\$200)$$

$$0 = .5 \times 500 + .5U(-\$200)$$

$$U(-\$200) = -500.$$

We can continue this process and obtain the utility equivalents of other dollar outcomes.

Appendix 1 : Simulation of Expected Utility

When we have obtained the mean and variance of the probability distribution of the present values and are able to specify the nature of the distribution (for example, when we assume it is normal), we can follow a simulation process to determine the expected utility if we know the utility function of the individual. Figure 11-3 shows the wealth distribution and the utility function.

We want to determine the utility of wealth with mean $\bar{Y}$ and standard deviation σ_Y.

The procedure we shall follow is to go to a table of random normal deviates (which may also be generated on a computer) and enter the table randomly. By taking a series of observations (that is, numbers from the table), we can determine the average utility of the wealth distribution.

Procedure

1. Take a number, say k, from a table of standard normal deviates.
2. Convert k to wealth: $Y = \bar{Y} + k\sigma_Y$.

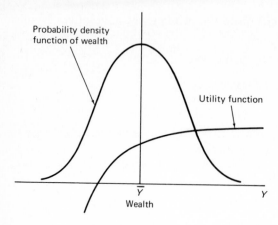

FIGURE 11-3

3. Go to Figure 11-3 and read the utility for Y wealth. This is one observation of utility.

4. Take n observations; obtain n utilities; divide the total of the n observations by n to obtain the mean utility of the wealth distribution.

Example

Assume that the mean wealth, $\bar{Y}$, equals $10,000 and the standard deviation of wealth, σ_Y, is $8,000.

We take a random normal deviate and find it to be $+1.2$. The wealth observation is

$$Y = \bar{Y} + k\sigma_Y$$

$$= \$10,000 + 1.2(\$8,000) = \$19,600 = \text{first observation of wealth.}$$

The next step is to measure the utility of $19,600 wealth. We see in Figure 11-4 that the utility measure is 7. This is our first observation of utility. We would repeat this process

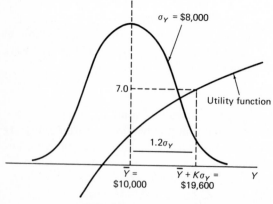

FIGURE 11-4

many times to obtain a series of observations that would be summed and divided by the number of observations to obtain the expected utility of the wealth distribution. Thus we can simulate the expected utility value of the wealth distribution.

Questions and Problems

11-1. The following utility function of Mr. Jay will be used for problems 11-1 and 11-2:

Dollars of Wealth	Utility Measure
−3,000	−3,000
−1,000	−1,000
−600	−500
−500	−350
0	0
100	100
500	150
1,000	200
2,000	350
4,000	500
10,000	1,000

Assume that there is a gamble which has .5 probability of $10,000 and .5 probability of $0.

Required: (a) What is the expected utility of the gamble? (b) What is the amount that Mr. Jay would be willing to accept for certain to cause him to be indifferent to the choice between the gamble and the certain amount? (c) What is the expected monetary value of the gamble? (d) What is the risk premium of the gamble?

11-2. Assume that there is a gamble which has a .5 probability of $4,000 and .5 probability of $1,000.

Required: (a) What is the expected utility of the gamble? (b) What is the amount that Mr. Jay would be willing to accept for certain to cause him to be indifferent to the choice between the gamble and the certain amount? (c) What is the expected monetary value of the gamble? What is the risk premium?

11-3. The following problem attempts to illustrate the simulation of the mean utility of a cash flow that has a normal probability density function.

The outcomes of a period are normally distributed with a mean of $100,000 and a standard deviation of $20,000. Four random deviations from the mean were obtained (in an actual simulation the number of observations would be much larger).

d
.40
1.35
− .83
2.50

The following values were obtained from the utility function:

Dollars	Utility Measures
0	0
83,400	10,000
108,000	15,000
110,000	16,000
127,000	19,000
150,000	20,000

Required: (a) Compute the dollar amounts of each of the four outcomes. (b) Using the utility function, determine the utility for each outcome. (c) Estimate the expected utility of the observations. (d) Estimate the certainty equivalent of the cash flow.

11-4. Assume the following utility function for the newly formed ABC Corporation.

Dollars	Utility Measure
−20,000	−400
−10,000	−100
0	0
7,200	80
8,600	90
10,000	100
18,600	140
20,000	150
30,000	190
35,800	200
40,000	220
60,000	240

a. Should the corporation accept an investment that requires an outlay of $10,000 and that will either involve a complete loss or generate cash flows of $30,000 within one week (each possibility has a .5 probability)?
b. What would be your recommendation if the probabilities were .65 of failure and .35 of success?

11-5. Assume the same utility function as in problem 11-4.

a. Should the ABC Corporation undertake the following investment? Assume that a .05 discount rate is appropriate.

Period	Cash Flow
0	−10,000
1	0 with .5 probability
	30,000 with .5 probability

b. What would be your recommendation if the probabilities were .6 of failure and .4 of success?

11-6. Assume the same utility function as in problem 11-4. The ABC Corporation has been offered an investment that costs $20,000. The investment has .5 probability of not generating any cash the first day and .5 probability of generating $30,000. It also can generate $0 or $30,000 with the same probabilities the second day. The amount received on the second day is statistically independent of the amount received on the first day. Should the firm accept the investment?

11-7. Assume the same situation as in problem 11-6, except that the transactions take place in successive years instead of days. The discount rate is .05. Should the firm accept the investment?

11-8. Assume the same investment as in problem 11-6, except that the cash flows of the second day will be the same as for the first day. Should the firm accept the investment?

11-9. Determine whether the following investment is acceptable. Explain briefly your computations and assumptions.

Period	Cash Flows
0	($1,000)
1	.5 probability of $2,100 cash flow
	.3 probability of $1.050
	.2 probability of $0

The firm has a cost of money of .05. The utility function of the corporation has the following values (interpolate if you need other values).

Money	Utility
−1,000	−300
0	0
500	50
1,000	70
1,050	75
1,300	85
1,500	90
2,000	100
2,100	101
3,000	125

11-10. The ABC Company can invest $1 million. The two possible payoffs occurring immediately are as follows:

Probability	Payoff
.5	$ 0
.5	2,600,000

   a. If you were in charge of making this decision would you accept? Explain.
   b. Assume that you can make two investments similar to that described above and own .5 of each investment. Would you accept this alternative? Do you prefer it to the possibility of investing the entire $1 million in one investment?

11-11. The IBC Company has the choice between two mutually exclusive investments. One requires an outlay of $10 million and has a net present value of $10,000. The second has an outlay of $500,000 and a net present value of $6,000. Both investments have a life of one year. The time value of money is .05.

   Assume certainty; which investment should the firm undertake? With uncertainty, does your answer change?

11-12. The Tin Can Company must choose between two plants. One is large and has sufficient capacity for working efficiently at the higher ranges of possible sales estimates. The other plant is smaller and is more efficient at lower ranges of sales, but is less efficient if sales are high. The net present values of the two plants are shown with different assumed levels of budgeted sales. The probability of reaching that level of sales is also shown.

Level of Expected Sales (as % of budgeted sales)	Probability	Present Value Large Plant	Present Value Small Plant
150	.10	$50,000,000	$40,000,000
100	.70	35,000,000	30,000,000
50	.20	(10,000,000)	10,000,000

Required: Which of the two plants should the company build based on the information presented?

Discussion Questions

11-A. A person may estimate the expected cash flows of year 5 to be $10,000. If this figure is used in the investment analysis, what assumption or assumptions are being made?

11-B. What is the maximum amount you would pay for the lottery of .5 probability of $1,000 and a .5 probability of $0? What does this imply about your utility function?

11-C. For you to be indifferent between the following two lotteries, what value of X must be inserted?

Lottery A	Lottery B
.5 probability of $1,000	1.0 probability of X
.5 probability of $0	

What does this imply about your utility function? Compare your value of X to the answer you gave to problem 11-B.

11-D. Would the utility function of a firm change after making an investment?

11-E. When is it reasonable to base decisions on the use of money (in the computations) and to ignore utility considerations?

11-F. In making a utility function for a corporation, how would you handle the situation where different corporate executives and owners have different utility functions?

11-G. If we did not try to incorporate utility considerations into the investment analysis, would the investment decisions of the firm still be affected by utility functions of the individual corporate executives, assuming some degree of decentralization?

11-H. If the firm is small enough for the president to make all the decisions, is it necessary to make a formal analysis using utility functions? Explain.

11-I. If we do not know the exact probabilities of the events that may occur, is it still reasonable to use the utility analysis? Is it reasonable to compute the expected monetary value?

11-J. Assume that a firm has two alternatives: (a) Plant A promises to earn a net present value of $10 million with certainty (assume this is a cost-plus government contract). Instead of plant A we could build a larger plant. (b) Plant B may earn a net present value of $50 million (this has a .5 probability) or it may have a negative net present value of $20 million (this event also has a .5 probability).

Which of the two plants do *you* prefer? Assume your firm's yearly earnings have averaged $5 million a year.

CHAPTER **12**

The Rate of Discount

The interest rate is not only an expression of the force of
nature: it also depends on the wisdom of men.

—*Pierre Massé,* Optimal Investment Decisions: Rules for
Action and Criteria for Choice *(Englewood Cliffs, N.J.:
Prentice-Hall, 1962, p. 15.*

In this chapter several alternative rates of discount that are used to evaluate
investments are discussed. An approach will be offered that separates the time-
value and risk calculations, and that can be used to evaluate risky investments
where time is a factor.

A satisfactory definition of a discount rate would be helpful in guiding the
internal investment policy of corporate management. The choice of investments
frequently represents a strategic decision for the management of a firm, since in
large part the choices made now will influence the future course of the firm's
development. It is not surprising to find that implicit in any definition of a
discount rate to guide investment policy is a judgment on the goals toward which
the firm is or should be striving. The goals determine the appropriate definition
of capital cost. Certainly we cannot assume without proof that seemingly different goals will lead to identical rates of discount.

The corporate goal that has been conventionally adopted in discussions of this
kind is that the corporation seeks to maximize the economic well-being of present
stockholders. There are at least two elements in maximizing the economic well-
being of stockholders. One is the expected cash proceeds that the stockholder
anticipates will result from stock ownership. These proceeds include dividends
and capital gains. In measuring the value of these receipts, adjustment must be
made for the timing of their realization. A second element that must be considered is the uncertainty associated with the expected cash flows.

It is recognized that corporate managements frequently have other goals that
are sometimes in conflict with the goal just described. Management may desire to
see the corporate organization expand; to ensure that its own tenure and ability
to choose its successors is not threatened; to extend or at least maintain the
realm in which it is free to make decisions for the organization without reference
to outside groups (be they government officials, minority stockholders, bankers,

life insurance companies, or labor union officials); to support what it considers to be desirable nonprofit institutions; to undertake activities in the name of the corporation for patriotic motives; or to achieve a high level of material benefits for itself. In attempting to work out a definition of a discount rate based on the goal of maximizing the economic interests of present stockholders, we do not mean to deny the existence or the importance of other goals. If other goals are in competition with the goal of maximizing present stockholders' economic interests, the development of an investment policy based on stockholders' interests may help us understand the extent to which the various goals are in conflict.

We will briefly describe the basic elements of computing the costs of different types of capital and the effect of changing capital structure on the weighted average cost of capital. We will then evaluate the use of the weighted average cost of capital as a discount rate for measuring the desirability of corporate investments.

The Sources of Cash

Funds to finance an investment proposal may be obtained by a firm in a variety of ways: by borrowing from banks; by allowing short-term liabilities to expand, by selling marketable securities such as government bonds, by selling other assets or parts of its business, by issuing additional securities (either bonds, preferred stock, or common stock), or by committing funds generated by operations. These are only some of the more important sources. For certain types of these sources of cash, such as bank loans, there is a generally accepted definition of the cost of funds obtained. For other sources, such as funds generated by operations, there is less agreement. Several definitions of the cost of capital from operations have been proposed, including the notion that funds from this source are free. We reject this notion.

The Cost of Retained Earnings

The costs associated with retaining some part of the current earnings are not always obvious. Occasionally corporate officials seem to take the position that these funds are free.[1] If the funds generated from retained earnings were free, any use of the funds within the corporation that benefited common stockholders would be justified. On the other hand, if there were a cost associated with the use of these funds within the corporation, it would not be sufficient to say that stockholders would benefit. The question must be asked, "Will the benefits be

---

[1] After interviewing the top officials of twenty companies in several different industries, G. Donaldson wrote, "The net conclusion is that the common practice of these twenty companies with respect to quantitative guides to investment decisions suggested a cost-free concept of retained earnings for the so-called mandatory investments in maintaining traditional product lines and a rough internal opportunity cost standard for 'voluntary' investment opportunities." [Gordon Donaldson, *Corporate Debt Capacity* (Boston: Graduate School of Business Administration, Harvard University, 1961), p. 62.]

great enough to cover the opportunity cost of the funds?" One suspects that this question is frequently not asked and that the corporate officials too often treat retained earnings as if they were a source of free funds.

If we stipulate the economic interests of present stockholders as overriding, then these funds are not free, and the cost associated with them must be measured by the opportunities foregone in using them in one way instead of in other possible ways. Essentially there are two kinds of opportunities for the use of corporate earnings. They may be retained within the corporation, or they may be distributed to stockholders.

If earnings (or some part of earnings) are retained within the corporation, stockholders are deprived of the current dividends that could have been paid with those earnings. This is a cost to the stockholders. On the other hand, there are some benefits, the valuation of which will depend on what the corporation does with the funds. Suppose they are retained by the corporation. If, as a result, there is an immediate and lasting increase in the value of the stock, that more than offsets the lower current dividend, stockholders will be better off than if the funds had not been retained and they had received the cash dividends.

Suppose that one accepts the propositions that retained earnings are not free but have a cost and that this cost should be measured by comparing the benefits stockholders would derive if the funds are retained within the corporation with the benefits they would derive from having the funds distributed. The difficult problem of deciding how to measure the relative size of the two sets of benefits in a particular instance still remains. If no objective measurement is provided, then the decision must be made on the basis of management's judgment. The theories of cost of capital we describe in this chapter provide possible approaches to measuring the cost of capital.

Management will also need to rely on its judgment to measure the benefits of the uses of capital funds. These funds need not be reinvested in long-lived assets in order to provide net benefits to stockholders. They may be used to reduce bank loans or bonded indebtedness, to start a training program for employees, or to add to the financial liquidity of the corporation by increasing the amount of cash on hand. If the use of the cash, whatever it may be, serves to increase the market value of the stock, it will serve to offset partially or completely the loss to the stockholder in not receiving a larger immediate dividend.

An example will illustrate the theory. Suppose a corporation whose capital structure consisted entirely of equity was considering an investment that would require an immediate cash outlay of $100,000. The officers of the corporation estimated that, if the investment proposal were accepted, the corporation would receive additional cash proceeds of $20,000 (after taxes) per year for perpetuity. The officials further estimated that, if the stock market is informed about the characteristics of this investment, the common stock of the company would immediately increase in value by $100,000. If the investment proposal were not accepted the company would be able to pay out an additional $100,000 in dividends. It would be to the advantage of stockholders to have the company accept the investment proposal.

The information given is sometimes used to estimate the cost of retained earnings for this investment. This estimate is the rate of discount that makes the present value of the expected cash flows equal to the change in the price of the common stock. In this example the present value of a perpetuity of $20,000 per year would equal $200,000 at 10 percent and would cost $100,000. Investments of this type will be advantageous to present stockholders, because they will result in an increase in the market price of the stock.

There are a number of problems with this approach. The estimated cost of retained earnings may vary from investment to investment, or from stockholder to stockholder. First, consider the effect of variation from investment to investment. The required rate of return may vary from one investment to another, depending on the risks and other characteristics of the investments. The return obtained for one investment cannot be used for a second investment. In fact, obtaining the return for any investment would be difficult, since we do not know with certainty how undertaking an investment will affect the value of the common stock. The arbitrary nature of the measure is not eliminated if the average cost of retained earnings is identified as the required rate of return for the company's existing assets (i.e., the discount rate that makes the expected cash proceeds from the existing assets equal to the market value of the firm). If an average cost of retained earnings is applied to a diverse group of investment projects to make accept and reject decisions, then stockholders' interests are likely to be harmed. This process will lead to accepting some undesirable investments whose required rates of return should exceed the cutoff rate, and to rejecting some desirable investments, whose required rates of return should be less than the average cutoff rate.

There may also be problems with the cost of retained earnings concept when there are differences in the income tax status of the firm's stockholders. Whether a particular stockholder will be better or worse off as a result of a somewhat smaller dividend and a somewhat larger rise in the price of the stock (or for that matter a smaller decrease in its value than might otherwise have taken place) will depend on the income tax rates on ordinary income and on capital gains to which the stockholder is subject. Stockholders differ widely in this regard. Some are subjected to high marginal tax rates, and others, such as pension funds and universities, are not subject to income taxes. Thus there is no one minimum yield at which stockholders are better off if the corporation reinvests earnings instead of paying greater dividends; rather, there are many groups of stockholders whose personal interests may be different.

An investor who is not subject to income taxes (for example, a university endowment fund or a pension fund) may be indifferent to the extra dollar in dividends and/or the extra dollar of capital gains. An investor who has to pay a 50 percent tax on ordinary income and a 20 percent tax on capital gains may be willing to sacrifice a dollar in dividends in order to gain less than a dollar in capital gains.

The fact that investors pay income taxes will tend to make obtaining new capital from stockholders more expensive to the stockholders than the retention of earnings by the corporation. This arises because the firm can retain $1 and have $1 to invest without the stockholder being subjected to personal income taxes. If $1 is given to stockholders (or if the stockholders earn it in some other manner) and the $1 is subjected to a personal income tax, after income taxes the investors will have less than $1. The return required by the investors for new money is apt to be somewhat higher than the return required for funds that are retained and that, thus, are not subject immediately to the personal income tax.

Assume a stockholder pays a .6 tax on marginal income and can earn a before-tax return of .10 and an after-tax .04 return on other investments of comparable operating risk. If a corporation has $100 that it can reinvest to earn .04 it will have $104 at the end of a year. If it then pays the $104 to the stockholders as a dividend, the stockholder will have $41.60 after personal income taxes. Alternatively, the corporation can pay the $100 immediately as a dividend and the stockholder will have $40 to invest. The stockholder will earn $1.60 after tax for the next year and again will end up with $41.60. If the firm can earn more than .04 for the year the stockholder will be better off with the firm reinvesting, than with it paying the money out as a dividend. This conclusion results from the deferring of personal income taxes.

Fortunately the firm will not have to accept investments inferior to those available to the stockholder if it can invest in identical or nearly identical opportunities as its stockholders. Thus, although the after-tax cost for the year to the stockholder in the preceding example would only be .04, the opportunity cost to the firm would be .10 if there are external investments available that give that return. Thanks to this opportunity-cost interpretation we can frequently bypass the question as to the tax rate of the investors in computing the cost of retained earnings. Nevertheless the strong incentive for a corporation to reinvest in the presence of high personal tax rates should be noted. This situation is probably a significant cause of a large number of corporate acquisitions.

The Internal Revenue Code is only one of many factors that create conflicts of interest among stockholders. At the same time some stockholders are attempting to increase their investment portfolios while others are withdrawing a part of their investments. Even if neither group was subject to taxes, the first would tend to prefer capital gains because it would thereby avoid the brokerage fees required to convert dividends into additional stock holdings. The second group would tend to prefer dividends so as to avoid the expenses and inconvenience of selling a part of its holdings periodically.

If the stock of corporations were distributed between investors in some random manner, the conflicts of interest between investors could be of great practical importance. However, the securities of most listed corporations undoubtedly tend to flow into the portfolios of investors whose personal or institutional investment goals are consistent with the known policies of the companies whose stock they hold. Thus conflicts of interest between stockholders of widely held corporations are greatly reduced by the ease with which stock may be sold.

A Theory of Stock Values

For the purpose of understanding the cost of equity capital, a useful theory of stock values is one which assumes that the price of a share of stock tends to be determined by the present value of the dividends which investors as a group expect to be paid by the company. This theory implies that under present institutional arrangements, the stockholder has an interest in earnings only because they affect future dividends or stock prices. As pointed out previously, because of personal income tax considerations, some investors prefer situations in which their stock-market gains can be realized in the form of capital gains rather than dividends. But, although a stock may for a time show increases in price because some investors come to look upon it as a potential source of capital gains, the stock cannot indefinitely continue to rise in price *only* on the basis of such expectations. If the expectations of capital gains are realized *only* because new groups of investors come to share similar expectations and to act on them, the situation may be described as a speculative boom, and it will end in a drastic decline in the price of stock as the supply of new investors gradually dries up. There is a theory that argues that there is always a "greater fool" who will purchase the stock; therefore one does not have to be concerned with the possibility of future dividends. The person holding the stock when it goes down is the fool. The other investors have speculated and won, at least with respect to this stock.

If the hopes of capital gains are to be based on a more solid footing, it must be because the stock eventually will become more valuable to some people for a reason other than faulty decisions of others, namely, the expectation of cash payments by the corporation.

To illustrate this approach to the theory of stock values, we may start with a very simple case in which a company is assumed to have a financial structure consisting solely of common stock. Suppose that by past behavior, announced policy, and an objective evaluation of the investment opportunities open to it, this company has established a firm expectation that its future dividends will continue to be paid at the constant rate of $6 per share per year. When the dividend per share is expected to be constant (and no stock dividends are anticipated), the cost of equity capital can be computed simply as the ratio of the expected dividend to the market price of the shares. In symbolic form, we have

$$r = \frac{D}{P_0},$$

where

r = cost of equity capital;
D = (constant) expected future dividend;
P_0 = current market price per share.

In the example described, if the market price per share is $50, the cost of capital would be estimated as 12 percent because this is the rate of discount implied by the market price per share and the expectation of the constant $6 per year dividend. It is important to note that we are not suggesting that the cost of equity capital is necessarily equal to the dividend price ratio. It turns out to be equal to this ratio only when the current dividend rate is expected to be continued into the indefinite future and when no stock dividends are expected.

More commonly, the market will expect some changes in future dividend rates. It can be shown that if the current dividend is expected to grow at a steady rate, the rate at which the market is discounting future dividends can be roughly approximated from the following expression:[2]

$$r = \frac{D_0}{P_0} + g,$$

where

r = cost of common stock capital (rate at which future dividends are being discounted) expressed as a decimal fraction;

D_0 = current dividend rate;

P_0 = current market price per share;

g = expected annual percentage rate of increase in future dividends, expressed as a decimal fraction, and r is greater than g.

The formula in the preceding paragraph assumes that the dividends of each period will increase by a constant percentage of the previous period's dividends and that the same discount rate is applicable to all future dividends. This formula does not explicitly consider expected capital gains or relate dividends to earnings. It is possible to modify the formula to include these elements if this seems desirable. For example, instead of including all future dividends, we could esti-

---

[2] To show that it is convenient mathematically to assume dividends are paid out and discounted continuously. If the initial dividend is D_0, and it is expected to increase at the rate of g per year, then the dividend in year t (that is, D_t) will be

$$D_t = D_0 e^{gt}.$$

By assumption, the current market price will be equal to the present value of this stream of expected dividends. If the (unknown) rate of discount is r, we can write

$$P_0 = \int_0^\infty D_t e^{-rt}\, dt.$$

Substituting and integrating, we have, provided $r > g$,

$$P_0 = \int_0^\infty D_0 e^{t(g-r)}\, dt = \frac{D_0}{r-g}.$$

The expression in the text is found by rearranging terms from the expression

$$P_0 = \frac{D_0}{r-g}.$$

See M. J. Gordon and E. Shapiro, "Capital Equipment Analysis: The Required Rate of Profit," *Management Science III*, October 1956, pp. 104–106.

mate the cost of capital on the basis of the dividends expected during some limited future period, and the expected price of the stock at the end of the period. If we assume discrete growth and discounting, consider only one future period, and assume a dividend is just about to be paid, the basic equation can be written as follows:

$$P_0 = D_0 + \frac{P_1}{1 + r},$$

where P_1 is the expected price one period from now, and the remaining symbols are defined as before. Rearranging terms, this reduces to the expression

$$r = \frac{D_0 + (P_1 - P_0)}{P_0 - D_0}.$$

In this form the role of capital gains becomes explicit; the estimate of the increase in the price of the stock up to some future date becomes a substitute for the estimate of expected dividends beyond that date.[3] But we may want to express P_0 in terms of future dividends. If we substitute

$$\left(D_1 + \frac{P_2}{1 + r} \right)$$

for P_1 in the expression

$$P = D_0 + \frac{P_1}{1 + r}$$

we obtain

$$P_0 = D_0 + \frac{1}{1 + r}\left(D_1 + \frac{P_2}{1 + r} \right) = D_0 + \frac{D_1}{1 + r} + \frac{P_2}{(1 + r)^2}.$$

If we continue to substitute for P_i we obtain a series

$$P_0 = D_0 + \frac{D_1}{1 + r} + \frac{D_2}{(1 + r)^2} + \cdots \infty.$$

In making these substitutions we make the additional assumption that the discount rate that is applicable now to all future dividends is the same discount rate that will be applicable at all future times.

Because the linkage between dividends and earnings is usually quite close,

---

[3] We could also define P_0 in terms of the dividend one period from now, assuming the present dividend has just been received.

$$P_0 = \frac{D_1 + P_1}{1 + r}$$

$$r = \frac{D_1 + (P_1 - P_0)}{P_0}$$

security analysts and others frequently concentrate their attention on estimates of future earnings. It is also possible to develop formulas for estimating the cost of capital that are expressed in terms of earnings instead of dividends. In so doing, it is important to keep in mind that retained earnings are of value to the ordinary investor only insofar as they constitute an economically profitable use of the company's funds.[4]

The formulas presented in the previous paragraphs should not be thought of as ways of estimating a company's cost of capital. Rather they are possible frameworks within which such estimates might be made. The constant growth rate for perpetuity is not a realistic assumption and should be modified for more accurate representation of a firm's value or cost of capital.

Changes in Stock Prices and the Cost of Equity Capital

We all know that stock prices fluctuate quite widely. Does this mean that we are faced with a cost for common stock that changes daily? The answer is a qualified yes.

Just as bond prices change from day to day as they reflect changes in the interest rate (thus changes in the cost of debt capital), changes in stock prices also will reflect changes in the cost of common stock. There is one prime difference, however, between bonds and stock. The interest payment on bonds is determined by contract and is relatively easily predicted. Common stock dividends are more difficult to predict. They are dependent to some extent on the earnings of the corporation, the cash available, and the decisions of the board of directors. In turn, the earnings of the corporation are dependent on numerous factors, such as general business conditions, the actions of competitors, and the desires of consumers. There are also the whims of the stock market, the waves of optimism and pessimism.

How do these factors affect the cost of capital? A change in expected dividends and earnings will cause the price of the stock to change, but there may *not* be a change in the cost of common stock capital. For example, if the price of a share of common stock is $10 and if future dividends of $1 per year are expected, the stock yields 10 percent. If conditions change and the expected dividends in the future, as seen by the market, are $.50 per year, the price of the stock may drop to $5. The cost of capital remains unchanged at 10 percent.

It is possible that attitudes toward the company, the industry, or the risks of business in general may change, or there may be a change in the amount of total funds available for investment in industry. In this case the market may still expect the $1 dividend to be earned into perpetuity, but the price of the stock may nevertheless change from $10 to $8. The indicated cost of capital has changed from 10 to 12.5 percent.

---

[4] On this point, see James E. Walter, "Dividend Policies and Common Stock Prices," *Journal of Finance*, XI (March, 1956), pp. 29–41.

It is, of course, impossible to determine with certainty what factors have caused a change in the price of a stock. Much work remains to be done in the area of isolating the reasons why the price of a share of stock changes.

Accumulated Depreciation and the Cost of Capital

There is some confusion about the relationships of depreciation expense to the generation of cash and of accumulated depreciation to the computation of the cost of capital.

The recognition of depreciation expense for purposes of measuring financial income does not affect the amount of cash available for investments. The two are completely independent. Charging more or less depreciation will not affect the amount of cash held by the firm. The write-off of the cost of a long-lived asset is an accounting expense that does not use cash, and since it does not generate cash, it does not affect the cash balance. However, the amount of depreciation expensed for tax purposes does affect the amount of cash because it affects the amount paid to the government.

In some cases the analyst may add depreciation back to income to compute the cash flow of the period. The same result, however, can be obtained by not subtracting depreciation expense in computing the cash flow.

Example

The revenue on a cash basis is $10,000, and the expenses utilizing cash are $6,000. The depreciation for the period is $1,800. One method of computing the cash flow is to exclude depreciation ($10,000 less 6,000 equals cash flow of $4,000). A second procedure adds depreciation back to income.

Cash revenue	$10,000
Less: Total expenses	7,800
Income	$ 2,200
Plus: Depreciation	1,800
Cash flow	$ 4,000

We can say that $1,800 of the fixed assets was converted into cash, and speak of the cash from depreciation. But this is inexact, because the cash came from operations. In any event we should distinguish between the origins of the cash and the sources of capital. Is accumulated depreciation a source of capital? Assume that the balance sheet at the start of the period was

Plant assets	$20,000	Capital stock	$20,000

At the end of the period the balance sheet would be

Cash		$ 4,000	Capital stock	$20,000
Plant assets	$20,000		Retained earnings	2,200
Less: Accumulated				
depreciation	1,800	18,200		
		$22,200		$22,200

The source of the capital of $22,200 is 100 percent stockholders' equity funds, and we do not have to concern ourselves with the amount of accumulated depreciation. The total net assets are $22,200, and the sources are fully accounted for by the capital stock and retained earnings.

Now assume that the depreciation expense for the period is $2,500 instead of $1,800. The cash flow would remain $4,000, but the income of the period would be reduced to $1,500, and the retained earnings would be $700 less than with the first computation. The end of the period balance sheet would be

Cash		$ 4,000	Capital stock	$20,000
Plant assets	$20,000		Retained earnings	1,500
Less: Accumulated				
depreciation	2,500	17,500		
		$21,500		$21,500

The source of the capital (or total assets) is still 100 percent stockholders' equity funds, and again we do not have to concern ourselves with the amount of accumulated depreciation. Assume we are tempted to include the $2,500 accumulated depreciation in the capital structure, and the $17,500 of plant assets is sold for $17,500 cash. What would the cost of capital now be? There is no accumulated depreciation, and it is apparent that the stockholders are the only source of capital.

If the accumulated depreciation is purposely overstated or understated, then the book value of the stockholders' equity will be incorrectly stated. This should lead to an adjustment of the book value if we were to use the book value. We prefer to use the market value of the stockholders' equity in computing a weighted average cost of capital.

The Cost of Raising Equity Capital by Selling Common Stock

A corporation can increase its equity capital by retaining earnings or by selling new common stock. The basic principles underlying the costs of capital under either method are the same. With no income taxes, if new common stock could be issued at a price equal to the market value of shares already outstanding, the costs would be the same under either method. In practice, the amount that can be realized per share from a new issue will be less than the market value of existing stock because of the need to price the new issue below the market price in order to attract buyers, and because of the various costs associated with floating a new issue. If the amount realized from a new issue is 20 percent less than the going market price, the cost of raising equity in this form will be 25 percent greater than the costs of retained earnings.

Example

Assume a situation where the firm has a cost of stock equity funds of .10. A dollar of earnings for perpetuity is currently worth $10. The firm will receive $8 of capital from each $10 of stock sold. It must earn $1 per year. This is a .125 return on the $8 received.

The .125 cost of the new capital is .25 higher compared to the .10 cost of retained earnings. The cost of issuance results in an increased cost of capital to the firm, but it may be felt that the present stockholders are not harmed by the addition of new stockholder capital because of the presence of highly profitable investments.

Another factor affecting the relative costs of retained earnings versus the issuing of new stock arises because of personal income taxes. Assume all stockholders are in the 60 percent marginal tax bracket. If the corporation pays a $1 dividend, the stockholders will have $.40 remaining after tax. If the stockholders can invest to earn 10 percent before tax they will receive $0.016 after each tax period. The corporation only has to earn .04 after corporate tax and pay it all as a dividend for the investor to be as well off with retention as with the $1 dividend. The cost of using the funds retained by the firm is lower than it would be if the firm must ask its stockholders for additional funds both because of the capital gains treatment and because of the deferral of personal taxes on dividends. The saving of transaction costs also reduces the cost of retained earnings compared to new common stock capital.

Cost of Long-Term Debt

The cost of long-term debt capital is the present effective interest rate for long-term securities of the specific firm being studied. This effective rate of interest may be a combination of three factors and may not be a valid indication of the time value of money. (The same observation would hold for the cost of common stock capital which we determined above.) These three factors are (1) Time value of money. (2) The use of the contractual interest payments, but because of uncertainty of payment the expected interest payments may be less than the contractual. (3) The investors may be risk averters and hence the amount they are willing to pay is less than they would pay for an amount equal to the expected value of the uncertain amounts. The last two factors make it difficult to use the measure of interest cost which is obtained from market prices to take into account only the time value of money.

The indicated contractual interest rate of an outstanding debt security may not be the effective rate of interest because the security may be selling at a premium or a discount. The effective rate of interest for an outstanding issue can be determined by comparing the current market price for the security with the remaining payment obligations. For example, the effective rate of interest for a bond outstanding can be found by finding the rate of interest which equates the market price to the present value of the amount due at maturity plus the present value of the series of interest payments.

Cost of Short-Term Debt

The cost of short-term debt is analogous to that of long-term debt in that there may be an explicit interest cost (as with a short-term bank loan).

There are several short-term liabilities that do not have explicit interest costs. Among these are taxes payable and wages payable. There are other short-term debts that may or may not have a cost if they are not paid promptly. For example, a trade creditor may offer terms of 2/10, $n/30$. There is no cost for not paying the bill in the first nine days, since the 2 percent discount may be taken at any time prior to the lapsing of ten days. If the discount is allowed to lapse, there is a 2 percent penalty assessed for the use of the funds for a maximum of twenty days. This is equivalent to an annual interest rate of approximately 36 percent. Some firms may allow the discount to lapse and then pay the bill some time after the thirty-day period. Here a cost is added, arising from the loss of credit standing, supplier ill will, and so on.

In the discussions on cash flows (Chapter 5) and income taxes (Chapter 6) it was suggested that any increase in noninterest-bearing liabilities should be subtracted from the increase in current assets required, and only the net amount (increase in current assets minus the increase in current liabilities) should be considered a cash outlay in computing the cash flows. This method of handling the noninterest-bearing liabilities leads to the conclusion that such liabilities should not be treated as a source of capital when computing the cost of capital.

If one did include the noninterest-bearing current liabilities as part of the capital structure when computing the cost of capital, then the total current assets required by the investment should be considered as an outlay made in the period during which the liabilities increase. Further, the value of a noninterest-bearing liability should be recorded at the present value of the amount to be paid.

The procedure that nets the current noninterest-bearing liabilities against current assets has been chosen in this book because it gives reasonable answers and simplifies both the computations and explanations of cash flows. Interest-bearing debt, long- and short-term, is included in the cost of capital calculation, but the cash flows arising from the issuance of this debt are conventionally excluded from the cash-flow calculations.

Debt and Income Taxes

When dividends are paid to stockholders, the effective cost of the equity funds can be determined by taking into consideration the amount of the dividend, the price of the stock, and the expected rate of change in the dividends. In computing the effective cost of debt, the interest payments must be adjusted to compensate for the fact that interest is deductible for tax purposes.

Example
Compute the average effective rate of interest, assuming that the yield of the debt outstanding is 10 percent, the tax rate for the corporation is 46 percent, and the corporation has taxable income.

Because the interest is deductible for corporate income tax purposes, $1 of interest will reduce taxes by $.46, and effective interest cost will therefore be $.54 per dollar of interest. The effective interest cost is .54 × 10 percent, or 5.4 percent, instead of the 10 percent yield of the debt. If a firm does not have taxable income, the effective cost of the interest payments becomes the contractual rate, not adjusted for income taxes. This possibility, if taken into consideration, would tend to make the effective interest cost higher than 5.4 percent. Also, the above calculation assumes the debt is selling at par.

If an investment proposal is to be financed by borrowing, is the interest rate on the specific loan the relevant discount rate for this investment? Would a second investment financed by common stock then have a different discount rate? If this approach were consistently followed, the cost of capital would be an erratic quantity, fluctuating up or down as the firm obtained additional increments of capital from varying sources. Although there are situations in which a particular investment can be related to a specific source of financing, more commonly there exists, on the one hand, a group of apparently desirable investment proposals and, on the other, a variety of sources of additional capital funds that, taken together, could supply the financing for the increased investment.

In taking the time value of money into account we do not in general advocate a procedure where the analysis would be influenced by the type of financing specific to the project. Recognizing, however, that there must be some stock equity capital if there is going to be debt issued and that these securities lead to payments that are treated differently from a tax standpoint, we want the after tax cost of capital to reflect the mixture of debt and common stock that will be used by the firm.

If the firm is using the after-tax borrowing rate to adjust for the time value of money, and some other procedure to adjust for risk, then the tax calculation should recognize that only part of the capital will lead to a tax shield. For example, suppose that a firm can borrow money at 10 percent before taxes and is subject to a 40 percent corporate tax rate. The after-tax cost of debt is 6 percent $[.10(1 - .4) = .06]$. But this is not the appropriate time value of money for the corporation. Suppose that the firm has a capital structure consisting of 40 percent debt and 60 percent equity. What is the after-tax time value of money to the corporation? Table 12-1 shows that the weighted average cost is .084.

TABLE 12-1.   *Illustrative Calculation of After-Tax Weighted-Average Cost*

Source of Capital	Before-Tax Time Value of Money	After-Tax Time Value of Money	Weights	Weighted After-Tax Time Values
Common stock	.10	.10	.6	.06
Debt	.10	.06	.4	.024
Totals			1.0	.084

Header over the four value columns: Time Value of Money for a Corporation

The 10 percent time value of money used for common stock is not meant to represent the cost of common stock equity capital but is a borrowing cost equivalent when there is no tax shield. The common stock time-value rate used in Table 12-1 does not reflect the costs of specific securities but rather the tax consequences and the basic cost of obtaining funds without an adjustment for risk, beyond that adjustment built into the cost of debt.

If we define k_0 to be the weighted average time value of money with a capital structure of L (L is the value of the debt divided by the value of total capital), then, if k_i is the borrowing rate,

$$k_0 = (1 - L)k_i + L(1 - t)k_i$$

$$k_0 = (1 - tL)k_i.$$

Examples:
A company with a tax rate of .48 uses .35 of debt that costs .10. We have for the after-tax cost of funds,

$$k_0 = (1 - .48 \times .35).10 = .0832.$$

In the example illustrated in Table 12-1, $t = .4$, $L = .4$, $k_i = .10$, and

$$k_0 = (1 - .40 \times .40).10 = .084.$$

Definition of Cost of Capital

Before discussing the complexities of the concept of the cost of capital, we shall state the definition of cost of capital that will be developed in this chapter. This procedure is chosen to give a compass that may assist the reader in following the necessarily complex explanation that will be discussed.

The cost of capital of a firm may be defined as a weighted average of the cost of each type of capital. The weight for each type of capital is the ratio of the market value of the securities representing that source of capital to the market value of all securities issued by the company. *The term* security *includes common and preferred stocks and all interest-bearing liabilities, including notes payable.*

Computing the Weighted Average Cost of Capital

Suppose the market value of a company's common stock is estimated at $45 million. The market value of its interest-bearing debt is estimated at $30 million, and the average before-tax yield on these liabilities is 10 percent per year, which is equivalent on an after-tax basis to 5.4 percent per year (equal to 10 percent times .54, assuming a 46 percent tax rate).

Assume that the company described in the preceding paragraph is currently paying a dividend of $8 per year and that the stock is selling at a price of $100. The rate of growth of the dividend is projected to be 6 percent per year. Thus the average cost of the common stock equity is

$$r = \frac{\$8}{\$100} + .06 = .08 + .06 = .14, \quad \text{or 14 percent}$$

The average cost of capital for the company as a whole could be estimated as shown in Table 12-2.

TABLE 12-2. *Estimate of Weighted Average Cost of Capital*

Capital Source	Proportion of Total Capital	After-Tax Cost	Weighted Cost
Equity	.60	.14	.084
Interest-bearing debt	.40	.054	.022
Average cost of capital			.106

The preceding example is expressed in terms of the rate of return required for present debt and the present common stock. If we were considering the raising of net capital to finance additional investments, it would be more accurate to speak in terms of the rate of return that would be required if a mixture of additional debt and common were to be issued. The word *average* that is used in the term *average cost of capital* refers to a weighted average of marginal costs for debt and stock.

The Optimum Capital Structure

There are times when a company will wish to consider a permanent change in its capital structure because management believes that changes in the relative cost of sources of capital, or changes in the business risks faced by the company, would make a different capital structure more desirable.

It may be that the minimum of the cost of capital curve is not a point but rather a range—that is, the average cost of a capital curve is flat—in fact, the entire curve may be horizontal. It has been argued that under certain conditions the entire curve is horizontal, and there is not one minimum cost of capital, but rather that all combinations of debt and common stock are equally desirable in the absence of income taxes.[5]

In discussing the concept of a minimum cost of capital, it is convenient to begin by imagining a company financed entirely by equity, and to consider the consequences of substituting increments of debt for the common stock equity.

At least two kinds of risks to which common stockholders are subject when debt is included in the capital structure of a company need to be distinguished for our purposes. These may be called the risk of bankruptcy, and the risk of increased leverage. By using average cost of capital of the firm, an attempt is made to take these risks into consideration.

---

[5] See F. Modigliani and M. H. Miller, "The Cost of Capital, Corporation Finance and the Theory of Investment," *American Economic Review*, Vol. **XLVIII**, June 1958, pp. 261–297.

A company financed only with funds obtained from stockholders may eventually have to cease operations because a combination of operating losses and poor investments has exhausted its funds, but debt increases the risk of bankruptcy. With debt it is possible equity holders may lose their interest in a company that may again become a profitable operation. It is frequently assumed that, with a well-managed and profitable company, the introduction of a small amount of nonequity capital presumably will not increase the risks of bankruptcy appreciably. Any increase in debt, however, increases the risks of bankruptcy. As the amount of debt rises, the risks of bankruptcy become greater, until the point is reached where the risk is substantial. Just what this point is may be difficult to specify because it varies, depending on the activities in which a company is engaged. Nevertheless it is well to remember that a very small increase in the chance that a firm may eventually become bankrupt can have a noticeable effect on the price that investors are willing to pay for its common stock, because if bankruptcy occurs, common stockholders are likely to lose their entire investment.

One advantage of debt capital comes from the financial leverage it provides for the remaining equity capital. An increase in the debt ratio, however, generally has two effects on the earnings per share available to common stockholders; it tends to change the average earnings per share; and it tends to increase the year-to-year variability of earnings per share (including negative earnings arising from bankruptcy or near bankruptcy). If expected earnings per share increase, this is likely to increase the price per share that investors are willing to pay; the increase in variability is likely to decrease the price per share that investors are willing to pay.

A second important advantage of debt is that interest is deductible for purposes of computing taxable income, whereas dividends on common stock are not deductible. With corporate tax rates close to .5 there is a very real incentive for firms to use debt as a major component of their capital structure.

There is an important nonfinancial cost associated with the use of debt. This category of costs is the result of limitations on management's freedom of action, which are usually included as part of the debt agreements. Provisions requiring that sinking funds be accumulated, limiting the conditions under which the corporation can acquire additional debt, and restricting the directors' freedom to declare dividends are examples. These limitations are frequently of great importance, but they are difficult to quantify, and they must be taken into account on a judgment basis.

It is impossible to give any simple rules for determining in advance the optimum capital structure for a particular firm.[6] Theoretically, the optimum

---

[6] It has been suggested that the average cost of capital of a company is not greatly affected by the company's capital structure because investors can adjust their own portfolios to either increase or decrease the leverage of the equities they own. See F. Modigliani and M. H. Miller, "The Cost of Capital, Corporation Finance and the Theory of Investment," *American Economic Review,* **XLVIII,** June 1958, pp. 261–297.

structure is reached when an additional debt issue, in substitute for stock equity, will result in a decrease in the price per share of the common stock. The capital structure just prior to the issue of that debt is the optimum capital structure. In determining whether a company's capital structure is optimum, management must to some extent rely on the intuitive judgment of well-informed persons.

It is important to keep in mind the fact that any increase in the percentage of debt used increases both the cost of the next dollar of debt and the expected return required by stockholders (there is more risk). If before the issuance of debt the debtholders required 10 percent and the stockholders required an expected return of 14 percent, after the issuance we can expect both of these costs to increase. Since the percentage of debt is also increasing we cannot predict the effect of the change on the weighted average cost of capital without more information.

Cost of Capital and the Discount Rate

It is sometimes stated that the cost of capital of a firm may be used to evaluate investments whose cash flows are perfectly correlated with the cash flows from the firm's present assets. With perfect correlation between the two sets of cash flows, the risk is the same. But if the timing of the cash flows is not also the same, the same discount rate cannot be used for both investments.

Consider a situation where some gambles have payoffs of either $0 or $1,000, both with .5 probability. Thus the expected payoff for all of the gambles is $500. All of the gambles are perfectly correlated, and the outcome of the gambles will be known immediately. Assume one of the gambles will pay off one year from now, and an investor is indifferent between this gamble and $400 for certain now. The choice of $400 implies an average cost of capital of .25. (The expected value of the payoff is $500 and a .25 rate of discount would equate the present value of $500 to $400.) A second gamble will pay off twenty years from today. If the discount rate of .25 is applied to the $500 expected value we obtain $5.75 (.0115 × $500). If the time value of money is .10, however, it is not clear that an investor would be indifferent between $5.75 and the gamble. The present value of $1,000 discounted at .10 is $148.64. This is what the gamble will be worth if the outcome is favorable. Multiplying by the .5 probability, we obtain an expected value of $74.32. Most persons would pay more than $5.75 for a lottery ticket that is equally likely to be worth $148.64 or zero.

The cost of capital combines in one discount rate an allowance for the time value of money and an allowance for risk. To apply the same cost of capital to cash flows that occur at different points in time, the magnitude of these allowances (i.e., the percent per unit of time) must remain constant over time.

Studies of the term structure of default-free interest rates suggest that the appropriate allowance for the time value of money is not necessarily constant for all future time periods. More importantly, the rate at which uncertainty is resolved is often not constant through time. In the previous example, all the uncertainty about the gamble will be resolved immediately. The discount rate of 25 percent for the first lottery represents the average value over one year of an allowance for the time value of money and an allowance for the risk of an uncertain event that will be resolved immediately. In this case we can easily separate the two components. The present value of $1,000 to be received in one year is $909, using .10 as the discount rate. This is the value of the gamble if the outcome is favorable. Multiplying by .5 we obtain an expected value of $454.50. This is $54.50 more than the value of the asset to the investor. This $54.50 difference represents the allowance for risk for an investment paying off at time one. If the investment paid off immediately the adjustment for risk would be (1.1)54.50 or $59.95, and the investment would be worth $440.05.

For the investment maturing in twenty years we compute the present value of $440.05 using .10 as the discount rate.

$$440.05(1.10)^{-20} = 65.41.$$

If we subtract $8.91 from the $74.32 expected present value, using .10 we again obtain $65.41. This value is likely to be a better estimate of value than the $5.75 obtained using .25 as the discount rate. ($8.91 = 59.95(1.1)^{-20}$)

If the benefits from all investments are perpetuities, the use of different discount rates, where the rates increase with increased risk, may give an evaluation of investments using their present values that is consistent with their risks. For example, if all investments have cash flows of $1,000 per year and if there are three investments with different risks (high, medium, and low), we can use a high discount factor (say, .20) with the high risk, a medium discount factor (say, .10) with the medium risk, and a low discount factor (say, .05) with the low risk. The three different present values we obtain are as follows:

	Discount Factor	Perpetual Cash Flow Present-Value Factors	Present Value of $1,000 per Year
High risk	.20	5	$ 5,000
Medium risk	.10	10	10,000
Low risk	.05	20	20,000

If there is another investment in the high-risk classification its cash flow (also a perpetuity) would be multiplied by the same factor of 5. Instead of being perpetuities the same general approach could be used if all the investments were one-period investments.

There is a $.50 discount per dollar of proceeds for risk as we move from the low- to the medium-risk investment, and a $.75 discount per dollar for risk as we move from the low- to the high-risk investment. These risk adjustments may not be correct, but at least the adjustment for risk is in the correct direction, and they apply in the same manner to all investments in the same risk class.

It is less obvious than with common stock, but the cost of corporate debt also includes an adjustment for risk, because there is generally the possibility of default. A bond yield of .07 is partially a result of time preference (say, .04) and partially a result of the risk of default. It may also include an allowance for the risk and dilution of value resulting from expected inflation.

As normally defined and computed, the cost of common stock equity funds and the yields of most debt instruments include an allowance for risk, but it does not necessarily follow that the use of a higher discount rate applied to future cash flows is a desirable way of determining the present value of an asset that is subject to risk.

The results of any evaluation of debt can be expressed in terms of yield. For example, suppose that a bond contract involves a promise to pay $50 per year for ten years and $1,000 at the end of the ten-year period. If a potential investor decides that he or she would pay no more than $371 for this bond, we may choose to describe the investor as willing to buy the bond if it is priced to yield 20 percent. This statement tells us nothing about how the investor actually decided what the bond was worth. Does the investor have a time value of money of 20 percent per year, or is it that he or she has an aversion to risk and fears a possible inability to collect interest and principal?

The use of high discount rates to allow for uncertainty makes a very special assumption about the nature of uncertainty. For example, suppose that we consider an investment to build and equip a plant for producing a new product. In some instances the major uncertainty may be related to the cost of constructing the plant, whereas the demand for the resulting output may be easily predictable in advance with very little uncertainty. This could be the case if the product to be made were to be sold in advance through a long-term sales contract, whereas the design, construction, and operation of the plant involved new or unusual engineering problems creating an unpredictable cost. The use of atomic energy to generate electric power is a tangible example of this situation. In such a situation the discounting of future revenues, themselves fairly certain, seems a poor way of allowing for the uncertainty about how much the fixed plant will cost. In another instance the main element of uncertainty may revolve around consumer acceptance of the product. The alternatives may be either a very high or a very low level of consumer acceptance, with a corresponding probability of either a series of years of very high cash proceeds or a series of years of little or no cash proceeds.

We shall use two examples to illustrate the difficulty of predicting the effect of using different discount rates in an attempt to take risk into consideration.

Example 1

Assume that we have two investments, the first more risky than the second. Do not be bothered by the vagueness of the description of the amount of risk. With the first investment we shall use a discount rate of .10, and with the second a discount rate of .20. The two investments have mean cash flows of $10,000 in years 1 and 50.

Note that the present value of the cash flows of year 1 of the less risky investment is 1.09 times as large as the cash flow of the more risky investment. However, the present value of

Year	Cash Flows	Present-Value Factor Using .10	Present Value Using .10	Present-Value Factor Using .20	Present Value Using .20
1	10,000	.9091	$9,091	.8333	$8,333
50	10,000	.0085	85	.0001	1

the cash flows of year 50 is approximately 85 times as large. The use of a larger rate of discount for a more risky investment may move the decision in the correct direction (that is, the riskier the investment, the lower the value of the future cash flows). However, it does this in an approximate and somewhat unpredictable manner. We cannot be sure of the impact of the risk discount added to the time value of money without considerable computation, and the effect of the risk discount will not be equal each year.

The use of a risk discount assumes that the risk difference between the two investments is increasing as we move farther into the future. As we have already mentioned, this assumption may not be correct. Even if the assumption is correct, we still need to inquire whether the discount factor appropriately measures the disadvantage of this risk.

This difficulty with the use of a risk discount (that is, a larger interest rate) to take risk into consideration is not limited to situations involving long time periods.

Example 2
Assume that we are given the opportunity to bet on a horse race being run today and the information we receive is so good that we consider the probability of obtaining $3 for each dollar invested to be .5. There remains a .5 probability of losing our entire investment, so we want to apply a large interest rate to take the risk into consideration. However, the benefits are zero time periods in the future. When the discount factor $(1 + r)^{-t}$ is computed for t equal to zero, we find the present-value factor is 1 and is independent of the choice of the discount rate, r.

We conclude that, for practical business decision-making, varying the rate of discount is not a good way of accomplishing the objective of taking risk into consideration. It is true that most persons would require a higher return for risky investments than for less risky investments; however, determining the exact amount the rate of discount should be increased for different types of risk in different time periods is a difficult task.

Summary of Weighted Average Cost of Capital

There are several conclusions that we can make concerning the use of a weighted average cost of capital. The weighted average cost of capital represents the average cost of funds to the firm. As such it reflects both the sources of capital and their uses.

Business managers quite properly want to know how different capital structures affect the cost of obtaining capital. They want to reduce the cost of obtaining new capital or even reduce the cost of the firm's present capital. In general, the stockholders of a firm will be better off if management can reduce the firm's weighted average cost of capital by changing its capital structure without changing its asset structure. For a given asset structure, the lower the cost of capital the better.

For a given capital structure, the weighted average cost of capital to a firm reflects the characteristics of the firm's assets, and particularly their average risk, but also the timing of the expected cash proceeds.

There is no reason to believe that any specific investment proposal being considered is exactly average with respect to risk or the timing of the cash proceeds. If investors knew the exact risk characteristics and timing of cash flows, they could define the risk-adjusted rate of discount that should be used. But if we change something, say the timing but not the risk, it is clear (as previously illustrated) that the same discount rate would not be used. Thus even where we say that the next investment has similar risk characteristics to the present investments of the firm, we cannot conclude that the same risk-adjusted discount rate should be used. When the risks of the different investments are different, the problem becomes even more complex.

The weighted average cost of capital represents an averaging of all risks of the firm. It would be incorrect to assume that the same rate of discount should be used for a marginal investment as required on the average for the present investments. Also, it should be recognized that if a firm accepts a substantial investment whose characteristics are very different from the average, the firm's cost of capital is likely to change as a result.

The weighted average cost of capital can be used to evaluate investments in much the same manner that the payback method can be used. It gives some insights, and, as long as it is not the final step in the analysis, it is not harmful. The basic problem is that it incorporates a risk adjustment, which is then inserted into a compound interest formula, and we do not know that risk compounds evenly through time for all investments at the same rate.

If desired, the present value of an investment can be computed using a weighted average cost of capital. Having done that calculation it is then necessary to consider the present values that result from the use of other discount rates. It may be that an investment with a positive present value should be rejected because of its risk characteristics or that an investment with a negative present value using the weighted average cost of capital should be accepted.

Default-free Rate of Discount

Assume that a reasonable person prefers $1 now rather than $1 in the future, and that there is a positive rate of discount. It is possible to have a situation where the discount rate is negative and we are satisfied to invest $1 now and get back less than $1 in the future just to be sure of getting something. Imagine a family with four children approaching college age. They might invest even with a negative discount rate, if holding cash was impractical.

There are many choices of discount rates that may be suggested for use in making investment decisions. The following are the two possibilities we shall consider in this section: (1) interest rate of government securities, and (2) interest rate of long-term bonds of the firm.

Before proceeding further, however, it is desirable to establish more clearly the characteristics we seek in selecting an interest rate. The term *risk-free* might be used to describe the interest rate. This is suggestive, but not strictly accurate. There are certain risks that cannot in practice be eliminated and that affect all interest-bearing securities to a greater or lesser extent. The interest rates we have in mind are those at which investors could lend money with no significant danger of default or at which they could borrow if their collateral were so good that their creditors would feel that there was negligible chance of default.

Even if the risk of default is practically negligible, there are other risks inherent in fixed-money debt instruments as long as there is uncertainty about the future changes that might take place in the economy. We shall describe these risks from the point of view of the lender. The counterparts of these risks also exist for a borrower.

One source of risk arises because of uncertainty about the future price level. Expectations about possible future price levels influence the market determination of interest rates. Lenders will tend to be hurt if the price level rises; hence they require a higher interest return with an expected price-level increase than with an expected price-level decrease, or with constant prices.

Another source of risk arises because of the possibility of changes in the level and term structure of interest rates. Normally, the interest rate on bonds will vary with the number of years to maturity even when there is no risk of default. Bonds that mature in a few years may have higher (or lower) yields than bonds that mature in the more distant future. If there is no risk of default, the lender can always be sure of earning the going yield by buying a bond of given maturity and holding it until it matures. The possibility exists, however, that some other strategy would result in earning a higher yield. If investors want to lend money for a five-year period and expect a decline in interest rates, they may be able to earn a higher yield by buying a fifteen- or twenty-year bond and selling it after five years than by buying a five-year bond and holding it to maturity. When this strategy is followed, however, there is no longer any guarantee that a certain minimum rate of interest will actually be earned.

A lender wishing to avoid the uncertainty that results from the possibility of changes in the term structure of interest rates may be unable to do so. This will happen if there is uncertainty about the amounts of cash that will be required on various future dates. An investment in short-term debt instruments, such as treasury bills, will lead to uncertainty about the rates that will be earned when the time for reinvesting these funds arises. An investment in longer-term securities will lead to uncertainty about the actual return that will be realized if the securities must be liquidated before they mature.

In spite of these limitations the interest rates on government debt constitute a reasonable choice of discount rates representing default-free lending opportunities. These rates represent actual market opportunities at which firms or individuals could lend money with essentially no risk of default.

Unfortunately, neither private corporations nor individuals can actually borrow money at these rates, even with the best available collateral. For various reasons the rates at which one could actually borrow for a given term would be higher than the rates at which the government can borrow for loans of the same maturity.

Borrowing Rate

Any individual or private business corporation that borrows money will find the interest rate it must pay will be greater than the default-free rate. An analysis of the discounting of debt-type cash flows is an interesting special problem that helps us to understand the discounting process, and it is worthwhile considering this problem, even when the difference between the interest rate promised on a debt and the default-free rate is not large enough to be material in relation to investment decisionmaking.

We shall ignore income tax considerations. Suppose that the interest rate on default-free one-year debts is 6 percent, and a private corporation offers to sell a bond that promises to repay $1,060 one year from now. If such a bond were offered by the federal government it could be sold for $1,000, because the obligations of the government are default-free. With a private corporation there is some possibility of default, although the possibility may be remote. Suppose that the potential buyers judge the probability distribution of future cash payments that would result from purchasing this bond to be as follows:

(1) Possible Cash Proceeds	(2) Probability	(3) Col. 1 × Col. 2
$1,060	.9990	$1,058.94
1,000	.0005	.50
500	.0003	.15
0	.0002	.00
	1.0000	Expected value $1,059.59

The bondholders view the bond contract as nearly default-free because they consider that there are only two chances out of 10,000 that they will receive nothing from the bond, and only one chance in a 1,000 that they will fail to receive the total amount promised. The bondholders, discounting the expected cash flows of $1,059.59 at the default-free rate of interest, would find the present value of the bond to be $999.61 ($1,059.59/1.06). If the potential purchasers were willing to buy the bond on the basis of the present value of its expected cash flows, they would offer $999.61 for it. It is customary to quote bond-yields on the basis of the payments promised, not the expected payments. On this basis it would be said that the bonds were sold to yield 6.04 percent ($1,060/1.0604 = $999.61).

One might question whether in fact potential buyers would pay $999.61 for the bond. Their expected return on a default-free government obligation would be just as high, although the most probable return on the corporation's bond is higher than on the government's. Suppose that the buyers offered to pay $998 for the bond, and the corporation sold it at that price. The present value of the expected cash flows is $999.61. The difference of $1.61 is a risk premium that serves to induce the bond buyers to buy this slightly risky asset instead of a default-free government bond.

It is interesting and relevant to note that the analysis made by a potential bond buyer is essentially the same as the analysis that the corporation would make in analyzing a risky investment. From the point of view of the buyer a bond is a risky investment. The future cash flows can be adjusted for timing by discounting at the default-free interest rate, but the expected present value is not the amount that would be paid for the asset. The value depends on the risks involved and on the risk attitudes of the purchaser.

Now let us look at the debt transaction from the point of view of the issuing corporation. Say the corporation receives $998. It is legally obligated to pay an amount whose most likely present value is $1,000. The corporation may agree with the bondholder's assessment of the possible cash proceeds of the bond and their probabilities. That is, the corporation recognizes that there is a small probability that it may be unable to meet its legal obligations under the contract. Even so it has received only $998 for entering into an obligation having a present value of expected cash payments of $999.61, for which the most likely consequences (probability .999) is that it will make payments whose present value is $1,000.

In analyzing the consequences of issuing the bond, the corporation should consider the reactions of the stockholders. The issuance of bonds may affect the risk premium stockholders use, and thus the market value of the common stock. Despite the incurrence of a liability that exceeds the cash received, the contract is not necessarily disadvantageous to the borrowing corporation. To balance the debt contract, it has received cash plus an intangible asset that we may call "increased liquidity." Why does the firm want increased liquidity? There may be several reasons, but we shall concentrate on one.

Assume that there is an advantageous investment with a positive expected net present value using the default-free rate. By expending the cash and the intangible asset called increased liquidity, the firm can acquire this investment. If the expected present value of the proceeds of the investment exceeds its cash cost plus its liquidity cost, the investment might be worthwhile. The financial accountant will record only the cash obtained from liability and the cash cost of the investment. The investment analyst should recognize that the asset is worth acquiring if the cash outlay plus intangible liquidity cost given up is less than the expected net present value plus a risk adjustment. Typically, the reason the firm is willing to incur a liability greater than the cash obtained is that it expects to use the cash to acquire an asset whose value is greater than the value of the liability.

If the firm has other assets, the decision about whether an investment is acceptable or not may have to be made on the basis of an analysis of its risk characteristics combined with the risk characteristics of the assets already owned by the firm. With uncertainty there are examples of undesirable investment whose expected net present value is positive, and of desirable investments whose expected net present value is negative. Life insurance is an example of the latter type.

If there is uncertainty, the discounting of future cash flows serves to place cash flows to be received at different points in time on a comparable basis relative to time. This process facilitates the making of investment decisions. But expected net present values cannot be used as a sole decision-making criterion when there is uncertainty.

Conclusions

When cash flows are discounted at a default-free interest rate, the resulting net present values adjust the cash flows for differences in timing, but not for risk. If any higher discount rate is used, there is an implicit risk allowance, and decision makers must ask themselves whether the appropriate risk allowance has been made. Some firms may prefer to use the rate at which they can borrow long-term funds as a discount rate. If their credit rating is good, this rate will not be far above the default-free rate, and it may be easier to explain and justify to management. Our theoretical preference is to use a default-free interest rate and make risk adjustments separately. For practical purposes we are willing to compromise. While we would continue to advocate the use of a default rate to compute a present value of a cash flow (not risk adjusted), we concede that for purposes of practical operational decision-making the use of the borrowing rate has a good deal of merit. It represents one estimate of opportunity cost, since the outstanding bonds could be retired or new bonds could be avoided (thus saving their cost). For a set of certain cash flows a firm would not want to invest using borrowed funds, unless the cost of the debt was less than the rate of return of the investment. With risky cash flows the conclusion is much more complex.

Even more important than the choice of a specific discount rate is the recognition that, when cash flows are uncertain, some investments may be undesirable, even though their expected cash flows have a positive net present value; whereas other investments may be desirable even with expected cash flows having a negative net present value. Because the risk characteristics of the investment will greatly influence the investment decision and the present-value calculation is viewed as only one information-input, it is most important that good investments should not be rejected by the use of a high rate of discount, so that they drop from consideration.

Questions and Problems

12-1. Assume that $1,000 is to be received thirty years from today. Compare the present values obtained using .05 and .20 as rates of discount.

12-2. The ABC Company has opened one hundred new stores. It has incurred a great deal of expenses associated with opening the stores, and the stores have not yet built up enough clientele to be profitable. On the other hand, the stores are operating at profit levels exceeding expectations, and there are indications that they will be very profitable in the future. It is obvious that the stock market has not yet digested this latter fact, and the stock of the company is currently depressed compared to management's appraisal of value. The company has the opportunity to acquire an additional fifty stores this year, but to do so will require new stockholder capital acquired from the market (it has borrowed all it feels it is prudent to borrow and cannot obtain more capital from its current stockholders). Without the new capital the stockholders can expect to earn an equivalent annual return of .15 on the current market value of their investment (assume there is $100 million or 1 million shares of stock outstanding). The stock is currently selling at $100 per share and paying $6 per share dividend. The earnings are $7.50 per share ($7.5 million in total).

The new investments would require $10 million to be obtained by issuing 100,000 new shares of common stock. The investment would return $1.2 million per year available for dividends for perpetuity. The stockholders desire a .08 return per year on their incremental investments.

Required: (a) Should the corporation issue the new shares and undertake the investment? (b) What would be your recommendation if the corporation had the necessary cash already available?

12-3. (*Continuation of 12-2.*)   Change the statement of the problem so that the present stockholders can expect to earn dividends of $6 per share or an equivalent annual return of .06 for perpetuity, unless the new investment is undertaken. Should the new investment be undertaken?

12-4. (*Continuation of 12-2.*)   Change the statement of the problem so that the present stockholders can expect to earn $8 million, or an equivalent return of .08 per year on the current market value of their investment, if the new investment is not undertaken. Should the new investment be undertaken?

12-5. The following facts apply to the ABC Company:

Cost of short-term loans   .05
Cost of long-term loans   .06
Cost of common stock capital   .10

	Book Value	Market Value
Current liabilities (noninterest-bearing)	$10,000,000	$10,000,000
Short-term loans (interest-bearing)	5,000,000	5,000,000
Accumulated depreciation	50,000,000	not applicable
Long-term debt	20,000,000	20,000,000
Common stock	25,000,000	75,000,000

a. Compute the average cost of capital. Assume the corporate income tax rate is .4.

b. Assume that as a result of a decrease in the income tax rate to .3, the market value of the common stock rises to $100 million with no change in the cost of common stock capital. Compute the new average cost of capital for the ABC Company.

12-6. A firm is financed by .2 long-term debt and .8 common stockholder capital. Assume that it has been established that both the common stockholders and the debtholders have a time value of money of .05. (We shall define this as being equal to their cost of capital.) The corporate tax rate is .4. Compute the average cost of capital.

12-7. The common stock of a company is selling at $50 per share and is paying a dividend of $2. The expected growth in dividends is .03 per year.
  Estimate the cost of common stock capital.

12-8. The ABC Company's stock is selling at $100 and the company is paying a $2 dividend. It has been paying the same amount for five years. The company has many desirable investments available; the cash needs exceed the cash it is generating. On the other hand, the company is earning $5 per share income and feels the stockholders should share in the prosperity of the company.
  The president has suggested an increase in the dividend from $2.00 to $2.06. The executive vice president has suggested that the corporation conserve its cash and instead of increasing the cash dividend rate it should issue a .03 stock dividend.
  There are currently 20 million shares of common stock outstanding.
  Required: What do you think the company should do?

12-9. The ABC Company is considering issuing $100 million of twenty-year bonds that will pay interest of .05 per year. This is the current long-term interest rate for comparable firms, and it is expected that the bonds will be issued at par. The tax rate is .4.
  a. Using the before-tax cash flows and the before-tax interest rate, compute the present value of the debt.
  b. Using the after-tax cash flows and the after-tax interest rate, compute the present value of the debt.
  c. Assume that the after-tax cost of capital is .10. Compute the present value of the debt.

12-10. The TCG Company has a before-tax operating income of $25 million and no debt. It is subject to an income tax rate of .4. The company allocates half of its after-tax income to dividends and half to retained earnings. It expects to continue dividing its after-tax income in the same proportions in future years. Its common stock is selling at 16.7 times current after-tax earnings. Each dollar of retained earnings generates on the average $.10 per year of additional before-tax income.
  Compute the TCG Company's cost of capital assuming 100 percent stock equity financing and no change in the earnings–price multiplier.

12-11. The corporate tax rate is cut to .3, but the TCG Company's cost of capital and its operating policies remain the same. How will the tax cut affect the market value of the company's stock?

12-12. The following balance sheet applies to the ABC Company.

Assets	
Current Assets	500,000
Long-Lived Assets	600,000
	1,100,000

Equities	
Current Liabilities	
Trade creditors	100,000
Bank loans	250,000
Long-Term Debt	300,000
Stock Equity:	
Preferred stock	100,000
Common stock	200,000
Retained earnings	150,000
	1,100,000

Assume the market value of the debt and stock are equal to the book values. The expected IRRs of the different securities to the investors (and also the costs to the firm) are

Bank loans	.10
Long term debt	.09
Preferred stock	.10
Common stock	.15

Compute the average cost of capital. Assume the income tax rate is .4.

12-13. The common stock of the BAC Company is selling at $100 per share and is currently paying a dividend of $2 per year. The expected growth in dividends is .04 per year. (a) Estimate the cost of common stock capital. (b) Assume that you computed the cost of common stock capital and obtained a figure of .03. What evidence would lead you to think that this estimate is too low to use in making investment decisions? (c) Assume that the expected growth in dividends of the BAC Company is .20 per year. Estimate the cost of capital. (d) Assume that the stock is paying a dividend of $2 per year and that this dividend is expected to grow by 10 percent per year. The cost of common stock capital is 8 percent. Estimate the current market price of the stock.

12-14. Assume that there are two investments of different risk. A return of .05 is required on one investment; on the other a return of .10 is required. Compare the present values obtained for each investment for expected cash flows of $1 billion one year, twenty years, and fifty years from now at the required rates of return.

12-15. Mr. Jones has a time value of money of .06. He is analyzing a common stock that is currently paying $2 per year dividend, but he expects the dividend to grow at a rate of .04 per year for perpetuity. (a) What is a reasonable estimate of price at which Mr. Jones might consider this common stock to be eligible for purchase (ignore risk considerations)? (b) What is a reasonable estimate of price if Mr. Jones expects the $2 dividend to decline at a rate of .04 per year?

12-16. Mr. Smith is reviewing a stock currently selling for $100 per share. He expects the price to increase to $102 in one year and the firm to issue a $2 dividend one year from now. Mr. Smith has a time value of money of .06. (a) What price per share might Mr. Smith be willing to pay? Ignore risk considerations. (b) If Mr. Smith purchased the stock, what return would he be expecting for his year's investment?

12-17. The ABC Company can borrow and lend funds at an interest rate of .08. It can invest $11 million in a risky project that on the average will lead to net cash flows of $1 million per year. A consultant has suggested that the firm use its cost of capital of .10 in computing the present value of the investment. The investment's life is extremely long. Insurance can be purchased that will guarantee the $1 million per year. Should the investment be undertaken? How much could the firm afford to pay for the insurance?

12-18. The ABC Company currently has outstanding $1 million of .05 debt with a maturity of two years. The only way it can finance a $500,000 investment would be by refinancing the $1 million with $1.5 million of .08 debt also maturing in two years. The investment would pay $55,000 in year 1 and $555,000 in year 2 (the investment has an IRR of .11). The firm has a cost of capital of .10. Debt costs and cash flows are on an after-tax basis.

cost of equity	.12 × .5 = .06
cost of debt	.08 × .5 = .04
	.10

Should the investment be accepted?

12-19. The ABC Company has issued a $1,000, .05 bond with a four-year life. The interest rate for default-free securities is now .05. Assume that the following probabilities of payment apply (the probability of collecting in a given year is statistically independent of whether or not a collection occurred in the previous year; missed collections are not made up):

Principal or Interest of Period	Probability of Collection	Probability of No Collection
1	1.0	.0
2	.9	.1
3	.6	.4
4	.5	.5

(a) Assume that you are willing to pay the expected present value; what amount would you pay for this bond? (b) If the investor pays the amount in (a), what is the approximate cost to the firm issuing the bond? (c) What is the market price of this investment likely to be?

12-20. The ABC Company has been offered a certain investment whose IRR is .05. It can borrow funds at .06, and the interest rate on government securities of a similar maturity is .04. There are no taxes. Should the investment be accepted?

12-21. The capital structure of the ABC Company is .8 stock and .2 long-term debt. Assume that investors have a time value of money of .05, and there is a corporate tax rate of .4. What is the appropriate rate of discount?

12-22. Assume that you have the choice between the following two investments:

Investment A	
Probability	Immediate Outcome
.5	$ 0
.5	1,000

The outcome of B will be known now, but the payoff is one year from now and consists of the following outcomes:

Investment B	
Probability	Outcome
.5	$ 0
.5	1,100

Required: Which investment do you prefer? What amount does B have to offer with .5 probability for you to be indifferent between the two investments?

12-23. (*Continuation of 12-22.*)   Assume that after ten years investment B pays an amount of $2,594 with .5 probability or $0 with .5 probability. Do you prefer A or B?

Discussion Questions

12-A. The CAB Company is currently paying a $2 dividend on its common stock. Assume that an investor thinks that the common stock will sell for $105 one year from now. The best alternative use of money (without risk) will earn .04. The maximum amount the investor is willing to pay for a share of CAB Company common is $100. Describe some possible reasons why the investor is not willing to pay more than $100 per share.

12-B. The ABC Company issued $1,000 bonds with a coupon interest rate of .05 per year at a price to yield .06 (the price was $885.30 per bond). The life of the bonds is twenty years.

Required: Give three different reasons as to why the bond yield is .06.

12-C. The ABC Company wants to use its cost of capital in evaluating investments. By a secret process it has succeeded in obtaining the forecasts of future dividends used by investors who currently purchase the stock. By equating the present value of these dividends to the price of the stock, it has obtained a number that it considers to be an estimator of the cost of common stock funds.

Required: Comment on the suitability of the measure obtained.

CHAPTER **13**

Accounting Concepts Consistent with Present-Value Calculations

What you're saying, then, is that just because all the professionals in the field believe it, it must be right. If this were really true, the world is flat.

—Joel Segall. From the Autumn 1969 Newsletter of the Graduate School of Business, University of Chicago.

Much of the economic analysis of evaluating prospective capital investments relies heavily on concepts such as cash flows and their net present value. This is in contrast to the usual accounting practice where the investment review emphasizes such concepts as revenue, depreciation, income, and return on investment. The purpose of this chapter is to show that the discounted cash-flow approach and the main accounting concepts can be reconciled, provided that the accounting concepts are appropriately defined.

We will consider two different methods that give identical net results. The first method includes all cash flows (including investment outlays) in the computation of depreciation and income. The second method excludes investment cash flows after the investment begins operations.

Economic Depreciation: Including All Cash Flows

If we are given the cash-flow stream associated with an asset and an appropriate interest rate, we can define the net present value of the cash flows associated with the asset during all succeeding time periods, and denote this present value as $V(t)$. $V(0)$ is the present value at time 0 (end of zero period) and $V(1)$ is the present value at time 1. $V(t)$ is after any new investment at time t.

The economic depreciation during period t will be defined as the change in present values during this period. That is, $D(t)$ is the depreciation of period t. $D(t)$ is defined as

$$D(t) = V(t-1) - V(t).$$

In the usual case, where the present values have declined over the period, depreciation will be a positive quantity. If the present values increase during the period, depreciation will be negative, and we shall refer to the negative value of depreciation as appreciation. If $N(t)$ is the cash flow of the t period (positive for inflows and negative for outflows), the income of the period is defined as the cash flow of the period minus the depreciation of the period. That is, if income is denoted by $Y(t)$ then

$$Y(t) = N(t) - D(t).$$

Return on investment can be defined as the ratio of the income of the period to the present value of the asset at the end of the previous period. If r is the discount rate used in this analysis, each period's return on investment will be equal to r. That is,

$$\frac{Y(t)}{V(t-1)} = r$$

if $V(t-1) \neq 0$.

The measure of depreciation expense being used in this section is not consistent with the conventional accounting definition, since $V(t)$ is affected by any additional investment. Because, the cash flows and depreciation are both affected by the same amount (and in opposite directions), the net income will be consistent with accounting measures of income.[1]

Consider two investments A and B where the cash flows of the one investment supply the cash needed to undertake the second investment. The appropriate rate of discount is 10 percent.

	Time		
	0	1	2
A	−17,355	10,000	10,000
B		−10,000	11,000
A + B	−17,355	0	21,000

Table 13-1 shows the computation of $V(t)$ for the joint investment A plus B. Exhibit 13-1 shows the computation of depreciation, income, and return on investment.

The returns on investment for both years are .10 which is also the internal rate of return of the joint investment.

The procedure described so far can be used without the necessity of distinguishing between cash flows from operations and investment-type cash flows. Investment-type cash flows result from acquiring or disposing of new assets. If this distinction is ignored, then $V(t)$ must be interpreted as the present value of the cash flows from all present assets and all planned additions and deletions in future periods. Similarly, $D(t)$ must be interpreted as the net depreciation of the

---

[1] This is not exact but will be close enough for purposes of this chapter. See H. Bierman, Jr., "A Further Study of Depreciation," *The Accounting Review*, April 1966, pp. 271–274.

TABLE 13-1.   *The Computation of V(t) for A + B (r = .10)*

		For V(0)		For V(1)	
Period	End-of-Period Cash Flow	Present-Value Factor	Present Value	Present-Value Factor	Present Value
1	0	.9091	0		
2	21,000	.8264	17,355	.9091	19,091
			V(0) = 17,355		V(1) = 19,091

EXHIBIT 13-1.   *Depreciation, Income, and Return on Investment*

For period 1 we have:

$D(1) = V(0) - V(1) = 17,355 - 19,091 = -1,736$
$Y(1) = N(1) - D(1) = 0 - (-1,736) = 1,736$

$$r = \frac{Y(1)}{V(0)} = \frac{1,736}{17,355} = .10.$$

For period 2 we have:

$D(2) = V(1) - V(2) = 19,091 - 0 = 19,091$
$Y(2) = N(2) - D(2) = 21,000 - 19,091 = 1,909$

$$r = \frac{Y(2)}{V(1)} = \frac{1,909}{19,091} = .10.$$

period, that is the decrease in value of the existing assets less the increase in asset values resulting from any net additions during the period. Thus, investment A decreased in value by $8,264 in period 1 (this amount is derived in the next section) but there is an additional investment of $10,000 thus, the value of D(1) is a negative $1,736. The asset value increased by $1,736.

Economic Depreciation: Excluding Investment Flows

The above procedure is operational. It does work. But the definition of depreciation that is used is not intuitively appealing, since depreciation is affected by the amount of investment made during the period. This "error" is washed out because the cash flows are also reduced by the amount of the investment and income is not affected.

The procedure to be illustrated aims at using a definition of depreciation that is more consistent with the definition that is used by accountants. Unfortunately, the introduction of this definition of depreciation does lead to some complexity. There is a real gain, however. Frequently, it is desirable to distinguish explicitly between cash flows from operations and investment-type cash flows. The basis for the distinction is that operational cash flows do not directly affect the cash flows of future periods but investment-type cash flows do. For example, an advertising outlay designed to increase future sales would be an investment; an advertising outlay designed to increase current sales only would be an operational cash flow. Also, the procedure allows the evaluation of discrete investments rather than requiring the evaluation of large sets of investments.

To implement the procedure, let $I(t)$ be defined as an investment type of cash flow occuring in period t. This is a negative cash flow that is incurred because the present value of the positive cash flows associated with the action is sufficiently large to warrant the expenditure. If there are investment-type cash flows encountered in period t, we have

$$I(t) + d(t) = V(t-1) - V(t),$$

or

$$d(t) = V(t-1) - V(t) - I(t),$$

where $I(t)$ is a negative quantity if there have been investment outlays, and $d(t)$ is net depreciation. Note that $d(t) = D(t) - I(t)$. The value of $I(t)$ is included, since $V(t)$ reflects the investment and the objective is to obtain a depreciation measure that is independent of $I(t)$.

Example

To illustrate these concepts, suppose that the discount rate is 10 percent and that interest is compounded annually. The cash flows associated with the hypothetical asset A are as follows. The cash flows occur at the end of each period.

Period	End-of-Period Cash Flow
0	−17,355
1	10,000
2	10,000

The calculations of the net present values of the remaining cash flows at various points in time are presented in Table 13-2. The calculations of depreciation, income, and return on investment are presented in Exhibit 13-2.

TABLE 13-2. Calculation of Net Present Value of an Asset at Various Points in Time ($r = .10$)

		For V(0)		For V(1)	
Period	End-of-Period Cash Flow	Present-Value Factor	Present Value	Present-Value Factor	Present Value
1	$10,000	.9091	9,091		
2	10,000	.8264	8,264	.9091	9,091
			$V(0) = \overline{17,355}$		$V(1) = \overline{9,091}$

EXHIBIT 13-2. *Depreciation, Income, and Return on Investment for Asset Described in Table 13-2*

For period 1

$$d(1) = 17,355 - 9,091 = 8,264$$

$$Y(1) = 10,000 - 8,264 = 1,736$$

$$r = Y(1)/V(0) = 1,736/17,355 = .10$$

For period 2

$$d(2) = 9.091 - 0 = 9,091$$

$$Y(2) = 10,000 - 9,091 = 909$$

$$r = Y(2)/V(1) = 909/9,091 = .10$$

The income of period 1 is \$1,736, which is exactly the same as with the previous procedure illustrated in Exhibit 13-1. The depreciation expense is now \$8,264, whereas it was previously a negative \$1,736, but this difference did not affect the income measures.

If we now consider investment B and define B to be essential to A, then the cash flows at time 2 are \$21,000 and we have (as previously computed)

$$V_0 = 17,355.$$

$$V_1 = 19,091.$$

$$V_2 = 0.$$

But now to compute $d(1)$, we have

$$d(1) = V(0) - V(1) - I(1),$$

where $I(1) = -10,000.$

$$d(1) = 17,355 - 19,091 - (-10,000) = \$8,264.$$

This depreciation expense measure is equal to that previously obtained (Exhibit 13-2) and is not affected by the new investment. Following the procedure of this section, an investment in the period does not affect the depreciation expense of the period.

Assets with Positive Present Values

In the preceding example we assumed that, before the first cash flow occurs, the net present value of the cash flows associated with the asset is 0. (The IRR of the investment is equal to the time value of money.) We shall now consider investment opportunities whose net present value is positive. How can we measure income and depreciation in such cases?

The example presented earlier will serve to illustrate this case if we assume that the appropriate time value factor for the firm is .05. As shown in Table 13-3, the net present value of the A investment is $1,239.

TABLE 13-3.   Computation of Net Present Value ($r = .05$)

Period	Cash Flow	Present-Value Factor (5%)	Present Value
0	−17,355	1.0000	−17,355
1	10,000	.9524	9,524
2	10,000	.9070	9,070
			Net Present Value 1,239

One solution is to recognize $1,239 of additional income at time 0, then act as if the asset cost $18,594 and depreciate that amount over its life. The 5 percent rate of interest woudl be used for discounting, and the return on investment each period after time 0 would be 5 percent. The computations are similar to those already illustrated (see Table 13-4 and Exhibit 13-3).

This procedure requires the adjustment of the cost of an asset to its value as well as the recording of income and acquisition. Because of the subjective nature of the inputs, many would object to the procedure.

TABLE 13-4.   Calculation of Net Present Value of an Asset ($r = .05$)

Period	End-of-Period Cash Flow	For $V(0)$ PV Factor	PV	For $V(1)$ PV Factor	PV
1	10,000	.9524	9,524		
2	10,000	.9070	9,070	.9524	9,524
			$V(0) = 18,594$		$V(1) = 9,524$

EXHIBIT 13-3.   Depreciation, Income, and Return on Investment for Asset Described in Table 13-4

For Period 1

$d(1) = 18,594 - 9,524 = 9,070$

$Y(1) = 10,000 - 9,070 = 930$

$r = 930/18,594 = .05$

For Period 2

$d(2) = 9,524 - 0 = 9,524$

$Y(2) = 10,000 - 9,524 = 476$

$r = 476/9,524 = .05$

An alternative approach would be to use the internal rate of return of the investment as the discount rate. If this is done for investment A, the computations would be identical to those shown in Table 13-2 and Exhibit 13-2.

The use of an asset's internal rate of return has the advantage of simplicity. But assets with identical cash flows except for the initial outlay would be recorded at values that are not equal to the present values that would be obtained using a common discount factor. For example, two investments with exactly the same benefit stream would be recorded differently if they cost different amounts (their internal rates of return would differ). This is, of course, consistent with generally accepted accounting practice. But it would lead to two identical benefit streams being recorded at different values and leading to different returns on investments. This practice would tend to reduce the usefulness of the return-on-investment calculation as a managerial control device. Suppose that two managers are in charge of the two assets. If both do as well as expected with their assets (that is, achieve the cash flows predicted for their assets), one will have a low return on investment and the other a higher return on investment. Thus, the return on investment measures not their operating ability, but the ability (or luck) of whoever originally uncovered the investment opportunities.

We can adjust the first procedure illustrated for those who do not want to recognize the unrealized appreciation as income. Suppose that the asset is carried on the books under two headings: (1) cost of the asset, and (2) the difference between the present value and the cost of the asset. The cost would be reduced each period by a depreciation expense computed by taking the change in the

TABLE 13-5.   *Computation of Incomes*

Period	Revenue	Depreciation (based on value)	Income (based on value)	Realized Gain	Income (based on cost)
1	$10,000	$ 9,070	$ 930	$ 806	$1,736
2	10,000	9,524	476	433	909
	20,000	$18,594	$1,406	$1,239	$2,645

TABLE 13-6.   *Computation of Realized Capital Gains**

Period	Depreciation (based on value)	Depreciation (based on cost)	Realized Gain
1	$ 9,070	$ 8,264	$ 806
2	9,524	9,091	433
	$18,594	$17,355	$1,239

* We could also have taken the difference in incomes resulting from the use of the two methods of depreciation. Identical results would be obtained.

present value of the cash flows, using the IRR (the interest rate that makes the present value of the investment equal to 0). The difference between the value and the cost would be reduced each year by an additional amount calculated so that the total of the two asset accounts equaled the value of the asset. These calculations are illustrated in Tables 13-5 and 13-6. The incomes and returns on investment for the investment in period 2 are shown in Exhibit 13-4.

The use of the IRR has the advantage of being somewhat more simple to compute and to present.

EXHIBIT 13-4. *Income and Return on Investment Calculations for Asset with Positive Net Present Value*

Period 2	
Revenue	$10,000
Less: Depreciation of original cost	9,091
Income (based on cost of asset)	909
Less: Reduction in unrealized capital gain of asset	433
Income (based on value of asset)	$ 476

$$\frac{\text{Income (based on cost of asset)}}{\text{Depreciated cost of asset}} = \frac{909}{9{,}091} = 10\%$$

$$\frac{\text{Income (based on value of asset)}}{\text{Depreciated value of asset}} = \frac{476}{9{,}524} = 5\%$$

Tax Effects

The preceding discussion applies if there are no income taxes, or if the cash flows and the discount rates used are on an after-tax basis. In general, given the present tax structure the value of an asset or investment opportunity will depend on the tax status of the investor. Thus it may be profitable for the investor who undertakes an investment to sell the resulting asset to another investor whose tax status is different. This concept is the basis for many tax shelters.

Consider an investment where there is an expenditure of $17,355 and then the investor receives $10,000 a year (before tax) for two years. The present value of the benefits is $18,594, using .05 as the discount rate. This is the value to a zero tax investor at time zero.

Suppose that the original investment has been made by A, that A is subject to a marginal tax rate of 40 percent on his taxable income, and that taxable income is computed using straight-line depreciation on the cost of the asset. Since A is subject to a tax rate of 40 percent, if the before-tax interest rate is .05, A's after-tax interest rate will be .03. Table 13-7 shows the present value of A's after-tax cash flows from the asset at a discount rate of .03, provided the asset is retained.

TABLE 13-7. *Value of an Asset to an Investor in the 40 Percent Tax Bracket if It Is Held*

Before-Tax Cash-Flow	Depreciation for Taxes	Taxable Income	Income Tax	After-Tax Cash Flow	Present-Value Factor (.03)	Present Value
10,000	8,677.5	1,322.5	529	9,471	.9709	9,195
10,000	8,677.5	1,322.5	529	9,471	.9426	8,927
20,000	17,355.0	2,645.0	1,058	18,942		18,122

Since the investment is worth $18,594 to the zero tax investor and only $18,122 to A, a sale by A is likely to occur (the gain to be taxed at the statutory rate for capital gains). If A receives an offer of $18,594 the capital gain would be $18,594 - 17,355 = \$1,239$. With a .20 capital gains tax ($248), A would net $18,346 which is larger than $18,122.

Valuation Not Affected by Taxes

Opportunities for transactions motivated by differences in tax status would be eliminated if taxable income were determined by using depreciation based on present value. When this convention is adopted, two investors who expect the same before-tax cash flows from an asset will assign it the same value at each point in time, even though each investor values the asset by discounting a different set of after-tax flows. This is consistent with P. A. Samuelson's definition of income.[2]

We will assume the same investment as above but will now assume a .10 before-tax interest rate. The investor is again subject to an income tax rate of 40 percent.

Taxable income is defined as the change in the present value of the future cash flows from an asset. If interest payments for such a taxpayer are tax deductible and the interest received is included in taxable income, such a taxpayer would use an after-tax rate of .06 if the before-tax interest rate was .10.

We previously computed (Exhibit 13-2) the incomes and depreciation of each year and obtained $V_0 = 17,355$ and $V_1 = 9,091$, $d(1) = 8,264$ and $d(2) = 9,091$ for a zero tax investor.

Using these depreciation expenses for taxes we obtain the results shown in Table 13-8.

In Table 13-9, the after-tax cash flows and the after-tax discount rate of .06 are used to calculate the value of the asset at various times. At each time, the value of the asset is the same on an after-tax basis as was computed on a before-tax basis for each year.

---

[2] See P. A. Samuelson, "Tax Deductibility of Economic Depreciation to Insure Invariant Valuation," *Journal of Political Economy*, 72, Dec. 1964, pp. 604–606.

TABLE 13-8. *Income Tax and After-Tax Cash Flows when Taxable Income is Defined in Present-Value Terms*

Period	End-of-Period Before-Tax Cash Flow	Depreciation	Income	Tax	End-of-Period After-Tax Cash Flow
1	$10,000	$8,264	$1,736	$694	$9,306
2	10,000	9,091	909	364	9,636

TABLE 13-9. *Calculation of Net Present Value of an Asset Based on After-Tax Cash Flows (r = .06)*

Period	End-of-Period Cash Flow	For V(0) PV Factor	PV	V(1) PV Factor	PV
1	$9,306	.9434	$8,779		
2	9,636	.8900	8,576	.9434	9,091
			V(0) $17,355	V(1)	9,091

Now consider the following investment shown in Table 13-10 and assume a zero tax investor whose cost of money is .10.

TABLE 13-10. *Zero Tax Investor*

Time	Cash Flow	Depreciation	Income	Beginning Investment	Return on Investment
0	−3,000				
1	1,300	1,000	300	3,000	.10
2	1,200	1,000	200	2,000	.10
3	1,100	1,000	100	1,000	.10

We see in Table 13-11 that the straight-line depreciation expense is equal to the economic depreciation. The net present value of the investment including the $3,000 outlay is zero before the outlay is made.

TABLE 13-11. *Present Values of Before-Tax Cash Flows*

Time	Cash Flow	Time 0 Present Value (using .10)	Time 1 Present Value (using .10)	Time 2 Present Value (using .10)
1	1,300	1,181.82		
2	1,200	991.74	1,090.91	
3	1,100	826.44	909.09	1,000.00
		3,000.00	2,000.00	1,000.00
Change in value:		Period 1 = 1,000	Period 2 = 1,000	Period 3 = 1,000

Now, assume the investor is taxed at 40 percent and straight line depreciation is used for taxes.

TABLE 13-12.   *Calculation of After-Tax Cash Flows*

Time	Cash Flow	Depreciation Expense	Income Before Tax	Tax	After Tax Cash Flow
1	1,300	1,000	300	120	1,180
2	1,200	1,000	200	80	1,120
3	1,100	1,000	100	40	1,060

The present value of the after-tax cash flows using the after-tax borrowing rate of .06 is shown in Table 13-13.

TABLE 13-13.   *Present Values with $t_c = .40$*

Time	Cash Flow	Time 0 Present Value (using .06)	Time 1 Present Value (using .06)	Time 2 Present Value (using .06)
1	1,180	1,113.20		
2	1,120	996.80	1,056.60	
3	1,060	890.00	943.40	1,000.00
		3,000.00	2,000.00	1,000.00

The present values at each moment in time are identically equal to the values obtained for the zero tax investor.

If the tax rate is changed but the same method of depreciation is used (economic depreciation) the present values of the investment will not be changed. The values are invariant to the tax rate if the depreciation expense used in the tax calculations is equal to the before tax change in value and if the after-tax discount rate used to accomplish the time discounting is equal to the market before-tax rate (the same for all investors) times the amount one minus the taxpayer's marginal tax rate.

With the method of depreciation illustrated transactions will not take place because of differentials in tax rates.

If the cost of the asset is less than $3,000, say $2,000, the procedure will still work if the asset is written up to its present value of $3,000 and if the tax depreciation expense is based on this $3,000 of present value.

Internal Rate of Return and Taxes
Let us assume a situation where an investment type of outlay may be deducted at the time the outlay is made rather than be depreciated over time.

We want to show that the internal rate of return after tax equals the internal rate of return before tax.

Assume the before tax cash flows are

$$C_0, C_1, C_2, \ldots C_N$$

where C_i is the cash flow of period i.

The after tax present value is:

$$\text{NPV} = (1 - t)C_0 + \frac{(1 - t)C_1}{1 + r} + \frac{(1 - t)C_2}{(1 + r)^2} + \cdots + \frac{(1 - t)C_n}{(1 + r)^n} = 0$$

where r is the internal rate of return.

Dividing both sides by $(1 - t)$ we obtain:

$$\text{NPV} = C_0 + \frac{C_1}{1 + r} + \frac{C_2}{(1 + r)^2} + \cdots + \frac{C_n}{(1 + r)^n} = 0$$

where r is the before tax internal rate of return.

The fact that the internal rate of return is not affected by the tax rate requires that C_0 and all subsequent cash flows be treated as taxable expenses or incomes in the years in which they occur.

Consider the following investment with an internal rate of return of .10.

Time	Before-Tax Cash Flow
0	-3,000
1	1,300
2	1,200
3	1,100

With immediate expensing and a .40 tax rate the cash flows and their present values would be:

Time	After-Tax Cash Flow	Present Value (.10)
0	-1,800	-1,800.00
1	780	709.09
2	720	595.04
3	660	495.87
	NPV =	0

The before- and after-tax internal rate of return are both .10. The internal rate of return is not affected by the tax rate.

The net present value would be reduced by an increase in the tax rate unless the rate of discount being used is the internal rate of return.

This analysis is also applicable to certain types of retirement funds, commonly known as IRA's and Keogh plans. The basic tax rules applicable to these plans are: 1) the cash invested in one of these funds is tax deductible in the year in which it is invested; 2) dividends, interest and capital gains realized by such a fund are not taxable as long as the money remains in the fund; and 3) cash withdrawn from such a fund is fully taxable in the year it is withdrawn. Suppose that the money invested in an IRA is used to purchase assets that provide an internal rate of return of 10 percent before taxes. Then the after-tax internal rate of return to the investor is also 10 percent. This is illustrated with the following simple example, for an investor in a 40 percent tax bracket and an asset whose IRR is 10 percent.

Time	Before Tax Cash Flow	After Tax Cash Flow
0	−3,000	−1,800
5	4,832	2,899

The after-tax cash flows will have a positive present value for any discount rate less than 10 percent. The present value calculation using a discount rate less than 10 percent explains why these investment-plans are so attractive.

Taking the Long-run Perspective without Neglecting the Short Run

Recently critics of the business scene have emphasized the tendency of business firms to focus on the short-run effects rather than the long-run consequences of decisions.[3] Part of the blame has been placed on graduate schools of business and their MBA programs, but this is an invalid accusation since for the past thirty years just about 100 percent of these schools have taught the use of internal rate of return and net present value (DCF and NPV) in making investment decisions. These are long-run perspectives. It is a very rare member of the academic community who would advocate focusing on the return on investment (ROI) of year 1 or year 2 for an investment with a life of twenty years. Unfortunately, managers do use such measures.

If the excessive focus on the short run was not learned at school, where was it learned? Partially it was learned on the job by observation of the paycheck (or more accurately the bonus payment) and a reading of the job agreement. A concern for short-run changes in the stock price also has motivated an excessive attention to the near-term effects of investments.

---

[3] See Robert H. Hayes and David A. Garvin, "Managing as if Tomorrow Mattered," *Harvard Business Review*, May–June 1982, pp. 70–79. Also, Robert H. Hayes and William J. Abernathy, "Managing Our Way to Economic Decline," *Harvard Business Review*, July–August 1980, pp. 67–77.

When corporations compensate top managers there is a tendency to reward a manager for:

a. increases in total earnings
b. improvements in ROI
c. improvements in earnings per share (EPS)

All things equal, it is both fair and desirable to reward managers who achieve increases in total earnings, improve ROI, and cause EPS to increase. It is only when we look closely at these measures that we see possible difficiencies in their use.

An intelligent operating officer will realize when a decision will benefit one of the above measures but will harm the firm. Then why is the bad decision made? Financial incentives geared to the short-run measures will cause the most conscientious managers to give serious consideration to an alternative which will benefit their take-home pay. Equally important is the fact that a decision which would harm the paycheck is likely to be rejected, even if the decision is likely to be beneficial in the long run.

It is unintelligent to offer rewards for a type of action and then think it immoral (or lacking in intelligence) when the managers act in a manner consistent with the incentives.

We will not suggest an abandonment of the short-term income measures but rather an adjustment in their calculation and an expansion to the use of other measures to supplement them. It would be more dramatic (and theoretically correct) to conclude that only measures that considered the entire life of the assets being used should be the basis of the performance measurement. But this approach would neglect the very natural desire of managers to know how both they and their subordinates are doing right now. We are naturally too impatient to wait until the year 2000 to find out how we did in 1985.

The Suggestion

The basic suggestion of this section is to convert the short-run measures of performance into long-run measures. This conversion will be accomplished using present-value depreciation. Present-value depreciation locks all the years together, so that if an investment is desirable, each year of life will show desirable performance measures.

Example

Assume a firm has .10 time value factor and uses straight-line depreciation. Consider an investment that has the following cash flows:

0	1	2	3	4
−200,000	50,000	60,000	100,000	171,875

With a .10 hurdle rate the investment is desirable on a discounted cash basis (it has an internal rate of return of .25). If the firm borrows the entire investment cost at an interest rate of .10 and the forecasts are realized, the following income statements will result if straight-line depreciation is used:

	Year			
	1	2	3	4
Revenue	50,000	60,000	100,000	171,875
Depreciation	50,000	50,000	50,000	50,000
Interest	24,000	15,000	10,000	5,000
Income	−20,000	−5,000	40,000	116,875

The first two years of operations have losses and if one focuses on total earnings, ROI, or earnings per share of the two early years the tendency will be to reject this investment. Only if one considers the entire life does the investment become desirable. This type of conflict situation is apt to arise whenever the benefits start low and increase through time.

We will first consider an accounting solution (there are several possible accounting solutions). Using the internal rate of return to compute present values, and defining $V(t)$ to be the present value at time t and $d(t)$ to be the present value depreciation for the tth period we have:

Time: t	$V(t)$	$d(t)$
0	200,000	
1	200,000	0
2	190,000	10,000
3	137,500	52,500
4	0	137,500
		200,000

$d(t)$ is equal to the change in value of the asset rather than the cost of the asset divided by the life or some other mechanical calculation. The income statements and returns on investment are now

	Year			
	1	2	3	4
Revenue	50,000	60,000	100,000	171,875
Depreciation	0	10,000	52,500	137,500
Income before				
Interest	50,000	50,000	47,500	34,375
Investment	200,000	200,000	190,000	137,500
ROI	.25	.25	.25	.25

The investment now favorably affects total earnings, ROI, and earnings per share of each year. Each year has an ROI equal to the internal rate of return of the investment.

We now reach a very important generalization. If an investment is economically desirable, the method of accounting used to evaluate performance should not indicate that any year's operations is not acceptable if the actual results are the same as the planned results. A method of accounting that shows bad performance measures when the performance is good is not acceptable accounting. Only if the actual results fall short of the forecasted should the measures of performance indicate less than acceptable performance.

A second solution to the problem illustrated above is to delay the performance evaluation (and bonus payment) until the end of the entire four-year planning horizon. This procedure would ensure that the short-run considerations would not be the crucial factor in analyzing the investment. The disadvantages are that managers want to track the progress being made to achieve goals and, secondly, that the wait for a bonus would be excessively long with long-lived investments.

Example

Assume a firm has a choice between two plants. One plant will be adequate for two years at which time an expansion, good for another four years, will be built. The other plant will be good for the entire six year period. The firm requires a return of .10 on its investments.

The expected cash flows are

	0	1	2	3	4	5	6
Plant A	−10,000	6,500	6,500 −44,966	18,000	18,000	18,000	18,000
Plant B	−36,566	6,500	6,500	18,000	18,000	18,000	18,000

Using straight-line depreciation and funds borrowed at a cost of .10 the income statements for the first two years will be:

	Plant A		Plant B	
	1	2	1	2
Revenue	6,500	6,500	6,500	6,500
Depreciation	5,000	5,000	6,094	6,094
Interest	1,000	500	3,600	3,000
Income	500	1,000	−3,194	−2,594

The income statements indicate a superiority for Plant A. There are positive incomes in both year 1 and year 2 while Plant B has two loss years. The managers with their bonus based on total income or earnings per share have a strong bias for Plant A. If the example is made more dramatic by moving the time of plant expansion for A to year 10, we can easily sense the incentive to exploit the possibility of achieving ten good years and letting the next manager worry about the plant expansion.

Now let us consider the economics of the two alternatives. Plant B costs $26,566 more at time 0 but saves $44,966 at time 2. By building Plant B, the firm earns .301 per year incrementally. Unless uncertainty is introduced it is clear that Plant B should be built if the company requires a .10 return on its investments.

The earnings-per-share incentives are identical to those of total earnings in this type of situation. Plant A will favorably affect earnings per share and Plant B will have an adverse effect for the first two years. In addition, the returns on investment for two years also point to Plant A as the preferred choice.

Thus a short run incentive approach will result in Plant A even though the discounted cash flow calculations make clear that in this situation Plant B is to be preferred.

The Suggestions

One suggestion is to require that all economically feasible alternatives be submitted to top management so that mutually exclusive investment decisions are not made at the operating level. Another possibility is for top management to consider the entire planning horizon rather than the year-by-year performance. This would imply that the size of a bonus would depend on more than the conventional accounting measure of the early years of operation. A comparison of the planned results and the actual results would be more important than the absolute value of accounting measures.

Following this proposal there would not be an incentive to choose A rather than B since both alternatives budget $6,500 of cash flows for the first two periods. If the actual results are $6,500 both investments will show identical performance.

The final suggestion is again to modify the method of accounting. Moving from straight-line depreciation to the use of present-value depreciation will modify B's results so that the losses of periods 1 and 2 are eliminated. The values at time 0, 1, and 2 and depreciations for periods 1 and 2 for plant B are:

Time	Plant B Value (Using .25)	Depreciation
0	36,566	
1	39,207	−2,641
2	42,509	−3,302

Plant B's internal rate of return of .25 is used as the discount rate.

The depreciation expenses are negative indicating the asset is becoming more valuable from time 0 to time 1 and from time 1 to time 2. Income statements for Plant B for the first two years are now:

	Year	
	1	2
Revenue	6,500	6,500
Depreciation	−2,641	−3,302
Income before Interest	9,141	9,802
Investment	36,566	39,207
ROI	.25	.25

Now investment B is more than competitive with investment A.

Conclusions

It is generally accepted accounting practice to use some method of depreciation accounting that is well-defined and is independent of the economic characteristics of the asset being depreciated. For tax purposes, the objective of depreciation accounting is to write the asset off as rapidly as possible (more exactly, to maximize the present value of the write-offs). For accounting purposes, the objective is to allocate the cost of the asset over its useful life. This chapter has suggested two alternative methods of defining depreciation. One method accomplishes the important objective of equating the return on investment of the asset to its internal rate of return. If we are willing to record an adjustment to the cost of the asset to its present value, the second method leads to the return on investment being equal to the time value factor (rate of discount defined to be appropriate) for the firm in each year of use. These procedures have the advantage of eliminating the types of distortions in the measurement of return on investment associated with the use of straight-line depreciation or accelerated depreciation when the cash flows do not decrease rapidly through time.

We know that investment decisions should be made using the available information for the entire life of the investment. The measures of performance should do likewise or distortions will be introduced if there is a focus on the short-run measures.

If the accounting measures are converted from conventional measures to economic measures significant improvements in the measures of performance result. They become reconciled to the economic measures of investment worth.

The severity of the distortions resulting from the use of conventional accounting were understated in the examples given in this chapter, since straight-line depreciation was used. If any of the accelerated depreciation methods were used the distortions would be even larger. The performance of the early years of use would appear even worse than indicated in the examples.

We have to move to a system of measuring performance where a desirable investment has desirable measures of performance as long as the actual results coincide with the forecasted results.

Questions and Problems

13-1. An asset costs $15,277 and will earn proceeds of $10,000 a year for two years. The cash is received at the end of each period. The time value of money is .20.

Required: (a) Compute the internal rate of return of the investment. (b) Compute the depreciations in value of the assets, the incomes, and returns on investment for the two years of life.

13-2. An asset cost $25,620 and will earn proceeds of $10,000 in year 1 and $20,000 in year 2. The time value of money is .10.

Required: (a) Compute the internal rate of return of the investment. (b) Compute the depreciations in value of the asset, the incomes, and returns on investment for the two years of life.

13-3. An asset costs $26,446 and will earn proceeds of $20,000 in year 1 and $10,000 in year 2. The time value of money is .10.

Required: (a) Compute the internal rate of return of the investment. (b) Compute the depreciations in value of the asset, the incomes, and returns on investment for the two years of life.

13-4. An asset costs $20,000 and earns proceeds of $11,000 in year 1 and $10,500 in year 2. The time value of money is .05.

Required: (a) Compute the internal rate of return of the investment. (b) Compute the depreciations in value of the asset, the incomes, and returns on investment for the two years of life.

13-5. An asset costs $20,000 and will earn proceeds of $12,000 in year 1 and $11,000 in year 2. The time value of money is .10.

Required: (a) Compute the internal rate of return of the investment. (b) Compute the depreciations in value of the asset, the incomes, and the returns on investment for the two years of life.

13-6. An asset costs $15,778 and will earn cash proceeds of $10,000 a year for two years, the first payment to be received two years from now. The sales will be made at the end of periods 1 and 2 and the collections at the end of periods 2 and 3. The time value of money is .10.

Required: Compute the depreciations, the incomes, and returns on investment for the life of the investment.

13-7. An asset costs $8,505 at time 0 and an additional $8,000 at time 1. It will earn proceeds of $10,000 a year for two years, the first payment to be received two years from now. The time value of money is .10.

Required: Compute the net depreciations, the incomes, and returns on investment for the life of the investment.

13-8. (*Continuing problem 13-7*).   What is the value of the investment at time 1 (after the second investment) if the actual investment outlay was only $5,000 at time 0 and $4,000 at time 1? What is the value at time 2? Assume that the expected benefits are unchanged.

13-9. The XYZ Company wants to know the cost of a new building it has constructed. It paid the builder an advance of $2 million and paid the remainder when the building was completed two years later (total amount paid to the builder was $3 million). (a) Determine the cost, assuming that the building was financed with .05 debentures. (b) Determine the cost, assuming that the building was financed entirely by stock.

13-10. An investment costs $14,059 and has expected cash flows of

0	1	2
−$14,059	$10,000	$5,000

The time value of money of the firm is .05. Management wants a system for reappraising capital budgeting decisions. (a) Assume that the accounting measures of expense (except for depreciation) and revenues would be the same as the preceding. Prepare statements of income and return on investment that would be reasonable tools for reappraisal of the decisions. (b) Assume that the cash flows just indicated apply, but the accounting measure of net revenue in period 1 is $14,762 and the net revenue in period 2 is $0. What is the depreciation of periods 1 and 2?

13-11a. Find the income, depreciation and return on investment, during periods one and two, using an interest rate of 25 percent. (No taxes are payable.)

Period	End of Period Before-Tax Cash Flows
0	−16,000
1	+16,000
2	− 7,000
3	+15,000

b. Assume a tax rate of 40 percent on income defined in present-value terms. What are the after-tax cash flows for periods one and two?

13-12. Consider the following before-tax cash flows.

0	1	2
− 100	0	+ 144

Suppose an investor is in the 60 percent tax bracket. Find the after-tax internal rate of return on this investment for each of the following circumstances.

a. The outlays come from after-tax funds. The taxes are paid using the present-value definition of income. (Assume a before-tax discount rate of 20 percent.)

b. The outlays come from after-tax funds. The proceeds are taxed using an income concept based on historical cost and straight-line depreciation.

c. The outlays come from before-tax funds and are tax-deductible. All proceeds are taxable when realized. (This is how some pension plans work.)

13-13. Consider the following before-tax cash flows.

Period	0	1	2
End of Period Cash Flow	−8,000	+15,000	−5,000

a. Find the income, and depreciation during period one, using present-value accounting. Assume no taxes and an interest rate of 6 percent in all periods.

b. Find the income and depreciation during period two, using present-value accounting. Assume no taxes and an interest rate of 6 percent in all periods.

c. Assume a tax rate of 25 percent on income defined in present-value terms. What are the after-tax cash flows for period *one* and *two*? (Assume the taxpayer has other taxable income in both periods.)

13-14. Given the following data:

Period	End of Period Before-Tax Cash Flows
0	−12,000
1	+12,000
2	− 6,000
3	+12,000

a. Find the income, depreciation and return on investment, during period one, using an interest rate of 12 percent. (No taxes are payable.)
b. Find the income, depreciation and return on investment during period two, using an interest rate of 12 percent. (No taxes are payable.)
c. Assume a tax rate of one third on income defined in present-value terms. What are the after-tax cash flows for periods one and two?

Discussion Question

13-A. The tax laws allow accelerated depreciation. Assume that an investment has equal cash flows in each year over its entire life.

Required: Without taxes, what timing of depreciation expense would you recommend to measure income appropriately? What does this imply about the tax depreciation deduction?

CHAPTER 14

A Manual

> But no one has ever won contemporary acclaim as a hero
> for wise economy and rationality, nor is his name celebrated
> in history books or attached to magnificent dams—our
> modern equivalent of pyramids.
>
> —*J. Hirschleifer, J. C. DeHaven, J. W. Milliman, Water
> Supply, Economics, Technology, and Policy. (The Rand
> Corporation, The University of Chicago Press, 1960), pp.
> v–vi.*

Each chapter adds additional complexities to the basic capital budgeting framework. Unfortunately, there is a very real danger of becoming immersed in excessive complexity and losing sight of some basic computations that can be very helpful in evaluating alternative investments. The objective of this chapter is to focus on the utilization of these basic calculations and to suggest that more complex calculations may be appropriate, but one should not ignore the basic calculations that are understandable and intuitively appealing.

We have attempted to make this chapter useful as the foundation for a capital budgeting manual. Its objective is to explain in detail some of the computations necessary to analyze investment proposals when the present-value method is used. No attempt is made to explain the theory behind the computations at this point. An attempt is made to give flexible procedures applicable to a wide range of situations.

The chapter is aimed at developing skill in the preparation of forms to be prepared or used by three different groups within the organization. In the first group are the sponsors of the project, the persons who are most familiar with what makes the project desirable and how it will operate. In the second group are the staff persons who must summarize the information obtained from the sponsors. The third group is top management, who must appraise and make the final investment decisions, using the information prepared for them as well as their experience and intuitive judgment.

This chapter focuses attention on the quantitative aspects of the investment decision, but it also allows for the presentation of descriptive material which tells in detail the pros and cons of different investment opportunities. It should be recognized that each computation requires assumptions about such things as the future level of general business activity, actions of competitors, costs of factors of production, and sales forecasts. Because there is a large amount of uncertainty connected with each of these factors, the resulting computations are, at best, only indications of future operating results.

The authors recognize that it is not possible to devise one set of forms that will be fully satisfactory to every company. The forms presented here are designed to illustrate the main calculations that would be desirable for an analysis of the cash flows that may result from an investment proposal. It is hoped that they will be useful in clarifying the application of the material discussed in earlier chapters and that they will provide a starting point from which a firm unfamiliar with the cash flow method of analyzing investments may proceed in devising administrative practices suitable for its special needs and its particular organizational structure.

The forms presented here can be used directly to compute absolute cash flows or to summarize the results of a relative cash-flow comparison. When the figures recorded are relative cash flows, it will ordinarily be necessary to use supplementary work sheets to perform the calculations. Some companies may prefer to have forms that allow space for at least two alternatives. The suggested forms can easily be revised to permit this procedure if it seems desirable.

The Capital Appropriations Request (Form A)

Suggestions from operating personnel on such problems as how to improve processes, replacement of equipment, and possible new products are, of course, desirable. The procedure described here attempts to ensure that all desirable suggestions are properly reviewed by higher levels of management and are given appropriate consideration. (Form A is on pp. 288–289.)

The sponsor of an investment project (outlays of over a given amount for plant, equipment, or other out-of-the-ordinary items may be classified as investment projects) should prepare Form A and the necessary supporting material. Because these forms are the basis of the quantitative analysis, they must be carefully prepared. It is recognized that many of the items on the forms are estimates, but they should be reasonable estimates. If the project is accepted, the estimates made on the forms will be reappraised after several periods of operations to determine whether they set forth objectives possible of attainment.

Technical assistance for filling out the forms should be available for the sponsor of the project. Because a staff person will have to process the data, it is desirable that contact be made with the Capital Budget Department early in the planning. A staff person should be assigned to assist in the preparation of the forms, to ensure that the data are ready for processing and that all alternatives have been considered. At the time the staff person is assigned to the project, a code number should be selected for the investment project so that references and files of information for the numerous investment projects can be easily identified and coordinated.

Explanations

A. Description and Justification Summary

The description and justification summary should give a brief statement of the nature of the project and of the type of benefits expected. For example: The purpose of this project is to replace a milling machine with a newer version in order to reduce labor costs per unit processed and to reduce the percentage of defective pieces. An incidental benefit is that there will be a 10 percent increase in capacity for this operation, but this benefit has not been quantified in the cash-flow analysis. Is the project to expand capacity, save labour, save energy, etc.?

B. Risk Analysis Summary

The purpose of the risk-analysis summary is to provide a basis for making a qualitative judgment of the risks to which the project is exposed. This may be done by describing under four main headings uncertain events which, if they occurred, would affect the value of the project to the company. The following classification of uncertain events might be used: (1) uncertain events whose occurrence would affect the cash flows of the project, but not the cash flows of other parts of the business; (2) uncertain events whose occurrence would affect the cash flows of the project and of other parts of the business in the same way; (3) uncertain events whose occurrence would have a favorable effect on the project but an unfavorable effect on the rest of the business (or an unfavorable effect on the project, but a favorable effect on the rest of the business); (4) the correlation of the project with the overall economy.

C. Cash-Flow Summary

The table heading for the cash-flow summary assumes that the cash-flow forecast will be based on the most probable outcome. If the forecast is actually made on this basis, the main assumptions about various uncertain contingencies should be explicitly described.

Frequently it will be desirable to prepare more than one cash-flow estimate, or to prepare the estimate on a different basis than the most probable outcome. In some respects the expected cash flow would be preferable. The expected cash flow is calculated by taking the sum of each possible outcome weighted by its probability. The calculation is likely to be worthwhile when the most probable outcome is also the best (or the worst) outcome. When net present values of better and worse outcomes are approximately symmetrically distributed around the most probable outcome, the latter can serve as a reasonable approximation to the expected outcome.

D. Summary of Economic Measures

1. *Most probable present values.* The first interest rate used represents the after-tax borrowing rate of the firm. The second rate represents an estimate of the average cost of capital. A graphical presentation of present values for all relevant interest rates should also be prepared.

2. *Internal rate of return.* The computation of the internal rate of return using the estimated cash flows gives the rate of interest for which the present value of the cash flows is equal to zero. The differences between the minimum acceptable return and the IRR gives one measure of the margin for error.

3. *Cash payback period.* The payback period of an investment may be an indication of the amount of risk, and is useful information. As a supplemental tool it is constructive. Used as the primary means of making accept or reject decisions, it is misleading. The payback period is the period of time required for the investors to recover their original investment.

4. *The effect on accounting income.* This is a measure that is computed by many companies. Management frequently wants to know the effect on income in the short run as well as the effect in the long run. The measure requires the preparation of pro-forma income statements.

Depreciation accounting becomes a crucial computation and component of the income computation. Unfortunately, conventional methods of depreciation accounting (straight-line or accelerated depreciation) can make a slow-starting, long-lived investment seem less desirable than it actually is by loading the early years with excessive depreciation and start-up expenses. It should be remembered that these methods are merely accounting conventions and may not be correct measures. However, the fact remains that the income statement will be affected by the accounting procedures, and management is interested in these effects.

E. Net Present Value Profile

This graph gives the net present value of the investment for different discount rates. It allows a delay in the choice of the rate of discount in the sense that management can inspect the figure and evaluate whether or not the investment is acceptable for a range of discount rates. For example, if the internal rate of return of the investment is 42 percent, we do not need to know the exact discount rate if the required rate of return is about 15 percent.

F. Net Present Value as Function of Life

The intersection of this graph with the horizontal axis gives a discounted payback break-even point. If the investment has a life equal to or greater than the intersection the firm at least breaks even on an economic basis.

The residual value of a project is the cash flows that will occur as a result of ending the project. Usually the size of the residual values will vary with the life of the project. Most projects have positive residual values resulting from liquidating working capital and selling unneeded fixed assets. Some projects may have negative residual values because of environmental factors (What will it cost to decommission a nuclear power plant?), the necessity to pay unemployment compensation, separation allowances, or to fund previously unfunded but vested pension benefits.

The chart showing net present values as a function of life should be clearly labeled to show whether it includes or excludes residual values. An analysis that

Form A

Capital Appropriations Request Form

Plant or division: Date:
Proposal: Code No.: _____

A. Description and Justification Summary:

B. Risk Analysis Summary:

C. Cash Flow Summary:
   Outlays are bracketed.   Estimated   Internal Rate
                             Life: _____   of Return: _____

Period	Most Probable Outcome		
	Dollars	Present Values Using	
	Cash Flows	Borrowing Rate ___ %	Cost of Capital ___ %
Total life			
Year 1			
Year 2			
Year 3			
Year 4			
Year 5			
Assuming life is 5 years			
Assuming life is 10 years			
Assuming life is 15 years			
Years 1–			

D. Summary of Economic Measures:
   1. Most probable present values using
      a. the after-tax borrowing rate (say 8%).
      b. the average cost of capital (say 15%).
   2. Internal rate of return _____.
   3. Cash payback period _____.
   4. The effect on accounting income in years:
      1
      2
      3

E. Net Present Value Profile

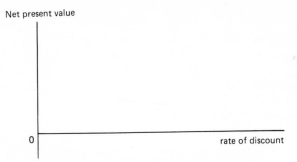

F. Net Present Value as Function of Life (discounted payback)

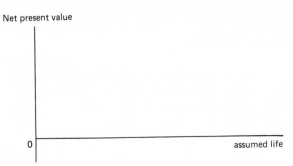

G. Approvals

Sponsor:_____   Prepared by_____

(Name)   (Title)   (Name)   (Title)

Routing	Initials	Date	Routing	Initials	Date
Engineering			R & D		
Production			Accounting		
Sales			Div. manager		
Market research					

excludes residual values is easier to prepare, since the cash-flow data previously estimated can be used. But such an analysis is incomplete. As a substitute for a complete analysis of residual values the sponsor might indicate whether they are likely to be large and whether they will be positive or negative. Of particular interest is the residual value associated with assuming a project life of zero years.

Residual values should always be calculated on an after-tax basis. The presence of corporate income taxes usually tends to increase the magnitude of the residual values.

G. Approvals

Space is provided in Form A to indicate the routing of the investment proposal from the original sponsor. The particular routing will, of course, vary from one organization to another. One of the main advantages of a systematic capital-budgeting procedure, however, is that it provides a framework for the coordination of planning in this area. For example, consider a proposal sponsored by the production manager for acquiring a new machine that will result in cost-saving and also in product improvements. An orderly routing of this proposal to the sales manager concerned will provide a routine mechanism for circulating information about the proposed product improvement. To take full advantage of the possibilities provided by systematic capital budgeting, the sales manager should be encouraged to attach a memorandum indicating whether or not the estimate of increased sales presented by the sponsor is reasonable, and include any other pertinent comments. The opportunities for consultation provided by this mechanism will frequently result in further improvements in the character of the investments actually submitted to the final authority. In any case it will provide valuable information for top management in weighting the important intangible factors almost invariably associated with an investment proposal. Later on, it can be used in comparing actual experience and costs with those predicted. This discipline will induce the sponsors to be more honest and precise in their estimates, and there will be less likelihood of overoptimism.

Estimating Cash Flows from Operations (Form A-1)

Section A

The sales figure should be the dollar value of sales expected to be recognized during the period under consideration. An adjustment for the timing of the actual collection of the cash receipts resulting from such sales is included by incorporating the change in Accounts Receivable under section C. If the product or products are partly substitutes for other products already produced by the company, an adjustment for the decline in cash proceeds resulting from the new product should be included under section D. The physical volume and price per unit underlying these calculations should also be included in a schedule.

Section B

In section B, the production cost estimates for each period should be those incurred for the *actual* rate of production expected during that period and *not* an estimated rate for the sales of the period. The actual rate of production during a period may be greater or less than the rate of sales, depending on whether inventories are increasing or decreasing. An adjustment for the cash flows resulting from the tax effect of inventory change is included in section E of Form A-1.

Section B should include all costs incurred because of the investment that would have been avoided if the investment had not been undertaken. Any cost that will be incurred, whether or not the investment is undertaken, should be excluded from this section. The value of the alternative uses of any resource for which the cost is unavoidable is discussed in section D.

Section C

In section C, adjustments are made for changes in cash tied up in working capital (other than partly or completely processed inventories). The procedures used in estimating these items are the same as procedures used in preparing cash budgets.

The increase in working cash balances should be the amount estimated as necessary to support the operations resulting from the investment. Excess cash reserves should not be included.

Ordinarily, the items in this section will total to a positive amount (indicating a use of cash) during periods in which the rate of operations is increasing. They will also show negative amounts (indicating a release of cash) during periods when the rate of operations is declining. Similarly, in a period of steady operations, this total will approach zero.

Section D

Most investment proposals will have some effect on the sales, costs, and use of resources in other parts of the organization. Section D is an attempt to allow for such influences. All estimates of cash flows should be on an after-tax basis. Frequently it will be extremely difficult to arrive at a satisfactory basis for estimating the items in this section because they are often difficult to measure, and wide differences of opinion may exist as to the importance of individual items. An example would be a new product that could partly substitute for an existing product of the firm. If no agreement can be reached as to the degree of substitution, the item may be listed as an intangible. There may be general agreement that sales of the old product will decrease, however, although the amount of the decrease may be in doubt. When some agreement can be reached as to the direction of the effect if not its size, it is usually wise to include an estimate of the minimal effect and to indicate in the intangible section of Form A that only a minimal estimate has been made and that there is disagreement as to the actual amount. In this case the estimate of the minimal decline in after-tax cash proceeds resulting from sales of the old product would be included under "Sales of other products."

Section E

Under section E, the item "increase in income taxes before allowing for depreciation" is computed and obtained from Schedule E. The tax rate used in that schedule should be the tax rate expected to apply in that year. The tax rate is applied to the taxable income (excluding the depreciation deduction) expected from the revenues and revenue deductions (associated with the investment) allowable for tax purposes. The tax section of the controller's department should be consulted in computing the taxable income to ensure that the assumptions made

Form A-1 *Cash Flows from Operations*

Proposal:

Code No._____

	Year 1 19__	Year 2 19__	Year 3 19__	Year 4 19__	Year 5 19__	Year 6 19__	Year 7 19__	Year 8 19__

A. Sales:

B. Expenses (except depreciation):
  Direct labor
  Materials
  Indirect labor
  Other manufacturing overhead
  Sales and promotion
  Administrative
  Other (include any investment-type outlays
    that are expensed for tax purposes in the period of outlay)

C. Increases (decreases) in current liabilities and
    nondepreciable assets (except finished inventory or work in process):
  Increase in accounts receivable
  Increase in inventory (supplies and raw material)
  Increase in working cash balances
  Decrease in current payables (subtract an increase)

D. Adjustments for cash flows in other parts of the business resulting from project:

Decrease in cash proceeds of other products

Cost of space utilized (cost of foregoing other uses)

Use of executive time

Other

E. Tax adjustments:

Increase in income taxes before allowing for depreciation (see Schedule E)

Tax savings from depreciation (subtract):

Outlays of cash $(B + C + D + E)$

F. After-tax cash flows from operations:

$[A - (B + C + D + E)]$

Form A-1 Schedule E: Computation of Income Tax (Without Allowing for Depreciation):

	Year 1 19__	Year 2 19__	Year 3 19__	Year 4 19__	Year 5 19__	Year 6 19__	Year 7 19__	Year 8 19__
Sales								
Deductions:								
Beginning inventory*								
Plus: Costs of production incurred†								
Total manufacturing costs								
Less: Ending inventory*								
Cost of goods sold								
Selling and promotion expenses								
Administrative expenses (directly associated with the project)								
Other								
Total deductions								
Amount subject to tax (sales less the total deductions)								
Increase in income taxes before allowing for depreciation (amount subject to tax times tax rate)								

* Includes work in process and finished goods.
† Excludes depreciation of the investment.

294

in preparing Schedule E are consistent with the method which will actually be used in preparing the tax returns.

Section F

Section F gives the after-tax cash flows from operations that result because of the investment. It should be inserted in column 1 of Form A-3 for further processing.

Computing the Annual Depreciation Charges (Form A-2)

Form A-2 is designed to compute the present value of the tax savings of the depreciation deductions.

Twice-Straight-Line Declining-Balance Method: No Salvage

When the twice-straight-line declining-balance method is used, the Internal Revenue Code allows the taxpayer to switch from this method to the straight-line method applied to the remaining book value and the remaining depreciable life. The switch should be made when the latter method is advantageous. The first step in computing the annual depreciation charges by this method is to determine in what year it will be advantageous to switch over. This can be done by dividing the expected life in years of the asset by 2, and adding 1 to the quotient. If the resulting number is an integer (whole number), it represents the year in which the switch takes place. If the resulting number is not an integer, the next largest integer is the year in which the switch takes place. For example, if the expected life is twenty years, the switch will take place in year 11, that is, $(20/2) + 1 = 11$. If the expected life is twenty-five years, the switch will take place in year 14, that is, $(25/2) + 1 = 13.5$.

If the expected life is n years, the first year's depreciation charge will be $2/n$ times the cost of the investment. The next year's depreciation charge is the preceding year's charge times $[1 - (2/n)]$, up until the year of the switch. The depreciation charge in the switch year and all subsequent years is simply the book value at the beginning of the switch year divided by the number of years of life remaining.[1]

Twice-Straight-Line Declining-Balance Method: With Salvage

Even though an asset has a positive expected salvage value, the first year's depreciation charge under this method is found by applying twice the straight-line rate to the book value of the asset (not the book value minus the expected salvage as in the straight-line or sum-of-the-year's-digits methods). Therefore, for the first few years of life the depreciation charge under this method will be the same whether or not the asset is expected to have any salvage value. The compu-

---

[1] The book value at the beginning of any year, up to and including the year in which the switch takes place, can be determined easily from the depreciation charge in the preceding year by multiplying that charge by $[(n/2) - 1]$, where n is the original life of the asset in years.

Form A-2:   *Computation of Annual Tax Savings from Depreciation*

Proposal:

Code No.:_____

Original Cost of Assets*_____   Expected Salvage Value_____

Expected Life of Assets_____   Depreciation Method_____

Year	(1) Depreciation Expense	(2) Tax Rate	(3) Tax Saving (1) × (2)	(4) Present- Value Factor	(5) Present Value of Saving (3) × (4)

* If the outlays are to be made over several periods, attach a schedule showing the timing of the outlays.

tations proceed either until the book value of the asset is equal to the expected salvage value or until it is advantageous to switch over to the straight-line method. However, if a switch takes place, the annual depreciation charge must then be figured by dividing the number of years of life remaining into the difference between the book value at the time of switch and the expected salvage.

Summarizing the Cash Flow Information and Computing Present Values (Form A-3)

Form A-3 is provided for the purpose of summarizing all the information on cash flows, and also to allow space for computing the present value of these cash flows by years.

If the sum of the present values of the net cash flows (total of column 5 of Form A-3) is positive, this means that the investment has passed the test of the present value of cash flows. It promises an internal rate of return greater than the company's rate of discount, thus warranting further consideration, and therefore would ordinarily be recommended to top management. Important exceptions to this rule may arise in the case of mutually exclusive investments (Is there another way of accomplishing the same objective that will be even more profitable?) or in cases where the investment has important intangible disadvantages. Similarly, investments with negative present values would not ordinarily be recommended to top management, but exceptions may occur in cases where the investment has important intangible advantages.

Instructions for Using Form A-3

General: Indicate outflows of cash (cash outlays) by bracketing the corresponding figures.

Column 1: This column is filled in from line F of Form A-1.

Column 2: Information for this column is obtained from Form A-2. Check to be sure that outlays charged to expense have been included in the appropriate line of Form A-1. Also include outlays for assets which are nondepreciable.

Column 3: This is the algebraic sum of columns 1 and 2. Enter this column in the appropriate column of Form A.

Column 4: Copy present-value factors from the appropriate column of Table A. The present-value factor for immediate outlays is always 1.000.

Column 5: This column is computed as the product of columns 3 and 4. If the entry in column 3 is bracketed, the entry on the same row in column 5 should also be bracketed to indicate net cash outlays. This column should also be entered into the appropriate column of Form A.

A Rough Cut for Uncertainty

One of the easiest procedures for introducing the consideration of uncertainty is to prepare two additional sets of forms A, A-1, A-2, and A-3. The basic set uses the most probable outcome. The two additional sets would use a pessimistic set of assumptions (say with a 5 percent probability that the actual results will be worse) and an optimistic set of assumptions (say with only a 10 percent probability that the actual results will be better than those contained in the calculations). If these two additional sets of forms are prepared there will be a 85 percent probability of the actual results being captured within the bounds that were established, and a 95 percent probability of exceeding the pessimistic estimate.

Form A-3:   *Summary of Cash Flows and Computation of Present Values*

Proposal:

Code No.:_____

Year	(1) Cash Flows from Operations	(2) Outlays for Assets	(3) Net Cash Flows (1) + (2)	(4) Present-Value Factors	(5) Present Value of Cash Flows (3) × (4)

Avoiding Errors Resulting from Improper Comparisons

Frequently the gains from making investments will be so large that no formal analysis is required to justify them. For example, a railroad must either replace a broken rail or abandon the line in which the broken rail occurs. The main danger to be avoided in analyzing such investments is the too-ready assumption that if only the present *necessary* investment is made, future cash flows will proceed indefinitely. If the investment is at all a borderline case, then what is required is a projection, not only of the present investment but also of the necessary additional investments that will be required in the future, thus making it possible to decide whether the whole series of these investments will be profitable. Otherwise, one may find oneself rebuilding an unprofitable road, rail by rail and tie by tie, with each small expenditure defended as absolutely necessary.

The sales and expenses estimates must always be on a comparative basis. That is, the estimates should attempt to measure the difference between what would occur if the investment under question were undertaken and if it were not undertaken. If the investment will reduce operating costs but not increase sales, then the appropriate entry for sales is 0. Similarly, if the investment will increase both sales and expenses, the amounts of increase of each should be estimated.

Because every estimate of cash flows involves an implied comparison, it is extremely important that a realistic situation be projected as the one likely to occur if the investment is not undertaken. The weakest professional football team would look good in a contest with an Ivy League college team, but no one would use the score of such a contest to judge the professional team's chances of winning the title in its own league. In the same way, an investment may look good if the cash-flow analysis is made by comparing its performance against an absurd and unprofitable alternative. Thus, in deciding whether to replace a five-year-old truck now with a new truck, we should not make the comparison as though a decision against replacement meant that the old truck would be operated for another ten years. Similarly, if operating the old truck is unprofitable from the viewpoint that using a common carrier would be less expensive, a decision to replace the old truck with a new model should probably be supplemented by comparing the costs of the new model with the costs of using a common carrier as well as with the costs of continuing to operate the old truck.

Because it is frequently difficult to decide in advance what alternative to the present investment is "realistic," it is important in such situations to try to analyze simultaneously all the significant available alternatives. If all available alternatives are considered, the choice of an unrealistic alternative as the common standard will not bias the results. Thus, if both replacing the old truck with a new model and using a common carrier are compared with the alternative of continuing to operate the old truck, it may become clear that, although buying a new truck may be preferable to continuing to operate the old one (that is, the present value of the cash outlays of the new truck will be less than those of the old truck), using a common carrier is better than buying the new truck (the present value of the cash outlays from using a common carrier is less than from buying a new truck).

Mutually exclusive investments are investments directly and adversely affecting the earning possibilities of each other (for example, ten different models of furnaces being considered when only one furnace is needed). With investments of this type the appropriate forms should be prepared for each investment. The net cash flow for each investment should be obtained and listed. Form A-3 can be used for this purpose. The investment with the highest present value is the most

desirable investment from the point of view of this one criterion. The best investment should be listed on Form A, but the fact that it is one of a set of mutually
exclusive investments should be indicated. If top management wants to review
the other possibilities, then the entire file of schedules should be presented with
this form as a cover sheet.

Using Depreciation Tables

Instead of computing the cash flows of each time period we can make use of
depreciation tables that give the present value of depreciation per dollar of
investment. These tables allow the use of the short-cut methods of evaluating
investments.

Assume the present value of depreciation for tax purposes is .546973. The
estimated life is twenty years, the rate of discount is .10, and the tax rate is .46.
The benefits will be a constant (before tax) $100,000 per year with an investment
that costs $800,000. The investment tax credit is .10. The computation steps are:

a. Compute the present value of the after-tax benefits as if there were no
depreciation tax shield:

$$100,000(1 - .46)8.5136 = 459,734.$$

b. Compute the present value of the tax savings assuming each dollar of depreciation expense has a present value of .546973:

$$800,000 \times .546973 \times .46 = 201,286.$$

c. Compute the investment tax credit:

$$800,000 \times .10 = 80,000.$$

d. Combine all the information to compute the net present value:

$$NPV = -800,000 + 459,734 + 201,286 + 80,000 = -58,980.$$

The net present value is negative and the investment should be rejected. The
above calculation assumes the investment tax credit does not reduce the tax
basis of the investment. The 1982 tax act requires that the tax basis be
reduced by half of the investment tax credit.

Bringing in Inflation

There is a very simple and theoretically correct way of bringing inflation considerations into the calculations. If the cash-flow forecasts reflect accurately the
firm's forecast of inflation, and if the discount rate is the nominal rate (the
observed cost of money), the net present value is a theoretically correct measure
of value. Thus if nominal dollars and a nominal discount rate are used, we have
taken inflation into consideration correctly.

But some managers will prefer to use real dollars and a real discount rate.

They can then vary the assumed rate of inflation and test the sensitivity of the decision to the inflation-rate assumption. This is not to imply that one could not accomplish the same type of analysis using nominal dollars and a nominal discount rate.

There follows a procedure for implementing the use of real dollars and a real discount rate.

The components of the nth years' cash flow should be multiplied by the factor $[(1 + i)/(1 + j)]^n$ where i is the rate of change in the price (or value) of the specific cash flow component and j is the inflation rate defined by the central office.

There are three basic situations:

$i = j$ in which case $(1 + i/1 + j) = 1$ and the cash-flow component of period 1 is a constant through time, relative to price-level changes. The real value does not change.

$i = 0$ in which case we have $(1 + i)/(1 + j) = 1/(1 + j)$, and the cash-flow component will decrease in real value through time if j is positive. Depreciation expense taken for taxes is a component that should be multiplied by $1/(1 + j)$ if real dollars are being used.

$i \gtrless j$ the price change for the component is different than the price level change. For example, if $i = .05$ and $j = .09$ we would have $(1 + i)/(1 + j) = 1.05/1.09$. If the expense of period one is $1,090, the expense of period two would be $1,050, and period three would be $1,011 if i and j stay constant.

The real dollars we obtain must be discounted using a real interest rate. If the time-value factor obtained from market measures is .15 and if the inflation rate is .09, the real interest rate is approximately .06, the difference between .15 and .09. More exactly the real rate is .055.

$$\text{Real Rate} = \frac{\text{Nominal Rate} - \text{Inflation Rate}}{1 + \text{Inflation Rate}} = \frac{.15 - .09}{1.09} = .055$$

If a $100 investment earns a .15 nominal return, the investor will have $115 at time 1. With .09 inflation the $115 is worth $115/1.09 = $105.50 in real terms. The investor has earned .055 real return.

Thus to use real dollars one should:

a. Multiply each period's nominal cash flow component by $[(1 + i)/(1 + j)]^n$ where n is the period where the cash flow takes place.
b. Estimate the appropriate real interest rate that is consistent with the market interest rates and the expected inflation.
c. Compute the net present value of the real cash-flow stream.

If there are no errors in calculation, the net present value obtained using this procedure will be equal to the net present value obtained using nominal dollars with a nominal discount rate.

Conclusions

This chapter has focused on the presentation of basic capital budgeting information. Two important reservations should be noted. First, we have avoided defining one discount rate as *the* hurdle rate. It is essential that management get to see a wide range of investments without good investments being cut off by lower levels of management because they did not meet an artificially high hurdle rate.

Second, the manual presented in this chapter does very little with risk analysis. Throughout the book suggestions will be made as to how to go about risk analysis. We have preferred not to offer a cookbook approach to risk analysis because we do not think the appropriate recipe currently exists. We would rather stick with the more detailed explanations scattered throughout the book than one recommendation. We do not recommend that risk be taken into account by adjusting upward the rate of discount for all investments.

Questions and Problems

There are no questions and problems for this chapter.

PART **THREE**

In this section we apply the more basic capital budgeting tools to different types of decisions that are more specialized than the first 14 chapters. Chapter 15 deals with buy versus lease, a specialized, but common, decision. Chapters 16–18 stretch one's imagination in thinking about investment decisions (investment timing, fluctuating rates of output and using additional information).

Chapter 19 acknowledges that complexities are introduced when a company makes investments in a foreign country.

Chapter 20 considers the special problems that arise when a government attempts to evaluate investments.

CHAPTER 15

Buy or Lease

Practical men, who believe themselves to be quite exempt from any intellectual influences, are usually the slaves of some defunct economist.

—*J. M. Keynes, The General Theory of Employment, Interest and Money (New York: Harcourt, Brace & Company, 1936), p. 383.*

When we use the term *lease* in this chapter, we shall be referring to a financial type of lease, that is, a lease where the firm has a legal obligation to continue making payments for a well-defined period of time. We are excluding from consideration the type of lease where an asset is acquired for a short period of time to fill a temporary need and then leasing is stopped. (A familiar example of this latter type of lease is the renting of an automobile at an airport.) We shall first deal with leases where there is a buy or lease option and the firm has already made the decision to acquire the asset. In this situation the buy or lease decision becomes a financing decision. We shall then discuss the situation where the firm must decide whether or not to buy, lease, or do nothing. We shall conclude that many financial leases are very similar to debt and should be treated in essentially the same manner as debt. A legally oriented person would be able to point out the differences between a lease and debt (especially when there is a failure to pay the required payments), but we shall concentrate on the similarities, and the decision maker can bring the differences into the analysis in a qualitative manner.

Borrow or Lease: The Financing Decision

We shall first assume a zero tax rate and analyze the financial aspects of the lease versus buy decision. Assume that a company is considering the lease or purchase of a piece of equipment. The firm has decided to acquire the equipment. The equipment will incur operating costs and will generate revenues that are unaffected by whether or not the equipment is leased or purchased. Thus for any lease or buy decision there will be many cash flows that are common to both decisions. There are, however, differences in the cash flows related to the method of financing the equipment. On the one hand, we have the cash flows associated with buying, and, on the other, the cash flows associated with leasing. Assume that the

00,000, and we can borrow the $100,000 at a cost of .05 per
 ~~;e~~ the equipment at a cost of $29,000 per year. Should we lease
 ~~;~~hat the equipment has an expected life of four years? Because
  acquire the asset, the only decision is the type of financing.

 ~~;~~y method of solving the buy versus lease decision with zero
taxes. Since ~~the~~ lease payments are $29,000 per year, the decision-maker can
make a phone call to the firm's bank and ask what payments would be required
annually for four years to repay a $100,000 loan. If the amount is less than
$29,000 (say, $28,201) then buy-borrow is more desirable than leasing (all other
things equal and zero taxes).

We can also compute the present value of the two alternatives. The present
value of the cash outlays with leasing is $29,000 times the present value of an
annuity for four periods using an interest rate of .05:

$29,000 \times 3.5460 = \$102,834.$

The present value of the immediate cash outlay associated with buying is
$100,000 and we again prefer buying (and borrowing). The present value of the
debt payments of $28,201 per year is also $100,000 if we use the borrowing rate of
.05.

If the discount rate used in the analysis is the same as the interest rate that the
firm would have to pay if it actually attempted to finance the purchase of the
asset by a loan, the particular loan repayment schedule chosen will not affect the
present value of the loan. Suppose that an amount K is borrowed, and interest of
k percent is paid on the principal plus accrued interest outstanding. Using k as
the discount rate, we find that the present value of the payments required to
repay the loan will always be K, whatever loan repayment schedule is chosen.

The purpose of this phase of the analysis is to determine whether the proposed
lease is financially attractive. Because the lease is presumed to require a contractually predetermined set of payments, it is reasonable to compare the lease with
an alternative type of financing available to the company that also required a
contractually predetermined set of payments, that is, a loan. In this analysis we
are only determining whether leasing or borrowing is preferable.

The conclusions to this point can be summarized as follows: We can buy a
piece of equipment for $100,000; it has an expected life of four years. The firm
could borrow the money to finance the purchase at an interest cost of 5 percent.
The equipment could also be acquired through a lease. If the annual lease payments were $29,000 per year for four years, there would be a financial cost
disadvantage to leasing, because the present value of the lease payments at 5
percent is larger than the amount that would have to be borrowed to finance the
purchase through borrowing. If the lease payments required were less than
$28,201, it could be shown that the lease would have a financial cost advantage.

Leasing and Financial Leverage

Suppose that an analysis along the lines described above led to the conclusion
that the lease had a financial cost advantage, but that the firm has the $100,000

cash available with which it can purchase the asset. One can imagine a company treasurer objecting as follows: "I agree that the lease incorporates very favorable financial terms. However, if we acquire the asset by leasing, we will be adding to the burden of fixed charges (including interest, debt repayment, other leases, and noncancellable overhead) that the company must bear. Entering into this lease would add to these fixed charges. For that reason I would prefer that we purchase the equipment outright if we decide to acquire it at all."

One can sympathize with the treasurer's desire not to increase fixed charges, and still disagree with the conclusion about the lease. The treasurer is correct in saying that, if the funds are used to purchase the asset, fixed financing charges will not increase. Fixed charges could also be kept constant, however, if the company leases the asset rather than buys it by applying the $100,000 available for purchase to a reduction in other fixed charges, say, by repaying some debt.

Accepting or rejecting a lease does not necessarily imply an increase or decrease in total fixed charges. A company can accept a financially advantageous lease without increasing its fixed charges if using debt would result in larger fixed charges. If the analysis indicates a financial disadvantage to the lease, and if the equipment is to be acquired at all, it should be bought. Whether the funds for the purchase should be obtained from debt, equity, or some mixture is a separate decision.

The analysis we have presented may be used to decide whether direct borrowing with an explicit debt security is more desirable or less desirable than leasing. We have not attempted to present an analysis here that proves debt is more or less attractive than other types of financing. We have kept the capital structure the same for both alternatives. Since a lease is debt, the buy alternative must also use debt to make the two alternatives comparable.

The analysis we have presented cannot be used to decide whether or not the asset should be acquired. Nor can it be used to decide whether the firm should have more or less financial leverage. If it has been decided that acquiring the use of the equipment is desirable, the analysis can be used to determine whether to buy or lease the equipment. The specific actions that should be taken will depend on whether or not additional financial leverage is desirable.

The analysis of this section is incomplete in several respects. It cannot tell us whether the equipment should be acquired at all, and it cannot tell us whether additional financial leverage is desirable.

In addition, the preceding analysis assumes a zero tax rate. It is necessary to take income taxes into consideration to make the analysis more realistic because income taxes will tend to influence the choice.

Buy or Lease with Taxes

Let us now consider the effects of a corporate income tax of 40 percent. With an income tax we shall want to put all cash flows on an after-tax basis, and because interest expense is deductible for tax purposes, we shall use an after-tax discount rate. If a discount rate of 5 percent was appropriate on a before-tax basis for borrowed funds, the corresponding after-tax rate can be assumed to be $(1 - .4)$ $.05 = .03$.

Because lease payments are a deductible expense in computing income subject to taxes, annual lease payments of $28,201 per year will become after-tax cash flows of $(1 - .4)$ $28,201, or $16,921, per year. The present value of the after-tax lease payments, using a 3 percent discount rate, will be $16,921 × 3.7171, or $62,897. This calculation can only be justified if the after-tax borrowing rate is being used.

The cost of the equipment is $100,000, and we shall consider borrowing that amount in order to finance purchase of the machine. The exact pattern of after-tax cash flows will depend on the debt repayment schedule. If the lender charges 5 percent per year, equal payments of $28,201 per year for four years would be one repayment schedule sufficient to repay the interest and principal on the loan. To put these cash flows on an after-tax basis for the borrower, we need to determine for each year how much of this amount will be considered a payment of interest and how much a repayment of principal. Only the interest expense portion is allowable as an expense for tax purposes. A different repayment schedule would lead to a different pattern of after-tax cash flows; but provided interest were computed on the remaining debt balance, the present value of the after-tax cash flows required to repay the principal and interest of the loan will always be $100,000. For example, suppose that the firm pays interest at $5,000 per year for four years and repays the principal in a lump sum at the end of the fourth year. The after-tax interest payments are $3,000 for each year. The present value of the debt is:

$$\$3,000 \times 3.7171 = \$\ 11,151$$
$$\$100,000 \times \ .88849 = \underline{\ \ \ \ 88,849}$$
$$\$100,000$$

We want to compute the cash flows of borrowing the funds to buy the equipment. If we subtract the present value of the positive cash flows associated with borrowing (plus $100,000) from the present value of the after-tax cash payments (a negative $100,000), we find that borrowing has a zero present value.

If we compare the $100,000 immediate cost of the asset with the $62,897 present value of the lease payments, there appears to be an advantage in favor of the lease, when taxes are taken into effect. However, depreciation tax deductions have not yet been considered. If the equipment is leased, the lessee cannot deduct depreciation. If the equipment is purchased, the right to deduct depreciation expense for tax purposes is obtained. With a tax rate of 40 percent, each dollar of depreciation expense will save $.40 of taxes. The present value of the tax savings resulting from depreciation will depend on the timing of the depreciation expense. If depreciation is charged on a straight-line basis over a four-year period, the value of the tax savings each year will be $10,000 (.4 × $25,000), and the present value of the tax savings will be $10,000 × 3.7171 = $37,171. Subtracting this from the cost of the investment gives a net present value of after-tax cash flows of

$62,829 for the borrow-and-buy decision. This is slightly less than the present value of the lease payments ($62,897).

If a more rapid method of depreciation were used, there would be a more clearly defined advantage in favor of buying. For example, if the twice-straight line, declining-balance method of depreciation were used, the present value of the tax savings could be computed, using Appendix Table D. With an interest rate of 3 percent and a life of four years, the present value of the tax deduction privilege is as follows: $100,000 × .4 × .946539 = $37,862. Subtracting this amount from $100,000 gives a net present value of $62,138 for buying and borrowing, which is $759 less than that for leasing.

The tax savings that result from charging depreciation if the asset is owned are not contractual in nature as are the other cash flows we are considering. Frequently, however, there is nearly as little uncertainty associated with the amount and timing of these cash flows as there would be in the case of a contract. Regardless of whether the particular piece of equipment performs as anticipated, the right to charge depreciation expense will generate tax savings as long as the firm as a whole has taxable income. Even if the firm does not have taxable income in any particular year, the tax-loss carry-forward and carry-back provisions of the law provide a high degree of assurance that tax savings will result, although their timing might change slightly. It should be remembered that there is also no guarantee that there will be enough revenues so that the full lease payments can be used to reduce taxes. The preceding analysis used the after tax borrowing rate. If any other discount rate is used the analysis is more complex.

One important difference in buying, compared to leasing, is that the firm that buys an asset owns the asset at the end of the time period of the lease. To the extent that the asset has net value at that time, this is also a net cash flow for the buy analysis. This difference will be illustrated when we discuss the buy–lease analysis for acquisition of land.

Is the Equipment Worth Acquiring?

In the previous sections we have shown that the present value of the cost (using twice-straight-line depreciation) of acquiring the equipment is $62,138 if it is bought, and $62,897 if leased. To decide whether it is worth buying the equipment, we need to compare the present value of the benefits with the net cost of $62,138.

Suppose that the equipment has a life of four years and would lead to before-tax cash savings of $30,000 per year. The after-tax cash savings are (1 − .4) × $30,000, or $18,000 per year. The present value of the tax savings that would result from the right to charge depreciation expense on the equipment has already been calculated and subtracted from the purchase price of the equipment, so these tax savings should not be considered again.

Using the after-tax interest rate of 3 percent, we find that the present value of the savings from operating the machine is

$18,000 × 3.7171 = $66,908.

Subtracting the present value of the costs of equipment from the present value of the savings, we have a net present value of $4,770 (that is, $66,908 − $62,138), indicating that we can accept the machine on a borrow-and-buy basis if we are willing to accept a return equal to the after-tax borrowing rate.

In situations such as this, we may be able to estimate the cost of acquiring the asset with a high degree of confidence, whereas the savings that would result from having the use of the asset are subject to considerable uncertainty. If the firm has not had experience with similar equipment, there may be some question as to whether the savings in cost per unit of product (or other measure of the rate of usage) will be as high as anticipated. In addition, there may be some uncertainty about the number of units of product that will be needed and about the equipment's anticipated life. For these and other reasons, a decision about whether or not the machine should be acquired will to a great extent depend upon management's judgments and risk preferences.

Risk Considerations in Lease versus Borrow Decisions

We began this chapter by suggesting that many leases are essentially financing instruments, comparable to debt contracts. It is desirable to consider the risks associated with the financial decisions (borrow or lease) we have been considering.

For practical purposes it may be reasonable, in some circumstances, to treat the financial cash flows as being free of any uncertainty. This assumption will not always be valid, as we shall see. If the likelihood of any substantial deviation from our predictions is very small, the time and cost involved in any detailed analysis of the uncertainties may not be worth the effort. The main justification for treating these financial cash flows as essentially certain for practical purposes is that their amounts and timing are largely determined by legal contracts that the firm acquiring the asset will have to fulfill. The lease contract determines the amounts and timing of the lease payments; the debt contract determines the amounts and timing of the debt repayments by the firm acquiring the asset. The depreciation expense charges allowed for tax purposes are not contractual, but they are fixed by law and in the presence of a large amount of other income and stable tax rates are reasonably certain.

Given a specific set of contracts, it might be possible to analyze the cash flows under various foreseeable alternatives. What would happen if the firm could not meet the legal requirements? Would it be declared bankrupt? Could the lease be terminated earlier? Could the loan be extended or renewed, or is it callable?

Possible changes in the corporate income tax rates are worth considering. If a decrease in the corporate income tax is anticipated, it will tend to raise the after-tax cash flows (benefits, net of costs) for any of the alternatives considered. The effect of this increase on the net present value of any alternative, however, will be somewhat offset by the fact that a decrease in tax rates will also tend to increase the appropriate after-tax discount rate and to decrease the value of the expense deductions, thus changing the relative desirability of buying or leasing. Some leases specify a minimum term and contain an option allowing the lessee to extend the lease for a longer time period. In these circumstances, uncertainty about how long the capital asset will be needed may influence the choice between leasing or buying.

The effects of these sources of uncertainty could be analyzed in detail if such an analysis were considered worthwhile. The following section illustrates such an analysis when there is uncertainty about how long the asset will be needed.

Leases with Uncertain Lives

Suppose that a piece of equipment is needed. The initial cost of the equipment, if it is bought, is $100,000. The equipment can be used for up to four years. After that time, a physical replacement would be necessary. The asset will be depreciated on a straight-line basis. If at any time the asset is no longer needed, it can be sold for its book value. The before-tax cost of borrowing is 5 percent, and a corporate income tax rate of 40 percent is applicable.

If the equipment is purchased, the cost will depend on how long it is used. Table 15-1 shows how the present value of the costs of owning the equipment will vary with the length of time that it is needed, assuming the salvage value of the equipment equals its book value.

TABLE 15-1.   *Present Values of Costs of Owning Equipment for t Years*

	Length of Time Equipment Is Owned (*t*)			
Item	1	2	3	4
Present value of purchase, outlays	$100,000	$100,000	$100,000	$100,000
Present value of tax shield from depreciation	9,709	19,135	28,286	37,171
Present value of salvage*	72,816	47,130	22,879	0
Net present value of costs	17,475	33,735	48,835	62,829

* Salvage for four successive years is as follows:

Year	Amount
1	75,000
2	50,000
3	25,000
4	0

Suppose that the equipment is also available on a lease basis. The lease requires rental payments of $28,333 per year [equal to (.6)($28,333) = $17,000 after taxes]. The lease is for a period of four years. It can be canceled by the lessee at the end of any annual period. There is a penalty of $5,000 if the lease is canceled at the end of the first year, but no penalty if canceled in later years. The lessor cannot cancel the lease.

Table 15-2 compares the present value of the costs of owning versus leasing for periods from one to four years.

TABLE 15-2.   *Present Values of Costs of Owning and Leasing*

	Number of Years Equipment Is Used			
	1	2	3	4
Owning	$17,475	$33,735	$48,835	$62,839
Leasing	19,417	32,529	48,086	63,191

If the equipment is used one year, the after-tax cost will be $17,000 plus 60 percent of the $5,000 or $20,000 with a present value of $19,417.

If it were certain how long the equipment would be needed, Table 15-2 could be used to decide whether to lease or buy. For example, if the equipment were needed for either one or four years, it would be less expensive to buy it. Suppose that four years is the most probable length of time the equipment will be needed. Although buying is less expensive if the equipment is needed for four years, it does not follow that buying is the best decision since there is some probability that the life will be different than four years.

Another approach is to calculate the expected present value of the two alternatives of buying or leasing. This requires assigning a probability to each year to reflect the likelihood that the equipment will be needed for that length of time, but not longer. Table 15-3 illustrates the necessary calculations for a hypothetical set of probabilities. On an expected present-value basis, the costs of leasing are less than the costs of buying. A change in probabilities might change the conclusion.

TABLE 15-3.   *Expected Present Values of Leasing versus Buying*

Number of Years Equipment Will Be Used	Probabilities	Buying		Leasing	
		Present Value of Costs	Probability × Present Value	Present Value of Costs	Probability × Present Value
1	.1	$17,475	$ 1,747	$19,417	$ 1,942
2	.2	33,735	6,747	32,529	6,506
3	.3	48,835	14,651	48,086	14,426
4	.4	62,839	25,136	63,191	25,276
	1.0		Expected PV = $48,281		Expected PV = $48,150

The Rate of Discount

Some analysts of the buy versus lease decision do not want to use the after-tax borrowing rate as the rate of discount. They argue that the residual value of the asset and the tax savings from depreciation deductions are not different than other cash flows associated with buy decisions and it is appropriate to test the sensitivity of the buy–lease decision to changing the rate of discount.

Leasing combines the elements of investment and financing. If we use a discount rate other than the after-tax cost of borrowing, the buy versus lease analysis becomes much more complex. The complexity arises because the debt flows are excluded from the buy analysis and included with the lease analysis. We want the two analyses to be comparable relative to the treatment of the debt flows and the tax deductions arising from the non-debt flows. The following analysis illustrates an approach to comparability by isolating debt effects in the lease, and excluding them from the cash flows to be discounted. The remaining cash flows are then compared to the buy cash flows at various interest rates.

Since depreciation is deductible if we buy, we want to isolate a deduction with leasing that is comparable to depreciation. With leasing the non-interest component of the lease payment is deductible (whereas with buying the principal payment associated with the debt is not deductible) and we shall treat this "principal" payment with leasing as being comparable to depreciation generated with the buy alternative. To compare the leasing and buy-borrow alternatives we will isolate out the cash flows that are not financing flows. These relevant flows are

a. Differences in the present value of the before-tax outlays of lease payments using the before-tax borrowing rate and the cost of the asset.
b. Differences in the depreciation tax shield of buying compared to the leasing counterpart of the depreciation tax deduction.
c. Investment tax credit (we will assume this is a neutral factor, since it may fall to either the lessee or lessor).
d. Residual value obtained if one buys.

Example

Assume an investment with a four-year life for tax depreciation purposes. The cost of buying is $100,000 and the asset can be leased for $31,547 per year. The borrowing interest rate is .10 and the tax rate is .40. The bank will lend $100,000 in return for four annual payments of $31,547.

The after-tax residual value at the end of four years is estimated to be $1,000. The debt amortization schedule for funds borrowed at .10 is

Time	Amount Owed	Interest	Principal*	Amount Owed End of Period
0	100,000	10,000	21,547	78,453
1	78,453	7,845	23,702	54,751
2	54,751	5,475	26,072	28,679
3	28,679	2,868	28,679	0

* Total amount paid is $31,547 each year. This column represents the "depreciation tax shield equivalent" of leasing or the implicit principal repayment.

Assuming straight-line depreciation, the tax savings of buy–borrow compared to leasing are

Period	Tax Deduction Buy Borrow	Tax Deduction Leasing*	Difference	Tax Rate	Tax Saving Cash Flow
1	25,000	21,547	3,453	.4	1,381
2	25,000	23,702	1,298	.4	519
3	25,000	26,072	−1,072	.4	−429
4	25,000	28,679	−3,679	.4	−1,472

* " Principai " payments treated as depreciation tax shield equivalents.

We can now prepare a table of cash flows of buy–borrow compared to leasing.

Period	Value of Buy–Borrow Depreciation Tax Savings Compared to Leasing	Residual Value	Cash Flows
1	1,381		1,381
2	519		519
3	−429		−429
4	−1,472	1,000	−472

Buy–borrow is more desirable than leasing for any positive rate of interest with the facts as given.

Now we assume that funds can be borrowed only at .12 resulting in an annual debt payment of \$32,924. The present value of the lease payments of \$31,547 using .12 as the discount rate is \$95,818. The debt amortization table for this amount of debt and a .12 interest rate is:

Period	Amount Owed Beginning of Period	Interest	Principal	Amount Owed End of Period
1	95,818	11,498	20,049	75,769
2	75,769	9,092	22,455	53,314
3	53,314	6,398	25,149	28,165
4	28,165	3,380	28,167	0*

* This is a rounding error.

There is $100,000 - 95,818 = 4,182$ less debt with leasing than with buying. We will take this as a positive flow for leasing at time 0. The relevant cash flows of buying and leasing are:

Period	Tax Deduction Buy–Borrow	Tax Deduction Leasing	Difference	Tax Rate	Tax Saving Cash Flow
1	25,000	20,049	4,951	.4	1,980
2	25,000	22,455	2,545	.4	1,018
3	25,000	25,149	−149	.4	−60
4	25,000	28,167	−3,167	.4	−1,267

We can now prepare a table of cash flows of buy-borrow compared to le.

Period	Value of Buy–Borrow Depreciation Tax Savings Compared to Leasing	Initial Value of Leasing and Residual Value of Buying	Cash Flows: Buy minus Lease
0		−4,182	−4,182
1	1,980		1,980
2	1,018		1,018
3	−60		−60
4	−1,267	+1,000	−267

Leasing is more desirable than buying at all positive interest rates. The advantage of the buy depreciation schedule cannot overcome the higher borrowing cost.

Leasing of Land

In making investment decisions we generally separate the cash outlay (the investment) from the financing (the source of the cash). The two are tied together by the use of a given rate of discount that measures the time value of money for the firm.

In leasing decisions involving land it may not always be possible to separate an investment from its financing, as they frequently become interwoven. In fact, in some situations it is not clear whether the land is being purchased or leased. Assume a situation where land is being leased but the company leasing the land can acquire the land for a nominal price at the end of twenty years. Are the lease payments for the use of the land, or are they for the use of money during the twenty-year period plus payments for the land?

We shall assume the following situation: Company A owns land and has offered to lease it to Company B at a cost of $80,242.65 per year for twenty years. After the twenty years A retains ownership of the land.

B is a very large, stable company, and A considers a lease with B to be the equivalent of a certain cash flow. Using the current long-term debt rate of .05, B finds the before-tax present value of the $80,242.65 per year to be $1 million.

A has offered to sell the land to B for $1 million. (A would not be taxed on this transaction.) Should B buy? B can obtain long-term funds at a cost of .05. These funds would have to be repaid at the end of twenty years. B's tax rate is .40, and B has taxable income.

B's analysis is as follows:

Cost of Leasing

The after-tax cost of leasing is obtained by multiplying the lease by the tax and present-value factors. The present value of an annuity for twenty periods using .03 is 14.8775.

After-tax cost of leasing = ($80,242.65) × .60 × 14.8755

$$= \$716,000.$$

Cost of Buying Land

The cost of buying is the immediate outlay of $1 million. The after-tax cost of leasing is less than the cost of buying. In considering the buy decision, however, we ignored the value of land at the end of the twenty years. The cash flow of the twentieth year may affect the decision.

We will compare the $716,000 after-tax cost of leasing with the $1 million after-tax cost of buying and compute the break-even value of land (at the end of twenty years). Let X be the value of the land after twenty years.

$$\$716,000 = \$1,000,000 - X(1 + .03)^{-20}$$

$$\$284,000 = .5537X$$

$$X = \$513,000.$$

Based on the after-tax computation, if the land is expected to have a value of less than $513,000, we should lease; otherwise we should buy. A change in the rate of discount would change the necessary residual value.

We can compare the two alternatives year by year. Assume that the land will be worth its present purchase price at the end of twenty years. The lease plan does not have a buy option.

With a balloon payment debt (constant interest payments) the after-tax cash flows (in dollars) are as follows:

	Year				
	1	2	3—19	20	
Lease	−$48,146	−$48,146	−$48,146	−$ 48,146	
Buy	− 30,000	− 30,000	− 30,000	− 30,000	interest
				− 1,000,000	repayment of debt
				+ 1,000,000	value of land
Difference (lease–buy)	−$18,146	−$18,146	−$18,146	−$18,146	

The $18,146 is the extra cost (per year) of leasing compared to buying. Assuming that the land does not depreciate in value through time, the advantage is clearly with buying. If the lease payments were $50,000 per year before tax, there would be indifference between buying and leasing.

Changing the timing of the debt repayment would not change the basic conclusion as long as the interest rate of the loan and the discount rate were equal.

Lease and Buy

There is an additional complication. Suppose that Company B can lease and then buy the land for $300,000 at the end of twenty years. A lease decision is preferable, based on the after-tax economic analysis. The Internal Revenue Service will probably object to the deduction of the lease payment for tax computations, however, and will consider a large part of the cash outlay as being a payment for the land (which it is).

Conclusions

Leasing of land is a possible method of financing the use of land. If we remove the mystery from the decision process, we find that leasing may be more desirable than purchasing if there exists a difference of opinion relative to the value of land upon termination of the lease. If Company A thinks the value of land will be increasing, it may lease to B at a price that seems low to B, if B thinks the value of the land will decrease. To the extent that the Internal Revenue Service allows lease payments for land to be deductible when there is an option to buy at a reduced price (that is, a price less than the expected market price) at the termination of the lease, there may be a tax advantage to leasing land. But this tax advantage cannot be automatically assumed, as it is likely that the lease payments will be interpreted to be a purchase payment, and thus not deductible for tax purposes.

Questions and Problems

Problems 15-1 to 15-6 are tied together and should be done consecutively. Assume a zero tax rate.

15-1. The ABC Company has contracted to make three lease payments of $10,000 each for the use of a piece of equipment. The first payment is to be made immediately and the other payments are to be made in successive years. Assume that the cost of debt is .05.

Required: Determine the debt equivalent of the lease payments.

15-2. Refer to problem 15-1. If we could borrow $28,000 and buy the equipment being leased, should we purchase it or lease it?

15-3. A piece of equipment cost $28,000 and has indicated cash flows of $10,200 a year for three years. The cash flows are received at the *beginning* of each year. With a time value of money of .10, is the investment desirable?

15-4. Assume that $18,000 could be borrowed with the funds being paid back as follows:

Period	
0	
1	$10,000
2	10,000

Refer to problem 15-3. Is the investment now desirable?

15-5. Refer to problem 15-3. If we could lease the equipment for $10,000 a year, with the first payment due immediately, would the equipment be desirable?

15-6. Refer to problem 15-3 and 15-4. If we could lease the equipment for $10,000 a year, would it be more desirable to buy and borrow or to lease the equipment?

15-7. The RSV Company can finance the purchase of a new building costing $1 million with a .05 bond that would pay $50,000 interest per year. Instead of buying the building, the company can lease it for $95,000 per year, the first payment being due one period from now. The building has an expected life of twenty years. The company has a zero tax rate.

Required: Should the company borrow and buy or lease?

15-8. The CDE Company is considering leasing a piece of equipment. There are three lease payments of $10,000 due at the end of each of the next three years. The equipment is expected to generate cash flows of $10,500 per year. Assume that the cost of debt is .05 and the income tax rate is .40.

Required: Combining the investment and its financing, prepare an analysis that shows the net present value of leasing.

15-9. Assume that the equipment of problem 15-8 can be purchased at a cost of $27,232.

Required: Should the equipment be purchased? Use sum-of-the-years'-digits method of depreciation for tax purposes. Use a discount rate of .03, but exclude the financing from the cash flows.

15-10. Assume that the life of a piece of equipment is uncertain, but that management believes that the probabilities of it having different lives and the present values of cash flows for buying and leasing for different assumed lives are as follows:

Assumed Life	Probability	Present Value (Buying)	Present Value (Leasing)
1	.2	−$20,000	−$ 2,000
2	.3	0	4,000
3	.4	20,000	10,000
4	.1	40,000	16,000
	1.0		

Required: Is it more desirable to buy or lease?

15-11. *The Rocky Boat Company*

The Rocky Boat Company is considering the purchase of a business machine. The alternative is to rent it. The purchase price of the machine is $100,000. The rental per year of the same machine is $30,000. The $30,000 includes all repairs and service. If the machine is purchased, a comparable service contract can be obtained for $1,000 a year.

The salesperson of the Business Machine Corporation has cited evidence indicating that the expected useful service life of this machine is five years.

The appropriate rate of discount of the firm is 5 percent per year. If rented, the company may cancel the lease arrangement with one month's notice.

Required: Prepare a comprehensive analysis for the controller of the Rocky Boat Company, indicating whether it is more desirable to purchase or rent. Assume a tax rate of zero.

15-12. The Rocky Boat Company (see problem 15-11) has purchased the machine on January 1, 1983. How should the machine be depreciated for tax purposes? Assume that a life of five years is acceptable to the Internal Revenue Service and that the tax is 52 percent. The net salvage value of the machinery is zero, because the removal costs are expected to be equal to the salvage proceeds. Use a .05 after-tax discount rate. (a) Prepare an analysis backing up your answer. (b) Recompute the investment decision of problem 15-11, taking income taxes into consideration and assuming that a five-year life is valid.

15-13. The Able Company was approached by a salesperson from the Rochester Machine Tool Corporation. Rochester had developed a machine that could mechanize an Able Company operation now performed by hand. The machine cost $30,000, had a life expectancy of three years, and could save Able Company $14,000 per year in labor costs. Able Company estimated that its hurdle rate was 10 percent. Its analysis of the cash flows that would result from using the machine is given in Table 15-4. Able Company was subject to a 50 percent corporate profit tax, and the machine would be depreciated on a straight-line basis for three years.

TABLE 15-4. *Cash Savings from Buying New Machine*

Annual reduction in labor expense	$14,000
Increased income tax liability before allowing for depreciation	−7,000
Tax saving from depreciation charge of $10,000 per year	5,000
Annual increase in cash flow from using machine	$12,000

Subjecting the purchase price and cash savings from using the machine to a present-value analysis, illustrated in Table 15-5, the Able Company decided it was not profitable to buy the machine.

When the Rochester Machine Tool salesperson heard of the decision, the machine was offered to Able on the basis of a three-year lease. The lease payments required were $11,223 per year. The salesperson pointed out that the extra $3,669 the company would pay if it leased the machine just covered the interest costs on the purchase price over a three-year period at 6 percent. Able figured that the lease payments of $11,223 were $2,777 less than the saving in labor cost. Half the difference would go to the government in extra taxes, but the company

TABLE 15-5.   *Cash Flow Analysis from Buying Machine*

Year	Cash Flow	Present-Value Factor (10% cost of capital)	Present Value
0	($30,000)	1.0000	−$30,000
1	12,000	.9091	10,909
2	12,000	.8264	9,917
3	12,000	.7513	9,016
	$ 6,000	—	−$ 158

would be ahead by $1,388 per year (half of $2,777) and no capital outlay was involved. They decided to lease the machine.

Only one Able executive disagreed. She felt that the company could borrow the money to pay for the machine from its regular banking connections and save even more money. Her calculations are presented in Table 15-6A, B. She was overruled because the other executives felt it was not wise for the company to incur any more debt.

Should Able buy or lease or neither?

TABLE 15-6 A.   *Cash Flows from Buying Machine and Borrowing Purchase Price from Bank at 6 Percent*

Item	Year 1	Year 2	Year 3
Reduction in labor expense	$14,000	$14,000	$14,000
Increased interest expense	−1,800	−1,235	− 635
Increase in income tax before allowing for depreciation	−6,100	−6,383	− 6,683
Tax savings from depreciation	5,000	5,000	5,000
Cash flows from operations	11,100	11,382	11,682
Repayment of loan principal	−9,423	−9,988	−10,589
Net cash flows	$ 1,677	$ 1,394	$ 1,093

TABLE 15-6 B.   *Comparison of Present Values from Leasing versus Buying and Borrowing*

Year	Lease Cash Flows*	Lease Present Values	Buy and Borrow Cash Flows†	Buy and Borrow Present Values	Present-Value Factors (10%)
1	$1,388	$1,262	$1,677	$1,525	.9091
2	1,388	1,147	1,394	1,152	.8264
3	1,388	1,043	1,093	821	.7513
	$4,164	$3,452	$4,164	$3,498	

* ($14,000 − 11,223) × .5 = $1,388.
† See Table 15-6A.

15-14. The ABC Company can purchase a new data-processing machine for $35,460 or rent it for four years at a cost of $10,000 per year. The estimated life is four years. The machine will result in a saving in clerical help of $11,000, compared to the present manual procedure. The corporation has a hurdle rate of .10 and a cost of available debt of .05. The incremental tax rate is .52. Assume that there is no investment tax credit. The following analysis was prepared for the two alternatives:

Buy			Year			
	0	1	2	3	4	Total
1. Outlay	−$35,460					
2. Savings before tax		$11,000	$11,000	$11,000	$11,000	
3. Depreciation*		17,730	8,865	4,432	4,432	
4. Taxable income (2 − 3)		(6,730)	2,135	6,568	6,568	
5. Tax on savings (.52 of income)		(3,500)	1,110	3,415	3,415	
6. Net cash flow (2 − 5)		14,500	9,890	7,585	7,585	
7. Present-value factors (using .10)		.9091	.8264	.7513	.6830	
8. Present values (6 × 7)	−$35,460	$13,182	$ 8,173	$ 5,699	$ 5,181	−$3,225

* Assume the depreciation of each year for tax purposes is computed, using the twice-straight-line method of depreciation.

Lease			Year		
	0	1	2	3	4
Gross savings		$11,000	$11,000	$11,000	$11,000
Lease payments		−10,000	−10,000	−10,000	−10,000
Savings before taxes		1,000	1,000	1,000	1,000
Income tax		520	520	520	520
Net savings		$ 480	$ 480	$ 480	$ 480

"Buy" was rejected because the net present value was minus $3,225. The lease alternative was accepted because the present value of the savings is positive for any positive rate of discount.

Required: Comment on the decision to lease. Prepare a report for the president of your firm on the relative merits of leasing and buying of depreciable assets and land.

15-15. The ABC Company has decided to acquire a piece of equipment but has not yet decided to buy or lease. The lease payments would be $33,670 paid annually at the end of each year. If purchased at a cost of $90,000 the equipment would be financed with debt costing .05, which can be repaid at any rate desired.

The life of the equipment is three years. The lease is a firm commitment to make three payments. There is no salvage value. Should the firm lease or buy–borrow? There are no taxes.

15-16. (*Continuing problem 15-15.*)   Assume that the firm has not yet decided to purchase (or lease) the equipment. The benefits (known with certainty) are $35,000 per year. The firm has a hurdle rate of .10. There are no taxes. The firm will use .05 debt if the asset is purchased. Should the firm buy or lease? The firm can still lease at $33,760 per year.

15-17. (*Continuing problem 15-15.*)   Assume that the lease terms are $33,049 and the firm can also borrow at .05 (the repayment would be $33,049 per year). Without taxes the firm is indifferent to borrowing and leasing. If the tax rate is .4, does this make buy–borrow or lease relatively more desirable?

15-18. The A Company can borrow funds at .10 (the after tax borrowing rate is .06). It has a marginal tax rate of .4. There is a 10% investment tax credit.

The company is considering buying equipment at a cost of $1,000,000 or leasing it at a cost of $101,853 per year for twenty years. The life of the equipment is twenty years with $80,000 expected salvage. The equipment can be depreciated for taxes using a twenty-year life. The implicit before-tax cost of the lease is .08 (the present value of $101,853 a year for twenty years is $1,000,000). $B(20, .06) = 11.4699$ $B(20, .08) = 9.8181$

PV of Deprec. (20, .06) SYD = .6768

PV of Deprec. (20, .08) SYD = .6061

Assume net salvage is taxed as ordinary income. The loan is equal payment debt.

Required:
  a. The after-tax cost of leasing (PV) is $_____.
  b. The net cost of buying (PV) is $_____.
  c. Assume the above equipment will save $170,000 per year (before tax). Should the equipment be acquired? Explain.

15-19. The RDV Company has a weighted average cost of capital of .15. Additionally, all of the facts applicable to the A Company (see 15-18) apply to RDV as well.

Required:
  a. The after-tax cost of leasing (PV) is $_____.
  b. The net cost of buying (PV) is $_____.
  c. Assume the above equipment will save $170,000 per year (before tax). Should the equipment be acquired? Explain.
  d. Assume that instead of equal payment debt, there is annual interest payments and a final period payment. How does this change the analysis?

15-20. The Railroad Company leases equipment. It has computed its weighted average cost of capital to be .11 and it requires a return equal to that on investments.

It charges for leased equipment based on cost of equipment and maintenance charges. The contracts are long-term contracts (four years) and the lease payments are to be constant each year.

The firm has computed its maintenance cost to be $3,000 in a year and increasing at a rate of 10% per year.

Management has requested that you compute an equal payment each year (payment at the end of each year) so that the firm will "earn an .11 return on its investment."

Required: Prepare a report with a recommendation as to how much should be charged per year for maintenance.

15-21. The Allen Company is faced with the decision whether to buy or rent data-processing equipment. The initial outlay for the equipment is $380,000 if purchased. The rentals are $100,000 per year and are cancelable on one month's notice by the Allen Company. Similar service contracts may be obtained if the equipment is purchased or rented.

The time value of money is 10 percent. The income tax rate is zero.

The best estimate of service life is five years, but an analysis of the life of equipment of a similar nature indicates that the life may be as follows:

Year	Probability (%)
1	0
2	1
3	2
4	25
5	40
6	30
7	2
8	0

Required: Should the equipment be purchased or rented?

15-22. The Fun City Chemical Corporation is considering a new machine. It has a life of five years. The machine would replace an older model that is less sophisticated. The new machine is expected to generate after-tax cash savings in the form of lower labor and material expense of $30,000 per year for five years, which is its economic life. The risk-adjusted present value of these cash flows is $115,000.

The Corporation is subject to a corporate tax rate of 40 percent. It has an arrangement with an equipment financing subsidiary of its lead bank through which it can make equipment collateral loans of up to seven years at an interest rate of $8\frac{3}{8}$ percent. The corporation considers that it has an optimal capital structure.

The equipment described above can be obtained through a five-year fixed commitment lease requiring payments of $42,350 per year. The first payment would be due one year from the date the equipment is delivered.

a. What is the debt equivalent of the lease?

b. If the equipment were available only through a lease, what action would you recommend?

15-23. (*Continuation of 15-22.*)   Suppose now that the equipment could also be purchased for $150,000. If purchased the equipment could be depreciated for tax purposes using the straight line method with a five year life and no salvage value. The investment tax credit does not apply. What action would you recommend?

15-24. The DC-95 is a typical data-cruncher model produced by KRUNCHEM, Inc. It sells for $1,000,000.

You have been hired as a pricing analyst for KRUNCHEM. Your boss is the marketing manager. Your first assignment is to estimate the after-tax cost that would be incurred by a typical customer who bought a DC-95 for $1,000,000. Assume the customer is a corporation paying income taxes at an average rate of 30 percent (the marginal rate is 52 percent). The customer's hurdle rate for new investments is 15 percent. It can borrow, on a long-term basis, at 10 percent.

The DC-95 is expected to have a salvage value of $100,000 in 10 years. Assume the difference between the cost and salvage value can be depreciated on a straight-line basis for ten years. There is no investment tax credit.

Find the after-tax cost of buying for the typical customer described above.

15-25. (*Continuation of 15-24.*)   The sales manager would rather lease machines than sell them. Your assignment is to develop a ten-year annual-payment lease such that the customer will save 5 percent after taxes by leasing rather than buying. (The lease will contain an option to buy the DC-95 in ten years for $100,000.) What annual payment should be specified in the lease?

Discussion Questions

15-A. Conventional wisdom says that high-tax entities should own assets and lease them to zero-tax entities.

Explain the conditions necessary for this position to be correct and the limitations in the conclusion.

Make clear your assumptions.

15-B. "To determine whether a contract is acceptable, discount the cash flows using the cost of capital." Is this reasonable if the contract is a debt contract? A lease contract?

CHAPTER 16

Investment Timing

Bill Shankly, manager of Liverpool's defending champions in the English Soccer League, comments: "The way some people talk about modern football [soccer], anyone would think the results of just one game was a matter of life and death. They don't understand. It's much more serious than that."
—*The New York Times, p. 7. January 13, 1974.*

In this chapter the term *timing* will be used to refer to decisions about when a new investment should be undertaken and when an investment should be terminated. For certain categories of investment decisions, the question of when to start is critical. An investment may seem desirable if the only alternatives considered are to accept or reject the investment now. If the alternative of undertaking the investment at a later time is possible, however, that may be preferable to accepting the investment now. In principle, the timing problem could be handled by considering a mutually exclusive set of alternatives: undertaking the investment now, or undertaking it one period from now, or two periods from now, and so on. But more efficient techniques for approaching this problem are available. We shall consider some of these in this chapter.

Frequently, in making investment decisions the useful life of the investment must be determined. This can be accomplished in at least two ways. First, the desirability of an investment may be affected by the estimate of its useful life. Thus the estimated profits from growing trees are critically affected by assumptions about when they will be harvested. Second, the decision to undertake an investment may require terminating an existing investment. Planting a new crop of trees may require harvesting the existing stand of trees; or buying a new car may require selling the old one. In these cases the salvage value of the existing investment, the costs incurred, and the revenues that might be received if it were not scrapped now will influence the decision of when to undertake the new investment.

In timing problems the relationships among the cost and revenue streams of the various alternatives are frequently complex. But the basic principles at work are not difficult to understand. To help focus on the basic principles, we begin with a simple example of a class of situations in which timing problems are important, but no investment decision is involved.

Basic Principles of When to Start and Stop a Process

In figure 16-1, the curve R represents the contribution to overhead (revenues minus variable costs) that will be generated at time t of a day if the business is operating. The line F represents the fixed costs that could be avoided if the business were not operating at time t. On the X axis time is measured from zero to twenty-four hours.

Let us first make the assumption that the business must operate continuously around the clock if it operates at all. For example, a private water works company may be obliged to operate twenty-four hours a day if it operates at all, even though the contribution to overhead produced during certain nighttime hours does not even cover the avoidable fixed costs of the time period. In these circumstances there is no timing problem, and it will be economically desirable to operate only if the total area under the R curve exceeds the total area under the F curve over the entire cycle of operations.

In some situations the manager is free to decide when to operate and when to shut down. For example, the owner of a supermarket may not be obliged to operate on a twenty-four-hour basis. In this situation, considering only explicit revenues and costs, the enterprise should operate only during the interval in which the contribution to overhead from operations exceeds the avoidable fixed costs of operating. In Figure 16-1 this interval extends from t_1 to t_2. The operations should start at t_1 and cease at t_2, since between these points $R \geq F$; in other words, the contribution exactly equals or is larger than the avoidable fixed costs.

The conclusion from these illustrations is that if there is a choice about when to start and stop an operation, it should be started when revenues equal costs and are rising; and it should be stopped when revenues equal costs and are falling.

As we shall see, this simple rule is really applicable to all the situations considered in this chapter. In applying the rule, the conceptual difficulties center on identifying the relevant revenues and costs.

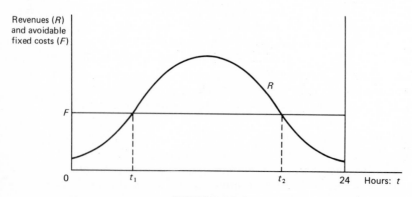

FIGURE 16-1

Growth-Type Investments[1]

Suppose that a firm owns a tract of land and is considering planting a crop of trees. It wishes to determine the net present value of that investment. Since the net present value will depend on when the trees are harvested, an estimate of that date is required. If the firm makes the investment, it is prepared to harvest the trees when the net present value of the investment is maximized.

Let

$f(t)$ = net revenue (net of all finishing expenses) obtainable if the trees are harvested in year t.

$f'(t)$ = slope of $f(t)$, that is, the rate at which the obtainable net revenue is changing with time.

i = market rate of interest.

C = cost of planting trees.

e^{-it} = present-value factor for time t.

P = net present value of the investment.

The net present value of the investment if the trees are harvested at time t is

$$P(t) = -C + e^{-it}f(t). \tag{1}$$

The determination of the optimum time to harvest the trees can be seen in Figure 16-2. The curve $f(t)$ begins at 0 and increases, rapidly at first, and then more gradually. The paths $a_0 a_1$ and $b_0 b_1$ are time-transformation curves that enable us to convert future values into present values at the assumed interest rate i. The present value of a_1 is a_0, and the present value of b_1 is b_0. The time transformations have a slope equal to i times their height. (Their heights are $a_0 e^{it}$ and

---

1 This section is based in part on Harold Bierman, Jr., "The Growth Period Decision," *Management Science,* 14, No. 6, Feb. 1968.

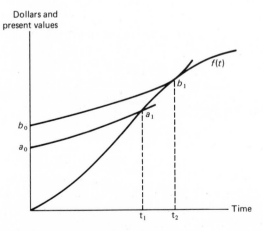

FIGURE 16-2

$b_0 e^{it}$.) the present value of the investment is maximized if the trees are harvested at t_2, when the value of the trees is b_1 and the net present value of the investment equals $(-C + b_0)$. At t_2 the $f(t)$ curve is tangent to the time-transformation curve. It follows that the slope of the $f(t)$ curve is $if(t_2)$ at t_2. Thus the value of t at which the present value of the investment is maximized must satisfy the condition that

$$f'(t) = if(t).$$ (2)

Recall that $f'(t)$ is the increase in the value of the trees per year. Thus the condition for an optimum is that the increase in the value of the trees must equal the interest rate times the value of the trees.

In terms of the criteria for stopping referred to in the previous section, the increase in the value of the trees if they are not harvested corresponds to the revenues, and the interest on the value of the trees corresponds to the fixed cost that can be avoided by harvesting.

The rule previously described for deciding when to harvest ignores the value of the land on which the trees are planted. If additional land of comparable quality is available in any desired amount at no cost, the economic value of the land is zero, and it need not be considered in deciding when to harvest trees growing on it.

Ordinarily, the value of the land must be considered. Suppose that if the trees were harvested the cleared land would be worth an amount $V(t)$ at time t. In that case the avoidable fixed costs incurred if the trees are allowed to grow include both the interest on the value of the standing trees and the interest on the value of the land. In these circumstances, a necessary condition that should be met when the trees are harvested is

$$f'(t) = i[f(t) + V(t)].$$ (3)

Of course, the value of the land depends on its best available use. For example, if the best use of the cleared land is for farming, then $V(t)$ should reflect the value of the land in that use.

Suppose, however, that the best use of the land is growing trees. Then, although equation (3) is still formally correct, it is not very helpful. When the trees are harvested depends on the value of the land; but the value of the land will depend on how often the trees growing on it can be harvested. In this case the value of the land must be determined on the assumption that the trees growing on it are harvested and replanted at intervals that maximize the value of the land.

We have already shown that the present value of one crop of trees, if they are harvested at the end of t years, is

$$P(t) = -C + f(t)e^{-it}.$$

Assume that the trees are replanted every T years and that we want to determine the optimum value of T. Let $V(T)$ be the present value of the land under these circumstances. Then $V(T)$ is determined as follows:

$$V(T) = P(T) + P(T)e^{-iT} + P(T)e^{-i2T} + P(T)e^{-i3T} + \cdots.$$

Summing this infinite series,

$$V(T) = \frac{P(T)}{1 - e^{-iT}} = \frac{-C + f(T)e^{-iT}}{1 - e^{-iT}}. \tag{4}$$

We want to select the value of T that maximizes $V(T)$. It can be shown that the value of T that maximizes $V(T)$ satisfies the following relationship:

$$f'(T) = i[f(T) + V(T)]. \tag{5}$$

In practice, the best way to determine the optimum value of T is by trial and error, using equation (4). Equation (5) is basically the same as equation (3), but in deriving equation (5) we have given an explicit method of determining the value of the land in its use for growing trees. Equation (5) can be interpreted as follows: a crop of trees should be allowed to grow until the annual increase in its value declines to the point where it is equal to the market interest rate times the sum of the value of the current stand of trees plus the present value of the future crops of trees that could be grown on the land if the present crop were harvested now.

Tree Farm Example

Suppose that the net realizable value of a crop of trees on a particular parcel of land as a function of their age is given by the following equation:

$$f(t) = -350 + 60t - .5t^2, \quad \text{for } 10 \le t \le 30. \tag{6}$$

Assuming a continuously compounded rate of interest of 5 percent per year, Table 16-1 shows the net realizable value of the trees from one growth cycle at various ages, their percentage rates of growth, and their present value. If the value of the land is ignored, the trees would be allowed to grow until the rate of increase in their value declines below 5 percent (in year 23). This is the age at which the present value of the realizable value of the trees is maximized.

Suppose, however, that after the trees were harvested the land could be sold for $500 or converted to some other use whose value was $500. In that case the amount realized when the trees were harvested would be $500 + f(t)$.

Table 16-2 shows the appropriate calculations in this case. Under these circumstances it would pay to harvest the trees when they are between the fourteenth and fifteenth year. After that time the rate of increase in the value of the trees is less than 5 percent of the amount that could be realized by cutting the trees and putting the land to some other use. This is also the age at which the present value of the land and trees is maximized.

If the most economical use of the land is to grow trees, the value of the land in this use must be determined. But the value of the land depends on the frequency at which crops are harvested and the costs of planting a new crop. Table 16-3 shows the value of the land when crops are harvested at various ages, if the cost of planting is $50. This is an application of equation (4). Harvesting in year 17 maximizes the present value of the land.

TABLE 16-1

Age of Trees t	Realizable Value f (t)	Annual Increment in Value f'(t)	Rate of Increase in Value f'(t)/f (t)	Present-Value Factor e^{-it}	Present Value $f(t)e^{-it}$
10	$200	$50	.2500	.6065	$121.30
11	250	49	.1960	.5770	144.25
12	298	48	.1611	.5448	162.35
13	346	47	.1358	.5220	180.61
14	392	46	.1173	.4966	194.67
15	438	45	.1027	.4724	206.91
16	482	44	.0913	.4493	216.56
17	526	43	.0817	.4274	224.81
18	568	42	.0739	.4066	230.95
19	610	41	.0672	.3867	235.89
20	650	40	.0615	.3679	239.14
21	690	39	.0565	.3499	241.43
22	728	38	.0522	.3329	242.35
23	766	37	.0483	.3166	242.52*
24	802	36	.0449	.3012	241.56
25	837	35	.0418	.2865	239.80
26	872	34	.0390	.2725	237.62

* Maximum present value.

TABLE 16-2

Age of Trees t	Realizable Value of Land and Trees 500 + f (t)	Annual Increment in Value f'(t)	Rate of Increase in Value $\frac{f'(t)}{500 + f(t)}$	Present-Value Factor e^{-it}	Present Value $e^{-it}[500 + f(t)]$
10	$ 700	$50	.0714	.6065	$424.55
11	750	49	.0653	.5770	432.75
12	798	48	.0602	.5448	434.75
13	846	47	.0556	.5220	441.61
14	892	46	.0516	.4966	442.97
15	938	45	.0480	.4724	443.11*
16	982	44	.0448	.4493	441.21
17	1,026	43	.0419	.4274	438.51
18	1,068	42	.0393	.4066	434.25
19	1,110	41	.0369	.3867	429.24
20	1,150	40	.0348	.3679	423.09
21	1,190	39	.0328	.3499	416.38

* Maximum present value.

TABLE 16-3

Age of Trees t	Net Present Value of One Crop of Trees Growing for t years $P(t) = -50 + e^{-it} f(t)$	Annuity Factor $\dfrac{1}{1 - e^{-it}}$	Value of Land $\dfrac{P(t)}{1 - e^{-it}} = V(t)$
10	$ 71.30	2.54	$181.10
11	94.25	2.36	222.82
12	112.35	2.20	246.81
13	130.61	2.09	273.25
14	144.67	1.99	287.39
15	156.91	1.90	297.41
16	166.56	1.82	302.46
17	174.81	1.75	305.29*
18	180.95	1.69	304.94
19	185.89	1.63	303.09
20	189.14	1.58	299.22

* Maximum present value.

Table 16-4 applies equation (5) to this situation. Both equations (4) and (5) result in an optimum life of seventeen years per crop (or slightly more if fractional years are allowed).

TABLE 16-4

t	V(t)	f(t)	f'(t)	$\dfrac{f'(t)}{V(t) + f(t)}$
10	$181.10	$200	50	.1312
11	222.82	250	49	.1036
12	246.81	298	48	.0881
13	273.25	346	47	.0759
14	287.39	392	46	.0677
15	297.39	438	45	.0612
16	302.46	482	44	.0561
17	305.29	526	43	.0517*
18	304.94	568	42	.0481
19	303.09	610	41	.0449
20	299.22	650	40	.0421

* Closest to .05.

Equipment Replacement

The question of when to replace an existing piece of equipment with another machine that will perform the same function is very similar to the question of when to harvest a crop of trees. One difference is that in the case of trees we are seeking to maximize the net present value of the revenues that we can receive from the land, whereas in the equipment-replacement problem we are seeking to minimize the net present value of the costs that will be incurred from owning and operating a sequence of machines.

In the machine problem, the costs incurred by retaining the existing machine are the costs of operating it for the current period (including any necessary repairs and maintenance), the decline in its salvage value during the current period, and the interest on the current salvage value of the existing machine. If the machine is retained for one additional period, we benefit by delaying for that length of time the costs of acquiring and oeprating all subsequent replacement machines. The magnitude of the latter cost is measured by the market interest rate times the present value of the costs of acquiring and operating all subsequent replacements. This present value will depend critically on how long each subsequent replacement equipment is retained. Thus the decision about when to replace the current machine requires an estimate of the economic value of its anticipated replacements, just as the decision about when to harvest a crop of trees depends on the future use that will be made of the land occupied by the trees.

The Strategy of Capacity Decisions

One of the most important decisions a corporation can make is the capacity decision. How large a plant should be built and when it should be built are two crucial decisions. An intelligent capacity strategy will greatly enhance a firm's profitability. Excess capacity and the resulting large capital costs lead to severe drops in profit. On the other hand, a shortage of capacity gives competition an opportunity to increase their share of the market and to come more rapidly down their learning curves.

We shall consider capacity strategy from several points of view, first, assuming a firm in isolation, and then considering a firm in a competitive environment. Elements of game theory will be used to illustrate the complexity of the decision.

The Basic Decision

The basic decision presents the problem of choosing the best of a set of mutually exclusive investments. Each of the alternatives provides a different timing for building capacity.

Consider the following two alternatives:

	0	1	2
A	−10,000		−14,400
B	−18,000		

With alternative A a small addition is made at time 0; then a second addition is made at time 2. With alternative B we build the same capacity at time 0 as we obtain over the two periods with alternative A.

Which alternative is better? Assume the firm has a time value factor of .20. The present value of A's outlays is $20,000 while B costs only $18,000. B is thus better than A, for in addition to costing less, B also supplies a cushion of capacity over the two-year planning period.

With a time value factor enough higher than .20 the preference could shift to A. For example, if the time-value factor is .40 the present value of A is $17,347. This causes A to be more desirable than B.

Performance Measurement and the Timing Decision

The timing decision for alternatives A and B was made on a straight economic basis (the maximization of the present value of the stockholder's position). It is well known that actual decisions are multidimensional with other factors being considered besides the net present value.

Assume the firm's time value factor is .20 so that B is more desirable than A. We now add the positive cash flows to the analysis.

	0	1	2	3	4
A	−10,000		−14,400		
		+6,000	+ 7,200	+8,800	+10,080
B	−18,000	+6,000	+ 7,200	+8,800	+10,080

Assume a four year life for the product being made and the use of straight-line depreciation. We have the following data for years 1 and 2 for the two investments (assuming a two-year life for the first unit of A and a four-year life for B):

	Year 1		Year 2	
	A	B	A	B
Revenues	6,000	6,000	7,200	7,200
Depreciation	5,000	4,500	5,000	4,500
Income	1,000	1,500	2,200	2,700
Investment	10,000	18,000	5,000	13,500
ROI	.10	.083	.44	.20

A is superior to B in both year 1 and year 2 based on income and return on investment. But with a 20 percent time value factor we know that B is better than A. The measure of performance being used is deficient. The cost of B includes the cost of excess capacity that will be used in periods after period 2. The first two periods should not be penalized for the acquisition of the excess capacity.

A shift to present-value depreciation solves the problem. It is inappropriate that the entire initial investment of B be considered an investment of the first two time periods. It should not be depreciated using straight-line depreciation. One way or another the performance measurement procedure must take these factors into consideration if the capacity decision is not to be distorted. Assume the following values and depreciation expenses are computed using B's internal rate of return of .252:

	Investment B	
Time	Value (.252)	Depreciation
0	18,010*	
1	16,550	1,460
2	13,520	3,030
3	8,050	5,470
4	0	8,050

* There is a rounding-off error.

The incomes and returns on investment of B are:

Year	Revenues	Present Value Depreciation	Income	Investment	ROI
1	6,000	1,460	4,540	18,010	.252
2	7,200	3,030	4,170	16,550	.252
3	8,880	5,470	3,410	13,520	.252
4	10,080	8,051	2,029	8,051	.252

A comparable method of income measurement for A would lead to an ROI of .20 for each year. Now B is not only to be preferred on an economic basis (a higher net-present value) but is also preferred using ROI for each year.

Competitors: Preempting the Market

The strategy of preempting the market is very attractive. In an expanding market a company builds before its competitors, thus making it unprofitable for others to build.

For example, assume there are 1,000,000 units of demand not being satisfied. It is expected that the cost of building capacity for 1,000,000 units per year is $10,000,000 and that the contribution margin per unit is $2. The life cycle of the product is expected to be ten years (we will assume for simplicity constant revenues over that period).

If 1,000,000 units per year can be sold, the net present value of the investment with a .10 time value factor (6.1466 is the annuity factor) is:

$$2,000,000 \ (6.1466) = \begin{array}{r} \$12,289,000 \\ -10,000,000 \\ \hline \end{array}$$

Net present value $ 2,289,000

Assume the market is not expected to exceed 1,000,000 units per year. Therefore, if the firm builds, a competitor building additional capacity would face the expectation of selling less than 1,000,000 units. Also, the possibility of a smaller contribution margin than $2 exists if competitors force the price down. From a strictly present-value-analysis basis the investment is not likely to be desirable given that a competitor is already building a plant of 1,000,000 units capacity.

The plans of competitors can thus affect the desirability of capacity expansion.

It is very likely that a firm and its competitors can lapse into a form of "prisoner's dilemma." Consider a situation where the net present value of firm A will be as follows:

Firm A's Net Present Value Conditional on B's Actions

	A Does Not Build	A Builds	Maximum Profits
B Does Not Build	1,000,000	2,289,000	2,289,000
B Builds	0	500,000	500,000

An analysis of the above table indicates that if B does not build, A is better off building and if B builds, A is better off building. A has a strong incentive to build.

Now consider Firm B's profits:

Firm B's Net Present Value Conditional on A's Actions

	A Does Not Build	A Builds
B Does Not Build	1,000,000	0
B Builds	2,289,000	500,000
Maximum Profits	2,289,000	500,000

The maximum profits for B occur when B builds if A builds, or if A does not build. B thus has a strong incentive to build.

Let us assume that both A and B build. If both firms build each firm will make profits of $500,000. This sum is less than the $1,000,000 of profits that both firms will earn if both firms do not build.

While both firms acting in their own interest should build, when they do so they will find that they have reached an inferior profit position.

A possible solution (but likely to be illegal in some countries) is for the firms to talk with each other to decide that not to build is preferable to both firms building. Still another possibility might be for the firms to merge, if that is legal.

If the firms cannot talk then it is likely that they will learn through time that certain actions will not be profitable.

For example, A may decide to build in the hope that B will not think that building is profitable. B will see, however, that $0 of net present value without building is less than $500,000 with building, and will decide to build. Firm A will regret the construction.

Now assume that A and B's profits are negative if both firms build. On a straight profit basis B should not build if A builds first. However, B might choose to teach A a lesson by building the capacity even though it is not needed. If A suffers losses from building excess capacity it might be satisfied with a more modest expansion in the next building cycle. An improved solution might be for both firms to build 500,000 units of capacity (the economics of this alternative are not given) and to share the market growth.

In some situations the capacity expansion will also result in changes in efficiency. The firm that does not expand and improve efficiency will be at a competitive disadvantage. This will also act as an incentive for B to expand when A expands.

The strategy of constructing preemptive capacity can backfire if the competitor feels that conceding the market can have adverse long-run effects, and thus reacts by building capacity even though the market will not absorb all the capacity of the industry.

Conclusion

The economic analysis of capacity expansion, without competitors, is a straightforward mutually exclusive investment decision until one considers the accounting measures of performance. These measures require adjustment so that there is not a conflict between the accounting measures and the economic measures of investment-desirability.

With shifts to considering strategy in a competitive situation the possibility of a prisoner's dilemma appears. The strategy of constructing preemptive capacity is balanced off by a strategy that attempts to teach the competitor that such a strategy is not profitable. Exact correct answers are lacking in a competitive situation, but we gain instead an appreciation of the degree of complexity that exists when there are competitors.

It is important to realize that the prices (and possibly costs) that exist before the capacity expansion might not be in effect after the capacity expansion. Observed prices and costs are not likely to be reliable indicators of price and costs when capacity and efficiencies are changed.

Questions and Problems

16-1. Trees growing in value at .15 per year are currently worth $1,000,000. The land itself (without the trees) is worth $5,000,000 now and one year from now. Money is worth .10. Should the trees be harvested now?

16-2. What is your answer to problem 16-1 if the trees are growing at .20 per year and money is worth .05?

16-3. High Voltage Electric Company has $10 million of debt outstanding which pays 7 percent interest annually. The maturity date of the securities is fifteen years from the present. There are $100,000 of bond issue costs and $200,000 of bond discount currently on the books.

Assume that a fifteen-year security could be issued which would yield 6 percent annually. The issue costs on the new issue would be $300,000, and the call premium on the old issue would be $500,000. (a) The company has a 10 percent cost of capital. Assume a zero tax rate. Should the old bonds be replaced with new securities? (b) Assume a discount rate of 7 percent. What would be your answer?

16-4. Referring to problem 16-3, how would your answer be affected by the possibility of interest rates decreasing in the future and the new bonds being issued for a thirty-year period?

16-5. Max A., the general manager of a mining company, is in need of advice. In answering, ignore uncertainty, and assume the cost of money is 10 percent. All data (including the cost of money) are in real after-tax dollars.

Dry Gulch is an operating mine. Ore can be produced and sold this year for a contribution of $200 per ton. However, if production is delayed a year, a contribution of $210 per ton could be realized. Would you recommend waiting? Explain.

16-6. (*Continuation of problem 16-5.*)   Wet Rock contains mineral deposits. Max plans to develop the property so that it can be mined, and then he will sell it to someone else to be mined. It will cost $1,000,000 and take about a year to get the property ready to sell. If development is started now, the property could be sold for $1,200,000 in one year. Max estimates the selling price will increase by 5 percent per year, but he anticipates no increase in development costs. Thus, the possible cash flows include the following:

Decision	0	1	2	3
Develop now	−1,000,000	1,200,000	0	0
Develop in 1 year		−1,000,000	1,260,000	0
Develop in 2 years			−1,000,000	1,323,000

If Max must develop the property now or next year, what should he do? Explain.

16-7. (*Continuation of 16-6.*)   Max decides not to develop the property referred to in problem 16-6. However, at the beginning of year 2, he suffers a heart attack, and takes a one-year's leave of absence. On returning at the end of year 2, he discovers that, in his absence, the property has been developed, but not yet sold. An offer to buy the property for $1,323,000 is in hand. Max is convinced that he can get 5 percent more by waiting another year. He feels the $1,000,000 expenditure was a sunk cost that should not affect his decision. He is inclined to wait at least another year. He wants your advice about when to sell, before making up his mind.

16-8. Woodrow owns a plot of land in the South. The land, with no timber on it, is worth $500. The $500 value of the land is based on its potential as residential land. At present, the land is forested. The timber on the land, is now ten years old and could be sold for $2000 now. However, Woodrow estimates that the value of the timber will increase by $500 per year for the foreseeable future. If Woodrow's objective is to earn a 10 percent return on his money, how many more years should he wait to harvest his timber? [For this question, assume $500 is the correct value of the land.]

16-9. (*Continuation of 16-8.*)   After the timber is harvested, it would cost $500 to plant another crop of timber. Ten years after planting, the crop would be worth $2,000 and would increase in value by $500 per year.

   Should Woodrow sell the land for residential purposes (value $500) after the present crop is harvested, or should he plant another crop?

16-10. The ABC Company has $10 million of debt outstanding, which pays .05 (that is, $500,000) interest annually. The maturity date of the securities is twenty years from the present.

   Assume that a new twenty-year security could be issued which would yield .04 per year. The issue costs would be $800,000, and the call premium on redemption of the old bonds is $100,000.

   Assume a zero tax rate for this company. The hurdle rate of the firm is .10.

   Required: Should the present bonds be refunded?

16-11. (*Continuing problem 16-10.*)   How would your answer be modified if the maturity date of the new issue were thirty years instead of twenty years?

16-12. The BCD Company has $10 million of debt outstanding, which pays .06 annually. The maturity date of the securities is twenty years from the present.

   Assume that new securities could be issued which would have the same maturity date. The issue costs of the new securities would be $2.7 million; there is no call premium on the present debt. Assume a zero tax rate.

   Required: Determine the rate of interest or yield rate of new securities at which the firm would just break even if they refunded. Determine to the nearest percent.

16-13. The York State Electric Corporation has $100 million of debentures outstanding, which are currently paying interest of 5.5 percent ($5.5 million) per year. The bonds mature in twenty-four years.

   It would be possible currently to issue thirty-year debentures of like characteristics that would yield 5 percent. The firm considers its cost of capital to be 8 percent. The marginal tax rate is .4.

   The analysis in Table 16-5 has been prepared.

   Required: Should the firm refund? Explain briefly.

16-14. The Bi-State Electric and Gas Corporation has $25 million of debentures outstanding, which are currently paying interest of 4.5 percent ($1.125 million) per year. The bonds mature in twenty-four years.

   It would be possible to currently issue thirty-year debentures of like character-

TABLE 16-5. York State Electric Refunding Calculations

	Before Taxes	After Taxes
Cash Outlays		
Premium at $50 per $1,000	$5,000,000	$3,000,000
Duplicate interest for thirty-day call period less interest received on principal at 1.4% due to temporary investment	300,000	180,000
Refunding expense (80% of $250,000, total expense of new issue based on remaining life of old issue of twenty-four years)	200,000	120,000
Call expense	50,000	30,000
Less tax saving due to immediate write-off of unamortized debt discount and expense		(20,000)
Total cash outlay of refunding		$3,310,000)
Interest Calculations		
Annual interest—old issue at 5.5%	$5,500,000	$3,300,000
Annual interest—new issue at 5%	5,000,000	3,000,000
		300,000
Total after-tax interest—old issue—discounted at 8% for twenty-four years* (present value factor = 10.5288)		34,700,000
Total after-tax interest—new issue—discounted at 8% for twenty-four years (present value factor = 10.5288)		31,600,000
Total after-tax discounted interest savings resulting from refunding		$3,100,000
Total after-tax cash outlay of refunding		3,310,000
Net savings due to refunding at effective interest rate of 5%		$ (210,000)

* The remaining life of the old issue.

istics that would yield 4 percent. The firm considers its hurdle rate to be 8 percent. The marginal tax rate is .50.

The following analysis has been prepared:

Cash Outlays	Before Taxes	After Taxes
Premium at $52 per $1,000	$1,300,000	$650,000
Duplicate interest for thirty-day call period less interest received on principal at 2% due to temporary investment	54,000	27,000
Refunding expense (80% of $220,000 total expense of new issue based on remaining life of old issue of twenty-four years)	176,000	88,000
Call expense	25,000	12,500
Less tax saving resulting from immediate write-off of unamortized debt discount and expense		−18,000
		$759,500

Required: Should the firm refund? Explain.

Discussion Questions

16-A. Why may a supermarket stay open during certain hours even though fixed operating costs are not recovered in these hours?

16-B. The formulation

$$f'(t) = rf(t) \quad \text{or} \quad r = \frac{f'(t)}{f(t)},$$

where r is the internal rate of return, is sometimes suggested (let growth continue until r is maximized). Using the example of the chapter, with land free, what does this imply about the growth period? What is the deficiency of the solution?

CHAPTER 17

Fluctuating Rates of Output

There is less in this than meets the eye.

—*Attributed to Tallulah Bankhead. Familiar Quotations by
J. Bartlett (1955).*

Special problems occur if a firm is faced with a choice of two or more types of equipment to produce a product, and if there will be fluctuations in the rate of output at which the equipment will be operated. The fluctuations in output may be the result of seasonal fluctuations in demand (which cannot be offset by storage), or the fluctuations may result because the rate of output needed is increasing or decreasing through time. We shall illustrate the case in which the fluctuations are due to seasonal factors. A similar, but more complicated, analysis would apply if demand were growing or falling. This analysis will assume the product cannot be inventoried. The opportunity to have inventory carried over to satisfy peak demand would make the analysis more complex.

When there are fluctuations in the rate of output, the amount of productive capacity needed will be determined by the peak rate of output required. The seasonal pattern will determine whether the average amount produced during the year is a high or low percentage of the available capacity.

Assume there are several types of equipment available, some types having higher fixed costs, but lower variable costs, than others. If only one type of equipment can be used, the average percentage of capacity used will influence the choice. For plants that operate at a high average percentage of capacity, equipment with high fixed costs and low variable costs is likely to have lower total costs. If the seasonal fluctuations are such that the plant operates at a low average percentage of capacity during the year, the equipment with lower fixed costs and higher variable costs is more likely to have lower total costs.

We will first determine which one of several types of equipment a firm should use if all the types of equipment can do the same task, but they have different costs for different levels of operations. Each type of equipment will have a fixed and variable cost component. The second problem to be solved is a situation where the production needs vary, and it is possible to buy one or more different types of equipment to service different levels of demand. Demand through time will be looked at as a pyramid where different horizontal slices of the pyramid can be serviced with different types of equipment. The objective will be to minimize the total cost for the year.

A Plant with One Type of Equipment

Suppose there is a choice between manual and semiautomatic equipment and that a plant is to be built in which only one type of equipment can be used. The product cannot be stored. The basic cost data on the equipment are as follow:

TABLE 17-1.   *Basic Data on Equipment Types*

Type	Capacity Per Machine (Units per year)	Annual Equivalent Fixed Costs Per Machine ($'s per year)	Variable Costs Per Unit ($'s per unit)	Annual Equivalent Fixed Costs Per Unit ($'s per unit)
Manual	40,000	$ 3,200	$1.00	$.08
Semiautomatic	100,000	$33,000	$0.50	$.33

We wish to compare the total costs of a plant containing either all manual equipment or all semiautomatic equipment. The total costs consist of the fixed costs and variable costs. In comparing fixed costs for the two types of machines we need to compare equal capacities. One way to do this is to restate the data in terms of fixed costs per unit of capacity by dividing the annual equivalent fixed costs per year per machine by the annual capacity of the machine. This gives the fixed cost per year for a capacity of one unit of output per year. On this basis the fixed cost per cent for the manual equipment is $3,200/40,000 = $.08 and the fixed cost per cent for the semiautomatic is $33,000/100,000 = $.33. The semiautomatic equipment has higher fixed costs than the manual; but this is offset by the fact that this type of equipment has lower variable costs.

If the equipment were to be operated at full capacity, the total costs of the semiautomatic equipment would be $0.33 + 0.50 = $0.83 per unit of output, while at full capacity the total costs of the manual equipment would be $.08 + 1.00 = $1.08 per unit of output. Thus at full capacity, the semiautomatic equipment is less costly. But if because of seasonal factors or because of their design characteristics, the equipment is not going to be operated at full capacity all year, the conclusion might be different. We can determine a breakeven average fraction of capacity (p) such that the total cost of the two types of machines will be the same. If the actual rate at which the plant will be operated is greater than p, semiautomatic equipment will be preferred; if it is less, manual equipment will be preferred. We assume the plant capacity is equal to a common multiple of the equipment capacities (say 4,000,000 units).

$$.08 + 1p = .33 + .5p \tag{1}$$

$$p = \frac{.25}{.5} = .5$$

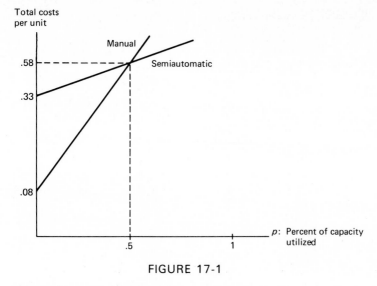

FIGURE 17-1

Figure 17-1 shows this analysis graphically. If the average fraction of capacity utilized exceeds the breakeven fraction of .5 then semiautomatic equipment is preferred. If it is less than .5 then manual equipment is less costly.

We could also solve for p using total costs as follows: If manual equipment is used 100 machines will be required to meet the capacity needs of 4,000,000 units: $(4,000,000/40,000) = 100$. The total annual fixed costs for 100 machines will be $100 \times \$3,200 = \$320,000$. If semiautomatic equipment is used, then 40 machines will be required $(4,000,000/100,000) = 40$. The total annual fixed costs will be $40 \times \$33,000 = \$1,320,000$. The breakeven quantity, Q, can be determined from the following equation:

$$320,000 + 1Q = 1,320,000 + .5Q \qquad (2)$$
$$Q = 1,000,000/.5$$
$$= 2,000,000.$$

Previously we solved for $p = .5$. With a capacity of four million units, a utilization factor of .5 implies a breakeven production level of 2,000,000 units per year.

To determine the capacity needed and the average percentage of capacity at which the plant will be operated, the seasonal pattern of production must be known. This information is contained in Table 17-2 for a hypothetical example.

Since the actual fraction of capacity to be utilized is .60, the semiautomatic plant would be preferred. At that level of utilization, since the indifference amount of utilization is .5, it has a lower total cost.

Assume the product cannot be inventoried. To determine the equipment capacity required we observe the highest rate of production that is required. In the third quarter 1,000,000 units must be produced. A plant that could produce 1,000,000 units in one quarter could produce 4,000,000 units in one year if it operated at a level rate. So the required capacity for the plant is 4,000,000 units

TABLE 17-2.   Seasonal Production Pattern

Period	Required Production (Units per Quarter)
January–March	200,000
April–June	600,000
July–September	1,000,000
October–December	600,000
Total annual production	2,400,000

per year. Because of seasonal fluctuations in demand, the actual output will be only 2,400,000 units per year. Therefore the average fraction of capacity utilized will be .60 or 60 percent.

Optimum Equipment Mix

So far we have assumed that only one type of equipment will be utilized. But in some circumstances several types of equipment can be used in the same plant or productive system. For example, a power-generating system may contain atomic energy generating capacity, fossil fuel capacity, and gas turbine capacity.

In designing a plant that contains several types of equipment, the objective is to have the correct amount of each type of equipment so as to minimize costs. Once a plant has been constructed, it must be operated in the most economical way possible. This requires utilizing the equipment with the lowest variable costs per unit to the maximum extent possible (that is, to its capacity) before resorting to equipment with higher variable costs per unit.

Suppose that we consider the problem of designing an optimum plant to meet the required rates of production specified in the previous example, where the required capacity of 4,000,000 units per year can be divided up among the two types of equipment—manual and semiautomatic in whatever amounts are considered desirable.

Note that three rates of production occur. In order of size they are 200,000, 600,000 and 1,000,000 of units per quarter. Based on these required rates of production the required capacity of the plant can be divided into three components. The first component represents the base demand of 200,000 per quarter (equivalent to 800,000 per year). The second component represents the increment in capacity necessary to increase production from 200,000 per quarter to the next level of 600,000 per quarter. So this component requires a capacity of 400,000 per quarter (equivalent to 1.6 million per year). The final component represents the increment in capacity necessary to increase production from 600,000 per quarter to 1,000,000 per quarter. This component, therefore also requires a capacity of 400,000 per quarter.

We now know that the plant will consist of three equipment components, one with a capacity of 800,000 units per year and two (not necessarily of the same type) with a capacity of 1.6 million units per year. To select the appropriate type of equipment for each of these components, we need to know for what part of the year each will be used. To determine this we must develop a production schedule for the plant. Table 17-3 represents a form that could be used for this purpose. Each row represents one quarter of the year. The first column shows the level of production required during each quarter. To determine a production schedule the available capacity must be assigned to meet the required production.

TABLE 17-3.   *Seasonal Production Schedule Form for Multiple Component Plant* (Units in Thousands)

		Equipment Component			
		1	2	3	
		Quarterly Capacity per Component			
		200	400	400	
	Required				Plant
Quarter	Production	Production per Component			Total
Jan.–March	200				
April–June	600				
July–Sept.	1,000				
Oct.–Dec.	600				
Total Annual Production	2,400				
Total Annual Capacity	4,000	800	1,600	1,600	4,000
Average Fraction of Capacity Used	.6				

At this stage we do not yet know what type of equipment will be used. The eligible types are those which are best for some value of *p*. The first component is determined by the need to meet the base demand, and this component will have variable costs at least as low as any other component. (If another component had lower variable costs it would be used before component 1.) Table 17-4 shows the status of the production plan when component 1 is used any time production is needed. Using only component 1 we can satisfy all of the required production in the first quarter, and part of the requirements of the other quarters. Since 200,000 units of component 1 can be used every quarter it will operate at 100 percent of capacity. This is larger than *p*, thus the optimal type of equipment for this component are two units of semiautomatic equipment. This equipment is less expensive when operated at or above 50 percent of capacity (*p*).

Table 17-5 shows the status of the production plan when equipment component 2 is assigned. It will have variable costs that are at least as low as the remaining equipment. It is not needed in the first quarter, but it is needed in the remaining three quarters. Since it will operate at 75 percent of capacity, semiautomatic equipment is also optimal for this component.

TABLE 17-4. *Step 1*
Seasonal Production Schedule for Multiple
Component Plant

		Equipment Component			
		1	2	3	
		Capacity per Component			
		200	400	400	
	Required				Plant
Quarter	Production	Production per Component			Total
Jan.–March	200	200			200
April–June	600	200			200
July–Sept.	1,000	200			200
Oct.–Dec.	600	200			200
Total Annual					
Production	2,400	800			800
Total Annual					
Capacity	4,000	800	1,600	1,600	4,000
Average Fraction					
of Capacity Used	.6	1.0	0	0	.20

TABLE 17-5. *Step 2*
Seasonal Production Schedule for Multiple
Component Plant

		Equipment Component			
		1	2	3	
		Capacity per Component			
		200	400	400	
	Required				Plant
Quarter	Production	Production of Components			Total
Jan.–March	200	200			200
April–June	600	200	400		600
July–Sept.	1,000	200	400		600
Oct.–Dec.	600	200	400		600
Total Annual					
Production	2,400	800	1,200		2,000
Total Annual					
Capacity	4,000	800	1,600	1,600	4,000
Average Fraction					
of Capacity Used	.6	1.0	.75	0	.50

In Table 17-5 we note that additional output beyond component 2 is required only in the third quarter. This output will be supplied by equipment component 3. This component will be used on average at only 25 percent of its capacity. Therefore manual equipment will be less expensive for this component. The final production plan is summarized in Table 17-6.

More Periods or More Equipment Types

The procedure illustrated can be used to handle problems with any number of periods or any number of equipment types if certain conditions are satisfied.

Two conditions are important with respect to the choice of periods. First, the periods must all be of equal length. Second, although the rate of production may vary from period to period, within any given period it must be constant.

These conditions can usually be satisfied by taking the shortest period of time during which production is constant as the period length. If day-to-day variations in production are relevant, then pick the day as the period-length, and divide the year into 365 one-day periods. Production in some periods can be zero.

If the number of periods is large it might be convenient to modify the production planning tables such as are exhibited in Table 17-3. As illustrated, they contain one line per period. With daily periods, this would make a very long table. A modification of Table 17-3 that is useful in this case is to design the table so that each line represents a different level of production. For example, in Table 17-6 there are two periods, the second and fourth quarters, in which the level of production is the same. Table 17-7 is an example of a production plan in which these two quarters have been combined into one line. The line for which required production is 600 per period represents two periods and for each component used the production per component is equal to the capacity of the component times two (the number of periods). If you plan to use this modification, carefully compare Tables 17-6 and 17-7.

It is necessary to pre-screen the equipment types and eliminate the equipment types that are more costly for every possible rate of production. To pre-screen the equipment types, first calculate their annual equivalent fixed costs *per unit of*

TABLE 17-6. *Final Version Seasonal Production Schedule for Multiple Component Plant*

Quarter	Required Production	Equipment Component 1 (Capacity 200)	Equipment Component 2 (Capacity 400)	Equipment Component 3 (Capacity 400)	Plant Total
		Production per Component			
Jan.–March	200	200			200
April–June	600	200	400		600
July–Sept.	1,000	200	400	400	1,000
Oct.–Dec.	600	200	400		600
Total Annual Production	2,400	800	1,200		2,400
Total Annual Capacity	4,000	800	1,600	1,600	4,000
Average Fraction of Capacity Used	.6	1.0	.75	.25	.60

TABLE 17-7. *Final Version Combining Quarters with Equal Production Seasonal Production Schedule for Multiple Component Plant*

No. of Periods	Per Period Required Production	Equipment Component 1 200	Equipment Component 2 400	Equipment Component 3 400	Plant Total
		Capacity per Component — Production per Component			
One	200	200			200
Two	600	400	800		1,200
One	1,000	200	400	400	1,000
Total Annual Production	2,400	800	1,200		2,400
Total Annual Capacity	4,000	800	1,600	1,600	4,000
Average Fraction of Capacity Used	.6	1.0	.75	.25	.60

capacity. Rank the equipment types by this measure from high fixed-cost types to low fixed-cost types. When this is done equipment type i will have higher fixed costs than equipment type $i + 1$. Screening involves the following steps.

1. If two types have the same fixed costs, eliminate the one with the higher variable cost. It should never be used.
2. If two types have the same fixed cost and the same variable cost, treat them as one type. They are economically identical.
3. Compare each adjacent pair of equipment types, starting with types 1 and 2, then with types 2 and 3, then types 3 and 4, and so on. In each of these comparisons, one type will have higher fixed costs than the other.
   a. If the type with the higher fixed costs also has higher variable costs than the other, eliminate it. It should never be selected.
   b. If the type with the higher fixed costs has lower variable costs, then find the breakeven fraction of capacity between the two types using equation (1). If the breakeven fraction is greater than one, then eliminate the type with the higher fixed costs.

After this screening has been completed, all inefficient types will have been eliminated and you will know the Optimum Utilization Range (OUR) for each type of equipment. The OUR for the first type of equipment is from 1.0 to the breakeven fraction between it and equipment type 2. For equipment type 2 the OUR is from its breakeven fraction with type 1 to its breakeven fraction with type 3.

Determination of Fixed Costs

Assume the manual equipment cost $18,081 per machine and is expected to last for ten years. The interest rate is 12 percent per year. We can determine the annual equivalent cost, F, to be:

$$FB(10, .12) = 18,081$$

$$5.650223F = 18,081$$

$$F = 3,200$$

This is consistent with the fixed cost used above for the manual equipment. For simplicity, taxes have been ignored in this example. When income taxes are relevant, the fixed and variable costs of the equipment should be put on an after-tax basis.

Conclusions

This chapter has illustrated a method of choosing the optimal mix of equipment types when output fluctuates. If desired, algebraic solutions can be prepared that arrive at the same solutions. If products can be stored, the solutions become complex and mathematical solutions are necessary.

Questions and Problems

17-1. A new plant is to be built to produce widgets. Three types of facilities are available: fully automated, semiautomated, and manual. All three facilities have the same expected life and produce widgets that are identical in every respect. Only the cost characteristics of the three types of facilities vary. The fixed and variable costs for each type of facility are shown in Table 17-8. All costs are on an after-tax basis, and fixed costs are expressed in terms of equivalent monthly after-tax flows, after allowing for tax savings from depreciation.

To prevent thefts, each widget is produced with the customer's name engraved on it. The name must be engraved before the widget is assembled.

TABLE 17-8.   *Cost Characteristics of Alternative Types of Widget Production Facilities*

Facility Type	Fixed Cost per Month for Enough Capacity to Produce One Widget per Month	Variable Cost per Widget
Fully automated	$20	$25
Semiautomated	14	35
Manual	6	60

This makes it impractical to maintain an inventory of completed widgets. Instead, production must take place after orders are received. Since demand follows a seasonal pattern, widget-production is seasonal as well. The anticipated seasonal pattern of demand (and production) is described in Table 17-8. The peak demand is 600 units per month, and a capacity sufficient to meet this peak demand is needed.

Suppose that the plant to be built can contain only one type of facility:

a. Using the demand forecast in Table 17-9, which type of facility should be chosen?

b. If Table 17-9 were modified by raising estimated demand in all months from March through August to 600 units per month, which type of facility should be chosen?

c. If peak demand (and therefore the required capacity) remained at 600 units per month (Q_{max}), how low would average monthly demand ($\bar{Q}$) have to fall before the manual facility would be chosen?

d. Let the total monthly cost of using the ith type of facility be

$$T_i = Q_{max} F_i + \bar{Q} V_i,$$ (1)

where

T_i = total monthly cost of the ith facility,
F_i = fixed cost per month for enough capacity to produce one widget per month using the ith facility,
V_i = variable cost per unit for the ith facility,
Q_{max} = maximum level of demand per month (equals required capacity),
$\bar{Q}$ = average level of demand (widgets per month).

TABLE 17-9. *Estimated Demand*

Month	Estimated Demand
January	100
February	100
March	300
April	400
May	600
June	500
July	400
August	400
September	300
October	200
November	200
December	100
Estimated annual demand	3,600 widgets/year

Average monthly demand $(\bar{Q}) = \dfrac{3,600}{12} = 300$ widgets per month

Make a rough graph with T_i on the vertical axis and $\bar{Q}$ on the horizontal axis. Sketch in equation (1) for each of the three facilities on this graph, using $Q_{max} = 600$ and the values of F_i and V_i from Table 17-8.

e. What generalizations can you make about the levels of $\bar{Q}$ at which each type of facility would be preferred?

f. The following equation was obtained from equation 1 by dividing both sides by Q_{max}, and letting $p = \bar{Q}/Q_{max}$.

$$\frac{T_i}{Q_{max}} = F_i + pV_i \tag{2}$$

Make a rough graph with T_i/Q_{max} as the vertical axis and p as the horizontal axis. Sketch in equation 2 on this graph for each of the three facilities, using the values of F_i and V_i from Table 17-8.

g. Does this graph suggest any further generalizations about the type of facility that would be preferred in problems of this type?

17-2. (*Continuing problem 17-1.*) Suppose that a widget plant can be constructed that contains more than one type of facility.

a. A widget plant has been constructed that contains six types of facilities. There are 100 units of capacity of each type. In terms of variable costs per widget, facility 1 has the lowest cost, facility 2 the next lowest cost, and so on. You are in charge of scheduling production in this plant and responsible for meeting each month's required production, while minimizing variable costs. Plan your production schedule by completing the following table to show for each month the number of units to be produced in each type of facility.

Month	Required Production	Amount to be Produced in Facility No.					
		1	2	3	4	5	6
Jan.	100						
Feb.	100						
March	300						
April	400						
May	600						
June	500						
July	400						
Aug.	400						
Sept.	300						
Oct.	200						
Nov.	200						
Dec.	100						
	3,600						

b. For each of the six types of facilities, compute the fraction of that facility's annual capacity which you plan to utilize.

c. If you were designing this plant and had available only the three types of facilities described in problem 17-1, how many units of capacity of each of the three types would you choose in order to minimize total costs? Of the year's production of 3,600 widgets, how many would be produced in each type of facility?

d. Compute the average total cost per month (averaged over a whole year) for the plant design you chose. Compare these costs with the best plant you could devise using only one type of facility.

17-3. The DEF Company uses a batch process method to produce product S. The product is very perishable so inventories are small, and production is geared closely to current sales. There are two seasons for product S, each season lasting six months. The DEF company has been producing and selling product S at the rate of 30 million units per month during the busy season–which lasts for six months. During the six-month slow season production and sales are only 10 million units per month.

The company is convinced it could sell an additional 5 million units per month during the six-month busy season if additional capacity were available. There is no question that these additional sales would be profitable. There is a question of what type of production equipment should be installed.

The company has a choice between two types of equipment. The batch process equipment is the same as the equipment currently in use. The continuous process equipment was developed a few years ago. Both types are known to be reliable and to produce equally high quality products. Cost data are given below.

Cost Item	Batch	Continuous
Equivalent annual fixed costs: Dollars per year per unit of capacity capable of producing one unit of product per month.	2.20	5.00
Variable costs of producing one unit of product.	0.90	0.50

a. What action would you recommend to the DEF Company if there were no costs savings or salvage values associated with scrapping existing batch capacity?

b. What action would you recommend if fixed costs of 1.00 per year per unit of capacity could be avoided by scrapping existing batch capacity?

17-4. The Giant Motor Car Company is considering the size that would be most desirable for its next assembly plant. We shall assume that there are the following two alternatives:

	Large Plant	Small Plant
Initial costs	$20,000,000	$4,000,000
Out-of-pocket cost savings per year, assuming the assembly of different numbers of cars per year		
100,000 cars		1,000,000
200,000 cars	0	
300,000 cars	2,000,000	
400,000 cars	4,000,000	

A forecast of car sales indicates the following demand for automobiles assembled in this plant:

First year after completion of the plant	100,000 cars
Second year after completion of the plant	200,000
Third year after completion of the plant	200,000
Fourth year after completion of the plant	300,000
Fifth year and thereafter for the expected life of the plant of twenty years	400,000

The company has a cost of money of 10 percent. For purposes of this problem assume an income tax rate of zero.

Required: Which one of the two plants is the more desirable?

17-5. Power Plant Design. A power system is to be constructed. Three types of generating equipment are available. Their costs are given in the following table. There are 8,760 hours in a year.

Type	Fixed Costs: Dollars Per Year Per KW of Capacity	Operating Costs: $ Per KW Hour of Electricity Produced
Nuclear	$200.00	$0.01
Coal	100.00	0.04
Gas	40.00	0.07

(A kilowatt hour of electricity is produced by operating a kilowatt hour of capacity for one hour.)

Suppose only one type of generating equipment could be used to supply an electrical need with the following characteristics:

Maximum Demand 1,000's of Kilowatts	500
Total Output Per Year, 1,000's KW hours	2,630,000

How much capacity should the plant have and which type of plant should be selected?

17-6. (*Continuation of 17-5*). Suppose more than one type of generating unit could be used to supply electrical needs with the following characteristics.

(1) Rate of Output 1,000's of KW's	(2) Hours Plant Operates at that Rate	(3) = (1) × (2) Total Output 1,000's of KW Hours
500	260	130,000
400	1,200	480,000
350	2,000	700,000
300	2,300	690,000
200	3,000	600,000
Totals	8,760	2,630,000

An economic design for this system will include the following:

Type of Equipment	Required Capacity 1,000 of KW's
4. Nuclear	_____
5. Coal	_____
6. Gas	_____

Discussion Questions

17-A. Distinguish between determining the optimum-sized plant and the optimum-sized firm.

17-B. Is it better to build a small plant and work it intensively (with overtime and double time) or build a large plant and sometimes have idle capacity?

CHAPTER **18**

Investment Decisions with Additional Information*

The chances of success of a given investment (whether of capital or labour) depend on the efficiency with which all those who work in the same firm cooperate with the factor in question.

—*J. R. Hicks, "The Theory of Uncertainty and Profit," Economica (London, May 1931), p. 185.*

Up to this point it has been assumed that the alternatives available to a decision maker are to accept or reject investment proposals. In this chapter we consider the possibility of obtaining more information before making a decision. When this possibility exists, the decision maker needs to compare the costs and benefits of additional information to decide if obtaining it is worthwhile. If additional information is collected the decision maker must combine the new information and the previously existing information to arrive at a decision. After a decision to accept a project has been made the possibility of doing a post audit arises. Post audits may be done by the decision-maker or by a higher level of management. The purpose of the post audit is to improve and possibly to control the decision-making process. The danger exists that the results of a post audit may be misinterpreted, so that it fails to achieve its objective or, in extreme cases, could lead to affecting adversely the decision-making process.

The three main topics considered in this chapter are (1) deciding if additional information is worthwhile; (2) using additional and prior information in decision-making; and (3) interpreting the results of post audits.

The analytical techniques illustrated in this chapter are based on formal statistical models. They are strictly applicable only to decision-making situations that conform to the assumptions underlying those models.

A substantial part of the chapter considers situations in which a single type of equipment can be installed in many different locations, and the possibility exists of obtaining additional information by trying the equipment in one location before deciding what to do about the other locations. Any procedure for screen-

* Parts of this chapter are based on an article by H. Bierman Jr. and Vithala R. Rao, "Investment Decisions with Sampling," that appeared in the Autumn, 1978 issue of *Financial Management.*

ing investment proposals, however, can be thought of as a procedure for deciding whether or not to obtain additional information.

Let us consider a procedure which is typical of the decision-making process in many companies. At each decision-making level before the final one, three alternatives may be possible; accept, reject, or send to a higher level. Sometimes rules are specified for the various levels. For example, at level 1, the accept alternative may not be available on proposals involving outlays of more than $10,000. At level 2 the accept alternative may not be available on proposals of more than $50,000. Rules such as this require that larger investments must be submitted to higher levels before an accept decision is possible. Since additional information and analysis is presumably available at each higher level, a decision (or requirement) to submit a proposal to a higher level may be interpreted as a decision to obtain additional information. Usually a proposal can be rejected at any level. Thus a decision at one level to submit a proposal to the next higher level implies there is not enough information to lead to a rejection decision. In some organizations that are structured in this way the final decision makers accept nearly all the proposals that come to them. For example, if an investment survives five possible reject decisions, it is assumed that the investment is a reasonable alternative.

The formal statistical models considered in this chapter may provide some insights into organizational situations like the one described above. Even if the assumptions of the particular statistical models used for illustration do not apply, some helpful generalizations are possible.

The Opportunity to Replicate

Multiplant firms have an opportunity to innovate sequentially that is frequently not available to firms with single plants (unless the single plant has multiple production lines). Consider the development of a new type of equipment in a multiplant company. The analysis for a single unit of equipment indicates a negative net present value. But there is some probability that the equipment would be successful and would have a positive present value in any subsequent use. In other words, there is uncertainty about the outcome but there is some probability that it would be a desirable investment. In such a situation, the possibility that the firm may miss out on a technological breakthrough may be sufficient motivation for trying the equipment as a sample investment.

If one unit of the equipment has a positive expected net present value, then some may argue that all the units should be acquired for the entire firm. On an expected value basis this is true. Under conditions of uncertainty and risk aversion, however, trying the investment on a small scale may help to determine if the forecasted good result will actually occur. If the result is good, then the remainder of the units can be purchased. The cost of this policy is delay of the investments, however, which may be a disadvantage.

An objective of this chapter is to emphasize that an apparently poor individual investment might be good when considered in the broader context of subsequent investments. We also want to show explicitly why the greater the uncertainty the better it is to obtain additional information, perhaps by trying an investment if the investment can be replicated (although we are not sure the investment should be undertaken until the calculations are made). Some managers will prefer to apply intuition, making the decision without the type of calculations that will be illustrated. The model, however, does incorporate the expert judgment of the decision maker into the decision process.[1] The decision will depend on the decision maker's evaluation of the probabilities of events rather than the intuitive judgment of the effect of the combination of probabilities and outcomes. Most important, the model allows the decision maker to focus on the relevant variables.

The Basic Model

The examples show the investment sampling process where the investment, although initially not desirable, may appear acceptable after considering the consequent opportunity of obtaining additional information and the possibility of sequential decisions. The chance of an improvement of the initially undesirable investment follows logically.

We shall assume initially that undertaking one investment would allow perfect information about what could happen if all the identical investments were undertaken. In a subsequent section, the analysis includes imperfect information. This complicates the analysis but does not change the basic logic of undertaking an investment with a negative expected net present value because of the information that can be obtained.

Figure 18-1 shows the basic model with the net present value of the profits lost by *not* undertaking the investment. V_0 is the random variable "net present value" with mean $\bar{V}_0$ for one unit of equipment, and V_b is the break-even present value.

---

[1] The methodology of decision calculus is useful in quantifying the experience and judgement of managers. See John D. C. Little, "Models and Managers: The Concept of Decision Calculus." *Management Science* (April 1970), pp. B466–85.

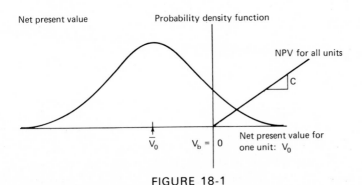

FIGURE 18-1

V_b is the value when V_0 is equal to zero, therefore, V_b is defined to be zero. C is the slope of the net present value curve for all units of investment.

Since the expected value of V_0, $\bar{V}_0$ is to the left of V_b, the correct decision seems to be to reject the investment. If the investment is rejected the present value is zero. But V_0 is a random variable with a probability density function. This is a "prior betting distribution." If we are certain that the net present value of the investment is $\bar{V}_0$ (the variance of the distribution is zero), then the investment would be rejected. If there is some probability that $V_0 > V_b$ then further analysis is required.

The value of C is crucially important because it defines the relationship of the net present value potential of all the equipment for different values of the random variable. C depends on the number of units of equipment in which the firm can feasibly invest. The more units of equipment the steeper the slope.

The profit potential for multiple investments, given an undesirable single investment, is a function of the slope of the net present value line (which in turn depends on the number of units of equipment), the variance of the probability density function, and the distance between $\bar{V}_0$ and V_b.

If $\bar{V}_0$ is less than 0 and if the value of V_0 is positive, the expected profits are

$$C \int_0^\infty V_0\, f(V_0)\, dV_0,$$

where $f(V_0)$ is the probability density function of V_0. The expected loss of undertaking one unit of investment if V_0 is less than V_b is

$$\int_{-\infty}^0 (-V_0) f(V_0)\, dV_0.$$

If the expected present value is positive the investment ought to be tried. Figure 18-2 shows the net present value if one investment is undertaken and then all investments are undertaken if the actual value of V_0 is greater than V_b. If the actual value of V_0 is less than V_b then no additional investments are undertaken.

Numerical Example

Consider an investment that costs $1,000,000. The outcome can either be e_1 or e_2 in all future years.

Event	Probability of Events	Outcome (a perpetuity)	Present Value	Net Present Value	Expected Present Value
e_1	.4	$150,000	$1,500,000	$500,000	200,000
e_2	.6	40,000	400,000	-600,000	-360,000
					-160,000

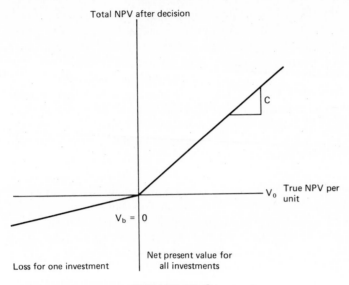

FIGURE 18-2

The time value factor (required return) is 10 percent. The expected present value of the benefits is \$840,000 (\$1,500,000 × .4 + \$400,000 × .6). Since the investment costs \$1,000,000 and the expected benefits are only \$840,000, the investment has a negative net present value of \$160,000, it should be rejected on an expected present-value basis.

The firm may have the opportunity to undertake eleven of these investments, however. There is a .4 probability that each unit of equipment will perform to produce a net present value of \$500,000 or \$5,500,000 in total. There is a .6 probability of eleven units losing \$600,000 per unit or \$6,600,000 in total. The expected value is negative (\$5,500,000 × 4 − \$6,600,000 × .6 = −\$1,760,000), and it would seem that the investment is not desirable. But we can modify the uncertainty by buying one item of equipment for a cost of \$1,000,000 and a negative expected value. Figure 18-3 shows the decision tree that evolves.

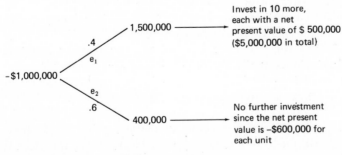

FIGURE 18-3

The firm invests in the ten additional units of equipment only if event e_1 occurs and the process proves to be feasible. If the process is feasible, each investment adds $500,000 of net present value. Multiplying the $500,000 by the 11 machines, we find the upper path leading to $5,500,000 of present value. The expected value of path e_1 for eleven units is: .4 ($5,500,000) = $2,200,000.

There is .6 probability that the first machine will lose $600,000. This will occur if the event is e_2. This is an expected cost of $360,000. Because the expected value of the e_1 path is $2,200,000 and the expected value of the e_2 path is −$360,000, we would advocate undertaking the single investment in the hope that we will find out that e_1 is the true state of the world. The expected net present value of trying an investment is $1,840,000.

If we changed the probabilities so that e_1 had a probability of .7 and e_2 a probability of .3, then $\bar{V}_0$, the expected NPV per unit of equipment, would be $170,000 (that is .7 × 500,000 − .3 × 600,000) per unit or $1,870,000 if all eleven units were accepted. Even though the investment is desirable, trying one unit first is still advisable if there is not a long time delay between investments. If all eleven units were undertaken there is a .4 probability that all the investments will turn out to be bad. The expected loss is eleven times as large as the loss from trying one unit. The expected loss from trying one unit is .3 × 600,000 or $180,000. If all eleven of the investments are undertaken the loss can be $6,600,000. The advantage of trying one unit is that the loss is limited to $600,000. It increases the expected net present value from $1,870,000 to $2,670,000 (that is .7 × 5,500,000 − .3 × 600,000). If there is no cost of delay the sampling of investments is desirable.

Sample Investment: Normal Prior Probability and Perfect Information

Assume now that the prior betting distribution of outcomes is normally distributed. (This assumption is not essential and is made only to simplify the arithmetic as we shift from the discrete to the continuous model.) Assume also that once the trial investment is undertaken we will know how the machine being considered will operate in the other environments of the company.

The prior distribution of outcomes (V_0) for the piece of equipment being considered has a normal distribution of net present values with a mean of ($\bar{V}_0$ = −$2,000) and a standard deviation of (σ_0 = $8,000). Since the distribution is for net present values, the break-even value (V_b)is equal to zero.

The expected net present value is a negative $2,000. If purchase of only one piece of equipment can be undertaken, the project would be rejected. However, assume that the firm uses 500 of these machines. For every dollar increase in net present value of one machine, the total net present value increases by $500. This is C.

Figure 18-4 shows the "betting distribution" on the net present value. If σ_0 equaled zero, and if management were sure that a net present value of −$2,000 would occur, then the project would be rejected. There is some probability,

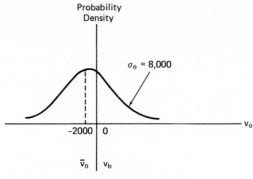

FIGURE 18-4

however, that the net present value will be positive. Define EVPI to be the expected value of perfect information, then

$$EVPI = C\sigma_0 L(D),$$

where

$$L(D) = \int_{+D}^{\infty} (Z - D)n(Z)\, dZ.$$

$n(Z)$ is the unit normal density function for the standardized random variable,

$$Z = \frac{V_0 - \bar{V}_0}{\sigma_0}, \quad \text{and} \quad D = \left| \frac{\bar{V}_0}{\sigma_0} \right|.$$

For example, we have

$$D = \left| \frac{-\$2,000}{\$8,000} \right| = .25,$$

and from a table of normal loss integrals $L(D) = .2863$.[2] The expected value of perfect information for 500 pieces of equipment is: $EVPI = 500(\$8,000) \times (.2863) = \$1,145,200$.

Define $L(D^*) = D + L(D)$, where D^* results from integrating more than $\frac{1}{2}$ the density function. The expected cost of undertaking the investment to find out the true value of V_0 is

$$E(L_0) = \int_{-\infty}^{0} (-V_0)f(V_0)\, dV_0 = \sigma_0 L(D^*).$$

For the example, we have

$$L(D^*) = .25 + .2863 = .5363 \quad \text{and} \quad E(L_0) = \$8,000\,(.5363) = \$4,290.$$

Since the expected value of the perfect information is $1,145,000 and the expected cost is only $4,290, the single investment with a negative expected value of $2,000 (considering only one machine) is acceptable.

[2] A table of loss integrals can be found in H. Bierman, C. Bonini, and W. Hausman, *Quantitative Analysis for Business Decisions*, Irwin, Sixth Edition 1981, p. 574.

If the firm could only undertake one unit of equipment:

$$C = \$1 \quad \text{and} \quad \text{EVPI} = \$8,000 \,(.2863) = \$2,290.$$

Now the expected cost is $4,290 and the expected value is $2,290. Thus, the expected net present value is a negative $2,000 (equal to the present value of one unit of investment) and the investment would be rejected. There must be

$$\frac{\$4,290}{\$2,290} = 1.87$$

units of investment for the firm to want to sample the investment of this example.

Delaying Other Investments

The sampling procedure (trying one investment before proceeding with the remainder) will result in the delay of other investments, adversely affecting their present value if they have positive present values.

Should these costs be considered? Consider first investments that would otherwise be rejected. If the alternative were to make all the investments now or do nothing, the firm would do nothing. The firm wants to obtain information as cheaply as possible, which is accomplished by undertaking a minimum-sized investment. While the expected value of this investment, taken by itself, is negative, the information that can be gathered justifies undertaking the investment. The fact that the other investments will be delayed is unfortunate, but it does not affect the basic sampling strategy. Delaying the investments decreases their net present value, but it also enables the firm to avoid investing funds in undesirable investments. On balance, the sampling of one investment is a desirable strategy if the investment would otherwise be rejected, and if the expected present value of all investments is positive.

Next consider a situation in which V_0 is greater than zero. If the alternatives were to accept all the investments now, or do nothing, the firm would accept all the investments now. In this case sampling may still be desirable. However in deciding whether to accept the investments now, or wait and collect additional information by sampling (or some other method) the expected decline in present value due to waiting should be considered as an additional cost.

In summary, delaying the start up of other investments should be considered as a cost of acquiring additional information if the investments would otherwise be accepted now. Delay is not a relevant cost if on the basis of the present information the investments would be rejected if they all had to be accepted now.

So far we have considered situations in which it may be desirable to obtain additional information. One way of collecting additional information is to sample. This is possible when there are many similar investments, and trying one may provide information about the value of the others. If additional information were costless and could be obtained instantly it would always be desirable whenever there was uncertainty about the investment's outcome. But in most situations obtaining information by sampling or further study takes time and money. The decision maker needs to compare the expected value of the additional information with its expected cost to determine whether it is better to decide now, or to wait while additional information is collected.

In the examples considered so far, if additional information is obtained it is decisive: there is no question about what decision should be made. Additional information is sometimes ambiguous. In the next section of the chapter we focus on the problem of combining prior information and additional information to make decisions.

Imperfect Information

Suppose it has been decided to obtain additional information before making a decision. The additional information can be in the form of a sample, as in the examples in the previous section, or a forecast prepared in some other way. Suppose that the additional information after being combined with the prior information does not eliminate all uncertainty. In this section we consider how the additional imperfect information should be used to make a decision.

Now assume that after the one investment is made, and the results observed, we still cannot be sure of the desirability of the investment; that is, the information obtained is imperfect. We will now assign a set of probabilities reflecting the reliability of the information. The conditional probabilities exist as shown in Table 18-1. Other probabilities are computed in the Appendix, p. 367.

TABLE 18-1. *Conditional Probabilities*

Observed Event	The actual state is:	
	Event e_1 (High Present Value)	Event e_2 (Low Present Value)
Investment seems to be profitable: G	.9	.2
Investment seems to be not profitable: B	.1	.8

If the investment actually is good, there is still a .1 probability that it may not appear profitable. If the investment actually is not good, there is a .2 probability that it may appear profitable. Extending the example to reflect an initial profitable probability of .4 and a .6 not-profitable probability, we will observe either profitable or not-profitable operations. The problem that has to be solved is whether or not it is desirable to go ahead and make the initial investment. The

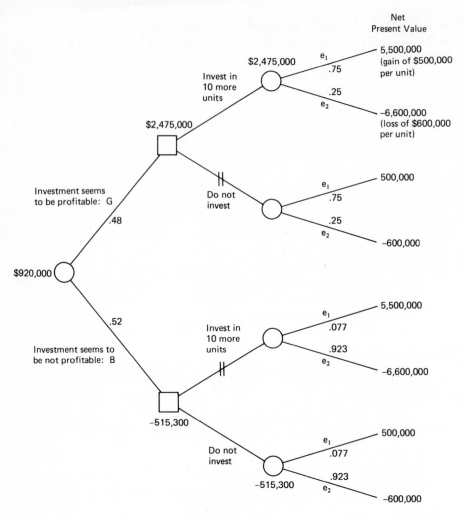

FIGURE 18-5

computations of the relevant revised probabilities are shown in the appendix to this chapter. Figure 18-5 shows the probabilities and the outcomes if purchase of one unit is undertaken to obtain information, and then the decision is whether or not to undertake the additional units.

In Figure 18-5 we have crossed out two inferior paths to simplify the presentation. The expectation of the G path and investing in ten more units is

Value of G path = .75($5,500,000) − .25($6,600,000) = $2,475,000.

The value of the B path and investing in only one unit is:

Value of B path = .077 ($500,000) − .923 ($600,000) = − $515,300.

There is .48 probability of G and .52 probability of B; thus the expected value of the process is (.48 × \$2,475,000 − .52 × 515,300) or \$920,044.

Where we once found that undertaking purchase of one or eleven units with negative expected values was undesirable, now that we can sample, we find that even with imperfect information it is desirable to try one unit. The expected present value is \$920,044.

Imperfect Information: The Normal Distribution

It is convenient to illustrate imperfect information using the normal probability distribution since the revision of the normal distribution is relatively easy to illustrate.

Assume that before obtaining additional information it is estimated that the investment proposal under consideration has an expected net present value of −\$540,000. The prior distribution has a standard deviation of \$300,000 and is assumed to be normally distributed. Without additional information, the decision would be to reject the proposal. Rather than rejecting the investment it has been decided to collect additional information. The new information will provide V_e, an unbiased estimate of the true net present value of the project, and will be normally distributed with a standard deviation σ_e of \$250,000. How favorable will the new information have to be in order to justify accepting the project?

It will be helpful to summarize the prior estimates before the new information becomes available in symbols. The expected value based on prior information is

$$\bar{V}_0 = E(V_0) = \int_{-\infty}^{\infty} V_0 \, f(V_0) \, dV_0 = -\$540,000$$

$\sigma_0 = \$300,000$. $f(V_0)$ is a normal probability density function.

Define V_e to be the value of the project as estimated only from the new information and V_r to be the revised value of the project as estimated from a combination of the prior information and the new information. It can be shown that under the assumptions made (normal prior, normal sample, unbiased estimate), that

$$V_r = \frac{\sigma_e^2 V_0 + \sigma_0^2 V_e}{\sigma_e^2 + \sigma_0^2}$$

$$= \frac{(250,000)^2(-540,000) + (300,000)^2 V_e}{250,000^2 + 300,000^2} = -221,311 + .5902 V_e.$$

Since V_r incorporates all of the available information, the correct approach is to accept the investment if V_r is greater than or equal to zero. In this example the revised estimate will be greater than zero if V_e is greater than \$375,000.

The critical value of V_e occurs when $V_r = 0$. Defining V_e^* to be the critical value of V_e and solving for it,

$$V_e^* = -\left(\frac{\sigma_e}{\sigma_0}\right)^2 \bar{V}_0.$$

In the example described above the formula yields

$$V_e = (250,000/300,000)^2(+540,000) = \$375,000.$$

If V_e turns out to be greater than \$375,000, we should accept the investment. If V_e turns out to be less than \$375,000 we should reject the investment.

The difficult aspect of the approach is obtaining the expected values and the standard deviations of the prior distribution and the sample distribution. In many situations only subjective estimates are available. The advantage of the model is that it incorporates the available information in a systematic manner into the decision process.

Post-Audit Bias[3]

It is generally agreed that after an investment is accepted the results of operations should be compared to the forecasted operations used as the basis of making the accept decision. Management would like to determine whether or not the forecasts on which decisions are based are biased. A forecast is said to be statistically biased if the average value of the forecast differs from the true value. A common fear of management is that the project sponsors responsible for a project may tend to be too optimistic, resulting in an upward bias in the forecasted net present value. We will describe post-audit bias as existing when the average of the present-value forecasts of the accepted investments exceeds the actual value of the investments' present value even though the forecasts are good (unbiased) forecasts.

The example used in the previous section will be helpful in considering the post-audit bias problem. There were two forecasts that could be used to make the decision, denoted V_e and V_r. We will refer to them as the sample forecast and the revised or posterior forecast, respectively. When the post audit is done by comparing the actual results with V_e, a post-audit bias problem is likely to be observed, even if the actual forecasts are not biased. When the post audit is done by comparing the actual results with V_r, there will be no post-audit bias problem. Using V_r, if a difference is observed, the possibility that the forecasts are biased should be investigated.

The post-audit bias as defined here results from the use of V_e, since the prior information is omitted from consideration. The actual results should be compared to the best information that was available for making the decision, the revised estimate of the net present value.

---

[3] For a more complete discussion of post-audit bias see Seymour Smidt, "A Bayesian Analysis of Project Selection and of Post-Audit Evaluations," *Journal of Finance* (June 1979), pp. 675–688.

Determining the Extent of the Post-Audit Bias

Suppose a forecast has been made. If the forecast exceeds the critical value V_e^* the investment proposal will be accepted, and this is a correct decision process. Only after the investment has been implemented however, will the true net present value, V_0 be known. The observed difference from the forecast can be defined as $(V_r - V_0)$ or if V_e is used as $(V_e - V_0)$. Since we assume $V_r = E(V_0)$ the expected bias resulting from the use of V_e is $(V_e - V_r)$. For the above example, if we have $V_e = \$1,000,000$, then

$$V_r = -221,311 + .5902 V_e$$

$$V_r = -221,311 + .5902(1,000,000) = 368,908.$$

The expected bias from the post-audit use of V_e is

$$V_e - V_r = 1,000,000 - 368,908 = \$631,092.$$

Since the forecast was greater than the prior mean, we should expect a systematic tendency for the forecast of $1,000,000 to be greater than the subsequently observed actual values (positive bias).

Conclusions

The existence of uncertainty not only raises the possibility that an investment that is acceptable may turn out to be undesirable, but also that an investment that seems to be unacceptable may turn out to be desirable if additional information is obtained. The value of the additional information must be balanced against the cost of the information.

After an investment has been accepted there is a need to evaluate the results of operating the investment compared to the forecasts used to make the investment decision. The possibility of post-audit bias arises in this situation if the forecast being used in the post audit does not incorporate all the relevant information—in particular if it leaves out prior information.

If post audits are done using forecasts that incorporate all of the information, there should be no post-audit bias. When such forecasts are used, and a bias is detected, it would indeed be a signal that corrective action to improve the forecasts may be appropriate.

Appendix. Calculations to Revise Probabilities

From Table 18-1 we obtain:

$$P(G|e_1) = .9 \qquad P(G|e_2) = .2 \qquad P(B|e_1) = .1$$

$$P(B|e_2) = .8$$

The joint probabilities are:

$$P(G, e_1) = P(G|e_1)P(e_1) = .9 \times .4 = .36$$

$$P(G, e_2) = P(G|e_2)P(e_2) = .2 \times .6 = .12$$

$$P(G) = \underline{.48}$$

$$P(B, e_1) = P(B|e_1)P(e_1) = .1 \times .4 = .04$$

$$P(B, e_2) = P(B|e_2)P(e_2) = .8 \times .6 = .48$$

$$P(B) = \underline{.52}$$

$$P(e_1|G) = \frac{.36}{.48} = .75 \qquad P(e_2|G) = .25$$

$$P(e_1|B) = \frac{.04}{.52} = .077 \qquad P(e_2|B) = .923$$

Questions and Problems

18-1. You are asked to provide statistical advice about capital budgeting decisions to the president of a corporation. For each project the president receives an estimate of its expected NPV from the division V.P. (denoted by V_0). He receives as well the standard deviation of the estimate (denoted σ_0). He also has or can obtain a separate estimate of the expected NPV from his corporate finance staff (denoted by V_e). The standard deviation of that estimate is denoted σ_e. The president wants to accept investments whose true NPV is positive and is willing to assume for decision-making purposes that V_0 and V_e are both *unbiased* normally distributed estimates of the true net present value.

The president has the following information already (in millions of dollars).

$$V_0 = .1 \qquad \sigma_e = .06 \qquad \sigma_0 = .08$$

He has instructed his corporate finance staff to obtain V_e. Since a prompt decision is needed, and he will be in Peking for three weeks, he has instructed his secretary to tell the division vice president to go ahead with the investment if V_e is greater than K, or to cancel it if V_e is less than K. The correct value of K is _____ (Show your calculations).

18-2. (*Continuation of 18-1.*)

For a third project the president already has the following information

$$V_0 = \$75,000 \qquad \sigma_e = \$1,000,000 \qquad \sigma_0 = \$150,000$$

The uncertainty about this project is all technological. The corporate research laboratory has assured the president that a $100,000 lab experiment could provide perfect information about the value of this project. What is the expected value of perfect information in this case? (Show your calculation.)

18-3. For the project referred to in question 18-2, the president could contract with an outside consultant to obtain an opinion about the value of project. The consultant's estimate will be unbiased, have a standard deviation of $100,000 and will cost $10,000. Which of the following alternatives is best?

a. Obtain perfect information from the lab.
b. Obtain imperfect information from the consultant.
c. Obtain information from both sources.
d. Accept the investment now.
e. Reject the investment now.

Show your calculations.

18-4. The Phil T. Rich Oil Company has a lease on the mineral deposits of a parcel of land. Geologists have provided the following opinions of what might be found if an exploratory well is drilled on this property.

Outcomes	Probability	PV of Resources Discovered (millions of dollars)
Only Gas Deposit	.18	5.0
Only Oil Deposit	.08	10.0
Both Oil and Gas	.02	15.0
Neither Oil nor Gas	.72	0
Total	1.00	

The possible gas deposits are in a geological formation approximately one mile below the surface. A well that stopped at this level could be drilled for $1.2 million ($0.8 million to set up the drill rig plus $0.4 million to drill the first mile.). The possible oil deposits are in a formation two miles below the surface. (The extra costs of drilling the second mile are $0.6 million if the drilling contractor is told before drilling begins, and $1.1 million if a decision is made after the well has already been drilled for the first mile.)

If Rich Oil does not spend at least $0.5 million exploring for oil on their property, its lease will expire at the end of the year.

Mr. Rich is considering the following alternatives:

a. Do nothing. Let the lease expire.
b. Drill for gas only.
c. Drill for gas. Then decide whether or not to continue to drill for oil.
d. Drill a two-mile deep well (This would find whatever gas or oil is on the property.).

The incremental costs (in millions of dollars) associated with each alternative are:

a. 0
b. 1.2
c. 1.2 (minimum) or 2.3 (maximum)
d. 1.8

In answering the following questions, assume that Rich Oil's objective is to maximize the expected net present value of its decision. For alternatives a, b, and d find the cost of the alternatives, the expected present value of the resources discovered, and the expected net present value of the alternative. Show all calculations. Which of the three actions is preferred?

18-5. (*Continuation of 18-4.*)

Based on his intuition, Mr. Rich has chosen alternative c. The drill is down to the $\frac{3}{4}$ mile level, and he is beginning to think carefully about the decision that will face him soon. He has rearranged the probability estimate provided by his geologists in the following form:

	Gas Present	Gas Not Present	Raw Totals
Oil Present	.02	.08	.10
Oil not Present	.18	.72	.90
Column Totals:	.20	.80	1.00

a. What is the best action for Mr. Rich if gas is found at the one mile level? Why?

b. What is the best action for Mr. Rich if gas is not found at the one mile level? Why?

18-6. (*Continuation of 18-4.*)

Asked to explain why he chose alternative c, Mr. Rich replied as follows:

"There were two advantages to that alternative. First I might find some gas. Second, I would find some information about the possibility of oil. Information is valuable in this business. I know I paid for the information. But it was worth it!"

Do you agree that *in this case*, the information is valuable? Explain. (It is acceptable, but not necessary, to calculate the value of the information to answer this question.)

Discussion Question

18-A. George Beardsley and Edwin Mansfield studied the experience of a giant multinational corporation in forecasting the profitability of new products. (*Journal of Business*, January, 1978). Specifically, the corporation recorded a forecast of the profitability of each new product at the time it was decided to produce the product. Each new product was post-audited nine years later, when its actual profitability was known. Beardsley and Mansfield found that "... the initial forecasts tend to be relatively optimistic in cases where actual profits were small and relatively pessimistic in cases where actual profits were large. Specifically, the forecasts underestimated the profitability of ... new products where they exceeded about $1 million, and overestimated the profitability of less profitable new products..." (pp. 130–131).

Two interpretations of these results are listed below. For each interpretation, indicate whether you believe the interpretation given is necessarily wrong or is not necessarily wrong (i.e., it could be correct). Give a brief explanation of your reasons.

1. The initial forecasts of new products whose true profitability was less than $1 million may be unbiased estimates of the true profitability of those new products.
2. The initial forecasts correspond to Bayesian revised forecasts that correctly incorporate relevant prior information.

CHAPTER **19**

Foreign Investments

"F.A.S.B 8 is the worst set of rules for foreign exchange accounting I have ever heard of—except for all the others anyone has ever shown me," a senior vice president of the Exxon Corporation once said.[1]

—*Deborah Rankin, The New York Times, May 8, 1978, p. D-1.*

We will define foreign investments as existing when the benefits to be derived through time are in a different currency than the currency of the initial investment. There is an implication that there will be at least two translations of currencies, one at the time of the initial investment and the second at the time that cash flows are returned to the country of the investing company.

In this chapter we will consider several complexities. The first is the necessity to consider the currency translation. The second is the necessity of considering the nature of the investment. This second problem is not unique to international investments, but is apt to occur more frequently in this setting. We then briefly discuss taxes, the remission of funds, and risk.

Currency Translation

Assume that two divisions are competing for funds. In one division an investment of $1,000,000 will return a 15 percent return, and in the second division a 35 percent return and a higher net present value can be earned. If these returns have been defined in terms of local currencies, then further adjustments are necessary.

Define

r to be the required rate of return of the parent company (say in dollars);
j to be the rate of devaluation of the currency of the investment;
k to be the rate of return that should be required in terms of the currency of the investment.

---

[1] One of "the others," F.A.S.B 52, has replaced F.A.S.B 8.

We want:

$$1 + r = \frac{1 + k}{1 + j},$$

or

$$k = r + j + rj.$$

Example

Assume the C Can Company requires an internal rate of return of .10. It is considering investing $1,000 in a country with a currency called "yen," which is devaluating its currency relative to the dollar at a rate of .20 per year. The $r = .10$, and $j = .20$, and

$$k = r + j + rj$$
$$= .10 + .20 + .02 = .32.$$

Assume that the current exchange rate is $1 for 1.20 yen and that one year from today the rate is expected to be $1 per 1.44 yen. If $1,000 is invested today the firm wants back $1,100 one year from today. That is, it must earn .32 on the investment of 1,200 yen or 1,584 yen.

$$1,200(1.32) = 1,584 \text{ yen.}$$

The 1,584 yen will be worth $1,100,

$$\frac{1,584}{1.44} = \$1,100,$$

and the firm will earn 10 percent on its initial investment of $1,000. In order to earn 10 percent in dollars the foreign subsidiary had to earn 32 percent in yen.

Now let us assume that the exchange rate next period will be $.8(1.20) = .96$ yen to a dollar and $j = -.20$. We now have

$$1 + k = (1 + r)(1 + j),$$

or

$$k = r + j + rj,$$

but

$$j = -.20,$$

and

$$k = .10 - .20 - .02 = -.12.$$

The investment of $1,000 and 1,200 yen now only has to return $1,200(1 - .12) = 1,056$ yen one year from now. The 1,056 yen will convert to $1,100 using the .96 conversion rate.

A Different Approach

The formulation

$$k = r + j + rj$$

is most useful as a device that reminds us that both the corporation's domestic required return and the change in the exchange rate must be considered in evaluating the investments of a foreign subsidiary. Also, the interaction term (rj) is not obvious, and the formulation reminds us of the necessity of including it.

Now we will switch to a more intuitive approach to the problem. Rather than computing an average percentage change in exchange rates or predicting one rate for all periods, the analyst will predict the exchange rate each period. The foreign currency will be converted to dollars to determine the net present value or internal rate of return of the investment. Assume the following cash flows and forecasted exchange rates exist.

Time	Yen	Conversion Rates	Dollars
0	−1,000,000	100 yen for $1	−$10,000
1	+ 100,000	80 yen for $1	+ 1,250
2	+1,100,000	50 yen for $1	+ 22,000

Using a 10 percent rate of discount the present value of the yen cash flow is zero. The present value of the dollar cash flow is $9,317.

$$
\begin{aligned}
-10,000 \times 1.0000 &= -10,000 \\
+ 1,250 \times .9091 &= 1,136 \\
+22,000 \times .8264 &= \underline{18,181} \\
&\ \ \underline{\$9,317}
\end{aligned}
$$

The internal rate of return moves from 10 percent in yen to 54 percent computed using dollars.

The Irrelevance of Future Plans

It is sometimes argued that only the analysis for the foreign currency should be done, since we are probably going to reinvest the yen in the same country when the yen is earned. Only the exchange rates when the cash flows are returned are alleged to be relevant.

The fact is that if the funds were returned to dollars they would have an internal rate of return of 54 percent (in the most recent example). If it is more desirable to leave the funds invested in the foreign land, that is a second decision.

There is one exception to the above conclusion. This exception occurs if the sequential foreign investments are economically linked. If one investment is made the second investment follows, and the second investment can only be made if the first investment is made. In these situations the two sequential investments should be treated as one alternative, and the cash flows converted into dollars only after the second investment is financed.

But if this limited situation does not exist, the analysis should be as if the exchange into dollars takes place for the first investment.

The Leverage Consideration

Frequently investments in foreign countries are made by forming subsidiary corporations. These subsidiaries frequently will have one or more partners and are financed heavily with debt. We argue that the additional leverage changes the required return. This conclusion assumes the existence of uncertainty.

Assume a situation where a firm is considering a $10,000 investment in a piece of equipment. The firm uses 10 percent as the rate of discount. There is uncertainty and possibility of two equally likely outcomes:

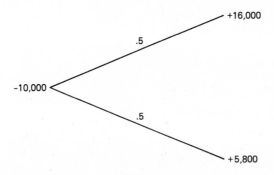

The expected outcome is $10,900 and the expected net present value is $-91. Using 10 percent the investment is not acceptable based on expected net present value.

Let us assume that the firm is financed with .4 debt and .6 common stock and the following costs apply:

	Capital Structure	Costs	Weighted Costs
Debt	.4	.06	.024
Common Stock	.6	.127	.076
Weighted Average Cost			.100

Right or wrong, assume the firm uses the average capital cost of 10 percent to evaluate investments.

While the equipment has been rejected in the United States there is an opportunity to buy it for a foreign subsidiary. Since the foreign subsidiary is financed with .5 debt, $5,000 is required as an investment by the parent.

The following stock equity cash flows will occur if the debt costs .07. We assume a 1 yen for 1 dollar exchange rate with no forecasted changes.

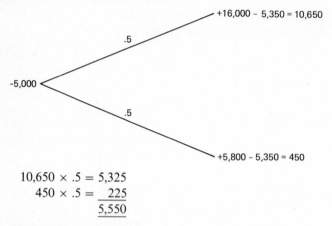

$$10,650 \times .5 = 5,325$$
$$450 \times .5 = \underline{225}$$
$$5,550$$

The $5,550 is a 11 percent return on the $5,000 investment and the investment is desirable, using the parent's discount rate of 10 percent. The expected net present value is $45. The switch in decisions is caused by the inclusion of more debt and the switch to the use of stock equity cash flows in the analysis of the foreign investment. Despite the increase in the cost of debt to .07, the investment is now deemed to be acceptable.

The investment of the $5,000 funds by the parent firm is being evaluated differently overseas than it is being evaluated domestically. Assume that we describe the problem so that the entire investment is domestic, but the subsidiary and its debt still exists. Most business analysts would reject the second analysis that says that the otherwise unacceptable investment is now acceptable. The investment is made to seem acceptable by the implicit inclusion of debt flows in the analysis and the switch to stock equity cash flows. It is far from obvious that 10 percent is the appropriate discount rate to evaluate the cash flows consisting of the $5,000 outlay followed by $5,550 of expected benefits one period later. We know that with .4 debt the stockholders required a .127 return. The subsidiary has .5 debt and if the analysis is to be done in terms of the cash flows to the stockholders then a return larger than .127 must be used.

In the above analysis the inclusion of the additional debt of the subsidiary was made obvious. Frequently in evaluating investments in foreign subsidiaries the inclusion of the debt is less obvious. The comparison is made by earning 10 percent on funds invested domestically or 15 percent on funds invested overseas. It is not made clear that the 15 percent return is on funds invested in the stock equity of a subsidiary and only results because of the additional debt that is incorporated in the analysis.

Taxes

The tax laws applicable to international trade are apt to change through time. Thus only general principles will be discussed in this section.

A primary tax issue is whether a tax paid in a foreign country will be treated as an expense (thus worth t_c per dollar as a deduction where t_c is the domestic corporate tax rate) or as a tax credit (thus worth $1 per dollar as a credit against taxes paid).

A second tax issue arises as to the extent of tax deferral that is feasible by not bringing back the earnings of the subsidiary to the home country. Tax deferral is a powerful incentive, and its possibility will greatly affect decision-making. Bringing back earnings and having them taxed compared to keeping them invested without being taxed are forms of mutually exclusive investments.

In some situations government rules will prevent the free flow of funds across national boundaries and thus further complicate decisions as to reinvest or commit additional funds.

Remission of Funds

Given legislation limiting the flow of funds, companies tend to develop strategies to facilitate the transfer of funds. Among these strategies are for the parent to supply capital in the form of debt so that payments of interest and principal accomplish the transfer, or inflate the intracompany transfer prices for materials or services. These manipulations also affect the taxes of the several jurisdictions under which the companies operate.

One of the simpler techniques for transferring funds is for the subsidiary to declare a cash dividend. Unfortunately institutional complexities may cause the firm to benefit from more roundabout strategies.

Foreign Investment and Risk

Foreign investment is a form of risk diversification. A foreign investment may be riskier than a domestic investment, but at the same time its overall effect on the risk of the corporation might be to reduce it.

For purposes of illustration assume that the variance of a domestic investment is 100, while the variance of a foreign investment is 250 (say there is a political risk).

The domestic investment is perfectly correlated with the current investments, however, while the foreign investment is independent of the current investments of the firm.

If the current variance of the firm's investments is 1,600, the variance of the firm with the domestic investment is

$$\text{Var (firm)} + \text{Var (investment)} + 2\sigma_{firm}\,\sigma_{investment}$$

$$1,600 + 100 + 2(40)(10) = 2,500.$$

With the foreign investment we have for the firm's variance,

$$1,600 + 250 = 1,850.$$

Even though the variance of the foreign investment is 2.5 times as large as the variance of the domestic investment, it has a significantly more desirable effect on the firm's risk.

The company's stockholders are also likely to benefit from the foreign diversification, since it is a form of diversification that is not likely to be implemented by the average stockholder of the firm.

Conclusion

Assume we start with two identical risk and return situations relative to the real investments in plant and equipment. One opportunity is domestic and the second is a foreign subsidiary. If the domestic investment is treated as a conventional investment and the basic investment cash flows are used but the foreign investment's cash flows are those of a residual investor (stockholder) a strong bias is introduced in the analysis for the foreign investment. There should be an upward switch in the required return if the stock equity cash flows are used instead of the investment cash flows.

Second, it should be remembered that the foreign currency must be translated back into the domestic currency in computing the present value or internal rate of return of the investment.

Questions and Problems

19-1. Company A required a .20 return on its domestic investments. It is considering investing in a foreign subsidiary. The foreign currency is being devalued at a rate of .15 per year. What rate of return should be required?

19-2. Company B requires a .15 return on its domestic investments. It is considering investing in a foreign subsidiary. The foreign currency is appreciating against the dollar. The dollar is depreciating at the rate of .10 per year. What rate of return should be required for an investment in the foreign country?

19-3. Assume an investment of $1,000 yen will pay $1,380 after one year. If 1 yen will buy $1 at the beginning of the year, and $1.15 yen will buy $1 at the end of the year, what return has been earned on the initial investment of $1?

19-4. Assume an investment of $1,000 yen will pay $1,035 after one year. If 1 yen will buy $1 at the beginning of the year, and .90 yen will buy $1 at the end of the year, what return has been earned on the initial investment of $1?

19-5. The following cash flows and exchange rates apply to an investment being considered by the C Company.

Time	Exchange Rate	Cash Flow
0	1.20 yen to $1	−12,000 yen
1	1.50 yen to $1	+ 1,200 yen
2	2.00 yen to $1	+13,200 yen

If the parent firm requires a return of 20 percent is the investment desirable?

19-6. The following cash flows and exchange rates apply to an investment being considered by the D Company:

Time	Exchange Rate	Cash Flow
0	1.20 yen to $1	−12,000 yen
1	.80 yen to $1	+ 1,200 yen
2	.50 yen to $1	+13,200 yen

If the parent company requires a return of 20 percent is the investment desirable?

19-7. The E Company is thinking of investing $10,000,000 in a foreign subsidiary (no exchange rate changes are expected). The investment is expected to earn 11 percent. The subsidiary is financed .6 with debt and .4 with common stock. The parent has a weighted average cost of capital of .10:

	Cost	Capital Structure	Weighted Cost
Debt	.08	.5	.04
Common Stock	.12	.5	.06
			.10

A return of .10 is required on investments. Assume the capital of the parent is $100,000,000 and the capital of the subsidiary is $50,000,000.

Required: Should the $10,000,000 be invested? Explain.

19-8. Assume the F Company makes decisions using expected monetary value, and has a 10 percent time-value factor.

It is considering the following investment:

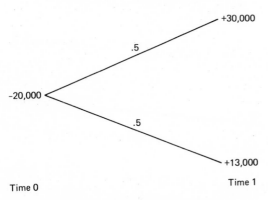

Time 0

Time 1

The expected monetary value at time 1 is $\frac{1}{2}(43,000) = \$21,500$. This is a 7.5 percent return on the investment of $20,000.

a. Should the investment be accepted?

b. Now assume the same investment is being considered by a subsidiary that is financed .7 by debt and .3 by common stock. The debt of the subsidiary costs .05. What expected return will the parent make on an investment of $6,000 in the subsidiary to purchase the equipment? Is the investment acceptable?

19-9. LDC is a poor but progressive country on the northern coast of a large continent in the Southern Hemisphere. The Prime Minister of LDC has to choose between two tax policies for foreign multinational corporations doing business in LDC. The estimated tax yields over the next four years are as follows:

Policy	Year				
	1	2	3	4	5
A	40	40	0	0	0
B	35	25	25	10	0

Both policies result in shifting the tax burden to foreigners. Whichever policy is adopted, the foreign multinational corporations will eventually learn how to avoid bearing the tax. Some new tax strategy will be required within five years. The Prime Minister has friends at major international banks who can invest excess funds (if any) at 10 percent or will lend money at that rate, if it can be repaid.

The Prime Minister wants your advice as to which tax policy she should choose. Explain.

20

Economic Evaluation of Private Investment Proposals: The Government's Point of View

Without development there is no profit, without profit no development.

—Joseph A. Schumpeter, Theory of Economic Development (Cambridge, Mass.: Harvard University Press, 1934), p. 154.

In the other chapters we have been concerned with methods of evaluating the economic worth of proposed investment projects from the point of view of the managers or owners of a business. An investment proposal that appears desirable to the business that proposes it may be considered to be unattractive from the point of view of a government. Similarly, a proposal that is unattractive to a business may be considered to be attractive to the government. The purpose of the present chapter is to introduce the reader to some of the differences between evaluating the economic impact of investment projects from a business point of view and from the point of view of a government agency.

Many executives in private business corporations will encounter situations in which to do their jobs effectively they must understand how investments are evaluated from a public economic point of view. In most countries today it is necessary to obtain approvals from one or more government agencies before an important business investment can be undertaken. A proposed investment must be justified not only to a board of directors but to officials from a finance ministry or a government planning office. These officials will be more interested in the cost and benefits from a public point of view than in the profitability to the corporation. Many principles of economic analysis relevant to evaluating investments from the point of view of the owners are also relevant to evaluating investments from a public economic viewpoint, however.

Businesses frequently have to give some attention to the effects an investment has on groups other than the owners of the business proposing it. For example, American businesses have been called upon to cooperate in helping to solve the balance of payments problems of the United States. It is not difficult to cite examples in which business investments that were economic from the point of view of the business organization proposing them were opposed by others because of water pollution, air pollution, or detrimental effects on scenic values.

The primary considerations to be incorporated in an evaluation of investments from a public economic point of view are

1. How large are the net benefits that would be derived from the proposed investment?
2. Who would receive the benefits?
3. By what means would the benefits become available to the recipients?

The first question refers to matters of economic efficiency. The second refers to matters of income distribution. The relevance of these two questions should be fairly clear. The relevance of the third question may be less apparent. The means by which benefits are distributed to a group may influence the satisfaction they derive from the benefits. It seems likely, for example, that both American farmers and countries that derive foreign exchange from exports of basic commodities would prefer an increase in income resulting from a higher price for the commodities they sell, to an equal increase in income in the form of a grant that has the characteristics of an unearned gift.

Although in principle the answers to all three questions are relevant to deciding on the value of a proposed investment, we shall concentrate in this chapter on the computations that must be made in order to measure the size of the net benefits.

In the following discussion we shall assume that we begin with an investment proposal that has already been analyzed from the point of view of its profitability to the owners of the business, using the procedures suggested earlier. The process of adjusting this analysis to a public economic point of view can be thought of as consisting of three basic steps.

In evaluating investments a business uses market prices to estimate the relevant cash flows. However, for a variety of reasons, market prices may not truly reflect opportunity costs of resources used or the opportunity value of the production. Whenever there is a systematic and material difference between the market price and these opportunity prices, the latter should be substituted for corresponding market prices.

A second type of adjustment is necessary when an investment is so large, relative to the markets in which its factors of production will be purchased or in which its products will be sold, that acceptance of the investment will appreciably change the relevant market price or opportunity price of one or more of the resources used or produced. When this is the case, neither the market prices, nor the opportunity costs that would have prevailed without the project, nor the prices with the project, will exactly measure the benefits or costs of accepting the project. In these circumstances we should use a price in between the price that would have prevailed without the project and the price that will prevail with it.

Some investment projects will lead to changes in the efficiency of other economic activities in the society. Such changes in efficiency may be beneficial or detrimental. In either case it is desirable to take them into account when evaluating the economic worth of investments from a public point of view.

The following sections discuss each of the preceding adjustments in some detail.

Discrepancies Between Market Prices and Opportunity Prices

The opportunity price or cost of a resource is the value of the resource used in its most valuable manner. In a competitive market there is a strong tendency for market prices to represent opportunity prices. Customers will tend to purchase additional units of a product whenever the value of the product to them is more than the price. Similarly, producers will tend to produce an additional unit whenever the price of an additional unit is greater than the extra cost of producing it (where cost is the opportunity cost of the factors of production). In equilibrium, under these conditions, the price of a commodity will measure both the value of an additional unit to customers and the incremental cost of producing it.

Monopoly Pricing

When a commodity is being produced under monopolistic (or oligopolistic) conditions, market prices are likely to differ from opportunity prices. A firm in a monopolistic position will find that it can increase its profits by pricing its products at something more than the extra cost of producing an additional unit. The market price will represent the marginal value of the commodity to the user, but not generally the cost of producing an additional unit.

If an investment proposal involves using factors of production purchased from a monopolistic firm operating within the government's boundaries, a better measure of the cost of the project, from a public economic point of view, can be obtained by substituting an estimate of the marginal cost of the products for the actual market prices.

Unemployed Resources

If in the absence of the project a resource would be unemployed, and if the resource cannot be stored, the appropriate opportunity price for using that resource in the project may be less than its market price. In some countries there is considerable unemployment and underemployment of resources, particularly unskilled labor. If a person who would otherwise be unemployed is put to work as a result of a new investment project, the wages paid may considerably overstate the true opportunity cost of using the person in this particular project. In fact, the opportunity to work may have a positive value taking into consideration the morale of the unemployed workers. With some particularly unpleasant or dangerous work the opportunity price may be greater than zero. More importantly, if labor must be induced to move from one location to another or be retrained, there may be some significant opportunity costs in employing the labor, even if the alternative would be to leave it unemployed. In addition to the direct cost of moving the workers, there may be costs associated with providing housing, schools, and various government facilities for the additional population at the new location. These are costs that might be avoided if the workers remained in their old location. Even allowing for such costs the market wage rates are likely to overestimate the opportunity cost of labor when there is chronic unemployment.

Foreign Exchange Shortages

So far we have considered cases in which the market price for using a resource was higher than its opportunity price. There are also important cases in which the market price of a resource is less than its opportunity cost. An important example involves the use of imported goods or services when there are fixed official exchange rates. The official exchange rate may not properly measure the opportunity price of foreign exchange. If a business imports a commodity, the price paid is likely to be the world market price converted to domestic prices at the official exchange rate. The opportunity cost for foreign exchange is a better estimate of the cost to the country of using foreign exchange in this way. Some projects may produce goods for export. The value of a foreign exchange earned by the exports may be underestimated when the official exchange rate is used. The investment project may produce goods that are not exported but are substitutes for imported goods. Such goods may save foreign exchange by reducing the amount that would have otherwise been imported. Again the value of the foreign exchange saving should be estimated by using an opportunity price for an exchange rate to compute the value of the imports rather than the official exchange rate. These discrepancies are reduced or eliminated when exchange rates are allowed to fluctuate freely.

Savings versus Consumption

Ordinarily, in attempting to evaluate an investment project we measure the extra income (the benefits less the costs) that would be generated by the project, but we do not concern ourselves with how this income would be used. A justification for stopping with a measure of income is that, if the recipients are free to allocate income in any manner they desire, the opportunity value of an additional dollar used for savings will have the same value as an additional dollar used for consumption. In some less-developed countries this assumption may not be valid at the national level. If the country's economic development is inhibited by low levels of savings and investment, the government may consider an increment of income saved and invested to be of greater value in promoting the economic interests of the country than an increment of income used for current consumption. In these circumstances the government may wish to measure how the income generated by a project is likely to be used. The proportion of income that goes into savings may be given more weight than the proportion going into current consumption. The additional value attached to income that is saved and reinvested can be thought of as an opportunity price for savings.

Taxes

A major difference between the way investments would be evaluated from the point of view of the business and from the public point of view is related to the treatment of taxes. The business will be concerned with the after-tax cash flows associated with the investment. This is correct from the public point of view if the taxes are really prices charged for services rendered to the business by government bodies. Examples are tax assessments covering services such as water, sewage, police, and fire protection. Such taxes need to be deducted, but they may require adjustment, as it is unlikely that they reflect the additional cost of providing the additional services used as a result of the investment. Expenditures reflecting the costs of providing such services are a proper deduction from the benefits of an investment from the public economic point of view.

Most tax payments, however, cannot usefully be thought of as payments for identifiable quantities of services rendered a particular business. A large fraction of taxes collected in a government's boundaries may be used for such things as health, education, and national defense (or paying for past wars). A business may benefit from such services in a general way, but there is not likely to be an identifiable relationship between the amount of taxes paid by the business and the amount of benefit received. Because this is the case, the costs and benefits of an investment should be analayzed on an individual basis with an attempt to measure the cost of the government services to be used and the contribution of the investment to the financing of these services.

We have previously mentioned that, if a country's ability to achieve its economic goals is inhibited because savings are too low to finance the desired level of investment, it may be reasonable to attach a high opportunity price to that portion of the project's income that is channeled into savings. Government savings might be used to finance either its own investment projects or those of the private sector. If a government devoted a proportion of its tax revenues to savings and if political or administrative complications did not prevent the effective use of these savings, the extra revenues generated by a new investment project might have more value in contributing to the country's economic goals than the same amount of funds retained in the hands of consumers. This analysis suggests that an opportunity price may in some situations be assigned to government tax revenues. This will increase the measure of benefits associated with investments that generate tax revenues.

Indivisibilities

If a project is so large that the operation of the project would change the market prices of one or more of the inputs purchased or of the products being produced, the net public benefits of the project may not be properly measured using market prices. This may be true even when the market prices represent the opportunity costs of using the resources consumed in the project and the opportunity values of the resources produced. This special evaluation problem arises if for some technological reason the investment must be undertaken on at least a certain minimum scale, large enough so that some of the relevant prices would change as a result of building the project. There are many situations where a series of small incremental investments is not feasible technologically. A jet airport runway must be of a certain minimum size; a dam cannot stop halfway across a river; and a railroad must have at least one set of tracks, preferably with reasonable starting and ending locations.

Suppose that a hydroelectric project results in a 25 percent increase in electric output and that a 50 percent reduction in the price of electricity results in a sufficient expansion of the use of electricity to absorb this extra power. Even if the new price of electricity appropriately measures both the marginal cost of producing an extra unit of electricity and the marginal value of the extra unit in its various uses, the benefits of the investment cannot be measured in terms of revenues collected. Under the assumptions given, accepting the project would lead to a 37.5 percent reduction in total revenues collected by the electric-power generating system. If revenues were used as a measure of the benefits, one might conclude that the 25 percent increase in output would lead to a reduction in total benefits.

One difficulty in this case arises because all the electricity is sold at a price that tells how much one small increment of electricity is worth when added to the existing supply. However, the project would add not one small increment to the supply but a very large increment. Consumers as a group should be willing to pay more for the output of the project. The value of this additional increment, expressed as a price per unit, will be an amount somewhere between the market price that would have prevailed without the project and the market price that prevails with it.

The appropriate measure of benefits in such cases is illustrated in Figure 20-1.

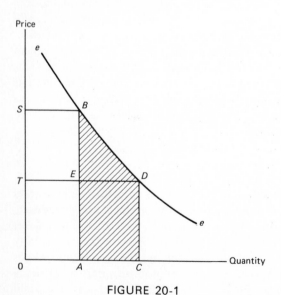

FIGURE 20-1

The vertical axis measures the price per unit, and the horizontal axis measures the rate of consumption in kilowatts per year. The curve *ee* is a market demand curve for electricity. Each point on the curve shows the quantity that would be sold at the corresponding price. Suppose that without the project a quantity *OA* would be produced (the marginal cost is *AB*) and sold at a price of *AB*. The total revenue collected under these circumstances is measured by the rectangle *OABS*. With the project, an additional quantity *AC* would be produced (with a marginal cost of *CD*). The market price will now be *CD* per unit. If all units are sold at that price, the total revenue collected with the new project would be measured by the rectangle *OCDT*. The additional amount that consumers are willing to pay for an increment of *AC* units of additional electricity, if the alternative were to do without this increment, is measured by the shaded area *ACDB*. It is this shaded area rather than the change in total revenues that properly measures the extra benefits from having this increment of electricity.

It is still necessary to subtract from these benefits an appropriate measure of the extra costs of providing this electricity. A problem similar to the revenue calculation occurs if a new investment project would materially change the prices of some of the resource inputs used in the project. Figure 20-2 represents an example of this sort. Suppose that in a country with only one steel mill it is proposed to build a second steel mill. Both the old and the new steel mills will require metallurgists. With just one steel mill *OG* metallurgists would be employed in the old mill at a salary of *GH*. The curve *ss* represents the potential supply of metallurgists at various salary levels. With the new mill, let us suppose that the total number who will be required in both the old and new mill increased by an amount *GI*. (The exact amount of the increase will depend on the demand curve of the product.) To increase the supply by this amount, it will be necessary

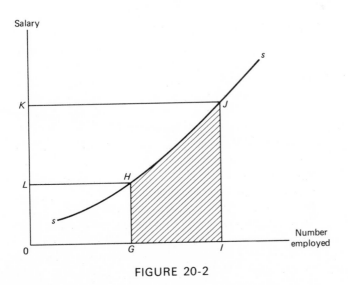

FIGURE 20-2

to pay a wage equal to *IJ*. The total wage bill for metallurgists with one steel mill is given by the area *OGHL*. The total wage bill for metallurgists with two steel mills is given by the area *OIJK*. The excess of the large area over the small area does not properly measure the extra cost to the country of obtaining the metallurgists required for the new mill, however. These extra costs are measured by the shaded area *GIJH*. The additional monetary payments that would in fact be paid to metallurgists if the new mill were built are transfers of income (in this case from the owners of the old steel mill to the metallurgists) in excess of the minimum needed to increase the supply of metallurgists. (For the minimum amount to take place, a discriminatory wage system would have to be used.) The actual wages would be used by a private owner of the mill, including the excess incentive to the workers; it should not be included in evaluating the new mill from the national economic point of view.

External Effects

An investment project may adversely affect the productivity of resources employed in other economic activities or the welfare of the population. To the extent that such changes are compensated for through market or legal institutional arrangement, their effect will tend to be included in the private benefit–cost evaluation of the investment. If the institutional arrangements do not provide for appropriate monetary compensation, these effects should be taken into account by incorporating implicit costs or benefits in evaluating the investment.

Suppose that a factory will produce a large amount of dirt and smoke. Consumers living where the dirt settles will spend more time dusting their furniture and more time and money cleaning clothes. Breathing the polluted air may even shorten their lives. In the absence of an appropriate tax on the factory that reduces its profit and compensates consumers for the additional expense and trouble, the smoke would be an uncompensated external diseconomy that should be taken into account in evaluating a project from the national point of view.

In other cases an investment may directly affect the productivity of resources employed in other enterprises. If a farmer installs drainage tiles on one field, the productivity of some of the neighbor's fields receiving the runoff may also be increased. An oil company drilling a wildcat well on its own land may provide valuable information about the possibility of oil on adjacent land that it does not control. Sometimes a drilling company is able to obtain compensation from its neighbors for the value of this information in the form of a payment toward the cost of the well, but generally there is no compensation for this type of information. A private utility may build a dam to generate electricity. An uncompensated effect of the dam might be to reduce the danger of flooding on downstream land. Unless it owned the land, the utility would not count this as a benefit derived from its investment. From a public point of view, decreased flood damage is a benefit attributable to the dam.

Investments by Governments

Governments facing investment decisions have exactly the same basic problem as business managers, that is, measuring the costs and benefits of each period and transforming them all back to the present so that one measure of value may be obtained.

Public servants do have a somewhat more difficult problem of measuring benefits because they know they should include the social benefits (and costs) of the project. The business manager may choose to take refuge in profit maximization of the firm and not include the social costs and benefits. (We are not saying that this position is desirable.)

Government projects are not without risk, so the government official is also faced with the necessity of making a risk analysis. The position of a national government is analogous to that of a well-diversified investor when it comes to evaluating project risk. Primary attention must be focused on the systematic risk of the project.

The choice of interest rate is an interesting problem.[1] The government has two basic choices:

1. Its borrowing rate.
2. The opportunity cost to the economy as measured by the cost of funds to business or the required return the firms are using.

The borrowing rate of the government is attractive because it is objectively measured and easily determined. Unfortunately, the rate itself is frequently a result of decisions of government (or near government) officials and may not reflect the opportunity cost of investments to the economy.

The second measure considered is the cost of funds to firms (or their required return); this measure is attractive, but again the information is difficult to obtain. Firms use a wide range of hurdle rates and frequently include risk adjustments. The rate used to take time value of money into account should not include a risk factor.

An added complication is the fact that business firms are taxed and government entities are not. Thus the investments of government should be placed on the same tax basis as the investments of corporations. This also means that the discount rate used by the government body should be on the same tax basis as the business firm.

For example, if we assume that investors require a return of .06 for both debt and stock, and if there is a .48 corporate tax rate, the following represents the cost of capital calculation if the firm uses 40% debt:

---

[1] For a comprehensive analysis of this problem see Robert C. Lind *et al*, *Discounting for Time and Risk in Energy Policy*, Resources for the Future, Inc., 1982.

	Before-Tax Required Return	Tax Rate	After-Tax Return to Cor- poration	Return to Investor	Tax Saving from Interest	After-Tax Cost to Cor- poration
Debt	.0600	.48	.0600	.0600	.0288	.0312
Stock	.1154	.48	.0600	.0600	—	.0600

	After-Tax Cost	Capital Structure	Weighted Average
Debt	.0312	.4	.0125
Stock	.0600	.6	.0360
			.0485

To make its discount rate equivalent, the government body would compute a before-tax required return. Thus its time value of money would be as follows:

	Before-Tax Required Return	Capital Structure	Weighted Average
Debt	.0600	.4	.024
Stock	.1154	.6	.069
			.093

Although the .093 required return is higher than the .0485 after-tax return of the business firms, it must be remembered that we are placing the government required return on a before-tax basis that is equal to the before-tax required return of the business firm. There is also a difference in the way benefits are measured. The private firm will apply its after-tax required return to the after-tax cash flows from the investment. If the government uses an equivalent before-tax discount rate, it should be applied to the before-tax benefits of the project.

The argument may be made that the required return of government should be lowered because the benefits of a business firm are incorrectly measured (omitting social costs) and the benefits of government enterprises are understated (omitting social benefits). These facts may require an adjustment, but the adjustment should not be in the form of changing the required time-value factor. Also, if either of the .06 required returns included a risk factor, this factor should be excluded by the government in discounting for time.

Cost–Benefit Analysis

The use of the term *cost–benefit analysis* to describe the valuation of government projects is widespread. Although the term might well refer to several different procedures, the usual interpretation is a ratio of the present value of benefits to the present value of costs. This is, of course, the same calculation that we described as the index of present value.

We were critical of the present-value index as a method of ranking investments and all the criticisms carry over to the cost–benefit calculation. Its use may be beneficial, however, if one or more of the following apply:

1. All investments are accepted whose benefit–cost ratio is greater than 1.
2. The best investment is "continuous" and we invest all the funds in it.
3. Only investments with benefit–cost ratios greater than 1 are accepted; then at least the government has chosen acceptable investments. (They may not be the best.)
4. The computation of the benefit–cost ratio initiated a calculation of the benefits and costs of the investment that would otherwise not be made.

Conclusions

It is apparent that different analyses of the desirability of investments may be appropriate for managerial decision-making and for decision-making where the objective is to take the public economic point of view into consideration. We have suggested several adjustments that might be made to the analysis prepared by the business manager. These adjustments generally require subjective judgments by the analyst.

The business manager might wish for a laissez-faire attitude on the part of government and for the government planners to allow any investment deemed desirable by persons willing to bet their fame or fortune, but the institutional fact remains that in most countries the considerations described in this chapter are relevant.

It is obvious that the manager should be aware of factors taken into consideration by the government planning organization when it attempts to decide whether or not a private investment project should be approved. In like manner the planning organization that is not aware of the factors considered by the business manager (or owner) in making investment decisions is at a severe disadvantage.

The discussion in this chapter of adjustments that can be made to investment project proposals to make them reflect the projects' effects on the economy should not be interpreted as a recommendation by the authors that governments should institute controls over private investment activity. A full discussion of this issue is beyond the scope of this book, although some points might be mentioned. Market prices may imperfectly measure the national economic benefits of a project, but it does not follow that a system of investment controls would be preferable. Market prices have the advantage of being relatively objective; their use facilitates decentralized decision-making and prompt adjustment to changed circumstances. At best, direct government controls have the disadvantage of adding to the time and expense needed to implement investment decisions. There is no guarantee that an attempt to estimate the public economic benefits of a project, requiring as it does a high level of analytical ability and a detailed knowledge of many sectors of the economy, possibly influenced by political considerations, will in practice produce an estimate that is consistently closer to the true measure than the unadjusted private estimate based on market prices.

Questions and Problems

20-1. There are three purchasers of a product; each is willing to pay the following amounts for one unit per period:

Purchaser	Price Purchaser is Willing to Pay
A	$10 (for first unit)
A	8 (for second unit)
B	7
C	5

There are four suppliers; each is willing to supply one unit per period at the following prices or higher:

Supplier	Price
W	$12
X	10
Y	9
Z	8 (for second unit)
Z	7 (for first unit)

Assume that the preceding prices for the suppliers also represent their marginal costs.

Required: (a) At what price would you expect the product to sell, and how many units would you expect to be sold per period? (b) What total (maximum) revenue would the purchasers of the product be willing to pay? At what total cost would the suppliers be willing to sell?

20-2. A major investment project will employ 100,000 workers. Presently 40,000 of these workers are employed, but the remainder are unemployed. Those that are employed are currently earning $20 million per year; it is expected that they will earn $60 million per year when the new project begins operation. The other workers will earn $30 million.

It will cost $2 million to retrain the workers for their new jobs and $1 million to move them to new living locations. The cost of new governmental and service facilities at their new location will be $10 million.

Required: Describe how the preceding information would be incorporated into the investment analysis from the point of view of the economy.

20-3. The exchange rate for a country is 2 yen for $1. A piece of equipment for an investment project will cost $100,000 or 200,000 yen. The country is short of dollars and wants to conserve its present supply. The planning board wants to choose between two alternative plans: (a) One suggestion is to use an effective exchange rate of 4 yen to $1. (b) Another suggestion is to use a higher discount rate for investments requiring the use of dollars than for investments using only domestic resources. For example, .08 could be used for the former and .04 for the latter. It is felt that there are current uses for dollars that will return, on a present-value basis, $2 for every $1 invested.

Required: How would you evaluate the desirability of the equipment?

20-4. The Airplane Company has a cost-plus-fixed-fee contract with the Air Force to build superjet transports. The government will buy any additional equipment that is needed and that is justified on a cost-saving basis.

The incremental tax rate for the company is .4.

The company has computed the following labor saving for a new piece of equipment that costs $18,334:

Time Period	
1	2
$10,000	$10,000 before tax
6,000	6,000 after tax

The company has an after-tax time value of money of .06, and the federal government has a before-tax time value of money of .05.

Required: Should the equipment be purchased?

20-5. Assume that the appropriate time discount for money is 5 percent on a before-tax basis and that the income tax rate is 40 percent. An investment opportunity is available requiring an outlay of $10,000 in year 0 and producing proceeds of $10,500 in year 1.

Required: Compute the present value on a before-tax and after-tax basis.

20-6. The before-tax cash flows are the same as in problem 20-5, but the outlay of $10,000 in period 0 is chargeable to expense for tax purposes in period 0.

Required: Compute the before-tax and after-tax cash flows.

20-7. The Eastern University has been offered a foundation grant of $2 million to establish a program in the administration of the arts. Although the program has been judged to be acceptable from an academic point of view, the president of the university does not want to accept the grant if it will drain resources from ongoing programs.

The following analysis of the program costs has been prepared:

	Annual Costs
Two professors of specialized interests	$ 60,000
Support of research personnel	40,000
Fringe benefits	9,000
Office space and other overhead	10,000
Student support	30,000
Administration	11,000
Overhead	20,000
Total	$180,000

Required: Should the president accept the grant?

20-8. The time value of money is 6 percent in country R and 8 percent in country P. Country P will not allow foreigners (from country R) to invest directly in country P. Country R is a rich country. Country P is poor. R has a foreign-aid program and it is considering two mutually exclusive proposals for helping country P. These are (a) make a gift of $5 million to country P; (b) make a $20 million loan to country P. Interest on the loan will be 5 percent, paid annually, with the principal to be repaid in a lump sum after twenty years.

You are a legislator in country R and you will have to vote for one or the other of these two proposals. Assume no uncertainty. Justify your answer, using the net present-value method.

Required: (a) Which alternative should you favor if you want to minimize the cost to country R of the aid it is providing to country P? (b) Which alternative should you favor if you want to maximize the benefit received by country P from R's foreign-aid program?

20-9. A state housing authority will lend funds at a cost of .05 to universities in the state to build student dormitories. The Private University has a proven need for dormitories, expected to cost $50,000,000, that would qualify it for the state loans. The board of trustees of Private has consistently followed a policy of borrowing no more than .4 of the cost of any facility and using the university's own resources for the remainder of the cost. There is $50,000,000 of endowment available (legally) for this type of construction, and members of the Board have argued that it should be used. Some argue that while $20,000,000 could be borrowed, they fear the degree of risk that would be associated with having a facility financed with 100 percent debt.

The current interest rate on long-term industrial bonds is .08 and long-term U.S. government bonds are earning .07.

Required: If you were advising the president of the university and the board of trustees, what would you recommend? What would you recommend if the university did not have the $20,000,000 of cash available for construction?

20-10. The U.S. Government has offered to assist a foreign government. For the construction of roads, it will lend $20,000,000 to be repaid forty years from now. For the first twenty years no interest will be paid, and then .03 interest will be paid per year (first payment twenty-one years from today).

The long-term borrowing rate for the U.S. Government is .07.

Required: A Senate committee is investigating the cost of foreign aid. Prepare a statement for the committee.

20-11. The present road between Town A and Town B was built fifty years ago and is poorly designed for modern autos. At present the traffic rate is 100,000 trips per year at an average cost (valuing time, fuel, etc.) of $100 per trip. If the road were rebuilt to modern standards it is estimated the traffic would increase to 1,000,000 trips per year, and the cost per trip would decline to $50.

Estimate the annual equivalent benefits of the rebuilt road. Assume the demand for road service is linear. (Hint: The "cost" per trip is analogous to the "price" on an ordinary demand curve.)

20-12. In evaluating the Alaskan Gas Pipeline two separate types of cost and benefit calculations are required. First, it is necessary to calculate the costs and benefits from the point of view of the corporation building the pipeline. Call these *private* costs and benefits. Second, it is necessary to calculate the costs and benefits from the point of view of the entire U.S. economy. Call these the *national* costs and benefits. For each of the following situations estimate what you consider to be the appropriate dollar measures of the private costs and of national costs. Explain the logic of your calculations. Assume all corporations are subject to a 40 percent tax rate, and all employed persons are subject to a 25 percent income tax rate.

During the intensive construction phase, 20,000 persons will be employed as welders on the pipeline project. Assume that all welders are paid the same wages, whether they are working on the project or elsewhere. Without the project, total employment of welders in the U.S. economy would be 100,000 persons earning an average of $16,000 per year. With the project, total employment of welders will be 110,000 persons and their average earnings will be $20,000 per year. Estimate the annual costs of employing welders during the intensive pipeline phase.

20-13. (*Continuation of 20-12.*)

During the intensive construction phase, 100,000 persons will be employed on the pipeline project in Alaska. Unemployment in the United States will decline by an equal amount. Some persons who are now unemployed will be hired directly to work on the pipeline. Other persons who are now employed will leave their present jobs to work on the pipeline, and presently unemployed persons will fill the positions they vacate.

All of the unemployed persons who will find jobs on the pipeline are now in forty-eight states south of the Canadian border. (There is no cyclical unemployment in Alaska.)

The average annual earnings of persons employed on the pipeline is $15,000 per year. The average income and expenditure of persons who are unemployed is

$4,000 per year. The cost of living is higher in Alaska mainly because of higher transportation and fuel costs. An unemployed person would need to spend $6,000 per year in Alaska to obtain the same standard of living that could have been obtained by spending $4,000 per year in the forty-eight states south of the Canadian border.

Estimate the annual employment costs per person that will be employed on the project.

20-14. (*Continuation of 20-12.*)

For each of the following items, indicate by a yes or no whether it should be included as a cost. Give a brief explanation.

Corporate income taxes that will be paid to the U.S. government.

Corporate income taxes that will be paid to the Canadian government.

Sales taxes that will be paid to the city of Fairbanks, Alaska.

Salaries for extra policemen that will be hired by the City of Fairbanks, Alaska to cope with traffic congestion that will be caused by the population increase resulting from the pipeline project.

Discussion Question

20-A. The country of Rajah has hired a firm of American consultants to decide on the desirability of a private corporation building a steel mill. The net annual benefits are computed to be $200 million before-taxes and $90 million on an after-tax basis. (The taxes are excise and income taxes.) The consultants computed the present value using the $90-million-a-year benefits.

Required: Comment on the computation of the annual benefits.

PART **FOUR**

In Part II the subject of uncertainty was introduced and the suggested solutions all involved subjective evaluations of risk. In this section we extend the subject to include the use of market measures of risk. From a theoretical point of view, this is a much more appealing approach to a solution. However, a practical manager whose goals extend beyond the market price of the firm's stock may want to adapt the theoretical solutions suggested in Chapters 23 and 24.

CHAPTER 21

An Overview of Capital Budgeting Under Uncertainty[1]

David Scott, Apollo 15 astronaut, on the blast-off: "You just sat there thinking that this piece of hardware had 400,000 components, all of them built by the lowest bidder."

—*Time, May 22, 1978, p. 81.*

We can expect that any manager concerned with investment decisions will sooner or later be forced to consider the fact that the outcomes of an investment are not known with certainty. Up to this point the solution to uncertainty-types of situations involved subjective evaluations by the decision maker as to the risk attitudes of the investor. The subjective nature of the decision process can be objected to since there is no exact set of rules for quantifying risk until we shift to allowing the market to place a price on risk. That is the direction in which this chapter is going. But first we will introduce a basic system for evaluating investments under conditions of uncertainty. The price for risk will be treated in a manner analogous with the way that a price for time value is treated.

We will briefly introduce the major elements of a useful approach to the capital budgeting decision under uncertainty. The objective will be to incorporate three factors into the calculations: the time value of money, the probability of an event occurring, and the value of a dollar received in a given state (condition of the world).

Prices With Certainty

Consider an investment that will pay $100 for certain after one time period and $200 after two time periods. If the appropriate time-value factor is .05, then we know that a dollar due in one time period is worth $\frac{1}{1.05} = .9524$ now. We can say that the "price" now of $1 due in one time period is .9524. In like manner the

---

[1] This chapter is adapted from a paper written by the authors titled "Capital Budgeting: A Review and a Forecast" published in *Bedrigfskunde*, January, 1976.

price now of $1 due in two time periods is .9070. Thus the present value of the proceeds from the investment is:

$100 × .9524 = $ 95
$200 × .9070 = $181
                        $276

In a situation of certainty, we would be willing to pay as much as $276 for the right to receive these proceeds.

If instead of earning $100 at time 1, the investment earned $146, we would merely substitute $146 for $100 in the above calculations. The .9524 would be unchanged, unless the time-value factor of .05 changed.

Prices With Uncertainty

We want to establish analogous "prices" for future dollars when uncertainty exists as for certainty. We will consider only a one-period horizon, where the only form of uncertainty that concerns us is uncertainty about the next period's cash flows. Consider an investment that has two possible cash flows next period. A tree diagram is a convenient way of illustrating the sequence of different possible outcomes that can occur. In this case, suppose there are two branches, with two different cash flows as illustrated. Each branch in the tree diagram represents a different possible "state of the world."

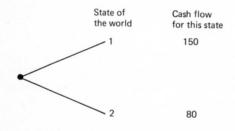

In the previous example we suggested the investment could be evaluated by multiplying the cash flow that would occur at time 1, $100, by a present-value factor, .9524, which represents the price of $1 in one period.

To evaluate investments under uncertainty, we suggest multiplying each of the possible cash flows that can occur by prices that represent the value now of a dollar to be received next period if a particular state of the world occurs. For example, suppose it was decided that $0.3204 was the right price for a dollar to be received next period if state 1 occurred, while if state 2 occurred, the price is $.6320. The investment evaluation process would be as follows:

(1)	(2)	(3)	(4)
	Value of a	Investment	
	Dollar Given	Cash Flow for	Risk-Adjusted
State i	State i	State i	Present Values
1	.3204	$150	$48.06
2	.6320	80	50.56
Totals	.9524		$98.62

Using this approach the total of the products in the last column—$98.62—would be the value of the cash proceeds.

To emphasize that this approach is a generalization of the use of present-value factors under conditions of uncertainty we recommend calling the prices in column 2 "risk-adjusted present-value factors" or RAPVFs. The total of the products of columns 2 and 3 in the last column is the "risk-adjusted present value of the investment."

Suppose an investment generates cash flows at time 1 of $100 for certain. Remember that a certain dollar received at time 1 should be discounted using .05 and is worth $(1.05)^{-1}$ or .9524.

State	RAPVF	Cash Flow	RAPV
1	.3204	$100	$32.04
2	.6320	100	63.20
Totals	.9524		$95.24

When the same cash flow is received in every state, the cash flows can be evaluated by summing up the RAPVFs over all states, and multiplying the total by the certain cash flow. The sum of the RAPVFs over all states is equal to the discount factor that would be applied to a certain cash flow. This approach can be generalized to cover multiperiod investments. As will be shown next, the RAPVFs must be estimated in a systematic fashion to obtain meaningful results.

The Three Factors

A risk-adjusted present-value factor can be considered to be the product of three terms: the probability that the state will occur; the present value of one dollar for certain; a risk-adjustment factor appropriate for that state. The probabilities must sum to 1 over all the states. Suppose, in our example, that the probability of the first state occurring is believed to be .7, and therefore the probability of the second state is .3. Using these values we can calculate an "expected" cash flow for the risky investment considered previously.

State	Cash Flow	Probability	Expected Cash Flow
1	150	.7	105
2	80	.3	24
Totals		1.0	129

The second term in the product is the present-value factor, the meaning of which has already been explained. Under the assumptions of this example, the present-value factor would be .9524 which corresponds to a one-period interest rate of 5 percent.

State	Expected Cash Flow	Present-Value Factor	Expected Present Value
1	105	.9524	100.00
2	24	.9524	22.86
	Total Expected Present Value		122.86

The third term in the product leading to the RAPVFs is the risk-adjustment factor. For a given state it represents the value of a dollar in the state. Each state has its own risk-adjustment factor. Just as present-value factors represent the price of certain dollars at different points in time, risk-adjustment factors represent the price of dollars in different states at the same point in time. These risk-adjustment factors do not consider either the time value of money or the probability of the event occurring. Ordinarily we would expect that an additional dollar would be less valuable in states in which we have larger incomes and wealth positions than in states in which we have smaller incomes and wealth positions. Therefore we would expect that the risk-adjustment factor would be below average in states in which most investors have above-average income and wealth, and above average in states in which they have below-average income and wealth. (Since the factors depend on income and wealth positions, the magnitudes of the outcomes may affect the values of the risk-adjustment factors if the outcomes are large relative to the decision-maker's income or wealth.)

Assume that state 1 in our example represents prosperity, and state 2 represents a severe depression. Assume a dollar in state 1 is worth $.48 at time 1 (the investor already has a cash surplus), and a dollar in state 2 is worth $2.212 (the investor is in desperate need for cash). These risk-adjustment factors are applied to the expected present value of the cash flows of each period. Continuing the calculations we again have a RAPV of $98.62.

State	Expected Present Value	Risk-Adjustment Factor	RAPV
1	$100.00	.4806	$48.06
2	22.86	2.2120	50.56
			$98.62

Multiplying the three components we obtain for the risk-adjusted present value factors for each state:

$.7 \times .9524 \times .4806 = .3204$

$.3 \times .9524 \times 2.212 = .6320$

which are the two "prices" we used previously.

We could also apply the risk-adjustment factors to the cash flows occurring in each state to obtain a risk-adjusted cash flow. These flows would be multiplied by present-value and probability factors to obtain RAPV. This would merely be changing the order of the calculations.

State	Cash Flow	Risk-Adjustment Factor	Risk-Adjusted Cash Flow
1	150	.4806	72.09
2	80	2.2120	176.96

Applying the probabilities and present-value factors to the risk-adjusted cash flows we again obtain $98.62.

State	Risk-Adjusted Cash Flow	Probability	Present-Value Factor	RAPV
1	72.09	.7	.9524	48.06
2	176.96	.3	.9524	50.56
				98.62

If an asset had a certain cash flow of $100 in each state the risk-adjusted present value of the asset is $95.24, which is consistent with our previous calculations, and the basic logic that a $100 for certain at time 1 is worth $95.24 at time 0.

State	Cash Flow	Proba-bility	Time-Value Factor	Risk-Adjustment Factor	RAPVF	RAPV
1	100	.7	.9524	.4806	.3204	32.04
2	100	.3	.9524	2.212	.6320	63.20
					.9524	95.24

The Expected Risk Adjustment

To insure that the risk-adjusted present value of a certain dollar is equal to the corresponding present-value factor, the expected value of the risk-adjustment factor over all states must be equal to unity. This requirement is satisfied in this example, as $.7 \times .4806 + .3 \times 2.212 = 1.00$. Logic requires, in a situation where claims can be readily traded, that this relationship exist, since we would expect a certain dollar to be worth a dollar.

It is important to recognize that the risk-adjusted present-value factor associated with a state depends on the income and wealth position of the typical investor in that state relative to other states at the same time. For relatively small outcomes it does not depend on the amount of cash generated by the asset during that state (where the cash flows generated by any one asset are a very small part of the income or wealth of a typical investor).

Countercyclical Assets

While most assets generate more cash flows during prosperity (state 1) than during depressions (state 2), some countercyclical assets may be available. Suppose there was a countercyclical asset available whose cash flow pattern was as follows:

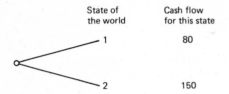

State of the world	Cash flow for this state
1	80
2	150

Using the RAPVF approach and the factors derived above, the value of this investment would be as follows:

State	RAPVF	Cash Flows	RAPV
1	.3204	80	25.63
2	.6320	150	94.80
Totals	.9524		120.43

Although the cash flows associated with this investment are uncertain and have a lower expected value than those of the first risky investment that we considered, the risk-adjusted present value of the investment is greater. This is because the investment generates more of its flows during the states of nature in which they are most needed. Assets like this have some of the characteristics of insurance, and are relatively attractive.

Application of the RAPV Approach

The risk-adjusted present-value approach described in the previous paragraphs is a generalization of the net present-value approach covered in the first section of this book. The RAPV approach can be applied in at least two different ways. A direct application would involve defining states of nature, determining the cash flows that would be generated by projects in each state, and estimating the

RAPVFs for each state. With these data the value of a proposed project could be determined. Sometimes this could be an extremely tedious method. The RAPV approach, however, even if not used to make the actual calculations, also offers some very useful insights into such vexing questions as how to compare the relative riskiness of two or more projects. The project which offers downside protection (thus has more valuable cash flows) has an edge.

These questions are explored in more detail in later chapters where the use of market measures of the RAPVFs is illustrated.

Questions and Problems

21-1. Evaluate the following investment assuming an interest rate of .10.

Time	Cash Flow
0	−8,000
1	10,000

21-2. (*Continuation of 21-1.*)   Instead of certain cash flows, assume the following time-1 outcomes exist:

Event	Probability	Outcome
e_1	.6	5,000
e_2	.4	17,500

Evaluate the investment assuming a zero risk adjustment.

21-3. (*Continuation of 21-1 and 21-2.*)   Assume a risk-adjustment factor of .8 applies to dollars received if event e_1 occurs. The discount rate for the certain cash flows is still .10.
   a. Determine the risk-adjustment factor for event e_2.
   b. Determine the RAPVFs for e_1 and e_2.

21-4. (*Continuation of previous problems.*)   Given all the previous facts evaluate the investment whose cash flows are described in 21-2.

21-5. Evaluate the following investment assuming an interest rate of .10 per period.

Time	Cash Flow
0	−11,000
1	+10,000
2	+5,000

21-6. (*Continuation of 21-5.*)   Instead of certain cash flows, assume the following possible outcomes exist:

	Period 1			Period 2	
Event	Probability	Outcome	Event	Probability	Outcome
e_1	.5	4,000	e_3	.4	6,500
e_2	.5	16,000	e_4	.6	4,000

The outcomes of period 2 are independent of the outcomes of period 1. Evaluate the investment assuming a zero risk adjustment.

21-7. (*Continuation of 21-5 and 21-6.*)   Assume the following risk-adjustment factors apply

e_1 .8 e_3 .9

a. Determine the risk-adjustment factors for events e_2 and e_4.
b. Determine the RAPVFs for all four of the events.

21-8. (*Continuation of previous three problems.*)   Given all the previous facts evaluate the investment.

CHAPTER 22

Introduction to Portfolio Analysis

If we have a correct theory but merely prate about it, pigeonhole it and do not put it into practice, then that theory, however good, is of no significance.

—*Mao Tse-Tung, On Practice (July, 1937) in Quotations from Chairman Mao Tse-Tung (New York. Bantam Books, Inc., 1967), p. 176.*

In this book the term *investment* refers to commitments of resources made in the hope of realizing benefits that are expected to occur over several time periods. These are the kinds of investments or capital expenditures ordinarily made by business organizations. However, in another context, the term *investment* is used to refer to the purchase and holding of marketable securities, particularly stocks and bonds.

There are certain similarities between these two activities that justify using the same term to refer to both. There are also important differences. Because the two kinds of "investment" are similar, certain analytical techniques originally developed for use in connection with investments in stocks and bonds are applicable to some extent to the long-term investments of business firms.

Normally, investors do not put all their money into the one best stock or bond. The disadvantage of concentrating investments is that if some unfavorable event occurs that affects the one investment, it may have a drastic effect on their total financial situation.

Stock market investors typically attempt to divide their assets into stocks of a number of different companies. When this strategy is followed, an unfavorable event affecting the value of any one company will have relatively less effect on the value of the entire portfolio, because much of the investment will be unaffected by the occurrence of such an event.

The collection of marketable stocks and bonds held by an individual investor is referred to as a *portfolio*. The *portfolio problem* might be defined as the problem of choosing a collection of securities that, taken together, has desirable characteristics with respect to risk and expected rate of return. The portfolio problem arises in the following way. Suppose that we agree on a reasonable way of measuring the expected rate of return and the risk of individual securities. Begin with a portfolio that consists entirely of one security. Now diversify the portfolio by adding a second security. How will this second security affect the expected rate of return and the risk of the portfolio? The objective is to construct a portfolio with desirable characteristics with respect to both risk and expected rate of return where there is a tradeoff between the two.

In much of what follows, the portfolio problem will be developed in a context in which the differences between investments in stocks and bonds on the one hand, and business capital expenditures on the other, are assumed to be of negligible importance. Before proceeding, however, it is desirable to mention briefly three of the differences between the types of investments.

One difference is the relevant time horizon and transaction costs. The transaction costs associated with purchasing or selling most stocks and bonds are a relatively small fraction of their value. Thus the holder of these assets can make decisions within the framework of a relatively short time-horizon. By contrast, the transaction costs associated with buying or selling the capital assets to which many business decisions refer may be a large fraction of their value. When acquisition of such assets is under consideration, the relevant time-horizon is often the life of the asset.

A second difference is the divisibility of the investments. One cannot buy half a steel mill, or two-thirds of a lathe; but one can buy securities that represent a very small fraction of a very large collection of assets. The assets themselves are not easily divisible, into convenient sizes for consumer ownership, but the securities are customarily issued in relatively small denominations so that investors can buy as many units as they need.

Another important difference is the nature of the dependency of the cash flows from the investments. The cash flows from a portfolio consisting of two securities can be obtained by adding the cash flows of the two securities. But the cash flow from a portfolio consisting of a blast furnace and a rolling mill under the same management is often greater than the total amount that could be earned from each of the assets by itself.

Rates of Return and Internal Rates of Return

In discussing securities and portfolios of securities, it is customary and useful to measure results in terms of "rates of return" and expected results in terms of "expected rates of return." In reference to investments in plant or equipment, we used the concept of an internal rate of return which is a related but distinct measure. To avoid confusion, we will define and illustrate these two concepts and point out some of the differences.

The internal rate of return (IRR) is defined as the discount rate that makes the present value of the cash proceeds expected from an investment equal to the present value of the cash outlays required by the investment. Ordinarily the cash proceeds referred to are the cash proceeds that are produced by the investment during its entire lifetime. The cash proceeds used are the cash proceeds that are expected to be received by one owner for as long as the investment is owned. The expected market value at the time it is sold is required to calculate the IRR. The market value of the asset does not enter into the calculation except at the beginning when the asset is purchased and at the end when it is sold. The adjective *internal* is used to describe this calculation because the calculation is based on *internal* information (cash flows) and not *external* information (market prices).

A distinct but related concept is that of a rate of return. Rates of return are always calculated for one period. The calculation requires the value of the asset at the beginning and at the end of the period as well as the cash flow received during the period. The rate of return of an asset is the ratio of the cash flows received from owning the asset during the period plus the change in the value of the asset during the period divided by the value of the asset at the beginning of the period. In symbols, if X_1 is the cash flow of the period and V_0 and V_1 are the values of the asset at the beginning and end of period one, then r_1, the rate of return on the asset during period 1, is calculated as:

$$r_1 = \frac{X_1 + V_1 - V_0}{V_0}$$

EXHIBIT 22-1. *Differences Between Rate-of-Return and Internal Rate-of-Return Calculations*

A. Asset Description

Time (End of Period)	0	1	2	3
Expected cash flows from asset	−100	20	20	120
Expected market value	100	110	105	0

B. IRR Calculation: Buy Asset for 100 at Time Zero and Sell at End of Period Indicated

Sell at End of Period	IRR	Required Calculation: Solve for r
1	30%	$-100 + \dfrac{20 + 110}{1 + r} = 0$
2	22.25%	$-100 + \dfrac{20}{1 + r} + \dfrac{20 + 105}{(1 + r)^2} = 0$
3	20%	$-100 + \dfrac{20}{1 + r} + \dfrac{20}{(1 + r)^2} + \dfrac{120}{(1 + r)^3} = 0$

C. Rate of Return Calculation

Period	Rate of Return	Rate of Return Calculation $r_t = \dfrac{X_t + (V_t - V_{t-1})}{V_{t-1}}$
1	30%	$r_1 = \dfrac{20 + (110 - 100)}{100}$
2	13.6%	$r_2 = \dfrac{20 + (105 - 110)}{110}$
3	14.3%	$r_3 = \dfrac{120 + (0 - 105)}{105}$

Exhibit 22-1 illustrates the calculation of these two measures for an asset whose life is three periods. Panel A in the exhibit gives the cash flows in each period (assume they occur at the end of the period) and the expected market value of the asset both at time zero and at the end of the next three periods. Panel B shows the results of the IRR calculations under three conditions: the asset is sold at the end of period 1, at the end of period 2 or at the end of period 3. Panel C shows the rate of return on the asset during each of the three periods.

One important conclusion is that if the asset is treated as having a life of one year, then the IRR of the asset and its expected rate of return during the first period will be the same. Perhaps for this reason, the measures are too often treated as identical. But except in that one period case, there is no simple relationship between the internal rate of return of the asset and the collection of single period rates of return. For example, the average rate of return is not equal to the IRR. (The average rate of return is $(.3 + .136 + .143)/3 = .193 = 19.3$ percent. The IRR $= 20$ percent.)

One important characteristic of the single period rate of return measure is that the rate of return of a portfolio is a value-weighted average of the rates of return of the assets in the portfolio. (The beginning of the period values of the assets are used as weights.) This statement is proved in a footnote for the two-asset case, but it could easily be generalized for any number of assets.[1]

When the IRR measure is used it is not true that the internal rate of return of a portfolio is equal to the weighted average of the internal rates of return of the assets comprising the portfolio unless all the assets have the same IRR or they all have a lifetime of one year. Some examples are illustrated in Exhibit 22-2.

Another important characteristic of one-period rates of returns is that they can be used as one period discount rates to determine the present value of an asset. This property can be illustrated using the asset described in Panel A of Exhibit 22-1. The expected rates of return on the asset for the next three periods are 30

---

[1] Let r_a, X_a, V_{a0} and V_{a1}, be the period one rate of return for asset a, its period one expected cash flow, and its beginning and ending values; comparable symbols are used for asset b. The weighted average return of a portfolio of both investments is:

$$R = \frac{r_a V_{a0} + r_b V_{b0}}{V_{a0} + V_{b0}}; \qquad r_a = \frac{X_a + V_{a1} - V_{a0}}{V_{a0}}; \qquad r_b = \frac{X_b + V_{b1} - V_{b0}}{V_{b0}}$$

Substituting the right hand side of the expressions for r_a and r_b into the expression for R we have:

$$R = \frac{X_a + V_{a1} - V_{a0} + X_b + V_{b1} - V_{b0}}{V_{a0} + V_{b0}}$$

Rearranging the numerator

$$R = \frac{(X_a + X_b) + (V_{a1} + V_{b1}) - (V_{a0} + V_{b0})}{V_{a0} + V_{b0}}$$

The right hand side of R is equal to the rate of return of the portfolio, since the first term in the numerator is the cash flow from the two assets, the next two terms measure the change in value during period one, and the denominator equals its value at the beginning of the period.

EXHIBIT 22-2. *Comparing the IRR of Individual Assets and of a Portfolio Formed by Their Combination*

Time (End of Period)	Asset Portfolio Cash Flows				
	0	1	2	3	IRR
Example 1					
Asset A	−100	20	20	120	20%
Asset B	−100	130			30%
Portfolio 1	−200	150	20	120	22.9%
Example 2					
Asset A	−100	20	20	120	20%
Asset B	−100	55	55	55	30%
Portfolio 2	−200	75	75	175	24.3%

percent, 13.6 percent, and 14.3 percent. Using these one period expected rates of return to discount the expected cash flows from the asset, we can calculate its present value as of time zero as follows:

$$PV = \frac{20}{1.3} + \frac{20}{(1.3)(1.136)} + \frac{120}{(1.3)(1.136)(1.143)}$$

$$= 15.385 + 13.543 + 71.091 = 100.$$

Introduction to the Portfolio Problem

With an individual investment we must consider risk or, more specifically, our attitudes toward the undesirable events that might occur. As soon as a firm has one asset or is considering the purchase of more than one asset, we must consider the risk not of the individual assets, but of the entire collection of assets.

Consider the following investment. (We shall call this investment A.)

Time		Rate of Return	Net Present Value (5%)
0	1		
− $400	$500	.25	76

Investment A has a rate of return (and IRR) of .25, and assuming a desired time value of money of .05 the investment is apparently acceptable. Now add the information that the $500 is an expectation and that for time 1 the outcomes are either $0 if event a_1 with .5 probability occurs, or $1,000 if event a_2 with .5 probability occurs.

Most of us would reject the investment. If you happen to find this investment acceptable, consider adding one or more zeros to each of the dollar amounts to increase the scale of the investment and then decide whether or not you find the investment acceptable.

Now consider a second investment (investment B) that has the following expected cash flows:

Time			
0	1	Rate of Return	Net Present Value (5%)
−$500	$500	.0	−24

This investment seems to be unacceptable, but again the $500 is an expectation. Assume that the dollar outcomes are $0 if event a_2 with .5 probability occurs, or $1,000 if event a_1 with .5 probability occurs.

Investment B with a rate of return of 0 is clearly undesirable if we consider it as an individual investment. When we combine A and B, however, we have an investment that most of us would find acceptable (see Figure 22-1) if we have a time-value factor of 5 percent.

The outcomes of the individual investment A and the individual investment B are uncertain. When we combine the investments, however, the uncertainty about the joint outcomes is eliminated. The factor at work to reduce the uncertainty of the sum of the investments is called the *covariance*. Whether event a_1 occurs or event a_2 occurs, the outcome of A + B is equal to $1,000. For example, if a_1 occurs, the outcome of A is 0, the outcome of B is $1,000, and the outcome of A + B is $0 + $1,000 = $1,000.

This additivity holds if the results of the investment are measured either in period 1 dollars or in expected net present values. In period 1 dollars the expected outcomes are $500 for A, $500 for B, and $1,000 for A + B. In expected net present values using .05 as a discount rate the amounts are $76 for A, −$24 for B, and $52 for A + B.

Additivity does not in general hold if internal rates of return are used. Based on expected period 1 dollars the internal rate of return of A is .25, of B is .0 and of A + B is .11. In the case of one-period investments, if the internal rates of return of A and B are weighted by the amounts invested, the expected value will equal the internal rate of return of the combination. Thus

$$\frac{400(.25) + 500(.0)}{900} = \frac{100}{900} = .11 = \text{expected rate of return of A + B.}$$

FIGURE 22-1

But this relationship between internal rates of return will not generally hold true if the cash flows extend over more than one period. However, expected present values are always additive.

To illustrate the two-period case suppose that the cash inflows in this example are to be received two periods from now as shown below.

Investment	Expected Cash Flows			IRR (%)
	0	1	2	
A	−400	0	500	11.8
B	−500	0	500	0.0
A + B	−900	0	1,000	5.4

The weighted average of internal rates of return of investments A and B (the returns weighted by the initial investments) is

$$\frac{400(.118) + 500(0)}{900} = .052.$$

This is not equal to the internal rate of return of the combined portfolio of A + B which is .054.

Variance and Covariance

The variance of a random variable X is equal to the expectation of the square of the differences from the mean:

$$\text{Var } (X) = E(X - \bar{X})^2 = E(X^2) - \bar{X}^2.$$

If we have two random variables X and Y, the variance of their sum is

$$\text{Var } (X + Y) = \text{Var } (X) + \text{Var } (Y) + 2 \text{ Cov } (X, Y).$$

The covariance between X and Y may be defined as

$$\text{Cov } (X, Y) = E[(X - \bar{X})(Y - \bar{Y})],$$

and it can be shown that

$$\text{Cov } (X, Y) = E(XY) - \bar{X}\bar{Y}.$$

For the one period example illustrated in Figure 22-1, if we let values of X represent the dollar outcomes of investment A, and values of Y represent the dollar outcomes of B, we would have the following computations:

a_i	$P(a_i)$	X	X^2	Y	Y^2	XY
a_1	.5	$0	$0	$1,000	$1,000,000	$0
a_2	.5	$1,000	$1,000,000	$0	0	0
			$E(X^2) = 500,000$		$E(Y^2) = 500,000$	$E(XY) = 0$

$$\text{Var } (X) = E(X^2) - \bar{X}^2 = 500{,}000 - 500^2 = 500{,}000 - 250{,}000 = 250{,}000$$

$$\text{Var } (Y) = E(Y^2) - \bar{Y}^2 = 500{,}000 - 500^2 = 500{,}000 - 250{,}000 = 250{,}000$$

$$\text{Cov } (X, Y) = E(XY) - \bar{X}\bar{Y} = 0 - (500)(500) = -250{,}000$$

$$\text{Var } (X + Y) = \text{Var } (X) + \text{Var } (Y) + 2 \text{ Cov } (X, Y)$$

$$= 250{,}000 + 250{,}000 + 2(-250{,}000) = 0.$$

Often the symbol σ_x^2 is used to denote the variance of X. The standard deviation is the square root of the variance and it is often denoted as σ_x.

The variance of the sum of the two investments is zero because of the large negative covariance. Although the preceding calculations use monetary values (to simplify the arithmetic), similar results would be obtained using net present values.

The covariance is a useful means of measuring how two random variables (say, the net present values of two investments) react to events. When the value of one investment outcome is large, will the other be large or small? Consider the two random variables X and Y.

Three basic relationships are illustrated in Figure 22-2. If we take the product of each pair of values for X and Y in all three situations, we would arrive at a positive amount for the sum or the average of these products. However, in situation 1 the higher the value of X, the higher the value of Y; in situation 2 the higher the value of X, the lower the value of Y; and in situation 3 the value of Y is not affected by the value of X. This difficulty (that all three situations have positive products) is solved by subtracting the mean of X and the mean of Y from the observed values of X and Y. The result is a shifting of the X and Y axes so that the average of the products is positive for situation 1, negative for situation 2, and zero for situation 3. This is shown in Figure 22-3.

If X and Y are statistically independent, then $E(XY) = \bar{X}\bar{Y}$ and Cov $(X, Y) = 0$. However, the covariance can also be equal to zero when there is not statistical independence.

The covariance is affected by the scale used to measure the variables. The correlation coefficient is invariant to scale and is obtained by dividing the covariance by the product of the two standard deviations

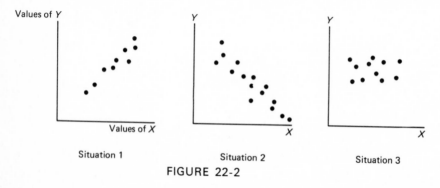

Situation 1   Situation 2   Situation 3

FIGURE 22-2

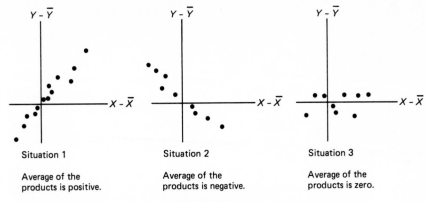

Situation 1

Average of the
products is positive.

Situation 2

Average of the
products is negative.

Situation 3

Average of the
products is zero.

FIGURE 22-3

$$\rho_{X,Y} = \frac{\text{Cov}(X, Y)}{\sigma_X \sigma_Y}.$$

The correlation coefficient $\rho_{X,Y}$ can take on values between -1 and 1 (see Figure 22-4).

The covariance may be written in terms of the correlation coefficient:

$$\text{Cov}(X, Y) = \rho_{X,Y} \sigma_X \sigma_Y.$$

If we have more than two variables, we have several covariances; for example,

$$\text{Var}(X_1 + X_2 + X_3) = \text{Var}(X_1) + \text{Var}(X_2) + \text{Var}(X_3) + 2\,\text{Cov}(X_1, X_2)$$
$$+ 2\,\text{Cov}(X_1, X_3) + 2\,\text{Cov}(X_2, X_3)$$

or, more generally,

$$\text{Var}\left(\sum_{k=1}^{n} X_k\right) = \sum_{k=1}^{n} \text{Var}(X_k) + 2 \sum_{k=1}^{n-1} \sum_{j=k+1}^{n} \text{Cov}(X_k, X_j).$$

We can let

$$\sigma_{ij} = \text{Cov}(X_i, X_j) \quad \text{if} \quad i \neq j,$$
$$\sigma_{ij} = \text{Var}(X_i) \quad \text{if} \quad i = j.$$

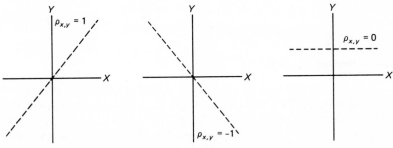

FIGURE 22-4

and then

$$\mathrm{Var}\left(\sum_{k=1}^{n} X_k\right) = \sum_{i=1}^{n} \sum_{j=1}^{n} \sigma_{ij}.$$

We shall now consider three variations of another basic investment situation. In the first example the covariance will be 0. The investments are statistically independent. (The correlation coefficient will be equal to zero.) In the second example the covariance will be negative. (The correlation coefficient will be equal to -1.) In the third example the covariance will be positive. (The correlation coefficient will be equal to 1.)

As the first example we present in Table 22-1 data on two investments, C and D. We assume that each of these investments would require an outlay of $1,000 and each could return one year later either $0 or $2,000. In each case the probability of the $0 return is .4, and the probability of the $2,000 return is .6. The investor is assumed to have a choice of either accepting investment C or investment D or both or rejecting both.

TABLE 22-1. *Subjective Probability Distributions of Returns from Two Investments*

Triggering Events for C	Triggering Events for D	Cash Flow of Period 1 (Both C and D)	Probability
e_1	e_3	$ \quad 0	.4
e_2	e_4	2,000	.6

It might appear that the two investments are identical. However, this may not be the case. Assume that with investment C the cash flow of $0 would occur if event e_1 occurred. The return of $2,000 would occur if event e_2 occurred. We assume that e_1 and e_2 are mutually exclusive and exhaustive events. With investment D the returns depend on events e_3 and e_4 .

To evaluate the consequences of accepting both investments C and D, we need additional information that has not yet been presented: the relationship between the events on which investment C depends and the events upon which investment D depends. We shall examine possible extreme cases of the relationship between the series of events.

Independent Investments

Case 1, the relationship illustrated in Table 22-2, is that in which the events that investment C depends on are statistically independent of the events on which investment D depends. In this context the term *statistical independence* means that the probability of any particular outcome for investment C is the same regardless of what the outcome is for investment D. The probabilities iisted in the table show the probability that both the event described by the column head and the event described by the row stub will occur. For example, if the outcome of investment D is $0 (that is, if e_3 has occurred), any of the two outcomes for investment C is possible, and each is relatively as likely as if the other outcome for D has occurred.

To help understand the implications of statistical independence more clearly, divide each of the two probabilities in row 1 (.16 and .24) by the row total of (.40). For example, for row 1, column 2, $.16 \div .40 = .40$. This is the conditional probability of event e_1, given that event e_3 has occurred. In symbolic terms, this conditional probability is expressed by $P(e_1 | e_3)$. We can also compute the conditional probabilities given that e_4 has occurred. The general mathematical relationship being used is

TABLE 22-2. *Joint Probability of Two Independent Investments: Case 1*

Investment D Outcomes		Investment C Outcomes		
		$0	$2,000	
		e_1	e_2	
$ 0	e_3	.16	.24	.40
2,000	e_4	.24	.36	.60
		.40	.60	1.00

$$P(e_i | e_j) = \frac{P(e_i, e_j)}{P(e_j)}.$$

where

$P(e_j)$ = probability of event e_j
$P(e_i | e_j)$ = conditional probability of event e_i, given that event e_j has occurred
$P(e_i, e_j)$ = joint probability of e_i and e_j; that is, the probability of events e_i and e_j both occurring.

In the context of the example,

$$P(e_1 | e_4) = \frac{.24}{.60} = .40, \qquad P(e_1 | e_3) = \frac{.16}{.40} = .40,$$

$$P(e_2 | e_4) = \frac{.36}{.60} = .60, \qquad P(e_2 | e_3) = \frac{.24}{.40} = .60.$$

It should be noted that the probability of e_1 does not depend on the outcome of investment D. In like manner we could show that the outcomes of investment

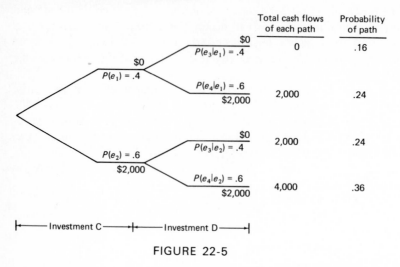

FIGURE 22-5

D are independent of the outcome of investment C (see Figure 22-5). Note that all the paths of investment D are independent of the path followed for investment C.

Let e_i be any event that determines the outcome of one investment, and let e_j be any event that determines the outcome of a second investment. If the events e_i and e_j are statistically independent, then $P(e_i | e_j) = P(e_i)$; that is, the probability of the event e_i given that e_j has occurred is equal to the probability of e_i. The probability of e_i is the same whether or not e_j has occurred. If this relationship holds for every possible pair of events that determines the outcomes of the two investments, the two investments are statistically independent.

We can summarize the results of undertaking both investments by combining the events that have equal monetary outcomes. The expected monetary value is obtained by weighting each outcome by its probability and summing.

(1) Cash Flow	(2) Probability of Cash Flow	(3) Col. 1 × Col. 2
$ 0	.16	$ 0
2,000	.48	960
4,000	.36	1,440
	Expected monetary value	$2,400

The expected values for each of the investments are $1,200. The variances of the investments are also equal. The computation of the variance of X, the outcomes for investment C, follows:

Event	Outcome X	$E(X)$	$X - E(X)$	$[X - E(X)]^2$	$P(X)$	$P(X)[X - E(X)]^2$
e_1	$ 0	$1,200	-$1,200	144×10^4	.4	57.6×10^4
e_2	2,000	1,200	800	64×10^4	.6	38.4×10^4
					Var $(X) = 96$	$\times 10^4$

Because the two investments are statistically independent, the covariance of their outcomes, Cov $(X, Y) = 0$. Thus the variance of the sum of their outcomes, $X + Y$, is Var $(X + Y) = $ Var $(X) + $ Var (Y):

Var $(X + Y) = 96 \times 10^4 + 96 \times 10^4 = 192 \times 10^4.$

The variance of the joint investment can also be computed using the basic definition of a variance. Let $Z = X + Y$.

Event	Outcome Z	E(Z)	Z − E(Z)	[Z − E(Z)]²	P(Z)	P(Z)[Z − E(Z)]²
$e_1\ e_3$	$ 0	$2,400	−$2,400	576×10^4	.16	92.16×10^4
$e_1\ e_4$	2,000	2,400	−400	16×10^4	.24	3.84×10^4
$e_2\ e_3$	2,000	2,400	−400	16×10^4	.24	3.84×10^4
$e_2\ e_4$	4,000	2,400	1,600	256×10^4	.36	92.16×10^4
					Var $(Z) = $ Var $(X + Y) = $	192.00×10^4

TABLE 22-3. *Joint Probability of Two Negatively Correlated Investments: Case 2*

Investment D Outcomes		Investment C Outcomes		
		$0	$2,000	
		e_1	e_2	
$ 0	e_3	.00	.40	.40
2,000	e_4	.40	.20	.60
		.40	.60	1.00

Negatively Correlated Investments

We shall use the term *negatively correlated investments* to refer to a situation where events affecting one investment in a desirable fashion will affect the second investment in an undesirable fashion.

In the second case, illustrated in Table 22-3 and Figure 22-6, it is assumed that there is a type of dependence between the returns of investment C and investment D; so if event e_3 occurs (investment D has a return of $0), we can be certain that event e_2 will have occurred (the return from investment C will be $2,000). If event e_1 occurs (investment C's return is $0), we can be certain that e_4 will then occur (investment D's return is $2,000). In this second case, there is uncertainty about which events may occur and about the return from either investment taken by itself. But if both investments are accepted, we can be certain that the total return will be at least $2,000.

The tree diagram for case 2 (Figure 22-6) is simplified by leaving off the branch with zero probability. Let $Z = X + Y$.

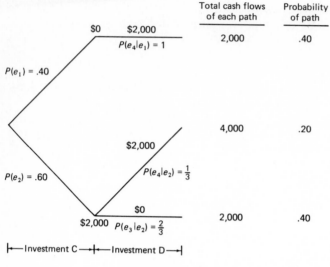

FIGURE 22-6

Event	Outcome Z	E(Z)	Z − E(Z)	[Z − E(Z)]²	P(Z)	P(Z)[Z − E(Z)]²
$e_1\ e_4$	\$2,000	\$2,400	−\$ 400	16×10^4	.4	6.4×10^4
$e_2\ e_3$	2,000	2,400	−400	16×10^4	.4	6.4×10^4
$e_2\ e_4$	4,000	2,400	1,600	256×10^4	.2	51.2×10^4
						64.0×10^4

The expected value of undertaking both is \$2,400 (\$2,000 × .8 + \$4,000 × .2) and the variance is \$640,000. In this case the two investments are negatively correlated. The correlation coefficient, ρ, is −.67 as we shall see. In general,

$$\text{Var}(Z) = \text{Var}(X + Y) = \text{Var}(X) + \text{Var}(Y) + 2\rho\sigma_X\sigma_Y.$$

Since in this case $\text{Var}(Z) = 64 \times 10^4$ and $\text{Var}(X) = \text{Var}(Y) = 96 \times 10^4$, we have

$$64 \times 10^4 = 96 \times 10^4 + 96 \times 10^4 + 2\rho96 \times 10^4,$$

$$-128 \times 10^4 = 2\rho96 \times 10^4,$$

$$\rho = -.67.$$

Positively Correlated Investments

The third case, illustrated in Table 22-4, is that in which the returns from the two investments have a type of risk-intensifying dependency. Under these circumstances the occurrence of event e_1 (\$0) guarantees that e_3 (\$0) will occur. Similarly, if the return from one of the investments is \$2,000, the return from the other will also be \$2,000. The returns are perfectly correlated.

TABLE 22-4. *Joint Probability of Two Positively Correlated Investments: Case 3*

Investment D Outcomes		Investment C Outcomes		
		$0 e_1	$2,000 e_2	
$ 0	e_3	.40	.00	.40
2,000	e_4	.00	.60	.60
		.40	.60	1.00

The tree diagram for case 3 is shown in Figure 22-7.

The expected value of undertaking both investments is $2,400 (that is, $4,000 × .6 + $0 × .4). The variance is calculated below.

Event	Outcome Z	E(Z)	Z − E(Z)	$[Z - E(Z)]^2$	P(Z)	$P(Z)[Z - E(Z)]^2$
e_1	$ 0	$2,400	−$2,400	576×10^4	.4	230.4×10^4
e_2	4,000	2,400	1,600	256×10^4	.6	153.6×10^4
					Var $(Z) =$ Var $(X + Y) =$	384.0×10^4

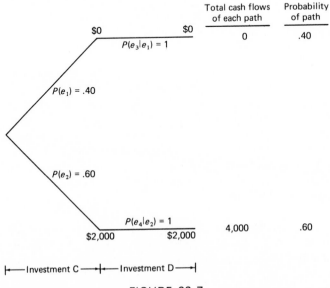

FIGURE 22-7

Summary of Example

In Table 22-5 all combinations of events that yield the same total cash flows are grouped together and the corresponding probabilities for each of the three cases described are presented in a single table. At the bottom of Table 22-5 several summary measures are presented.

TABLE 22-5. *Summary of the Results of the Three Cases*

Total Cash Flows	Probabilities		
	Case 1	Case 2	Case 3
$ 0	.16	.00	.40
2,000	.48	.80	.00
4,000	.36	.20	.60
	1.00	1.00	1.0
Expected cash flow	$2,400	$2,400	$2,400
Variance (σ^2)	1,920,000	640,000	3,840,000
σ	1,388	800	1,959
Coefficient of variation $\sigma/E(Z)$	.58	.33	.82

The standard deviation (σ) is a measure of the risk, because it measures the spread of the possible outcomes. The expected outcome [$E(Z)$] is a measure of the value of the benefits. We can divide the standard deviation by the expected return in order to relate the risk measure to expected benefits. The resulting measure is called the coefficient of variation by statisticians:

$$\text{``Risk'' per dollar of expected return} = \frac{\sigma}{E(Z)}.$$

If two different sets of investments require the same outlay and have the same expected return, the variance or standard deviation of the return from each set is a useful measure of the amount of risk. It will normally be the case, however, that the standard deviation of investments will vary with the size of the investment, and the size of the standard deviation may not be a very satisfactory measure of the riskiness of an investment set. In Table 22-5, the three cases outlined require the same outlay and also have the same expected return, so one could make comparisons using the standard deviation. Case 2 has the least amount of risk associated with it; case 3 has the greatest amount of risk (using σ as the measure of risk).

We have also computed the coefficient of variation in order to relate the standard deviation to the expected value of the investment. Because the expected values are the same, this additional measure adds little information in this special situation.

In practice, events that tend to stimulate general business conditions will tend to increase the returns from most investments. Similarly, events that affect the operations of a particular company are likely to increase or decrease the returns of most projects in that particular company. These factors will tend to introduce a situation analogous to case 3 between the returns of individual investment projects within a company.

Conclusions

The main point made in this chapter is that the riskiness of a single investment cannot be evaluated in a meaningful way by looking only at the possible outcomes of the investment taken by itself. In evaluating the riskiness to a corporation of a new asset to be acquired by the corporation, one should take into account how it will affect the dispersion of possible outcomes for the corporation as a whole. Similarly the common stock of a particular corporation is seldom the sole asset in the portfolio of an investor. The majority of the common stock of large corporations is held by institutions whose portfolios contain dozens and sometimes hundreds of other stocks. Even among individual investors, those who have substantial portfolios are likely to exhibit a significant degree of diversification.

The corporation should take into consideration the nature of the risk associated with the investment and its interaction with the risks of other investments. The process by which risk is incorporated into the decision can be complex. The existence of security markets helps simplify the decision process tremendously, however. Assuming investors who are able and willing to diversify, the only risk components that need be taken into account by the corporation (from the point of view of stockholders) are those that the investors cannot eliminate by diversification. This suggests that many investments that have been traditionally considered to be highly risky, such as exploring for new reserves of oil, may turn out to be relatively riskless. Methods of adjusting for risk when a firm is owned by stockholders who have diversified stock portfolios are presented in the next two chapters.

Corporate management may wish to apply a significant risk premium to large investments that could jeopardize the existence of the firm. If managers have special skills and experience that make them more valuable to their present employer than to other firms, and if they derive a large fraction of their income from this employment, they are less able than most stockholders to diversify against events that could threaten the continued existence of the firm.

If we drop the assumption of a large publicly owned firm, we can no longer assume that an investor has attained diversification. Now, the investor may be adversely affected by a decision. The corporation may try to take into consideration the affairs of this investor; but this is very difficult, because the investor may be either seeking large gains, no matter how risky, or attempting to avoid risk.

Questions and Problems

22-1. Two investments have the following characteristics for a commitment of an outlay of $800:

	Expected Net Present Value	Variance
Investment A	$1,000	$100
Investment B	2,000	900

Required: For an outlay of $800 in each of the two investments ($1,600 in total),
   a. Compute the expected benefits (return).
   b. Compute the variance of the returns if the correlation coefficient is .8.
   c. Compute the variance of the returns if the correlation coefficient is −.8.
   d. Compute the variance of the returns if the investments are independent.

22-2. The outcomes of investment A are as follows:

Event	Outcome	Probability
e_1	$200	.4
e_2	100	.5
e_3	−100	.1

Required: Compute the expectation and variance of the investment.

22-3. All you are told about an investment is that there is an outlay of $100 and that the returns (net of outlay) have an expectation of $120 and a variance of $7,600.
   Required: Would you accept this investment? Explain.

22-4. Two investments have the following net returns for the two events indicated:

		Net Present Value of Investment	
Event	Probability	A	B
e_1	.6	$600	−$100
e_2	.4	−400	500

Required: (a) Compute the expectation and variance of the NPV of each investment and the covariance of the two investments. (b) Compute the correlation coefficient of the two investments.

22-5. (*Continuing problem 22-4.*) What is the expected value and variance of the net present value of investment in both A and B?

22-6. An investment X has the following net present value for the two events indicated:

Event	Probability	Net Present Value
e_1	.6	$500
e_2	.4	100

Required: Compute the expectation and variance of the net present value of investment in X.

22-7. Two investments whose outcomes are statistically independent have the following net present values with the indicated probabilities:

		Investment	
Event	Probability	R	S
e_1	.4	-$400	$500
e_2	.6	600	-100

Required: (a) Compute the expected net present value and variance of each of the two investments. (b) Compute the covariance and correlation coefficient of the two investments. (c) Compute expected NPV and variance of the NPV's if investment is made in both R and S.

22-8. An investment has the following outcomes and probabilities;

-$ 500	.24
100	.16
500	.36
1,100	.24

Required: Compute the expectation and variance of the outcomes from this investment.

22-9. Mr. J. R. Nilson is the chairman of the Investment Committee, of the endowment of Llenroc University. The university's endowment consists of 65 percent common stock and 35 percent fixed income securities. Mr. Nilson believes that a 68 percent symmetrical confidence interval for the rate of return on the common stock portion of the portfolio is from −4 percent to 26 percent. If the fixed income securities were certain to yield 7 percent,

   a. Find the expected rate of return of the University's portfolio.
   b. Find its standard deviation.
   c. What action would be required to change the expected rate of return of the University's portfolio to 10 percent?

Discussion Questions

22-A. The ABC Book Company is considering investing $3 million in an advanced teaching mechanism. If the advanced mechanism is successful, the company expects the investment to have a net present value of $4 million. If it is unsuccessful, the investment has a negative net present value of $2 million. The probability of success is .7 and failure .3. A loss of $2 million would be very material to this firm.

The company is also considering investing $1 million in a new method of producing books. The method has a .4 probability of being workable. If the method works, the net present value of this investment is computed to be $2 million if the teaching mechanism fails and $0 if the teaching mechanism is successful. If the method of producing books is not successful, there will be a net loss of $1 million resulting from this investment, with a successful teaching mechanism; and the company will break even on this investment if the teaching mechanism is not successful. (See Table 22-6.)

TABLE 22-6.   *Payoffs of $1 Million Investment in Book Production*

Book Production Method Successful	Teaching Mechanism Successful	
	Yes	No
Yes	0	$2,000,000
No	−$1,000,000	0

Required: Should the company undertake the advanced mechanism or both of the investments?

CHAPTER 23

The Capital Asset Pricing Model

One would hope ... that some day satisfactory solutions will be found to the pervasive and fundamental problem. At present, however, the problem of uncertainty is clouded by uncertainty.

—*Robert Dorfman, A. Maass et al. Design of Water Resource Systems.* (Cambridge, Mass.: Harvard University Press, 1962) p. 158.

In principle, there is a clear criterion for determining whether the financial community considers an investment worthwhile. Worthwhile investments increase the wealth of the owners of the firm's securities.

For example, suppose that the stock of a particular company is currently quoted at $50 per share. During the next year management will have to make a decision about a major investment opportunity, and the outcome of this decision will become known to the financial community shortly after the decision is made. Management believes that if it rejects this investment opportunity the company will be able to pay a dividend of $5 per share, its stock will sell for $53 per share one year from now, and a stockholder will have a total value of $58 per share. If the investment opportunity is accepted, however, the company will be able to pay a dividend of only $3 per share (because a larger quantity of cash and retained earnings will be required to help finance the investment), but the price per share at the end of the year will be $57, reflecting the market's recognition of the earnings potential from the new investment. This is a total of $60. Ignoring the important complication of personal taxes, stockholder's wealth will be $2 per share greater if the company accepts the investment than if it rejects it.

In practice, it is not easy to implement this criterion. The major difficulty is predicting how an investment decision will affect the price of a company's stock. Given the present state of knowledge, a totally satisfactory procedure for making such predictions cannot be given. However, we believe that procedures can be suggested that will be helpful in practice to managers.

The necessary tasks can be broken down into two parts: (1) determine the main factors that influence stock prices, and (2) determine the relationship between investment projects and these factors.

The present chapter is concerned with the theory of stock prices. Many of the basic ideas underlying the theory are simple, intuitively appealing, and have been known for a long time. What makes the theory important and relevant are the relatively recent developments that enable us to restate these old ideas into mathematical terms. As a result, it is now possible to quantify some of the factors that affect stock prices and the value of real investments.

The basic ideas are as follows: most investors dislike risk. Other things being equal, most investors would prefer higher returns to lower returns. Whenever it is possible to reduce risk without reducing expected returns, it follows that investors will attempt to do this. It will be assumed that the standard deviation of the rate of return from a portfolio of securities is a reasonable measure of risk. Thus there is an incentive to use diversification to reduce the standard deviation of a portfolio. For example, if the rates of return from two securities have the same expected value and are independent, it can be shown that a portfolio consisting of both securities in appropriate proportions will have a lower risk than any portfolio which consists of only one of the securities.

To the extent that the rates of return from different securities are not highly correlated, risk-averse investors who diversify their holdings can reduce their total risk. However, to the extent that rates of return from different securities are correlated with one another and thus tend to fluctuate more or less in unison, diversification does not lead to complete risk elimination.

We find it useful to break down risk into two components: (1) risk that can be eliminated by diversification, which is termed *unsystematic* risk, and (2) risk that is still present with an efficient portfolio (all unsystematic risk has been eliminated), which is termed *systematic* risk. The latter reflects how the investments in the portfolio are correlated with the market.

If the costs of diversification are relatively low, investors will not be willing to pay more for a security simply because it carries a relatively low burden of unsystematic risk (which can be diversified away). Similarly, securities that carry a large amount of unsystematic risk will not suffer a serious price disadvantage.

To anticipate the conclusions of this chapter, to the extent that security prices are determined by the activities of the investors who can diversify their portfolios at low cost, the prices of securities will be set in such a way that differentials in expected rates of return will reflect primarily differences in the amount of systematic risk to which the securities are exposed.

Market Portfolio

Investors whose objective is to achieve the maximum amount of diversification would include in their portfolio every security available. Securities are defined here to include common stock and any other security for which there is a market. Thus warrants, convertible bonds, and preferred stock issues would be included in this portfolio.

In deciding how to allocate their assets, the investors do not attempt to anticipate future changes in the value of each security, but use the existing market valuations. Thus, if the outstanding common stock of company X represented .035 percent of the value of the equity of all companies, the stock would represent

.035 percent of the value of the portfolio. The investor would literally be buying a share in the capital market; we shall call the resulting investment the *market portfolio*.

We shall assume that, because of the diversification characteristics of the market portfolio and the risk aversion of most investors, the prices of the securities in the market portfolio have adjusted so that an investor could not earn a higher rate of return for the same or a lower level of risk in some other form of investment. The level of risk associated with the market portfolio may be too high or too low for a particular investor, however. We next consider how investors can vary the level of risk to which they are exposed and still invest in the market portfolio.

Capital Market Line

Suppose that r_f represents the rate of return that could be earned on a government security maturing one period from now. For an investor with a one-period planning horizon, there would be no default risk associated with owning a one-period government security. We shall call such a government security a *default-free asset*, since we are considering only the risk of default. Now consider the possible portfolios that could be constructed by taking combinations of the market portfolio and these government securities. Suppose that our hypothetical investors devoted a proportion α of their assets to the market portfolio and a proportion $1 - \alpha$ to this government security. Assume that the fraction α is between 0 and 1. Denote by $\bar{r}_m$ the expected rate of return from $1 invested in the market portfolio. Similarly, let σ_m denote the standard deviation of the rate of return r_m from the market portfolio. The expected rate of return on the investors' portfolio, $\bar{r}_p$, is given by

$$\bar{r}_p = (1 - \alpha)r_f + \alpha\bar{r}_m$$
$$= r_f + \alpha[\bar{r}_m - r_f], \tag{1}$$

and the standard deviation of the rate of return on their portfolio is given by

$$\sigma_p = \alpha\sigma_m. \tag{2}$$

If equation (2) is solved for α and that quantity substituted into equation 1, the resulting relationship between the expected rate of return of a portfolio and its standard deviation (when the portfolio is a mixture of the market portfolio and a default-free asset) can be rewritten as

$$\bar{r}_p = r_f + \left[\frac{\bar{r}_m - r_f}{\sigma_m}\right]\sigma_p. \tag{3}$$

A graphical representation of the relationship in equation (3) is shown in Figure 23-1. Line *AD* is the *capital market line*.

If an investor chose an α of 0 all the funds would be held in government securities and the expected return would be r_f and σ_p would be 0. This corresponds to point A in Figure 23-1. If an investor chose an α of 1, all the funds

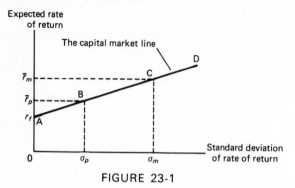

Expected rate of return

FIGURE 23-1

would be held in the market portfolio and the expected return would be $\bar{r}_m$ and σ_p would equal σ_m. This corresponds to point C in Figure 23-1. An investor could also reach any point on the straight line from A to C by picking an appropriate value of α between 0 and 1. The points to the right of point C on the market line correspond to values of α that are greater than 1. To reach such points, an investor must be able to borrow at the rate r_f. Suppose that this were the case and that an investor was willing to absorb a level of risk corresponding to a value of $\sigma_p = 2\sigma_m$. The investor could buy \$2 worth of the market portfolio for every dollar of equity owned. The necessary funds would be obtained by borrowing. In effect, the investor would be buying the market portfolio on a 50 percent margin at an interest rate of r_f. The investor's expected return is given by equation 1 with α equal to 2. Similarly, the standard deviation of return of the portfolio is given by inserting $\alpha = 2$ into equation (2). Since both equations apply, it follows that equation (3) is also applicable.

The capital market line applies only to a very special category of portfolios, those consisting of mixtures of the market portfolio and of riskless assets.

Security Market Line

The capital market line illustrates the relationships between the risk and expected return that investors could realize by varying the proportion of the riskless asset and the market portfolio in their personal portfolios.

Let us assume that investors try to adjust the composition of their portfolios in an effort to obtain a better combination of risk and expected return. Investors might vary the composition of their portfolios by increasing or decreasing their holdings of a particular risky security. If it were possible to achieve a better risk–return relationship by this technique then the market would not be in equilibrium and some investors would act to take advantage of the opportunity.

Assume the market is in equilibrium and that v represents the equilibrium price of a security. The rate of return that will be earned by holding the security for one period will be

$$r^* = \frac{w}{v} - 1, \qquad (4)$$

where w is the sum of the dividends that will be received plus the end-of-period value of the security, and r^* is the rate of return on the equilibrium value of the security. The expectation of r^*, denoted by

$$\bar{r}^* = \frac{\bar{w}}{v} - 1, \tag{5}$$

is called the required rate of return. If the market is in equilibrium, the required rate of return must satisfy the following relationship:

$$\bar{r}^* = r_f + \frac{\bar{r}_m - r_f}{\sigma_m^2} \text{ Cov } (r^*, r_m). \tag{6}$$

We will define lambda to be equal to

$$\lambda = \frac{\bar{r}_m - r_f}{\sigma_m^2},$$

and, substituting in equation (6), we obtain

$$\bar{r}^* = r_f + \lambda \text{ Cov } (r^*, r_m). \tag{7}$$

Equations (6) and (7) measure the required rate of return from an asset, which may be any security or any portfolio of securities. On the right-hand side of the equation, Cov (r^*, r_m) is the covariance between the rates of return on the equilibrium value of the security and the market portfolio, and λ is the market's return–risk tradeoff rate for the period.

If the covariance between the rate of return from the individual security and the rate of return on the market portfolio is zero, then the equilibrium expected rate of return on the given security will equal the rate of return on a one-period default-free asset, even if the particular security has a rate of return whose standard deviation is greater than zero. In fact, if a security could be found whose correlation with the market was negative, then its equilibrium expected rate of return could be less than the return received from a one-period default-free asset. Negatively correlated investments are difficult to find.

For some purposes, it is convenient to compare the Cov (r^*, r_m) for a particular security with the variance of the market portfolio by taking the ratio of these two quantities. This ratio, called the *beta coefficient* of the security, is

$$\beta = \frac{\text{Cov } (r^*, r_m)}{\sigma_m^2}. \tag{8}$$

A beta coefficient of unity indicates that a security has the same amount of systematic risk per dollar of its value as the market portfolio. A beta coefficient greater (less) than unity indicates the security is riskier (safer) than the market portfolio.

Required Rate of Return versus Cost of Capital[1]

Suppose that a one-period investment is available whose cost is c. The end-of-period-1 cash flow from the investment is x. Therefore the rate of return on cost for the investment is

$$r = \frac{x}{c} - 1,$$

and the expected rate of return on cost is

$$\bar{r} = \frac{\bar{x}}{c} - 1,$$

where $\bar{x}$ is the expected end-of-period-1 cash flow.

In capital budgeting practice a commonly used criterion for making accept or reject decisions is to compare the expected rate of return on cost for an investment with the firm's weighted average cost of capital (WACC). The WACC represents the required rate of return for the firm as a whole, and as its name suggests, is an average. Those who advocate this procedure recommend accepting the investment of its expected rate of return on cost exceeds or is equal to the firm's cost of capital. That is, accept if $r \geq$ WACC.

Figure 23-2 shows both the WACC and the required-return lines. The two lines imply different investment criteria; in each case the line is the boundary between the accept region (above the line) and the reject region (below the line).

For investments B and D both criteria lead to the same decisions. For investments A, C, and E, contradictory recommendations would result. Investments A and E would be rejected by the WACC criterion—but would be acceptable using the capital asset pricing model approach, even though E yields less than the default-free return. Investment C would be accepted using the WACC, but rejected using the CAPM approach.

Figure 23-2 illustrates one important limitation of the WACC approach: the fact that it does not take into account variations in the riskiness of different projects. The WACC approach tends to reject some low-risk projects like A that should be accepted because their rates of return are more than enough to compensate for their risk. The WACC approach tends to lead to the acceptance of high-risk projects, like C, whose expected rates of return are greater than the WACC, but not enough greater to compensate for the risk of the project.

Figure 23-2 illustrates a firm with a WACC of .15 and a Beta of 1.1.

Making Investment Decisions

The theory of stock prices presented in this chapter can be applied to investment decisions if the assets in question have a life of only one period. We illustrate

---

[1] The analysis in this section is adapted from Mark E. Rubinstein, "A Mean-Variance Synthesis of Corporate Financial Theory," *Journal of Finance*, XXVIII (March 1973), pp. 167–181.

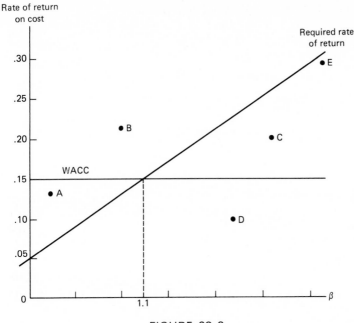

FIGURE 23-2

these applications here. The next chapter will illustrate how the theory can be applied to assets whose lives extend over multiple periods.

If the investment opportunities are economically independent, an accept or reject decision must be made for each investment. In this instance the criterion that should be used to make the decision is to compare the risk-adjusted present value of the cash flows from the investment with its cost c. Let v be the risk-adjusted present value. If $v - c$ is greater than or equal to zero, the investment should be accepted. If it is negative, it should be rejected. The quantity $(v - c)$ is the risk-adjusted counterpart, under conditions of uncertainty, of the net present value of the investment. Thus $v - c$ will be called the risk-adjusted net present value, RANPV.

To find the risk-adjusted present value of the cash proceeds we use the relationship,

$$v = \bar{y} - \lambda \, \text{Cov} \, (y, r_m), \tag{9}$$

where $y = x/(1 + r_f)$.

The appendix to this chapter shows how equation (9) is derived from equation (7).

Example 1

Suppose that r_f is .08 and that the following facts apply to a one-period investment where two events may occur.

Event n	Probability of Event: p	Value of r_m	Cash Flow x
1	.8	.20	432
2	.2	.00	108

From this we can compute $\bar{r}_m$ and σ_m^2.

n	p	r_m	pr_m	$r_m - \bar{r}_m$	$(r_m - \bar{r}_m)^2$	$p(r_m - \bar{r}_m)^2$
1	.8	.20	.16	.04	.0016	.00128
2	.2	.00	0	−.16	.0256	.00512
			$\bar{r}_m = .16$			$\sigma_m^2 = .00640$

The value of λ is

$$\lambda = \frac{\bar{r}_m - r_f}{\sigma_m^2} = \frac{.16 - .08}{.0064} = 12.5.$$

If event 1 occurs the cash flows are \$432, and if event 2 occurs the cash flows are \$108. The covariance between r_m and y, which is, by definition,

$$\sum p(y - \bar{y})(r_m - \bar{r}_m),$$

can be shown to equal[2]

$$\sum py(r_m - \bar{r}_m).$$

The latter expression, which is computationally simpler, is used in the examples. The computations of $\bar{y}$ and Cov (y, r_m) follow:

n	x	y	p	py	$(r_m - \bar{r}_m)$	$py(r_m - \bar{r}_m)$
1	432	400	.8	320	.04	12.8
2	108	100	.2	20	−.16	−3.2
				$\bar{y} = 340$		Cov $(y, r_m) =$ 9.6

We can now compute v:

$$v = \bar{y} - \lambda \, \text{Cov} \, (y, r_m)$$

$$= 340 - (12.5)(9.60) = 340 - 120 = \$220.$$

If the alternatives were to accept or reject, this investment would be acceptable if its cost were less than \$220.

---

[2] $\sum p(y - \bar{y})(r_m - \bar{r}_m) = \sum py(r_m - \bar{r}_m) - \sum p\bar{y}(r_m - \bar{r}_m)$

and

$\sum p\bar{y}(r_m - \bar{r}_m) = \bar{y}(r_m - \bar{r}_m) = 0$

therefore

$\sum p(y - \bar{y})(r_m - \bar{r}_m) = \sum py(r_m - \bar{r}_m)$

A Simplified Calculation: A State Preference Approach

The preceding calculation can be simplified by explicitly using a state preference approach to valuation. Let us define $s(n)$ to be the value today of an investment that will pay $1 at time 1 if node n occurs. For $n = 1$, the value of $s(1)$ can be computed as follows.

n	x	y	p	py	$(r_m - \bar{r}_m)$	$py(r_m - \bar{r}_m)$
1	1	.92593	.8	.74074	.04	.02963
2	0	0	.2	0	−.16	0
				$\bar{y} = .74074$		Cov $(y, r_m) = .02963$

$$s(1) = \bar{y} - \lambda \text{ Cov } (y, r_m)$$

$$= .74074 - (12.5)(.02963) = .74074 - .37037 = .37037.$$

A similar calculation for $n = 2$ will show that

$$s(2) = .55556.$$

To generalize these results let $p(n)$ be the probability of node n, and $r_m(n)$ the value of r_m at that node. Suppose an investment pays one dollar at time 1 if node n occurs and nothing otherwise. The present value of the expected cash flows from such an investment will be

$$\bar{y} = \frac{p(n)}{1 + r_f}.$$

The covariance between y and r_m for such an investment will be[3]

$$\text{Cov } (y, r_m) = \frac{p(n)}{1 + r_f} [r_m(n) - \bar{r}_m].$$

Substituting the values for $\bar{y}$ and Cov (y, r_m) in equation (9), the value of such an investment will be

$$s(n) = \frac{p(n)}{1 + r_f} [1 - \lambda(r_m(n) - \bar{r}_m)]. \tag{10}$$

For example, $s(1)$ could be calculated directly using equation (10).

$$s(1) = \frac{.8}{1.08} [1 - (12.5)(.20 - .16)]$$

$$= (.74074)(1 - .5) = .37037.$$

Equation (10) is extremely important, since it simplifies the computation of RAPV. The value $s(n)$ is a time-risk transformation factor that enables us to compute the risk-adjusted present value of a dollar at node n one time period

[3] Remember that Cov $= \sum py(r_m - \bar{r}_m)$ and $y = 1/(1 + r_f)$ at node n, and zero elsewhere.

later. It is not dependent on there only being two outcomes. While v gives the risk-adjusted present value of all outcomes stemming from one node, $s(n)$ gives the risk-adjusted present value of one path stemming from a node.

To find the risk-adjusted present value of the investment we multiply the values of $s(n)$ by the cash flows and sum:

Event	$s(n)$	x	$xs(n)$
1	.3704	432	160
2	.5556	108	60
	.9260		$v = \$220$

This value of v agrees with the number obtained previously by using equation (9). Equations (10) and (9) lead to the same solution, but (10) has the advantage of being easier to compute. A price is being placed on the value of a dollar in each state (event) that can take place.

Example 2

We will now consider an investment in which, again, two possible events may occur (labeled events 3 and 4). The value of r_f is now .03. The following facts apply:

Event: n	p	r_m	x
3	.3	.20	206
4	.7	.00	103

From this we can compute $\bar{r}_m$ and σ_m^2.

n	p	r_m	pr_m	$r_m - \bar{r}_m$	$(r_m - \bar{r}_m)^2$	$p(r_m - \bar{r}_m)^2$
3	.3	.20	.06	.14	.0196	.00588
4	.7	.00	.00	−.06	.0036	.00252
			$\bar{r}_m = .06$			$\sigma_m^2 = .00840$

The value of lambda is

$$\lambda = \frac{\bar{r}_m - r_f}{\sigma_m^2} = \frac{.06 - .03}{.0084} = 3.5714.$$

Using equation (10),

$$s(3) = \frac{p(n)}{1 + r_f}\left[1 - \lambda(r_m(n) - \bar{r}_m)\right] = \frac{.3}{1.03}\left[1 - 3.5714(.14)\right]$$

$$= .14563.$$

$$s(4) = \frac{.7}{1.03}\left[1 - 3.5714(-.06)\right] = .82524.$$

The risk-adjusted present value of the investment is

Event	$s(n)$	x	$xs(n)$
3	.1456	206	30
4	.8252	103	85
	.9708		$v = \$115$

The following calculations using the covariance also give $115.

n	p	x	y	py	$r_m - \bar{r}_m$	$py(r_m - \bar{r}_m)$
3	.3	206	200	60	.14	8.4
4	.7	103	100	70	−.06	−4.2
				$\bar{y} = 130$		Cov $(y, r_m) = $ 4.2

The value of v is again $115:

$$v = \bar{y} - \lambda \operatorname{Cov}(y, r_m) = 130 - 3.5714(4.20) = 130 - 15 = \$115.$$

Instead of using equation (10) the values of $s(n)$ can be computed using equation (9) if we make the assumption that x is $1 with node n and zero otherwise. For example, for $n = 3$ we would have

n	p	x	y	py	$(r_m - \bar{r}_m)$	$py(r_m - \bar{r}_m)$
3	.3	1	.9709	.2913	.14	.0408
4	.7	0	0	0	−.06	0
				$\bar{y} = .2913$		Cov $(y, r_m) = $ .0408

$$v = s(3) = \bar{y} - \lambda \operatorname{Cov}(y, r_m)$$

$$= .2913 - 3.5714(.0408) = .1456.$$

Comparable calculations for $s(4)$ again give a value of .8252.

If the investment earns cash flows of $1 with event 3 *and* event 4 we would expect the risk-adjusted present value to be $1/1.03 = \$.97087$, since there is zero risk ($1 will be received no matter what event occurs). Using the values of $s(3)$ and $s(4)$ we obtain $.97087 for the RAPV.

Event	$s(n)$	x	$xs(n)$
3	.14563	$1	.14563
4	.82524	1	.82524
			$\$.97087$

The .97087 is equal to $(1 + r_f)^{-1} = (1.03)^{-1}$.

Conclusions

With risky cash flows we have to take both the time value and risk of the cash flows into consideration. We find that the values obtained from the use of equation (10) can be used as "prices" or transformation factors to find the risk-adjusted present value of cash flows to be received one period from now.

In the next chapter we will apply the models of this chapter to multiperiod investments.

Appendix

We want to show that equation (9) follows from equation (7).

$$v = \bar{y} - \lambda \, \text{Cov} \, (y, r_m). \tag{9}$$

Starting with equation (7) we have

$$\bar{r}^* = r_f + \lambda \, \text{Cov} \, (r^*, r_m).$$

We can substitute $\bar{x}/v - 1$ for $\bar{r}^*$, $x/v - 1$ for r^*, and then solve the equation for v. In doing this we take advantage of the fact that for any constant v,

$$\text{Cov} \left(\frac{x}{v} - 1, r_m \right) = \frac{1}{v} \, \text{Cov} \, (x, r_m).$$

Making these substitutions, equation (7) becomes

$$\frac{\bar{x}}{v} - 1 = r_f + \lambda \left(\frac{1}{v} \right) \text{Cov} \, (x, r_m).$$

Adding one to both sides and multiplying by v gives

$$\bar{x} = (1 + r_f)v + \lambda \, \text{Cov} \, (x, r_m);$$

therefore, solving for v,

$$v = \frac{\bar{x} - \lambda \, \text{Cov} \, (x, r_m)}{1 + r_f}. \tag{7.A}$$

Note that by definition

$$\frac{\bar{x}}{1 + r_f} = \bar{y}.$$

Also, since $y = x/(1 + r_f)$, it follows that

$$\text{Cov} \, (x, r_m) = (1 + r_f) \, \text{Cov} \left(\frac{x}{1 + r_f}, r_m \right)$$

$$= (1 + r_f) \, \text{Cov} \, (y, r_m).$$

Substituting these expressions into (7.A) gives

$$v = \frac{\bar{x}}{1 + r_f} - \lambda \frac{\text{Cov}(x, r_m)}{1 + r_f}$$

$$= \bar{y} - \lambda \frac{(1 + r_f) \, \text{Cov}(y, r_m)}{1 + r_f}$$

$$= \bar{y} - \lambda \, \text{Cov}(y, r_m),$$

which is the desired result.

Questions and Problems

For problems 23-1 through 23-9, assume that $\bar{r}_m = .14$, $r_f = .08$, and $\sigma_m = .12$.

23-1. If an investor put half her funds in the market portfolio and half in treasury bills,
  a. What rate of return would you expect her to earn?
  b. What is the standard deviation of returns from her portfolio?
  c. Draw a rough graph with expected return on the vertical axis and standard deviation of return on the horizontal axis. Plot the market portfolio at point C and the investor's portfolio at point B on this graph.
  d. Find the slope of the capital market line.

23-2. If an investor wished to hold a portfolio consisting only of treasury bills and shares in the market portfolio, and he wanted an expected return of .12 per year, what proportion of his funds should be invested in the market portfolio? What is the standard deviation of returns from this portfolio?

23-3. On January 1, M.B. University had an endowment worth $100 million. Of this amount $25 million was invested in treasury bills, and $75 million was invested in the market portfolio. By the following December 31, MBU had earned $2 million in interest, and had received dividends of $3 million. These amounts were considered as "income" and used to pay the current expenses of the university. Except for "rolling over" treasury bills, no portfolio transactions were undertaken. Although on December 31 MBU's portfolio still held the same number of shares in the market portfolio, the market value of these shares had declined to $60 million because of a general decline in stock prices.
  a. What was the expected annual rate of return on MBU's portfolio on January 1, and its standard deviation?
  b. What was the actual rate of return earned?

23-4. (*Continuing problem 23-3.*) If no shift has occurred in the capital market line, what rate of return would be expected from the portfolio held by MBU on December 31?
  If MBU wished to modify the composition of its December 31 portfolio so that the expected rate of return was the same as that of its January 1 portfolio, what transactions would be necessary?

23-5. (*Continuing problem 23-3.*)
  a. By how many standard deviations did the realized return on MBU's portfolio fall short of its expected return?
  b. If the distribution of rates of return can be approximated by a normal distribution, what is the probability of earning as little as this or less?

23-6. Suppose that it were possible for an investor to borrow at 8 percent per year as much as $.75 for every dollar of stock he owned "free and clear." Could an investor having $100,000 in cash devise a portfolio consisting only of shares in the market portfolio and treasury bills for which the expected rate of return was 17 percent?

If it is possible, describe the transactions that would be necessary; if not, explain why it is impossible.

23-7. A retired doctor wants to hold a portfolio consisting only of debt and stock in the market portfolio. She also wants the assurance that, even if the return on the market portfolio were two standard deviations below normal, the rate of return on her portfolio would be no less than -5 percent. What portfolio would you recommend for her?

23-8. The covariance between the rate of return of a stock and the rate of return of the market index is .0192. What is the required rate of return of this stock?

23-9. What is the beta coefficient of the common stock described in problem 23-8?

23-10. If an investment is expected to temporarily depress both accounting income and the current market price of the stock, should the investment be undertaken if it is expected to have a beneficial long-run effect on stock prices?

23-11. Assume the following facts:

	Default-Free Investment	Market Investment
Expected return	.07	.10
Standard deviation	0	.02

Compute the portfolio expected return and risk (standard deviation) if the investment is split .6 in the market portfolio and .4 in the default-free investment.

23-12. (*Continuing problem 23-11.*) For the information given determine the equations for the capital market line and the security market line for the investment. What are the slopes of the two lines?

23-13. (*Continuing problem 23-11.*) Assume that there is an investment j with a covariance of .00064 with the market. Determine the expected return required by the market.

23-14. (*Continuing problem 23-13.*) If the investment currently has an expected return of .15, what would you expect to happen?

23-15. (*Continuing problem 23-13.*) If the covariance of the investment with the market were $-.00064$, what would be the expected return required by the market?

23-16. For the information given in problem 23-13, compute the β of the investment. Using the β, compute the expected return required by the market.

23-17. If the β of a security is large, what does this imply about the expected change in value of the stock for small changes in the value of the market portfolio?

23-18. A risky one-period investment requires an immediate outlay of $1,000. The possible proceeds, which will be received in one period, are listed below along with their probabilities and the corresponding RAPVF's.

Outcome Number	RAPVF	Probability of Outcome	Cash Proceeds
n	$s(n)$	p	x
1	.15	.2	2,000
2	.40	.5	1,500
3	.35	.3	500

a. Find the expected cash flow from the investment.
b. Find the expected rate of return (on the cost) of the investment.
c. Find the required rate of return of the investment.
d. Find R_f.

23-19. The following data apply to the next two questions.

$$R_f = .085$$

State	Probability of State	Rate of Return on Market, Given State
1	.2	.36
2	.4	.21
3	.3	.16
4	.1	$-.04$

a. Find λ.
b. Find the RAPVF's for states 2 and 3, using the Capital Asset Pricing Model (CAPM).

23-20. A security analyst believes that the rate of return that can be earned on default free securities during the next year is .08, and that the possible one-period rates of return that can be realized from holding the "market" portfolio, and their probabilities are as follows:

Rate of Return	Probability
.30	.30
.20	.40
.10	.25
−.10	.05

a. What is the expected rate of return on the market portfolio?

b. What is the variance of the rate of return on the market portfolio? (You can round to the nearest percent.)

The portfolio manager is responsible for a $100 million pension fund that must be divided between the market portfolio and default free securities.

c. How much of each should be held to achieve an expected rate of return of 15 percent on the pension portfolio?

d. What would be the standard deviation of the rate of return on the pension portfolio if its expected rate of return was 15 percent?

23-21. Assume the default free rate, r_f, is .11 and the following additional data

Outcome Number	Probability of Outcome	Rate of Return on Market Portfolio
n	p	r_m
1	.6	.25
2	.4	.05

a. Find λ.

b. Find the risk-adjusted present value factors (RAPVF's) for each of the outcomes.

23-22. A risky one-period investment requires an immediate outlay of $150. The possible proceeds, which will be received in one period, are listed below along with their probabilities and the corresponding RAPVF's.

Outcome Number	RAPVF	Probability of Outcome	Cash Proceeds
n	$s(n)$	p	x
1	.2175	.6	300
2	.4014	.3	200
3	.3070	.1	100
	.9259		

a. Find the RANPV of the investment.

b. Find the expected rate of return (on the cost) of the investment.

c. Find the required rate of return of the investment.

d. Find r_f.

CHAPTER **24**

Application of the Risk-Adjusted Present-Value Method to Multiperiod Investments

Theories that are right only 50 percent of the time are less economical than coin-flipping.

—*George J. Stigler, The Theory of Price (New York: Macmillan Publishing Co., Inc., 1966), p. 6. (Professor Stigler assumes decisions with two outcomes.)*

Chapter 21 introduced the general approach to capital budgeting under uncertainty that will be implemented in this chapter. The approach is an extension of the present-value method to conditions of uncertainty. When we assumed certainty we applied present-value factors to future cash flows to find present-value equivalents. For example, with a .10 time-value factor we applied a present-value factor of .9091 to a cash flow of period 1 and .8264 to a cash flow of period 2 to find present-value equivalents.

The procedure with uncertainty is analogous. Prices are determined that take into consideration both time value and risk. The prices are time-value and risk-transformation factors that are analogous to the present-value factors used in the certainty situation. In this chapter the prices will be determined using the capital asset pricing model and the methods of calculation of Chapter 23. Alternative methods of determining prices (RAPVFs) could be used.

To implement this approach a number of steps are necessary. First, the approach must be generalized to handle multi-period assets. Second, practical methods of determining the relevant risk-adjusted present-value factors are needed. Third, methods of combining estimates of the cash flows of a proposed project for each state with the RAPVFs for that state must be determined. Each of these steps will be considered in this chapter.

The capital asset pricing model was introduced, and its application to one-period investments illustrated, in Chapter 23. The present chapter suggests methods of using such models to evaluate multiperiod investments. A risk-adjusted net present value factor (RAPFV) will be computed for each possible event (or tree diagram node), and this price will be applied to the cash flow of that node.

Figure 24-1 shows the probabilities and the market returns for a two-period

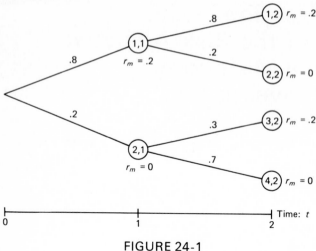

FIGURE 24-1

investment. The tree diagram provides a useful framework for analysis. For simplicity only two outcomes are allowed for each node.

Note that if a bad year occurs, the probability of a second bad year is high. The states of nature have been selected so that the market return can be only .2 or 0. Reference to Chapter 23 will show that the market return-risk tradeoff (λ) depends on the state of nature. Figure 24-1 combines the two one-period examples of Chapter 23 to make up a single two-period investment.

We will assume (consistent with the previous chapter) that

$r = .08$ for the first time period.
$r = .08$ for the second time period if starting from node (1, 1).
$r = .03$ for the second time period if starting from node (2, 1).

Each node is numbered with two numbers separated by a comma. The first number is the node number (starting from the top) and the second number is the time period. Thus node (3, 2) is node 3 in time period 2. There is only one path through the tree diagram from the origin to a particular node.

In Chapter 23 we define $s(n)$ to be the risk-adjusted present-value factor (RAPVF) for the nth node, and determined $s(1)$ to be .3707 and $s(2)$ to be .5552 for the first example and $s(3)$ to be .1459 and $s(4)$ to be .8253 for the second example. The cash flows are discounted one period.

Using the symbolism for multiperiod investments, $s(n, t)$, where n is the node number and t the time period, and the values from Chapter 23 we have

$s(1, 1) = .3707.$ $s(2, 2) = .5552.$
$s(2, 1) = .5552.$ $s(3, 2) = .1459.$
$s(1, 2) = .3707.$ $s(4, 2) = .8253.$

While we could use the $s(n, t)$ factors for single periods, it is somewhat easier to compute RAPVFs that transform the cash flows to values at time zero. Define

$S(n, t)$ to be the risk-adjusted present value at time zero of one dollar received at node n and time t. For the example we have

$S(1, 1) = s(1, 1) = .3707.$
$S(2, 1) = s(2, 1) = .5552.$
$S(1, 2) = s(1, 1) \times s(1, 2) = .3707 \times .3707 = .1374.$
$S(2, 2) = s(1, 1) \times s(2, 2) = .3707 \times .5552 = .2058.$
$S(3, 2) = s(2, 1) \times s(3, 2) = .5552 \times .1459 = .0810.$
$S(4, 2) = s(2, 1) \times s(4, 2) = .5552 \times .8253 = .4582.$

The logic of multiplying $s(2, 1)$ times $s(3, 2)$ to obtain $S(3, 2)$ is the same logic whereby we multiply .9091 times .9091 (where .9091 is the present value of $1 due in one time period) to obtain the present value of $1 due in two time periods. If a dollar at node $(3, 2)$ is worth .1459 at time 1, then it is worth .5552 times .1459 or .0810 at time zero, thus $S(3, 2) = .0810$.

Applying the RAPVFs

Now that we have determined the $S(n, t)$'s, the evaluation of an investment is exactly analogous to the net present value calculation. Figure 24-2 shows the cash flows of an investment that costs $300. The facts of Figure 24-1 also apply to Figure 24-2.

The risk-adjusted present value is

Node (n, t)	$S(n, t)$	Cash Flow	RAPV
(1, 1)	.3707	432	160
(2, 1)	.5552	108	60
(1, 2)	.1374	432	58
(2, 2)	.2058	108	22
(3, 2)	.0810	206	17
(4, 2)	.4582	103	47
			RAPV = $364

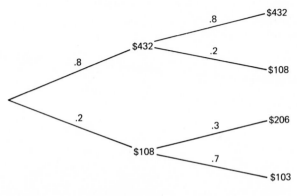

FIGURE 24-2

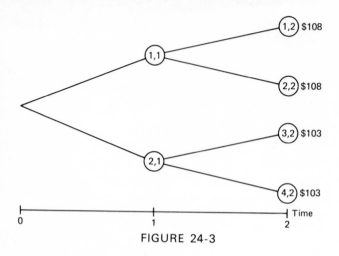

FIGURE 24-3

Since the risk-adjusted present value is $364 and the cost is only $300 the investment is acceptable.

In a world of uncertainty, the same term structure of interest rates could be used to evaluate different assets. Similarly, in a world of uncertainty the same RAPVFs could be used to evaluate many different assets. In the next example we use the RAPVFs previously derived to evaluate a new asset.

A Second Example

Assume that an investment will generate $108 at nodes 1 and 2 of period 2, and $103 at nodes 3 and 4. These cash flows are represented in Figure 24-3. If node 1 occurs during period 1, the firm will know that it is to receive $108 for certain in period 2. It will also know the period 2 default-free interest rate, which will be 8 percent in that case. So the future cash flows will be worth $100 at the end of period 1, at node 1.

If node 2 occurs during period 1, the firm will know that it is to receive only $103 for certain in period 2. It will also know the period 2 default-free interest rate, which will be 3 percent in that case. So the future cash flows will be worth $100 at the end of period 1, at node 2.

The value of the asset one period from now looks like this:

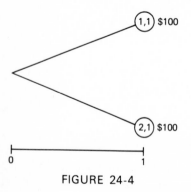

FIGURE 24-4

Since the interest rate in period 1 is 8 percent, we would expect the asset to be worth $100/1.08 = 92.59$.

The same answer could be reached using risk-adjusted present-value factors on the period 2 cash flows.

Node (n, t)	$S(n, t)$	Cash Flows	RAPV
(1, 1)	.37037	0	0.00
(2, 1)	.55556	0	0.00
(1, 2)	.13717	108	14.81
(2, 2)	.20576	108	22.22
(3, 2)	.08091	103	8.33
(4, 2)	.45847	103	47.22
			$92.59

Alternatively, we could apply RAPVFs to the end-of-period one-asset values.

Node	$S(n, t)$	$v(n, t)$	RAPV
(1, 1)	.37037	100	37.037
(2, 1)	.55556	100	55.556
			$92.593

In principle the application of the capital asset pricing model illustrated above enables us to compute risk-adjusted present-value factors for different nodes through time. While the presence of risk precludes the conventional compound interest calculations directly, indirectly we are taking into account the time value of money as well as the risk of the investment.

Once the RAPVFs have been computed, the calculations of the net value of an investment are analogous to the calculations that are made under the assumption of certainty. If the RAPV is greater than the cost of the investment, the investment is acceptable.

Limitations of the Model

The procedure described above is intended to illustrate a basic approach to taking time value and risk into consideration. In practical applications some modifications are desirable. The version of the capital asset pricing model described in this and the preceding chapters implicitly assumes that the one-period rate of return on the market portfolio is normally distributed. Alternatively, the model could be derived by assuming investors have quadratic utility functions. Unfortunately, the use of a quadratic utility function introduces new problems.

The normal probability distribution is an acceptable approximation if the period in question is relatively short, for example, a month. But complications arise if the model is used with a constant variance per period for many periods or for long periods of time. The normal distribution is unbounded. Thus positive probabilities are assigned negative stock prices, even though, with limited liability on common equity, negative stock prices are not possible. If the time period is very short the probability of a zero (or negative) stock price is so small that the normal approximation is useful.

One simple method of correcting this problem is to assume that $\ln (1 + r_m)$ is normally distributed. As r_m approaches its lower limit of -100 percent, $(1 + r_m)$ approaches zero and $\ln (1 + r_m)$ approaches minus infinity. This assumption leads to better descriptions of the behavior of the market portfolio for long periods of time.

One other important limitation is that the CAPM considers only systematic risk. Unsystematic risk is important to undiversified investors and managers.

Supershares

If the magnitude and timing of the cash flows generated by an asset are known with certainty, the relevant present-value factors can be found each day in the financial pages of the newspaper. For example, the present value of $1,000 due with certainty in one year is equal to the price of a $1,000 one-year treasury bill. Unfortunately, there are no securities that promise to pay off a fixed amount at a predetermined time, if and only if the range of increase in the value of the market portfolio is within a certain prefixed range. But Nils Hakansson and others have suggested methods of marketing such securities.[1] Hakansson calls such securities "supershares." It has been predicted that there would be a substantial demand by investors for such securities, if they were available. If supershares were available, readers would be able to dispense with a table of RAPVFs and instead obtain accurate and relevant values from the financial tables of their newspapers.

It is also possible to determine the value of a RAPVF from the prices of options on a stock market index.[2] Such options are now being traded in financial markets, although only for short time horizons.

Conclusions

Each passing year leads to better and more complex tools for coping with the difficult problem of capital budgeting under uncertainty. The use of RAPVFs is one path that holds promise for a wide range of circumstances. However, it is important to note that the procedure implicitly assumes there are markets for the buying and selling of rights to dollars for different states (that is, different events in given time periods). In the absence of these extensive markets, it is reasonable for corporate managers to apply factors reflecting their own (or their corporation's) risk aversions.

[1] Nils H. Hakansson, "The Purchasing Power Fund: A New Kind of Financial Intermediary," *Financial Analysts Journal*, November–December 1976, pp. 49–59.

[2] D. T. Breeden and R. H. Litzenberger "Prices of State-Contingent Claims Implicit in Option Prices," *Journal of Business*, October, 1978. R. W. Banz and M. H. Miller, "Prices for State-Contingent Claims: Some Estimates and Applications," *Journal of Business*, October 1978.

Problems

24-1. The following information applies to a one-period investment.

n	p	r_m	x
1	.3	.25	1,300
2	.7	.05	300

Assuming that $r_f = .06$, find the RAPV of the investment.

24-2. The following information applies to a one-period investment with $r_f = .06$. Find its RAPV.

n	p	r_m	x
1	.2	.25	1,900
2	.1	.25	100
3	.4	.05	600
4	.3	.05	-100

Compare the RAPV of this investment with the RAPV of the investment described in problem 24-1.

24-3. The following information applies to a two-period investment with $r_f = .06$. Find v.

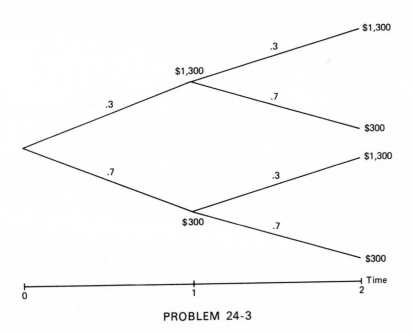

PROBLEM 24-3

t	n	p(n)	r_m	x
1	1	.3	.25	1,300
1	2	.7	.05	300
2	1	.09	.25	1,300
2	2	.21	.05	300
2	3	.21	.25	1,300
2	4	.49	.05	300

The tree diagram for this investment is as follows, with the cash proceeds for each time period shown on the appropriate branch.

24-4. The following information applies to a two-period investment with $r_f = .06$. Find v.

t	n	p(n)	r_m	x
1	1	.3	.25	1,300
1	2	.7	.05	300
2	1	.09	.25	1,300
2	2	.21	.05	1,300
2	3	.21	.25	300
2	4	.49	.05	300

The tree diagram for this investment is as follows, with cash proceeds for each time period shown on the appropriate branch.

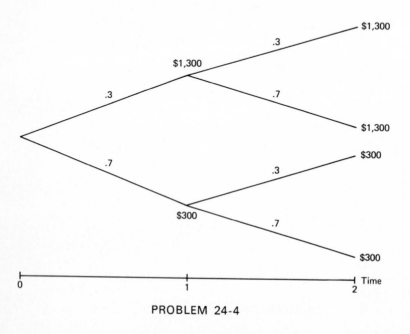

PROBLEM 24-4

24-5. The following information applies to a two-period investment with $r_f =$ .06. Find v.

t	n	$p(n)$	r_m	x
1	1	.3	.25	1,300
1	2	.7	.05	300
2	1	.09	.25	1,600
2	2	.21	.05	600
2	3	.21	.25	1,000
2	4	.49	.05	0

The tree diagram for this investment is as follows, with cash proceeds for each time period shown on the appropriate branch.

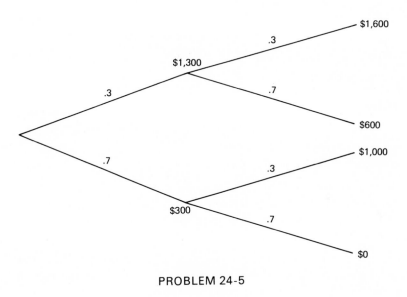

PROBLEM 24-5

24-6. In the following figure, there are two numbers near the middle of each branch. The first is a one period RAPVF for that branch. The second (in parentheses) is the conditional probability of the branch given the previous node. Numbers at the end of each branch are cash flows that will occur if the event corresponding to the branch occurs.

Data in the following figure apply to questions 24-6 through 24-8.

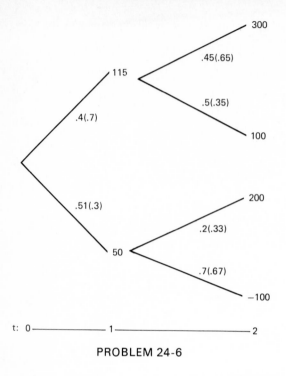

t: 0 ———————— 1 ———————————— 2

PROBLEM 24-6

Find the RAPV at time zero of an asset that will generate all of the cash flows described in the tree diagram for this problem.

24-7. (*Continuation of 24-6.*)
Find the required rate of return on the asset during period 1.

24-8. (*Continuation of 24-6.*)
Express the value of the asset at $t = 0$ in terms of the present discounted value of its expected future cash flows. (Hint: Use required rates of return as discount rates.)

24-9. An asset is expected to generate cash flows of $500 per year for three years. The covariances between the cash flows and the return on the market portfolio in various years are given in the following table.

Table of Values of Cov (X_t, R_{mt})

	R_{m_1}	R_{m_2}	R_{m_3}
X_1	8	0	0
X_2	8	8	0
X_3	8	8	8

If $R_f = .10$ and $\lambda = 10$ for the next three years, what is the risk-adjusted present value of the asset now, using the CAPM?

24-10. The following tree diagram gives values of $s(n, t)$ single period RAPVF's.

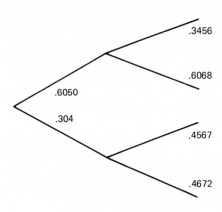

.3456

.6068

.6050

.304

.4567

.4672

PROBLEM 24-10

a. Complete the following table.

t	n	S(n, t)
1	1	.6050
1	2	.3040
2	1	
2	2	
2	3	
2	4	

b. Find the RAPV of one dollar at time 2 if "good times" occur. (Odd numbered nodes are "good times.")

CASE 1

The Oneida Tomato Company*

The following letter was received by one of the authors from Mr. Walter Payne, the chief executive officer of Oneida Tomato, a food processing firm, in response to a request to make a case presentation to a capital budgeting class.

I think I am probably the wrong person to speak before your Capital Budgeting class as we are totally unscientific when it comes to this subject. When making capital investment decisions we generally do not give serious consideration to the payback analysis and then compare this payback with alternative uses of capital. Our long-term marketing objectives tend to be the overriding consideration when we decide where to invest capital dollars. In many cases we know that the payback is going to be extremely poor for a number of years, but we make the investment anyway if it is necessary to reach our long-term market penetration goals.

In summary, capital budgeting plays second fiddle to the strategic business policy decisions that are of overriding importance in a company such as ours devoted to marketing branded consumer products. I would probably end up contradicting much of your course material and adding little that would be of value in terms of capital budgeting. In many industries, I am sure that a more scientific approach than we use is a valuable management tool. For better or worse, we have never considered it to be particularly significant in our decision-making process.

Oneida is primarily engaged in processing and distributing tomatoes. After some persuasion, the chief executive, Mr. Walter Payne, who is also the founder of the company, was persuaded to describe a capital budgeting decision recently faced by his firm.

The Oneida Tomato Company obtained most of its raw material from the section of the country in which the company had started and where most of its processing plants were located. Sales were also concentrated in that region. Mr. Payne was convinced that the success of the company depended on developing national distribution; he believed that substantial economies in advertising costs could be obtained if the company became a national advertiser. Weather conditions caused substantial variation from year-to-year in the supply of tomatoes available in any single region of the country. Accordingly, he felt it imperative to develop sources of supply in several regions of the country.

The investment decision that Mr. Payne discussed with the class was the construction of a new tomato processing plant in the Southeast, a region of the country in which Oneida had no previous processing facilities.

Suppose that you are in charge of a study to evaluate this investment. The results of the study will be presented to Mr. Payne before he makes the final decision on this project. Outline the topics that you think should be included in the study. What information would need to be collected to do the study? To what extent would the results of the study depend on judgement? To what extent would they depend on quantitative data? Do you think the results could be expressed in terms of expected cash flows? Explain.

---

* Names of persons, places and things in this case have been changed to preserve confidentiality.

CASE **2**

Wellesley Woolen Company

The Wellesley Woolen Company was an old, established, Massachusetts textile company. It specialized in woolens used in high-style garments.

The controller stated that the company had not made a major investment decision in recent years. Machines were modernized, but were not frequently replaced. In fact, almost all the machines had been purchased over fifteen years ago.

Another member of top management stated, "The woolen industry is intensely competitive. This is illustrated by the fact that mills must work three shifts in order to make a profit. The Wellesley Woolen Company has been able to exist by limiting capital expenditures to modifications of equipment. A large number of the machines now owned were purchased secondhand. The advantages of more modern equipment are that it is somewhat faster, has larger cards, and requires less maintenance. These savings do not justify the purchase of new equipment. Firms that have bought new equipment have run into difficulties. For example, a new Southern mill was recently closed because the owners couldn't pay for the capital equipment they had purchased."

A seller of texile machinery justified the policy of the Wellesley Woolen Company. The larger number of textile firms going out of business created an extensive market in secondhand textile equipment. This machinery was only slightly less efficient than more recent equipment. In fact, much of the used equipment was built after World War II. Prior to 1950 much of the secondhand equipment had been shipped to foreign markets, but in recent years this market had greatly disappeared. For example, the South American textile manufacturers would rather buy new German textile machinery than secondhand American machinery. They considered the German machinery more efficient and less likely to break down.

One problem encountered by textile machinery salesmen was the reluctance of textile manufacturers to accept radical changes in machinery. They preferred small changes because this did not create new problems of maintenance and repair. They also preferred to have all machines of one type to simplify the spare-parts problem.

Required: Does Wellesley Woolen have an investment decision?

CASE **3**

Norwalk Screw Company

The Norwalk Screw Company was located in Norwalk, Connecticut. It was a privately held corporation and capital expenditures were financed entirely out of funds generated by operations.

In choosing among different investment possibilities, management relied heavily on its experience. Because management generally had between fifteen and forty years' experience, the capital budgeting computations frequently were not made for specific decisions, although a capital budget was prepared.

An example of an investment decision that was decided affirmatively was the purchase of a zinc plater. The plater was purchased for $20,000. It increased capacity, eliminated expensive subcontracting, and reduced direct labor on this particular plating process from two workers to one. Management was very satisfied with the purchase. Equipment used in the manufacture of screws generally had a long life. It rarely became obsolete, although it was modified and improved.

A decision to be made was whether or not to operate a truck instead of using common carriers in the states of Connecticut and Rhode Island. The traffic manager prepared an analysis of costs and pounds of product transported during December (see Exhibits 1 and 2). The product transported included raw material, finished goods, and product requiring outside work.

EXHIBIT 1
Norwalk Screw Company. Inter-Works Communication

      TO: Controller

SUBJECT: Truck Operation in Rhode Island & Connecticut

The New England Motor Rate Bureau is increasing the trucking rates 6 percent effective March 10th. In an effort to avoid this increase and other future increases we are planning to operate our own truck on a limited scale in the states of Rhode Island and Connecticut.

At the present time we are planning to use our two and one-half ton truck to start this operation. Connecticut has been selected as the major point due to the fact that we have a round-trip movement to Shelton, Connecticut. Each day we have considerable tonnage going to Shelton and coming back to our plant from there. In addition, we have good accounts at New Haven, New Britain, and Hartford which would enable us to load approximately 5,000 pounds each day. Coming to our plant we also have freight from Bridgeport, Hartford, Torrington, and Providence. The freight from Providence is ideal in that it consists of set-up boxes and a class 1 commodity which would ride perfectly over a load of screws or coils of brass.

EXHIBIT 2

Norwalk Screw Company. Analysis of Shipments in Rhode Island and Connecticut (Pounds of Freight)

Month of December	Shelton Out	Shelton In	New Britain Out	Hartford Out	Hartford In	Pawtucket Out	New Haven Out	Bridgeport In	Middleton In	Torrington In	Waterville In	Providence In
1	3,000	5,000					1,628					
2	2,662	5,475	2,552									
5	5,000	4,494										
6	3,791	4,412	459	783	2,935				306			600
7	624	940	519				57		1,010			
8	5,673	2,977						2,954	128			2,000
9	1,530	1,075	3,701		831							
12	4,123	5,297					522					
13	704	3,288	430	319	1,360	443			22			
14	2,279	2,206			1,057			2,730				
15	1,928	2,180	2,870	47	374				608			2,000
16	2,773	2,935		1,035	365							1,700
19	5,000	1,090			217				145	3,500		
20	4,052	1,900		1,022	210					3,000		
21	5,000	815			50				247		4,000	
27	4,953	4,825			48							
28	3,400	5,000				1,584						
29	2,112	1,532	2,015								3,500	
30		1,161	4,951		384						3,500	

Figures based on actual shipping and receiving during the month of December show that we paid $1,761.81 for both shipping and receiving charges covering nineteen shipping and receiving days, an average of $92.72 per day or $463.60 per week.

Based on an average round trip of 280 miles per day at $.06 a mile for gas, oil, depreciation, etc., it would cost us $16.80 per day or $84 a week. The driver's wages would be approximately $100 per week based on forty hours at $1.82 per hour and ten hours overtime at $2.73 per hour. Our cost weekly would be $184 against $463.60 via common carrier or a saving of $279.60 per week and $14,259.60 per year.

The service would by no means be limited to the points mentioned above and would be a very flexible operation to satisfy our customers' and our needs. Eventually it could develop into our using our own larger trucks over a greater area. This operation is scheduled to start March 1.

Your comments will be appreciated.

> Very truly yours,
> R. Smith
> Traffic Manager

The analysis of the traffic manager indicated large savings, but the controller rejected the plan.

The cost of a new two and one-half ton truck was $5,000. The company already owned one truck of this type and a pickup truck. Both of these vehicles were driven by one man.

The controller stated: "We generally reject if payback is more than two years." This is the usual approach to investments when the decision can be based on payback or return. Obviously, many investment decisions are made on other bases.

Required: What action should the controller take, based on Mr. Smith's letter?

The Calculating Energy Saver

Joe Sharp, a famous history professor, heated his home with fuel oil. In an average winter he used 800 gallons of oil. Joe felt it was his patriotic duty to reduce his fuel consumption by adding additional insulation to his house. Also, he thought it might save him some money. Two alternatives were available. Method one cost $1,000 and would reduce fuel consumption by 12 percent. Method two would cost $1,500 and would reduce his fuel consumption by 15 percent. Fuel oil costs $1.20 a gallon now. Assume a real discount rate of 3 percent, and an increase of 1 percent per year in the real price of fuel oil. Joe expects to sell his house in twenty years and move to a warm climate.

1. Measure and compare the investment worth of both methods using the following: Payback, IRR, NPV, Equivalent Annual Return, and Cost Benefit Ratio.
2. Which method of insulation do you think is best for Joe? Why?
3. Which measure would you use to explain your preference to Joe? Why? (Assume he was not familiar with any of the measures.)

The Super Project

In March 1967 Mr. Crosby Sanberg, Manager, Financial Analysis at General Foods Corporation, told a casewriter, "What I learned about incremental analysis at the Business School doesn't always work." He was convinced that under some circumstances "sunk costs" were relevant to capital project evaluations. He was also concerned that financial and accounting systems did not provide an accurate estimate of "incremental costs and revenues" and that this was one of the most difficult problems in measuring the value of capital investment proposals. Mr. Sanberg used the Super project[1] as an example.

Super was a new instant dessert, based on a flavored, water-soluble, agglomerated powder. Although a four-flavor line would be introduced, it was estimated that chocolate would account for 80 percent of total sales.

General Foods was organized along product lines in the United States. Foreign operations were under a separate division. Major U.S. product divisions included Post, Kool-Aid, Maxwell House, Jell-O, and Birds Eye. Financial data for General Foods are given in Exhibit 1, 2, and 3.

The capital investment project request for Super involved $200,000 as follows:

Building modifications	$ 80,000
Machinery and equipment	120,000
	$200,000

Part of the expenditure was required for modifying an existing building, where Jell-O was manufactured. Available capacity of a Jell-O agglomerator[2] would be used in the manufacture of Super, so that no cost for the key machine was included in the project. The $120,000 machinery and equipment item represented packaging machinery.

The Market

The total dessert market was defined as including powdered desserts, ice creams, pie fillings, and cake mixes. According to a Nielsen survey, powdered desserts constituted a significant and growing segment of the market; their 1966 market share had increased over the preceding year. Results of the Nielsen survey follow:

---

[1] The name and nature of this new product have been disguised to avoid the disclosure of confidential information.

[2] Agglomeration is a process by which the processed powder is passed through a steam bath and then dried. This "fluffs up" the powder particles and increases solubility.

EXHIBIT 1
The Super Project: Consolidated Balance Sheet of General Foods Corporation Fiscal Year Ended April 1, 1967 (In millions of dollars)

Assets	
Cash	$ 20
Marketable securities	89
Receivables	180
Inventories	261
Prepaid expenses	14
Current assets	$564
Land, buildings, equipment (at cost, less depreciation)	$332
Long-term receivables and sundry assets	7
Goodwill	26
Total	$929

Liabilities and Stockholders' Equity	
Notes payable	$ 22
Accounts payable	86
Accrued liabilities	73
Accrued income taxes	57
Current liabilities	$238
Long-term notes	39
$3\frac{3}{8}$% debentures	22
Other noncurrent liabilities	10
Deferred investment tax credit	9
Stockholders' equity	
Common stock issued	164
Retained earnings	449
Common stock held in treasury, at cost	(2)
Stockholders' equity	$611
TOTAL	$929
Common stock—shares outstanding at year-end	25,127,007

EXHIBIT 2
The Super Project: Common Stock Prices of General Foods Corporation 1958–67

Year	Price Range
1958	$ 24–$39\frac{3}{4}$
1959	$37\frac{1}{8}$–$53\frac{7}{8}$
1960	$49\frac{1}{8}$–$75\frac{1}{2}$
1961	$68\frac{5}{8}$–$107\frac{3}{4}$
1962	$57\frac{3}{4}$–96
1963	$77\frac{5}{8}$–$90\frac{1}{2}$
1964	$78\frac{1}{4}$–$93\frac{1}{4}$
1965	$77\frac{1}{2}$–$89\frac{7}{8}$
1966	$62\frac{3}{4}$–83
1967	$65\frac{1}{4}$–$81\frac{3}{4}$

EXHIBIT 3

The Super Project: Ten-Year Summary of Statistical Data of General Foods Corporation, 1958–67
(All dollar amounts in millions, except assets per employee and figures on a share basis)

Fiscal Years	1958	1959	1960	1961	1962	1963	1964	1965	1966	1967
Earnings										
Sales to customers (net)	$1,009	$1,053	$1,087	$1,160	$1,189	$1,216	$1,338	$1,478	$1,555	$1,652
Cost of sales	724	734	725	764	769	769	838	937	965	1,012
Marketing, administrative and general expenses	181	205	236	261	267	274	322	362	406	449
Earnings before income taxes	$ 105	$ 115	$ 130	$ 138	$ 156	$ 170	$ 179	$ 177	$ 185	$ 193
Taxes on income	57	61	69	71	84	91	95	91	91	94
Net earnings	$ 48	$ 54	$ 61	$ 67	$ 72	$ 79	$ 84	$ 86	$ 94	$ 99
Dividends on common shares	24	28	32	35	40	45	50	50	53	55
Retained earnings—current year	24	26	29	32	32	34	34	36	41	44
Net earnings per common share	$ 1.99	$ 2.21	$ 2.48	$ 2.69	$ 2.90	$ 3.14	$ 3.33	$ 3.44	$ 3.73	$ 3.93
Dividends per common share	$ 1.00	$ 1.15	$ 1.30	$ 1.40	$ 1.60	$ 1.80	$ 2.00	$ 2.00	$ 2.10	$ 2.20
Assets, Liabilities, and Stockholders' Equity										
Inventories	$ 169	$ 149	$ 157	$ 189	$ 183	$ 205	$ 256	$ 214	$ 261	$ 261
Other current assets	144	180	200	171	204	206	180	230	266	303
Current liabilities	107	107	126	123	142	162	202	173	219	238
Working capital	$ 206	$ 222	$ 230	$ 237	$ 245	$ 249	$ 234	$ 271	$ 308	$ 326
Land, buildings, equipment, gross	$ 203	$ 221	$ 247	$ 289	$ 328	$ 375	$ 436	$ 477	$ 517	$ 569
Land, buildings, equipment, net	125	132	148	173	193	233	264	283	308	332
Long-term debt	49	44	40	37	35	34	23	37	54	61
Stockholders' equity	$ 287	$ 315	$ 347	$ 384	$ 419	$ 454	$ 490	$ 527	$ 569	$ 611
Stockholders' equity per common share	$11.78	$12.87	$14.07	$15.46	$16.80	$18.17	$19.53	$20.99	$22.64	$24.32
Capital Program										
Capital additions	$ 28	$ 24	$ 35	$ 40	$ 42	$ 57	$ 70	$ 54	$ 65	$ 59
Depreciation	11	14	15	18	21	24	26	29	32	34
Employment Data										
Wages, salaries, and benefits	$ 128	$ 138	$ 147	$ 162	$ 171	$ 180	$ 195	$ 204	$ 218	$ 237
Number of employees (in thousands)	21	22	22	25	28	28	30	30	30	32
Assets per employee (in thousands)	$ 21	$ 22	$ 23	$ 22	$ 22	$ 23	$ 24	$ 25	$ 29	$ 29

Per share figures calculated on shares outstanding at year-end and adjusted for 2-for-1 stock split in August 1960.

Dessert Market
August–September 1966 Compared with August–September 1965

	Market Share August–September 1966	% Change from August–September 1965	
		Share	Volume
"Jell-O"	19.0%	+3.6	+40.0
"Tasty"	4.0	+4.0	(new)
Total Powders	25.3	+7.6	+62.0
Pie Fillings and Cake Mixes	32.0	−3.9	(no change)
Ice Cream	42.7	−3.4	+5.0
Total Market	100.0%		+13.0

On the basis of test market experience, General Foods expected Super to capture a 10 percent share of the total dessert market. Eighty percent of the expected volume of Super would come from a growth in total market share or growth in the total powdered segment, and 20 percent would come from erosion of "Jell-O" sales.

Production Facilities

Test market volume was packaged on an existing line, inadequate to handle long-run requirements. Filling and packaging equipment to be purchased had a capacity of 1.9 million units on a two-shift, five-day work-week basis. This represented considerable excess capacity, since 1968 requirements were expected to reach 1.1 million units, and the national potential was regarded as 1.6 million units. However, the extra capacity resulted from purchasing standard equipment, and a more economical alternative did not exist.

Capital Budgeting Procedure

Capital investment project proposals submitted under procedures covered in The General Foods Accounting and Financial Manual are identified as falling into one of the following classifications:

1. Safety and Convenience
2. Quality
3. Increase Profit
4. Other

These classifications served as a basis for establishing different procedures and criteria for accepting projects. For example, the Super project fell in the third classification, "increase profit." Criteria for evaluating projects are given in Exhibit 4. In discussing these criteria, Mr. Sanberg noted that the payback and return guidelines were not used as "cut-off" measures. Mr. Sanberg added: "Payback and return on investment are rarely the only measure of acceptability. Criteria vary significantly by type of project. A relatively high return might be required for a new product in a new business category. On the other hand, a much lower return might be acceptable for a new product entry which represented a continuing effort to maintain leadership in an existing business by, for example, filling out the product line."

EXHIBIT 4
The Super Project: Criteria for Evaluating Projects by
General Foods Corporation

The basic criteria to be applied in evaluating projects within each of the classifications are set forth in the following schedule:

Purpose of Project

A. *Safety and Convenience:*

1. Projects required for reasons of safety, sanitation, health, public convenience, or other over-riding reason with no reasonable alternatives. Examples: sprinkler systems, elevators, fire escapes, smoke control, waste disposal, treatment of water pollution, etc.

2. Additional nonproductive space requirements for which there are no financial criteria. Examples: office space, laboratories, service areas (kitchens, rest rooms, etc.)

B. *Quality:*

Projects designed primarily to improve quality.

C. *Increase Profit:*

1. Projects that are justified primarily by reduced costs.

2. Projects that are designed primarily to increase production capacity for an existing product.

Payback and ROFE Criteria

Payback–return on funds projections not required but the request must clearly demonstrate the *immediate* need for the project and the lack or inadequacy of alternative solutions.

Requests for nonproductive facilities, such as warehouses, laboratories, and offices should indicate the advantages of owning rather than leasing, unless no possibility to lease exists. In those cases where the company owns a group of integrated facilities and wherein the introduction of rented or leased properties might complicate the long-range planning or development of the area, owning rather than leasing is recommended. If the project is designed to improve customer service (such as market-centered warehouses) this factor is to be noted on the project request.

If Payback and ROFE cannot be computed, it must be clearly demonstrated that the improvement is identifiable and desirable.

Projects with a Payback period *up to ten years* and a ten-year return *on* funds *as low as 20%* PBT are considered worthy of consideration, provided (1) the end product involved is believed to be a reasonably permanent part of our line or (2) the facilities involved are so flexible that they may be usable for successor products.

Projects for a proven product where the risk of mortality is small, such as coffee, Jell-O Gelatin, and cereals, should assure a payback in *no more than ten years*, and a

3. Projects designed to provide facilities to manufacture and distribute a new product or product line.

D. *Other:*

This category includes projects which by definition are excluded from the three preceding categories. Examples: standby facilities intended to insure uninterrupted production, additional equipment not expected to improve profits or product quality and not required for reasons of safety and convenience, equipment to satisfy marketing requirements, etc.

ten-year PBT return on funds of *no less* than 20%.

Because of the greater risk involved such projects should show a high potential return *on* funds (not less than a ten-year PBT return of 40%) Payback period, however, might be as much as *ten years* because of losses incurred during the market development period.*

While standards of return may be difficult to set, some calculation of financial benefits should be made where possible.

Estimates of payback and return on funds employed were required for each profit-increasing project requiring a total of $50,000 or more of new capital funds and expense before taxes. The payback period was the length of time required for the project to repay the investment from the date the project became operational. In calculating the repayment period, only incremental income and expenses related to the project were used.

Return on funds employed (ROFE) was calculated by dividing ten-year average profit before taxes by the ten-year average funds employed. Funds employed included incremental net fixed assets plus or minus related working capital. Start-up costs and any profits or losses incurred prior to the time when the project became operational were included in the first profit- and loss-period in the financial evaluation calculation.

Capital Budgeting Atmosphere

A General Foods accounting executive commented on the atmosphere within which capital projects were reviewed as follows: "Our problem is not one of capital rationing. Our problem is to find enough good solid projects to employ capital at an attractive return on investment. Of course, the rate of capital inputs must be balanced against a steady growth in earnings per share. The short-term impact of capital investments is usually an increase in the capital base without an immediate realization of profit potential. This is particularly true in the case of new products.

"The food industry should show a continuous growth. A cyclical industry can afford to let its profits vary. We want to expand faster than the gross national product. The key to our capital budgeting is to integrate the plans of our eight divisions into a balanced company plan which meets our overall growth objectives. Most new products show a loss in the first two or three years, but our divisions are big enough to introduce new products without showing a loss."

---

* These criteria apply to the United States and Canada only. Profit-increasing capital projects in other areas in categories c1 and c2 should offer at least a ten-year PBT return of 24% to compensate for the greater risk involved. Likewise, foreign operation projects in the c3 category should offer a ten-year PBT return of at least 48%.

Documentation for the Super Project

Exhibits 5 and 6 document the financial evaluation of the Super project. Exhibit 5 is the summary appropriation request prepared to justify the project to management and to secure management's authorization to expend funds on a capital project. Exhibit 6 presents the backup detail. Cost of the market test was included as "Other" expense in the first period because a new product had to pay for its test market expense, even though this might be a sunk cost at the time capital funds were requested. The "Adjustments" item represented erosion of the Jell-O market and was calculated by multiplying the volume of erosion times a variable profit contribution. In the preparation of Exhibit 6, costs of acquiring packaging machinery were included but no cost was attributed to the 50 percent of the capacity of a Jell-O agglomerator to be used for the Super project because the *General Foods Accounting and Financial Manual* requested that capital projects be prepared on an incremental basis as follows:

"The incremental concept requires that project requests, profit projections, and funds-employed statements include only items of income and expense and investment in assets which will be realized, incurred, or made directly as a result of, or are attributed to, the new project."

Exchange of Memos on the Super Project

After receiving the paper work on the Super project, Mr. Sanberg studied the situation and wrote a memorandum arguing that the principle of the preceding quotation should not be applied to the Super project. His superior agreed with the memorandum and forwarded it to the corporate controller with the covering note contained in Appendix I. The controller's reply is given in Appendix II.

EXHIBIT 5
The Super Project: Capital Project Request Form of General Foods Corporation

NY 1292-A 12-63
PTD. IN U.S.A.

December 23, 1966
Date

"Super" Facilities   66-42
Project Title & Number

New Request ☒   Supplement ☐

Jell-O Division—St. Louis
Division & Location

Expansion-New Product ☐ A
Purpose
☐ R

Project Description
To provide facilities for production of Super, chocolate dessert. This project included finishing a packaging room in addition to filling and packaging equipment.

Summary of Investment	
New capital funds required	$200M
Expense before taxes	—
Less: trade-in or salvage, if any	—
Total this request	$200M
Previously appropriated	—
Total project cost	$200M

Financial Justification*	
ROFE (PBT basis). 10 yr. average	62.9%
Payback April, F'68 Feb. F'75	6.83
Period from to	yrs.
Not required	☐
* Based on total project cost and working funds of	$510M

Estimated expenditure rate	
Quarter ending Mar. F19 67	$160M
Quarter ending June F19 68	40M
Quarter ending F19	
Quarter ending F19	
Remainder	

Other information	
Major ☐ Specific ☐ Blanket ☐ ordinary	
Included in annual program Yes ☐ No ☐	
Percent of engineering completed	80%
Estimated start-up costs	$15M
Estimated start-up date	April

Level of approval required
☐ Board   ☐ Chairman
☐ Exec. V.P.   ☐ Gen. Mgr.

Signatures		
		Date
Director Corp. Eng.		
Director B & A		
General Manager		
Vice President		
Exec. Vice President		
President		
Chairman		

For Division Use—Signatures	
Name and Title	Date

(Instructions for this form are on page 468)

Instructions for Capital Project Request Form NY 1292–A

The purpose of this form is to secure management's authorization to commit or expend funds on a capital project. Refer to Accounting and Financial Manual Statement No. 19 for information regarding projects to which this form applies.

New Request—Supplement
Check the appropriate box.

Purpose
Identify the primary purpose of the project in accordance with the classifications established in Accounting and Financial Statement No. 19, i.e., Sanitation, Health and Public Convenience, Nonproductive Space, Safety, Quality, Reduce Cost, Expansion–Existing Products, Expansion–New Products, Other (specify). Also indicate in the appropriate box whether the equipment represents an addition or a replacement.

Project Description
Comments should be in sufficient detail to enable Corporate Management to appraise the benefits of the project. Where necessary, supplemental data should be attached to provide complete background for project evaluation.

Summary of Investment
New Capital Funds Required.   Show gross cost of assets to be acquired.

Expense Before Taxes.   Show incremental expense resulting from project.

Trade-in or Salvage.   Show the amount expected to be realized on trade-in or sale of a replaced asset.

Previously Appropriated.   When requesting a supplement to an approved project, show the amount previously appropriated even though authorization was given in a prior year.

Financial Justification
ROFE.   Show the return on funds employed (PBT basis) as calculated on Financial Evaluation Form NY 1292-C or 1292-F. The appropriate Financial Evaluation Form is to be attached to this form.

Not Required.   Where financial benefits are not applicable or required or are not expected, check the box provided. The nonfinancial benefits should be explained in the comments.

In the space provided, show the sum of The Total Project Cost plus Total Working Funds (line 20, Form NY 1292-C or line 5, Form NY 1292-F) in either of the first three periods, whichever is higher.

Estimated Expenditure Rate
Expenditures are to be reported in accordance with accounting treatment of the asset and related expense portion of the project. Insert estimated quarterly expenditures beginning with the quarter in which the first expenditure will be made. The balance of authorized funds unspent after the fourth quarter should be reported in total.

Other Information

Check whether the project is a major, specific ordinary, or blanket, and whether or not the project was included in the Annual Program. Show estimated percentage of engineering completed; this is intended to give management an indication of the degree of reliability of the funds requested. Indicate the estimated start-up costs as shown on line 32 of Financial Evaluation Form NY 1292-C. Insert anticipated start-up date for the project; if start-up is to be staggered, explain in comments.

Level of Approval Required

Check the appropriate box.

EXHIBIT 6
The Super Project: Financial Evaluation Form of General Foods Corporation
(Dollar figures in thousands)

NY 1292-C 10-64
PTD. IN U.S.A.

Jell-O	St. Louis	The Super Project	67–89	Date
Division	Location	Project Title	Project No.	Supplement No.

Project Request Detail	1st per.	2nd per.	per.	per.	per.	per.
1. Land	$ 80					
2. Buildings	120					
3. Machinery & Equipment						
4. Engineering						
5. Other (Explain)						
6. Expense Portion (Before Tax)						
7. Sub-Total	$200					
8. Less: Salvage Value (Old Asset)						
9. Total Project Cost*	$200					
10. Less: Taxes on Exp. Portion						
11. Net Project Cost	$200					

Funds Employed	1st per. F 68	2nd per. F 69	3rd per. F 70	4th per. F 71	5th per. F 72	6th per. F 73	7th per. F 74	8th per. F 75	9th per. F 76	10th per. F 77	11th per.	10-yr. avg.
12. Net Project Cost (Line 11)	$200	200	200	200	200	200	200	200	200	200		
13. Deduct Depreciation (Com.)	19	37	54	70	85	98	110	121	131	140		
14. Capital Funds Employed	$181	163	146	130	115	102	90	79	69	60		113
15. Cash	124	134	142	157	160	160	169	169	178	178		157
16. Receivables												
17. Inventories	207	222	237	251	266	266	281	281	296	296		260
18. Prepaid & Deferred Exp.												
19. Less Current Liabilities	(2)	(82)	(108)	(138)	(185)	(184)	(195)	(195)	(207)	(207)		(150)
20. Total Working Funds (15 Thru 19)	329	274	271	264	241	242	255	255	267	267		267
21. Total New Funds Employed (14 + 20)	$510	437	417	394	356	344	345	334	336	327		380

Return on New Funds Employed—10-yr. avg.

	PAT (C ÷ A)	PBT (B ÷ A)
A. New Funds Employed (Line 21)	$380	$380
B. Profit Before Taxes (Line 35)		$239
C. Net Profit (Line 37)	$115	
D. Calculated Return	30.2%	62.0%

Payback Years from Operational Date

Part Year Calculation for First Period	— yrs.
Number of Full Years to Pay Back	6.00 yrs.
Part Year Calculation for Last Period	0.83 yrs.
Total Years to Pay Back	6.83 yrs.

Profit and Loss

22. Unit Volume (in thousands)	1100	1200	1300	1400	1500	1500	1600	1600	1700	1700	1460
23. Gross Sales	$2200	2400	2600	2800	3000	3000	3200	3200	3400	3400	2920
24. Deductions	88	96	104	112	120	120	128	128	136	136	117
25. Net Sales	2112	2304	2496	2688	2880	2880	3072	3072	3264	3264	2803
26. Cost of Goods Sold	1100	1200	1300	1400	1500	1500	1600	1600	1700	1700	1460
27. Gross Profit	1012	1104	1196	1288	1380	1380	1472	1472	1564	1564	1343
Gross Profit % Net Sales	%										
28. Advertising Expense	1100	1050	1000	900	700	700	730	730	750	750	841
29. Selling Expense											
30. Gen. and Admin. Costs											
31. Research Expense	15										2
32. Start-up Costs	360										36
33. Other (Explain) Test Mkt.	180										
34. Adjustments (Explain) Erosion		200	210	220	230	230	240	240	250	250	225
35. Profit Before Taxes	$(643)	(146)	(14)	168	450	450	502	502	564	564	239
36. Taxes	(334)	(76)	(7)	87	234	234	261	261	293	293	125
36A. Add: Investment Credit	(1)	(1)	(1)	(1)	(1)	(1)	(1)	(1)	—	—	(1)
37. Net Profit	(308)	(69)	(6)	82	217	217	242	242	271	271	115
38. Cumulative Net Profit	$(308)	(377)	(383)	(301)	(84)	133	375	617	888	1159	
39. New Funds to Repay (21 less 38)	$818	814	800	695	440	211	(30)	(283)	(552)	(832)	

See Accounting & Financial Manual Policy No. 19 for Instructions.

* Same as Project Request

Instructions for Preparation of Form NY 1292-C
Financial Evaluation

This form is to be submitted to Corporate Budget and Analysis with each profit-increasing capital project request requiring $50,000 or more of capital funds and expense before taxes.

Note that the ten-year term has been divided into eleven periods. The first period is to end on the March 31st following the operational date of the project, and the P & L projection may thereby encompass any number of months from one to twelve, e.g., if the project becomes operational on November 1, 1964, the first period for P & L purposes would be 5 months (November 1, 1964 through March 31, 1965). The next nine periods would be fiscal years (F '66, F '67, etc.) and the eleventh period would be 7 months (April 1, 1974 through October 30, 1974). This has been done primarily to facilitate reporting of projected and actual P & L data by providing for fiscal years. See categorized instructions below for more specific details.

Project Request Detail.   *Lines 1 through 11* show the breakdown of the Net Project Cost to be used in the financial evaluation. *Line 8* is to show the amount expected to be realized on trade-in or sale of a replaced asset. *Line 9* should be the same as the "Total Project Cost" shown on Form NY 1292-A, Capital Project Request. Space has been provided for capital expenditures related to this project which are projected to take place subsequent to the first period. Indicate in such space the additional costs only; do not accumulate them.

Funds Employed

Capital Funds Employed.   *Line 12* will show the net project cost appearing on line 11 as a constant for the first ten periods except in any period in which additional expenditures are incurred; in that event show the accumulated amounts of line 11 in such period and in all future periods.

Deduct cumulative depreciation on *line 13*. Depreciation is to be computed on an incremental basis, i.e., the net increase in depreciation over present depreciation on assets being replaced. In the first period depreciation will be computed at one half of the first year's annual rate; no depreciation is to be taken in the eleventh period. Depreciation rates are to be the same as those used for accounting purposes. *Exception:* When the depreciation rate used for accounting purposes differs materially from the rate for tax purposes, the higher rate should be used. A variation will be considered material when the first full year's depreciation on a book basis varies 20% or more from the first full year's depreciation on a tax basis.

The ten-year average of Capital Funds Employed shall be computed by adding line 14 in each of the first ten periods and dividing the total by ten.

Total Working Funds.   Refer to Financial Policy No. 21 as a guide in computing new working fund requirements. Items which are not on a formula basis and which are normally computed on a five-quarter average shall be handled proportionately in the first period. For example, since the period involved may be less than 12 months, the average would be computed on the number of quarters involved. Generally, the balances should be approximately the same as they would be if the first period were a full year.

Cash, based on a formula which theorizes a two weeks' supply (2/52nds), should follow the same theory. If the first period is for three months, two-thirteenths (2/13ths) should be used; if it is for 5 months, two-twenty-firsts (2/21sts) should be used, and so forth.

Current liabilities are to include one half of the tax expense as the tax liability. The ten-year averages of Working Funds shall be computed by adding each line across for the first ten periods and dividing each total by ten.

Profit and Loss Projection

P & L Categories (Lines 22 through 37).   Reflect only the incremental amounts which will result from the proposed project; exclude all allocated charges. Include the P & L results expected in the individual periods comprising the first ten years of the life of the project. Refer to the second paragraph of these instructions regarding the fractional years' calculations during the first and eleventh periods.

Any loss or gain on the sale of a replaced asset (see line 8) shall be included in line 33.

As indicated in the caption Capital Funds Employed, no depreciation is to be taken in the eleventh period.

The ten-year averages of the P & L items shall be computed by adding each line across for the eleven periods (10 full years from the operational date) and dividing the total by ten.

Adjustments (Line 34).   Show the adjustment necessary, on a before-tax basis, to indicate any adverse or favorable incremental effect the proposed project will have on any other products currently being produced by the corporation.

Investment Credit is to be included on Line 36-A. The Investment Credit will be spread over eight years, or fractions thereof, as an addition to PAT.

Return on New Funds Employed.   Ten-year average returns are to be calculated for PAT (projects requiring Board approval only) and PBT. The PAT return is calculated by dividing average PAT (line 37) by average new funds employed (line 21); the PBT return is derived by dividing average PBT (line 35) by average new funds employed (line 21).

Payback Years From Operational Date

Part Year Calculation For First Period.   Divide number of months in the first period by twelve. If five months are involved, the calculation is $5/12 = .4$ years.

Number of Full Years to Pay Back.   Determined by the last period, excluding the first period, in which an amount is shown on line 39.

Part Year Calculation For Last Period.   Divide amount still to be repaid at the end of the last full period (line 39) by net profit plus the *annual* depreciation in the following year when payback is completed.

Total Years to Pay Back.   Sum of full and part years.

APPENDIX I

TO: J. C. Kresslin, Corporate Controller

FROM: J. E. Hooting, Director, Corporate Budgets and Analysis

March 2, 1967

Super Project

At the time we reviewed the Super project, I indicated to you that the return on invest-ment looked significantly different if an allocation of the agglomerator and building, originally justified as a Jello-O project, were included in the Super investment. The pro rata allocation of these facilities, based on the share of capacity used, triples the initial gross investment in Super facilities from $200,000 to about $672,000.

I am forwarding a memorandum from Crosby Sanberg summarizing the results of three analyses evaluating the project on an:

I. Incremental basis
II. Facilities-used basis
III. Fully allocated facilities and costs basis

Crosby has calculated a ten-year average ROFE using these techniques.
Please read Crosby's memo before continuing with my note.

Crosby concludes that the fully allocated basis, or some variation of it, is necessary to understand the long-range potential of the project.

I agree. We launch a new project because of its potential to increase our sales and earning power for many years into the future. We must be mindful of short-term conse-quences, as indicated by an incremental analysis, but we must also have a long-range frame of reference if we are really to understand what we are committing ourselves to. This long-range frame of reference is best approximated by looking at fully allocated invest-ment and "accounted" profits, which recognize fully allocated costs because, in fact, over the long run all costs are variable unless some major change occurs in the structure of the business.

Our current GF preoccupation with only the incremental costs and investment causes some real anomalies that confuse our decision-making. Super is a good example. On an incremental basis the project looks particularly attractive because by using a share of the excess capacity built on the coat tails of the lucrative Jell-O project, the incremental investment in Super is low. If the excess Jell-O capacity did not exist, would the project be any less attractive? In the short term, perhaps yes because it would entail higher initial risk, but in the long term it is not a better project just because it fits a facility that is temporarily unused.

Looking at this point from a different angle, if the project exceeded our investment hurdle rate on a short-term basis but fell below it on a long-term basis (and Super comes close to doing this), should we reject the project? I say yes because over the long run as "fixed" costs become variable and as we have to commit new capital to support the business, the continuing ROFE will go under water.

In sum, we have to look at new project proposals from both the long-range and the short-term point of view. We plan to refine our techniques of using a fully allocated basis as a long-term point of reference and will hammer out a policy recommendation for your consideration. We would appreciate any comments you may have.

TO: J. W. Hooting, Director, Corporate Budgets and Analysis

FROM: C. Sanberg, Manager, Financial Analysis

February 17, 1967

Super Project: A Case Example of
Investment Evaluation Techniques

This will review the merits of alternative techniques of evaluating capital investment decisions using the Super project as an example. The purpose of the review is to provide an illustration of the problems and limitations inherent in using incremental ROFE and payback and thereby provide a rationale for adopting new techniques.

Alternative Techniques

The alternative techniques to be reviewed are differentiated by the level of revenue and investment charged to the Super project in figuring a payback and ROFE, starting with incremental revenues and investment. Data related to the alternative techniques outlined below are summarized [at the end of this appendix].

Alternative I Incremental Basis

Method. The Super project as originally evaluated considered only incremental revenue and investment, which could be directly identified with the decision to produce Super. Incremental fixed capital ($200M) basically included packaging equipment.

Result. On this basis the project paid back in seven years with a ROFE of 63 percent.

Discussion. Although it is General Foods' current policy to evaluate capital projects on an incremental basis, this technique does not apply to the Super project. The reason is that Super extensively utilizes existing facilities, which are readily adaptable to known future alternative uses.

Super should be charged with the "opportunity loss" of agglomerating capacity and building space. Because of Super the opportunity is lost to use a portion of agglomerating capacity for Jell-O and other products that could potentially be agglomerated. In addition, the opportunity is lost to use the building space for existing or new product volume expansion. To the extent there is an opportunity loss of existing facilities, new facilities must be built to accommodate future expansion. In other words, because the business is expanding Super utilizes facilities that are adaptable to predictable alternative uses.

Alternative II Facilities-Used Basis

Method. Recognizing that Super will use half of an existing agglomerator and two-thirds of an existing building, which were justified earlier in the Jell-O project, we added Super's pro rata share of these facilities ($453M) to the incremental capital. Overhead costs directly related to these existing facilities were also subtracted from incremental revenue on a shared basis.

Result. ROFE 34%.

Discussion. Although the existing facilities utilized by Super are not incremental to this project, they are relevant to the evaluation of the project because potentially they can be put to alternative uses. Despite a high return on an incremental basis, if the ROFE on a project was unattractive after consideration of the shared use of existing facilities, the project would be questionable. Under these circumstances, we might look for a more profitable product for the facilities.

In summary, the facilities-used basis is a useful way of putting various projects on a common ground for purposes of *relative* evaluation. One product using existing capacity should not necessarily be judged to be more attractive than another practically identical product which necessitates an investment in additional facilities.

Alternative III Fully Allocated Basis

Method. Further recognizing that individual decisions to expand inevitably add to a higher overhead base, we increased the costs and investment base developed in Alternative II by a provision for overhead expenses and overhead capital. These increases were made in year five of the 10-year evaluation period, on the theory that at this point a number of decisions would result in more fixed costs and facilities. Overhead expenses included manufacturing costs, plus selling and general administrative costs on a per unit basis equivalent to Jell-O. Overhead capital included a share of the distribution system assets ($40M).

Result. ROFE 25%

Discussion. Charging Super with an overhead burden recognizes that overhead costs in the long run increase in proportion to the level of business activity, even though decisions to spend more overhead dollars are made separately from decisions to increase volume and provide the incremental facilities to support the higher volume level. To illustrate, the Division—F1968 Financial Plan budgets about a 75% increase in headquarters' overhead spending in F1968 over F1964. A contributing factor was the decision to increase the sales force by 50% to meet the demands of a growing and increasingly complex business. To further illustrate, about half the capital projects in the F1968 three-year Financial Plan are in the "non-payback" category. This group of projects comprised largely "overhead facilities" (warehouses, utilities, etc.), which are not directly related to the manufacture of products but are necessary components of the total business. These facilities are made necessary by an increase in total business activity as a result of the cumulative effect of many decisions taken in the past.

The Super project is a significant decision which will most likely add to more overhead dollars as illustrated above. Super volume doubles the powdered dessert business category; it increases the Division businesses by 10%. Furthermore, Super requires a new production technology: agglomeration and packaging on a high-speed line.

Conclusions

1. The incremental basis for evaluating a project is an inadequate measure of a project's worth when existing facilities, with a known future use, will be utilized extensively.
2. A fully allocated basis of reviewing major new product proposals recognizes that overheads increase in proportion to the size and complexity of the business and provides the best long-range projection of the financial consequences.

Alternative Evaluations of Super Project
(Figures based on 10-year averages; in thousands of dollars)

	I Incremental Basis	II Facilities- Used Basis	III Fully Associated Basis
INVESTMENT:			
Working capital	$267	$267	$267
Fixed capital			
Gross	200	653	672
Net	113	358	367
Total net investment	380	625	634
Profit before taxes:[1]	239	211	157
ROFE:	63%	34%	25%
Jell-O Project			
Building	$200 × $\frac{2}{3}$ = $133		
Agglomerator	640 × $\frac{1}{2}$ = 320		
	$453		

[1] Note: Assumes 20% of Super volume will replace existing Jell-O business.

APPENDIX II

TO: Mr. J. E. Hooting, Director, Corporate Budgets and Analysis

FROM: Mr. J. C. Kresslin, Corporate Controller

SUBJECT: SUPER PROJECT

March 7, 1967

On March 2 you sent me a note describing Crosby Sanberg's and your thoughts about evaluating the Super project. In this memo you suggest that the project should be appraised on the basis of fully allocated facilities and production costs.

In order to continue the dialogue, I am raising a couple of questions below.

It seems to me that in a situation such as you describe for Super, the real question is a *management decision* as to whether to go ahead with the Super project or not go ahead. Or to put it another way, are we better off in the aggregate if we use half the agglomerator and two-thirds of an existing building for Super, or are we not, on the basis of our current knowledge?

It might be assumed that, for example, half of the agglomerator is being used and half is not and that a minimum economical size agglomerator was necessary for Jell-O and, consequently, should be justified by the Jell-O project itself. If we find a way to utilize it sooner by producing Super on it, aren't we better off in the aggregate, and the different ROFE figure for the super project by itself become somewhat irrelevant? A similar point of view might be applied to the portion of the building. Or if we charge the Super project with half an agglomerator and two-thirds of an existing building, should we then go back and relieve the Jell-O projects of these costs in evaluating the management's original proposal?

To put it another way, since we are faced with making decisions at a certain time on the basis of what we then know, I see very little value in looking at the Super project all by itself. Better we should look at the total situation before and after to see how we fare.

As to allocated production costs, the point is not so clear. Undoubtedly, over the long haul, the selling prices will need to be determined on the basis of a satisfactory margin over fully allocated costs. Perhaps this should be an additional requirement in the course of evaluating capital projects, since we seem to have been surprised at the low margins for "Tasty" after allocating all costs to the product.

I look forward to discussing this subject with you and with Crosby at some length.

478

CASE **6**

Fall River Lumber Company

In considering the purchase of equipment for debarking logs, the Financial Analysis Department of the Fall River Lumber Company prepared the following report.

Proposed Debarking Installation for Flakeboard Plant

Introduction

The flakeboard plant is using peeled aspen so that our finished board will have a light-colored appearance. This lighter appearance is felt to be necessary by the Sales Department if we wish to continue to point our product toward a higher-quality market.

Moreover, as the plant's operating efficiency is a direct function of the life of its flaker knives, the peeled wood will contribute somewhat to increasing this life by eliminating the abrasive action caused by the sand and dirt that is often found within the bark.

However, the primary consideration in maintaining an adequate knife life is that the moisture content in the aspen be sufficient (above 35 percent air dry) to act as a cooling agent on the flaker knives.

If the aspen supplied to the plant is too dry, the flaker knives heat up, thereby becoming dull, and the plant's operations are impaired. Past experience has demonstrated to us that the difference in flaker knife life is almost insignificant between using *freshly peeled aspen* and *freshly unpeeled aspen*, but quite significant between using *dry peeled aspen* and *freshly peeled aspen*.

In the initial stages of operations, the plant used fresh "hand-peeled" aspen direct from the wood dealers. However, because the hand peeling (commonly known as sap peeling) season lasts only during the trees' annual growth period (a six-week period from spring to early summer), it is only during this time that a sufficient volume (2 cords per person per day) can be maintained. Out of season this type of production drops to $\frac{1}{2}$ cord per person per day, thus becoming uneconomical. Although a sufficient year's supply of aspen could possibly be bought during the six-week sap-peeling season, the wood would dry out in storage and the problem of flaker knife life again becomes the critical factor.

Chemical debarking must be ruled out as a possibility because the wood becomes too dry in the one-year period that is required for the tree to die and the bark to fall off.

Thus the use of some kind of mechanical debarking equipment that would ensure a year-round supply of peeled wood with the correct moisture characteristics becomes necessary if we wish to continue producing our lighter-colored flakeboard.

Alternative Solutions

The following proposals exist as a possible means of supplying peeled aspen to the flakeboard plant:

1. Installing permanent debarking facilities at Fall River employing King or Elmo equipment.
2. Utilizing portable debarkers at Fall River, such as the Leswork.

Recommendations

This study recommends installing a King debarker out in the woodyard. In addition, it recommends the use of mechanical feeding accessories and a bark burner. The estimated savings would be $40,000 per year compared to our present portable Leswork installation. The total estimated investment would be $70,000. The return on this investment would be at the rate of 57 percent, or payback in one and three-quarters years.

Summary of Findings

The problem as outlined in the introduction of this study of determining the most economical and sound engineering method of debarking aspen for the flakeboard plant is complicated.

Basically, it boils down to balancing our rate of production required to supply the flakeboard operations against a capital investment and estimated debarking cost per cord that we are willing to pay for.

Certain assumptions were made. The main ones, subject to the most variability, are

1. The estimated useful life of the debarkers.
2. The estimated repair and maintenance costs.
3. The machine production per hour.

The alternative of *buying peeled wood* is not recommended and such rejection is based mainly on the following considerations:

1. The wide diversity in the location of the aspen stands, creating a difficult peeling set-up in the field.
2. The uncertain supply in the winter season.
3. The higher operating costs for the wood dealer necessitated by his increased handling and depreciation expenses.
4. The possible legal problems arising from buying and renting debarkers to the wood dealers.
5. The reluctance of the wood dealers to debark in the field.
6. The uncertainty of getting clean wood.

Rejection of *portable debarkers at Fall River* is primarily based on a pure cost consideration. To maintain our estimated production requirements of 1 million square feet per month in the flakeboard plant would necessitate reinvesting in portable debarkers at a rate that would more than offset the initial low investment cost. The low production inherent in these debarkers means running them at their capacity practically around the clock and thereby quickly reaching their estimated life of 5,000 cords.

The choice lies between buying a King debarker, either new or used, or an Elmo. A used King is rejected because its return on investment is less than that of a new King. Both the Elmo and King are substantially the same machine as far as the efficiency in debarking the wood goes. However, the rugged design of the Elmo has kept its repair and maintenance charges well under that of the King. While there are over one hundred King installations in operation, certain companies, such as the United States Paper Company of Flint, Michigan, are replacing their King with Elmos, as the latter seemed to hold up better. Nevertheless, the economic advantage evidenced by the higher rate of return of the new King as compared to the Elmo, 57 percent versus 49 percent (see Table 3), takes into consideration this more rugged design of the Elmo; yet this report still concludes that the King investment is the more advantageous for our requirements.

It is well to mention that the inherent savings of using an Elmo or a King debarker lie not only with the increased production (both over twice the hourly capacity of a Leswork), which lowers the total unit cost per cord of wood debarked, but also with the longer estimated life of the machines. The savings are not a result of an overall reduction in manpower.

Although the debarkers themselves do not require operating labor, the machine's higher productive capacities require that such men be utilized as spotters on the infeed and outfeed conveying equipment.

The economics of the study are summarized in Tables 1 to 4. The first three compare the operating costs and investments of a King, an Elmo, and a Leswork debarking install-ation. Table 4 summarizes the return-on-investment data of the King and Elmo install-ations as compared to our present Leswork operations.

Location

The location of a debarker installation is an important factor in determining the efficiency of its operation. The installation could be placed in one of two places:

1. Adjacent to the flakeboard plant, or
2. Out in the woodyard.

Wood handling is a major consideration to this location decision, in particular supply-ing the infeed side of the debarker. On the outfeed side, stacking the slick debarked logs is also a job. If the sticks are maintained with a minimum end-to-end spacing on the infeed conveyor, full utilization of the debarker is obtained. This requires production equipment. With the debarker in the woodyard, the crane could be utilized in unloading the trucks directly onto the infeed-line deck conveyors leading into the debarker, thereby producing at rated capacity. If the volume of trucks is too high at any one period, the crane could stack the wood in ranks adjacent to the infeed table, and in a slack period feed the debarker from these ranks. Whereas, if the crane were brought into the plant site, this would cut down on the yard efficiency for stacking wood when the debarker is not in use. The only other solution would be to use a Cary Lift in place of the crane. However, this means an increased investment of $22,000.

TABLE 1.   *Cost Estimates for Flakeboard Plant Debarkers*

	King (New)	King (Used)	Elmo	Leswork*
Debarker cost (with power)	$23,200	$16,000	$44,000	$4,000
Accessories (conveyors and deck, etc.)	37,425	27,700	52,000	—
Installation	9,650	14,600	9,800	300
Total investment	$70,275	$58,300	$105,800	$4,300
Fixed costs per cord	$0.82	$1.08	$0.74	$0.95
Variable costs per cord	1.16	1.32	0.72	2.87
Total estimated cost per cord	$1.98	$2.40	$1.46	$3.82

* Present Fall River operations (estimated three Lesworks required to meet production demands).

Other advantages of locating the debarker installation in the woodyard are the follow-ing:

1. More space, thereby allowing for flexibility of operations.
2. Possible future infeed application utilizing a "hot" pond. This type of wood handling

TABLE 2. Analysis of Total Investment Estimate for Flakeboard Plant Debarkers

Type of Debarker		King (New)	King (Used)	Elmo	Leswork
Debarker (with power)		$23,200	$16,000*	$ 44,000	$4,000
Building		$(7,000)†	$(4,500)†	$(No	
Infeed and outfeed conveyors		9,000	6,000	exact	
Cross chain conveyor		10,000	10,000	breakdown	
Bark conveyor		5,000	3,500	given,	
Starting equipment		1,425	1,200	similar	
Cary Lift		(21,400)†		to new	
Bark burner		10,000	3,000	King	
Special roll conveyor and flipper			2,000	equip.)	
Spare parts		2,000	2,000		
Total accessories		$37,425	$27,700	$ 52,000	$ —
Dismantling old King equipment and accessories		$ —	$ 5,000	$ —	$ —
Freight—In		250	200	400	50
Power line to woodyard					
2,100-foot wire at $2/foot	$4,200				
22 poles on 100-foot intervals at $100/pole	2,200	6,400	6,400	6,400	
Labor and materials to install equipment (3 men, 3 days)		3,000	3,000	3,000	250
Total installation		$ 9,650	$14,600	$ 9,800	$ 300
Total investment		$70,725	$58,300	$105,800	$4,300

* Estimated.

† Not included in totals for accessories.

TABLE 3. *Analysis of Cost Estimates per Cord for Fall River Flakeboard Plant Debarkers*

Type of Machine	Elmo	King (New)	King (Used)	Leswork (Fall River)
Estimated life*	20,000 hours 5 years	14,000 hours 3¼ years	10,000 hours 2¼ years	2,000 hours ¼ year
Rated capacity—rough cords per hour	9	7	6	2¼
Fixed costs per cord		Cost estimate per cord		
Depreciation charges: $\dfrac{\text{total equipment cost}}{\text{tot. est. life} \times \text{rated cap.}}$ $\dfrac{\$106,000}{20,000 \text{ hr} \times 9 \text{ cords/hr}}$ (sample calculation)	$0.59	$0.71	$0.96	$0.90
Interest, taxes, insurance: avg. annual invest. × 10% $\dfrac{\$106,000 \times .1}{2 \times 4,000 \text{ hr/yr} \times 9 \text{ cd/hr}}$ 9 cords/hr	0.15	0.11	0.12	0.05
Total fixed costs	$0.74	$0.82	$1.08	$0.90
Variable costs per cord				
Repairs and upkeep	$0.05†	$0.32†	$0.37†	$0.05
Maintenance (½ hr/8-hr shift) $\dfrac{\$.125 \text{ hr}}{\text{rated capacity}}$ (routine lubrication and adjust.)	0.01	0.02	0.02	0.05
Operating labor: $\dfrac{2 \text{ men} \times \text{hourly wage} \times 113\%‡}{\text{rated capacity}}$ $\dfrac{2 \text{ men} \times \$2/\text{hr} \times 113\%}{9 \text{ cords/hr}}$	0.05	0.65	0.75	1.67
Operating supplies and power: 50% hr/rated capacity	0.06	0.07	0.08	0.10
Bark hauling: $\dfrac{\$4/\text{truck/hr} \times 1 \text{ hr/load}}{4 \text{ cords/truck load}}$	—	—	—	1.00
Bark burning	0.10	0.10	0.10	—
Total variable costs	$0.72	$1.16	$1.32	$2.87
Total estimated cost per rough cord	$1.46	$1.98	$2.40	$3.82

* Estimated life based on 16 hr/day × 5 days/wk × 50 wk/yr = 4,000 hr/yr × 5 yr = 20,000 hr.
† Estimated from actual operations at Great Falls Paper Company (Elmo) and Paper Products (King installation).
‡ Thirteen percent increased for Social Security, workmen's compensation, retirement benefits.

TABLE 4. *Estimated Return on Investment Comparing Proposed Debarkers with Present Leswork Debarker*

	With Bark Burner*		
	Elmo	King (New)	King (Used)
Estimated savings per rough cord	$ 2.63	$ 1.84	$ 1.42
Estimated required rough cords/year† (59 cords/day × 360 days)	22,000	22,000	22,000
Estimated total savings per year	$ 52,000	$40,000	$31,000
Estimated total investment	$106,000	$70,000	$58,000
Estimated return on investment	49%	57%	54%
Payback period	2 years	1¾ years	1⅘ years

	Without Bark Burner		
	Elmo	King (New)	King (Used)
Estimated savings per rough cord	$ 1.55	$ 1.05	$ 0.68
Estimated required rough cords/year† (59 cords/day × 360 days)	22,000	22,000	22,000
Estimated total savings per year	$34,000	$23,000	$15,000
Estimated total investment	$96,000	$60,000	$48,000
Estimated return on investment	35%	38%	31%
Payback period	3 years	2½ years	3¼ years

* Cost of bark burner including installation is $10,000.

† Based on production requirements of fifty finished cords per day, which provides for 1 million square feet of board per month and a 15 percent bark loss.

appears to be the most practical way of solving loading into King-type debarkers. The wood is simply dumped into the pond, which has impellers submerged in the water. If the sticks are not in contact with the water for more than half an hour, the moisture content of the wood is not affected.

3. Ease of installation, because there would be no interference with the existing supply of wood to the plant.

The principal advantage to locating near the flakeboard plant site is the reduced material handling on the outfeed end. Instead of stacking the wood on trailers for hauling to the plant or in ranks for inventory, it could be fed directly to the flakers. However, this means that the debarking operation is dependent *directly* on the flakeboard plant's operations, for if the plant shuts down so must the debarker. Otherwise, if the debarker would run when the plant was down, the material handling would increase, since the peeled wood would have to be set off. Out in the woodyard this would not be the case. Wood racks mounted on rails or the present trailers could be placed under the outfeed end conveyor and easily removed sideways away from the flow of materials when each rack has been filled.

Bark Disposal

Another important aspect in a debarking operation is the problem of bark disposal. The bark could possibly be

1. Burned in a regular "bark burner."

2. Utilized as fuel at our boiler house, provided the necessary adapting equipment was installed.
3. Possibly pressed into logs and sold as fireplace wood.
4. Hauled away and dumped as refuse.

This study compares returns with and without a bark burner. (See Table 4.)

If the efficiency of burning is high enough to prevent excessive smoke, the investment in such a piece of equipment would pay for itself by the savings ($1 per rough cord × 22,000 cords per year = $22,000) resulting from eliminating hauling to the dump.

Discussion of Alternative Solutions

1. *Portable Debarkers at Fall River*. It is possible to utilize *a series* of Leswork portable debarkers for the flakeboard plant's wood requirements. At the present time we are barking approximately forty-five rough cords per day ($2\frac{1}{4}$ rough cords per hour × 20 hours per day). This appears to be maximum capacity for these debarkers. Assuming a 15 percent bark loss and a 2 percent wood loss, this results in a production of thirty-seven finished cords per day (45 × .83). This is enough capacity for 750,000 square feet of board per month (assuming 1.5 finished cords per 1,000 square feet). Basing our wood requirements at a minimum of 1 million square feet per month, we would need a production of about fifty finished cords per day. Thus it would be necessary to invest in a minimum of two more debarkers (one for reserve) to fulfill our minimum production requirements. This would be an investment of $12,000 (3 × $4,000), excluding the necessary conveying accessories. However, based on an estimated life of 2,000 hours or 5,000 cords, two thirds of this investment would theoretically be replaced approximately every four months or one-third year.

$$\left(\frac{5,000 \text{ cords}}{45 \text{ cd/day} \times 30 \text{ days/mo}} = 3.7 \text{ mo} \right)$$

Thus a $12,000 initial investment becomes a $28,000 yearly investment.

Expanding this investment to a comparable figure with the King and Elmo debarkers, the following result is seen:

Type	Elmo	King (New)	Portable Leswork
Estimated life	5 years	$3\frac{1}{2}$ years	4 years
Total investment	$106,000	$70,000	$112,000

2. *Permanent Debarking Facilities*. In considering permanent debarking facilities for the Fall River flakeboard operations, the first question that must be answered is what type of bark-removal operation is feasible. Some principal methods of bark removal apart from manual labor with a spud or draw knife are the following:

a. By means of friction by tumbling or rotating action, such as the rotating cylindrical drum at Williamsburg.
b. By hydraulic pressure.
c. By shear principle.
d. By the rosser head, or cutter head, principle, such as the present Leswork debarker.

An attempt to debark some aspen in the Williamsburg drum was not successful because the wood was not dry enough to experience sufficient friction for effective bark removal.

Since the flakeboard operations demand this higher moisture content in the wood, this generally recognized quick, cheap bark-removal system cannot be utilized.

A hydraulic pressure debarker is ruled out chiefly on the grounds of the water pollution problem it would create.

The basic feature of a King-type debarker consists of a blunt-edge pressure elastically against the log, which then penetrates the bark down into the cell-forming cambium layer between the bark and wood. Tangential pressure against the bark produces shear stresses between bark and wood sufficient to overcome the strength of the cambium layer. The principal feature of such a machine is the removal of bark at a substantially low wood loss. The trade names of debarkers of this type are the King and the Elmo. Both of these debarkers could be used for our flakeboard operations.

The rosser, or cutter head, principle is employed on the Leswork machine we are now using. While these machines remove the bark sufficiently, the wood loss appears to be higher than with the King type. In addition, as these machines are portable, production is not as great as on the King machines. As an example, the Leswork debarks between 2 to $2\frac{1}{2}$ rough cords per hour as compared to 5 to 10 rough cords per hour on the King. Nevertheless, the Leswork is a proven debarker that could be utilized in our operations.

Both the King and the Elmo have been utilized in flakeboard operations. It is generally felt that the King does an excellent job in debarking, but the maintenance requirements are high. Moreover, there seems to be more of a problem debarking wood with varying diameters with the King than with the Elmo. (Our operations use wood ranging from 4 to 15 inches in diameter.)

Because the Elmo has been designed for more rugged operations, its weight is approximately $2\frac{1}{2}$ times the King (22,000 pounds versus 9,000 pounds). Simultaneously, its cost is $20,000 more ($44,000 versus $24,000).

The rating of a debarker is dependent on the number of sticks per cord, the percentage of bark removal required, and the infeed system to the debarker. In addition, under wintertime conditions it is necessary to slow down the debarker in order to maintain the same percentage of bark removal. For this study, the average rated capacity of the King and Elmo debarkers was based on automatic conveying accessories. It should be kept in mind that manual feeding to either of these debarkers would tend to reduce their rated capacity.

Required: Assume a zero tax rate and a time value of money of .05. What decision should the firm make.

CASE 7
Jacobs Division*

Mr. Richard Soderberg, Financial Analyst for the Jacobs Division of MacFadden Chemical Company, was reviewing several complex issues relating to a new product introduction being considered for investment purposes in the ensuing year, 1974. The project, involving a specialty coating material, qualified for investment according to company guidelines. The Jacobs Division Manager, Mr. Reynolds, was fearful, however, that the project might be too "risky." Moreover, Mr. Soderberg believed the only practical way to sell what he regarded as an attractive opportunity would place the product in a weak competitive position over the long run. Finally, he was concerned that the estimates employed in the probabilistic analysis were little better than educated guesses.

MacFadden Chemical Company was one of the ten largest in the world with sales in excess of $1 billion. Its volume had grown steady at the rate of 10% per year throughout the post war period until 1957. Sales and earnings had grown more rapidly. Beginning in 1957, the chemical industry began to experience overcapacity particularly in basic materials. Price cutting ensued. Also, more funds had to be spent in marketing and research to remain competitive. As a consequence, sales and profits were adversely affected. The company achieved only modest growth in sales of 4% in the 1960's and an overall decline in profits. Certain shortages began developing in the economy in 1972; by 1973, sales had risen 60% and profits over 100% as the result of price increases and near-capacity operations. Most observers believed that the "shortage boom" would be only a short respite from the intensively competitive conditions of the last decade.

There were eleven operating divisions of MacFadden, organized into three groups. Each division had a multiplicity of products centered around one chemical, such as fluoride, sulphur, or petroleum. The Jacobs Division was an exception. It was the newest and smallest division with sales of $30 million. Secondly, its products were all specialty industrial products, such as dyes, adhesives and finishes, purchased in relatively small lots by a great diversity of industrial customers. No single product had sales in excess of $5 million and many had only $100,000 or so in volume. There were 150 basic products in the division, each with several minor variations. Finally, it was one of the more rapidly growing divisions—12% per year prior to 1973—with a high return on total assets net of depreciation of 13%.

In capital budgeting analysis, there were some corporate wide guidelines for new investment opportunities: 8% for cost reduction projects, 12% for expansion of facilities, and 16% for new products or processes. Returns were measured in terms of discounted cash flows (internal rate). All calculations were estimated after taxes. Mr. Soderberg believed that these rates and methods were typical of the chemical industry.

Mr. Reynolds, however, tended to demand higher rates for projects in his division, even though its earning's growth-stability in the past marked it as one of the more reliable

* Copyright © 1984 by The Colgate Darden Graduate School of Business Administration of the University of Virginia and by Robert F. Vandell, The Charles C. Abbott Professor of Business Administration. This case was prepared by Professor Vandell and is used with his permission.

sectors of MacFadden's operations. Mr. Reynolds had three reasons for wanting to see better returns. First, one of the key variables used in appraising management performance of MacFadden was the growth of residual income (market share, profit margins, etc. were also considered). Residual income was the division's profits after allocated taxes minus a 10% capital charge on total net assets (assets after depreciation). Mr. Reynolds did not like the idea of investing in projects that were too close to the target rate of earnings imbedded in the residual income calculation. Next, many new projects had high start-up costs. Even though they made attractive returns over the long run, these projects hurt overall earnings performance in the short run. " Don't tell me what its (a project's) discounted rate of return is, tell me whether we're going to improve our return on total net assets within three years," Mr. Reynolds was known to say. Finally, Mr. Reynolds was skeptical of estimates. " I don't know what's going to happen here on this project, but I'll bet we overstate returns by 2 to 5% on average," was a typical comment by him. As a result, Mr. Reynolds tended to look for at least 4% in return more than the company standards before he became enthusiastic about the project. " You've got to be hardnosed about taking risk," he said, " By demanding a decent return for riskier opportunities, we've a better chance to grow and prosper."

Mr. Soderberg knew that Mr. Reynolds' views were reflected in actions at decision-making levels throughout the division. Projects that did not have fairly promising return prospects relative to Mr. Reynolds' standards tended to be dropped from analysis or shelved fairly early in the decision process. While this was hard to estimate, Mr. Soderberg guessed that almost as many projects with returns meeting the company hurdle rates were abandoned in this division as were ultimately approved. In fact, the projects submitted were usually so promising Mr. Reynolds rarely said no to a proposal. His capital budgets, in turn, were accepted virtually unchanged at higher management levels, unless top management happened to be unusually pessimistic about business and money prospects.

A new production-process project was often under study for several years after research had developed a " test tube " idea. The properties of the product had to be evaluated in relation to market needs, competition and the like. A diversity of possible applications tended to complicate this analysis. At the same time, technological studies were under way examining material sources, plant location, manufacturing process alternatives, scale economics, and so on. A myriad of feasible alternatives existed, only some of which could be actively explored. These activities often involved outlays in excess of several hundred thousand dollars before any real feel for the potential of the project could be ascertained realistically. A project manager was assigned to any major project to coordinate this work. " For every dollar of new capital approved, I bet we spend $.30 on business analysis of opportunities," observed Mr. Soderberg, " and that doesn't count the money we spend on research."

The project that concerned Mr. Soderberg at the moment had been dubbed Silicone-X. The product was a special-purpose coating that added slipperiness to a surface. The coating would be used on a variety of products to reduce friction by increasing slide. The uniqueness lay in its hardness, adhesiveness (to the applied surface), and durability. It could be used in almost any application where lubricants might be imperfect in eliminating friction between moving parts. There were a great diversity of situations where Silicone-X might be useful. In terms of maket, the product was likely to have a large number of buyers, each ordering small quantities. Only a few firms were likely to buy in yearly amounts larger than 5,000 pounds.

" Test tube batches " of Silicone-X had been tested in a variety of applications inside and outside Jacobs. Comments were universally favorable, although an upper price limit of $2 per pound seemed likely to be the maximum possible. Lower prices were, of course, considered attractive, but this was unlikely to produce larger volume. For planning purposes a price of $1.90 per pound was used.

Demand was harder to estimate because of the variety of possible applications. Market-research people had estimated a first-year demand of 1,000,000 to 2,000,000 pounds with 1,200,000 sited as the most likely. Mr. Soderberg empathized with the problem of the market researchers. They had tried to do a systematic job of looking at the segments of most probable application, but the data was not good. "They could spend another year studying it, and state their opinions more confidently. But we wouldn't find them more believable. The estimates are educated guesses by smart people. However, they are also pretty wild stabs in the dark. They won't rule out the possibility of demand as low as 500,000 lbs, and 2,000,000 lbs is not a ceiling to possibility." Once the product was established, however, growth was considered to be pretty good.

Once the product became established, however, demand was likely to grow at a healthy rate—perhaps 10% per year. However, the industries served were likely to be cyclical with swings in volume requirements of plus or minus 20% depending on market conditions.

There was no patent protection on Silicone-X, and the technological know-how involved in the manufacturing process could be duplicated by others in time (perhaps twelve months). "Someone is certainly going to get interest in this product when sales volume reaches $3,000,000 and it's essentially a commodity," observed Mr. Soderberg.

"The product life is likely to be pretty good. We think demand should level off after 8 to 10 years, but the odds are very much against someone developing a cheaper or markedly superior substitute," claimed Mr. Vorst, the Project Manager. As most equipment required for the project was likely to wear out and need replacement after 15 years, give or take a few, this seemed like a natural point to terminate an analysis.

"Fortunately the cost estimates look pretty solid. Basic chemicals, of course, do fluctuate in purchase price, but we have a captive source with stable manufacturing costs. We can probably negotiate a long term transfer price with Wilson (another MacFadden Division) although this is not the time (sharply higher prices for an apparently temporary period) to do so," added Mr. Vorst.

In his preliminary analysis, Mr. Soderberg tended to use net present-value calculations and in this case the discount rate would be 20%. "We can always convert the data to a discounted cash flow rate when we have to do so," said he. "We also work with most likely estimates. Until we get down to the bitter end, there are too many alternatives to consider, and we can't afford probabilistic measures or fancy simulations. A conservative definition of most likely values is probably good enough for most of the subsidiary analyses. We've probably made over 200 present-value calculations using our computer programs just to get to this decision point, and heaven knows how many quick and dirt paybacks," observed Mr. Soderberg.

Mr. Soderberg went on to say, "We've made a raft of pretty important decisions that affect the attractiveness of this project. Lord knows, some of them are bound to be wrong—I hope not critically so. In any case, these decisions are behind us. They're buried so deep in the assumptions, no one can find them, and top management wouldn't have time to look at them anyway."

Mr. Soderberg was down to two alternatives: a labor intensive limited capacity solution and a capital intensive solution. "The analysis all points in one direction," he said, "but I have the feeling it's going to be the worst one for the long run."

The labor-intensive method involved an initial plant- and equipment-outlay of $900,000. This alternative only had a capacity to service 1.5 million pounds. "Even if the project bombs out, we won't lose much. The equipment is very adaptable. We could find uses for about half of it. We could probably sell the balance for $200,000, and let our tax write-offs cover most of the rest. We should salvage the working capital part without trouble. It's the start-up costs and losses that we'll encounter until we decide that the project is no good that are our real risks," summarized Mr. Soderberg. "We can at least get this project on stream in one year's time. In the first year we'll be lucky to satisfy half the possible demand, and spending $50,000 debugging the process." Exhibit 1 shows Mr. Soderberg's analysis of the labor-intensive alternative. The calculations showed a small net present value when discounted at 20%. Mr. Soderberg noted, however, that there was a sizeable net present value if an 8% discount rate was used. The positive present values when related to the negative present values looked particularly attractive.

The capital intensive method involved a much more sizeable outlay—$3,300,000—for plant and equipment. Manufacturing costs would, however, be reduced by $.35 per unit and fixed costs by $100,000, excluding depreciation, which would increase (depreciation would be over a longer period). The capital-intensive plant was designed to handle 2.0 million pounds, the lowest volume for which appropriate equipment could be acquired. The equipment was more specialized. Only $400,000 of this machinery might be redeployed to other company activities. The balance probably had a salvage value of $800,000. It would take two years to get the plant on stream, and the first operating year volume was likely going to be low—perhaps 700,000 pounds at the most. Debugging costs were likely to be $100,000.

Exhibit 2 presents Mr. Soderberg's analysis of the capital-intensive method. At 20% discount rate, the capital-intensive project had a sizeable negative present value, and appeared much worse than the labor-intensive alternative. However, at an 8% discount rate it looked significantly better.

To gain some perspective, Mr. Soderberg estimated the internal rate on the incremental investment under the labor intensive method in Exhibit 3. The internal rate was slightly above 14%. As a cost-reduction opportunity, this rate was attractive, but partly because of the expanded capacity. As a part of a new product opportunity, it was unattractive. Mr. Soderberg was not sure how he should look at the project.

Several things concerned Mr. Soderberg about this analysis. Mr. Reynolds would only look at the total return. Thus, the capital intensive project would not qualify. Yet it seemed the safest way to start the program based on a breakeven analysis (see Exhibit 4). The capital intensive alternative only needed a demand of 325,900 pounds to break even, whereas the labor-intensive method required 540,000 pounds of sales volume.

Mr. Soderberg was also concerned that competition might develop in the future, and that price cutting would ensue. If the price per pound fell by 20¢, the labor-intensive method would not break even unless 900,000 pounds was sold, and, of course, Jacobs would be sharing the market with a competitor. A competitor, of course, would—once the market was established—build a capital intensive plant, and be in a good position to cut prices by even more than 20¢. In short, there was a risk, given the labor-intensive solution, that Jacobs could not remain competitive with Silicone-X. The better the demand proved to be, the more serious this risk would become.

Once the market was established, Jacobs could build a capital intensive facility. Almost none of the labor intensive equipment would be useful in the new plant. The new plant would still cost $3,300,000, and Jacobs would have to write off losses on the labor-intensive facility.

The labor-intensive facility would be difficult to expand economically. It would cost $50,000 for each 100,000 pounds of additional capacity (only practical in 250,000 pound increments). An additional 100,000 pounds of capacity in the capital intensive unit could be added for $25,000 in contrast.

Pricing strategy was also an element. At $1.90 a pound, Jacobs would invite com-

EXHIBIT 1
Jacobs Division: Analysis of Labor Intensive Alternative Silicone-X

				Year			
	0	1	2	3	4	5–15	Terminal 15
Investments:							
Plant & Equipment	$ 900,000						
Working Capital		$ 140,000	$ 14,000	$ 15,000	$ 17,000	$ 20,000	$381,000
Demand in Pounds		1,200,000	1,320,000	1,452,000	1,597,000	n.a.	
Capacity in Pounds		600,000	1,500,000	1,500,000	1,500,000	1,500,000	
Units Sold		600,000	1,320,000	1,452,000	1,500,000	1,500,000	
Sales Price Limit		1.90	1.90	1.90	1.90	1.90	
Variable Costs per Unit:							
Manufacture		1.30	1.30	1.30	1.30	1.30	
Marketing		.10	.10	.10	.10	.10	
Marketing Total		1.40	1.40	1.40	1.40	1.40	
Contribution Per Unit		.50	.50	.50	.50	.50	
Contribution in Dollars:		300,000	660,000	726,000	750,000	750,000	
Fixed Costs		210,000	210,000	210,000	210,000	210,000	
Depreciation		60,000	60,000	60,000	60,000	60,000	
Start-up Costs		50,000	0	0	0	0	
Total Fixed Costs		320,000	270,000	270,000	270,000	270,000	
Profit Before Tax		(20,000)	390,000	456,000	480,000	480,000	
Profit After Tax at 50%		(10,000)	195,000	228,000	240,000	240,000	
Cash Flow Operations		50,000	255,000	288,000	300,000	300,000	
Total Cash Flow	$(900,000)	$ (90,000)	$ 241,000	$ 273,000	$ 283,000	$ 280,000	$381,000
Net PV at 20%	(900,000)	(75,000)	167,400	158,000	136,500	584,300	24,700

Net Present Value $95,900 at 20%

| Net PV at 8% | (900,000) | (83,300) | 206,600 | 216,700 | 208,000 | 1,469,300 | 120,100 |

Net Present Value $1,237,400 at 8%

491

EXHIBIT 2
Jacobs Division: Analysis of Capital Intensive Alternative Silicone-X

					Year				Terminal Year
	0	1	2	3	4	5	6	7–15	15
Investments:									
Plant & Equipment	$1,900,000	$1,400,000							$ (962,000)
Working Capital			$ 160,000	$ 11,000	$ 17,000	$ 20,000	$ 24,000	$ 30,000	(422,000)
Demand in Pounds			1,320,000	1,452,000	1,597,000	1,757,000	1,933,000	2,125,000	
Capacity in Pounds			700,000	2,000,000	2,000,000	2,000,000	2,000,000	2,000,000	
Units Sold			700,000	1,452,000	1,597,000	1,757,000	1,933,000	2,000,000	
Sales Price/Unit			1.90	1.90	1.90	1.90	1.90		
Variable Costs Per Unit:									
Manufacture			.95	.95	.95	.95	.95		
Selling			.10	.10	.10	.10	.10		
			1.05	1.05	1.05	1.05	1.05		
Contribution Per Unit			.85	.85	.85	.85	.85		
Contribution in Dollars:			595,000	1,234,200	1,357,500	1,493,500	1,643,100	1,700,000	
Fixed Costs			110,000	110,000	110,000	110,000	110,000	110,000	
Depreciation			167,000	167,000	167,000	167,000	167,000	167,000	
Start-up Costs			100,000	0	0	0	0	0	
Total Fixed Cost			377,000	277,000	277,000	277,000	277,000	277,000	
Profit Before Tax			218,000	957,200	1,080,500	1,216,500	1,366,100	1,423,000	
Profit After Tax at 50%			109,000	478,600	540,200	608,200	683,000	711,500	
Cash Flow Operations			276,000	645,600	707,200	775,200	850,000	878,500	
Total Cash Flow	($1,900,000)	($1,400,000)	$ 116,000	$ 634,600	$ 690,200	$ 755,200	$ 826,000	$ 848,500	$1,384,000
Present Value at 20%	($1,900,000)	($1,166,700)	80,600	366,900	332,900	303,500	276,600	1,144,800	89,800
			Net Present Value at 20% = ($471,600)						
Present Value at 8%	($1,900,000)	($1,296,300)	99,500	503,300	507,300	514,000	520,500	3,338,200	436,300
			Net Present Value at 8% = $2,722,800						

petition. Competitors would be satisfied with a lower rate of return—perhaps 12%—in an established market. At somewhat lower prices, Jacobs might discourage competition. The project could not be "sold" at lower prices (that is, even the labor-intensive alternative would not provide a rate of return of 20%).

In short, it began to appear to Mr. Soderberg as if the use of a high discount rate forced the company to make riskier decisions and enhanced the prospects of realizing lower rates of return than forecast.

He was also concerned by the fact that the proposals did not consider expansion opportunities. The labor-intensive alternative would look better if 500,000 pounds of capacity were added as soon as demand warranted this action. In two years' time, expansion, and, for that matter cost reduction could be justified using lower rates of return.

EXHIBIT 3
Jacobs Division: Incremental Return on Investment Capital Intensive Alternative

Year	Labor Intensive Cash Flow	Capital Intensive Cash Flow	Difference	PV at 14%
0	$(900,000)	$(1,900,000)	$(1,000,000)	$(1,000,000)
1	(90,000)	(1,400,000)	(1,310,000)	(1,149,100)
2	241,000	66,000	(175,000)	(134,700)
3	273,000	644,600	371,600	220,000
4	283,000	690,200	407,200	241,500
5	280,000	755,200	475,200	246,500
6	280,000	871,000	551,000	251,000
7–15	280,000	883,500	573,500	1,212,000
15	381,000	1,284,000	903,000	126,500
			Net Present Value	$ 14,700

EXHIBIT 4
Breakeven Analysis Silicone X

Normal	Labor Intensive	Capital Intensive
Fixed Costs		
Operations	210,000	110,000
Depreciation	60,000	167,000
Total	270,000	277,000
Contribution per Unit	.50	.85
Units to Break Even	540,000	325,900
Price Competitive		
Contribution per Unit	.30	.65
Units to Break Even	900,000	426,200

Molecular Compounds Corporation (Abridged)

The Molecular Compounds Corporation manufactured a wide variety of products in the chemical field and related areas, ranging from industrial chemicals through consumer goods. During the 1950's, MOCOM's sales had grown over 60%, reaching a level in excess of $700 million in 1962. Net income had withstood the pressures of competition within the chemical industry with the result that per-share earnings had also risen about 60% during this time. This rise occurred despite additional profit erosion caused by increased depreciation charges and higher allocations for research and development (see Exhibit 1). The corporate executive group was extremely anxious to match or exceed this growth record in the decade from 1960 to 1970. Toward this end, it had instructed the financial and planning staff to reevaluate the methods of financial analysis to insure that adequate investments were being made.

Developments in the chemical industry had contributed to executive concern about MOCOM's growth prospects. Recently, a number of successful, large firms—e.g., Standard Oil Company (New Jersey), Goodyear Tire and Rubber Company, W. R. Grace and Company, and the Borden Company—had entered the field and had aggressively sought to share in the chemical and allied products market, which had sales of $30 billion in 1961. There were already 10 firms, primarily in chemicals, with sales of over $300 million and numerous smaller firms with significant sales in narrower segments of the market. Each of these firms was tending to diversify further. Some of the substantial postwar expansion had led to overcapacity. All this meant increased competition among giants for available demand. In particular, price-cutting in established products had squeezed margins considerably without generating much new volume. Sales and earnings also seemed likely to become more volatile, especially as foreign competition became more important.

At the same time, the industry was becoming increasingly mature. Some segments still retained the dynamic growth patterns that had been evident during the introduction of petrochemicals and plastics. However, more firms were spending more on research to achieve a strong position in these fields, and existing competitive advantages were proving more tenuous. In total, the balance had shifted toward a higher proportion of products with limited prospects for growing demand.

These factors led MOCOM's top management to conclude that it would be necessary to secure full and effective utilization of available capital resources if the firm was to achieve continued rapid growth. The increased size and complexity of MOCOM's operations, however, made such an objective all the more difficult to achieve. A recent drop in the

EXHIBIT 1
Molecular   Compounds   Corporation: Market
Price, Earnings and Dividends per Share 1947–
March 1962

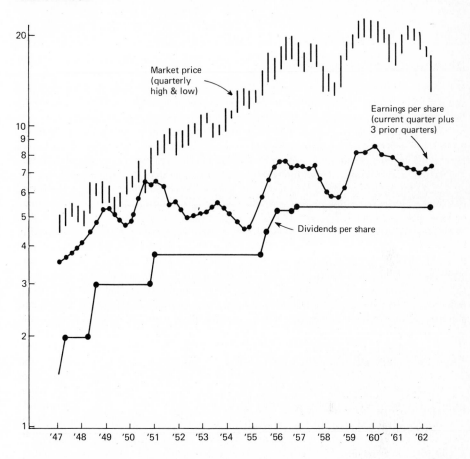

amount of capital expenditures submitted for approval had thus been the cause of considerable concern.

Partially because of these considerations, the members of MOCOM's financial and planning staff were considering a revision in the company's budgeting procedure in early 1962. In their judgment, the most significant revision would eliminate the 12% (after tax) minimum return on investment criterion or "cutoff" rate. This rate had been used to evaluate all projects since the existing procedures had been introduced in the middle 1950's. The essence of the argument for elimination of the rate was that the existing system was overstructured. For example, some executives argued that a cutoff rate tended to discourage submission of low-return but relatively riskless projects in which MOCOM could profitably invest. In short, the elimination of the artificial restraint of a cutoff rate might encourage operating personnel to submit any project that appeared worthwhile.

Other members of the planning staff, however, thought that a cutoff rate (preferably 12%, but certainly no lower than 6% or 7%) was essential as a management tool. They believed that with no formal guideline the divisions would create their own rules and procedures, many of which would be more stringent than the 12% rate currently set by the corporation. There remained, however, considerable disagreement as to just what cutoff rate should be used and how it should be administered in order to stimulate satisfactory growth.

Decentralized Management

MOCOM was organized into 11 autonomous divisions. Each division was self-supporting and contained its own staff groups. Division executives were held responsible for planning the course of their divisions and for operating them successfully. Although plans and problems were discussed regularly with headquarters personnel, central management's greatest influence arose through performance-appraisal. Performance was evaluated by a number of financial methods as well as by less formal factors. Top corporate management considered, for example, a division's return on investment (operating income, less an allocation for corporate overhead and for depreciation on the division's assets, divided by the sum of gross fixed investment and gross working capital), its operating percentages (income as a percentage of sales, etc.), and growth trends.

Through these evaluations, top management communicated its desires and criticisms in ways, sometimes subtle, that appeared to have a profound effect upon divisional attitudes and orientations. While unquestionably misinterpretations and other misunderstandings arose, top management considered that this planning system worked more successfully than would a more formal set of policies, goals, and operating directives. Nevertheless, the influence of performance evaluations on subsequent actions was a cause for modest concern because of the difficulty of comparing actual success against relative differences in available opportunities.

Any adjustments in the capital budgeting process would have to take existing division-headquarters relationships into account.

Existing Capital Budgeting Procedures

The fundamental objective of the company's current capital budgeting process was to maximize corporate growth and especially the growth of earnings per share. This objective would permit the payment of a fair and, it was hoped, growing dividend to stockholders; and, subject to the vagaries of the stock market, would create conditions favorable for significant capital appreciation.

Although each division was responsible for generating projects, all divisions were expected to abide by the 12% cutoff rate which was applied by the divisional financial analyst following procedures set by the central planning staff. Projects below that rate were actively discouraged and usually rejected, even though they required less than $150,000 and could consequently be approved by divisional management without central management review.

About 40% of the corporation's total capital expenditures were included in the division budgets and were not reviewed by headquarters, although this percentage varied from division to division. Projects requiring an investment of more than $150,000 were forwarded to the financial and planning staff, which reviewed the request on behalf of the capital budget review committee. This committee, consisting of the corporation's president, the executive vice president, two divisional managers, and two central staff vice presidents,

EXHIBIT 2
Molecular Compounds Corporation: "Cost of Equity" (eps/MP) 1947–March 1962

gave final[1] approval to projects in excess of the size divisional management could approve. In addition, if any project smaller than $150,000 and returning less than 12% seemed particularly attractive, division management could request the capital budget review committee to waive the cutoff requirement.

The 12% cutoff rate had been selected after an extensive investigation, which considered a wide variety of possibly relevant considerations. The four most important were: (1) *Growth expectations.* Over the previous 50 years the company's earnings per share had increased 7% to 8% a year. It was assumed that the stockholders expected that this rate of growth would be maintained and in addition that a dividend yield of at least 3% would be

---

[1] In certain instances approval by the board of directors was also required.

provided.[2] A combination of these two figures (dividends per share divided by market price, plus "growth") yielded a cost of equity capital of 10% or 11%. Twelve percent was selected to allow a slight margin for error in the budgeting process. (2) *Cost of capital.* From an actual balance sheet, a weighted average cost of capital, including debt (estimated interest charges) and equity (estimated earnings per share/market price), was calculated. This measurement turned out to be substantially lower than 12%. (3) *Industry standards.* Cutoff rates used by other companies in MOCOM's industries were investigated and found to be roughly around 12%. (4) *Feasibility.* Management believed that the 12% rate was quite practical, since it would not generate more projects than the firm could absorb. As there seemed to be no sound, rigorous basis for making the necessary final judgment, a 12% cutoff rate (after taxes) was accepted because it seemed about right.

The corporation also had installed a standard method of computing return on investment. After experimentation with several financial measures, management chose a net after-tax cash-flow present-value technique. In this measurement present-valued cash outflows were subtracted from present-valued cash inflows (including an estimate for recovery) to arrive at a net present-value figure. From alternative investments, the one showing the highest net present value was selected, all other factors being equivalent. Other measurements, such as internal rate of return (that rate which makes the net present value equal to zero), after-tax return on gross investment, payback years in present-value dollar terms, and profits as a percentage of sales, were used as supplementary guides.

Returns were also measured on an expected-value basis. Division personnel were supposed to consider various alternative outcomes and calculate related cash flows. They then assigned probabilities to the flows and used the probabilities as weights to obtain an expected present-value figure. This adjustment was intended to correct the "most likely" estimate for skewed probability distributions in which the "expected" result differed from the most likely estimate.

Problems with the Existing System

The central planning and financial staff acted as consultants to the divisions in their planning and capital budget preparation, in addition to reporting to the corporate headquarters and providing the reports, plans, and analyses top management needed. Many of the analysts had worked in one or another of the divisions before they transferred to the central staff group. The staff thus considered themselves fairly familiar with the attitudes of the divisions and with the informal methods that existed on local levels to supplement the formal capital budgeting procedure.

As a result of their visits and work in the field, the planning staff began to suspect that the existing capital budgeting system was possibly choking off investments at the extremes of the opportunity spectrum. At the least, the planning group believed that too few low-risk, low-return and too few high-risk, high-return projects were being submitted to the capital budget review committee. For example, very few projects were ever submitted that were as low as the cutoff rate of 12%. The average internal return rate seemed to be between 17% and 20% on low-risk projects and went up much higher for any request that had a major risk associated with it.

Moreover, the capital budget review committee rarely rejected a project. "When one is rejected," an executive of the central staff remarked, "you can hear the anguished cries

---

[2] Growth in earnings per share is more frequently used as an indication of future trends in market price than is a measurement of actual historical market price growth in order to avoid the influence of temporary moods of the market.

through the whole building." Some members of the financial and planning group considered this situation evidence that few borderline projects were being submitted for top-level consideration. As a consequence top corporate management was unable to exercise significant influence on the allocation of funds within the company. "It's not the obvious investments that top management should consider," commented one analyst, "since anyone can decide these. They should be concerned with the marginal projects which are at present being screened out all along the line."

While it was less clear-cut, there was also evidence that very few projects were being rejected at lower echelons. This condition further suggested that only those projects which were relatively certain to receive final approval were even flowing into the beginning of the decisional pipeline. The criteria used by the divisions to screen possible attractive opportunities were not always known, but they appeared to be, oftentimes, more cautious than top management wished. The negative decisions, then, were commonly made at the source of the idea, at a level in the organization quite removed from direct communication with the capital budget review committee.

Equally important, screening criteria at intermediate levels were known to differ from division to division and probably from person to person. For example, a number of executives were known to use a cutoff rate of 15% based upon after-tax return on gross investment (a cutoff criterion used within the company prior to 1956) in evaluation of projects. Unquestionably, other standards were employed wherever they seemed appropriate to individuals.

Although central management had established the minimum return standard of 12%, it had not otherwise provided guidelines on any formal basis, leaving a number of very critical judgments to the discretion of operating personnel. For example, the central staff had developed no rules to suggest how much, if any, return premium was desired as risks increased on project opportunities. Because attitudes toward risk probably differed markedly from individual to individual, and by individual from year to year and from project to project, the planning staff found it almost impossible to determine what real criteria were affecting the negative investment decisions.

In composite, these negative decisions were probably quite significant. First of all, some executives were afraid that MOCOM might be underspending relative to its ability. MOCOM's top management believed that the company had sufficient sources of funds to support a substantial increase in the rate of plant expenditures. The company's debt-to-capitalization ratio ranged between 25% and 30%, well below levels considered safe. Management believed that the firm could borrow nearly $100 million more at favorable interest terms. This potential source of funds, combined with a large after-tax income and a substantial depreciation throwoff, practically insured that even extremely large capital budgets could be sustained over a number of years without recourse to common stock financing. Indeed, in recent years internally generated funds alone had proved adequate to meet normal dividend and capital expenditure demands for funds.

There was good evidence that many favorable opportunities were never submitted. For example, the question of the effectiveness of the capital budgeting system was raised in a dramatic way in 1960, when the limit on projects that could be included in division budgets changed from $75,000 to $150,000. The number of projects included in the division budgets increased substantially, and it appeared that the dollar volume of projects requiring investments of between $100,000 and $150,000 would be about four times its previous level.

Second, top management's influence on the strategic balance of overall expenditures was limited. While they might suggest directions for expansion or encourage increased outlays for certain divisions, top executives were perforce limited to selecting from projects submitted. Their lack of familiarity with the specific details of projects lost in the screening process made it difficult for them to offer suggestions.

There was also a comparative absence of considerations relating to strategic balancing of capital expenditures in the divisions and smaller operating subdivisions. Even division managers, for example, were typically several echelons removed from the active management of the products and plants they supervised. At lower levels, points of view became more parochial.

Finally, several types of projects were clearly being overlooked. One category included very safe projects promising a return of between 5% or 6% and 12%. These investments typically were in the cost-reduction area and generally promised to continue producing savings long after the nominal 15 years used in calculating the economic value of the project. For example, this type of project would include such installations as power plants, plants for producing basic materials, and improvements in basic heavy equipment. An increase in outlays for these projects might tend to dampen existing cyclical earnings swings.

There seemed to be an equal lack of projects at the other extreme, the high-risk and high-return ventures. In this category were new products which faced great uncertainties in the market but which, if they succeeded, could provide MOCOM with handsome profits.

The problem with the high-risk projects, as the financial and planning group saw it, was the extent of the risk to the division or plant managers. "It is hard to get a division manager," noted one of the central staff analysts, "to commit himself and his division to a project which requires new assets equal to a major percent of the assets he has allocated to him at present. The risk (probability of success or failure) to him and to his division is the same as the risk to the corporation, but the extent of the risk (the seriousness of failure) is greater. If he guesses wrong and the project is a dud, he's got to do some explaining to show why his return on assets has dropped. But the potential returns are so great that the company could afford to have a bunch of duds for each one which pans out and still come off ahead." In essence, the planning staff believed that the utility curves of the division managers were quite different from the utility curve of the corporation as a whole. At lower organizational levels, this problem appeared even more severe.

When the central financial office staff began to investigate the capital budgeting procedure, they decided to look for samples of projects which had not been submitted to the capital budget review committee but which, they felt, should have been. It was difficult to locate such projects, since few detailed records existed for most projects that had not been submitted. In addition, divisional managements were naturally reluctant to admit that they might have rejected desirable opportunities. The planning staff did discover some instances of projects in the two groups, however, and one example from each group is included in Appendices A and B. The first is a low-risk, low-return project; the second is one of high risk and high return.

After studying the material in Appendix A, a member of the central planning office said:

This is an example of the type of project which I think we are unwisely discouraging by our cutoff rate. I think that at least this project should have been submitted to the capital budget review committee to give them a look at it. After all, the situation is comparatively riskless. First, we are supplying only part of our capacity. Earnings should therefore be quite stable on the bottom side. Second, the product and the process are what you might call mature. Although there is an oversupply at present, I think that in the future the price might well go up rather than down as forecast. Demand is growing; yet the economic performance will discourage entry or expansion until rates improve. People have been stung in the business so far, and I don't think that there will be much more new entry. The existing price, I am informed by people who follow the market, is very probably at or near its foreseeable future floor. An upturn in the economy may alone increase the level significantly. Third, the life of this project is extremely long. Once they get the plant up, it will go on producing chlorine year after year. No significant maintenance is required for at least 25 years. Plants built as early as 1900 are still operating. At a low discount rate, returns after 15 years still have a significant present value. And fourth, this project requires a minimum of manpower and is a sure thing to produce pretty much as estimated. It is a tried and tested method. People know how to design and build it with a minimum of engineering effort. Once it's going, very little expensive talent will be required to keep it going or to work out the bugs. If it's men and not money which we're trying to save, I think we should look at more projects like this. The product is enduring and basic. Its usage is likely to continue to grow somewhat faster than the economy, even though the sources of demand may continue to change.

Commenting on Appendix B, the same person said:

The division manager's criticisms of the report are, in my view anyway, pretty well justified. Certainly some of the estimates look a little strange. But, you know, maybe they did have something. After all, in the chemical industry you never really know what's going to happen with a new product of this type until you actually build the plant. You can't get enough of the stuff out of a test tube to really start selling it, or even test it thoroughly. And you can't really be sure what quality product you'll get out of the plant until you build one and see. It's a trick business and I think that some of the spirit of the 1930's has gone. Maybe there's too much analysis today. Thirty years ago that plant probably would have been built and on stream by now. They would have found the resin didn't work completely where they thought it would, but they would have had enough to really experiment with and would have found other uses. Now, by our delay, competitors have had that much more time to catch up. Maybe one of them will build a plant and capture the market with a similar product.

Even though those estimates are probably a little inflated, the plant could have done satisfactorily. And if maybe one out of every four or five paid on the scale the division thought this one would, the company could afford to lose the other three or four and still be better off. But it's hard for the divisions to see that problem because they have to shoulder the risk for the failure of their projects.

In any case, there is no look at bottomside risk. What would we lose if the product proved to be a complete bust? I'm sure it would be a lot less than $7 million! Also, there's no talk of technological or product risk. My guess is that it would be comparatively low for an end product in the chemical industry. I'm not sure how to get more of these proposals either more completely analyzed or up to the top so the capital budget review committee can look at them.

Note: By mid-1962, this project had not yet been submitted for consideration at the headquarters level.

APPENDIX A

Excerpts from a report by the Division Planning Manager to the Division Manager, Basic Chemical Division, Molecular Compounds Corporation (dated April 1961).

SUBJECT: Proposed chlor-alkali plant requiring investment of $2,695,000.

Basis of the Study. After consideration of a wide variety of other alternatives, the proposal as presented includes only the most favorable conditions for plant location and assumes that all the products and by-products will be used within the company and that the plant will operate at capacity. We believe that this latter assumption is justified because the chlorine plant will produce only 75% of the corporation's chlorine requirements. Less certainty, however, exists with regard to the utilization of some of the by-products of the process, and in preparing these estimates we have assumed that internal requirements for these products will not absorb the entire production until 1965. Thereafter complete captive use seems highly probable.

The process for producing chlorine which we have selected is one which has long been known, and there is little likelihood that it will be made obsolete by a major change in the technology of chlorine production during the life of the plant. Raw material figures were selected on the most economical basis. In most cases this selection process could be easily accomplished by a comparison of delivered prices to output efficiency (i.e., make or buy) since usually only one possible process existed for the " make " alternative. (Data omitted.)

The figures for the investment and for the recovery in the sixteenth year include the necessary investment in working capital as well as in fixed capacity.

The savings through our making chlorine rather than buying it have been estimated to decrease over the years because we anticipate that the price for chlorine on the market will undergo a gradual decline. At present the market is intensely competitive, but because the processes and markets for chlorine are relatively mature no new entries are anticipated which would result in a major price reduction. Purchase price estimates were obtained from the central purchasing staff.

Conclusions

1. The economic performance of a chlor-alkali plant under the selected conditions is discouraging. At the target rate the net present value is a *minus* $653,000. (Exhibit A-1.) The Discounted Cash Flow return is about 5%.
2. The economic performance is not affected to a major degree by the variations of unit costs of utilities for the range studied.
3. A reasonable reduction in any single item (e.g., new fixed investment, plant cost, or product-distribution cost) does not improve the economic performance of the project a sufficient amount to make it attractive.
4. Even a reasonable reduction of two factors combined (new fixed investment and plant cost) does not make the project attractive.
5. It becomes evident that *all* factors entering into the economic analysis of a chlor-alkali installation must be optimum simultaneously in order for the project to approach economic acceptability. Thus the investment and plant cost must be held to a minimum, the plant must be located close to a dependable source of cheap salt brine, must have all products (chlorine, caustic soda, and hydrogen) consumed at the plant location, and must have low-cost steam and electric power available.

Comment. The economic performance of a chlor-alkali plant is not particularly attractive. As long as the product demand pattern, salt supply, and power costs remain substantially as set forth in this report, it is questionable that realistic reductions could be made which would be of sufficient magnitude to revise the economic performance of the project to an attractive level.

Recommendations

1. No further attempts should be made to refine estimates of investment and operation costs for a chlor-alkali plant unless new and reliable information becomes available.
2. If the MOCOM captive demand patterns for chlorine and caustic soda should change from that as presently envisioned to one closer to optimum, additional economic evaluations would be in order.

EXHIBIT A-1
Molecular Compounds Corporation: Present Value of Proposed Chlor-Alkali Plant at 12%
(Dollar figures in thousands)

Year	0	1	2	3	4	5	6	7	8	9	10	11	12	13	14	15	16
Capital investment including working capital	—	$(343)	$(2,063)	$(238)	$ (51)												$136
Manufacturing costs				$529	$529	$529	$529	$529	$529	$529	$529	$529	$529	$529	$529	$529	Recovery of Working Capital
Other costs				128	128	128	128	128	128	128	128	128	128	128	128	128	
Total costs				$ 657	$657	$657	$657	$657	$657	$657	$657	$657	$657	$657	$657	$657	
Purchase cost				1,024	1,059	1.000	991	990	986	980	978	974	972	965	960	957	
Net savings				367	402	343	334	333	329	323	321	317	315	308	303	300	
Depreciation expense				$ 365	$338	$309	$281	$253	$225	$197	$169	$141	$113	$ 84	$ 56	$ 28	
Before-tax savings				2	64	34	53	80	104	126	152	176	202	224	247	272	
After-tax savings				1	31	16	25	38	50	60	73	84	97	108	119	131	
Cash flow		(343)	(2,063)	128	328	325	306	291	275	257	242	225	210	192	175	159	136
12% discount factor	1.000	.893	.797	.712	.636	.567	.507	.452	.404	.361	.322	.287	.257	.229	.205	.183	.163
Annual present value of cash flow		$(306)	$(1.644)	$ 92	$202	$184	$155	$132	$111	$ 93	$ 78	$ 65	$ 54	$ 44	$ 36	29	22

Accumulated Present Value of: outflows (1950)

inflows 1297

Net Present Value (653)

APPENDIX B

I. Excerpts from a report by the Division Planning Manager to the Division General Manager, Industrial Products Division, Molecular Compounds Corporation (dated February 1961).

SUBJECT: Proposed plant for the manufacture of water-soluble resins, to be constructed in several stages with initial capacity of 15,500,000 pounds per year requiring an initial fixed investment of $7,370,000.

Basis of the Study

Sales Justification. About 3 billion pounds of water-soluble or water-dispersal resins are sold today in the United States. By 1970 the sales of these products (which include such natural products as starches and modified starches, glue, casein, and locust bean gum, and organic substitutes similar to our product) are expected to be about 4 billion pounds.

Our product, because of its potentially low price and desirable properties, should permit us to sell about 15,500,000 pounds per year by 1963, as estimated by the following schedule:

Grade	Expected Sales Estimated 1963 (lbs.)	Estimated Potential Market (lbs.)	% of Potential Market
A	5,250,000	100,950,000	5.2
B	1,250,000	25,440,000	4.9
C	7,300,000	130,000,000	5.6
D	1,700,000	55,420,000	3.1

We have an excellent but of course not invulnerable patent position. Although several patents are held by competitors, our patent program covering process, compositions, and uses—as well as our advanced research position in the industry—should give us a very strong position in the market for this resin for many years. We believe that the company is relatively invulnerable to backward integration by potential customers since in general the use of the product by any one firm is not large enough to justify the required capital investment.

In reaching our estimates of potential sales volume for this product, we have been in contact with a number of possible users for the compound. On the basis of their test applications and uses we have customers who have expressed interest in purchasing about 4 million pounds a year, assuming that all quality specifications can be met. Our projections of volume are based on our estimates of the markets in which our tests have shown our product to offer effective substitutability, because of either a significant price saving, or because of important superior qualities on a competitive pricing basis.

Our most optimistic sales estimates assume only that we will sell 155,000,000 pounds per year by 1970. (Exhibit B-1.) This is a little less than 4% penetration into the 4-billion-pound market. Our sales of 15,500,000 pounds in 1963 will be the base on which we will build to make our product the major synthetic water-soluble resin.

Cost Justification. Our analysis [not included in this case] shows that the most economical plant alternative is to build a plant for an expected annual volume of 15,500,000

EXHIBIT B-1
Molecular Compounds Corporation: Price and Volume Ranges for Proposed Plant for Manufacture of Water Soluble Resins

	Volume Sold (thousands of pounds)			Price		
	Probable	High	Low	Probable	High	Low
1962	7,500	15,000	2,800	$0.69	$0.83	$0.65
1963	15,000	31,400	4,650	0.65	0.81	0.59
1964	25,500	53,000	6,700	0.60	0.77	0.53
1965	38,250	73,500	9,500	0.58	0.72	0.48
1966	49,700	92,300	11,650	0.54	0.71	0.45
1967	59,100	108,100	13,900	0.52	0.70	0.40
1968	68,500	125,800	16,250	0.47	0.65	0.38
1969	76,900	135,400	18,800	0.46	0.64	0.36
1970	85,300	155,000	21,150	0.46	0.64	0.35
1971	85,300	155,000	21,150	0.46	0.64	0.35
1972	85,300	155,000	21,150	0.46	0.64	0.35
1973	85,300	155,000	21,150	0.46	0.64	0.35
1974	85,300	155,000	21,150	0.46	0.64	0.35
1975	85,300	155,000	21,150	0.46	0.64	0.35
1976	85,300	155,000	21,150	0.46	0.64	0.35

pounds in such a manner that expanded facilities can be easily added up to a total of 60,000,000 pounds annual capacity. The initial cost of the 15.5-million-pound plant is estimated at $7,370,000, with the expansion possible in two stages. The first stage would bring capacity up to 25,500,000 pounds per year at a cost of $1,000,000 and the second stage would be to full expansion of 60 million pounds at a cost of $3,500,000.

In preparing our operating costs, we have estimated that the per unit manufacturing cost would vary from 31¢ at a volume of 3,000,000 pounds per year down to 20¢ at a volume of 50,000,000 to 60,000,000 pounds. Distribution costs have been estimated to be relatively constant at 1.5¢ per pound since we anticipate selling this product with our existing sales force and most of the incremental cost will be for shipping and packaging. The overhead costs on an incremental basis are expected to be $250,000 per year at a minimum and a maximum of $375,000 when capacity is reached.

Working capital investment (based on one month's receivables and one month's inventory) has been estimated at about 20% of the cost of goods sold.

Depreciation is calculated on the sum-of-the-years'-digits method.

Conclusions

Using the proposed facilities and operating schedule, comparisons were made between a number of possible marketing results. We worked with a most probable case, a conservative sales volume with high prices and low prices. Price and volume estimates are included in Exhibit B-1. Calculations for the most probable case are included as a sample in Exhibit B-2. Our most probable estimate produced a net present-value cash flow of $29,555,000 at 12% and a discounted cash flow return of about 50%. The results of the various calculations are summarized below and have been assigned relative probabilities.

EXHIBIT B-2
Molecular Compounds Corporation: Most Probable Present Value at 12%, of Proposed Plant for Manufacture of Water Soluble Resins
(Dollar figure in thousands)

Calendar year	1961	1962	1963	1964	1965	1966	1967	1968	1969	1970	1971	1972	1973	1974	1975	1976	1977
Project year	0	1	2	3	4	5	6	7	8	9	10	11	12	13	14	15	16
New fixed investment	$(2,800)	$(4,570)		$(1,000)		$(3,500)											$2,450
Working capital (20% cost of goods sold)	(50)	(465)	(310)	(500)	(408)	(305)	(376)	(36)									
Total investment	$(2,850)	$(5,035)	$(310)	$(1,500)	$(408)	$(3,805)	$(376)	$(36)									
Volume (in thousands of lbs.)		7,500	15,500	25,500	38,250	49,700	59,100	60,000	60,000	60,000	60,000	60,000	60,000	60,000	60,000	60,000	
Sales ($000)		$5,175	$10,075	$15,300	$22,185	$26,838	$30,732	$28,200	$27,600	$27,600	$27,600	$27,600	$27,600	$27,600	$27,600	$27,600	
Cost of goods sold		$2,325	$3,875	$6,375	$8,415	$9,940	$11,820	$12,000	$12,000	$12,000	$12,000	$12,000	$12,000	$12,000	$12,000	$12,000	
Distribution at $15 per thous. lbs.		113	233	383	574	746	887	900	900	900	900	900	900	900	900	900	
All other costs		250	275	300	350	350	375	375	375	375	375	375	375	375	375	375	
Total costs		$2,688	$4,383	$7,058	$9,339	$11,036	$13,082	$13,275	$13,275	$13,275	$13,275	$13,275	$13,275	$13,275	$13,275	$13,275	
Operating income		$2,487	$5,692	$8,242	$12,846	$15,802	$17,650	$14,925	$14,325	$14,325	$14,325	$14,325	$14,325	$14,325	$14,325	$14,325	
Depreciation (sum-of-the-years'-digits)		921	860	941	869	1,380	1,254	1,129	1,004	878	753	627	502	376	251	125	
Income before tax		$1,566	$4,832	$7,301	$11,977	$14,422	$16,396	$13,796	$13,321	$13,447	$13,572	$13,698	$13,823	$13,949	$14,074	$14,200	
Income after tax		752	2,319	3,504	5,749	6,923	7,870	6,622	6,394	6,455	6,515	6,575	6,635	6,696	6,756	6,816	
Annual cash income		1,673	3,179	4,445	6,618	8,303	9,124	7,751	7,398	7,333	7,268	7,202	7,137	7,072	7,007	6,941	
Annual cash flow	$(2,850)	$(3,362)	2,869	2,945	6,210	4,498	8,748	7,715	7,398	7,333	7,268	7,202	7,137	7,072	7,007	6,941	2,450
12% present-value factors	1.00	.893	.797	.712	.636	.567	.507	.452	.404	.361	.322	.287	.257	.229	.205	.183	.163
Annual present value	$(2,850)	$(3,002)	$ 2,287	$ 2,097	$ 3,950	$ 2,550	$ 4,435	$ 3,487	$ 2,989	$ 2,647	$ 2,340	$ 2,067	$ 1,834	$ 1,619	$ 1,436	$ 1,270	$ 399

Accumulated Present Value of outflows (5,852)
inflows 35,407
Net Present Value 29,555

Unit Cost

1962	$0.31
1963	0.25
1964	0.25
1965	$0.22
1966	0.20

Capacity
1961—15,500,000 lbs
1964—25,500,000
1966—60,000,000

Case	Net PV at 12% (000)	Internal Rate of Return	Probability	Expected Net PV at 12% (000)	Expected Internal Rate of Return
Most probable	$29,555	50 + %	.40	$11,822	20%
Conservative sales volume— high price	10,006	33%	.10	1,001	3
Conservative sales volume— low price	(1,170)	9	.25	(293)	2
Optimistic sales volume—high price	68,260	100 + %	.10	6,826	10
Optimistic sales volume—low price	24,904	50 + %	.15	3,736	8
Totals, expected amounts			1.00	$23,092	43%

All our estimates were well above the demanded cutoff rate except the one instance when a low volume would be combined with a low price. Even weighting this likelihood heavily did not alter the final figure significantly, since the expected return is over 40% and the net expected PV is over $23 million.

Recommendations

This planning department believes that the substantial returns this project offers make the investment of $7,370,000 well worth the risk and recommends that this facility be included in the annual appropriations request.

II. Excerpts from a Memorandum from the Division Manager, Industrial Products Division, Molecular Compounds Corporation, to the Division Planning Manager.

SUBJECT: Memorandum report on water-soluble resin plant.

I am returning your proposal to you for further testing and analysis. I do not feel that the market potential and objectives for the market share and sales volume have been explicitly enough explored. To extrapolate to 155 million pounds on the basis of a few containers sent to potential customers seems slightly unrealistic. It also seems clear that to compare this volume with the four-billion-pound total market is unrealistic. I doubt that our product is comparable to all water-soluble and water-dispersal resins. It is essential to determine in exactly what areas our resin is competitive and how well it can be expected to compete by virtue of its physical and cost characteristics. Once this analysis has been made and combined with more extensive tests of consumer acceptance, it may be possible to estimate the returns of this project without the great variation which is evident in this proposal.

With regard to the estimates, according to my quick calculations, a 10% change in volume, price and cost would decrease the net PV at 12% by about $12 million. (Exhibit B-3.) I would expect that a 30% change in these factors would thus bring us down to the

EXHIBIT B-3
Molecular Compounds Corporation: Effect on Most Probable
Present Value of a 10% Decrease in Volume and a Seven-Cent
Decrease in Unit Gross Margin
(Dollar figures in thousands)

Year	Most Probable Results		Effect of 10% Decrease in Volume		Effect of Decrease of Seven Cents in Unit Gross Margin	
	Gross Margin	Volume (thousands of pounds)	Decrease (thousands of pounds)	Loss in Gross Margin ($000)	New Volume (thousands of pounds)	Loss in Gross Margin ($000)
1	$0.38	7,500	750	$ 285	6,750	$ 472
2	0.40	15,500	1,550	620	13,950	976
3	0.35	25,500	2,550	893	22,950	1,606
4	0.36	38,250	3,825	1,377	34,425	2,410
5	0.34	49,700	4,970	1,690	44,730	3,131
6	0.32	59,100	5,910	1,891	53,190	3,723
7	0.27	60,000	6,000	1,620	54,000	3,780
8	0.26	60,000	6,000	1,560	54,000	3,780
9	0.26	60,000	6,000	1,560	54,000	3,780
10	0.26	60,000	6,000	1,560	54,000	3,780
11	0.26	60,000	6,000	1,560	54,000	3,780
12	0.26	60,000	6,000	1,560	54,000	3,780
13	0.26	60,000	6,000	1,560	54,000	3,780
14	0.26	60,000	6,000	1,560	54,000	3,780
15	0.26	60,000	6,000	1,560	54,000	3,780
				$20,856		$46,338
				(A)		(B)

Year	Decrease in Cash Flow		Present Value Factor At 12%	Decrease in Present Value
	Before-Tax (A + B)	After-Tax		
1	$ 757	$ 363	0.893	$ 324
2	1,596	766	0.797	610
3	2,499	1,200	0.712	854
4	3,787	1,818	0.636	1,156
5	4,821	2,314	0.567	1,312
6	5,614	2,695	0.507	1,366
7	5,400	2,592	0.452	1,172
8	5,340	2,563	0.404	1,035
9	5,340	2,563	0.361	925
10	5,340	2,563	0.322	825
11	5,340	2,563	0.287	736
12	5,340	2,563	0.257	659
13	5,340	2,563	0.229	587
14	5,340	2,563	0.205	525
15	5,340	2,563	0.183	469
	$67,194	$32,252		$12,555

breakeven at 12% if not lower. I do not feel, with a new product which is going to have to replace a well-established set of products and customer-producer relationships, that it is unreasonable to expect the revenues might be some 50% lower than estimated or that costs of production would be 30% higher. The reason this factor is not evident in the analysis is that the probable and the low prices are so close together and the high price is extremely high. This estimate, I think, must result in some distortion from what the possible cases might actually be.

To advance with a $7 million project on the basis of such figures does not seem to me reasonable in this rather poor business atmosphere. I do not feel that this project can be counted on to be of advantage to the company's return on investment.

CASE **9**

Arkansas Petroleum Company*

In May 1974, Mr. Warren Edwards, Financial Vice President of the Arkansas Petroleum Company, was concerned with a number of issues that had been raised recently about the company's capital budgeting policies and procedures. His task was to develop new methods of capital budgeting more appropriate to emerging circumstances.

Arkansas Petroleum Company was a significant domestic oil company with sales of approximately $2.0 billion. The Arkansas Company brand was well known in the midwest, where 90% of its sales were concentrated. Arkansas was diversified outside oil (mostly petrochemicals and coal) and fully integrated. However, crude production represented only 15% of refinery needs, and refined products (about 10%) were purchased. Its strength lay at the marketing end of the process, where it enjoyed a strong 12% market share in its limited regional markets.

Up until 1974, top management determined an overall corporate hurdle rate, based upon the firm's estimated historic average cost of capital, and applied this rate as a minimum return on investment criteria for all operating divisions.

In evaluating an investment opportunity, an operating unit would discount cash inflows and outflows at the hurdle rate. Projects with present values ratios greater than 1 (present value of inflows divided by present value of outflows) were given further consideration. A number of projects could not be evaluated exclusively on economic grounds (e.g., office buildings, antipollution devices, security systems), and some projects with inadequate net present value ratios were submitted and approved. Most projects were, however, justified on economic grounds. Riskier projects might not be approved even if their present-value ratio, based on expected value calculations, was above 1. While there were no firm guidelines, management tended to use a net present-value ratio of 1 only for very low-risk projects. Moderate-risk projects tended to be evaluated against a standard of a 1.2 present-value ratio, and high-risk project usually required a ratio of 1.5. These guidelines were rather fuzzily applied, because of different views about risk. In any case, project economics was only one factor considered in any evaluation.

Capital availability had never been a problem prior to 1974. Arkansas benefited from high cash flows, as the result of depletion allowances. Dividend payouts were low relative to earnings so that retained earnings were favorable. Additional needs had been financed by long term borrowings. No new equity financings were necessary. However, the debt proportion in the capital structure had risen steadily from 18.2% in 1960 to 46.8% at the end of 1973. Lenders had begun signaling management that the present debt/ratio was about as high as the firm could go without seriously jeopardizing bond ratings, or their equivalent, for new issues. Indeed, with the increase in interest costs, coverage ratios were considered very low, already, and the debt proportions might have to be further reduced.

* Copyright © 1984 by the Colgate Darden Graduate School of Business Administration of the University of Virginia and by Robert F. Vandell, the Charles C. Abbott Professor of Business Administration. This case was prepared by Professor Vandell and is used with his permission.

511

Mr. Edwards had decided to have a moratorium on new debt issues for at least one year to allow the equity proportion of the capital structure to grow.

In the period 1960 to 1973, financings had been achieved as follows (dollar figures in millions):

Sources		Applications	
Depletion/Depreciation	$ 489	New Plant	$1359
Retained Earnings	307	Working Capital	210
Net Debt Financing	773		$1569
Total	$1569		

The major sources of capital had all come under pressure recently. As the result of changes in the law with regard to depletion, the percentage of noncash charges divided by gross plant had been declining. Congress was considering even more restrictive depletion allowances, and Mr. Edwards was fearful some adverse decisions might lie ahead. Profits after taxes but before interest as a percentage of capital structure had until recently been declining, whereas interest and dividends had been rising. As a result, retained earnings were squeezed (relative to the dollar value of the capital structure). While price increases, relating to the oil crisis, had reversed this trend, Mr. Edwards was fearful this situation might be temporary. The moratorium on borrowing removed an important source of capital.

At the same time demand for capital was rising as a percentage of gross plant. Some needs related to environment requirements. Inflation had increased the cost of new investments. And the present energy shortage was expected to increase pressures for new investment. Arkansas thus expected to need to raise sizeable amounts of new capital externally to finance its growth. Equity funds would have to be raised for the first time. However, equity markets for Arkansas' stock, as measured by the ratio of market price to estimated twelve-months' future earnings were at their lowest post-war levels. Capital from this source was certainly not attractive.

The funds-forecast for the next three years (1975–1977) was (in millions of dollars):

Sources		Applications	
Depletion/Depreciation	$ 216	Capital Expenditures	$1620
Retained Earnings	163	Working Capital	214
Total	$ 379		$1834
Short Fall	$1455		

The shortage of funds was large compared with Arkansas' net worth at the end of 1973 of $1,019 million.

During the period, Arkansas' cost of capital had declined until 1970. In part this reflected the increased use of debt financing, and in part a rise in the price earnings ratio helped. By 1973, however, a precipitous decline in the price-earnings ratio, coupled with a higher average of cost of interest, had increased the capital charge as shown in Exhibit 1.

Management believed that these costs understated the real cost of money to the firm, because historically Arkansas' growth rate was about 3% above the average for all firms. Management added 3% to the capital cost to recognize the performance superior expected by creditors and stockholders. Some individuals believed that the 3% should apply only to equity capital.

EXHIBIT 1
Arkansas Petroleum Company: Cost of Capital Calculations, Representative Years

	Weight	Cost After Tax	Weighted Cost
1960			
Debt	.182	4.3%	.78
Common Stock	.818	8.5%	6.95
		Weighted Average	7.73%
1965			
Debt	.325	4.8%	1.56
Common Stock	.675	7.1%	4.79
		Weighted Average	6.35%
1970			
Debt	.436	5.7%	2.49
Common Stock	.564	5.5%	3.10
		Weighted Average	5.59%
1973			
Debt	.468	6.0%	2.81%
Common Stock	.532	11.1%	5.91%
		Weighted Average	8.72%

NOTE: The after-tax cost of debt funds represented the average interest of outstanding long term debt, stated on an after tax basis. Tax rates averaged about 30 percent of reported income over the period.

Equity cost was determined by dividing a trendline measure of earnings per share for the year by the average of monthly closing prices for the common stock.

Management did not adjust its hurdle rates, year by year, to recognize changes in the cost of capital. However, the hurdle rate had declined from 11% in 1960 to 9% in 1970. Under 1973 conditions, a 12% hurdle rate seemed more appropriate to Mr. Edwards, although the effective rate was still 9%.

Mr. Edwards was not, however, satisfied with this conclusion. The price-earnings ratio for Arkansas stock had since fallen to 6.9 × earnings per share, suggesting an equity cost of 14.4%. Moreover, equity funds would be the main source of capital in the next year or so. He wondered perhaps if this implied that a 17% to 18% hurdle rate might be more appropriate. Clearly the choice of the hurdle rate would affect the amount of expenditures considered attractive, and perhaps their mix as well.

Mr. Edwards was further troubled by the comment made by Arkansas' primary investment banker to the effect, new equity issues would be very difficult to place in the depressed market conditions and prevailing mood, and might be impossible. It seemed to Mr. Edwards that cost of capital measures were pretty meaningless if capital was unavailable or restricted in quantity. In any case, his measure did not consider the underpricing and issuing costs of raising equity funds, a figure that might be 6–7% of the issue in today's market.

The weighted average-cost calculation in Mr. Edwards' mind was backward looking. He wondered whether he should be projecting future capital mixes and their related costs in determining an appropriate hurdle rate. For instance, new debt funds might cost 9.5% to 10.0% at the moment, and if any refinancing were required the marginal cost of the incremental debt funds would be higher. Weighted average debt costs still reflected some financings in the early 1950's when interest rates were 4%.

Related to this question was how far in the future to project. Forecasting market prices for common equities for six months was problematic enough, let alone trying to anticipate what these prices might become in several years' time. The present moratorium on debt would drastically affect capital costs this year, but over time the impact would diminish. He was uncertain what sort of planning horizon was appropriate, especially given the firm's current unique circumstances.

In recent years Mr. Edwards was concerned by the growth in importance of "non-productive investments", that is, the necessary investments that did not add to earning power or avoid erosion of earning power directly. In the early 1960's these nonproductive investments amounted to about 10% of the total new fund commitments. Today, largely as a result of environmental laws and pressures, they had increased to 20%. Mr. Edwards believed that in order to earn 12% on all new capital investments, Arkansas now had to earn at least 15% (12% ÷ .8) on its productive investments. This issue needed resolution.

At the time the present-value ratio had been adopted for evaluating projects, management was completely satisfied with the intellectual relevance of a hurdle rate, as an expression of the opportunity cost of money. While the notion that the average cost of capital represented this opportunity cost had been debated and its measurement was never considered wholly scientific, it had been accepted. Circumstances had now changed, however. It looked to be difficult, if not impossible, to fund all desirable expenditures in the future because of the prevailing capital scarcity. Mr. Edwards wondered what the relevant notion of hurdle rate should be during periods of capital scarcity and internal fund rationing.

Recently, one of his assistants, Robert Drew, had raised a question about how the hurdle rate should be used. Two years ago, in recognition of inflation, Arkansas had adjusted its methods of present-value calculations. In effect, future cash flows were adjusted to reflect the effects of inflation. Estimates of the rates of inflation for various items (e.g., labor costs, prices, construction costs) were supplied by the firm's economic department and plugged into future cash flows. The net cash flows in future years were then deflated by an estimate of the cost of living index to put them in current (common dollar) terms. The common dollar cash flows were then discounted at the hurdle rate to determine the net present-value ratio for the project. Mr. Drew argued that the last step was wrong. Cost of capital had risen to reflect investors views of inflation. (That is, the investor was seeking the same common dollar rate of return as in the past, and to do so had to add to this basic rate, roughly, the rate of inflation to determine satisfactory return on investment opportunities.) If this was so the double step of deflating the value of future cash flows and discounting at a hurdle rate, reflecting inflation expectations, overcompensated for inflation. Mr. Edwards believed that Mr. Drew was right in part, but doubted if money-costs yet fully considered inflation expectations. In one sense, this was troublesome, for considering inflationary effects was certainly appropriate in evaluating investment opportunities, yet a procedure that dealt with them incorrectly would only increase confusion and misinformation. To the extent inflation did in fact influence money-costs, it also meant that capital would remain expensive, or could become more costly.

Even if the appropriate hurdle rate was clear cut, how the rate should be used within the company in evaluating projects was not. As noted, Arkansas historically had used one rate to discount all projects in all phases of its operations. This practice had come under increasing attack.

Perhaps, Robert Charles, President of the pipeline company presented these views most vigorously:

Each phase of our business is different, must compete differently, and must draw on capital differently. Pipelines are a regulated industry, and the return on our total capital is limited to about 7%. In most cases, this return is highly certain. The throughput and the profit margins are contracted for on a long-term basis to assure a satisfactory rate of return (by major oil companies who depend on the suppliers). We are not as deeply into pipelines as our competitors, primarily because it is almost impossible to justify an investment with our present single hurdle rate system. This unique constraint adds to our production costs, and in the end weakens our profit margins on sales, and our long-run competitive position.

Given the recognized safety of the investment, many independent pipeline companies can raise most of the capital needed from the debt markets. In projects comparable to the ones we would consider, 85% to 90% of the necessary capital is raised through the debt markets at interest rates reflecting at least A quality. If we could do the same, notice what this would do to our capital costs (using 1973 data):

	Weight	Cost	Weighted Cost
Debt	.85	6.0%	5.10
Equity	.15	11.1%	1.67
		Total	6.77%

Even at today's high capital costs, pipeline projects develop favorable present value ratios. I contrast this with the exploratory drilling division where risks are high and where independents are financed primarily by equity funds (i.e., 11.1%). In my book, their hurdle rate should reflect the cost of equity funds.

There is another subtlety. Our corporate tax rate is 30% on average because of heavy write-offs on exploratory drilling. However, the tax savings are heavily concentrated in one or two operating divisions. The rest of us pay about 50% of our income in taxes. The firm's interest costs before taxes are 8.7%. This should mean that the after-tax cost of interest is only 4.35% for pipelines. Considering taxes properly materially reduces our division's weighted cost of capital (to 5.37%).

In short, I believe that we are really rationing equity funds. We should be seeking a constant rate of return on equity. Those of use who benefit from lower risk, and hence can trade on our equity more extensively, should not be penalized because our ability to earn on our assets is restricted in ways not detrimental to very favorable capacity to achieve high returns on our equity, when stated comparably to our competition.

Implicit in Mr. Charles' arguments, as Mr. Edwards understood it, each division in the company would have a different hurdle rate. The costs of the various forms of capital would remain the same (except perhaps for the tax element). However, the mix of capital used would change in the calculation. Low-risk operations would use leverage more extensively, while the high risk divisions would have little or no debt funds. Thus, lower risk divisions would have lower hurdle rates.

Mr. Charles' views were supported by several other division managers. Opposition was just as strong, however, particularly from the divisions whose hurdle rate might be increased. George Pritchett, Division Manager of the Exploratory Drilling Division, expressed his opinion as follows:

Money is all green. We should be putting our money where the returns are best. A single hurdle rate may deprive the underprofitable divisions of investments in order to channel more funds into profitable divisions. But isn't this the aim of the process?

We don't finance each division separately. The corporation raises capital based on its overall prospects and record. The diversification of the company probably helps keep our capital costs down and enables us to borrow more in total than the sum of the capabilities of each division separately. As a result, developing separate hurdle rates is both unrealistic and misleading. All our stockholders want from us is to invest our funds wisely in order to increase the value of their stock. This happens when we pick the most promising projects, irrespective of their source.

Several years ago we installed probability calculations in our project evaluations in order to determine the expected value of projects. I thought the purpose of this calculation was to take risk and uncertainties fully into account. Multiple hurdle rates will only confuse things by adding a second dimension to our risk appraisals in a way that will obscure the meaning of the basic calculation.

Mr. Charles countered these arguments as follows:

In considering how much to loan us, lenders will consider the composition of risks. If money flows into safer investments over time, their willingness to lend us funds will tend to increase. While multiple hurdle rates may not reflect capital structure changes on a day-to-day basis, over time they will reflect prospects more realistically.

Our stockholders are just as much concerned with risk. If they perceive our business as being more risky than other companies, they will not pay as high a price for our earnings. Perhaps this is why our price earnings ratio is below the industry average most of the time.

Probability calculations leading to expected value measures of the return potential of projects measure average prospects. They do not consider the dispersion around the expected value. Projects with high dispersion should be less attractive.

It is not a question of whether we adjust for risk—we already do. We look for higher present-value ratios before we fund riskier projects. The only question in my mind is whether we make these adjustments systematically or not. If we attribute a capital structure to a division or, for that matter, to a project so that the rate of return on equity represents equivalent risks, then we are in a position to pick the projects with the best returns on imputed equity.

At the moment, as I understand it, our real problem is an inadequate and very costly supply of equity funds. If we are really rationing equity capital, then we should be striving for the best returns on equity for the risk. Multiple hurdle rates achieve this objective.

As he listened to these and several similar arguments over the course of several months, Mr. Edwards became increasingly concerned with several other considerations. First, the corporate strategy directed the company towards increasing its integration, particularly towards developing strong crude oil production. One effect of using multiple hurdle rates would be making it more difficult to justify exploratory drilling proposals, since the required rate of return would be increased. In contrast, pipeline investments had a relatively low priority, since they were more in the nature of cost reduction. Drilling and marketing investments tended to build the overall strength of the firm more. Perhaps multiple hurdle rates were the right idea, but the notion that they should be based on capital costs rather than strategic considerations was wrong. On the other hand, perhaps multiple rates based on capital costs should be used, but, in allocating funds, higher net present-value ratios should be used for screening projects in divisions that were less strategically important. (Theory was certainly not clear on how to achieve strategic objectives when allocating capital, in Mr. Edwards' mind.)

When the present-value ratio replaced the discounted rate of return as the primary economic screening tool, it had been adopted because it was considered an ideal tool for the economic rationing of capital. Capital rationing was now a more material problem for Arkansas. Using a single measure of the cost of money (hurdle rate or discount factor) made the present-value ratio results consistent at least in economic terms. If Arkansas adopted multiple rates for discounting cash flows, Mr. Edwards was afraid the calculation would lose its meaning. A present-value ratio of 1.2 to 1 would not mean the same thing from division to division. To him, a screening criterion had to be consistent and understandable, or its usefulness would decrease.

Finally, Mr. Edwards was concerned with the problems of attributing capital structures to divisions. In the marketing division, for example, a new gas station might be 100% financed either by lease or debt arrangement. This was feasible only because the corporation guaranteed the debt. New gas stations, in Mr. Edwards' mind, were fairly risky, perhaps warranting only a 20% debt structure on average. The financing conventions in this division would make this point difficult to sell. And, in any case, Mr. Edwards considered debt-capacity decisions very difficult to make for the corporation as a whole, let alone for each of its divisions. At best, judgments would be very crude.

Mr. Edwards had two bright young MBA's working for him, and he had discussed the problem of multiple hurdle rates at length with them. Their views differed.

William Lombard stressed that he had learned at his school that the investment decision should never be mixed with the financing decision. A firm should decide what its investments should be, and then how to finance them most efficiently. If leverage were added to a present-value calculation it would distort the results. Use of multiple hurdle rates was simply a way of mixing financings with investment analysis. He also believed that a single rate left the risk-decision clean cut. Management could simply adjust its standard (demanded present-value ratio) as risks increased.

Thomas Gamble, in contrast, noted that the weighted average cost of capital calculation tended to represent an average market reaction to a mixture of risks. Lower than average risk projects should probably be accepted even though they did not meet a weighted average criterion. Higher than normal risk projects should provide a return premium. While the multiple hurdle rate system was a crude way of achieving this end, it at least was a step in the right direction. Moreover, he believed that the objective of a firm should be to maximize return on equity funds. Since equity funds were and would remain the chief scarce resource being allocated in the foreseeable future, a multiple rate system would tend to maximize returns to stockholders better than a single rate system. The company in effect was still using a single rate and that was its desired rate of return (e.g., 11.1%) on equity funds allocated to divisions and projects.

Mr. Edwards had one further factor to consider. A recently concluded study, reviewing the actual results against forecasts for new investments made 5 to 10 years ago, produced disturbing results. Although the methodology might be debatable, the results nevertheless seemed consistent with his impressions. The real returns on projects, according to the study, were running about three percentage points less than originally forecast on average. In certain divisions and for certain types of projects, results were much worse.

In particular, prices, either for purchased items like foreign crude, (30% of Arkansas' total) or for finished products like gasoline had been difficult to estimate, with serious repercussions on the accuracy of forecasts. The recent Arab oil embargo, related price increases, etc., would only make these forecasts more uncertain in the future.

Mr. Edwards wondered whether this evidence should be used to penalize projects from certain divisions, with persisting estimating problems and if so how penalties might be put into force, without distorting the usefulness of economic evaluating activities.

Mr. Edwards had no hope that all the issues before him could be resolved systematically. He did want, however, to institute a pragmatic system of appropriate hurdle rates (or one rate) which would tend to facilitate better judgments under the new circumstances faced by Arkansas. He knew that his final resolutions of these issues would not only have to be convincing to himself but understandable and convincing to top management, the division managers, and the individual analysts in the operating divisions.

There were sufficient funds on hand to fund the 1974 capital budget. The capital budgeting process for 1975 would begin with the submission of plans and expenditure proposals in September 1974, by division managers. Some divisions had already begun the planning process. If any changes were to be made in the budgeting analysis, the screening criteria, etc., the announcements would have to be made very shortly.

Community Edison Company

Background

Community Edison (ComEd) is a regulated public utility which produces and sells electricity. ComEd's management has been told by its engineers that some additional equipment must be installed to meet the growth in demand from its customers. The required equipment will cost $100,000. To raise the capital necessary to purchase the equipment, ComEd needs to assure its capital suppliers that the present value of the incremental after-tax cash flows that will result from using this new equipment will at least equal the cost of the equipment, when discounted at 15 percent. In order to get the required after-tax cash flows, ComEd will need to devise an appropriate price schedule, which must be approved by a government agency known as the Public Service Commission (PSC). The PSC will not approve a price schedule if the return on investment (ROI) in any year is more than 15 percent. In calculating the ROI the PSC uses after-tax accounting earnings divided by the beginning of the year accounting value of the assets.

Additional Facts

A unit of electricity is called a megawatt hour (MWH). The essential facts are:

Demand:	Year 1	60 MWH
	Year 2	120 MWH
Cost of Equipment		$100,000
Life of Equipment		2 years
Operating costs		zero
Salvage value		zero
Income Tax Rate		40 percent

The same financial statements are used by ComEd for income taxes and for financial reporting, and by the PSC for computing ROI's.

General Problem

ComEd's general problem is to find a price schedule that will satisfy the requirements of its capital suppliers and of the PSC. The capital suppliers will be satisfied if the present value of the after-tax cash flows discounted at 15 percent is at least $100,000. The PSC will be satisfied if the return on investment is less than or equal to 15 percent each year. There is more than one price schedule that satisfies both of these conditions.

The problem of choosing an appropriate price schedule was discussed at a recent meeting of the Board of Directors of ComEd. Some directors felt that since the equipment needed would last two years, it should be depreciated by an equal amount in each year.

Another group of directors felt that investor confidence would be enhanced if the before-tax revenues of the company were constant from year to year. They favored a financial plan that would achieve this objective. A third group of directors felt that public relations would be improved if ComEd could stabilize the price per unit charged for electricity. The financial vice president, Mr. Moneypenny, stated that any one of these objectives was feasible, but not all three. The board agreed that at the next meeting they would review the financial implications of meeting each set of objectives.

Prepare three versions of the following table for Mr. Moneypenny. Each version should satisfy the objectives of one set of directors.

	Year 1	2	Totals
1. Units Sales (MWH)	60	120	
2. Price per unit ($/MWH)			
3. Revenues ($)			
4. Depreciation ($)			100,000
5. Before-Tax Income ($)			
6. Income Tax ($)			
7. After-Tax Income ($)			
8. After-Tax Cash Flow ($)			
9. Beginning of Period Investment ($)	100,000		
10. ROI	.15	.15	
11. PV of ATCF ($)			100,000

CASE **11**

The Algone Case

Memorandum
>   TO: Y. P. Student
>   Economic Evaluation Manager
>   Wedoodit Chemical Corporation
> FROM: I. M. Selfmade, President

As you know, the research and development department of our company has developed a new product that we are considering marketing under the brand name of Algone. Algone is an unstable liquid that must be kept under pressure at an extremely low temperature, of approximately $-200°$F. Above this temperature it decomposes within a few minutes. Algone has only one important known commercial application. When a quarter pound of Algone is sprayed through a specially designed applicator onto the feathers of a freshly killed chicken, the feathers completely disappear within seconds. There are no harmful side effects and the product has been approved for use by the Food and Drug Administration.

Wedoodit Chemical is considering two alternative means of exploiting this new product. One possibility is to sell the exclusive rights to the patent to the Chiselem Corporation, which would produce and market Algone. The alternative is for Wedoodit to build a plant to produce the product itself. Chiselem has offered us a straight cash payment of $1 million for the patent rights.

The attached memoranda from the Market Research Manager and the Engineering Manager provide a basis for evaluating the profit potential of Algone if Wedoodit undertakes to manufacture and market the product itself. As economic evaluation manager, you are expected to specify the type of equipment that would be needed for the most profitable manufacturing facility to produce Algone, to present cash flow estimates for the operation of the facility, and to make a recommendation as to whether or not Wedoodit should sell its patent rights to Algone.

As you know, we have estimated our cost of capital to be 8 percent, and it is company policy to exploit all available investment opportunities that can earn us at least that much.

We are subject to income taxes of 54 percent on incremental income, consisting of 52 percent federal and 2 percent state corporate income tax rates.

Memorandum
>   TO: I. M. Selfmade
>   President
>   Wedoodit Chemical Corporation
>   FROM: V. Gotfigures
>   Market Research Manager
> SUBJECT: Market Potential for Algone

Total Market

The only significant potential commercial use for Algone is to remove feathers from chickens (broilers) being processed for market. This requires $\frac{1}{4}$ pound of Algone per bird. Approximately 2 billion chickens are consumed in the United States each year. Poultry consumption has been growing rapidly in the last decade as a result of improved technology and lower costs. However, no further growth in this market is expected. The effects of increased population will be offset by growing competition from turkeys and increased consumption of beef as a result of higher consumer incomes.

About half of the poultry are processed in plants in very low cost labor areas where Algone would be more expensive than other means of removing feathers, or in plants whose layout is not easily converted to this process. Therefore, we expect the total market potential for this process to amount to 1 billion birds per year for the foreseeable future. This would require 250 million pounds of Algone annually, or about 1 million pounds per working day (based on a five-day week and fifty working weeks in the year).

Market Share

Although Algone is patented, news of our discovery has already leaked out to competitors, who are developing similar products not covered by our patents. We are certain to have competitors soon after we begin production. The high capital costs of producing this product and the large potential market will prevent any one firm from dominating the market. We expect to be able to gain and hold 10 percent of the total U.S. market, equivalent to 25 million pounds annually.

Price

Because alternative means of removing chicken feathers are easily available, a market demand for Algone would be very elastic at prices above 12 cents per pound. It is difficult to know how low the price might go, as this would depend on the costs of our competitors and the danger the industry might overexpand, making the business unprofitable for all concerned. Prices below 8 cents per pound would almost certainly be unprofitable. We estimate the price level will fluctuate around 10 cents, and recommend using that figure for planning purposes. All price quotations are F.O.B. our plant; customers to absorb freight.

Fluctuations in Demand

Fluctuations in demand are particularly important because Algone is an unstable compound. It cannot be stored except at prohibitive costs. The product must be shipped the same day it is produced. The effective market area for our plant will be limited to those customers who can receive product no more than twenty-four hours after it leaves the plant. The plant will have to operate Saturday through Thursday, because product shipped on Friday would be received on Saturday and would partly decompose by Monday. Poultry processing plants do not operate Saturdays or Sundays.

Poultry consumption does not fluctuate very much seasonally. But poultry processing *plants* normally operate only a half-day on Friday. Our production of Algone would be correspondingly lower on Thursdays.

Thus a plant that expects to have an average daily output of 100,000 lb should expect a product fluctuation as follows:

Day of Week	Daily Production (lb)
Sunday through Wednesday	111,000
Thursday	55,000
Average daily production	100,000

Memorandum
    TO: I. M. Selfmade
FROM: W. E. Triedit
          Manager of Engineering
          Design and Pilot Plant Operations Department
          Wedoodit Chemical Corporation

A plant location has been selected for the Algone project in consultation with Market Research and Traffic Departments. Land and associated development costs (nondepreciable) would be $100,000. We hold a ninety-day option on the site.

Two methods of producing Algone have been devised and pilot plant tested. Summary cost figures follow:

Method	Equipment and Installation per 1,000 Lb of Daily Capacity	Variable Material and Operating Expense per 1,000 Lb of Algone Produced
A	$80,000	$ 5
B	$34,000	$45

Either type of equipment would last for ten years and the costs of equipment and installation would be entirely depreciable. No salvage is expected. Variable costs do not include any depreciation and are on a before-tax basis.

In addition to the equipment listed, capital costs for office, shipping, and miscellaneous utilities would amount to $20,000 per 1,000 pounds of maximum daily output. The various costs of operating these facilities are included in the variable costs of methods A and B.

It would be possible to design a plant that would include a provision for producing Algone by both methods A and B in whatever proportions seem desirable. For example, a 50,000-pound daily maximum production could be achieved in a facility having a capacity of 30,000 pounds using method A and 20,000 pounds using method B. There are no significant shutdown or start-up costs for either method of production.

A plant with a daily output capacity up to 125,000 pounds per day could expect fixed costs (for property taxes, insurance, plant guards, etc.) of about $100,000 per year (excluding depreciation). These costs would all require cash outlays and could be charged to expense for income tax purposes. A plant this size would also require working capital (inventories, accounts receivable, and cash) of about $50,000.

CASE **12**

Bokaro Steel Plant

In 1963 the United States Steel Corporation completed for the U.S. government "A Techno-Economic Survey of a Proposed Integrated Steel Plant at Bokaro, Bihar State, India."

The following quotations are taken from the study:

Profitability—Operations of the plant at Step I levels alone would be unprofitable even though operations are projected at full capacity following completion of start-up.... Each year of the projected period produces a cash deficit which reaches $270 million in 10 years or an average annual deficit of $27 million.

Presumably, government of India loans will cover these deficits.

Upon examination of the profitability of Bokaro it is evident that the heavy burden of excise duties and large interest payments on loans are the greatest influences on the results. Production costs on the other hand indicate that Bokaro could be a relatively low-cost steel producer based upon the facilities proposed and the assumptions made with respect to raw materials, manpower and managerial control.

The projected Bokaro expansion in Step II to 2.5 million ingot tons, with operations beginning four years after start of Step I production, will result in profitable operations when close to 100 percent of capacity is reached and will remain profitable thereafter.

Since the government of India is assumed to own the mill, it is relevant to mention that during the twenty-year period an estimated $1.0 billion of revenue would accrue to the government of India from the Bokaro operation, through excise duties on ingots, finished steel products, and coal chemical by-products. Income taxes paid by Bokaro would give the government an estimated $0.5 billion. In addition, the "surcharge," of difference between the retention price and selling price, would amount to about $1.2 billion during the same period and would accrue to the government.

The selling price is the price paid by a plant's customers, the retention price the amount it is permitted to keep. Both are set by the government.

Required: Discuss how the items described should affect the analysis of the Bokaro steel plant.

The Eatwell Company

The Eatwell Company is considering the purchase of a new machine to replace one currently in use. The new machine would cost $100,000 and be depreciated over a four-year period on a straight-line basis. It would have no salvage value. Ignore the investment tax credit in making your analysis.

Let us suppose that the new equipment whose purchase is proposed is to be used to replace an older machine that is fully depreciated and has no salvage value. The older machine could be continued in use for another four years, if this were economically desirable. Either machine could be used to produce a part that is a component of one of the company's products. The company's engineering department estimates that the use of the proposed new machine would most likely result in a reduction of $.25 per unit in the manufacturing cost of the component. This cost-reduction calculation takes into consideration savings in direct labor, material, and variable overhead, on a before-tax basis; the cost attributed to depreciation in the new machine is not included in this calculation.

There is some chance that the savings may not be as great as anticipated. The engineering department considers that there is .1 probability the machine produces savings of $.15 per unit, and it further believes that there is .9 probability that savings of $.25 per unit will actually be realized.

Because the total savings that will be realized will depend on the number of units produced, the sales department of the company was asked to estimate total sales for the next four years for the product. The product has an established and stable market. The sales department expected that demand would continue at the present rate for the next four years, in which case total sales would amount to 600,000 units, but added an important qualification. It was known that a competitor was about to introduce a product that might be more satisfactory than the company's product to some consumers. If the competitive product is successful, unit sales for the four-year period might be only 400,000. The sales department, however, believed the probability is only .3 that the competitor's product would be successful.

TABLE 1. *Joint Probabilities of Possible Outcomes Associated with Use of New Equipment*

Unit Cost Reduction	Unit Sales 400,000	Unit Sales 600,000	Marginal Probability
$.25	.27	.63	.90
.15	.03	.07	.10
Marginal probability	.30	.70	1.00

TABLE 2. *Annual After-Tax Savings Before Depreciation*

Event	Unit Cost Reduction	Unit Sales for Four Years	(1) Prob-ability	(2) Total Before Taxes	(3) Savings After Taxes Col. 2 × .6	(4) Annual After-Tax Savings Col. 3 × ¼	(5) Expec-tation Col. 1 × Col. 4
e_1	$.25	600,000	.63	$150,000	$90,000	$22,500	$14,175
e_2	.25	400,000	.27	100,000	60,000	15,000	4,050
e_3	.15	600,000	.07	90,000	54,000	13,500	945
e_4	.15	400,000	.03	60,000	36,000	9,000	270
			1.00				19,440

Considering both the engineering and technical uncertainties connected with the pro-posed new equipment, four possible outcomes (events) need to be considered. These out-comes and their probabilities are given in Table 1. The joint probabilities were calculated on the assumption that the unit cost reduction achieved by the machine would be sta-tistically independent of the unit sales of the product. The assumption seems reasonable in this instance.

The financial consequences of these four outcomes are described in Table 2, assuming a .4 tax rate.

Although the cash inflows that might result from using the new equipment are uncer-tain, the cash outflows associated with a decision to acquire the new equipment, and the tax savings from depreciation, are not uncertain (see Table 2).

The Eatwell Company produces about one hundred different food products, which are distributed through retail foodstores. The machine in question would be used to help manufacture one of these products. The product in question accounts for about 3 percent of sales and of net profits.

Eatwell has a capital structure consisting of 80 percent equity and 20 percent debt. It is able to borrow money on a long-term basis at 5 percent (before taxes). The financial committee estimates that the company's average cost of capital is 10 percent.

The company has no established policy as to the minimum acceptable level of return. It feels that both profitability and risk need to be considered in deciding whether or not an investment is desirable.

Should Eatwell purchase this new machine? What data would you use to defend your judgment?

Rokal Company

The Rokal Company is a small regional hardware wholesaler. In recent years the company has been earning approximately $500,000 per year after taxes. Approximately half the earnings have been paid out as dividends. The stock is closely held by descendants of the founder, many of whom rely on their dividends for a substantial part of their personal income. The board of directors of the company consists of the principal stockholders or their representatives, including the president. Day-to-day management of the company is concentrated in the hands of the president, Mr. John Chalishan, who, it is generally agreed, is the only family member capable of effectively running the business. The board is consulted on important policy matters. Their main objective is to have the company maintain a stable dividend, with some growth if possible.

Recently, several of the board members have become concerned about the possible dangers to dividend stability arising from the fact that management is so heavily concentrated in the hands of the president. In case of a serious sickness or unexpected death, there would be no one else capable of quickly and effectively taking over the management. The board recognized that, in time, an effective professional manager could be found to replace Mr. Chalishan. It also recognized that the company would suffer some financial impairment if it operated without an experienced and energetic head for the six to twenty-four months that would be required to find a new president. The ability of the company to pay its regular dividend during such an interim period was questionable.

The possibility of hiring a potential replacement now was considered but rejected. A person of the necessary experience and ability would be expensive; and would have no real future with the company if Mr. Chalishan, who was only forty-seven years old, remained in good health; thus a new addition might become a source of friction and factionalism.

The board members finally concluded that the purchase of an insurance policy on Mr. Chalishan's life in the amount of $500,000 would be the best way of handling this risk. Inquiries with an insurance broker indicated that a single payment of $15,000 would provide a five-year term policy on Mr. Chalishan's life, assuming he passed the usual medical examination. The policy provided for renewal if desired with no subsequent medical examination.

When the subject was raised at a board meeting, Mr. Chalishan reacted rather coolly and asked to have the subject tabled until the next meeting. This was done. At the subsequent meeting Mr. Chalishan presented an analysis of the proposed life insurance policy as an investment, which he felt it was. He recommended that the proposal should be rejected on the grounds that it was an obviously unprofitable investment. He presented Table 1 to justify his opinion.

Required: Can the purchase of a life insurance policy be treated as an investment? Why or why not? Is it reasonable for the Rokal Company to purchase this policy?

TABLE 1. *Analysis of Life Insurance Policy As an Investment*

		A. Present-Value Analysis			
Year	Cash Flow	Probability*	Expected Cash Flow	Present-Value Factor†	Present Value
0	−$ 15,000	1.000		1.0000	−$15,000
1	500,000	.005	$2,500	.9524	2,381
2	500,000	.005	2,500	.9070	2,268
3	500,000	.005	2,500	.8638	2,160
4	500,000	.005	2,500	.8227	2,057
5	500,000	.005	2,500	.7835	1,959
				Net present value −	4,177

B. Internal Rate of Return Analysis

The discounted cash flow IRR on the expected cash flows
associated with this policy is approximately minus 6 percent.

* Probability based on mortality experience for males of like age and occupation.
† Using a 5 percent discount rate.

Appendix Tables

TABLE A. *Present Value of $1.00* $ $(1 + r)^{-n}$*

n/r	1.0%	2.0%	3.0%	4.0%	5.0%	6%	7%	8%	9%	10%	11%	12%	13%	14%	15%
1	.9901	.9804	.9709	.9615	.9524	.9434	.9346	.9259	.9174	.9091	.9009	.8929	.8850	.8772	.8696
2	.9803	.9612	.9426	.9246	.9070	.8900	.8734	.8573	.8417	.8264	.8116	.7972	.7831	.7695	.7561
3	.9706	.9423	.9151	.8890	.8638	.8396	.8163	.7938	.7722	.7513	.7312	.7118	.6931	.6750	.6575
4	.9610	.9238	.8885	.8548	.8227	.7921	.7629	.7350	.7084	.6830	.6587	.6355	.6133	.5921	.5718
5	.9515	.9057	.8626	.8219	.7835	.7473	.7130	.6806	.6499	.6209	.5935	.5674	.5428	.5194	.4972
6	.9420	.8880	.8375	.7903	.7462	.7050	.6663	.6302	.5963	.5645	.5346	.5066	.4803	.4556	.4323
7	.9327	.8706	.8131	.7599	.7107	.6651	.6227	.5835	.5470	.5132	.4817	.4523	.4251	.3996	.3759
8	.9235	.8535	.7894	.7307	.6768	.6274	.5820	.5403	.5019	.4665	.4339	.4039	.3762	.3506	.3269
9	.9143	.8368	.7664	.7026	.6446	.5919	.5439	.5002	.4604	.4241	.3909	.3606	.3329	.3075	.2843
10	.9053	.8203	.7441	.6756	.6139	.5584	.5083	.4632.	.4224	.3855	.3522	.3220	.2946	.2697	.2472
11	.8963	.8043	.7224	.6496	.5847	.5268	.4751	.4289	.3875	.3505	.3173	.2875	.2607	.2366	.2149
12	.8874	.7885	.7014	.6246	.5568	.4970	.4440	.3971	.3555	.3186	.2858	.2567	.2307	.2076	.1869
13	.8787	.7730	.6810	.6006	.5303	.4688	.4150	.3677	.3262	.2897	.2575	.2292	.2042	.1821	.1625
14	.8700	.7579	.6611	.5775	.5051	.4423	.3878	.3405	.2992	.2633	.2320	.2046	.1807	.1597	.1413
15	.8613	.7430	.6419	.5553	.4810	.4173	.3624	.3152	.2745	.2394	.2090	.1827	.1599	.1401	.1229
16	.8528	.7284	.6232	.5339	.4581	.3936	.3387	.2919	.2519	.2176	.1883	.1631	.1415	.1229	.1069
17	.8444	.7142	.6050	.5134	.4363	.3714	.3166	.2703	.2311	.1978	.1696	.1456	.1252	.1078	.0929
18	.8360	.7002	.5874	.4936	.4155	.3503	.2959	.2502	.2120	.1799	.1528	.1300	.1108	.0946	.0808
19	.8277	.6864	.5703	.4746	.3957	.3305	.2765	.2317	.1945	.1635	.1377	.1161	.0981	.0829	.0703
20	.8195	.6730	.5537	.4564	.3769	.3118	.2584	.2145	.1784	.1486	.1240	.1037	.0868	.0728	.0611
21	.8114	.6598	.5375	.4388	.3589	.2942	.2415	.1987	.1637	.1351	.1117	.0926	.0768	.0638	.0531
22	.8034	.6468	.5219	.4220	.3418	.2775	.2257	.1839	.1502	.1228	.1007	.0826	.0680	.0560	.0462
23	.7954	.6342	.5067	.4057	.3256	.2618	.2109	.1703	.1378	.1117	.0907	.0738	.0601	.0491	.0402
24	.7876	.6217	.4919	.3901	.3101	.2470	.1971	.1577	.1264	.1015	.0817	.0659	.0532	.0431	.0349
25	.7798	.6095	.4776	.3751	.2953	.2330	.1842	.1460	.1160	.0923	.0736	.0588	.0471	.0378	.0304
26	.7720	.5976	.4637	.3607	.2812	.2198	.1722	.1352	.1064	.0839	.0663	.0525	.0417	.0331	.0264
27	.7644	.5859	.4502	.3468	.2678	.2074	.1609	.1252	.0976	.0763	.0597	.0469	.0369	.0291	.0230
28	.7568	.5744	.4371	.3335	.2551	.1956	.1504	.1159	.0895	.0693	.0538	.0419	.0326	.0255	.0200
29	.7493	.5631	.4243	.3207	.2429	.1846	.1406	.1073	.0822	.0630	.0485	.0374	.0289	.0224	.0174
30	.7419	.5521	.4120	.3083	.2314	.1741	.1314	.0994	.0754	.0573	.0437	.0334	.0256	.0196	.0151
35	.7059	.5000	.3554	.2534	.1813	.1301	.0937	.0676	.0490	.0356	.0259	.0189	.0139	.0102	.0075
40	.6717	.4529	.3066	.2083	.1420	.0972	.0668	.0460	.0318	.0221	.0154	.0107	.0075	.0053	.0037
45	.6391	.410	.2644	.1713	.1112	.0727	.0476	.0313	.0207	.0137	.0091	.0061	.0041	.0027	.0019
50	.6080	.3715	.2281	.1407	.0872	.0543	.0339	.0213	.0134	.0085	.0054	.0035	.0022	.0014	.0009

* r is the rate of discount and n is the number of time periods.

TABLE A. Present Value of $1.00 (cont'd)

n/r	16%	18%	20%	22%	24%	26%	28%	30%	32%	34%	36%	38%	40%	45%	50%
1	.8621	.8475	.8333	.8197	.8065	.7937	.7813	.7692	.7576	.7463	.7353	.7246	.7143	.6897	.6667
2	.7432	.7182	.6944	.6719	.6504	.6299	.6104	.5917	.5739	.5569	.5407	.5251	.5102	.4756	.4444
3	.6407	.6086	.5787	.5507	.5245	.4999	.4768	.4552	.4348	.4156	.3975	.3805	.3644	.3280	.2963
4	.5523	.5158	.4823	.4514	.4230	.3968	.3725	.3501	.3294	.3102	.2923	.2757	.2603	.2262	.1975
5	.4761	.4371	.4019	.3700	.3411	.3149	.2910	.2693	.2495	.2315	.2149	.1998	.1859	.1560	.1317
6	.4104	.3704	.3349	.3033	.2751	.2499	.2274	.2072	.1890	.1727	.1580	.1448	.1328	.1076	.0878
7	.3538	.3139	.2791	.2486	.2218	.1983	.1776	.1594	.1432	.1289	.1162	.1049	.0949	.0742	.0585
8	.3050	.2660	.2326	.2038	.1789	.1574	.1388	.1226	.1085	.0962	.0854	.0760	.0678	.0512	.0390
9	.2630	.2255	.1938	.1670	.1443	.1249	.1084	.0943	.0822	.0718	.0628	.0551	.0484	.0353	.0260
10	.2267	.1911	.1615	.1369	.1164	.0992	.0847	.0725	.0623	.0536	.0462	.0399	.0346	.0243	.0173
11	.1954	.1619	.1346	.1122	.0938	.0787	.0662	.0558	.0472	.0400	.0340	.0289	.0247	.0168	.0116
12	.1685	.1372	.1122	.0920	.0757	.0625	.0517	.0429	.0357	.0298	.0250	.0210	.0176	.0116	.0077
13	.1452	.1163	.0935	.0754	.0610	.0496	.0404	.0330	.0271	.0223	.0184	.0152	.0126	.0080	.0051
14	.1252	.0985	.0779	.0618	.0492	.0393	.0316	.0253	.0205	.0166	.0135	.0110	.0090	.0055	.0034
15	.1079	.0835	.0649	.0507	.0397	.0312	.0247	.0195	.0155	.0124	.0099	.0080	.0064	.0038	.0023
16	.0930	.0708	.0541	.0415	.0320	.0248	.0193	.0150	.0118	.0093	.0073	.0058	.0046	.0026	.0015
17	.0802	.0600	.0451	.0340	.0258	.0197	.0150	.0116	.0089	.0069	.0054	.0042	.0033	.0018	.0010
18	.0691	.0508	.0376	.0279	.0208	.0156	.0118	.0089	.0068	.0052	.0039	.0030	.0023	.0012	.0007
19	.0596	.0431	.0313	.0229	.0168	.0124	.0092	.0068	.0051	.0038	.0029	.0022	.0017	.0009	.0005
20	.0514	.0365	.0261	.0187	.0135	.0098	.0072	.0053	.0039	.0029	.0021	.0016	.0012	.0006	.0003
21	.0443	.0309	.0217	.0154	.0109	.0078	.0056	.0040	.0029	.0021	.0016	.0012	.0009	.0004	.0002
22	.0382	.0262	.0181	.0126	.0088	.0062	.0044	.0031	.0022	.0016	.0012	.0008	.0006	.0003	.0001
23	.0329	.0222	.0151	.0103	.0071	.0049	.0034	.0024	.0017	.0012	.0008	.0006	.0004	.0002	.0001
24	.0284	.0188	.0126	.0085	.0057	.0039	.0027	.0018	.0013	.0009	.0006	.0004	.0003	.0001	.0001
25	.0245	.0160	.0105	.0069	.0046	.0031	.0021	.0014	.0010	.0007	.0005	.0003	.0002	.0001	.0000
26	.0211	.0135	.0087	.0057	.0037	.0025	.0016	.0011	.0007	.0005	.0003	.0002	.0002	.0001	
27	.0182	.0115	.0073	.0047	.0030	.0019	.0013	.0008	.0006	.0004	.0002	.0002	.0001	.0000	
28	.0157	.0097	.0061	.0038	.0024	.0015	.0010	.0006	.0004	.0003	.0002	.0001	.0001		
29	.0135	.0082	.0051	.0031	.0020	.0012	.0008	.0005	.0003	.0002	.0001	.0001	.0001		
30	.0116	.0070	.0042	.0026	.0016	.0010	.0006	.0004	.0002	.0002	.0001	.0001	.0000		
35	.0055	.0030	.0017	.0009	.0005	.0003	.0002	.0001	.0001	.0000	.0000	.0000			
40	.0026	.0013	.0007	.0004	.0002	.0001	.0001	.0000	.0000						
45	.0013	.0006	.0003	.0001	.0001	.0000	.0000								
50	.0006	.0003	.0001	.0000	.0000										

TABLE B. Present Value of $1 Received per Period $\dfrac{1-(1+r)^{-n}}{r}$

n/r	1.0%	2.0%	3.0%	4.0%	5.0%	6%	7%	8%	9%	10%	11%	12%	13%	14%	15%
1	.9901	.9804	.9709	.9615	.9524	.9434	.9346	.9259	.9174	.9091	.9009	.8929	.8850	.8772	.8696
2	1.9704	1.9416	1.9135	1.8861	1.8594	1.8334	1.8080	1.7833	1.7591	1.7355	1.7125	1.6901	1.6681	1.6467	1.6257
3	2.9410	2.8839	2.8286	2.7751	2.7232	2.6730	2.6243	2.5771	2.5313	2.4869	2.4437	2.4018	2.3612	2.3216	2.2832
4	3.9020	3.8077	3.7171	3.6299	3.5459	3.4651	3.3872	3.3121	3.2397	3.1699	3.1024	3.0373	2.9745	2.9137	2.8550
5	4.8534	4.7135	4.5797	4.4518	4.3295	4.2124	4.1002	3.9927	3.8897	3.7908	3.6959	3.6048	3.5172	3.4331	3.3522
6	5.7955	5.6014	5.4172	5.2421	5.0757	4.9173	4.7665	4.6229	4.4859	4.3553	4.2305	4.1114	3.9975	3.8887	3.7845
7	6.7282	6.4720	6.2303	6.0020	5.7864	5.5824	5.3893	5.2064	5.0330	4.8684	4.7122	4.5638	4.4226	4.2883	4.1604
8	7.6517	7.3255	7.0197	6.7327	6.4632	6.2098	5.9713	5.7466	5.5348	5.3349	5.1461	4.9676	4.7988	4.6389	4.4873
9	8.5660	8.1622	7.7861	7.4353	7.1078	6.8017	6.5152	6.2469	5.9952	5.7590	5.5370	5.3282	5.1317	4.9464	4.7716
10	9.4713	8.9826	8.5302	8.1109	7.7217	7.3601	7.0236	6.7101	6.4177	6.1446	5.8892	5.6502	5.4262	5.2161	5.0188
11	10.3676	9.7868	9.2526	8.7605	8.3064	7.8869	7.4987	7.1390	6.8051	6.4951	6.2065	5.9377	5.6869	5.4527	5.2337
12	11.2551	10.5753	9.9540	9.3851	8.8632	8.3838	7.9427	7.5361	7.1607	6.8137	6.4924	6.1944	5.9176	5.6603	5.4206
13	12.1337	11.3484	10.6350	9.9856	9.3936	8.8527	8.3577	7.9038	7.4869	7.1034	6.7499	6.4235	6.1218	5.8424	5.5831
14	13.0037	12.1062	11.2961	10.5631	9.8986	9.2950	8.7455	8.2442	7.7862	7.3667	6.9819	6.6282	6.3025	6.0021	5.7245
15	13.8650	12.8493	11.9379	11.1184	10.3797	9.7122	9.1079	8.5595	8.0607	7.6061	7.1909	6.8109	6.4624	6.1422	5.8474
16	14.7179	13.5777	12.5611	11.6523	10.8378	10.1059	9.4466	8.8514	8.3126	7.8237	7.3792	6.9740	6.6039	6.2651	5.9542
17	15.5622	14.2919	13.1661	12.1657	11.2741	10.4773	9.7632	9.1216	8.5436	8.0216	7.5488	7.1196	6.7291	6.3729	6.0472
18	16.3983	14.9920	13.7535	12.6593	11.6896	10.8276	10.0591	9.3719	8.7556	8.2014	7.7016	7.2497	6.8399	6.4674	6.1280
19	17.2260	15.6785	14.3238	13.1339	12.0853	11.1581	10.3356	9.6036	8.9501	8.3649	7.8393	7.3658	6.9380	6.5504	6.1982
20	18.0455	16.3514	14.8775	13.5903	12.4622	11.4699	10.5940	9.8181	9.1285	8.5136	7.9633	7.4694	7.0248	6.6231	6.2593
21	18.8570	17.0112	15.4150	14.0292	12.8211	11.7641	10.8355	10.0168	9.2922	8.6487	8.0751	7.5620	7.1015	6.6870	6.3125
22	19.6604	17.6580	15.9369	14.4511	13.1630	12.0416	11.0612	10.2007	9.4424	8.7715	8.1757	7.6446	7.1695	6.7429	6.3587
23	20.4558	18.2922	16.4436	14.8568	13.4886	12.3034	11.2722	10.3711	9.5802	8.8832	8.2664	7.7184	7.2297	6.7921	6.3988
24	21.2434	18.9139	16.9355	15.2470	13.7986	12.5504	11.4693	10.5288	9.7066	8.9847	8.3481	7.7843	7.2829	6.8351	6.4338
25	22.0232	19.5235	17.4131	15.6221	14.0939	12.7834	11.6536	10.6748	9.8226	9.0770	8.4217	7.8431	7.3300	6.8729	6.4641
26	22.7952	20.1210	17.8768	15.9828	14.3752	13.0032	11.8258	10.8100	9.9290	9.1609	8.4881	7.8957	7.3717	6.9061	6.4906
27	23.5596	20.7069	18.3270	16.3296	14.6430	13.2105	11.9867	10.9352	10.0266	9.2372	8.5478	7.9426	7.4086	6.9352	6.5135
28	24.3164	21.2813	18.7641	16.6631	14.8981	13.4062	12.1371	11.0511	10.1161	9.3066	8.6016	7.9844	7.4412	6.9607	6.5335
29	25.0658	21.8444	19.1884	16.9837	15.1411	13.5907	12.2777	11.1584	10.1983	9.3696	8.6501	8.0218	7.4701	6.9830	6.5509
30	25.8077	22.3965	19.6004	17.2920	15.3724	13.7648	12.4090	11.2578	10.2737	9.4269	8.6938	8.0552	7.4957	7.0027	6.5660
31	26.5423	22.9377	20.0004	17.5885	15.5928	13.9291	12.5318	11.3498	10.3428	9.4790	8.7331	8.0850	7.5183	7.0199	6.5791
32	27.2696	23.4683	20.3888	17.8735	15.8027	14.0840	12.6466	11.4350	10.4062	9.5264	8.7686	8.1116	7.5383	7.0350	6.5905
33	27.9897	23.9886	20.7658	18.1476	16.0025	14.2302	12.7538	11.5139	10.4644	9.5694	8.8005	8.1354	7.5560	7.0482	6.6005
34	28.7027	24.4986	21.1318	18.4112	16.1929	14.3681	12.8540	11.5869	10.5178	9.6086	8.8293	8.1566	7.5717	7.0599	6.6091
35	29.4086	24.9986	21.4872	18.6646	16.3742	14.4982	12.9477	11.6546	10.5668	9.6442	8.8552	8.1755	7.5856	7.0700	6.6166
40	32.8347	27.3555	23.1148	19.7928	17.1591	15.0463	13.3317	11.9246	10.7574	9.7791	8.9511	8.2438	7.6344	7.1050	6.6418
45	36.0945	29.4902	24.5187	20.7200	17.7741	15.4558	13.6055	12.1084	10.8812	9.8628	9.0079	8.2825	7.6609	7.1232	6.6543
50	39.1961	31.4236	25.7298	21.4822	18.2559	15.7619	13.8007	12.2335	10.9617	9.9148	9.0417	8.3045	7.6752	7.1327	6.6605

TABLE B. Present Value of $1 Received per Period (cont'd)

n/r	16%	18%	20%	22%	24%	26%	28%	30%	32%	34%	36%	38%	40%	45%	50%
1	.8621	.8475	.8333	.8197	.8065	.7937	.7813	.7692	.7576	.7463	.7353	.7246	.7143	.6897	.6667
2	1.6052	1.5656	1.5278	1.4915	1.4568	1.4235	1.3916	1.3609	1.3315	1.3032	1.2760	1.2497	1.2245	1.1653	1.1111
3	2.2459	2.1743	2.1065	2.0422	1.9813	1.9234	1.8684	1.8161	1.7663	1.7188	1.6735	1.6302	1.5889	1.4933	1.4074
4	2.7982	2.6901	2.5887	2.4936	2.4043	2.3202	2.2410	2.1662	2.0957	2.0290	1.9658	1.9060	1.8492	1.7195	1.6049
5	3.2743	3.1272	2.9906	2.8636	2.7454	2.6351	2.5320	2.4356	2.3452	2.2604	2.1807	2.1058	2.0352	1.8755	1.7366
6	3.6847	3.4976	3.3255	3.1669	3.0205	2.8850	2.7594	2.6427	2.5342	2.4331	2.3388	2.2506	2.1680	1.9831	1.8244
7	4.0386	3.8115	3.6046	3.4155	3.2423	3.0833	2.9370	2.8021	2.6775	2.5620	2.4550	2.3555	2.2628	2.0573	1.8829
8	4.3436	4.0776	3.8372	3.6193	3.4212	3.2407	3.0758	2.9247	2.7860	2.6582	2.5404	2.4315	2.3306	2.1085	1.9220
9	4.6065	4.3030	4.0310	3.7863	3.5655	3.3657	3.1842	3.0190	2.8681	2.7300	2.6033	2.4866	2.3790	2.1438	1.9480
10	4.8332	4.4941	4.1925	3.9232	3.6819	3.4648	3.2689	3.0915	2.9304	2.7836	2.6495	2.5265	2.4136	2.1681	1.9653
11	5.0286	4.6560	4.3271	4.0354	3.7757	3.5435	3.3351	3.1473	2.9776	2.8236	2.6834	2.5555	2.4383	2.1849	1.9769
12	5.1971	4.7932	4.4392	4.1274	3.8514	3.6059	3.3868	3.1903	3.0133	2.8534	2.7084	2.5764	2.4559	2.1965	1.9845
13	5.3423	4.9095	4.5327	4.2028	3.9124	3.6555	3.4272	3.2233	3.0404	2.8757	2.7268	2.5916	2.4685	2.2045	1.9897
14	5.4675	5.0081	4.6106	4.2646	3.9616	3.6949	3.4587	3.2487	3.0609	2.8923	2.7403	2.6026	2.4775	2.2100	1.9931
15	5.5755	5.0916	4.6755	4.3152	4.0013	3.7261	3.4834	3.2682	3.0764	2.9047	2.7502	2.6106	2.4839	2.2138	1.9954
16	5.6685	5.1624	4.7296	4.3567	4.0333	3.7509	3.5026	3.2832	3.0882	2.9140	2.7575	2.6164	2.4885	2.2164	1.9970
17	5.7487	5.2223	4.7746	4.3908	4.0591	3.7705	3.5177	3.2948	3.0971	2.9209	2.7629	2.6206	2.4918	2.2182	1.9980
18	5.8178	5.2732	4.8122	4.4187	4.0799	3.7861	3.5294	3.3037	3.1039	2.9260	2.7668	2.6236	2.4941	2.2195	1.9986
19	5.8775	5.3162	4.8435	4.4415	4.0967	3.7985	3.5386	3.3105	3.1090	2.9299	2.7697	2.6258	2.4958	2.2203	1.9991
20	5.9288	5.3527	4.8696	4.4603	4.1103	3.8083	3.5458	3.3158	3.1129	2.9327	2.7718	2.6274	2.4970	2.2209	1.9994
21	5.9731	5.3837	4.8913	4.4756	4.1212	3.8161	3.5514	3.3198	3.1158	2.9349	2.7734	2.6285	2.4979	2.2213	1.9996
22	6.0113	5.4099	4.9094	4.4882	4.1300	3.8223	3.5558	3.3230	3.1180	2.9365	2.7746	2.6294	2.4985	2.2216	1.9997
23	6.0442	5.4321	4.9245	4.4985	4.1371	3.8273	3.5592	3.3253	3.1197	2.9377	2.7754	2.6300	2.4989	2.2218	1.9998
24	6.0726	5.4509	4.9371	4.5070	4.1428	3.8312	3.5619	3.3272	3.1210	2.9386	2.7760	2.6304	2.4992	2.2219	1.9999
25	6.0971	5.4669	4.9476	4.5139	4.1474	3.8342	3.5640	3.3286	3.1220	2.9392	2.7765	2.6307	2.4994	2.2220	1.9999
26	6.1182	5.4804	4.9563	4.5196	4.1511	3.8367	3.5656	3.3297	3.1227	2.9397	2.7768	2.6310	2.4996	2.2221	1.9999
27	6.1364	5.4919	4.9636	4.5243	4.1542	3.8387	3.5669	3.3305	3.1233	2.9401	2.7771	2.6311	2.4997	2.2221	2.0000
28	6.1520	5.5016	4.9697	4.5281	4.1566	3.8402	3.5679	3.3312	3.1237	2.9404	2.7773	2.6313	2.4998	2.2222	2.0000
29	6.1656	5.5098	4.9747	4.5312	4.1585	3.8414	3.5687	3.3316	3.1240	2.9406	2.7774	2.6313	2.4999	2.2222	2.0000
30	6.1772	5.5168	4.9789	4.5338	4.1601	3.8424	3.5693	3.3321	3.1242	2.9407	2.7775	2.6314	2.4999	2.2222	2.0000
31	6.1872	5.5227	4.9824	4.5359	4.1614	3.8432	3.5697	3.3324	3.1244	2.9408	2.7776	2.6315	2.4999	2.2222	2.0000
32	6.1959	5.5277	4.9854	4.5376	4.1624	3.8438	3.5701	3.3326	3.1246	2.9409	2.7776	2.6315	2.4999	2.2222	2.0000
33	6.2034	5.5320	4.9878	4.5390	4.1632	3.8443	3.5704	3.3328	3.1247	2.9410	2.7777	2.6315	2.5000	2.2222	2.0000
34	6.2098	5.5356	4.9898	4.5402	4.1639	3.8447	3.5706	3.3329	3.1248	2.9410	2.7777	2.6315	2.5000	2.2222	2.0000
35	6.2153	5.5386	4.9915	4.5411	4.1644	3.8450	3.5708	3.3330	3.1248	2.9411	2.7777	2.6315	2.5000	2.2222	2.0000
40	6.2335	5.5482	4.9966	4.5439	4.1659	3.8458	3.5712	3.3332	3.1250	2.9412	2.7778	2.6316	2.5000	2.2222	2.0000
45	6.2421	5.5523	4.9986	4.5449	4.1664	3.8460	3.5714	3.3333	3.1250	2.9412	2.7778	2.6316	2.5000	2.2222	2.0000
50	6.2463	5.5541	4.9995	4.5452	4.1666	3.8461	3.5714	3.3333	3.1250	2.9412	2.7778	2.6316	2.5000	2.2222	2.0000

TABLE C.   *Present Value of Depreciation of $1.00 of Assets Under ACRS*

Discount Rate	Class Life			
	3 years	5 years	10 years	15 years
.01	.979156	.969618	.949194	.928486
.02	.959001	.940615	.902132	.864282
.03	.939507	.912912	.858479	.806496
.04	.920645	.886436	.817933	.754358
.05	.902386	.861118	.780223	.707203
.06	.884707	.836893	.745105	.664453
.07	.867582	.813701	.712360	.625607
.08	.850988	.791487	.681788	.590226
.09	.834904	.770198	.653211	.557930
.10	.819309	.749784	.626466	.528385
.11	.804183	.730201	.601407	.501299
.12	.789507	.711404	.577900	.476415
.13	.775263	.693353	.555825	.453508
.14	.761435	.676010	.535071	.432377
.15	.748007	.659340	.515539	.412848
.16	.734962	.643309	.497136	.394764
.18	.709968	.613040	.463395	.362398
.20	.686343	.584973	.433263	.334347
.22	.663987	.558903	.406251	.309873
.24	.642812	.534647	.381947	.288384
.26	.622733	.512045	.360003	.269403
.28	.603676	.490950	.340122	.252545
.30	.585571	.471233	.322053	.237492
.32	.568356	.452778	.305581	.223985
.34	.551971	.435479	.290520	.211810
.36	.536364	.419244	.276710	.200787
.38	.521485	.403986	.264014	.190769
.40	.507289	.389629	.252312	.181628
.45	.474517	.357238	.226755	.161956
.50	.445185	.329136	.205493	.145871

TABLE D. *Present Value of Depreciation Charges from $1.00 of Assets Depreciated over n Years, Using the Twice Straight-Line Declining Balance Depreciation Method, Discounting at r Percent per Year, Assuming No Salvage Value**

n	1%	2%	3%	4%	5%
3	.985753	.971890	.958397	.945260	.932465
4	.981570	.963759	.946539	.929883	.913765
5	.977620	.956126	.935471	.915611	.896505
6	.973593	.948394	.924329	.901332	.879339
7	.969722	.941004	.913741	.887838	.863203
8	.965781	.933528	.903095	.874349	.847170
9	.961962	.926325	.892896	.861498	.831973
10	.958088	.919063	.882674	.848693	.816918
11	.954316	.912033	.872833	.836432	.802576
12	.950500	.904965	.862998	.824248	.788403
13	.946772	.898100	.853497	.812540	.774853
14	.943010	.891213	.844023	.800930	.761488
15	.939326	.884508	.834848	.789745	.748676
16	.935615	.877793	.825713	.778670	.736058
17	.931974	.871243	.816850	.767980	.723936
18	.928312	.864693	.808038	.757408	.712010
19	.924714	.858295	.799475	.747187	.700533
20	.921098	.851904	.790970	.737088	.689251
21	.917543	.845654	.782695	.727311	.678378
22	.913973	.839416	.774483	.717659	.667697
23	.910459	.833309	.766484	.708302	.657388
24	.906935	.827220	.758552	.699071	.647267
25	.903462	.821253	.750819	.690114	.637488
26	.899982	.815306	.743155	.681281	.627890
27	.896550	.809476	.735677	.672703	.618607
28	.893112	.803668	.728269	.664247	.609498
29	.889721	.797971	.721036	.656027	.600680
30	.886326	.792298	.713874	.647927	.592029
31	.882974	.786729	.706876	.640049	.583647
32	.879620	.781187	.699949	.632287	.575425
33	.876309	.775744	.693178	.624731	.567452
34	.872995	.770330	.686477	.617289	.559631
35	.869722	.765009	.679923	.610041	.552042
36	.866449	.759718	.673438	.602902	.544599
37	.863214	.754516	.667093	.595945	.537370
38	.859981	.749344	.660816	.589094	.530281
39	.856784	.744259	.654672	.582414	.523391
40	.853589	.739204	.648595	.575837	.516633
41	.850430	.734231	.642643	.569420	.510063
42	.847273	.729289	.636757	.563101	.503617
43	.844150	.724426	.630991	.556934	.497346
44	.841031	.719594	.625289	.550862	.491193
45	.837945	.714838	.619701	.544933	.485204
46	.834863	.710113	.614176	.539095	.479328
47	.831813	.705461	.608760	.533391	.473604
48	.828767	.700840	.603405	.527776	.467988
49	.825752	.696289	.598153	.522287	.462514
50	.822742	.691769	.592961	.516883	.457143

TABLE D.   *Twice Straight-Line Declining Balance (cont'd)*

n	6%	7%	8%	9%	10%
3	.919999	.907850	.896007	.884459	.873195
4	.898161	.883049	.868405	.854212	.840448
5	.878113	.860399	.843330	.826873	.810998
6	.858291	.838135	.818819	.800297	.782525
7	.839757	.817424	.796132	.775819	.756424
8	.821445	.797073	.773962	.752024	.731181
9	.804178	.777979	.753259	.729907	.707825
10	.787165	.759267	.733076	.708455	.685282
11	.771038	.741615	.714123	.688399	.664295
12	.755187	.724354	.695683	.668981	.644070
13	.740105	.708006	.678296	.650747	.625155
14	.725308	.692046	.661403	.633114	.606944
15	.711188	.676885	.645423	.616490	.589849
16	.697352	.662101	.629912	.600443	.573398
17	.684121	.648022	.615200	.585272	.557908
18	.671167	.634304	.600928	.570615	.543003
19	.658756	.621213	.587360	.556731	.528930
20	.646613	.608464	.574202	.543320	.515386
21	.634960	.596275	.561668	.530587	.502568
22	.623565	.584409	.549515	.518288	.490228
23	.612613	.573046	.537917	.506587	.478522
24	.601907	.561985	.526671	.495281	.467249
25	.591605	.551378	.515921	.484505	.456532
26	.581536	.541054	.505496	.474090	.446205
27	.571835	.531140	.495515	.464146	.436369
28	.562355	.521489	.485834	.454531	.426886
29	.553212	.512211	.476552	.445336	.417837
30	.544278	.503178	.467546	.436441	.409106
31	.535651	.494483	.458901	.427921	.400760
32	.527222	.486017	.450509	.419674	.392703
33	.519076	.477859	.442442	.411764	.384988
34	.511116	.469914	.434610	.404104	.377534
35	.503416	.462249	.427071	.396746	.370386
36	.495891	.454783	.419749	.389616	.363474
37	.488606	.447573	.412693	.382758	.356836
38	.481485	.440547	.405836	.376109	.350413
39	.474586	.433757	.399221	.369706	.344236
40	.467841	.427138	.392791	.363494	.338254
41	.461301	.420735	.386580	.357504	.332493
42	.454907	.414491	.380540	.351689	.326910
43	.448702	.408445	.374701	.346076	.321527
44	.442633	.402549	.369018	.340624	.316306
45	.436740	.396834	.363520	.335354	.311265
46	.430976	.391258	.358166	.330233	.306373
47	.425374	.385850	.352981	.325279	.301644
48	.419894	.380571	.347930	.320460	.297051
49	.414565	.375446	.343034	.315794	.292607
50	.409349	.370443	.338262	.311254	.288288

* Values tabled are $D(n, r) = \sum\limits_{i=1}^{n} \dfrac{d_i}{(1+r)^i}$

where $d_i = \begin{cases} (2/n)(1 - 2/n)^{i-1} & \text{for } i < k \\ \dfrac{(1 - 2/n)^{k-1}}{n + 1 - k} & \text{for } i > k \end{cases}$ and k is the smallest integer greater than or equal to $(n/2 + 1)$

TABLE D. *Twice Straight-Line Decline Balance (cont'd)*

n	11%	12%	13%	14%	15%
3	.862205	.851479	.841009	.830785	.820799
4	.827096	.814139	.801561	.789345	.777477
5	.795677	.780884	.766593	.752782	.739427
6	.765462	.749069	.733311	.718155	.703569
7	.737891	.720170	.703213	.686975	.671415
8	.711362	.692499	.674530	.657399	.641054
9	.686922	.667114	.648326	.630487	.613533
10	.663444	.642841	.623381	.604978	.587558
11	.641678	.620426	.600432	.581597	.563831
12	.620795	.599014	.578601	.559443	.541436
13	.601339	.579138	.558408	.539018	.520855
14	.582687	.560159	.539199	.519662	.501419
15	.565240	.542468	.521351	.501731	.483465
16	.548517	.525574	.504369	.484727	.466494
17	.532823	.509768	.488526	.468906	.450743
18	.517778	.494669	.473441	.453890	.435837
19	.503615	.480496	.459318	.439865	.421946
20	.490034	.466948	.445860	.426537	.408781
21	.477215	.454194	.433219	.414046	.396465
22	.464915	.441993	.421160	.402160	.384774
23	.453276	.430474	.409799	.390984	.373799
24	.442102	.419446	.398950	.380335	.363365
25	.431503	.409008	.388700	.370291	.353538
26	.421320	.399004	.378899	.360707	.344178
27	.411640	.389513	.369616	.351643	.335337
28	.402333	.380407	.360728	.342981	.326903
29	.393467	.371749	.352289	.334766	.318913
30	.384935	.363433	.344200	.326906	.311278
31	.376792	.355509	.336501	.319432	.304026
32	.368948	.347891	.329112	.312271	.297087
33	.361449	.340617	.322065	.305446	.290478
34	.354219	.333617	.315293	.298897	.284144
35	.347294	.326919	.308820	.292643	.278100
36	.340612	.320467	.302593	.286633	.272297
37	.334201	.314283	.296630	.280882	.266747
38	.328010	.308319	.290887	.275348	.261413
39	.322061	.302594	.285377	.270043	.256300
40	.316309	.297067	.280063	.264932	.251379
41	.310775	.291752	.274957	.260023	.246655
42	.305420	.286616	.270028	.255288	.242101
43	.300261	.281670	.265284	.250732	.237722
44	.295264	.276886	.260699	.246333	.233496
45	.290443	.272273	.256280	.242095	.229425
46	.285770	.267806	.252005	.237998	.225492
47	.281255	.263492	.247879	.234044	.221698
48	.276876	.259312	.243882	.230218	.218029
49	.272641	.255271	.240021	.226521	.214484
50	.268529	.251351	.236277	.222940	.211052

TABLE D.   *Twice Straight-Line Declining Balance (cont'd)*

n	16%	17%	18%	19%	20%
3	.811044	.801511	.792194	.783085	.774177
4	.765944	.754731	.743827	.733220	.722897
5	.726509	.714007	.701903	.690179	.678819
6	.689524	.675993	.662949	.650369	.638231
7	.656495	.642180	.628435	.615231	.602537
8	.625447	.610531	.596266	.582613	.569537
9	.597406	.582052	.567419	.553463	.540141
10	.571048	.555386	.540513	.526374	.512921
11	.547053	.531189	.516172	.501941	.488440
12	.524488	.508516	.493443	.479202	.465728
13	.503814	.487801	.472734	.458535	.445137
14	.484356	.468368	.453365	.439263	.425989
15	.466428	.450508	.435606	.421633	.408508
16	.449534	.433726	.418965	.405154	.392209
17	.433891	.418222	.403621	.389989	.377236
18	419128	.403626	.389212	.375779	.363236
19	.405398	.390077	.375859	.362632	.350301
20	.392417	.377297	.363290	.350281	.338171
21	.380295	.365382	.351588	.338798	.326907
22	.368814	.354118	.340548	.327981	.316315
23	.358052	.343575	.330225	.317880	.306431
24	.347840	.333588	.320464	.308341	.297111
25	.338234	.324205	.311301	.299395	.288377
26	.329101	.315298	.302616	.290926	.280118
27	.320483	.306900	.294434	.282955	.272349
28	.312275	.298913	.286662	.275390	.264984
29	.304506	.291359	.279316	.268244	.258031
30	.297092	.284160	.272323	.261448	.251423
31	.290056	.277331	.265693	.255008	.245164
32	.283330	.270810	.259368	.248870	.239203
33	.276930	.264609	.253355	.243037	.233540
34	.270802	.258676	.247608	.237465	.228135
35	.264956	.253020	.242131	.232157	.222986
36	.259350	.247600	.236887	.227078	.218062
37	.253991	.242420	.231876	.222226	.213360
38	.248844	.237449	.227070	.217576	.208855
39	.243913	.232689	.222469	.213124	.204544
40	.239170	.228112	.218049	.208850	.200407
41	.234618	.223722	.213809	.204750	.196439
42	.230234	.219495	.209729	.200808	.192625
43	.226018	.215432	.205808	.197019	.188960
44	.221953	.211515	.202030	.193371	.185432
45	.218038	.207745	.198394	.189859	.182037
46	.214257	.204105	.194885	.186473	.178764
47	.210611	.200596	.191503	.183208	.175610
48	.207086	.197205	.188235	.180056	.172565
49	.203682	.193930	.185081	.177013	.169625
50	.200387	.190762	.182030	.174071	.166785

TABLE E. e^{-x}

x	0	.01	.02	.03	.04
0	1.000000	.990050	.980199	.970446	.960789
.10	.904837	.895834	.886920	.878095	.869358
.20	.818731	.810584	.802519	.794534	.786628
.30	.740818	.733447	.726149	.718924	.711770
.40	.670320	.663650	.657047	.650509	.644036
.50	.606531	.600496	.594521	.588605	.582748
.60	.548812	.543351	.537944	.532592	.527292
.70	.496585	.491644	.486752	.481909	.477114
.80	.449329	.444858	.440432	.436049	.431711
.90	.406570	.402524	.398519	.394554	.390628
1.00	.367879	.364219	.360595	.357007	.353455
1.10	.332871	.329559	.326280	.323033	.319819
1.20	.301194	.298197	.295230	.292293	.289384
1.30	.272532	.269820	.267135	.264477	.261846
1.40	.246597	.244143	.241714	.239309	.236928
1.50	.223130	.220910	.218712	.216536	.214381
1.60	.201897	.199888	.197899	.195930	.193980
1.70	.182684	.180866	.179066	.177284	.175520
1.80	.165299	.163654	.162026	.160414	.158817
1.90	.149569	.148080	.146607	.145148	.143704
2.00	.135335	.133989	.132655	.131336	.130029
2.10	.122456	.121238	.120032	.118837	.117655
2.20	.110803	.109701	.108609	.107528	.106459
2.30	.100259	.099261	.098274	.097296	.096328
2.40	.090718	.089815	.088922	.088037	.087161
2.50	.082085	.081268	.080460	.079659	.078866
2.60	.074274	.073535	.072803	.072078	.071361
2.70	.067206	.066537	.065875	.065219	.064570
2.80	.060810	.060205	.059606	.059013	.058426
2.90	.055023	.054476	.053934	.053397	.052866
3.00	.049787	.049292	.048801	.048316	.047835
3.10	.045049	.044601	.044157	.043718	.043283
3.20	.040762	.040357	.039955	.039557	.039164
3.30	.036883	.036516	.036153	.035793	.035437
3.40	.033373	.033041	.032712	.032387	.032065
3.50	.030197	.029897	.029599	.029305	.029013
3.60	.027324	.027052	.026783	.026516	.026252
3.70	.024724	.024478	.024234	.023993	.023754
3.80	.022371	.022148	.021928	.021710	.021494
3.90	.020242	.020041	.019841	.019644	.019448
4.00	.018316	.018133	.017953	.017774	.017597
4.10	.016573	.016408	.016245	.016083	.015923
4.20	.014996	.014846	.014699	.014552	.014408
4.30	.013569	.013434	.013300	.013168	.013037
4.40	.012277	.012155	.012034	.011914	.011796
4.50	.011109	.010998	.010889	.010781	.010673
4.60	.010052	.009952	.009853	.009755	.009658
4.70	.009095	.009005	.008915	.008826	.008739
4.80	.008230	.008148	.008067	.007987	.007907
4.90	.007447	.007372	.007299	.007227	.007155

TABLE E. e^{-x} (cont'd)

x	.05	.06	.07	.08	.09
0	.951229	.941765	.932394	.923116	.913931
.10	.860708	.852144	.843665	.835270	.826959
.20	.778801	.771052	.763379	.755784	.748264
.30	.704688	.697676	.690734	.683861	.677057
.40	.637628	.631284	.625002	.618783	.612626
.50	.576950	.571209	.565525	.559898	.554327
.60	.522046	.516851	.511709	.506617	.501576
.70	.472367	.467666	.463013	.458406	.453845
.80	.427415	.423162	.418952	.414783	.410656
.90	.386741	.382893	.379083	.375311	.371577
1.00	.349938	.346456	.343009	.339596	.336216
1.10	.316637	.313486	.310367	.307279	.304221
1.20	.286505	.283654	.280832	.278037	.275271
1.30	.259240	.256661	.254107	.251579	.249075
1.40	.234570	.232236	.229925	.227638	.225373
1.50	.212248	.210136	.208045	.205975	.203926
1.60	.192050	.190139	.188247	.186374	.184520
1.70	.173774	.172045	.170333	.168638	.166960
1.80	.157237	.155673	.154124	.152590	.151072
1.90	.142274	.140858	.139457	.138069	.136695
2.00	.128735	.127454	.126186	124930	.123687
2.10	.116484	.115325	.114178	.113042	.111917
2.20	.105399	.104350	.103312	.102284	.101266
2.30	.095369	.094420	.093481	.092551	.091630
2.40	.086294	.085435	.084585	.083743	.082910
2.50	.078082	.077305	.076536	.075774	.075020
2.60	.070651	.069948	.069252	.068563	.067881
2.70	.063928	.063292	.062662	.062039	.061421
2.80	.057844	.057269	.056699	.056135	.055576
2.90	.052340	.051819	.051303	.050793	.050287
3.00	.047359	.046888	.046421	.045959	.045502
3.10	.042852	.042426	.042004	.041586	.041172
3.20	.038774	.038388	.038006	.037628	.037254
3.30	.035084	.034735	.034390	.034047	.033709
3.40	.031746	.031430	.031117	.030807	.030501
3.50	.028725	.028439	.028156	.027876	.027598
3.60	.025991	.025733	.025476	.025223	.024972
3.70	.023518	.023284	.023052	.022823	.022596
3.80	.021280	.021068	.020858	.020651	.020445
3.90	.019255	.019063	.018873	.018686	.018500
4.00	.017422	.017249	.017077	.016907	.016739
4.10	.015764	.015608	.015452	.015299	.015146
4.20	.014264	.014122	.013982	.013843	.013705
4.30	.012907	.012778	.012651	.012525	.012401
4.40	.011679	.011562	.011447	.011333	.011221
4.50	.010567	.010462	.010358	.010255	.010153
4.60	.009562	.009466	.009372	.009279	.009187
4.70	.008652	.008566	.008480	.008396	.008312
4.80	.007828	.007750	.007673	.007597	.007521
4.90	.007083	.007013	.006943	.006874	.006806

Index